ICME-13 Monographs

Series Editor

Gabriele Kaiser, Faculty of Education, Didactics of Mathematics, Universität Hamburg, Hamburg, Germany

Each volume in the series presents state-of-the art research on a particular topic in mathematics education and reflects the international debate as broadly as possible, while also incorporating insights into lesser-known areas of the discussion. Each volume is based on the discussions and presentations during the ICME-13 congress and includes the best papers from one of the ICME-13 Topical Study Groups, Discussion Groups or presentations from the thematic afternoon.

More information about this series at http://www.springer.com/series/15585

Gabriele Kaiser · Norma Presmeg
Editors

Compendium for Early Career Researchers in Mathematics Education

Editors
Gabriele Kaiser
Faculty of Education
Universität Hamburg
Hamburg, Germany

Norma Presmeg
Mathematics Department
Illinois State University
Normal, IL, USA

ISSN 2520-8322 ISSN 2520-8330 (electronic)
ICME-13 Monographs
ISBN 978-3-030-15635-0 ISBN 978-3-030-15636-7 (eBook)
https://doi.org/10.1007/978-3-030-15636-7

Library of Congress Control Number: 2019934361

© The Editor(s) (if applicable) and The Author(s) 2019. This book is an open access publication.
Open Access This book is licensed under the terms of the Creative Commons Attribution 4.0 International License (http://creativecommons.org/licenses/by/4.0/), which permits use, sharing, adaptation, distribution and reproduction in any medium or format, as long as you give appropriate credit to the original author(s) and the source, provide a link to the Creative Commons license and indicate if changes were made.
The images or other third party material in this book are included in the book's Creative Commons license, unless indicated otherwise in a credit line to the material. If material is not included in the book's Creative Commons license and your intended use is not permitted by statutory regulation or exceeds the permitted use, you will need to obtain permission directly from the copyright holder.
The use of general descriptive names, registered names, trademarks, service marks, etc. in this publication does not imply, even in the absence of a specific statement, that such names are exempt from the relevant protective laws and regulations and therefore free for general use.
The publisher, the authors and the editors are safe to assume that the advice and information in this book are believed to be true and accurate at the date of publication. Neither the publisher nor the authors or the editors give a warranty, expressed or implied, with respect to the material contained herein or for any errors or omissions that may have been made. The publisher remains neutral with regard to jurisdictional claims in published maps and institutional affiliations.

This Springer imprint is published by the registered company Springer Nature Switzerland AG
The registered company address is: Gewerbestrasse 11, 6330 Cham, Switzerland

Preface

Early career researchers represent the future of the field, insofar as they will shape the further development of research within the field. Hence the importance, for the future of high-quality research in the field of mathematics education, of supporting and encouraging new scholars as they enter this community of researchers. It has now become common for large international and national conferences, and not only those in mathematics education, to offer specific activities for early career researchers in order to introduce them to the important research methods within the field, to provide them with surveys and overviews on topics significant to the field and to introduce them to academic writing and publishing. Overall, these activities aim to induct early career researchers into the community, help them become *au fait* with its research standards and provide insight on the state-of-the-art results achieved so far by those who have already worked in this community for a long time and who are identified as experts in the field.

At the 13th International Congress on Mathematical Education (ICME-13), which took place from 24 to 31 July 2016, an Early Career Researcher Day was therefore organized to take place directly before the congress on 24 July 2016, which attracted 450 participants. This Compendium and its chapters are based on workshops that were presented as part of this activity, with a few additional chapters on important themes in mathematics education.

Although the Early Career Researcher Day, and ICME-13 itself, followed the structure of summer schools in general and special workshops from various networks (e.g. the European Researchers on Mathematics Education, or activities of the German community), the question arises whether early career researchers need specific offerings or, in general, why the programme was structured in such a way, and why we structured the Compendium as it is.

We have seen in the last two decades a strong development towards higher quality standards of research in mathematics education. Rigorous standards of quality need to be met in carrying out research in fulfilment of the requirements for a Ph.D., or at post-doc level. One of these requirements is to have a clear conceptual framework including reference to well-known theories from mathematics education, either as home-grown theories, or invoking those borrowed from other disciplines.

The standards concerning methodologies have also been raised as the field matures. One aspect of this concern with standards of methodology is the increasing importance of large-scale studies in mathematics education. The high standards of psychometric research have long been unquestioned, but what are the implications when the methods of social and naturalistic research are also recognized as having significance is answering current questions of research in the field? This development leads to the question of what constitutes quality, both in qualitatively and in quantitatively oriented research. It is recognized that qualitative and quantitative methods have different goals, differ in their applicability, and above all, answer different questions in mathematics education research. While qualitative research often enables depth of perception of *why* a certain phenomenon is happening, quantitative research addresses the question of *how widespread* such a phenomenon is. Both kinds of research have their place, and they may complement each other.

The quality standards of objectivity, reliability and validity common in statistical research are not questioned, but what does that mean for qualitatively oriented research focusing quite often on a single case, with no chance of repetition or control groups? Various mixed methods approaches may offer one kind of solution; however, these questions are essential for the future development of research in mathematics education.

With the proliferation of journals and conference proceedings, dissemination of research results through publication has assumed increasing importance in recent years, with growing publication possibilities. Publishing a study nowadays needs to fulfil many requirements concerning the clarity of the theoretical framework and the methodology used. What is the role of home-grown standards in publishing? Do we wish to fulfil the standards implemented by psychometric research? Do we wish to orient towards educational research standards, which are often more qualitatively oriented? It is not by accident that we use the standards of the American Psychological Association (APA) for referencing in many journals of mathematics education.

The Early Career Researcher Day at ICME-13 and its outcome, the Compendium for Early Career Researchers in Mathematics Education, are characterized by a combination of presentations on methodological approaches and theoretical perspectives shaping the field in mathematics education research. Overall, the book provides a state-of-the-art overview of important theories from mathematics education and the broad variety of empirical approaches currently widely used in mathematics education research. This Compendium supports early career researchers in selecting adequate theoretical approaches and adopting the most appropriate methodological approaches for their own research. Furthermore, it helps early career researchers in mathematics education to avoid common pitfalls and problems while writing up their research and it provides them with an overview of the most important journals for research in mathematics education, helping them to select the right venue for publishing and disseminating their work. The strong emphasis on academic writing and publishing, supported by descriptions of the major journals in mathematics education by their (former or associate) editors, offers strong insight into the theoretical and empirical bases of research in mathematics education for early career researchers in this field. Such knowledge is necessary for new and seasoned researchers alike, for the production of high-quality research papers in mathematics education.

We would like to thank Armin Jentsch and Thorsten Scheiner, who were strongly involved in organising the Early Career Researcher Day at ICME-13 and shaped it with their ideas. Furthermore, we thank Ferdinando Arzarello, who welcomed the participants in his role as ICMI-president. We hope that this Compendium for Early Career Researchers in Mathematics Education will foster further similar activities and support the development of an international network for Early Career Researchers in Mathematics Education.

Hamburg, Germany Gabriele Kaiser
Normal, USA Norma Presmeg

Contents

Part I Empirical Methods

1. **Argumentation Analysis for Early Career Researchers** 3
   Christine Knipping and David A. Reid

2. **Topic-Specific Design Research: An Introduction** 33
   Koeno Gravemeijer and Susanne Prediger

3. **A Naturalistic Paradigm: An Introduction to Using Ethnographic Methods for Research in Mathematics Education** 59
   Judit N. Moschkovich

4. **An Introduction to Grounded Theory with a Special Focus on Axial Coding and the Coding Paradigm** 81
   Maike Vollstedt and Sebastian Rezat

5. **Interactional Analysis: A Method for Analysing Mathematical Learning Processes in Interactions** 101
   Marcus Schütte, Rachel-Ann Friesen and Judith Jung

6. **Planning and Conducting Mixed Methods Studies in Mathematics Educational Research** 131
   Nils Buchholtz

7. **The Research Pentagon: A Diagram with Which to Think About Research** 153
   Angelika Bikner-Ahsbahs

8. **Qualitative Text Analysis: A Systematic Approach** 181
   Udo Kuckartz

9. **Problematising Video as Data in Three Video-based Research Projects in Mathematics Education** 199
   Man Ching Esther Chan, Carmel Mesiti and David Clarke

Part II Important Mathematics Educational Themes

10 Approaching Proof in the Classroom Through the Logic
    of Inquiry 221
    Ferdinando Arzarello and Carlotta Soldano

11 A Friendly Introduction to "Knowledge in Pieces": Modeling
    Types of Knowledge and Their Roles in Learning 245
    Andrea A. diSessa

12 Task Design Frameworks in Mathematics Education Research:
    An Example of a Domain-Specific Frame for Algebra Learning
    with Technological Tools 265
    Carolyn Kieran

13 Gender and Mathematics Education: An Overview 289
    Gilah C. Leder

14 Theoretical Aspects of Doing Research in Mathematics
    Education: An Argument for Coherence 309
    Stephen Lerman

15 The Professional Development of Mathematics Teachers 325
    Björn Schwarz and Gabriele Kaiser

**Part III Academic Writing and Academic Publishing:
Academic Writing**

16 Pleasures, Power, and Pitfalls of Writing up Mathematics
    Education Research 347
    Norma Presmeg and Jeremy Kilpatrick

17 Scholarly Writing 359
    Helen J. Forgasz

**Part IV Academic Writing and Academic Publishing: Description
of Major Journals in Mathematics Education**

18 *Educational Studies in Mathematics*: Shaping the Field 377
    Merrilyn Goos

19 *For the Learning of Mathematics*: An Introduction
    to the Journal and the Writing Within It 393
    Richard Barwell and David A. Reid

20 *The International Journal of Science and Mathematics Education*:
    A Beginner's Guide to Writing for Publication 407
    Peter Liljedahl

21 *Journal for Research in Mathematics Education*: Practical Guides for Promoting and Disseminating Significant Research in Mathematics Education................................ 425
Jinfa Cai, Stephen Hwang and Victoria Robison

22 *The Journal of Mathematical Behavior* 443
Carolyn A. Maher, Elizabeth Uptegrove and Louise C. Wilkinson

23 Publishing in the *Journal of Mathematics Teacher Education* 455
Despina Potari

24 Towards Article Acceptance: Avoiding Common Pitfalls in Submissions to *Mathematical Thinking and Learning* 467
Lyn D. English

25 *ZDM Mathematics Education*—Its Development and Characteristics..................................... 481
Gabriele Kaiser

Part V Looking Ahead

26 What Makes for Powerful Classrooms, and How Can We Support Teachers in Creating Them? A Story of Research and Practice, Productively Intertwined 495
Alan H. Schoenfeld

27 If We Want to Get Ahead, We Should Transcend Dualisms and Foster Paradigm Pluralism 511
Thorsten Scheiner

Contributors

Ferdinando Arzarello Dipartimento di Matematica "Giuseppe Peano", Università di Torino, Turin, Italy

Richard Barwell University of Ottawa, Ottawa, Canada

Angelika Bikner-Ahsbahs University of Bremen, Bremen, Germany

Nils Buchholtz University of Oslo, Oslo, Norway

Jinfa Cai University of Delaware, Newark, USA

Man Ching Esther Chan Melbourne Graduate School of Education, The University of Melbourne, Melbourne, VIC, Australia

David Clarke Melbourne Graduate School of Education, The University of Melbourne, Melbourne, VIC, Australia

Andrea A. diSessa University of California, Berkeley, CA, USA

Lyn D. English Queensland University of Technology, Brisbane, Australia

Helen J. Forgasz Monash University, Melbourne, VIC, Australia

Rachel-Ann Friesen Technische Universität Dresden, Dresden, Germany

Merrilyn Goos University of Limerick, Limerick, Ireland

Koeno Gravemeijer Eindhoven University of Technology, Eindhoven, The Netherlands

Stephen Hwang University of Delaware, Newark, USA

Judith Jung Technische Universität Dresden, Dresden, Germany

Gabriele Kaiser University of Hamburg, Hamburg, Germany

Carolyn Kieran Département de Mathématiques, Université du Québec à Montréal, Montréal, QC, Canada

Jeremy Kilpatrick University of Georgia, Athens, GA, USA

Christine Knipping Universität Bremen, Bremen, Germany

Udo Kuckartz Philipps-University Marburg, Marburg, Germany

Gilah C. Leder Monash University, Melbourne, VIC, Australia;
La Trobe University, Melbourne, VIC, Australia

Stephen Lerman London South Bank University, London, UK

Peter Liljedahl Simon Fraser University, Burnaby, Canada

Carolyn A. Maher Rutgers University, New Brunswick, NJ, USA

Carmel Mesiti Melbourne Graduate School of Education, The University of Melbourne, Melbourne, VIC, Australia

Judit N. Moschkovich University of California, Santa Cruz, CA, USA

Despina Potari National and Kapodistrian University of Athens, Athens, Greece

Susanne Prediger Technical University Dortmund, Dortmund, Germany

Norma Presmeg Mathematics Department, Illinois State University, Normal, IL, USA

David A. Reid University of Bremen, Bremen, Germany

Sebastian Rezat University of Paderborn, Paderborn, Germany

Victoria Robison University of Delaware, Newark, USA

Thorsten Scheiner Institute for Learning Sciences & Teacher Education, Australian Catholic University, Brisbane, Australia;
The University of Auckland, Auckland, New Zealand

Alan H. Schoenfeld University of California, Berkeley, USA

Marcus Schütte Technische Universität Dresden, Dresden, Germany

Björn Schwarz University of Vechta, Vechta, Germany

Carlotta Soldano Dipartimento di Filosofia e Scienze dell'educazione, Università di Torino, Turin, Italy

Elizabeth Uptegrove Rutgers University, New Brunswick, NJ, USA

Maike Vollstedt University of Bremen, Bremen, Germany

Louise C. Wilkinson Syracuse University, Syracuse, NY, USA

Part I
Empirical Methods

Chapter 1
Argumentation Analysis for Early Career Researchers

Christine Knipping and David A. Reid

Abstract Proving processes in mathematics classrooms follow their own peculiar rationale, which raises the question of how to reconstruct and analyse the complex argumentative structures that arise in classroom discussion. In this chapter we describe a method of analysis of argumentation processes in the mathematics class, following the structure of our workshop at the ICME-13 *Early Career Researcher Day*. The method builds on Toulmin's theory of argumentation (Toulmin 1958) and allows the description of both global argumentation structures and local argumentations. A three stage process is followed: reconstructing the sequencing and meaning of classroom talk; analysing local argumentations and global argumentation structures; and finally comparing these argumentation structures and revealing their rationale. The second stage involves two moves, first analysing local arguments on the basis of Toulmin's functional model of argumentation, and second analysing the global argumentative structure of the proving process. We provide an example of the use of the method to analyse a transcript from a mathematics classroom.

Keywords Argumentation · Argumentation processes · Argumentation structures · Proof · Proving · Mathematics classrooms · Model of argumentation

1.1 Toulmin's Functional Model of Argumentation

We make use of Toulmin's (1958) functional model of argumentation which has the important characteristic that it was developed to reconstruct arguments in different fields, such as law or medicine. As Toulmin (1958) investigates the functional

---

C. Knipping (✉)
Universität Bremen, Fachbereich 03 - AG Didaktik der Mathematik, MZH 6120, Bibliothekstraße 5, 28359 Bremen, Germany
e-mail: knipping@uni-bremen.de

D. A. Reid
Universität Bremen, Fachbereich 3, Bibliothekstraße 5, 28359 Bremen, Germany
e-mail: dreid@uni-bremen.de

© The Author(s) 2019
G. Kaiser and N. Presmeg (eds.), *Compendium for Early Career Researchers in Mathematics Education*, ICME-13 Monographs,
https://doi.org/10.1007/978-3-030-15636-7_1

structure of rational arguments in general, he asks "What, then, is involved in establishing conclusions by the production of arguments?" (p. 97). Toulmin's first answer is that facts (data) might be cited to support the conclusion. He illustrates this by the following example. If we assert that 'Harry's hair is not black', we might ground this on "our personal knowledge that it is in fact red" (p. 97). We produce a datum that we consider as an evident fact to justify our assertion (conclusion). If this is accepted, this very simple step, datum—conclusion, can represent a rational argument.

But this step, its nature and justification, can be challenged, actually or potentially, and therefore it is often explicitly justified. Instead of additional information, an explanation of a more general style, by rules, principles or inference-licenses has to be formulated (p. 98). Toulmin's second answer addresses this type of challenge. A 'warrant' might be given to establish the "bearing on the conclusion of the data already produced" (p. 98). These warrants "act as bridges, and authorize the sort of step to which our particular argument commits us" (p. 98). In the example above the implicit warrant of the argument is 'If anything is red, it will not also be black." (p. 98). While Toulmin acknowledges that the distinction between data and warrants may not always be clear, their functions are distinct, "in one situation to convey a piece of information, in another to authorise a step in an argument" (p. 99). In fact, the same statement might serve as either datum or warrant or both at once, depending on context (p. 99), but according to Toulmin the distinction between datum, warrant, and the conclusion or claim provides the elements for the "skeleton of a pattern for analyzing arguments" (p. 99, see Fig. 1.1). In the following we use "claim" in cases where data and warrants have not yet been provided, and "conclusion" when they have been.

Toulmin adds several other elements to this skeleton, only one of which is discussed here. Both the datum and the warrant of an argument can be questioned. If a datum requires support, a new argument in which it is the conclusion can be developed. If a warrant is in doubt, a statement Toulmin calls a "backing" can be offered to support it.

Figure 1.2 shows a single step in an argument in terms of Toulmin's model. From the data $c^2 = b^2 - 2ab + a^2 + 2ab$ it concludes that $c^2 = b^2 + a^2$. Such a step is typical in algebraic proofs of the Pythagorean Theorem. The warrant for it consists of several standard principles of arithmetic, and these are normally in an algebraic proof left implicit, but can be reconstructed in a straightforward way. Implicit warrants are marked with dotted outlines.

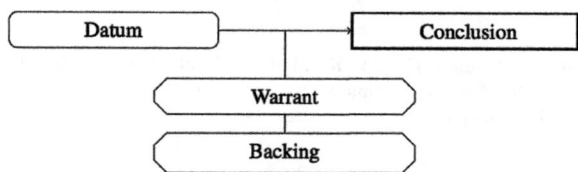

Fig. 1.1 Toulmin Model (In our diagrams Data are enclosed in rectangles with rounded corners, Warrants and Backings in rectangles with angled corners, and Conclusions in plain rectangles.)

Fig. 1.2 Datum, warrant and conclusion for the final step in a proof

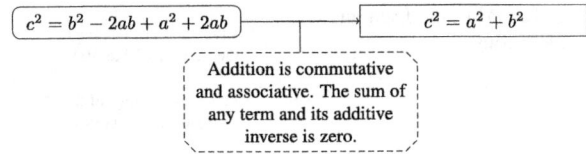

Toulmin states, "The data we cite if a claim is challenged depend on the warrants we are prepared to operate with in that field, and the warrants to which we commit ourselves are implicit in the particular steps from data to claims we are prepared to take and to admit" (p. 100). Therefore careful analyses of the types of warrants (and backings) that are employed explicitly or implicitly in concrete classroom situations, allow us to reconstruct the kinds of mathematical justifications students and teacher together operate on. In particular, the comparison of warrants and backings in different arguments can reveal what sort of argument types are used in proving processes in mathematics classrooms.

For example, in Fig. 1.2, we supply an implicit warrant based on mathematical properties of addition. In a different context the warrant for this argument might have been geometrical, interpreting $2ab$ as the area of a rectangle (or two triangles), or syntactical not interpreting the symbols at all, operating on them purely formally. Any of these types of warrants (and backings) could occur in a classroom and indicate the *field* of justifications in which the students and teacher operate.

Other researchers (e.g., Inglis et al. 2007) make use of other elements in Toulmin's model, including "modal qualifiers" and "rebuttals". Many arguments do not establish their conclusions with complete certainty, and in such arguments we find qualifiers like "probably" and "possibly" as well as rebuttals that identify cases where the conclusion does not hold. Inglis et al. consider the arguments of postgraduate university students in mathematics and find that modal qualifiers play an important role in their mathematical argumentations. In our work in schools, however, we find that the mathematical argumentations produced are often quite different from what advanced mathematics students produce, and as a result we usually do not find it necessary to make use of any elements in the Toulmin model beyond data, conclusions, warrants and backings. We add one element, however, which we call "refutation". A refutation differs from a rebuttal in that a rebuttal is local to a step in an argument and specifies exceptions to the conclusion. A refutation completely negates some part of the argument. In a finished argumentation refuted conclusions would have no place, but as we are concerned with representing the entire argumentation that occurred, it is important for us to include refutations and the arguments they refute, as part of the context of the remainder of the argumentation, even if there is no direct link to be made between the refuted argument and other parts of the argumentation. Aberdein (2006) proposes extending Toulmin's rebuttal element to encompass refutations, but for our purposes we prefer to limit rebuttals to Toulmin's original role, of specifying circumstances where the conclusion does not hold.

It is possible for a step in an argument to make use of several data, and to lead to more than one conclusion. Figure 1.3 shows such a step, in which the two data in

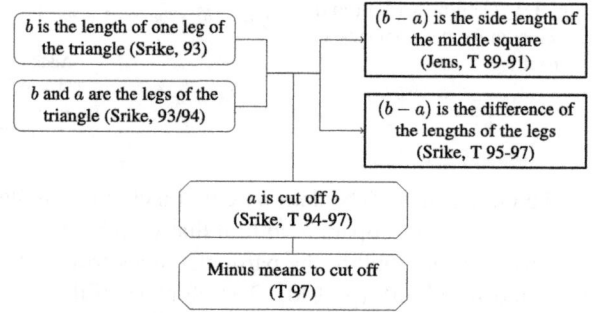

Fig. 1.3 Multiple Data and Conclusions

combination are used to arrive first at a conclusion about the side length of a square, and later at a conclusion about the difference in the lengths of the legs of a right triangle.

An important way in which we use the Toulmin model that extends it significantly, is our application of it not only to single steps in argumentations, but also as a tool to explore the global structure of an argumentation. In the next section we describe this distinction in more detail.

1.2 Local and Global Arguments

Toulmin (1958) notes "an argument is like an organism. It has both a gross, anatomical structure and a finer, as-it-were physiological one" (p. 94). Toulmin's aim is to explore the fine structure, but in considering classroom argumentations both argumentative forms must be reconstructed. Toulmin's model is useful for reconstructing a step of an argument, which allows us to single out distinct arguments in the proving process (for example as in Figs. 1.2 and 1.3). We call these "argumentation steps" or *local arguments*. But it is also necessary to lay out the structure of the argument as a whole (the anatomical structure), which we call *global argument* or the argumentation "structure" of the proving process.

Between the global argument or the argumentation structure of the entire proving process and the local level of the argumentation steps there is an intermediate level we call an "argumentation stream". An argumentation stream consists of a number of argumentation steps that are connected, and which lead to a final target conclusion. The written proof in the right hand side of Fig. 1.4 provides a simple example. The argument presented on the blackboard, reconstructed as a chain of argumentation steps, is shown in Fig. 1.5 (Additional data and analysis can be found in Knipping 2003). The final conclusion ($c^2 = a^2 + b^2$), a formulation of the Pythagorean Theorem, is the target conclusion of the argument. The argument can be reconstructed as a simple chain of conclusions beginning with a datum "$c^2 = (b-a)^2 + 4\text{rwD}$" that has been taken from the drawing on the blackboard. This datum leads to a conclusion: $c^2 = (b-a)^2 + 2ab$, but no warrant is explicitly

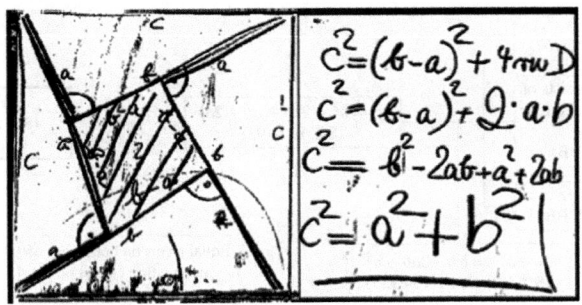

Fig. 1.4 A written proof of the Pythagorean Theorem

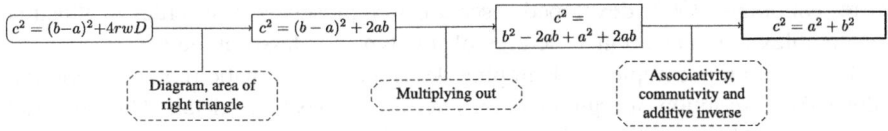

Fig. 1.5 Functional reconstruction of the written proof presented in Fig. 1.4 (The target conclusion is outlined with a thicker line than conclusions that are recycled as data for subsequent steps.)

given to support this inference. The information in the diagram (adjacent sides of the right triangle are a and b) and implicit calculations of the area of the four right triangles implicitly support this claim. The next two steps are also based on implicit warrants. In Fig. 1.4 we include reconstructed possible implicit warrants for each step; they are marked by a box with a dashed line. Note that the statement "$c^2 = (b - a)^2 + 2ab$" is not only the conclusion of one step but also the datum of another. Finally the target conclusion: $c^2 = a^2 + b^2$ is established.

This type of argument can be characterised as a chain of statements, each one deduced from the preceding one on logical and mathematical grounds. This has been described by Duval as "Recyclage" (Duval 1995, pp. 246–248) Once a statement has been established as a conclusion it functions as a datum, an established true fact, in the next step. Aberdein (2006) calls this way of combining single steps "Sequential" and he describes four other ways steps could be combined. As we show in the following, our empirical research on classroom argumentation provides examples of Aberdein's ways of combining steps, as well as other ways.

Figure 1.6 shows another argumentation stream, involving verbal argumentation leading up to the written proof shown in Fig. 1.4. It combines the features of multiple data for an argumentation step and the chaining of steps in which the conclusion of one step becomes a datum for the next.

As discussed earlier, the functional model of Toulmin, which is helpful for reconstructing argumentation steps and streams, is not adequate for more complex argumentation structures. Analyzing proving processes in classrooms requires a different model for capturing the global structure of the argumentations developed

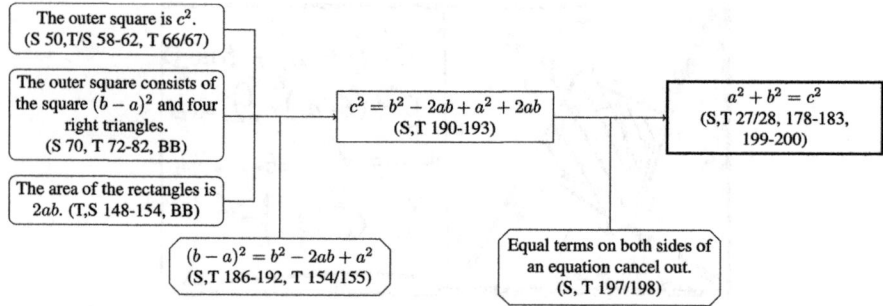

Fig. 1.6 An argumentation stream from verbal argumentation

there. Knipping (2003) developed a schematic representation in order to illustrate the complex argumentation structures of this type of classroom talk.

To address this complexity Knipping developed a schematic representation that allows the description of argumentations at different levels of detail. This approach differs from Aberdein's (2006) as he reduces the complexity of the argumentation by a process of folding that results in a single step that includes all the assumptions (initial data and warrants) of the full argumentation, but which hides the relationships between these assumptions. Knipping's approach also differs from that taken by van Eemeren et al. (1987) who developed two different ways of representing the structures of everyday written argumentations, in that she makes the role of warrants more visible. We illustrate below how Knipping's method makes the global argumentation visible while preserving the relationships in the local steps.

Argumentation streams are combined to make up the global argumentation structure. To represent these structures, it is necessary to lose some information. The function of each element is retained but the details are not. Figure 1.7 shows how the argumentation stream in Fig. 1.6 is reduced to a schematic diagram (shown to the right).

These schematically represented streams are then combined to represent the global argumentation structure, as shown in Fig. 1.8. The shaded area is the argumentation stream shown in Fig. 1.6.

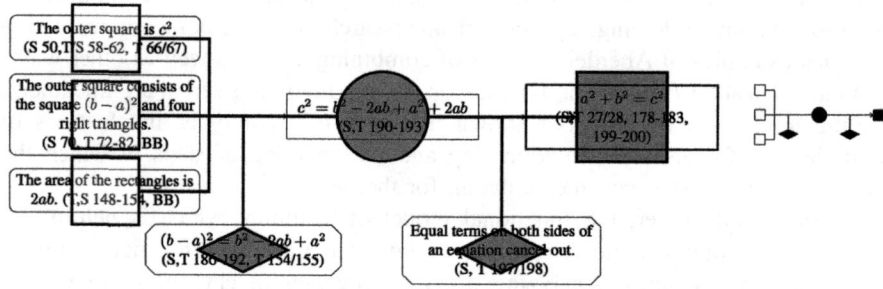

Fig. 1.7 The argumentation stream from Fig. 1.6 reduced to a functional schematic

Fig. 1.8 The argumentation structure of a classroom proving process

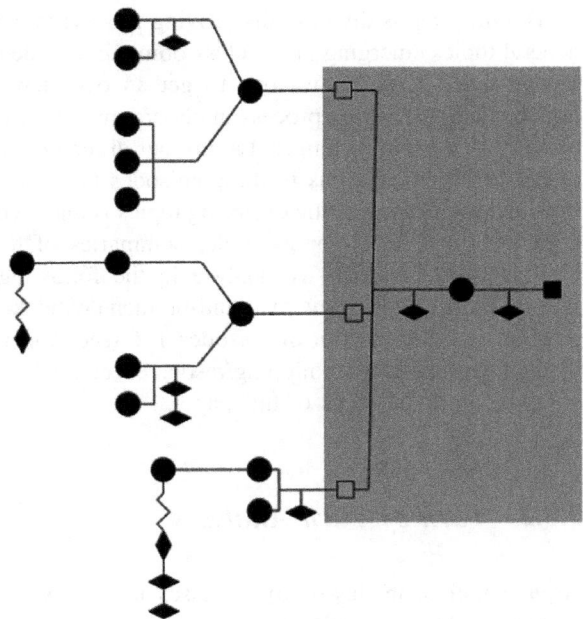

1.3 Reconstructing Arguments in Classrooms

To reconstruct arguments in classrooms we follow a three stage process:

1. reconstructing the sequencing and meaning of classroom talk (including identifying episodes and interpreting the transcripts);
2. analysing arguments and argumentation structures (reconstructing steps of local arguments and short sequences of steps which form "streams"; reconstructing the global structure); and
3. comparing local argumentations and comparing global argumentation structures, and revealing their rationale.

We illustrate below each of these stages by discussing episodes of a proving process that occurred in Ms. James' grade 9 (age 14–15 years) classroom in Canada. The class was trying to explain why two diagonals that are perpendicular and bisect each other define a rhombus. The students had discovered and verified empirically that the quadrilateral produced is a rhombus using dynamic geometry software.

1.3.1 Reconstructing the Sequencing and Meaning of Classroom Talk

Reconstructing the sequencing and meaning of classroom talk on proof and proving involves first dividing the proving process into episodes, followed by turn analysis of the transcript, identifying data, conclusions and warrants.

The first step is dividing the proving process into episodes. This means that the general topics emerging in the classroom talk are identified and their sequencing is reconstructed. This allows one to get an overview of the different steps in the argumentation. Proving process in classrooms can occur over long periods of time, from 20 to 40 min or longer. Laying out different episodes of the process helps to make the argumentations in these episodes more accessible to analysis. Once the flow and sequencing of the emerging topics is made visible the reconstruction of the arguments can start. For example, summaries of the episodes in the classroom proving process which we analyse in the following are reconstructed first (see Appendix A, http://www.math.uni-bremen.de/didaktik/ma/knipping/resources_en.html). The full transcript of episodes 1–6 (see Appendix B, http://www.math.uni-bremen.de/didaktik/ma/knipping/resources_en.html) is the basis for further analyses, which are the focus of this paper.

1.3.2 Turn by Turn Analyses

Argumentations in classroom processes are mostly expressed orally and by a group of participants. Generally arguments are produced by several students together, guided by the teacher. As Herbst showed (2002), it is the teacher who mostly takes responsibility for the structure and correctness of the argument, but students contribute to the argument, so there is a division of labour in the class. Argumentations are co-produced; the teacher and the students together produce the overall argument. Their turns are mutually dependent on each other; their public meanings evolve in response to each other. The argument forms in relation to these emerging meanings. So, in order to reconstruct the structure of an argument first the meanings of each individual turn put forward in class have to be reconstructed. As Krummheuer and Brandt state:

> Expressions do not a priori have a meaning that is shared by all participants, rather they only get this meaning through interaction. In concrete situations of negotiation the participants search for a shared semantic platform. [*Äußerungen besitzen "a priori keine von allen Beteiligten geteilte gemeinsame Bedeutung, sondern erhalten diese erst in der Interaktion. In konkreten Situationen des Verhandelns bzw. Aushandelns wird nach einer solchen gemeinsamen semantischen Bedeutungsplattform gesucht"*]. (2001, p. 14, our translation)

Because meanings emerge through interaction, reconstructing meanings necessarily involves some reconstruction of the process by which they emerge. Generally statements of classroom talk are incomplete, ambiguous and marked by deictic[1]

---

[1] In linguistics, a deictic term is an expression, for example a pronoun, that gets its meaning from its context. The meaning of "this" depends on what is being pointed to. The meaning of "I" depends on who is speaking. In philosophy the word "indexical" is used to express the same idea.

terms. Deictic terms are replaced as much as possible in the reconstruction of the argumentation. For example, in Episode 1 the following exchange occurs:

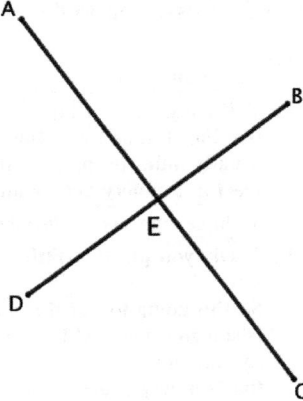

Fig. 1.9 The teacher's initial diagram (letters were not included)

Line	
1	T: [I am going to add] to my diagram [see Fig. 1.9] as I go. How do you usually indicate that two things meet at a ninety degree angle?
2	Multiple students: [indecipherable]
3	Teacher: Ok, you put that little square. So I'm going to put that in there [she marks angle AEB with a little square] and that's ninety degrees. Now if that's ninety, due to supplementary angles —
4	Multiple students: they're all ninety
5	Teacher: we know that they're all ninety. Good, thank you

Words like "that", "they" refer to objects that everyone involved knows the reference for, but for us in reconstructing the argument these references must be made explicit, so "that" in "if that's ninety" would be replaced by "angle ABC" or some other precise reference.

This exchange also includes an argument in which a statement is formulated as a question. The teacher's question "How do you usually indicate that two things meet at a ninety degree angle?" is answered by the students in a way the teacher reacts to by marking the ninety degree angle with a little square. We find that such exchanges occur often in classrooms. In the reconstruction of the argument we reconstruct such questions as statements, so that their grammatical form is no longer visible, but their function in the argument is clearer. For example, this exchange is reconstructed as the two statements "To indicate an angle is a 90° angle it is marked with a little square. (T-1-3)" and "Angle AEB is marked with a little square (T-3)".

Because the focus of the analysis is the argumentative structure of the classroom talk the reconstruction of the meanings of statements in the turn by turn analysis must consider the argumentative function of the statements: datum, conclusion, warrant, etc. These functions are identified in the next step of analysis. Utterances are primarily reconstructed according to their function within the collectively emerging argumentation, not with respect to subjective intentions and meanings as in interaction analyses. The reconstructed turns from the above exchange, and the functions assigned to them, are shown here:

	Actual utterances	Reconstructions	
1	T: [I am going to add] to my diagram [see Fig. 1.9] as I go. **How do you usually indicate that two things meet at a ninety degree angle?**	The diagonals are perpendicular (T-1)	D
2	Multiple students: [indecipherable]		
3	T: Ok, **you put that little square.** So **I'm going to put that in there** [she marks angle AEB with a little square] and **that's ninety degrees.** Now if **that's ninety, due to supplementary angles** —	To indicate an angle is a 90° angle it is marked with a little square. (T-1-3)	W
		Angle AEB is marked with a little square. (T-3)	C
		Angle AEB is a 90° angle. (T-3)	D
		"due to supplementary angles" (T-3)	W
4	MS: **they're all ninety**	All angles around E are 90° angles (MS-4)	C
5	T: we know that **they're all ninety.** Good, thank you	All angles around E are 90° angles. (T-5)	C

In Knipping's (2003, 2004) analyses of classroom processes focusing first on conclusions turned out to be an effective step in reconstructing argumentations. It is helpful to begin by identifying what statement the participants are trying to justify, the claim that gains the status of a conclusion by their argument. So, before actually analysing the complete argument we look for conclusions and claims. For example, in the short excerpt above, the statement "they're all ninety" made by the students in line 4 and repeated by the teacher in line 5, is a conclusion. Having identified this conclusion we can now look for the data and warrant leading to it.

In line 3 the teacher says "Now if that's ninety, due to supplementary angles" and then waits for the students to answer. Here we can identify a datum "that's ninety" and a warrant "due to supplementary angles". This can be diagrammed as shown in Fig. 1.10.

It is interesting that in this case both the warrant and the datum are given explicitly. Typically, reconstructed arguments in secondary level classroom proving processes are often incomplete, as was the case with the written proof in Fig. 1.4.

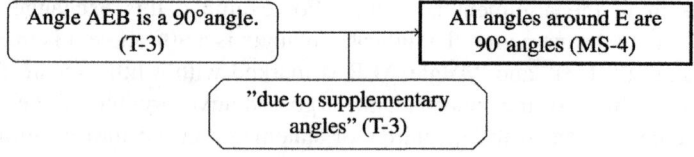

Fig. 1.10 Diagram of argumentation step in transcript lines 3–5

The warrant is often not given, but it can usually be assumed or taken as implicit, as the transition from datum to conclusion must be justified somehow. In our argumentation analyses we usually do not add implicit warrants, but leave them implicit in the reconstruction. This is meant to illustrate the implicitness of both the argumentation and warrant. This allows the comparison of the degree of explicitness in different argumentation structures. In cases where we do want to talk about an implicit warrant we place it in a dashed box (as in Fig. 1.5).

Readers may find it interesting to work through Appendix B at this point and attempt to identify in each turn statements that might be data, conclusions, and warrants.

1.3.3 Analysing Arguments and Argumentation Structures

In the following we describe in detail the moves in the reconstruction of local arguments, then of intermediate argumentation streams, and then of global argumentation structures. This method for reconstructing arguments, argumentation streams and argumentation structures was developed by Knipping (2003, 2008).

1.3.3.1 Functional Reconstruction of Local Arguments

Having identified statements that might be data, conclusions, and warrants in each turn, the next move is to group these statements together into argumentation steps. As noted above, warrants are often implicit, and it is rare to find backings. We occasionally come across arguments where the datum has been left implicit. In such cases the warrant is present, however, so in the reconstruction the datum is left implicit, and the argument consists of the warrant and the conclusion (see Knipping 2003).

Analysing students' and teachers' utterances in the class according to this functional model allows us to reconstruct argumentations evolving in the classroom talk. In our analyses only utterances that are publicly (in the class) accepted or constituted as a statement are taken into account. The teacher's attention to some utterances and deferment of others can play a major role in this. This is not surprising given Herbst's (2002) findings that in general only the teacher takes responsibility for the truth of statements. Where alternative argumentations or attempts at an argument are publicly acknowledged, they are also considered in our analyses, although the focus is on the main structure of the argumentation.

Episode 1 provides an example where we do not consider some arguments part of the main stream of the argumentation. In Fig. 1.11 the argument relates to a convention for showing mathematical properties in diagrams. In contrast, the argument in Fig. 1.10 includes statements about the properties themselves. Only the argument in Fig. 1.10 is later connected into the main structure of the

Fig. 1.11 Diagram of an argumentation step related to mathematical conventions in Episode 1

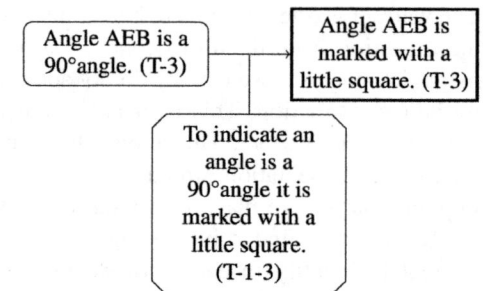

argumentation, and even in cases where the same statement occurs in arguments of both kinds (such as "Angle AEB is a 90° angle. (T-3)"), we do not connect them.

Above we indicate how to reconstruct local arguments or argumentation steps, as many researchers in mathematics education have done (see for example Inglis et al. 2007; Krummheuer and Brandt 2001; Fukawa-Connelly 2014). As the literature on reconstructing local arguments is already extensive and easily accessible we do not discuss this further here, but leave the interested reader to look up some of this literature. The reader may also wish to do a functional reconstruction of the local arguments in the transcript given in the appendix for this paper by themselves and we encourage readers to discuss their reconstructions with other researchers or more experienced colleagues. In the next section we move on to describing the process of reconstructing intermediate argumentation streams.

1.3.3.2 Functional Reconstruction of Intermediate Argumentation Streams

Having reconstructed individual steps in the argumentation, the next move is to link these together into streams, but looking for connections between them. Some connections may already have been noticed, for example when the same statement has been identified as both conclusion and as data, because it plays these two roles in two steps of the argumentation. However, it often occurs that these connections are hidden, because two equivalent statements made at two different times play these two roles, and until the equivalent statements are identified the connection remains hidden. For example, in Episode 3, lines 28 and 29, the teacher says "that is the same length as that, is the same length as that, is the same length as that" referring to the perimeter of the figure, and later "AB is equal to BC, is equal to CD, is equal AD" referring to the same segments by name. If the first statement is identified as data leading to the conclusion "Rhombus" and the second is identified as a conclusion of an argument based on congruent triangles, but they are not recognised as being equivalent, then the connection between two steps in the argument may not be made.

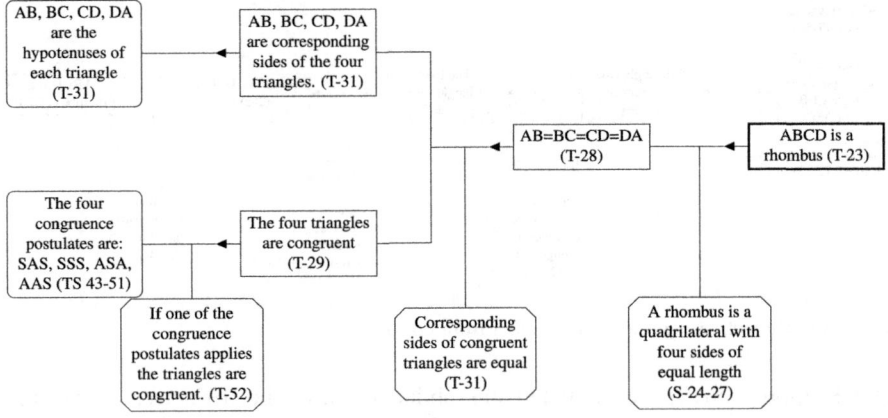

Fig. 1.12 Abductive argumentation stream from episodes 3-5

28	T: four sides of equal length. If I can prove that is the same length as that, is the same length as that, is the same length as that [refers to the perimeter of figure]. If I can prove that, I'm done. Rhombus
29	T: So that's your goal. To prove that and if you want, you can throw in some letters, prove that AB is equal to BC, is equal to CD, is equal AD. Now every single time we did one of these proofs we were looking for congruent triangles. Because if those triangles in that shape are congruent, what would we know about their sides?

These lines also provide an example of a difficulty that emerges in argumentations generally, that of deciding the level of detail that is needed. The statement "AB is equal to BC, is equal to CD, is equal AD" can be interpreted as three statements: "AB is equal to BC", "BC is equal to CD", "CD is equal to AD". Whether it makes sense to do so depends on how this statement is used elsewhere. In our reconstruction of this proving process, we tried fitting both interpretations of the statement into argumentation streams, before deciding that it was used as a single statement in the argumentation.

Figure 1.12 shows the reconstructed argumentation stream that occurs in episodes 3-5. This stream is interesting because the statements that occur first, on the left, were made last, and vice versa. In classroom proving processes such an abductive stream sometimes occurs, where the argument goes backwards from the intended conclusions to the data needed to deduce that conclusion. For a general description of abductive reasoning see Reid (2018) and for references to other representations of abduction using the Toulmin scheme see Papadaki et al. (2019).

In the classroom contexts presented here there are linguistic markers of what is going on. Abduction is indicated by statements that begin for example with "If I can" (see transcript in Appendix B). The phrase "If I can" suggests that the speaker is thinking about establishing a statement that has not yet been established, but which could, if established act as data in the argument. Identifying abductions in argumentation is not simple. In prior analyses of this stream (for example in Reid

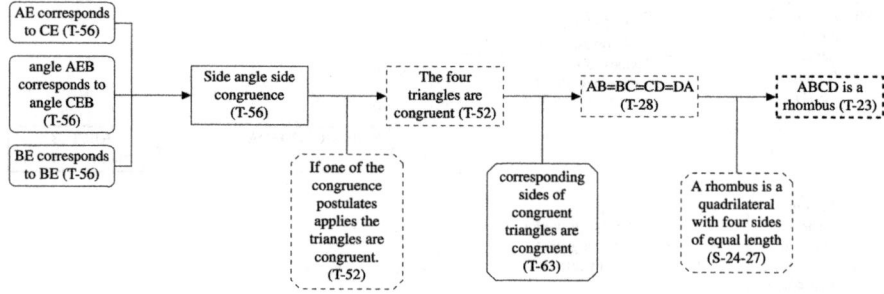

Fig. 1.13 Deductive argumentation stream from episode 6

and Knipping 2010) we conflated this abduction with the deductive stream that follows it, misled by the occurrences of the same statements in both streams. Deductive streams are much easier to understand and to recognise in classroom contexts. In a classroom proving process, where the main flow of the argument is deductive, it makes sense to diagram abductions as if they were deductions, but marking them with arrows showing the flow of the argument in the opposite direction.

Figure 1.13 shows the reconstruction of the deductive argumentation stream that corresponds to the abductive stream in Fig. 1.12. The starting data in Fig. 1.13, from transcript line 56, corresponds to the data hypothesised at the chronological end of the abduction, from transcript lines 43–51. In the deductive stream some steps are left implicit (marked with dashed outlines) as they have already been stated during the abductive stream.

In this section we demonstrate the reconstruction of argumentation streams. Looking for connections between local arguments, i.e., individual steps in the argumentation, reveals connected streams of argumentation. These can be of different types, as we show above. Abduction and deduction are two examples which illustrate that the functional reconstruction of arguments incorporates far more than just the restoration of logically sound deductive arguments. This illustrates the utility of Toulmin's functional model for reconstructing arguments. Because he set out to produce a model of argument that was flexible enough to capture many different types of argument, his model can be used in many different situations.

It can be difficult to observe and represent deductive arguments arising in students' talk or classroom discourses. Revealing and portraying abductions is generally considerably harder as we note above. Both lead to an understanding of different *schemes* of argumentation (as discussed by Godden and Walton 2007; Knipping and Reid 2013; Metaxas et al. 2009, 2016; Metaxas 2015; Aberdein forthcoming; Walton and Reed 2005). In the next section we look at how reconstructing the global argumentation structures of proving processes in classrooms can also lead to understanding different types of argumentation schemes.

1.3.3.3 Reconstructing the Argumentation Structure of Proving Processes in Class

The argumentation streams shown in Figs. 1.12 and 1.13 and those containing the steps shown in Figs. 1.10 and 1.11, as well as those for episodes 7–10, can be combined into a global argumentation structure, shown in Fig. 1.14. Small shapes (rectangles, circles and diamonds) correspond to the shapes used in representing argumentation streams so that corresponding statements can be identified, and more importantly, so that the function of each statement in the argumentation is clear. The colouring of the shapes can indicate statements with special functions, for example, here white rectangles represent initial data and in Fig. 1.8 they represent target conclusions of intermediate stages within the global argumentation.

The two regions marked in grey are the argumentation streams shown in Figs. 1.12 and 1.13. The wavy line connecting the two grey regions shows two equivalent statements discussed above, from transcript line 56 and transcript lines 43–51, where the abduction triggered the deduction.

As is usual for classroom proving processes, this argumentation structure is complex. Three parallel argumentation streams lead to the conclusion "AB = BC = CD = DA" from which the final conclusion is drawn. A fourth argument, proposed by one of the students, leads directly to the conclusion "ABCD is a rhombus", but this faulty argument was refuted by the teacher (shown by a zigzag, see Reid et al. 2011).

Representing argumentation structures, classifying and analysing them is not the end goal of this method. As in Knipping (2003) the goals is to compare

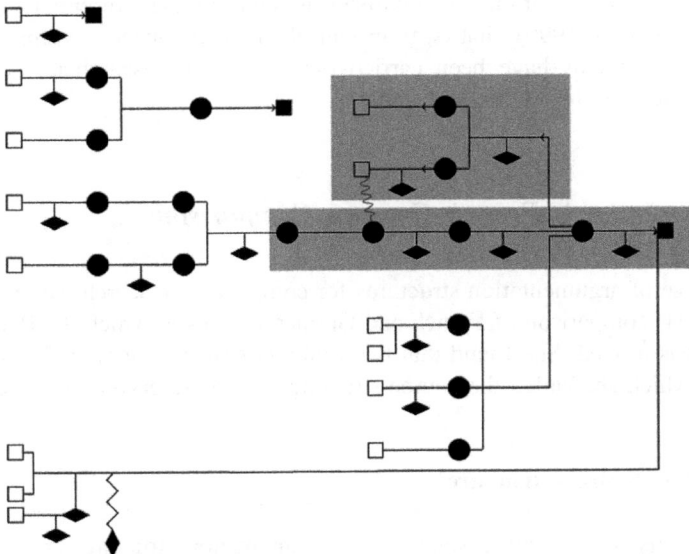

Fig. 1.14 The global argumentation structure in Ms James' lesson

argumentation structures in order to reveal differences in the rationale of proving (and other argumentation) processes in mathematics classrooms. Comparison of these structures can reveal, for example, differences in the goals of the teaching, that might not have otherwise been observed. In the next section we examine several such comparisons of argumentation structures in more detail.

1.4 Comparing Argumentation Structures and Revealing Their Rationale

A goal of reconstructing global argumentation structures is comparing the structures that are observed in different contents in order to reveal differences in the goals of teaching, in the nature of the warrants accepted, or other aspects of the context of the argumentation. In other words, the goal of analysing argumentation structures is not only to understand better the nature of argumentation in mathematics classrooms but also to better understand mathematics classrooms overall.

Krummheuer (2007) considers comparison as a methodological principle that provides a reliable method of revealing characteristics of teaching in mathematics classrooms. As with Glaser and Strauss (1967), for Krummheuer comparative analysis represents a central activity that allows empirical control of the heuristic generation of theory. In this approach comparisons occur continuously, "the comparison of interpretations of different observed parts of reality represents a main activity on nearly every level of analysis: from the first interpreting approach to the later more theoretical reflection" (Krummheuer 2007, p. 71, describing Strauss and Corbin 1990). The aim of these comparisons is "conceptual representativeness" (see Strauss and Corbin 1990), that is, to ground theoretical concepts within the data.

Such comparisons have been carried out by several researchers, and in this section we review their work and findings.

1.4.1 Knipping's French-German Comparison

The first use of argumentation structures for comparative research was Knipping's (2003, 2004) comparison of French and German lessons in which the Pythagorean theorem was proved. She found that two different structures emerged in these two contexts, which she called the source-structure and the reservoir-structure.

1.4.1.1 The Source-Structure

In proving discourses with a source-like argumentation structure, arguments and ideas arise from a variety of origins, like water welling up from many springs.

The teacher encourages the students to formulate conjectures that are examined together in class. In some cases this means that students propose conjectures that are unconnected to the overall structure. More than one justification of a statement is appreciated and encouraged by the teacher. This diversity of justifications results in an argumentation structure with parallel streams in which intermediate statements are justified in various ways. False conjectures are eventually refuted, but they are valued as fruitful in the meantime. In argumentations with a source-structure a funneling effect becomes apparent. Towards the end of the argumentation only one chain of statements is developed in contrast to the beginning where many parallel arguments are considered. The structure has these characteristic features:

- Parallel arguments for the same conclusion.
- Argumentation steps that have more than one datum, each of which is the conclusion of an argumentation stream.
- The presence of refutations in the argumentation structure.

The source-structure is also characterised by argumentation steps that lack explicit warrants or data. While this also occurs in the other types of argumentation structure, it is frequent in the source-structure.

In Fig. 1.15 the typical features of the source-structure are evident. There are parallel arguments for the same conclusion (AS-1 and AS-2; AS-3 and the first part of AS-5), there are argumentation steps that have more than one datum (AS-8), and there are refutations (in AS-3 and AS-6, marked ↯).

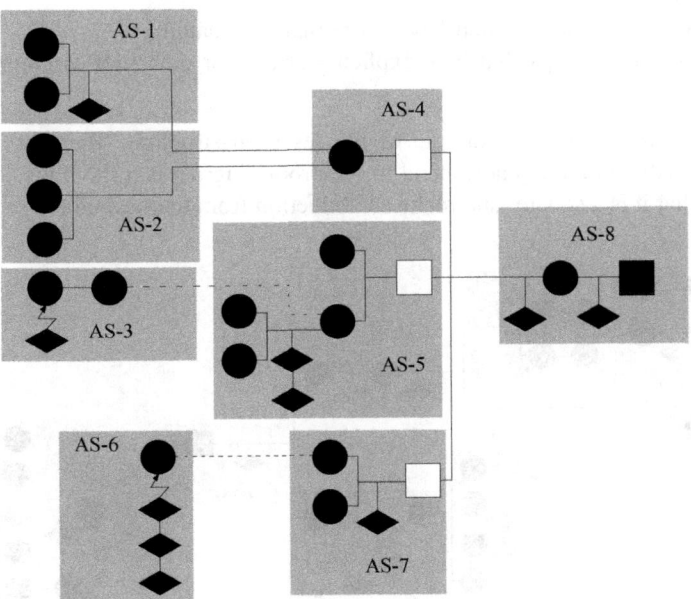

Fig. 1.15 The source-structure in a German classroom (Reid and Knipping 2010, p. 185)

1.4.1.2 The Reservoir-Structure

Argumentations with a reservoir-structure flow towards intermediate target-conclusions that structure the whole argumentation into parts that are distinct and self-contained. The statements that mark the transition from the first to the second part of the proving discourse (shown as rectangles) are like reservoirs that hold and purify water before allowing it to flow on to the next stage. Most of the features listed above as characteristic of the source-structure are missing in the reservoir-structure, with the exception of argumentation steps which have more than one datum each of which is the conclusion of an argumentation stream. Argumentation steps that lack explicit warrants or data occur, but less often than in the source-structure.

The most important feature of the reservoir-structure, which distinguishes it from a simple chain of deductive arguments, is that the reasoning sometimes moves backwards in the logical structure and then forward again. Initial deductions lead to desired conclusions that then demand further support by data. Through an abduction possible data are identified that, if they could be established, would lead to the desired conclusion (indicated by the dashed line in Fig. 1.16). Once these data are confirmed further deductions lead reliably to the desired conclusion. This characterizes a self-contained argumentation-reservoir that flows both forward towards, and backwards from, a target-conclusion.

In summary, the reservoir-structure has these characteristic features:

- Abductive steps to identify data from which desired conclusions can be deduced.
- Argumentation steps which have more than one datum.
- Argumentation steps that lack explicit warrants or data (not as common as in source-structure).

Figure 1.16 shows an example of the reservoir-structure. The class has concluded (in AS-1) that a quadrilateral in the proof diagram is a rhombus. They wish to prove that it is a square, and make an abduction from the desired result that it is a

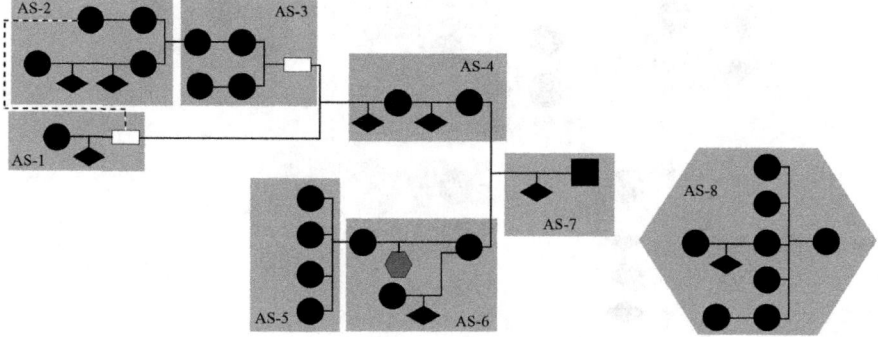

Fig. 1.16 Reservoir-structure from a French classroom (Reid and Knipping 2010, p. 186)

square, the datum that it is a rhombus, and the general rule that if a rhombus has a right angle it is a square, to conclude that the quadrilateral should have a right angle. This becomes the target-conclusion in the argumentation streams AS-2 and AS-3. The three streams AS-1, AS-2 and AS-3 form a reservoir in which the argumentation remains until it is sufficiently clarified to proceed. A closed structure can also be found in the second part of the process, formed by AS-5, AS-6 and AS-7. In contrast to the reservoir in the first part, the argumentation in the second part only flows forwards.

1.4.1.3 Comparison

Knipping found the reservoir-structure in all three of the mathematics lessons she observed in France, and the source-structure in all three of the classrooms she observed in Germany. She concluded that different classroom cultures exist when proving the Pythagorean Theorem. She hypothesised that these differences are due to different cultural traditions of reasoning.

In the German context she characterized that approach to proving as more *intuitive-visual*, in which the teacher does not want to break the proof down into deductive parts, but wants the students to come to their own understanding starting from the figure given. The teacher wants them to *see* the general statement, including its justification, from the given proof figure. In the complete proof discourse she encourages the students to make up their own arguments. This means their conjectures and different arguments are valued as fruitful and discussed in public.

She characterized the proving processes in the French classrooms as more *conceptual*. In these argumentations the conclusions are deduced from concepts. Data can be illustrated and formulated on the basis of figures, but the conclusions drawn from them are arrived at conceptually. The giving of reasons, i.e. warrants or backings, is central in this kind of argumentation. These lead to conclusions that can be recycled, i.e. used in the next argumentation step as data.

1.4.2 Knipping and Reid's Spiral Versus Source Comparison

Knipping and Reid (2013) compared a structure they observed in a Canadian classroom (the same one analysed above) with the source-structure Knipping observed in the French classrooms. They call this new structure a spiral-structure.

1.4.2.1 Spiral-Structure

In a proving process with a spiral argumentation structure the final conclusion is proven in many ways. First one approach is taken, then another and another. Each approach can stand on its own, independent of the others. Students suggest some approaches and the teacher proposes others. Faulty arguments may be refuted by students or the teacher. Some student contributions do not lead to the conclusion and result in disconnected argumentation streams.

The global argumentation structure depicted in Fig. 1.17 shows the spiral argumentation structure from Ms James' class as Knipping and Reid presented it in 2010. Note that there are several changes in comparison to the structure for the same lesson, shown in Fig. 1.14. Most significantly, the abductive stream was not observed in the earlier analysis. In both figures, however, several features characteristic of the spiral argumentation structure are evident:

- Parallel arguments for the same conclusion (AS-B, AS-D, AS-E).
- Argumentation steps that have more than one datum, each of which is the conclusion of an argumentation stream (the final conclusions of AS-B and AS-E).
- The presence of refutations in the argumentation structure (AS-D).
- Argumentation streams that do not connect to the main structure (AS-C).

Both the source-structure and the spiral-structure were observed in classrooms where a teacher took a prominent role in guiding the students through a proving processes. Therefore, it is not surprising that these argumentation structures have several similar characteristic features, including parallel arguments, argumentation

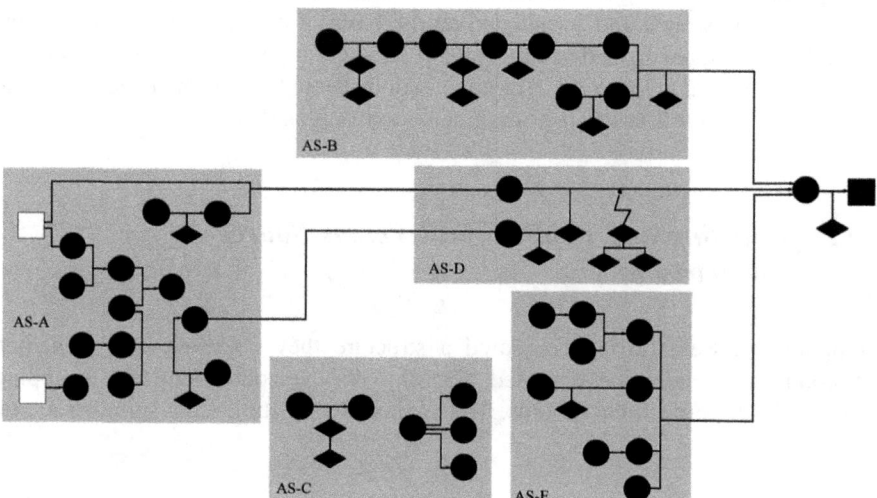

Fig. 1.17 Spiral-structure from Ms James' classroom (Reid and Knipping 2010, p. 188)

steps that have more than one datum, and the presence of refutations. However, a closer comparison reveals that they differ in how these features play out in the global structure.

1.4.2.2 Comparison

One of the main distinctions between the spiral-structure and the source-structure is the location of the parallel arguments. In the source-structure the parallel arguments occur at the start of the proving process (AS-1 and AS-2 in Fig. 1.15). The teacher invites input at this stage, but once the basis for the proof is established, the teacher guides the class to the conclusion through an argumentation that no longer has parallel arguments. In the spiral-structure, however, the conclusions of the parallel arguments are almost the final conclusion in the entire structure. In fact, two of the three parallel arguments in Fig. 1.17 (AS-B and AS-E) could stand alone as proofs of the conclusion. Having proven the result in one way, the teacher goes back and proves it again in a different way. And she values students' attempts to prove the conclusion using other approaches. The source-structure and the spiral-structure differ also in the kinds of refutations they involve and in the inclusion or omission of warrants.

Examining the argumentation structures in these two classrooms allows us to describe their characteristic features, and by comparing them we can understand the different ways these features occur. We see the parallel arguments, refutations and omitted warrants in both, but we see these features occurring differently. Looking more closely at the features of the local arguments helps to explain these differences, and reveals an important distinction between the rationales of the proving processes taking place. In the German classroom, we find in the local arguments a focus on interpreting the given figure. The activity is essentially one of unpacking the data in the figure and expressing it verbally. It is not clear how this could be transferred to proving another theorem, unless a similar complex figure were provided. We suspect this is inevitable in a class focussing on the Pythagorean Theorem.

In contrast, in Mrs James's class the focus is more on proving. The result itself is relatively uninteresting, but the recycling of conclusions as data, the provision of warrants, the fact that the same result can be proven in different ways, and bringing different prior knowledge to bear, are all important. Student contributions are valued, even when flawed, and the argumentation, especially in AS-B, served as a model for the students when proving similar claims in subsequent lessons.

The source structure and the spiral structure are interesting to compare because they have many characteristic features in common, including parallel arguments, argumentation steps that have more than one datum, refutations, and unconnected argumentation streams. There are differences in how these features play out in the global structures, however, and to explain these differences Knipping and Reid (2013) focus again on local arguments, and the goals of teaching.

1.4.3 Abductions in the Reservoir-Structure Versus Ms James' Lesson

As mentioned above, abductions are found in argumentations with a reservoir-structure, such as the one shown in Fig. 1.16. The re-analysis above of Ms James' lesson also revealed an abduction and it is interesting to compare them. In the lessons Knipping (2003) analyses that have a reservoir-structure, the abductions are fairly direct. The datum that is sought leads in a single step to the desired conclusion. However, the argument needed to establish the datum involves several steps. In contrast, the abduction that occurred in Ms James' classroom goes back several steps, to several possible congruence conditions that are quickly established. Once the needed data have been established, the deductions corresponding to the abductive steps are quickly done. In other words, in the French classrooms the abduction does not parallel most of the deduction that follows it. A datum is identified that in needed, and this becomes the target conclusion of an argumentation stream that begins from other, already known, data. In Ms James' lesson, however, the abduction involves several steps, and parallels closely the deduction that follows it. In fact, many statements in the deduction are left implicit because they have already been made provisionally in the abduction.

The abduction in Ms James' class could be seen as an example of what Boero et al. (1996) call 'cognitive unity' in which there is a strong link between an abductive process of conjecturing and a deductive process of proving the conjecture. In the argumentation we describe above, the abductive argumentation stream produces a conjecture: that one of the congruence postulate will apply to the triangles in the diagram. This conjecture is quickly verified, and then used to deduce several intermediate claims made in the abductive argumentation. Because the abduction has traversed the same arguments as the deductive stream, but in reverse order, very little new effort is needed to produce the deductive stream. As noted above, much of it can be left implicit because the statements needed have already been made.

1.4.4 Shinno's Research

Shinno (2017) analysed a lesson sequence on square roots that was intended to introduce irrational numbers in a ninth-grade classroom. Reconstructing the argumentation allowed him to obtain a deeper understanding of the process by which students come to a new concept of number. The global argumentation structure he reconstructed is shown in Fig. 1.18. In AS2 a square of area 10 is constructed geometrically. The conclusion of AS6 is that $\sqrt{10}$ is an irrational number. In AS5 the conclusion is that $\sqrt{10}$ cannot be expressed as a fraction. AS3 and AS4 establish that fractions can be expressed as repeating decimals and vice versa. The global argumentation structure has several features of a reservoir-structure, such as

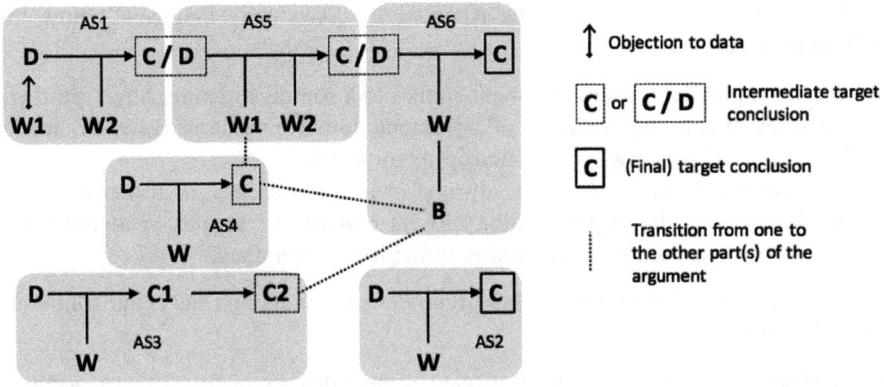

Fig. 1.18 Shinno's global argumentation structure (Shinno 2017, p. 199)

intermediate target conclusions, but also has arguments in support of warrants and backings, a feature only rarely present in the other structures. As Shinno notes "AS3 and AS4 can be considered as mathematical underpinnings for AS5 and AS6. These statements are essential for students to understand the meaning of the proof of irrationality of $\sqrt{10}$." (p. 199). What Shinno calls an "objection to data" in AS1, is a refutation of the datum "the solution of $x^2 = 10$ is 3.1622777" based on a warrant that the product of the final digits must be 0 for the square to be a whole number.

In comparing his global argumentation structure to those described by Reid and Knipping (2010) Shinno observed two novel features: arguments in support of warrants and backings, and the seemingly disconnected AS2, which is nonetheless important to the argument in some non-discursive way (p. 199).

1.4.5 Cramer's Comparisons

Cramer (2018) analyses the argumentations of a group of high school students working in a small group on a wide variety of tasks over a school year. This context allows her to compare the structures of their argumentations between tasks and over time. She categorises their argumentations into several categories, based on the obstacles faced by the students in participating in the argumentation. Her categories include: No real obstacles; Academic language, Rationality, Discourse-ethics.

In the category "No real obstacles" the argumentation diagrams have the following characteristics:

- The reasoning diagrams are rather long and warrants are often made explicit.
- Most learners are involved in the argumentation and the teacher does not play a major role.
- The structure can be characterized as a source-structure.

Argumentation structures in the category of "Academic language" show the following features:

- There are parallel lines of argument similar to a source-structure; however, there are often breaks within lines of argumentation. Refutations are often made. Warrants and backings are explicit in many cases.
- The target conclusions come always from the teacher and the teacher's involvement in the argumentation always consists of simple, scattered utterances. The wording of utterances is difficult to understand.

In the category "Rationality" the argumentation diagrams have the following characteristics:

- In many cases, there are unconnected arguments. Frequently, these occur in connection with refutations. The teacher and the students take responsibility for the argumentation to varying degrees.

Cramer's comparison of the argumentation diagrams in the "Discourse Ethics" category reveals the following properties:

- The arguments are rather short. Often refutations occur. Warrants are often left out.
- Many arguments are strongly guided by the teacher.

Cramer observes that refutations are discernible in most of the argumentation diagrams. She suggests that this can be seen as an indication that there is some confusion about the knowledge base the students had in common. The students evidently started partly from different assumptions. This may have been made the development of collective argumentation more difficult.

The argumentations analysed by Cramer (2018) illustrate in yet another way how argumentation structures can be of very different kinds in mathematics teaching and learning processes. They demonstrate the relevance and value of detailed reconstructions of argumentation structures, using the methods outlined above, based on and extending the Toulmin model.

1.4.6 Potari and Psycharis' Comparisons

Potari and Psycharis (2018) explore prospective mathematics teacher (PMT) argumentation while interpreting classroom incidents and find "different argumentation structures and types of warrants, backings and rebuttals in the process of PMTs' interpretations of students' mathematical activity." (p. 169). They compared PMT's argumentations to the source-structure and spiral-structure and adapted the methods described above to analyze PMTs' interpretations of critical incidents they identified when reflecting on lessons the PMTs observed or taught. These comparisons were enhanced by using Nardi et al.'s (2012) classifications of different types of warrants. Comparing argumentation structures allowed Potari and Psycharis to reveal potential shifts in PMTs' interpretations of classroom phenomena. They found that some of the teachers' argumentations have "… similar features as the spiral argumentation structure of Knipping and Reid (2015). This is because it involves parallel arguments that could stand alone leading to the final claims, warrants, and backings that adequately justify the claims, and refutations of the main claims." (p. 222). Comparing PMT's argumentations over time they saw different argumentation structures and types of warrants, backings, and rebuttals. The later argumentations were richer and the PMTs could support their claims in different independent ways. So the reconstruction of argumentation structures and types allowed the researchers to describe PMTs' developments in teacher education over time.

1.4.7 *Papadaki, Reid and Knipping's Comparisons*

Papadaki et al. (2019) compare the role of abduction in the argumentations structure from Ms James' class (described above) to the abductions that occurred in a geometry teaching experiment in Papadaki's research (2017). While in both cases the students involved were using dynamic geometry software to generate conjectures and then engaging in argumentations in a whole class context, the main foci of the lessons were quite different and this is reflected in the argumentation structures. Is Ms James' class, the abduction occurs as part of a mainly deductive proving process. Producing a proof is the goal of the lesson and the abduction is used to identify data needed in the proof. In Papadaki's research, however, the process is primarily one of making conjectures, which can be supported but not proven. The task the students were given asks them to make a hypothesis, and does not provide a framework in which they could prove their hypotheses. The abduction is used to arrive at hypotheses, from which some consequences are deduced. The only proofs that are produced are disproof of false hypotheses. Hence, the overall argumentation is abductive with deductive elements. One consequence of this, visible in the argumentation structures, is that the looping seen in Fig. 1.14, resulting from the backward flowing abductions, does not occur in Papadaki's structures. The flow of the argumentation is all in one direction, whether it is deductive or abductive.

1.5 Concluding Remarks

Proving processes in mathematics classrooms follow their own peculiar rationale, which raises the question of how to reconstruct and analyse the complex argumentative structures that arise in classroom discussion. Toulmin's functional model of argument allows us to reconstruct arguments in mathematics classrooms at the local level, and above we described how these local arguments can be connected together into a global structure. By comparing these argumentation structures we can describe their characteristic features, and understand the different ways these features occur. Attention to both the local and the global levels are essential to understanding proving processes in the classroom. Examining argumentation structures provides a tool to better understand the different ways in which teachers teach proof in actual classrooms and how students in those classrooms come to an understanding of proof and proving.

The value of looking at the production of arguments in class has been recognised in mathematics education for some time (at least since Krummheuer 1995) as a way of bringing to light the relevance of argumentation for learning processes in general and for mathematics learning in particular. In this chapter, we reference a range of recent research in the area of argumentation analyses in mathematics education that makes use of the methods we describe. This research illustrates the value of reconstructing argumentation and argumentation structures in classroom contexts, as a way of looking at teaching and learning processes. In this chapter we attempted to tease out particularly the value of reconstructing argumentation structures and comparing these structures. The recent research in this area allows us to get deeper insights into a variety of significant fields in mathematics education, for example,

- students' processes of learning and understanding concepts (see e.g., Shinno, Papadaki)
- learning and teaching proving in the mathematics class (Knipping and Reid, Cramer)
- interpretation of classroom phenomena by teachers and their developments in this respect (Potari and Psycharis, Erkek and Bostan).

The focus on reconstructing and comparing argumentation structures in recent years has pushed the research in all these areas forward towards a deeper understanding of students' and teachers' practices. It has also pointed at areas and points that require further attention and research. For example, the relation between abduction and deduction, which has been researched by our Italian colleagues for a long time (see Boero et al. 1996) within the theoretical frame of cognitive unity, can be examined from a new perspective in view of comparative studies of argumentation structures. Also, our comparisons demonstrate that abduction can play different roles in argumentation, which has been clear for a long time in the philosophical and linguistic literature (see, e.g., Eco 1983). Yet it makes a difference to show empirically that significant qualitative differences between roles of abduction occur in classrooms, and that abduction occurs at times when we did not particularly expect it.

Another recent trend in mathematics education has been to look at argumentation schemes (Metaxas et al. 2016). Colleagues call for using theoretical frameworks from other fields, e.g., linguistics, rhetoric, philosophy, and so on, to develop theoretical categorisations of "argumentation schemes" for analysing argumentation processes in the context of mathematics learning and teaching. The examination of argumentation schemes has been a tradition in rhetoric and philosophy for hundreds or thousands of years. Recently this tradition has been rediscovered in the philosophy of mathematics. Specifically, a branch called the philosophy of mathematical practice has evolved in the last two decades (we are thinking of the work of Bart van Kerkhove, Andrew Aberdein, and others). Working with argumentation theory, communication theory and pragmatics this philosophy of mathematical practice has developed very promising new frameworks to look at mathematical practices. These researchers are also engaging in interdisciplinary work with mathematics educators (see Aberdein and Dove 2013; Inglis and Aberdein 2014; Aberdein forthcoming). This seems to be a very fruitful and promising direction for future research.

References

Aberdein, A. (2019 forthcoming). Evidence, proofs, and derivations. *ZDM Mathematics Education, 52*(4).

Aberdein, A. (2006). Managing informal mathematical knowledge: Techniques from informal logic. In J.M. Borwein, & W.M. Farmer (Eds.), *Mathematical knowledge management* (Vol. 4108, pp. 208–221). Lecture notes in artificial intelligence. Berlin: Springer.

Aberdein, A., & Dove, I. J. (Eds.). (2013). *The argument of mathematics*. New York: Springer.

Arzarello, F., & Sabena, C. (2011). Semiotic and theoretic control in argumentation and proof activities. *Educational Studies in Mathematics, 77*(2–3), 189–206.

Ayalon, M., & Even, R. (2016). Factors shaping students' opportunities to engage in argumentative activity. *International Journal of Science and Mathematics Education, 14*(3), 575–601.

Boero, P., Garuti, R., Lemut, E., & Mariotti M.A. (1996). Challenging the traditional school approach to theorems: A hypothesis about the cognitive unity of theorems. In L. Puig & A. Gutierrez (Eds.), *Proceedings of the Twentieth Conference of the International Group for the Psychology of Mathematics Education* (Vol. 2, pp. 113–120). Valencia, Spain: PME.

Conner, A., Singletary, L. M., Smith, R. C., Wagner, P. A., & Francisco, R. T. (2014a). Teacher support for collective argumentation: A framework for examining how teachers support students' engagement in mathematical activities. *Educational Studies in Mathematics, 86*(3), 401–429.

Conner, A., Singletary, L. M., Smith, R. C., Wagner, P. A., & Francisco, R. T. (2014b). Identifying kinds of reasoning in collective argumentation. *Mathematical Thinking and Learning, 16*(3), 181–200.

Cramer, J. (2018). *Mathematisches Argumentieren als Diskurs: Eine theoretische und empirische Betrachtung diskursiver Hindernisse*. Wiesbaden: Springer Spektrum.

Duval, R. (1995). *Sémiosis et pensée humaine. Registres sémiotiques et apprentissages intellectuels*. Bern: Peter Lang.

Eco, U. (1983). Horns, hooves, insteps: Some hypotheses on three types of abduction. In U. Eco & T. Sebeok (Eds.), *The sign of three: Dupin, Holmes, Peirce* (pp. 198–220). Bloomington, IN: Indiana University Press.

Fukawa-Connelly, T. (2014). Using Toulmin analysis to analyse an instructor's proof presentation in abstract algebra. *International Journal of Mathematical Education in Science and Technology, 45*(1), 75–88.

Garuti, R., Boero, P., & Lemut, E. (1998). Cognitive unity of theorems and difficulty of proof. In A. Olivier & K. Newstead (Eds.), *Proceedings of the 22nd Conference of the International Group for the Psychology of Mathematics Education* (Vol. 2, pp. 345–352). Stellenbosch: University of Stellenbosch.

Glaser, B. G., & Strauss, A. L. (1967). *The discovery of grounded theory: Strategies for qualitative research*. Aldine: Chicago.
Godden, D., & Walton, D. (2007). Advances in the theory of argumentation schemes and critical questions. *Informal Logic, 27,* 267–292.
Herbst, P. G. (2002). Engaging students in proving: A double bind on the teacher. *Journal for Research in Mathematics Education, 33*(3), 176–203.
Inglis, M., & Aberdein, A. (2014). Beauty is not simplicity: an analysis of mathematicians' proof appraisals. *Philosophia Mathematica, 23*(1), 87–109.
Inglis, M., Mejía-Ramos, J. P., & Simpson, A. (2007). Modeling mathematical argumentation: The importance of qualification. *Educational Studies in Mathematics, 66,* 3–31.
Knipping, C. (2003). *Beweisprozesse in der Unterrichtspraxis: Vergleichende Analysen von Mathematikunterricht in Deutschland und Frankreich*. Hildesheim: Franzbecker Verlag.
Knipping, C. (2004). Argumentations in proving discourses in mathematics classrooms. In G. Törner et al. (Eds.), Developments in mathematics education in German-speaking countries. Selected Papers from the Annual Conference on Didactics of Mathematics, Ludwigsburg, 5–9 March 2001 (pp. 73–84). Hildesheim: Franzbecker Verlag.
Knipping, C. (2008). A method for revealing structures of argumentations in classroom proving processes. *ZDM Mathematics Education, 40,* 427–441.
Knipping, C., & Reid, D. (2013). Revealing structures of argumentations in classroom proving processes. In A. Aberdein & I. J. Dove (Eds.), *The argument of mathematics* (pp. 119–146). New York: Springer.
Knipping, C., & Reid, D. (2015). Reconstructing argumentation structures: A perspective on proving processes in secondary mathematics classroom interactions. In A. Bikner-Ahsbahs, C. Knipping & N. Presmeg (Eds.) *Approaches to qualitative research in mathematics education.* (pp. 75–101). Berlin: Springer.
Krummheuer, G. (1995). The ethnography of argumentation. In P. Cobb & H. Bauersfeld (Eds.), *The emergence of mathematical meaning: Interaction in classroom cultures*. Hillsdale: Lawrence Erlbaum.
Krummheuer, G. (2007). Argumentation and participation in the primary mathematics classroom: Two episodes and related theoretical abductions. *Journal of Mathematical Behavior, 26*(1), 60–82.
Krummheuer, G., & Brandt, B. (2001). *Paraphrase und Traduction. Partizipationstheoretische Elemente einer Interaktionstheorie des Mathematiklernens in der Grundschule*. Weinheim: Beltz.
Metaxas, N. (2015). Mathematical argumentation of students participating in a mathematics–information technology project. *International Research in Education, 3*(1), 82–92.
Metaxas, N., Potari, D., & Zachariades, T. (2009). Studying teachers' pedagogical argumentation. In M. Tzekaki, M. Kaldrimidou, & H. Sakonidis (Eds.), *Proceedings of the 33rd Conference of the International Group for the Psychology of Mathematics Education* (Vol. 4, pp. 121–128). Thessaloniki: PME.
Metaxas, N., Potari, D., & Zachariades, T. (2016). Analysis of a teacher's pedagogical arguments using Toulmin's model and argumentation schemes. *Educational Studies in Mathematics, 93*(3), 383–397.
Nardi, E., Biza, E., & Zachariades, T. (2012). 'Warrant' revisited: Integrating mathematics teachers' pedagogical and epistemological considerations into Toulmin's model for argumentation. *Educational Studies in Mathematics, 79,* 157–173.
Papadaki, C. (2017). Hide and think: Limiting the obvious and challenging the mind in geometry In *CERME 10-Tenth Congress of the European Society for Research in Mathematics Education* (pp. 706–713).
Papadaki, C., Reid, D., & Knipping, C. (2019). Abduction in argumentation: Two representations that reveal its different functions. In Presentation to TSG 1, CERME-11, Utrecht, NL. To appear in the proceedings.

Potari, D., & Psycharis, G. (2018). Prospective mathematics teacher argumentation while interpreting classroom incidents. *Educating prospective secondary mathematics teachers* (pp. 169–187). Cham, Switzerland: Springer.

Reid, D.A. (2018). Abductive reasoning in mathematics education: Approaches to and theorisations of a complex idea. *Eurasia Journal of Mathematics, Science and Technology Education, 14*(9), em1584. https://doi.org/10.29333/ejmste/92552.

Reid, D., & Knipping, C. (2010). *Proof in mathematics education: Research, learning and teaching*. Rotterdam: Sense.

Reid, D., Knipping, C., & Crosby, M. (2011). Refutations and the logic of practice. *PNA, 6*(1), 1–10. HANDLE: http://hdl.handle.net/10481/16011.

Shinno, Y. (2017). Reconstructing a lesson sequence introducing an irrational number as a global argumentation structure, In Kaur, B., Ho, W.K., Toh, T.L., & Choy, B.H. (Eds.). *Proceedings of the 41st Conference of the International Group for the Psychology of Mathematics Education* (Vol. 4, pp. 193–200). Singapore: PME.

Strauss, A., & Corbin, J. (1990). *Basics of qualitative research: Grounded theory procedures and techniques*. Newbury Park: Sage.

Toulmin, S. E. (1958). *The uses of argument*. Cambridge, UK: Cambridge University Press.

Tsujiyama, Y. (2012). Characterization of proving processes in school mathematics based on Toulmin's concept of field. In *Pre-Proceedings of ICME12*, (pp. 2875–2884).

van Eemeren, F. H., Grootendoorst, R., & Kruiger, T. (1987). *Handbook of argumentation theory: A critical survey of classical backgrounds and modern studies*. Dordrecht: Foris Publications.

Walton, D., & Reed, C. (2005). Argumentation schemes and enthymemes. *Synthese, 145*, 339–370.

Walton, D., Reed, C., & Macagno, F. (2008). *Argumentation schemes*. Cambridge: Cambridge University Press.

Yackel, E. (2001). Explanation, justification and argumentation in mathematics classrooms. In M. van den Heuvel-Panhuizen (Ed.), *Proceedings of the 25th International Conference on the Psychology of Mathematics Education* (Vol. 1, pp. 9–23). Utrecht: IGPME.

Open Access This chapter is licensed under the terms of the Creative Commons Attribution 4.0 International License (http://creativecommons.org/licenses/by/4.0/), which permits use, sharing, adaptation, distribution and reproduction in any medium or format, as long as you give appropriate credit to the original author(s) and the source, provide a link to the Creative Commons license and indicate if changes were made.

The images or other third party material in this chapter are included in the chapter's Creative Commons license, unless indicated otherwise in a credit line to the material. If material is not included in the chapter's Creative Commons license and your intended use is not permitted by statutory regulation or exceeds the permitted use, you will need to obtain permission directly from the copyright holder.

Chapter 2
Topic-Specific Design Research: An Introduction

Koeno Gravemeijer and Susanne Prediger

Abstract Design research has become a powerful research methodology of increasing relevance in mathematics education research. This chapter provides an overview and selected insights for novice researchers who want to find out if this research methodology is suitable for their own projects, and what possible research outcomes can look like. As topic-specificity is the feature that distinguishes didactical design research from generic educational design research, different models for topic-specific design research are presented.

Keywords Design research · Design experiment · Learning processes · Realistic mathematics education · Structuring the learning content

2.1 Introduction

Design research is a research methodology that has grown during the last 30 years, starting with early work in the 1980 and 1990s (Cobb and Steffe 1983; Gravemeijer and Koster 1988; Wittmann 1995; Artigue 1992; see Prediger et al. 2015, for a historical overview). In this chapter, we present its main ideas and common features, but also different versions of design research. We focus on topic-specific design research aiming at local instruction theories for different mathematical topics.

In this chapter, we present design research with its aims, common characteristics and usual procedures (Sect. 2.2) and offer insights into two example projects (Sect. 2.3). Section 2.4 provides categories for reflection on design research.

K. Gravemeijer (✉)
Eindhoven University of Technology, Eindhoven, The Netherlands
e-mail: koeno@gravemeijer.nl

S. Prediger
Technical University Dortmund, Dortmund, Germany
e-mail: prediger@math.uni-dortmund.de

© The Authors(s) 2019
G. Kaiser and N. Presmeg (eds.), *Compendium for Early Career Researchers in Mathematics Education*, ICME-13 Monographs,
https://doi.org/10.1007/978-3-030-15636-7_2

2.2 What Is Design Research?

2.2.1 Dual Aims and Common Characteristics

Design research combines *instructional design* (aiming at developing teaching-learning arrangements for classrooms) and *educational research* (aiming at investigating and understanding the initiated teaching learning processes, and what brings this process about). Instead of executing those activities in sequence, design-researchers perform both simultaneously and intertwine them in several cycles in order to reach the dual aims (Cobb et al. 2003; Kelly et al. 2008; Van den Akker et al. 2006).

Even if design research approaches can differ in their concrete realization, they usually share five common characteristics (Cobb et al. 2003; Prediger et al. 2015). They are

(1) *interventionist*, i.e., the intent of design research is to create and study new forms of instruction, in this sense, it must be intended to intervene in the classroom practices (interventionist) rather than just to involve observation of regular classroom practices (naturalistic);
(2) *theory generative*, i.e., the goal of design research is to generate theories about the process of learning and the means of supporting that learning (see above); generating theories here means both developing and refining theories in terms of inventing categories and generating hypotheses (but rarely 'testing hypotheses' in the narrow sense of experimental psychology);
(3) *prospective and reflective*, i.e., design experiments create conditions for developing theory (prospective), however, these theories are in turn the subject of critical examination (reflective);
(4) *iterative*, i.e., theory is developed in an iteration of cycles of conjecturing, testing, and revising;
(5) *pragmatic roots and humble theories*, i.e., design experiments accept the complexity of the classroom as a research setting, and theories are domain- or even topic-specific and are meant to have practical implications.

2.2.2 General Structure of a Design Experiment

These characteristics are realized by design experiments (Cobb et al. 2003). Very roughly speaking, what design researchers do in design experiments is not very different from what teachers do as reflective practitioners, but researchers combine this practice with theory development.

We may observe that what teachers do when teaching a lesson involves three kinds of activity:

- *preparing,* the teacher designs or selects instructional activities with an eye on the learning goals;
- *enacting,* the instructional activities are enacted and the teacher observes the students' actions and utterances with an eye on the intended learning process;
- *reflecting,* the teacher analyzes what has transpired in the classroom, contrasts this with what was anticipated, and revises or adapts the instructional activities.

Typically, reflective practitioners search for the best solution to a concrete practical problem (possibly in an action research mode, e.g., Breen 2003). In retrospect, they might ask themselves, what have I learned? However, teachers rarely start out with the aim of learning from a specific lesson. Moreover, if that would be a teacher's goal, he or she would have to consider how to facilitate reaching that goal, for instance, by explicating the goals and expectations about the learning process in advance, and considering how to keep track of the learning of the students and the factors that might influence that learning.

Likewise, these are important considerations for design researchers. In design research the overriding goal is to contribute to theory development that transcends an individual classroom or lesson. Design researchers may also aim at solving concrete problems, but the aims always include gaining insights into the learning processes, the means of support and typical obstacles and conditions of success (Cobb et al. 2003; Bakker and van Eerde 2015). As design researchers want to make a contribution to the scientific community, an additional feature comes to the fore, that of ensuring a sound empirical and theoretical basis as support for theoretical claims, which may emerge from the design experiment.

Summarizing, we may argue that at its core, design research resembles what reflective practitioners do when designing, enacting and reflecting on individual lessons. However, the goal of generating empirically grounded theory brings a host of demands that are not part of everyday teaching. We elaborate this point in the following, by showing how the three phases, preparing, enacting and reflecting, are worked out in design research.

Preparing for the Design Experiment

In preparation for the design experiment, the researchers need to clarify the learning goals and the instructional starting points, and to develop a conjectured, or provisional, local instruction theory. Such a local instruction theory includes theories about a possible learning process, and theories about possible means of supporting that learning process. Further decisions will have to be made about the theoretical intent of the design experiment and about data gathering and data analysis.

As a rule, the research team cannot simply adopt the educational goals that are current in a given domain—as in general these goals may be determined largely by history and tradition. The researchers will have to problematize the topic under consideration from a disciplinary perspective, search for the core ideas in the given domain, and establish what the most relevant or useful goals are (Gravemeijer and Cobb 2006).

In order to be able to develop a conjectured local instruction theory, one also has to consider the instructional starting points. The focus here is to understand the consequences of earlier instruction, upon which one can build in the further design experiment cycles.

Once the potential end points and the instructional starting points are established, the design research team can start to formulate the conjectured local instruction theory. The term *conjectured* is used as the expectation is that this theory will be revised under the influence of how the students' thinking and understanding evolves when the planned (and later revised) instructional activities are enacted in the classroom. Simon's (1995) conception of a hypothetical learning trajectory may serve as a paradigm here. The enactment of the instructional activities is always tightly interwoven with the envisioned classroom culture and the proactive role of the teacher, so this must be part of the planning as well.

We may further note, that even though one of the primary aims of a design experiment is to support the constitution of an empirically grounded local instruction theory, another aim might be to study classroom events as instances of more encompassing issues. Such issues are, for instance, the role of symbolizing and modeling or the proactive role of the teacher. In practice, this type of aim may be identified prior to the design experiment, during the experiment, or even afterwards.

As part of the preparation, decisions have to be made about the types of data that need to be generated in the course of the experiment. A general guideline here is that the data have to make it possible to address the issues that were identified as research goals at the start of the design experiment.

Next to data gathering one also has to consider how the data are to be interpreted. Here the theoretical frameworks may play a dual role. We may take the emergent perspective on the classroom culture (Yackel and Cobb 1996) as an example. On the one hand, the concepts of social norms and socio-mathematical norms reveal what norms to aim for in order to make the design experiment successful. On the other hand, the same framework offers an interpretative framework for analyzing classroom discourse and communication.

Enacting the Design Experiment

The second phase consists of actually conducting the design experiment. At the heart of the design experiment lies a cyclic process of (re)designing, and testing instructional activities and other aspects of the design. The scope of such a cycle may vary over research projects, from individual activities or lessons, to a complete course. In each cycle, the research team conducts an anticipatory thought experiment by envisioning how the proposed instructional activities might be realized in interaction in the classroom, and what students might learn as they participate in them. During the enactment of the instructional activities in the classroom, and afterwards, the research team tries to analyze the actual process of the students' participation and learning. On the basis of this analysis, the research team later makes decisions about the validity of the conjectures that underlay the instructional activities, and about the consequences for the next activity. This often also implies an adaptation of the local instruction theory.

Reflecting on the Design Experiment, the Retrospective Analysis

One of the primary aims of a design experiment is typically to contribute to the development of a local instruction theory. Other goals may concern more encompassing issues. The manner in which the retrospective analysis is conducted will vary, as differences in theoretical frameworks and objectives will result in differences in the retrospective analyses. Instead of trying to offer a general description, we return to this issue in the discussion of the cases presented as examples.

2.2.3 Differences Between Various Design Research Approaches

Most design research approaches can be subsumed under the three main steps of preparing, enacting, and reflecting, as sketched in Sect. 2.3, and exhibiting the five characteristics presented in Sect. 2.2. However, design research approaches take a large variability of forms, depending on their origin, their actual context, and the specific needs they are supposed to fulfill. Hence, literature of the last decades pays tribute to this variety (e.g., Kelly et al. 2008; Plomp and Nieveen 2013; Van den Akker et al. 2006, for educational design research in different domains). Surveying the field in mathematics education, Prediger et al. (2015) have classified the differences with respect to the following:

- *age groups*: These may vary from Kindergarten to university mathematics.
- *the reasons for doing design research:* Design research approaches vary in their prioritization of the dual aims, focusing more towards solving practical problems or more towards generating theory and understanding the teaching learning processes.
- *the type of results:* Depending on the prioritization of aims, the former purpose may aim at producing artifacts that can be used directly in classrooms. In contrast, the latter may aim at local instruction theories or more general insights, and is often embedded in a larger research program.
- *the scale of the design project:* This may vary from the nano level (of individuals and single tasks), through the micro level (classrooms and teaching units), the meso level (e.g. school-specific curriculum), the macro level (e.g. national syllabi or core objectives) up to the supra level (international or internationally comparative aspects), as specified by Van den Akker (2013, p. 55).
- *the background theory:* Finally, implicit or explicit *background theories* on teaching and learning will strongly influence both the conception and the results of research, e.g., socio-constructivism will lead to other decisions in design and analytic focus than a purely individualistic background theory.

Here, we add an additional source of variation, the degree to which the design research takes into account the *topic-specificity* of the instructional design and the research.

2.2.4 Striving for Topic-Specific Design Research Rather Than Only Generic Educational Design Research

Design research approaches are successfully applied in generic educational research as well as in different subject matter didactics, such as mathematics education research. The collection of 51 case studies involving design research (Plomp and Nieveen 2013) shows that both versions are insightful. Whereas generic design research projects mostly focus on specific design principles or design elements (e.g., How can the use of tutorial computer systems enhance students' motivation for independent work?), many subject matter education research projects pose more didactical questions, concerning the specific mathematical topics to be learned.

In topic-specific design research, which is the theme of this chapter, didactical issues are put at the center. These concern both the question of *how* to teach a given topic and the question of *what* should be taught and *in which structure* (i.e. sequencing order and sense making relations). These questions are treated in all three phases, starting with the preparation phase. It is important to emphasize that the choice of the topic itself is not an empirical question. But the empirical part of topic-specific design research can provide new insights into the structure of the topic to be learned (Hußmann and Prediger 2016). In the following sections, we explain what we mean by this kind of topic-specificity, because we consider it an important quality within the areas of subject matter research.

Apart from promoting topic-specific design research, we take the position that, in general, topic-independent principles must be enriched by very concrete, topic-specific design research striving for local instruction theory on the concrete topic. The design research aims at finding concrete ways of realization as well as specialized knowledge regarding typical, topic-specific learning and teaching processes, organized in hypothetical learning trajectories, as explained in Sect. 2.2.

Although some elements of the local theories are of course transferable to the next topic (e.g., from algebraic expressions to fractions), this transfer is usually investigated in a subsequent topic-specific design research project.

2.3 Learning from Examples of Topic-Specific Design Research

In this section, two projects are presented briefly, in order to provide insights into the processes and typical outcomes. Although sharing the topic-specificity (see Sect. 1.4) and the strong focus on learning processes (Prediger et al. 2015), these projects are different in terms of interesting aspects: Firstly, both examples offer guidelines for instructional design as a significant part of design research, although in different forms. Secondly, both examples have an open eye for what is happening in the design experiment, however, in significantly different ways. The second example on fruitful starting points and obstacles for students' learning pathways, focuses on what the underlying difficulties are and how those can be addressed, following a highly structured approach. The first example aims at developing a local instruction theory from scratch; there is no history of teaching this topic to the given age group. In this sense the research project is exploratory. It aims at finding out which opportunities arise and what possibilities emerge, what ingenuity the students bring to the table and how this can be utilized in the design of highly innovative instruction.

2.3.1 Exploratory Design Research—An Example Project for Instantaneous Speed in Grade 5

In this section, a design research project on instantaneous speed in 5th Grade, carried out as a Ph.D. study by de Beer (2016), is presented as an example of exploratory design research. The section starts with a brief introduction to the design research tradition in which this research project was embedded, namely, Realistic Mathematics Education (RME).

Realistic Mathematics Education as a Research Tradition

Design research in the RME tradition has its roots in Freudenthal's (1973) proposal to organize mathematics education as a process of guided reinvention. Analyzing instructional sequences that tried to do justice to this principle, Treffers (1987) formulated the domain-specific theory for realistic mathematics education implicit in those sequences. This theory was later cast in terms of three instructional design heuristics (Gravemeijer 2004), guided reinvention, didactical phenomenology, and emergent modeling—which are discussed later in this chapter.

The aim of RME is that students be enabled to construct their own mathematics under their own steam. However, the goal is not for the students to construct idiosyncratic mathematics; the mathematics the students construct has to be compatible with the conventional mathematics of the wider society. Thus the teacher has to support students in building on their own knowledge and ideas, while at the same time keeping an eye on the endpoints for which he or she is aiming. This goal points to an interactive process in which the teacher adapts to the students' thinking. To support such a process, RME design research aims at developing local instruction theories, which can function as frameworks of reference for teachers. On the basis of these frameworks, teachers may develop hypothetical learning trajectories (Simon 1995), tailored to their preferences, their goals and their classrooms. In line with this conception, RME design research aims at developing theory about student learning, together with theories about the means of support—such as instructional activities, tasks and tools, and a fitting classroom culture. Thus the goal in RME design research is not just the development of instruction that fits the idea of guided reinvention, for a given topic. Key is also to come to understand how that instruction works. In relation to this point we may observe that there are often a number of key insights that emerge during one or more research projects. Such insights may emerge in all three phases of a research project.

Being open to new insights is critical here. In relation to this openness, we may refer to Smaling's (1992) methodological conception of objectivity. Smaling (1992) argues that there are two components of objectivity, (1) avoiding distortion, and (2), *"letting the object speak"*. Design research aiming at new insights, relies heavily on the latter—of course without neglecting the need to avoid distortion.

As indicated above, a design research project on instantaneous speed in Grade 5 is presented here as an example of exploratory design research within this research tradition. This research project consisted of a series of design experiments, which were extensively reported on by de Beer (2016). Here, we do not describe the individual design experiments, but try to give a more general overview. We use the three phases of a design experiment to structure our elucidation, even though there were actually three design experiments, and thus for each experiment, three of cycles of preparation, enactment, and retrospective analysis, were completed.

Preparing for the Design Experiment on Instantaneous Speed

In the preparation phase, we established the starting points, the potential end points and the preliminary local instruction theory. In conventional education, instantaneous speed is approached by taking the limit of average speed for a time interval approaching zero. This is of course beyond the reach of primary school students. We therefore aimed at an informal conception of instantaneous speed. Following Kaput and Schorr (2007), we further inferred that interactive dynamic computer representations might offer support.

While preparing for the experiment, we drew on the RME instructional design heuristics concerning guided reinvention, didactical phenomenology and emergent modeling (Gravemeijer 1999).

Guided reinvention. Though there is a tradition in RME of describing goals as procedures in relation to the reinvention of algorithms, our interest has shifted towards mathematical relations and conceptual understanding (Gravemeijer in preparation). In case of the local instruction theory on speed, we may characterize the goal for the students as developing a framework of mathematical relations, which involve co-variance, tangent lines, rise-over-run, and eventually, speed as a variable. But at the start of the design experiment on instantaneous speed, it was not clear what would be within the reach of 5th grade students. The belief that understanding speed is closely linked to graphing, however, provided a clear direction for the design. When following the guided reinvention design recommendation to look at the history, we also found strong links between trying to come to grips with speed and the use of graphs. We further made a connection with a historical definition of speed, which preceded the notion of average speed.

Around 1335, William Heytesbury reasoned that one could define instantaneous speed on the basis of the distance that would be traveled if the speed would stay constant for a given period of time (Clagett 1959).

Didactical phenomenology. The didactical-phenomenology design heuristic advises the researcher-designer to look for the phenomena that are organized by the tool, concept, or procedure one wants the students to reinvent (Freudenthal 1991). In our case, the phenomenon of moving objects presents itself as an obvious candidate. As researchers, however, we were concerned that the students' use of the language learned at school in connection with motion might make it very difficult to establish the students' actual understanding of speed. Looking for an alternative we found various descriptions in the literature, of students reasoning about the speed with which the water level in glassware rises (e.g., Swan 1985). On the basis of this characterization, we inferred that they have a basic understanding of the relation between the width of the glass and the rising speed, and of the relation of the latter with the shape of the corresponding graph. In terms of the didactical phenomenology design heuristic, the changing water height became the phenomenon that could be organized by the tool (a graph), and the concept (speed) we wanted the students to reinvent.

Emergent modeling. The emergent modeling design heuristic was not elaborated at the start of the design experiment. Nevertheless, the idea that the visual representations of changing water heights had to play a central role, was already indicted by the other design heuristics. Modeling was given a more prominent place in the 2nd design experiment cycle, when we decided to integrate the idea of modeling-based learning. Consequently modeling changing water heights received a more prominent place. Gradually we started to realize that the initial model and the final model could respectively be described as _model of_ changing water heights, and, _model for_ reasoning about the rising speed (Gravemeijer 1999), while 'the' model could be loosely defined as 'visual representations of the filling process'.

Enacting the Design Experiment on Instantaneous Speed

As we felt we did not know enough of the students' starting points, we started with a number of one-on-one teaching experiments to get a sense of potential starting points. Those one-on-one teaching experiments showed us that the students were quite able to reason about cylindrical glasses. They realized that the water would rise with a constant speed, and they effortlessly drew linear graphs to illustrate this. With cocktail glasses of conic shape, however, they ran into problems. They initially believed that the water height in the cocktail glass would develop similarly to the cylindrical glass. When they were shown a computer simulation of how the glass filled up, they quickly realized that the rising speed slowed down when the water level went up. They also realized the logic behind it; as the glass got wider the rising speed would go down. As a rule, however, the students in the sample were unable to draw a seemingly correct graph. Our explanation for this was that the students had virtually no experience with drawing graphs. All they had was some experience with interpreting segmented line graphs.

Reflecting on these findings, we connected Heytesbury's idea of "speed staying the same" to the notion of constant speed. In other words, the (instantaneous) rising speed at a given point (at given width) in an arbitrary glass could be equated with the constant speed in a cylindrical glass of precisely that width. In line with this idea, we decided to ask the students, when the rising speeds in a cylindrical and a cocktail glass would be the same. Once this link was established, we would elaborate on it. The linear graph of the fitting cylindrical glass would not only show the speed at a point, but might also be developed as the tangent line at that point, with help of dynamic computer software (Fig. 2.1).

The end point we would be aiming for, therefore concerned the idea of the tangent line at a point of a height versus time graph, signifying the constant speed that would correspond with the instantaneous speed at that point.

Conceptually, the conjectured learning process starts from the students' informal understanding of instantaneous speed, builds on their insight that the rising speed at a given height is defined by the width of the glass at that height, deepens that insight by equating the instantaneous speed with a constant speed that corresponds with that width, and expressing this speed with a linear graph corresponding with a tangent line to the graph of water height versus time.

In deviation from the ideal of short micro-design cycles in which adaptations occur during each design experiment, adaptations were mainly made in between subsequent design experiments. The research conditions did not allow for changes on the spot. Moreover the design experiments had to be carried out in a limited series of lessons, as the topic of instantaneous speed was not part of the regular curriculum.

Because we were not clear about how the students were thinking in the first teaching experiment, we borrowed the idea of modeling-based learning (MbL) from science education (Louca and Zacharia 2012), which aims at engaging students in the socially mediated development and use of an explanatory model. In doing so, we tried to foster that the students would express their thinking with their models. This attention to modeling resulted in the second teaching experiment being better aligned with the RME design heuristic of emergent modeling.

The students were asked to make drawings that would show how the rising speed in a cocktail glass would develop, and next to improve on them. As expected, the students initially came up with realistic drawings that had the character of snapshots (Fig. 2.2).

Fig. 2.1 Computer software linking constant speed in an imaginary cylindrical glass with a tangent line

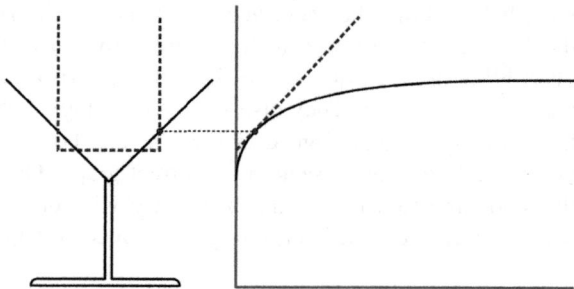

Fig. 2.2 One student's snapshots showing how the water level changed over time: "It goes up increasing more and more slowly"

In subsequent lessons the representations were discussed and the students were asked to make minimalist models with only the necessary elements to describe the situation. This resulted in a pivotal episode—on which we reported earlier (de Beer et al. 2015).

In a whole class discussion in one of the two classrooms in the 3rd design experiment, some students drew a segmented line graph on the white board to model how the water level changed over time (see Fig. 2.3).

When the teacher asked the class if they could find the speed in this graph, a student remarked that a straight line did not fit his understanding of how the cocktail glass fills up. He argued, that "it should go a bit bent", and he drew a curve (Fig. 2.4).

The student explained that at a certain moment, the graph would almost not rise any more. Reactions by other students in the classroom suggested that they agreed with this line of reasoning. The students in the parallel classroom did not come up with the idea of a curved graph by themselves. Here the teacher introduced the idea of shrinking the intervals in discrete graphs. On the basis of this suggestion, these students too came to see the curved continuous graph as an adequate model for

Fig. 2.3 Segmented line graph as a model of changing water heights

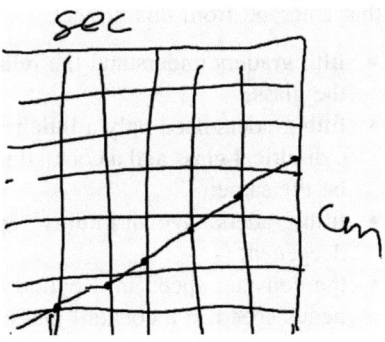

Fig. 2.4 Curve as improvement on the straight line

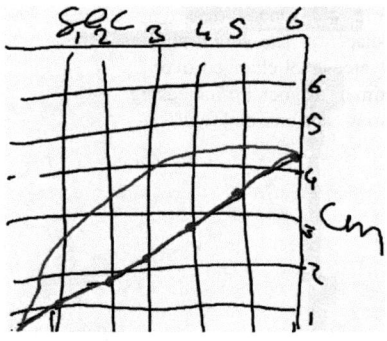

describing changing speed. In retrospect, we believe that the discrepancy between the segmented line graphs and the constantly diminishing speed may be exploited to support other students in reinventing the curved graph.

Retrospective Analysis

As explained above, abduction played an important role in the retrospective analysis (de Beer et al. 2015). The retrospective analysis was based on the comparative method of Glaser and Strauss (1967), and more specifically on the elaboration of this method by Cobb and Whitenack (1996). The analysis consisted of two steps: First formulating *conjectures of what happened* and testing those conjectures against the available data, and second, formulating *conjectures of why this happened*, which were also tested against the data. Although all data were taken into account, especially the transcriptions of whole-class discussions and the students' products proved valuable in formulating and testing conjectures.

This two-step analysis was carried out after each design experiment, each time the findings of the earlier experiment informed the following one, building on the conjectures that were corroborated, and revising conjectures that were rejected. The latter were used to improve the design, and to generate new explanatory conjectures. We do not have enough room to work out the potential local instruction theory that emerged for this design experiment. We do believe, however, that the gist of it can be deducted from the above account. A more detailed description can be found in the thesis of de Beer (2016). Instead, here we highlight the key insights that emerged from this project:

- fifth graders understand the relation between the rising speed and the width of the glass;
- fifth graders need only a little reflection time to realize that the rising speed in a cylindrical glass and a cocktail glass would be the same, when the widths would be the same;
- fifth graders have an intuitive conception of instantaneous speed, which can be deepened;
- the constant speed in a cylindrical glass may be used to specify the instantaneous speed in a cocktail glass;

- the tangent line signifying the instantaneous speed at a point of a water-height versus time graph, may be developed from the graph of the constant speed of a cylindrical glass with the appropriate width.

In light of the above findings we may speak of a fruitful series of design experiments. Even though the research was exploratory, the findings appear to have significant implications for the way speed is addressed in primary school. Currently the curriculum focuses on average speed, which results in a merely shaky understanding. The research, however, indicates that fifth grade students have an intuitive notion of instantaneous speed, which can be expanded. This result suggests that it might be advisable to shift the focus from average speed to instantaneous speed in primary school. Deepening the students' understanding of instantaneous speed should then be complemented with a more thorough treatment of constant speed than is now common. This challenge to the current school curriculum underscores the power of exploratory design research that adheres to the methodological prescription of "letting the object speak" (Smaling 1992). In concluding this section, we may further point to the central role of the RME instructional design heuristics in supporting the design work of the researchers.

2.3.2 Structuring Learning Trajectories—An Example Project on Exponential Growth for Grade 10

Exponential growth is one of the most complex topics in Grade 10, as students must connect all their knowledge about various models and representations for functional relationships (Confrey and Smith 1995). In this section, a design research project is sketched, which focused on a fine-grained analysis of which aspects are to be learned on exponential growth and how they can be structured into a learning trajectory (foundations of the project are given by Hußmann and Prediger 2016; further elaborated by Thiel-Schneider 2018).

The design followed the general design heuristic of emergent modelling (Sect. 2.1), starting from everyday experiences in meaningful contexts and developing the formal connections and their characteristics by horizontal and vertical mathematization (Gravemeijer 1999). However, little was known on how to structure the various aspects in the teaching-learning arrangement.

In the following, the general research framework and selected results from the project are presented. This example shows that although they refer to similar backgrounds, different concrete versions of topic-specific process-focused design research are possible and develop slightly different terminologies. We decided to keep the terminology that was used in the context of the research example under consideration.

Research Framework

The project was conducted within the FUNKEN-model of topic-specific Didactical Design Research that was developed within the FUNKEN-graduate-school for

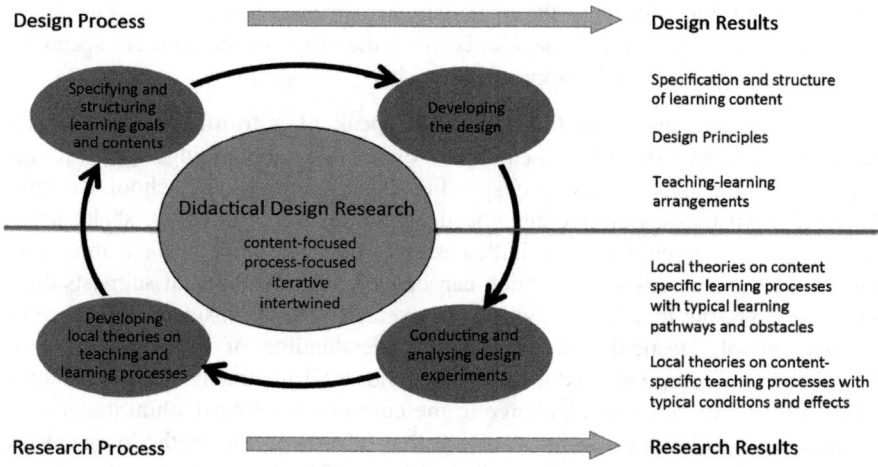

Fig. 2.5 Four working areas for topic-specific Didactical Design Research in the FUNKEN-model (Prediger et al. 2012; translated by Prediger and Zwetzschler 2013)

more than twenty design research projects in nine subject matter didactic disciplines (Prediger et al. 2012; Prediger and Zwetzschler 2013; following main ideas of Gravemeijer and Cobb 2006).

Like other design research approaches, the model relies on the *iterative* interplay between designing teaching-learning arrangements, conducting design experiments, and empirically analyzing the teaching-learning processes. Specific to the FUNKEN-model are the four working areas shown in Fig. 2.5, in which the three typical working areas (developing the design, conducting and analyzing the design experiments, and developing local theories) are enhanced by a forth one, *specifying and structuring the learning content,* which is often too implicit and which is a core focus of endeavour for each topic-specific project (see Sect. 2.4). As the framework is *content-focused* on topic-specific aspects, the specification and structuring of learning goals and content are treated as one of four *intertwined* working areas.[1]

Expected *research outcomes* consist of empirical insights and contributions to local theories on learning and teaching processes of the treated topic (here mainly for identifying fruitful starting points and explaining typical misconceptions on students' learning pathways concerning the topic of exponential growth) and hypotheses on necessary connections to be drawn in the learning trajectories. *Expected design outcomes* comprise the specified and structured mathematical

---

[1]The FUNKEN-model chooses the term working area instead of phases in order to highlight the iterative interplay and highly intertwined character of these areas, which cannot always be separated chronologically.

content (here exponential growth), the topic-specifically refined design principles (here for emergent modeling) and the prototypic teaching-learning arrangement.[2]

Leading Questions for the Specifying and Structuring the Learning Content

The working area of specifying and structuring the learning content has proven to be crucial also for many other Design Research projects within the FUNKEN graduate school (Prediger et al. 2012; Hußmann and Prediger 2016). The working area developed into a specific way to establish contributions to theory: although there is no schematic recipe for conducting it, the recurring questions listed in Table 2.1 can provide some guidance.

The prospective elaboration can start on the *formal level:* the concepts and theorems relevant for a topic are specified and the logical connections between them are explored for determining logically possible trajectories through the network of definitions and theorems. However, the didactical decision about a suitable instructional sequence of concepts and theorems cannot be determined purely on the formal level. Instead, the priority is on the *semantic level* on which the big ideas and basic mental models are identified and structured into a hypothetical learning trajectory. This work on the semantic level is informed by design principles such as horizontal and vertical mathematization. The semantic level is elaborated iteratively together with the *concrete level* (in which the sequence is realized in a teaching learning arrangement based on suitable contexts and instructional activities) and the *empirical level* which draws upon the design experiments and their retrospective analysis. Hence, the prospective elaboration encompasses the formal, semantic and concrete levels, the retrospective analysis encompasses the empirical, concrete and semantic levels, each tightly interwoven and oriented to the questions in Table 2.1.

Specifying and Structuring on the Formal, Semantic, and Concrete Levels for the Topic of Exponential Growth

For the design research study on exponential growth explored by Hußmann and Prediger (2016), Thiel-Schneider (2018) for Grade 10, characterizing the topic as exponential growth rather than as exponential functions is already a decision on the *semantic level*: Exponential functions should be treated in modelling contexts, following the *big idea* of functions as describing and predicting processes and changes (cf. Schweiger 2006). Hence, the basic mental models contain those of functional relationships, the correspondence model (each x corresponds to a y, e.g., for each year, the stock of a measure can be determined) and the covariation model (asking for the variation in y when x varies, e.g., the change of the measure per month) (Confrey and Smith 1995).

---

[2] In the FUNKEN-model, the terminology was slightly adapted: as the structured learning content is not always a unidimensional hypothetical trajectory, this term is chosen to distinguish the pure structure of the content from its realization by tasks and support means in the teaching-learning arrangement. The local theory is not called local instruction theory but local theory on teaching and learning processes in order to avoid the misunderstanding that instruction is restricted to teaching.

Table 2.1 Typical questions on four levels for specifying and structuring the content (without assuming completeness) (Hußmann and Prediger 2016)

		Specifying the content (selecting aspects and their backgrounds)	Structuring the content (relating and sequencing aspects, including connecting points for long-term processes)
Prospective Elaboration	Formal level	• Which concepts and theorems have to be acquired? • Which procedures have to be acquired, and how are they justified formally?	• How can the concepts, theorems, justifications and procedures be structured in logical trajectories? • Which connections are crucial, which are contingent? • How can the network between concepts, theorems, justifications and procedures be elaborated?	Retrospective Analysis
	Semantic level	• What are the underlying big ideas behind the concepts, theorems and procedures? • Which basic mental models and (graphical, verbal, numerical and algebraic) representations are crucial for constructing meaning?	• How do the underlying ideas and meanings relate to each other and to earlier and later learning content? • How can the meanings be successively constructed by horizontal mathematization in the intended learning trajectories? • Which trajectories of vertical mathematization have to be elicited in order to initiate the invention / discovery of core ideas, concepts, theorems and procedures? • How can the intended learning trajectories be sequenced with respect to the logical structure?	
	Concrete level	• Which core questions and core ideas can guide the development of the concepts, theorems, and procedures? • In which context situations and by which problems can the core questions and ideas be treated exemplarily for re-inventing the content?	• How can the meanings be successively constructed in situations in the intended learning trajectories? • How can the intended learning trajectories be sequenced with respect to the problem structure? • Which trajectories of horizontal mathematization have to be elicited in order to initiate the invention / discovery of core ideas, concepts, theorems and procedures?	
	Empirical level	• Which typical individual perspectives of students (conceptions, ideas, knowledge, ...) can be expected? • How do they relate to the intended perspectives (resources vs. obstacles)? • What are origins of typical obstacles or idiosyncratic conceptions?	• Which critical points in students' learning pathways are most crucial (obstacles, turning points,...)? • Which typical preconceptions or previous knowledge can serve as fruitful starting points? • How can the intended learning trajectory be re-sequenced with respect to students' starting points and obstacles?	

For the realization on the *concrete level*, the bank context of assets and compound interests was chosen, as this context carries main features of exponential growth, is realizable for students and relevant for their later lives.

The complexity of the topic of exponential growth consists in coordinating the different characterizations (here restricted to discrete functions). The function $f : \mathbb{N} \to \mathbb{R}^+$ is exponential, if it can be expressed in the form

(C1) $f(x+1) = \lambda \cdot f(x)$ (constantly multiplicative growth)
(C2$_p$) $f(x+1) = f(x) + p \cdot f(x)$ (constantly proportionally additive growth)
(C3) $f(x) = a \cdot b^x$ (direct determination)

Although on the *formal level*, these characterizations are equivalent and can be easily transformed into each other, they bear huge differences on the semantic level (Confrey and Smith 1995; Thompson 2011): students connect (C1) and (C2) mainly to the covariance model as they characterize the pattern of growth, and they connect (C3) mainly to the correspondence model as the formula can be used for determining $f(x)$ for a value of x. The bank context of interests resonates with (C2), the growth by constantly adding the same proportion (percentage) each year. Deriving (C3) from (C2) requires attention to the correspondence model via (C1) as it builds upon repeated multiplication.

Based on this roughly sketched prospective elaboration, a hypothetical learning trajectory was composed in which students can discover the characterizing features while exploring the growth of assets. The horizontal mathematization was supported by tables as major representation, the vertical mathematization was triggered by prompts to schematize the identified recursive pattern into an explicit formula in order to determine assets after 30 years.

Specifying and Structuring Exponential Growth Iteratively on the Empirical, Concrete, and Semantic Levels

The iterative design experiment cycles with tenth graders were conducted along the developed hypothetical learning trajectory and retrospective analysis on the empirical, concrete, and semantic levels.

Students' knowledge of percentages proved to be a suitable starting point for their learning pathways. In each cycle, the activities were optimized so that more students could discover the main aspects and connect them to each other.

For the *empirical* contribution to structuring the learning content, one empirical finding was most influential (Hußmann and Prediger 2016; other aspects presented by Thiel-Schneider 2018). Although characterization C1 and C2 are easily transformable to each other on the formal level, many students showed a compartmentalized understanding of different characterizations, hence an obstacle on the *semantic level*: For many students, C1 was activated only for integral exponents, completely separate from C2 which was used only for decimal exponents. This compartmentalization produced mistakes such as confusing the growth factor 1.02 (corresponding to 2%) with the constantly doubling growth (corresponding to 200%) (Hußmann and Prediger 2016).

Thus, the restructuring of the learning trajectory had to take more intensively into account the transition between the two characterizations. The iterative refinement of the learning trajectory focused on this transition and how it could be

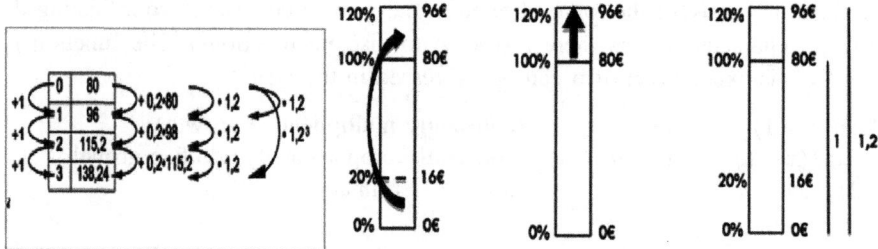

Fig. 2.6 Transition between additive and multiplicative perspective on constant growth in tables and in the graphical representation: In the percent bar, adding 20% is scaling up by 1.2

enhanced by relating different representations (Fig. 2.6). For this purpose, the percent bar had to be included in order to support the transition from constantly proportionally additive growth to constantly multiplicative growth, not only on the formal, but also on the semantic level: In the percent bars, adding 20% can be made visible to be semantically equivalent to scaling by 1.2 (Fig. 2.7), as adding 20% corresponds to scaling to 120%, i.e., scaling by 1.2. For several years, this leads to repeated multiplication with a cumulative factor $(1 + p)^n$ for n years.

Once the graphical representation was introduced, the learning trajectory could be reorganized so that multiplicative and additive perspectives were first adopted separately and then deliberately connected. In a further cycle, it was decided to treat integer growth factors only after the connection of both perspectives.

Although this limited insight into the project cannot account for all findings on students' learning pathways (see Thiel-Schneider 2018 for more details), Fig. 2.7 shows how typical outcomes may appear: By the iterative interplay of all four working areas and levels, the hypothetical learning trajectory (with all the corresponding activities) was enriched and consolidated.

As often appears, the learning trajectory is not a unidimensional one, but takes the character of a multi-facetted landscape, showing the characterizations, representations, core ideas and models to work on in each step. Although there is not the space to explain the details of the compressed, non-self-explanatory Fig. 2.7, it can give an impression of the *kinds* of results. This landscape is a major design outcome, but also a substantially refined analytical tool as it allows the researcher to map students' learning pathways as navigations within and around the structure.

One way of realizing the learning trajectory in a teaching-learning arrangement with all activities, tasks and representations was elaborated into a textbook chapter (Thiel-Schneider and Hußmann 2017), but of course, other realizations are also possible. On the theoretical level, the investigation of learning pathways contributed to the problems of compartmentalization of thinking and the necessity of building bridges.

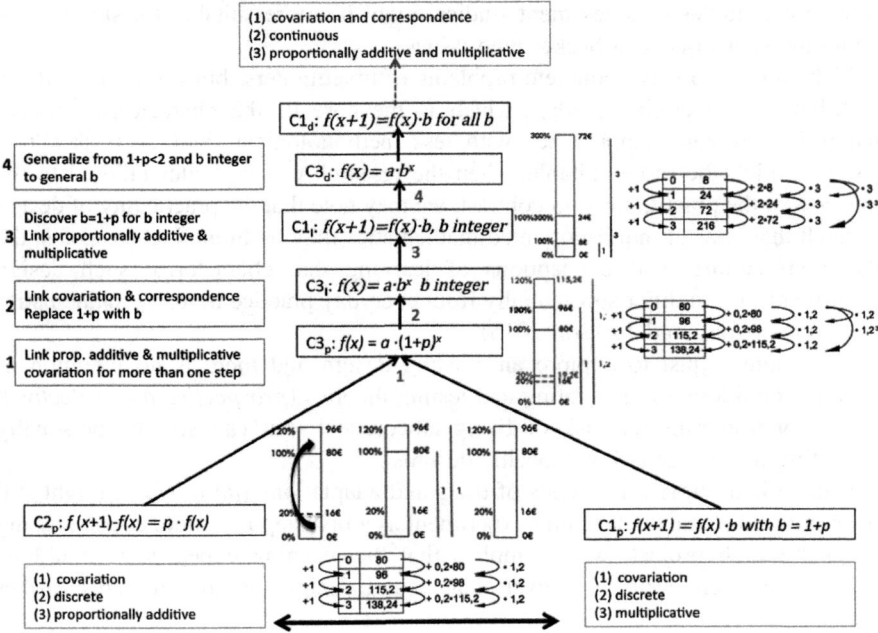

Fig. 2.7 Revised intended learning trajectory for exponential growth (Hußmann and Prediger 2016; more elaborated by Thiel-Schneider 2018)

2.4 Looking Back

The sketched examples of design research Ph.D.-projects in Sect. 2.2 portray what design research may look like, and what is involved in topic-specific design research. In connection with this we may also mention the highly interesting book by Bakker (2018) which offers further insightful advice, especially for young researchers.

2.4.1 When Is Topic-Specific Design Research a Suitable Methodology?

Design research is not a panacea for all sorts of research questions. For many educational challenges, other research approaches are better suited. In the following we briefly sketch a series of considerations, using the features of design experiments as described by Cobb et al. (2003) as a framework of reference.

If the aim, for instance, is not to change classroom practices (which is the core of the *interventionist* characteristic), *naturalistic research* approaches such as observation studies of assessment studies might be more suitable for simply analyzing the status quo and background issues.

If the aim is to solve concrete problems of practitioners, but not necessarily to contribute to generating theory (which is the core of the characteristic *theory generative*), research approaches with less methodological rigor such as *action research* might be more suitable. Then the research can be better tailored to the concerns of the practitioners. In contrast, we may note that the practicality of design research that aims at inquiry oriented mathematics may be limited as the goals, the classroom culture, and conceptions of learning that characterize such design experiments, often differ substantially from everyday practice in many mathematics classrooms (Cobb and Jackson 2015).

If the aim is just to explore an existing design and there is no intention of creating conditions for generating and testing theories (*prospective and reflective*), the exploration runs the risk of being atheoretical (but can still be personally interesting for learning about specific designs).

If there is no time for a series of trials and adaptations (*iterative*), it might still make sense to frame the teaching experiment as a first step in a more encompassing design research project, which implies that the teaching experiment should be analyzed as such. Mark, however, that sound design research requires further cycles.

If the aim is to validate a narrow and very clear hypothesis, a *randomized controlled trial* with valid measures for the intended learning gains might be more suitable. Mark, however, that the applicability of the findings in arbitrary classrooms may be limited (Gravemeijer 2016).

If the aim is to validate or refute 'grand theories', a *randomized controlled trial* might again be more fitting. However, the feasibility of judging grand theories in experimental designs might be overrated. Instead, design research aims for more humble, topic-specific, theories that have practical implications (*pragmatic roots and humble theories*).

2.4.2 Meeting Major Methodological Concerns

Critique on the lack of methodological sophistication of design research focuses on issues of generalizability, applicability in everyday practice, and a lack of standardization of methodological procedures. Even though we may argue that methodological approaches must vary because the design researchers' aims vary, there are of course various considerations that have to be taken into account in many variations of design research (see also Bakker 2018).

Background Theories and Assumptions

One of the critiques of design research is that the research question often takes the form of a how-to question, e.g., 'How to shape instruction on topic X?' For many scholars, such a research question is inadequate, because almost any answer would suffice. However, there is always an educational philosophy and a theoretical background against which such a question is posed. In mathematics education, part of the educational philosophy is often that the students should learn with understanding. Additionally, RME requires that the students experience mathematics as an activity, and learn by reinventing mathematics. Such starting points offer the boundary conditions within which the 'how-question' is to be answered. Background theories, such as socio-constructivism or cognitive theory, also significantly influence both the design and the way data are interpreted. The former implies that design researchers should explicate their educational philosophy and their background theories. In a more general sense, it may be argued that researchers have to be clear about their goals, their theoretical stance, and their analysis. The presented example projects show how a concrete project can be embedded in a broader framework, which helps to make the basic assumptions explicit.

Interpretive Framework

An important aspect of the methodological control of the empirical working area concerns the translation of observations of classroom events into scientific data. To make this translation, an interpretive framework is needed. An example of such an interpretative framework is the so-called emergent perspective of Yackel and Cobb (1996), which encompasses norms, practices and beliefs, or Vergnaud's (1996) theory of conceptual fields, which encompasses individuals' concepts-in-action and their relation to the concepts in view (applied, e.g., by Prediger and Zwetzschler 2013). The need for such a framework may be elucidated by observing that it makes a huge difference whether student utterance are to be viewed as a result of the students' own thinking, or as a result of the students efforts to imitate what the teacher has shown. Similarly, RME theory can function as an interpretative framework for interpreting student activity in light of the intended reinvention process.

Argumentative Grammar

Another critique is that design research lacks an argumentative grammar, which offers schemes of argumentation that link data to analysis, and to final claims and assertions (Kelly 2004). In response to Kelly's (2004) call for an argumentative grammar, Cobb et al. (2015) proposed the employment of the following requirements:

- demonstrate that the participants would not have developed particular forms of reasoning but for their participation in the design experiment;
- document how each successive form of reasoning emerged as a reorganization of prior forms of reasoning;
- specify the aspects of the learning ecology that were necessary, rather than contingent, in supporting the emergence of these successive forms of reasoning.

These three components closely relate to our conception of a local instruction theory (and are further explored by Bakker 2018). As the nature of design research is to explore innovative local instruction theories, the first requirement of the argumentative grammar is usually catered for. The second requirement may be linked to the fact that the local instruction theory is meant to function as a framework of reference for teachers, which requires that teachers have to be able to adapt the theory to their situation. We may argue that this is possible only if teachers who want to use the local instruction theory understand how successive forms of students' reasoning emerge as a reorganization of prior forms of reasoning along their learning pathways. The third requirement touches upon the conception of a local instruction theory as encompassing theories about a possible learning process, and theories about possible means of supporting that learning process. However, it asks for a broader description, which also incorporates the specificities of the classroom and what occurred in the classroom during the teaching experiment, and how these aspects influenced the emergence of the successive forms of reasoning.

A Holistic Approach

Most important for us seems to be those considerations that refer to the interplay of experiment and the process of theorizing. Ecological validity requires that the applied theories and the resulting theoretical contributions have to take into account the complexity of classrooms. This aspect requires a different approach than the reductionist approach of the sciences in which phenomena are disassembled in individual variables whose interdependencies can be researched systematically—especially by testing hypotheses.

In this respect, we may refer to Gould (2004) who depicts a complementary way of knowing; the more holistic approach of the humanities, in which, in his view, *concilience* plays a large part: "the validation of a theory by the 'jumping together' of otherwise disparate facts into a unitary explanation" (p. 192). The underlying idea of grasping how things work resonates with Maxwell's (2004) *process-oriented conception of causal explanation*, "that sees causality as fundamentally referring to the actual causal mechanisms and processes that are involved in particular events and situations" (p. 4). We may translate this conception into the recommendation to researchers to search for the underlying mechanisms, and a holistic view that unites seemingly disparate facts.

Summing up, design research provides a research methodology for all who want to combine aims of improving teaching with generating theories which can underpin the teaching. Although the research process can never be easily schematized, procedures and structures have been developed that support the challenging and creative parts of topic-specific design research, also for novices.

References

Artigue, M. (1992). Didactical engineering. In R. Douady & A. Mercier (Eds.), *Recherches en Didactique des Mathématiques. Selected papers* (pp. 41–70). Grenoble: La Pensèe Sauvage.

Bakker, A. (2018). *Design research in education: A practical guide for early career researchers.* London: Routledge.

Bakker, A., & Van Eerde, H. A. A. (2015). An introduction to design based research with an example from statistics education. In A. Bikner-Ahsbahs, C. Knipping, & N. Presmeg (Eds.), *Doing qualitative research: Methodology and methods in mathematics education* (pp. 429–466). New York: Springer.

Breen, C. (2003). Mathematics teachers as researchers: Living on the edge? In A. J. Bishop, C. Keitel, J. Kilpatrick, & F. K. S. Leung (Eds.), *Second international handbook of mathematics education* (pp. 523–544). Dordrecht: Kluwer.

Clagett, M. (1959). *Science of mechanics in the middle ages*. Madison: University of Wisconsin Press.

Cobb, P., & Steffe, L. P. (1983). The constructivist researcher as teacher and model builder. *Journal for Research in Mathematics Education, 14*(2), 83–95.

Cobb, P., & Whitenack, J. W. (1996). A method for conducting longitudinal analyses of classroom videorecordings and transcripts. *Educational Studies in Mathematics, 30*(3), 213–228.

Cobb, P., & Jackson, K. (2015). Supporting teachers' use of research-based instructional sequences. *ZDM Mathematics Education, 47*(6), 1027–1038.

Cobb, P., Jackson, K., & Dunlap, C. (2015). Design research: An analysis and critique. In L. English & D. Kirshner (Eds.), *Handbook of international research in mathematics education* (pp. 481–503). New York: Taylor & Francis.

Cobb, P., Confrey, J., diSessa, A., Lehrer, R., & Schauble, L. (2003). Design experiments in education research. *Educational Researcher, 32*(1), 9–13.

Confrey, J., & Smith, E. (1995). Splitting, covariation, and their role in the development of exponential functions. *Journal for Research in Mathematics Education, 26*(1), 66–86.

de Beer, H. (2016). *Exploring Instantaneous speed in grade 5. A design research* (PhD thesis). Eindhoven University of Technology, the Netherlands.

de Beer, H., Gravemeijer, K., & van Eijck, M. (2015). Discrete and continuous reasoning about change in primary school classrooms. *ZDM Mathematics Education, 47*(6), 981–996.

Freudenthal, H. (1973). *Mathematics as an educational task*. Dordecht: Reidel.

Freudenthal, H. (1991). *Revisiting mathematics education*. Dordrecht: Kluwer.

Glaser, B., & Strauss, A. (1967). *The discovery of grounded theory: Strategies for qualitative research (third paperback printing 2008)*. New Brunswick: Aldine Transaction.

Gould, S. J. (2004). *The hedgehog, the fox, and the magister's pox*. London: Vintage.

Gravemeijer, K. (1999). How emergent models may foster the constitution of formal mathematics. *Mathematical Thinking and Learning, 1*(2), 155–177.

Gravemeijer, K. (2004). Local instruction theories as means of support for teachers in reform mathematics education. *Mathematical thinking and learning, 6*(2), 105–128.

Gravemeijer, K. (2016). Design-research-based curriculum innovation. *Quadrante, XXV*(2), 7–23.

Gravemeijer, K. (in preparation). A socio-constructivist elaboration of RME. In M. van den Heuvel-Panhuizen, P. Drijvers, M. Doorman, & M. van Zanten (Eds.), *Book 1: Reflections from inside on the Netherlands didactic tradition in mathematics education*.

Gravemeijer, K., & Cobb, P. (2006). Design research from a learning design perspective. In J. Akker, K. Gravemeijer, S. McKenney, & N. Nieveen (Eds.), *Educational design research* (pp. 45–85). London: Routledge.

Gravemeijer, K., & Koster, K. (Eds.). (1988). *Onderzoek, ontwikkeling en ontwikkelingsonderzoek*. Utrecht: Vakgroep OW&OC.

Hußmann, S., & Prediger, S. (2016). Specifying and structuring mathematical topics—a four-level approach for combining formal, semantic, concrete, and empirical levels exemplified for exponential growth. *Journal für Mathematik-Didaktik, 37*(S1), 33–67.

Kaput, J., & Schorr, R. (2007). Changing representational infrastructures changes most everything: The case of SimCalc, algebra and calculus. In G. Blume & K. Heid (Eds.), *Research on technology in the learning and teaching of mathematics* (pp. 21–253). Mahwah: Erlbaum.

Kelly, A. (2004). Design research in education: Yes, but is it methodological? *Journal of the Learning Sciences, 13*(1), 115–128.

Kelly, A. E., Lesh, R. A., & Baek, J. Y. (Eds.). (2008). *Handbook of design research methods in education: Innovations in science, technology, engineering, and mathematics learning and teaching.* New York: Routledge.

Louca, L. T., & Zacharia, Z. C. (2012). Modeling-based learning in science education: Cognitive, metacognitive, social, material and epistemological contributions. *Educational Review, 64*(4), 471–492.

Maxwell, J. A. (2004). Causal explanation, qualitative research, and scientific inquiry in education. *Educational Researcher, 33*(2), 3–11.

Plomp, T., & Nieveen, N. (Eds.). (2013). *Educational design research*. Enschede: SLO.

Prediger, S., & Zwetzschler, L. (2013). Topic-specific design research with a focus on learning processes: The case of understanding algebraic equivalence in grade 8. In T. Plomp & N. Nieveen (Eds.), *Educational design research: Illustrative cases* (pp. 407–424). Enschede: SLO, Netherlands Institute for Curriculum Development.

Prediger, S., Gravemeijer, K., & Confrey, J. (2015). Design research with a focus on learning processes—an overview on achievements and challenges. *ZDM Mathematics Education, 47*(6), 877–891. https://doi.org/10.1007/s11858-015-0722-3.

Prediger, S., Link, M., Hinz, R., Hußmann, S., Thiele, J., & Ralle, B. (2012). Lehr-Lernprozesse initiieren und erforschen—Fachdidaktische Entwicklungsforschung im Dortmunder Modell [Initiating and researching teaching learning processes—Didactical design research in the Dortmund model]. *Der mathematische und naturwissenschaftliche Unterricht, 65*(8), 452–457.

Schweiger, F. (2006). Fundamental ideas. A bridge between mathematics and mathematics education. In J. Maaß & W. Schlöglmann (Eds.), *New mathematics education research and practice* (pp. 63–73). Rotterdam: Sense.

Simon, M. A. (1995). Reconstructing mathematics pedagogy from a constructivist perspective. *Journal for Research in Mathematics Education, 26*(2), 114–145.

Smaling, A. (1992). Varieties of methodological intersubjectivity—the relations with qualitative and quantitative research, and with objectivity. *Quality & Quantity, 26*(2), 169–180. https://doi.org/10.1007/BF02273552.

Swan, M. (Ed.). (1985). *The language of functions and graphs: An examination module for secondary schools*. Nottingham: Shell Centre for Mathematical Education.

Thiel-Schneider, A. (2018). *Zum Begriff des exponentiellen Wachstums: Entwicklung und Erforschung von Lehr-Lernprozessen in sinnstiftenden Kontexten aus inferentialistischer Perspektive*. Wiesbaden: Springer.

Thiel-Schneider, A., & Hußmann, S. (2017). Geldanlagen—Wachsendes Wachstum vergleichen. In S. Prediger, B. Barzel, S. Hußmann, & T. Leuders (Eds.), *Mathewerkstatt 10 [Textbook for Grade 10]* (pp. 61–94). Berlin: Cornelsen.

Thompson, W. (2011). Quantitative reasoning and mathematical modeling. In L. L. Hatfield, S. Chaimberlain, & S. Belbaise (Eds.), *New perspectives and directions for colloborative reseach in mathematics education* (pp. 33–57). Laramie: University of Wyoming.

Treffers, A. (1987). *Three dimensions: a model of goal and theory description in mathematics instruction—The Wiskobas project*. Dordrecht: Kluwer Academic Publishers.

Van den Akker, J. (2013). Curricular development research as a specimen of educational design research. In T. Plomp & N. Nieveen (Eds.), *Educational design research: illustrative cases* (pp. 52–71). Enschede: SLO, Netherlands Institute for Curriculum Development.

Van den Akker, J., Gravemeijer, K., McKenney, S., & Nieveen, N. (Eds.). (2006). *Educational Design Research*. London: Routledge.

Vergnaud, G. (1996). The theory of conceptual fields. In L. P. Steffe & P. Nesher (Eds.), *Theories of mathematical learning* (pp. 219–239). Mahwah, NY: Lawrence Erlbaum.

Wittmann, E. C. (1995). Mathematics education as a "design science". *Educational Studies in Mathematics, 29*(4), 355–374.

Yackel, E., & Cobb, P. (1996). Sociomathematical norms, argumentation, and autonomy in mathematics. *Journal for Research in Mathematics Education, 27*(4), 458–477.

Open Access This chapter is licensed under the terms of the Creative Commons Attribution 4.0 International License (http://creativecommons.org/licenses/by/4.0/), which permits use, sharing, adaptation, distribution and reproduction in any medium or format, as long as you give appropriate credit to the original author(s) and the source, provide a link to the Creative Commons license and indicate if changes were made.

The images or other third party material in this chapter are included in the chapter's Creative Commons license, unless indicated otherwise in a credit line to the material. If material is not included in the chapter's Creative Commons license and your intended use is not permitted by statutory regulation or exceeds the permitted use, you will need to obtain permission directly from the copyright holder.

Chapter 3
A Naturalistic Paradigm: An Introduction to Using Ethnographic Methods for Research in Mathematics Education

Judit N. Moschkovich

Abstract This chapter provides an introduction to integrating a naturalistic paradigm and ethnographic methods into research in mathematics education. The chapter addresses methodological issues specific to designing and conducting research in mathematics education framed by a naturalistic paradigm that includes ethnographic methods and, in particular, using video as an ethnographic research methodology. The theoretical perspective used in this chapter is based on assumptions summarized in a chapter by Moschkovich and Brenner (Handbook of research design in mathematics and science education, Lawrence Erlbaum Associates, Mahwah, pp. 457–486, 2000). This chapter focuses on describing and illustrating an ethnographic stance and the design of ecologically valid mathematical tasks, and summarizes design issues for ethnographic research, in particular using video.

Keywords Mathematics education · Methodology · Ethnographic methods · Video

3.1 Introduction

This chapter provides an introduction to integrating a naturalistic paradigm and ethnographic methods into research in mathematics education. The chapter considers methodological issues specific to designing and conducting research in mathematics education that is framed by a naturalistic paradigm and uses ethnographic methods, paying particular attention to using video as an ethnographic research methodology.

Early researchers in mathematics education should be interested in these methodological approaches for several reasons. A naturalist paradigm and

---

J. N. Moschkovich (✉)
University of California, Santa Cruz, CA, USA
e-mail: jmoschko@ucsc.edu

© The Author(s) 2019
G. Kaiser and N. Presmeg (eds.), *Compendium for Early Career Researchers in Mathematics Education*, ICME-13 Monographs,
https://doi.org/10.1007/978-3-030-15636-7_3

ethnographic methods expand the set of methodological tools for research on mathematics learning and teaching beyond techniques such as clinical interviews or "think-aloud" sessions to include activity in natural settings, as students work in pairs or groups. Ethnographic methods provide systematic ways to collect and analyze data in natural settings, which might seem daunting in their messiness. And ethnographic methods can be used to design more ecologically valid tasks for subsequent data collection using clinical interviews or 'think-aloud' sessions.

Ethnographic methods are not new to research in mathematics education and have been used by researchers outside the classroom (for examples see work in the references by Brenner 1985, 1998; Civil 2002; Civil and Bernier 2006; González et al. 2001; and others) as well as inside the classroom to document and study classroom activity focusing on the teachers or the learners. This chapter uses my own research as an example and thus focuses on learners' activity in classrooms. However, there are many other ways, settings, and foci for research using ethnographic methods.

The chapter focuses on the following questions:

1. *What is a naturalistic paradigm?* What principles guide research studies using a naturalistic paradigm? How can a naturalistic paradigm be combined with other research approaches to explore questions about mathematical thinking and learning?
2. *What are ethnographic methods?* What is the difference between doing 'an ethnography' and using ethnographic methods? How can researchers use ethnographic methods to investigate aspects of mathematical thinking and learning? What are central methodological concepts related to ethnographic methods?
3. *How can video be used as an ethnographic research methodology?*
4. *How can we analyze student mathematical activity using a naturalistic paradigm and ethnographic methods?*

The theoretical perspective used in this chapter is based on the assumptions summarized in the chapter by Moschkovich and Brenner (2000), in which we described how to integrate a naturalistic paradigm into research on mathematics and science cognition and learning. This chapter also uses several important concepts such as a definition of context by Lave (1988, p. 462), and illustrates two concepts discussed by Moschkovich and Brenner (2000), an ethnographic stance (p. 474) and ecological validity for cognitive tasks (p. 466) (each of these is discussed in detail in Sect. 3.2 of this chapter).

The term "methodology" is sometimes misunderstood to refer only to "methods," when, in fact, theory and methods are intricately related, mutually constructive, and informing of each other. Methodology includes the underlying theoretical assumptions about cognition and learning: what cognition and learning are; when and where cognition and learning occur; and how to document, describe, and explain them. I will use the term "methodology" to refer to theory and methods together.

The dictionary definition of paradigm is a philosophical or theoretical framework. Integrating a naturalistic paradigm into research involves using both theory and methods that reflect, or are at least consonant with, that naturalistic paradigm.

Methodology is assumed to be theory plus methods, not a collection of methods but an epistemological stance towards multiple aspects of research: Theory informs research questions, research design, and data analysis (i.e., selecting lessons, transcribing, focus for different analyses). For example, video or interviews are not techniques but data sources that can be used from multiple theoretical stances. Similarly, data collection or analysis techniques such as discourse or protocol analysis are also framed by a researcher's stance or paradigm. Research design decisions depend on having clear and focused research questions and imagining what data would look like that might answer particular research questions. Since no researcher or research study can cover everything, each study needs to focus on what that one study can do well.

3.2 A Naturalistic Paradigm[1]

Ethnographic methods are framed by a naturalistic paradigm, which is different than that of experimental design. However, the design and analysis processes are still systematic and have to be consistent with the theoretical framing for a study. In the chapter by Moschkovich and Brenner (2000), we described a naturalistic paradigm as follows:

> The naturalistic paradigm that undergirds our work is an emergent paradigm about the nature of the research enterprise (Lincoln and Guba 1985; Erlandson et al. 1993). This paradigm arose in contrast to positivistic traditions in which the scientific method was considered the route to discovering an objective reality. The naturalistic paradigm assumes that meaning is constructed by both participants and observers so that, in effect, there are multiple realities (Erlandson et al. 1993). Because these multiple versions of reality are shaped by both theoretical and value frameworks, it is not possible to achieve pure objectivity. (Guba 1990). (p. 459)

We also described the goal of the naturalistic research enterprise according to Guba (1990) as follows: "to identify the variety of constructions that exist and bring them into as much consensus as possible" (p. 26). To fulfill this purpose, naturalistic research takes a holistic view in order to examine these various constructions in relation to each other as they interact in their own contexts. Naturalistic research is not synonymous with qualitative research, although qualitative methods tend to be the preferred methods used in the naturalistic paradigm (Erlandson et al. 1993; Guba 1993), the naturalistic paradigm is inherent in some qualitative traditions, but not all (for more details see Jacob 1987).

Using this paradigm implies that design and analysis are conducted from an ethnographic stance, that context is defined as a complex, multifaceted, and interactional phenomenon and that design considers the ecological validity

---

[1]This section is largely based on a previous publication co-authored with M. Brenner (Moschkovich and Brenner 2000).

(Bronfenbrenner 1977; Cole et al. 1978) for mathematical tasks used in a study. In the next sections I address each of these three aspects of a naturalistic paradigm.

3.2.1 An Ethnographic Stance

The theoretical stance can be summarized as the assumption that meaning is socially constructed and negotiated in practice. The research principles include considering multiple viewpoints, studying cognition in context, and connecting theory generation and verification. It is important when using ethnographic methods not to simply use the methods divorced from the naturalistic paradigm that frames these methods.

Naturalistic and cognitive (or experimental) methods can be combined in complementary ways and can be integrated into mathematics education studies, but this integration and combination must be carefully considered during all aspects of research, designing a study, collecting data, and analyzing data. For example, the mathematics content of most interest may not always be visible in "natural" settings, so researchers may need to combine data from a "natural" setting and a more structured situation that includes an intervention, a quasi-experiment, or a design experiment (Brown 1992). Nonetheless, to understand the process of learning from the naturalistic research stance, it is essential to include at least some data from a "natural" setting, such as a classroom or other complex setting, in the research design. The third section of the chapter describes this design process in more detail.

A naturalistic paradigm is not defined by the methods used or the place where data are collected but, more importantly, by a theoretical stance and a set of research principles. The theoretical stance assumes that meaning is socially constructed and negotiated in practice and uses several research principles such as considering multiple viewpoints, studying cognition in context, and connecting theory generation and verification. This stance and these principles do not exist on their own; they are tied in complex ways to several disciplines and traditions and draw meaning from these disciplines. A naturalistic paradigm and the accompanying ethnographic methods are couched within the practices of an academic discipline also and take their meaning from these practices.

A naturalistic paradigm and an ethnographic stance can be summarized by the following principles: (1) Consider multiple points of view and (2) Study cognitive activity in context. These two principles derive from ethnography, a methodology (not a collection of methods) connected closely to the theoretical principles of anthropology, such as the centrality of the concept of culture (Spindler and Spindler 1987). Definitions of culture[2] are contested and vary across academic disciplines.

---

[2]There is no one definition of culture, however anthropologists typically agree that it involves learning that people do as members of human groups as they learn to "interpret experience and generate behavior (Spradley 1979), that it is an action or a process, not a thing, and that it includes both explicit (reported) and tacit (common sense, not reported directly) meaning making. Here I

A definition of culture or an account of debates around its definition is beyond the scope of this chapter. However, educational anthropology and cultural psychology provide some assumptions to ground studies in mathematics education.

First and foremost, we cannot assume "cultural uniformity or a set of harmonious and homogeneous set of shared practices" (Garcia and González 1995, p. 237) about *any* cultural group. To avoid 'essentializing' cultural practices Gutiérrez and Rogoff (2003) propose that we focus not on individual traits but on what they call "repertoires of practice" using the assumptions that individuals develop, communities change, and learners have access to multiple practices. They argue that we should "neither attribute static qualities to cultural communities nor assume that each individual within such communities shares in similar ways those practices that have evolved over generations" (Lee et al. 2003).

3.2.2 Ecological Validity

Ecological validity in psychological studies (Bronfenbrenner 1977; Cole et al. 1978) ensures that participants' reasoning is examined on cognitive tasks that are connected to regular cultural practices, in or out of school. Cultural psychology has shown that, when this is not the case, participants look less competent that they actually are (Cole et al. 1978). It is most important to use ecological validity when designing cognitive tasks,[3] as described by Cole et al. Bronfenbrenner (1977) suggests that for a study to be considered ecologically valid it should be designed to meet three conditions:

> First, it must maintain the integrity of the real-life situations it is designed to investigate. Second, it must be faithful to the larger social and cultural contexts from which the subjects came. Third, the analysis must be consistent with the participants' definition of the situation. (p. 35)

Cole et al. (1978) recommend that "the analysis of any behaviour should begin with a descriptive analysis of at least one real world scene" (p. 4). This descriptive analysis informs the design of experiments (or quasi-experiments) that preserve some aspects of the real-world setting while modifying others. A study can start with observations in a setting where cognitive phenomena occur regularly without intervention. To explore further the cognitive phenomena observed in the natural setting originally, researchers then design interviews, quasi-experiments, tests, and interventions, based on those observations.

---

am not referring to culture as a factor or a variable (such as socioeconomic status, ethnicity, or gender) but to the concept of culture: the assumption that everyone participates in multiple cultural practices and that these cultural practices play a role in thinking, reasoning, and learning.

[3]The design of ecologically valid mathematics tasks is addressed in detail in other publications (i.e. Lave 1988; see Moschkovich and Brenner 2000 for other references).

When considering whether a task is ecologically valid, context is not assumed to be a unilateral experience. Traditional task analyses of mathematics problems conducted by experts assume that learners know what experts know and thus use an impoverished notion of context, defined by how an expert sees and interprets a task. In contrast, a more complex notion of context adds depth to how we see and interpret mathematical tasks.

3.2.3 Context

Lave (1988) provides a definition for *context* and distinguishes it from the *setting*. For Lave, a setting is the physical and social environment.[4] A description of a setting includes the objects, people, and activities that are present. In contrast, Lave defines context as the relationship between a setting and how participants interpret the setting, including how participants interpret, view, or understand artifacts (documented by how participants use and/or communicate about their activity with an artifact). A description of context would analyze more deeply the different interpretations or views that a setting and an artifact (as well as the practices that take place in a setting) may have for different participants.

A description of context delves more deeply into the *different meanings that a setting and the practices taking place in a setting have for different participants.* Context is thus not a single entity, such as a place, but instead it is:

> ... an identifiable, durable framework for activity, with properties that transcend the experience of individuals, exist prior to them, and are entirely beyond their control. On the other hand, context is experienced differently by different individuals. (p. 151)

For example, using Lave's (1988) definitions of context and setting, an algebra word problem is an artifact—not a context—that can create or support different contexts; such contexts depend on how different people, for example, understand or view an algebra word problem in person:

- A kinder-gardener may view an algebra words problem as a bunch of scribbles on a page.
- A high school student may see a word problem as a task to solve using practices learned in school, other ways that a high school student might understand or view an algebra word problem would include affective aspects of activity, such as a negative or positive emotional reaction, depending on that student's past experiences with word problems.
- A mathematics instructor might see or view an algebra word problem as a way to show their students how to apply an important mathematical idea or technique to a concrete situation.

---

[4]Lave uses the term "arena" to refer to "setting" and defines "setting" as the "repeatedly experienced, personally ordered and edited version" (Lave 1988, p. 151) of an arena.

One way to address the importance of context is to study mathematical thinking and learning in the settings in which it naturally and regularly occurs without intervention. The naturalistic paradigm and ethnographic research methods were developed to study activity within such "natural" settings and here they have much to offer mathematics education research. A naturalistic paradigm provides a road map for understanding learners in their own terms and highlighting the potential in what they know, rather than only comparing their knowledge to that of an expert, and analyzing the unexpected structure of novices' knowledge, the alternative understandings held by learners (Confrey 1990), or the potential for progress in students' initial conceptions (Moschkovich 1992, 1999).

3.3 Research Design Issues for Ethnographic Data Collection

In this section I summarize issues to consider for ethnographic data collection. Even if the research design is not full blown ethnography, a study can use a mixed tool kit that includes some ethnographic methods such as participant observation or open-ended interviewing. First, a note that using ethnographic methods is not the same as writing an ethnography and that an ethnography involves much more than using ethnographic methods (Moschkovich and Brenner 2000):

> Ethnography is a methodology that is intricately related to the theoretical principles of anthropology, such as the centrality of culture:

> …many people, who are quite innocent of anthropology as a discipline and who have only vague notions of cultural process, claim to be doing ethnography. We have nothing against anyone doing qualitative, field site evaluation, participant or non-participant observation, descriptive journalism, or anything else if it is well done. It will produce some tangible result and may be useful, but it should not be called ethnography unless it is, and it is not ethnography unless it uses some model of cultural process in both the gathering and interpretation of data. (Spindler and Spindler 1987, p. 151)

A central question to consider in designing a study is what types of research questions can be answered with ethnographic methods and what types cannot be answered with ethnographic methods. For example, in contrast to experimental design, ethnographic methods cannot answer cause and effect questions but leave room for new research questions as they emerge during a study. Participant observation can also shape or focus the research questions asked (as well as inform the design of interviews or cognitive tasks for clinical interviews).

Other design issues for ethnographic data collection include the following:

(1) When will classroom data be collected or what will be the time frame? For example, during the first weeks of a school year it is suitable to look at how the 'culture' of the classroom is established, or later in the year, how does the classroom culture appear once the classroom routines have already been established?

(2) Will the unit of analysis be a full topic or a full curriculum unit?
(3) How much data will be collected? How will decisions be made about how much data will be enough[5]?
(4) Who or what is the focus of the data collection: the teacher, groups of students, individual students, the whole class, etc.?

One of the central goals of using ethnographic methods is to identify the issues for the participants (Spradley 1979). However, ethnographic methods also help the analyst to raise issues that the participants may not have been aware of themselves. There are many different ways to collect data when using ethnographic methods. Two broad ethnographic methods used for data collection are participant observation and open ended interviewing. Important distinctions are the differences between what people say they do (self-reports, interviews), what people are observed doing (observation), and what the researcher concludes from participation in an activity (participant observation).

Other design issues include making decisions about what supporting data are needed to answer the research questions, for example, copies of student work, hand-outs, student grades, test scores, etc. The design also needs to consider what kind of background information will be collected on students or teachers. If interviewing, decisions will need to be made regarding whether it will happen daily, after a natural grouping of data, group debriefing, etc. and whether the interviews will be clinical interviews, pair discussions, group discussions after taping, etc. If interviews are conducted with students, then decisions will need to be made about the tasks used (i.e. complementary cognitive tasks, ecologically valid tasks, etc.).

3.4 Video as an Ethnographic Research Methodology

Using video data to document mathematical activity is more than a matter of using a particular research method, it is a matter of methodology. Like other methods, video is a research method that is theory laden and that can be used from multiple theoretical stances. Uses of video data as an ethnographic method are multiple and varied. Video can be used to record, examine, and analyse many different types of phenomena and for multiple purposes. The data collection and analysis can focus on children's activity (i.e. mathematical explaining, engagement, etc.), or on examining patterns or trends in teaching practices, or record and examine participant structures in a classroom. Some researchers archive video data for a second analysis at a later time. In the next section I focus on issues involved in using video to document mathematical activity among learners, and describe some issues particular to using video.

---

[5]A useful concept is data saturation (Glaser and Strauss 1967; Strauss and Corbin 1990).

3.4.1 Advantages and Disadvantages of Using Video Data

There are both advantages and disadvantages to using video data. Video data have several advantages when used to document learning and teaching. Video data may capture "more" of what happens in a classroom than other forms of data collection such as student and teacher self-reports, interviews, or questionnaires. Video data make it possible to capture both teacher and student activity, sometimes simultaneously. Overall, video data have the potential to capture more than what one set of eyes and ears can notice and record in real time.

However, video data also have disadvantages for documenting learning and teaching when compared to other methods of collecting data. Video data capture 'less' of what happens in a classroom than other forms of data collection because the researcher must make choices that limit what is and what is not recorded. Researchers choose whether to pan across a room, focus on the teacher, focus on students, or fix on one group of students. In contrast to observations, what activity is captured and what activity missed, is determined by camera location, rather than a trained observer's reaction to events as they unfold. It is important to remember that video data, like any other type of data, have limitations. Video data are not equivalent to direct observational data nor do they provide an 'objective' or 'realistic' view of a setting or the activity in any setting. Video data reflect deletions and selections, capture only one particular perspective, and this perspective is one that no participant could have had (Hall 2000) and the analyst decides what perspective to present (Goldman 2014).

Researchers working from a naturalistic paradigm (Moschkovich and Brenner 2000) recommend that video data not stand alone but instead be interpreted and framed by other kinds of data. Other types of data such as observations, field notes, supporting materials, and contextual information are necessary for making meaning for recorded video data. The analysis of classroom activity needs to be couched and framed by other types of data: the teacher's goals, textbook use, district policies, preceding lessons, information about the students, etc., and this is especially important for cross-cultural work:

> Contextualizing recorded behaviour is important in understanding the meaning behind that behaviour, and it is especially important when coding across cultures (Erickson 1986). Similar behaviours may have different meanings and comparisons can be problematic. (Ulewicz and Beatty 2001, p. 13)

Several problems have been documented when using and analysing video data (Ulewicz and Beatty 2001; Derry et al. 2010; Tobin et al. 1989). For example, viewers may sometimes develop an exaggerated sense of confidence about what they know about a classroom after watching just a short video clip (Brenner, personal communication; Tobin et al. 1989; Ulewicz and Beatty 2001, and my own personal experiences). Assessment of mathematics teaching through video data have been documented to have a tendency to focus only on negative aspects, but researchers have found that a process of social moderation or discussion along with coding "allowed scorers to overcome their tendency to focus only on negative aspects of performance and to acknowledge positive aspects" (Frederiksen et al. 1998, p. 255).

In my own experience showing, discussing, and coding video, it is common for viewers to focus on what is wrong in a lesson or what a student is doing wrong, rather than on how a lesson is working well or what a student is doing well. Because video slows action down, every participant on tape may seem both less and more competent than in real time. As we watch video, we have more time to notice how participants mis-speak or make mistakes than we would have if we were observing in real time, thus making them appear *less* competent. As we watch video, we also have more time to notice and really think about what participants said and did, potentially making them look *more* competent than in real time. The ways that analysts perceive a participant's competence or lack of competence is framed and informed by the theoretical framework we use to analyse video data.

3.4.2 *Transcription and Translation as Theory*

There are several stages of design decisions to make when using video as part of the ethnographic methods for a research study: collecting, preparing, describing, and analysing. Preparing video includes using content logs, writing memos, selecting segments to transcribe, and transcribing/subtitling. I will focus on issues related to the preparing stage, especially transcribing and translating, because these are crucial for using video from a naturalistic paradigm and as part of a toolkit of ethnographic methods.

Transcription and transcript quality are heavily loaded with theory (Ochs 1979; Poland 2002). Researchers make many decisions about transcripts that are based on their theoretical frameworks and on the particular research questions for a study. For example, decisions regarding what to include in transcripts and which transcript conventions to use are informed by theory. Whether a transcript will include or not gestures, emotions, inscriptions, body posture, and description of the scene (Hall 2000; Poland 2002; McDermott and Gospodinoff 1978), will depend on whether these aspects of activity are relevant or not to the particular research questions. Similarly, selecting transcript conventions and deciding whether overlapping utterances, intonation, and pauses are included or not in a transcript depends on whether these aspects are relevant to the research questions and analysis for which the transcript and video will be used. And whether and how aspects of activity are relevant (or not) to the research questions depends on the theoretical framework. Rather than asking whether a transcript is done, finished, or complete, we should first ask what purposes and research questions the current transcript is serving and what theoretical perspective frames the study. Only then can we decide whether the current transcript is sufficiently detailed (in terms of what information it includes)

3 A Naturalistic Paradigm: An Introduction to Using Ethnographic... 69

and systematic (in terms of how this information was recorded and represented) for those specific purposes and research questions.[6]

Two aspects of conversations and features of talk that may be relevant to documenting mathematical activity are intonation and the use of gestures.[7] Perceiving a student as uncertain or hesitant because of intonation patterns may have an impact on how both researchers and teachers perceive student contributions in mathematics classrooms. For example, intonation patterns vary across languages and among dialects:

> Perhaps the most prominent feature distinguishing Chicano English from other varieties of American English is its use of certain intonation patterns. These intonation patterns often strike other English speakers as uncertain or hesitant. (Finegan and Besnier 1989, p. 407)

Translation presents a challenge all its own. Translation is not simply a copy of the original utterance but in another language. Translating between national and social languages necessarily involves interpretation. It seems impossible to translate without putting some piece of ourselves in the new utterance—translators are not simply empty vessels when we translate. There seems to be no way to translate an utterance and be certain that the original utterance carried *exactly* that meaning.

When participants use two languages, it is important for researchers to decide how to display translations. There are several reasons that make it crucial that the original utterances be displayed regardless of the language of these utterances or whether the intended audience speaks that language. First, the original utterances need to be available for inspection so that the analysis and the translations are transparent to all readers. The choice of whether they appear in the text of an analysis or in an appendix is up to the analyst. Second, displaying only translations privileges the language of the translation (usually English for international publications) and perpetuates views of the world as principally monolingual. Subtitles can be useful (even for monolingual utterances), since not everyone can hear what the analyst hears after hours of repeated listening.

3.4.3 Analysing Mathematical Activity

In closing this section, I would like to raise an issue related to analysing mathematical activity using video, a focus on the negative aspects of human activity in video data and *how* we use video data to document learners' mathematical activity. The focus on the negative when looking at videotapes is a danger that applies not only to analyses of teaching but also to how we view learners' mathematical

---

[6]Transcript quality ranges over a wide spectrum and transcripts need to be labelled according to the stage of development. I have used labels such as rough transcript, working transcript, and "done for now" transcript, because a transcript is never really finished.

[7]Students' use of gestures to convey mathematical meaning has been documented in multiple studies (for example De Freitas and Sinclair 2012; Edwards 2009; Edwards et al. 2009).

activity. It is a common experience for viewers to focus on what a student is doing wrong, rather than on what a student is doing well. Because a focus only on negative aspects or performance has been documented as a problem when looking at videotapes (Frederiksen et al. 1998), video data should be used carefully to document competence, proficiency, or other evaluative analysis of either teacher or student activity.

3.5 Analyzing Mathematical Activity Using a Naturalistic Paradigm and Ethnographic Methods

In this section I use my own work as one example of a way to analyse student mathematical activity using a naturalistic paradigm and ethnographic methods[8] and focus on describing how I have used an ethnographic stance and ecological validity to design mathematical tasks.

3.5.1 An Ethno-Mathematical Perspective as an Example of an Ethnographic Stance

I use an ethno-mathematical perspective (a particular version of the more general ethnographic stance described earlier) to frame the description of mathematical activity among bilingual learners. An ethno-mathematical perspective expands the kinds of activities considered mathematical beyond the mathematics found in textbooks or learned in schools (D'Ambrosio 1985, 1991; Nunes et al. 1993). This perspective emphasizes that "mathematical activity" is not a unitary category but is manifested in different ways in different settings. Moreover, mathematical activity is not always immediately evident to the participants or the analyst but, instead, is uncovered during analysis. Using this perspective focuses data analysis on uncovering the mathematical structure in what participants are *actually* doing and saying. It focuses the analysis on specifying what mathematical concepts and conceptions students are grappling with, even when these mathematical concepts and conceptions may not be immediately evident to participants or sound like textbook definitions of academic mathematics, thus making students' own mathematical activity more visible. Taking an ethno-mathematics stance means that students' mathematical activity in the classroom is seen not as a deviant or novice version of academic/school mathematical practices but instead as a particular case of students' everyday activity, where participants use social and cognitive resources to make sense of situations.

---

[8]For more detailed examples see Moschkovich (1996, 1998, 2008, 2011).

When focusing on mathematical reasoning (Moschkovich 2011), I have used several criteria for selecting segments to transcribe:

- *Mathematical topic, problem or task*: I select all segments where student activity focuses on a particular mathematical topic, problem, or task.
- *Mathematical concepts and conceptions discussed*: Sometimes students discuss and use mathematical ideas other than those intended in the problem or task. For example, I select all segments where student seem to use proportional reasoning, even if that was not the intention of the problem.
- *Mathematical discourse activity*: I select all segments were students were engaged in a particular discourse activity such as explaining, comparing answers, disagreeing, etc.
- *Markers of understanding*: I select segments where participants themselves mark that they understand or don't understand, for example saying "I really get this now! Or "I don't get this..."
- *Communication breaks down*: I select segments when communication seems to break down and participants say, for example "What do you mean?"

Below are some questions I have used for analysing mathematical activity:

1. Are students participating in mathematical practices? If yes, which ones?
2. Does student activity reflect mathematical competence? If yes, which aspects of mathematical competence does student activity reflect?
3. Are there any "big" mathematical ideas evident in student activity (students need not be conscious of the mathematics themselves)? If yes, which ones? If not, which "big math ideas" do I see as relevant to this discussion?

3.5.2 Two Studies as Examples of Using an Ethnographic Stance and Designing Ecologically Valid Tasks

The typical design for my research projects is a cycle that combines classroom observation and discussion between pairs of students. The central design is a cycle of classroom observations for several weeks, videotaping lessons and small groups, designing ecologically valid tasks for what I call "peer discussion sessions," and videotaping those discussion sessions between pairs of students outside of the classroom. The discussion session problems are designed to be ecologically valid and target conceptions documented in the classroom observations. The "peer discussion sessions" are structured to support dialogue and discussion of not only answers but also conjectures, predictions, and justifications. This design cycle is based on studies of mathematics at work, for example tailors in Liberia (Brenner 1985, 1998; Lave 1997), but I use it to study mathematical reasoning in school.

The classroom data collection includes long term classroom observations (4–6 weeks minimum). I use those observations for multiple purposes: to get to know the students and the teacher, document and understand classroom routines and practices, document mathematical reasoning in the classroom, generate my own conjectures about student conceptions, and as the basis for designing ecologically valid tasks that target conceptions documented in the classroom observations. I also video tape whole class discussion and selected small group conversations for one or two focus small groups. I work in close collaboration with the teacher in making many of the design decisions.

The peer discussion sessions are for pairs of students who work on problems targeting student conceptions documented in the classroom. The students produce written work and their discussions are video-taped. These peer discussion sessions provide a quieter setting for data collection, a task focused on particular ideas, and structured discussions.

For this research project, I collected a large set of data in an eighth-grade bilingual mathematics classroom. The class was conducted mostly in English, with some discussions and explanations in Spanish. The teacher used Spanish mostly when she was addressing students who were seen as Spanish dominant. Some students spoke mainly English, some students used both languages, and some students spoke mainly in Spanish.

Classroom observations and videotaping were conducted during two curriculum units from *Connected Mathematics*, "Variables and Patterns" and "Moving Straight Ahead." Data collected included videotapes of whole-class discussions and at one student group for every lesson, as well as videotaped problem-solving sessions in pairs. I analysed one classroom discussion that occurred during the unit "Moving Straight Ahead" (Moschkovich 2008) between two students, Carlos and David, and their teacher. For that analysis, I focused on two classroom discussions, one in their small group and another a few months later as a whole class. Although the analysis focused on the transcripts from those two discussion, I used the long-term classroom observations and field notes to develop an overall sense of the classroom, to contextualize the two students' work on those two days, and to document the source of local ways of talking about the graphs.

For example, I describe this class as one where students expected to make sense of their work, discussed their work with peers, and also used the teacher as a resource in their discussions. Students took on some of the responsibility for explaining and understanding solutions and engaged in serious and extended discussion of their solutions. The small group discussions seemed to be important to the students. Nevertheless, while the students shared responsibility for explaining solutions, they sometimes also tended to rely on the teacher as the authority for evaluating a solution.

The teacher and students used multiple meanings for the phrase "I went by…" to describe the scales on graphs (e.g., 'I went by ones' or 'I went by twos'). Using an ethnographic stance, the analysis focused on the ways that the participants themselves used those phrases, not on any one canonical meaning. The graphs, verbal descriptions, gestures, and the multiple meanings generated during the discussion

3 A Naturalistic Paradigm: An Introduction to Using Ethnographic...

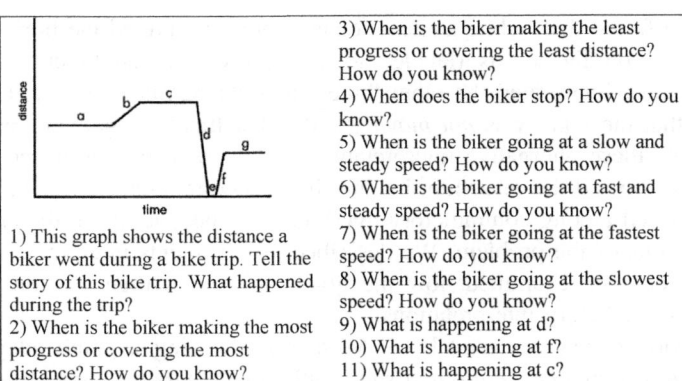

Fig. 3.1 The problem students discussed in pairs

were all resources for socially constructing interpretations of the graphs. These phrases and their meanings were locally situated, not only in this particular discussion, but also in the history of the classroom and lesson. The classroom observations (and observations in other classrooms) provided the data necessary to contextualize those phrases as not just used by these two students and as not just unusual or strange but part of the local classroom ecology.

For another analysis, I used only the peer discussion data, but that analysis was still informed by the classroom observations. In that paper (Moschkovich et al. 2017), we analyzed eight peer discussion sessions that involved four pairs of bilingual students (two discussion sessions per pair). During the peer discussion sessions, pairs of students answered questions about a distance versus time graph and an imagined bicycle trip.[9] The students were working on a problem with twelve questions about a distance vs. time graph depicting the motion of an imagined biker (shown in Fig. 3.1). The first question asked the students to tell a story about a bike trip corresponding to the graph. Questions two through eight asked students to identify when the biker was going fastest, slowest, or stopped. Questions nine through twelve asked what was happening for particular segments of the graph.

This paper is an example of using an ethnographic stance, in this case to analyze not classroom data but the data from pair discussion outside of a classroom using an ecologically valid task. For the analysis, we used the pairs as the unit of analysis, coded video with transcripts for student conceptions, counted and summarized conceptions for each pair, and made comparisons across pairs of students. Using an ethnographic stance, the chapter describes how pairs of students generated multiple interpretations of the horizontal segments on the graph in Fig. 3.1, a distance-time graph depicting the motion of a biker. Assuming the biker moves along a line, all horizontal segments on this graph represent that the biker was stationary. In this

---

[9]While the student pairs worked together on the task, the first author of the paper observed silently and then asked follow-up questions in order to clarify student responses and understand students' assumptions about the goals of the task.

analysis we found that, while students consistently interpreted the horizontal segment located on the *x*-axis (labeled *e*) as representing the biker *not moving*, sometimes they interpreted the other three horizontal segments (*a*, *c*, and *g*), representing that the biker was *not moving* and, other times, as *moving*. We did not view any of these alternative interpretations of the segments as misconceptions. Instead, we showed the reasoning behind these interpretations and described how students shifted among contradictory interpretations depending on the affordances and constraints of the problem. We described how students interpreted horizontal segments and then examined how the graph and the written text mediated the students' contradictory interpretations.

This problem was designed by J. Moschkovich using a graph adapted from *Investigations in number, data, and space,* 4th grade, "Graphs" unit (Russell et al. 1997) and questions used in this classroom's text/unit from *Connected Mathematics Project* (Lappan et al. 1998). The questions were presented in both English and Spanish. The problem was designed using both previous research and curriculum materials with several goals in mind. First, the central goal for the task was not to assess student learning during the curriculum unit but, instead, to explore student conceptual understandings, especially as they discussed their answers with a peer. Second, the problem was designed to be an ecologically valid task (Moschkovich and Brenner 2000) for the activity in this classroom. The graph and the questions were designed to parallel the form and content of questions in the units from *Connected Mathematics Project* (Lappan et al. 1998) that were used in this classroom.

The questions were constructed using terms and phrases commonly used in the classroom and in the unit text, such as "steady pace," "most progress," "least progress," etc. Previous research has shown that learners face difficulties in developing qualitative understandings of graphs, so another goal for the task was to elicit students' qualitative reasoning and conceptual understanding, rather than computational skills, so the graph and questions contain no numbers. Although the graph may appear "strange" (the trip does not start at the origin, segment *d* can be interpreted in multiple ways), these aspects of the graph are not considered defects of the task design, but instead, as characteristics of an interesting, challenging, and open ended task hypothesized to generate multiple conjectures and stimulate discussion between the students solving the problem.

The introduction to the peer discussion sessions included a description of the guidelines for how the student pairs were to discuss and record their responses. The students were instructed to provide answers and explanations for each problem. To structure dialogue and discussion, the students followed an instructional sequence similar to the Itakura method for classroom discussions in science (Hatano 1988; Inagaki 1981; Inagaki and Hatano 1977). Students were asked to discuss their answers and agree on an answer with their partner before writing their final answer on paper. To promote the discussion of different conjectures, students were told that they did not have to agree on their initial choices, and that their individual choices would be recorded on the videotape, but that they had to agree on their final answers.

Each pair participated in two peer discussion sessions, separated by approximately eight weeks, where they worked on the problem in Fig. 3.1. Each session lasted between 45 min and 1 h. During the interval between discussion sessions, these students participated in an eight-week curriculum unit on graphing and everyday motion from *Connected Mathematics Project* (Lappan et al. 1998) titled "Moving Straight Ahead." The peer-discussion sessions were videotaped, transcribed, and coded. Students' written work was collected and included in the analysis.

For the purpose of that analysis, we treated the pair of students as the unit of analysis. In order to describe how pairs of students interpreted horizontal segments in the graph, we compared what students wrote as their final answer on a shared answer sheet with the video and transcripts of the discussion that took place between students as they worked towards consensus. In that analysis, we focused on the students' interpretations of the horizontal segments a, c, e and g, not only because different pairs interpreted these segments differently, but also because within each pair, the statements students made about horizontal segments were often conflicting.

Since mathematical reasoning activity involves coordinating multiple semiotic resources, the analysis included attention to the variety of semiotic tools that students used such as the graph, the written text, student's written responses, and spoken language (including terms referring to parts of the graph, terms used during classroom lessons, and terms borrowed from the text in the written questions). Finally, we found that in order to understand how the student pairs were interpreting horizontal segments in the graph, it was crucial to understand the problem context not as a given (or from an expert's perspective), but from the students' perspective and as co-constructed by the pair.

The development of our coding scheme for analyzing the students' discussion was motivated by a concern with staying "close" to students' interpretations, a focus on the specifics of how student interpretations were mediated by a particular problem context, and an emphasis on interpretation as a productive reasoning practice. The first stage of our three-step coding process involved identifying and paraphrasing utterances that referred to any of the seven labeled line segments of the graph. At this stage, in order to increase reliability, the second and third authors coded utterances independently and then compared codes. The three authors discussed any uncertainties in coding, revisited any discrepancies, and reviewed transcript coding in conjunction with the original video data. Only utterances that were clearly referring to a particular segment were retained in the analysis. The second stage involved compiling paraphrased utterances that could be attributed to each of the horizontal line segments on the graph (segments a, c, e, and g, where our definition of "horizontal" is "parallel to or on the x-axis"). The third stage involved deriving and using two super-ordinate headings to group clusters of utterances. For example, the responses "stayed where he was" and "didn't move at all" and "he stopped" were clustered under the heading *not moving* and responses such as "started going again" or "going fast and steady" were clustered under the heading *moving*. After coding, clustering, and quantifying student utterances by pairs, we returned to the transcripts, video, and written data to examine in more detail any relationships between these clustered target utterances and the problem context associated with these utterances, to uncover what elements of the problem context students were referring to.

3.6 Learning to Use Ethnographic Methods

In closing, I suggest several ways that early career researchers can learn to use ethnographic methods for research in mathematics education. Although reading foundational texts is necessary, it is not sufficient. Reading can be supplemented by taking a methodology course, but that is also not enough. The optimal way to learn and develop expertise is to apprentice with mentors or more experienced peers. One can also collect tips from experienced researchers and listen to their stories. It is important to actually work at designing a project or study that would include using ethnographic methods as part of the overall research design and have that design critiqued and improved by experienced researchers.

Below are a few suggested discussion questions to consider:

1. Collect ideas from colleagues for how novice researchers can learn to use ethnographic methods.
2. Imagine and describe a small project or study that you think could be designed using ethnographic methods as part of the overall research design.

    (a) Focus on a few research questions and how the ethnographic methods will address those questions: What are the purposes of this ethnographic data collection, verifying or generating theory, gathering evidence, generating hypotheses, justifying a claim or claims?
    (b) How will the ethnographic methods be combined with other methods?
    (c) How will you make decisions regarding what ethnographic data to collect?

References

Brenner, M. E. (1985). The practice of arithmetic in Liberian schools. *Anthropology and Education Quarterly, 16*(3), 177–186.
Brenner, M. E. (1998). Adding cognition to the formula for culturally relevant instruction in mathematics. *Anthropology and Education Quarterly, 29*(2), 214–244.
Bronfenbrenner, U. (1977). Toward an experimental ecology of human development. *American psychologist, 32*(7), 513.

Brown, A. L. (1992). Design experiments: Theoretical and methodological challenges in creating complex interventions in classroom settings. *The Journal of the Learning Sciences, 2*, 171–178.

Civil, M. (2002). Culture and mathematics: A community approach. *Journal of Intercultural Studies, 23*(2), 133–148.

Civil, M., & Bernier, E. (2006). Exploring images of parental participation in mathematics education: challenges and possibilities. *Mathematical Thinking and Learning, 8*(3), 309–330.

Cole, M., Hood, L., & McDermott, R. P. (1978). Ecological niche picking: Ecological invalidity as an axiom of cognitive psychology. *Unpublished manuscript. Laboratory of Comparative Human Cognition, Rockefeller University, New York.*

Confrey, J. (1990). A review of the research on student conceptions in mathematics, science, and programming. *Review of Research in Education, 16*, 3–56.

D'Ambrosio, U. (1985). *Socio-cultural bases for mathematics education.* Campinas, Brazil: UNICAMP.

D'Ambrosio, U. (1991). Ethno-mathematics and its place in the history and pedagogy of mathematics. In M. Harris (Ed.), *Schools, mathematics and work* (pp. 15–25). Bristol, PA: Falmer Press.

De Freitas, E., & Sinclair, N. (2012). Diagram, gesture, agency: Theorizing embodiment in the mathematics classroom. *Educational Studies in Mathematics, 80*(1–2), 133–152.

Derry, S. J., Pea, R. D., Barron, B., Engle, R. A., Erickson, F., Goldman, R., et al. (2010). Conducting video research in the learning sciences: Guidance on selection, analysis, technology, and ethics. *The Journal of the Learning Sciences, 19*(1), 3–53.

Edwards, L. D. (2009). Gestures and conceptual integration in mathematical talk. *Educational Studies in Mathematics, 70*(2), 127–141.

Edwards, L., Radford, L., & Arzarello, F. (Eds.). (2009). *Gestures and multimodality in the construction of mathematical meaning.* Dordrecht, The Netherlands: Springer.

Erickson, F. (1986). Qualitative methods in research on teaching. In M. Wittrock (Ed.), *Handbook of research on teaching* (3rd ed., pp. 119–161). New York, NY: MacMillan.

Erlandson, D. A., Harris, E. L., Skipper, B. L., & Allen, S. D. (1993). *Doing naturalistic inquiry: A guide to methods.* Newbury Park, CA: Sage Publications.

Finegan, E., & Besnier, N. (1989). *Language: its structure and use.* NY: Harcourt Brace Jovanovich.

Frederiksen, J. R., Sipusic, M., Sherin, M., & Wolfe, E. W. (1998). Video portfolio assessment: Creating a framework for viewing the functions of teaching. *Educational Assessment, 5*(4), 225–297.

Garcia, E., & Gonzalez, R. (1995). Issues in systemic reform for culturally and linguistically diverse students. *Teachers College Record, 96*(3), 418–431.

Glaser, R., & Strauss, A. (1967). *The discovery of grounded theory.* Chicago: Aldine.

Goldman, R. (2014). *Points of viewing children's thinking.* Psychology Press.

González, N., Andrade, R., Civil, M., & Moll, L. (2001). Bridging funds of distributed knowledge: Creating zones of practices in mathematics. *Journal of Education for Students Placed at Risk, 6*(1–2), 115–132.

Guba, E. G. (1990). The alternative paradigm dialog. In E. G. Guba (Ed.), *The paradigm dialog* (pp. 17–31). Newbury Park, CA: Sage Publications.

Guba, E. G. (1993). Foreword. In D. A. Erlandson, E. L. Harris, B. L. Skipper, & S. D. Allen (Eds.), *Doing naturalistic inquiry: A guide to methods* (pp. ix–xv). Newbury Park, CA: Sage Publications.

Gutiérrez, K. D., & Rogoff, B. (2003). Cultural ways of learning: Individual traits or repertoires of practice. *Educational Researcher, 32*(5), 19–25.

Hall, R. (2000). Video recording as theory. In R. Lesh & A. Kelly (Eds.), *Handbook of research design in mathematics and science education* (pp. 647–664). Mahwah, NJ: Lawrence Erlbaum Associates.

Hatano, G. (1988). Social and motivational bases for mathematical understanding. In G. Saxe & M. Gearhart (Eds.), *Children's mathematics* (Vol. 41). New directions for child development. SF: Jossey-Bass.

Inagaki, K. (1981). Facilitation of knowledge integration through classroom discussion. *The Quarterly Newsletter of the laboratory of Comparative Human Cognition, 3*(2), 26–28.

Inagaki, K., & Hatano, G. (1977). Amplification of cognitive motivation and its effect on epistemic observation. *American Educational Research Journal, 14,* 485–491.

Jacob, E. (1987). Qualitative research traditions: A review. *Review of Educational Research, 57,* 1–50.

Lappan, G., Fey, J. T., Fitzgerald, W. M., Friel, S. N., & Phillips, E. D. (1998). *Connected mathematics.* White Plains, NY: Dale Seymour Publications.

Lave, J. (1988). *Cognition in practice.* New York: Cambridge University Press.

Lave, J. (1997). The culture of acquisition and the practice of understanding. *Situated cognition: Social, semiotic, and psychological perspectives* (pp. 63–82).

Lee, C. D., Spencer, M. B., & Harpalani, V. (2003). Every shut eye ain't sleep: Studying how people live culturally. *Educational Researcher, 32*(5), 6–13.

Lincoln, Y., & Guba, E. (1985). *Naturalistic inquiry.* Beverly Hills, CA: Sage Publications.

McDermott, R., Gospodinoff, K., & Aron, J. (1978). Criteria for an ethnographically adequate description of concerted activities and their contexts. *Semiotica, 24,* 245–275.

Moschkovich, J. N. (1992). Students' use of the x-intercept: An instance of a transitional conception. In W. Geeslin & K. Graham (Eds.), *Proceedings of the Sixteenth Meeting of the International Group for the Psychology of Mathematics Education* (Vol. 2, pp. 128–135). Durham, NH: Program Committee of the 16th PME Conference.

Moschkovich, J. N. (1996). Moving up and getting steeper: Negotiating shared descriptions of linear graphs. *The Journal of the Learning Sciences, 5*(3), 239–277.

Moschkovich, J. N. (1998). Resources for refining conceptions: Case studies in the domain of linear functions. *The Journal of the Learning Sciences, 7*(2), 209–237.

Moschkovich, J. N. (1999). Students' use of the x-intercept as an instance of a transitional conception. *Educational Studies in Mathematics, 37,* 169–197.

Moschkovich, J. N. (2008). I went by twos, he went by one: Multiple interpretations of inscriptions as resources for mathematical discussions. *The Journal of the Learning Sciences, 17*(4), 551–587.

Moschkovich, J. N. (2011). Ecological approaches to transnational research on mathematical reasoning. In R. Kitchen & M. Civil (Eds.), *Transnational and borderland studies in mathematics education* (pp. 1–22). New York, NY: Routledge, Taylor & Francis.

Moschkovich, J. N., & Brenner, M. (2000). Integrating a naturalistic paradigm into research on mathematics and science cognition and learning. In R. Lesh & A. Kelly (Eds.), *Handbook of research design in mathematics and science education* (pp. 457–486). Mahwah, NJ: Lawrence Erlbaum Associates.

Moschkovich, J., Zahner, W., & Ball, T. (2017). Reading a graph of motion: How multiple textual resources mediate student interpretations of horizontal segments. In J. Langman & H. Hansen-Thomas (Eds.), *Discourse Analytic perspectives on STEM education: Exploring interaction and learning in the multilingual classroom* (pp. 31–51). New York, NY: Springer.

Nunes, T., Schliemann, A., & Carraher, D. (1993). *Street mathematics and school mathematics.* Cambridge, UK: Cambridge University Press.

Ochs, E. (1979). Transcription as theory. In E. Ochs & B. Schieffelin (Eds.), *Developmental pragmatics* (pp. 41–72). New York, NY: Academic Press.

Poland, B. (2002). Transcription quality. In J. Gubrium & J. Hosltein (Eds.), *Handbook of interview research context and method.* Thousand oaks, CA: Sage.

Russell, S., Tierney, C., Mokros, J., & Goodrow, A. (1997). *Investigations in number, data, and space* (Fourth grade, Graphs unit). Palo Alto, CA: Dale Seymour Publications.

Spindler, G., & Spindler, L. (1987). Ethnography: An anthropological view. In G. Spindler (Ed.), *Education and cultural process* (pp. 151–156). Prospect Heights, IL: Waveland.

Spradley, J. P. (1979). *The ethnographic interview*. Fort Worth, TX: Harcourt Brace Jovanovich.
Strauss, A., & Corbin, J. M. (1990). *Basics of qualitative research: Grounded theory procedures and techniques*. Sage Publications, Inc.
Tobin, J., Wu, D., & Davidson, D. (1989). *Preschool in three cultures: Japan, Chain, and the United States*. New Haven, CT: Yale University Press.
Ulewicz, M., & Beatty, A. (Eds.). (2001). *The power of video in international comparative research in education*. Washington DC: National Academy Press.

Open Access This chapter is licensed under the terms of the Creative Commons Attribution 4.0 International License (http://creativecommons.org/licenses/by/4.0/), which permits use, sharing, adaptation, distribution and reproduction in any medium or format, as long as you give appropriate credit to the original author(s) and the source, provide a link to the Creative Commons license and indicate if changes were made.

The images or other third party material in this chapter are included in the chapter's Creative Commons license, unless indicated otherwise in a credit line to the material. If material is not included in the chapter's Creative Commons license and your intended use is not permitted by statutory regulation or exceeds the permitted use, you will need to obtain permission directly from the copyright holder.

Chapter 4
An Introduction to Grounded Theory with a Special Focus on Axial Coding and the Coding Paradigm

Maike Vollstedt and Sebastian Rezat

Abstract In this chapter we introduce grounded theory methodology and methods. In particular we clarify which research questions are appropriate for a grounded theory study and give an overview of the main techniques and procedures, such as the coding procedures, theoretical sensitivity, theoretical sampling, and theoretical saturation. We further discuss the role of theory within grounded theory and provide examples of studies in which the coding paradigm of grounded theory has been altered in order to be better suitable for applications in mathematics education. In our exposition we mainly refer to grounded theory techniques and procedures according to Strauss and Corbin (Basics of qualitative research: Grounded theory procedures and techniques, Sage Publications, Thousand Oaks, 1990), but also include other approaches in the discussion in order to point out the particularities of the approach by Strauss and Corbin.

Keywords Grounded theory · Coding procedures · Coding paradigm · Coding families · Theoretical sensitivity

4.1 Introduction

In 1967, sociologists Barney Glaser and Anselm Strauss published their seminal book "The discovery of grounded theory: Strategies for qualitative research" (Glaser and Strauss 1967), which lays the foundation for one of the most prominent and influential qualitative research methodologies in the social sciences and beyond. With their focus on theory development, they dissociate themselves from mere theory verification and the concomitant separation of the context of theory

---

M. Vollstedt (✉)
University of Bremen, Bremen, Germany
e-mail: vollstedt@math.uni-bremen.de

S. Rezat
University of Paderborn, Paderborn, Germany
e-mail: srezat@math.uni-paderborn.de

© The Author(s) 2019
G. Kaiser and N. Presmeg (eds.), *Compendium for Early Career Researchers in Mathematics Education*, ICME-13 Monographs,
https://doi.org/10.1007/978-3-030-15636-7_4

discovery and the context of theory justification, which was the prominent scientific method at that time. With their approach to qualitative research, they also go beyond the mere description of phenomena. Originally, the book was written as a book for young researchers. One of its main intentions was to legitimate qualitative research (Mey and Mruck 2011).

Quite soon after their joint publication in 1967, Glaser and Strauss developed grounded theory in different directions and started to argue their own understanding of grounded theory methodology and methods apart from each other in different ways, Glaser primarily on his own, Strauss also together with Juliet Corbin (Glaser 1978; Strauss 1987; Strauss and Corbin 1990). Later, students of Glaser and Strauss further developed the different interpretations of grounded theory methodology so that today there is a second generation of grounded theory researchers, namely Juliet Corbin, Adele E. Clarke, and Kathy Charmaz (Morse et al. 2009). As those further developments of grounded theory resulted in different research methodologies, it has been suggested to talk about grounded theory methodologies in plural or at least to acknowledge that there are numerous *modi operandi* involving grounded theory methods in different fields of research as well as different national traditions (Mey and Mruck 2011). In Germany, for instance, it is still most common to work with the grounded theory methodology version that was published by Strauss and Corbin in 1990 (German translation from 1996). The second generation's developments are still hardly noticed.

As this chapter is an introduction to grounded theory methodology and methods, our aim is to outline the common core of the different approaches to grounded theory. Therefore, we give a short introduction to grounded theory as a methodology (Sect. 4.2) and its techniques and procedures (Sect. 4.3). We further discuss an issue that lies at the heart of grounded theory, namely the role of theory within the methodology (Sect. 4.4). There, we also describe some examples of studies that used grounded theory as the main methodology, but took a specific stance to theory development in using the methodology.

4.2 A Short Positioning of Grounded Theory

This section provides a short overview of grounded theory as a methodology. We aim to answer two questions: 1. What is a grounded theory? 2. What kind of research questions are appropriate for a grounded theory study?

4.2.1 What Is Grounded Theory?

There is no simple answer to this question as the term *grounded theory* adheres to different research elements. In the first place, grounded theory is a methodology, which is characterized by the iterative process and the interrelatedness of planning, data collection, data analysis, and theory development. Grounded theory further provides a particular set of systematic methods, which support abstraction from the data in order to develop a theory that is grounded in the empirical data. These methods include different coding procedures, which are based on the method of constant comparison. New data are gathered continuously and new cases are included in the analysis based on their potential contribution to the further development and refinement of the evolving theory. This sampling method is called *theoretical sampling*. The iterative process of data collection according to theoretical sampling, data analysis, and theory development is continued until new data do not contribute any longer to a substantial development of the theory, i.e. until *theoretical saturation* is achieved. The theory that is the product of this process is also referred to as *grounded theory*. The quality of a grounded theory is not evaluated according to the standard criteria of test theory, i.e. objectivity, reliability and validity, but according to criteria such as credibility, plausibility, and trustworthiness.

4.2.2 What Kind of Research Questions Are Appropriate for a Grounded Theory Study?

According to the usual scientific procedure, the research question is at the outset of any scientific endeavour. It is the essence of what the researcher wants to know. The overall purpose of the study is to find an answer to the research question. Methodology and related methods are but a vehicle to find the (possibly best) answer to the research question. Ideally, it should be the research question that determines the methodology and not vice versa. Thus, it is important to ask what kind of research questions are appropriate for a grounded theory study. The character of the research question will influence the methodology and the choice of methods. We will try to characterize the kind of questions to which grounded theory could probably provide a good answer.

The overarching goal of grounded theory is to develop theory. Therefore, grounded theory studies may be carried out related to research phenomena or objects, which lack a (sufficient) theoretical foundation. It may be, that no theory exists for the phenomena under study or that the existing theories are insufficient in that

- they lack important concepts;
- the relationships among the concepts are not elaborated enough;
- the relevance of the concepts and their relationships has not been corroborated for the population or the context under study.

Due to the origins of grounded theory in the social sciences, the main epistemological interest lies in predicting and explaining behavior in social interaction. Thus, Strauss and Corbin (1990) stress the orientation towards action and processes of grounded theory research questions.

4.3 A Short Introduction to the Methods and Techniques of Grounded Theory

The methods and techniques of grounded theory make use of different elements: some relate to the collection, some to the evaluation of data, and some refer to the research process. The following section gives a short introduction to the most important methods and techniques to make the start of working with grounded theory easier for a newcomer to this vast field. A more detailed description of the procedures and techniques can be found in the original literature describing grounded theory (e.g., Glaser 1978; Strauss 1987; Strauss and Corbin 1990). Note that technical terms and procedures may differ (slightly) when adhering to literature from different traditions of grounded theory. Even within one tradition of grounded theory, the methodology may also change over time (see Sect. 4.3.3.2 for an example with relation to the coding paradigm proposed by Strauss and Corbin 1990 and Corbin and Strauss 2015 respectively). To gain a more practical idea about the application of grounded theory, we suggest looking at Vollstedt (2015) for an example of the application of grounded theory methods in an international comparative study in mathematics education carried out in Germany and Hong Kong.

4.3.1 Theoretical Sensitivity and Sensitizing Concepts

When starting to work with grounded theory, there is no fixed theory at hand with which to evaluate the data. On the contrary, the researcher moves into an open field of study with many unclear aspects. As described above, important concepts are missing, and/or their relationship is not elaborated enough. The longer the researcher will have worked in this field, the clearer those unclear aspects will (hopefully) become. In order to make sense of the data, an important ability of the researcher is theoretical sensitivity. The notion of theoretical sensitivity is closely linked to grounded theory and Glaser (1978) even devoted a whole book to this issue. Corbin and Strauss (2015) describe sensitivity as "having insights as well as being tuned into and being able to pick up on relevant issues, events, and happenings during collection and analysis of the data" (p. 78). According to Glaser with the assistance of Holton (2004) the essence of theoretical sensitivity is the "ability to generate concepts from data and to relate them according to normal models of theory in general" (para. 43). They further sum up a number of single abilities that characterize the theoretical sensitivity of a researcher. These are "the personal and temperamental bent to maintain analytic distance, tolerate confusion and regression while remaining open, trusting to preconscious processing and to conceptual emergence [...] the ability to develop theoretical insight into the area of research combined with the ability to make something of these insights [...] the ability to conceptualize and organize, make abstract connections, visualize and think multivariately" (para. 43).

The opinions about how a researcher might develop theoretical sensitivity differ between the two founders of grounded theory and are in fact one of the main differences between their approaches. While Glaser (with the assistance of Holton 2004) suggests that the "first step in gaining theoretical sensitivity is to enter the research setting with as few predetermined ideas as possible" (para. 43), Strauss and Corbin (1990) name different sources of theoretical sensitivity: these are respective literature, the professional and personal experience of the researcher as well as the analytical process itself. However, the researcher is not supposed to follow the beaten track of the literature or his/her personal experience, but to question these and go beyond in order to get novel theoretical insight. In "Basics of qualitative research" Strauss and Corbin (1990) describe techniques to foster theoretical sensitivity. These are questioning, analyzing single words, phrases or sentences, and comparing, thus techniques, which pervade grounded theory in general.

4.3.2 Interdependence of Data Collection, Analysis, and Development of Theory

One characteristic of grounded theory is that data collection, data analysis, and theory development are not successive steps in the research procedure but are intertwined and interdependent. Thus, action in terms of data collection and reflexion in terms of data analysis and theory development always alternate. Data collection and analysis initialize the process of theory development. Further cycles of data collection and analysis are guided by theoretical sampling and serve to specify the research focus on the one hand, and to develop hypotheses and theory on the other. Theoretical sampling denotes a cumulative sampling method, in which the selection of new cases that are to be included in the analysis is guided by the unfolding theory. In this context "cases" does not necessarily mean "people". Corbin and Strauss (2015) point out that "it is concepts and not people, per se, that are sampled" (p. 135). The authors point out that the goal of theoretical sampling might vary throughout the process of theory development. In the beginning of the process, cases are selected, because they are likely to enable the discovery of new relevant concepts. Later on, cases are selected because they are likely to contribute to the differentiation, elaboration, consolidation, and validation of categories in terms of their properties, their dimensions, or their interrelations (see the next section for the development of concepts and categories).

Theoretical sampling and the development of theory are continued until *theoretical saturation* is achieved, i.e., new data do not seem to contribute any longer to the elaboration of categories. The relations between the categories are well developed and validated (Strauss and Corbin 1990).

4.3.3 Data Analysis

The overarching goal of data analysis in the grounded theory methodology is theory development. In order to achieve this goal, the collected data are evaluated by applying different ways of coding as the core process. Coding in grounded theory methodology is a process of conceptual abstraction by assigning general concepts (codes) to singular incidences in the data.

After having collected some (not necessarily all) data, the evaluation process may begin. Depending on which line of grounded theory methodology one follows, the different kinds of coding that are applied may vary in nomenclature as well as procedures (Glaser 1978; Mey and Mruck 2011; Strauss and Corbin 1990; Teppo 2015). Glaser (1978) discriminates between substantive coding, which consists of open and selective coding, and theoretical coding. In contrast, Strauss and Corbin (1990) differentiate between three kinds of coding procedures that are needed to develop a grounded theory from the data: open, axial, and selective coding. These procedures are not to be misunderstood as being precise procedures that are easily distinguishable. On the contrary, the procedures are neither clear-cut, nor do they easily define phases that chronologically come one after the other. They embody rather different ways of working with the data that can be combined with each other and between which the researcher can move back and forth if needed (Mey and Mruck 2011).

The following sections give a brief overview of open, axial, and selective coding following Strauss and Corbin (1990). Section 4.4 then focusses on the role of theory in grounded theory with a special focus on axial coding and the coding paradigm.

4.3.3.1 Open Coding

Although the different procedures of coding do not occur in a strict sequence, open coding is usually the first approach to the data. Core elements of open coding are posing sensitizing questions and constantly comparing data and codes.

Open coding is the part of data analysis that focuses on the conceptualisation and categorisation of phenomena through an intensive analysis of the data. In this first step of open coding, the data are broken up into smaller parts that are deeply analysed. The aim of this analysis is to grasp the core idea of each part and to develop a code to describe it. Open codes can be either developed in vivo, i.e. directly from the data using descriptions that also are derived from or close to the data, or with reference to technical literature referring, e.g., to theories from mathematics education, educational psychology, or other relevant areas of study.

In a second step then, these smaller analytical parts are compared with respect to similarities and differences. Similar parts can be labelled with the same code. Strauss and Corbin (1990) use the terms *concept* and *category* to denote a phenomenon that is categorized and conceptualized by assigning it to one code (*concept*) or concepts of higher order (*category*). This means that the concepts developed are then related to other concepts so that categories of a higher order emerge so that different dimensions of the category can be described. During the process of developing the dimensions of categories, theoretically relevant characteristics of every category are determined and explicated in the code descriptions (Mey and Mruck 2011).

The overall goal of open coding is to develop a wealth of codes with which to describe the data. To reach this goal, sensitizing questions are posed regarding the data when they are being analysed. This finally leads to new discoveries (Strauss and Corbin 1990). The following list shows some of the questions that offer rich answers for the interpretation of the data (Böhm 2004; Mey and Mruck 2011; Strauss and Corbin 1990):

- What?—Which phenomenon is described?
- Who?—Which people are involved? Which roles do they embody, or which ones are assigned to them?
- How?—Which aspects of the phenomenon are dealt with? Which are left out?
- When? How long? Where?—In what way is the spaciotemporal dimension biographically relevant or important for single actions?
- Why?—Which justifications are given or deducible?
- Whereby?—Which strategies are used?
- What for?—Which consequences are anticipated?

To pose those sensitizing questions, the researcher uses his/her personal and professional experience as well as knowledge that was gained from the relevant literature. All those resources are used in a creative manner of free association (Strauss and Corbin 1990) to interpret the data and to develop codes to describe the interpretation found. Thus, the researcher's own and other people's presuppositions in relation to the phenomenon are questioned and investigated.

4.3.3.2 Axial Coding

To develop a grounded theory, the emerging relationships between the elaborated concepts need to be integrated into an overarching framework with one core category. Glaser (1978) calls this process *theoretical coding*; Strauss and Corbin (1990) differentiate between *axial coding* and *selective coding*, but themselves emphasize that there is not much of a difference, except at the level of abstraction.

According to Strauss and Corbin (1990), axial coding is needed to investigate the relationships between concepts and categories that have been developed in the open coding process. As people act and interact with other people, they possess different strategies to handle their interpretations of the situations in which they are involved. Their acting as well as the pursuit of their strategies have consequences. Explanations contain conditions that have an impact on one's actions and interaction as well as the consequences that result from these (Strauss and Corbin 1990). To work out the relations between the categories, Strauss and Corbin (1990) suggest examining the data and the codes based on a coding paradigm that focuses on and relates causal conditions, context, intervening conditions, action/interaction strategies, and consequences. These perspectives on the data help to detect relations between concepts and categories in order to relate them on a meta level. Strauss and Corbin (1990) perceive the coding paradigm as an obligatory element of a grounded theory: if the coding paradigm was not used in theory development, the theory would miss density and precision.

One of the most difficult questions for a researcher new to the field of grounded theory is as follows: How does the coding paradigm work? After having broken up the data in the process of open coding, they are joined together in a new way in the process of axial coding as links are worked out between a category and its subcategories. The focus of axial coding is on a category (the phenomenon) in relation to the following aspects. First, causal conditions specify the phenomenon with respect to incidents or occurrences that result in appearance or development of a phenomenon. Second, the context is the specific set of characteristics in which the phenomenon is embedded. Simultaneously, the context also characterizes the special set of conditions in which action/interaction strategies take place to overcome, handle or react to a certain phenomenon. Third, intervening strategies are the broad and general conditions that influence action/interaction strategies. These comprise, for instance, time, space, culture, socioeconomic status, technological status, career, history, and individual biography. Fourth, action or interaction strategies are directed towards the phenomenon. No matter whether the research is about individuals, groups or collectives, there is always action or interaction that is directed towards the phenomenon, to handle or to overcome it, to perform it, or to react to it. The phenomenon always appears in a certain context or under specific circumstances. The interactional component is related to the self of the acting person as well as to other interactions. And finally, action and interaction that are performed or—on the contrary—are not performed as an answer to or to overcome a phenomenon, lead to results and consequences. These are neither always predictable nor intended, and also the default of an action/interaction leads to results and consequences. Consequences can be real or hypothetical in the present or in the future. In addition, consequences can change their frame of reference as in one point of time they can be consequences of an action/interaction, whereas at a later point of time, they can be part of causal conditions for another phenomenon. Note that in the fourth edition of the "Basics of qualitative research", Corbin and Strauss (2015) reduced the coding paradigm to the three main features "conditions", "actions-interactions", and "consequences or outcomes".

As Glaser, Strauss, and his colleagues were social scientists, the aspects chosen for their coding paradigm do not necessarily meet the necessities for educational research. Thus, there have been researchers who have changed the procedure of axial coding such that they in general followed the idea to look for relations between the phenomena described in the categories that were developed in the process of open coding but changed the aspects in the coding paradigm to look for those relations. We take a deeper look at the coding paradigm and its possibilities of amendment in Sect. 4.4.

4.3.3.3 Selective Coding

The goal of selective coding is to integrate the different categories that have been developed, elaborated, and mutually related during axial coding into one cohesive theory. To reach this goal, the results from axial coding are further elaborated, integrated, and validated. Thus, selective coding is quite similar to axial coding, but it is carried out on a more abstract level. The categories are theoretically integrated into a consistent overarching theory as they are subsumed under a core category that is linked to all other categories that were established in axial coding. As Teppo (2015, with reference to Corbin and Strauss 2008, p. 14) points out, the questions that have to be answered are "what is the research all about?" and "what seems to be going on here?". Thus, selective coding is the process of choosing the core category and relating it with the other categories from axial coding. In addition, these relations need to be validated and some categories might need to be refined and further elaborated. The core category described "the central phenomenon around which all the other categories are integrated" (Strauss and Corbin 1990, p. 116). If the core category is found, the story line of the research is set or, as Vollstedt (2015) writes, the path is detected that leads the way through all the trees so that the wood can finally be seen. Having detected the core category, the researcher knows the central phenomenon of his/her research and can finally answer the research question. The product of this research process finally appears: the grounded theory that arose from the data.

4.3.3.4 Memos and Diagrams

A further central rule of grounded theory methodology is to interrupt the coding process again and again to write down memos: "Stop coding and record a memo on your ideas", as Glaser and Strauss (1967, p. 113) put it. In general, memos are very special types of written notes as they keep track of the analytical process and the directions for the analyst. Thus, they not only describe the phenomena they are about, but move on a meta level by being analytical and conceptual and help the researcher to step back from the material to see it from an analytical distance (Strauss and Corbin 1990). Glaser (with the assistance of Holton 2004, para. 61) writes: "Memos are theoretical notes about the data and the conceptual connections between categories. The writing of theoretical memos is the core stage in the process of generating theory. If the analyst skips this stage by going directly to sorting or writing up, after coding, he/she is not doing GT" [i.e., grounded theory].

There are different kinds of memos like memos on methodical decisions, planning steps, case selection, or interpretative team sessions. The most important variant for the development of a grounded theory is writing memos that contain code notes and theoretical notes. In the process of data analysis, codes can be elaborated so that code notes can be further developed into theoretical notes (see Strauss and Corbin 1990 for a detailed description). Although it is tempting not to write memos in the analytical process, "writing memos and doing diagrams are important elements of analysis and never should be considered superfluous, regardless of how pressed for time the analyst might be" (Strauss and Corbin 1998, p. 218). Thus, writing memos should accompany the whole analytical process from the development of the first code to the final grounded theory. Memos are written only for the analyst in order to keep track of the analytical "process, thoughts, feelings, and directions of the research and researcher—in fact, the entire gestalt of the research process" (Strauss and Corbin 1998, p. 218). Hence, they are hardly seen by people other than the researchers involved, but are nevertheless of high importance, also from the perspective of quality criteria. As mentioned above, the quality of a grounded theory can be judged—among other criteria—with reference to credibility, plausibility, and trustworthiness. Memos are needed to argue and prove the development of the grounded theory from the data and are thus a crucial aspect to draw back to when writing down the theory. In addition, Strauss and Corbin also warn "if memos and diagrams are sparsely done, then the final product theory might lack conceptual density and integration. At the end, it is impossible for the analyst to reconstruct the details of the research without memos" (Strauss and Corbin 1998, p. 218).

Supplementary to written memos, diagrams also help the researcher to find relations between concepts and develop the grounded theory from the data. Strauss and Corbin (1998) define diagrams as "visual devices that depict the relationships among concepts" (p. 217). Thus, diagrams are needed to link concepts graphically, which is especially helpful for instance to illustrate the relations between the different elements of the coding paradigm (cf. Vollstedt 2015 for a concrete example).

4.4 The Role of Theory Within Grounded Theory and the Coding Paradigm

From its origins, there has been a conflict inherent in the grounded theory methodology, which relates to the role of theory. The main idea of grounded theory and one of its hallmarks is that categories, concepts, and finally theory 'emerge' from the data. In "The discovery of grounded theory" the researcher is therefore advised to "ignore the literature of theory and fact on the area under study, in order to assure that the emergence of categories will not be contaminated" (Glaser and Strauss 1967, p. 37). However, Glaser and Strauss also admit that "of course, the researcher does not approach reality as a *tabula rasa*. He must have a perspective that will help him see relevant data and abstract significant categories from his scrutiny of the data" (Glaser and Strauss 1967, p. 3). Thus, they acknowledge that in modern epistemology it is taken for granted that the world is always perceived through theoretical lenses and related conceptual networks, and empirical observation therefore is always influenced by the theoretical and conceptual knowledge of the observer. Thus, the inherent conflict in terms of the role of theory in grounded theory is, if it is possible that theory only "emerges" from the data or if theory is actually "forced" on the data. This has in fact been a major issue of debate between the two founders of grounded theory—Glaser and Strauss—which finally led to their separation and constitutes the fundamental difference between the two approaches to grounded theory today (Kelle 2005).

In order to resolve this conflict between an unbiased emerging of theory and the inevitably theory-laden perspective of the researcher, Glaser and Strauss introduce the notion of *theoretical sensitivity*. In later works, the *coding families* (Glaser 1978) and the *coding paradigm* (Strauss and Corbin 1990) can also be seen as answers to the same problem.

The coding families (Glaser 1978) are sets of general sociological concepts organized into loosely connected frameworks, which are supposed to foster the theoretical sensitivity of the researcher in order to support the development of theory from the data. Some illustrative examples of coding families are provided in Table 4.1. Glaser's (1978) original list is much more detailed and extensive.

Strauss and Corbin (1990) offer a general model, which they denote as "coding paradigm", and which is supposed to provide a general frame for analyzing relationships between the categories and concepts. The coding paradigm has already been described in more detail in Sect. 4.3.3.2.

Although the coding families and the coding paradigm are only very general and widely accepted perspectives on social reality, it is important to be aware that the coding families and the coding paradigm are themselves theoretical framings or orientations, which are utilized within grounded theory in order to develop theory. Thus, the development of theory is not independent, but is structured by the theoretical assumptions and relations provided by the coding families and the coding paradigm. Both encompass a particular perspective on social reality.

Due to the sociological background of Glaser and Strauss, the epistemological interest of grounded theory lies in predicting and explaining behavior and social processes. Accordingly, the coding paradigm focuses on action and interaction in social contexts and related strategies (Tiefel 2005). The causal assumptions that are

Table 4.1 Some examples from Glaser's (1978, pp. 73–82) coding families

Families	Examples
The Six C's	Causes (sources, reasons, explanations, accountings or anticipated consequences), Context or Ambiance, Contingencies, Consequences (outcomes, efforts, functions, predictions, anticipated/unanticipated), Covariances, Conditions or Qualifiers
Process	Stage, Staging, Phases, Phasing, Progressions etc.
Degree	Limit, Range, Intensity, Extent, Amount, Polarity, Extreme, Boundary, Rank, Grades, Continuum, Probability, Possibility, etc.
Dimension	Dimensions, Elements, Divisions, Piece of, Properties of, etc.
Identity-Self	Self-image, Self-concept, Self-worth, Self-evaluation, Identity, etc.
Means-goal	End, Purpose, Goal, Anticipated consequences, Products
Cultural	Social norms, Social values, Social belief, Social Sentiments
Theoretical	Parsimony, Scope, Integration, Density, Conceptual level, Relationship to data, Relationship to other theory, Clarity, Fit, Relevance, Modifiability, etc.

inherent in the coding paradigm structure the development of theory as a whole. Accordingly, Kelle (2005) advises researchers, which "may feel that this approach goes contrary to their requirements and would be well advised to construct an own coding paradigm rooted in their own theoretical tradition" (para. 21). Tiefel (2005) also argues that especially in educational research, the coding paradigm of grounded theory is not universally applicable. She even goes one step further and suggests an alternated coding paradigm, which captures dimensions of individual construction of meaning in the dialectic between the individual and the social context (see Sect. 4.4.1.1). In mathematics education research, there are also studies that are based on a grounded theory methodology, but which altered the coding paradigm according to their needs. Two examples are presented in Sects. 4.4.1.2 and 4.4.1.3.

4.4.1 Examples from Studies in Which the Coding Paradigm Was Changed

The following section provides a little insight into three studies in which the coding paradigm was altered. Tiefel (2005, cf. Sect. 4.4.1.1) offers an amendment for learning and educational science; Vollstedt (2011, cf. Sect. 4.4.1.2) and Rezat (2009, cf. Sect. 4.4.1.3) are studies from mathematics education.

4.4.1.1 A Modification of the Coding Paradigm from the Perspective of Learning and Educational Theory

As Tiefel (2005) explicates, Strauss and Corbin offer with their coding procedures a technique that relates structures, actions, and subjectivity with each other. A special focus is put on the processes involved. Being sociologists, their spotlight is primarily on the prediction and explanation of (social) action and (societal) processes. The phenomena that they are especially interested in are, thus, closely linked to a pragmatistic understanding of an activistic significance of objects, which is raised by people's action or work and which can be changed by interaction and over time. Thus, in this disciplinary context, theories that are grounded in data aim at the explanation of conditions, meanings and significances, as well as procedures that influence people in different situations and areas of their active construction of the world.

Tiefel (2005) continues that educational science also defines the analysis of interdependencies between biographic and structural processes by means of selected contexts and situations. Nevertheless, its cognitive interest focuses rather on the desire to understand individual decisions and actions. Thus, research in educational science also concentrates rather on the reconstruction of biographical processes in their interdependence with social relativities. Thus, in her research on processes of learning and education as well as the professional biography of an educational consultant, Tiefel (2005) developed a coding paradigm for processes of learning and education with a special focus on questions of understanding. She proposes the following three perspectives:

- Perspective of meaning (especially referring to the reconstruction of the self-perception): How does the informant present him-/herself? What does the person say about him-/herself? What is not mentioned? Which orientations (norms, values, sciences, commonplaces etc.) are relevant for the informant?
- Perspective of structure (especially referring to the reconstruction of the world view): Which conditions are shown as important or relevant for the possibilities and the spheres of action of the self? Which ideas, positions, and assumptions give orientation? Which social relations, institutional or social/historical connections are marked as being important for the self?
- Courses of action: Which activities/interactions does the informant describe? Which options are noticed and how are they dealt with? Are the strategies rather active or passive, target-oriented or tentative seeking?

Tiefel's (2005) suggestion for the modification of the coding paradigm with respect to learning and educational sciences is probably closer to the needs of many researchers in mathematics education than Strauss and Corbin's (1990) coding paradigm. However, there are still areas where it does not provide the structure needed to grasp the relevant information to answer the research questions. Therefore, the following two sections provide insight into two studies that further adapted the coding paradigms to their needs to be able to develop a dense grounded theory.

4.4.1.2 Personal Meaning When Dealing with Mathematics in a School Context

The claim for meaning in education has been raised for many years and meaningful learning is assumed to be a central impetus (Biller 1991) as well as one of the major goals (Vinner 2007) of education. Hence, one of the challenges of education in general as well as of mathematics education in particular is to find convincing answers to the quest for meaning. Subsequently, to make learning meaningful for the students, we need to ask the students what is meaningful to them rather than imposing some kind of meaning that might be meaningful from a normative perspective, but can hardly be related to the students' biography (Meyer 2008). Howson (2005) therefore distinguishes between two different aspects of meaning, "namely, those relating to relevance and personal significance (e.g., 'What is the point of this for me?') and those referring to the objective sense intended (i.e., signification and referents)" (p. 18). Hence, "even if students have constructed a certain meaning of a concept, that concept may still not yet be 'meaningful' for him or her in the sense of relevance to his/her life in general" (Kilpatrick et al. 2005, p. 14). In her research, Vollstedt (2011) therefore took the students' perspective when she was interested in the aspects of the learning process that make learning mathematics meaningful for them. To emphasize the focus on the learner's perspective, the term *personal meaning* was coined to designate those aspects that are personally relevant for the students, i.e., the first aspect of meaning that was described by Howson above (cf. also Vollstedt and Duchhardt, in press).

One aim of the study was to develop a grounded theory about what personal meanings students construct when they are involved with mathematical contents in a school context. A second aim was to put a special focus on the role of the cultural background of the classroom situation. Therefore, the interview study was conducted in Germany and in Hong Kong. The two places were chosen as examples of a Western and a Confucian Heritage Culture (CHC, cf. Leung et al. 2006) to make sure to have quite distinct cultural backgrounds for teaching and learning mathematics.

Data gathered for the study comprised video recordings of three mathematics classrooms (9th and 10th grade) for one week in each place together with field notes taken by the researcher. The videos were used for a sequence of stimulated recall (Gass and Mackey 2000) at the beginning of each interview with volunteers from the classes (see Vollstedt 2011 or 2015 for further details).

In the process of axial coding it turned out that neither Strauss and Corbin's (1990) nor Tiefel's (2005) coding paradigm really fitted the data and the research questions. Therefore, the coding paradigm was also adapted to the individual needs of Vollstedt's study in the following way: At first, there was a long and intense discussion with fellow researchers from the *Graduate Research Group on Educational Experience and Learner Development* at the University of Hamburg about how personal meaning might be constructed, and which aspects seemed to be relevant for its construction. In the final model it is assumed that there is an individual in a certain situation in which he/she is dealing with mathematics in a school context, e.g., the student Johanna is studying mathematics at home. The situational context, i.e., the context of the learning situation in terms of topic as well as classroom situation/home, is a crucial factor for the construction of personal meaning and of particular importance in this study as there was a special focus on cultural background of the teaching and learning situation. In this situation, there are certain preliminaries that are part of Johanna, such as her personal background, i.e., aspects that cannot be influenced by herself, including her socio-economic or migration background. In addition, personal traits, i.e., aspects that concern her self, are relevant. They comprise concepts that are discussed in various scientific fields such as educational psychology (self-concept, self-efficacy), mathematics education (beliefs), and educational science (developmental tasks). Based on these preliminaries, Johanna then constructs personal meaning with relation to the learning content and context. Depending on the result of this construction, different consequences can occur. Johanna might for instance appraise the situation with respect to her personal goals so that different actions might follow, e.g., she might not understand the contents she is dealing with and will therefore ask her neighbour for help. Or she might think that mathematics is not as important as spending time with her friends so that she will stop working on her tasks.

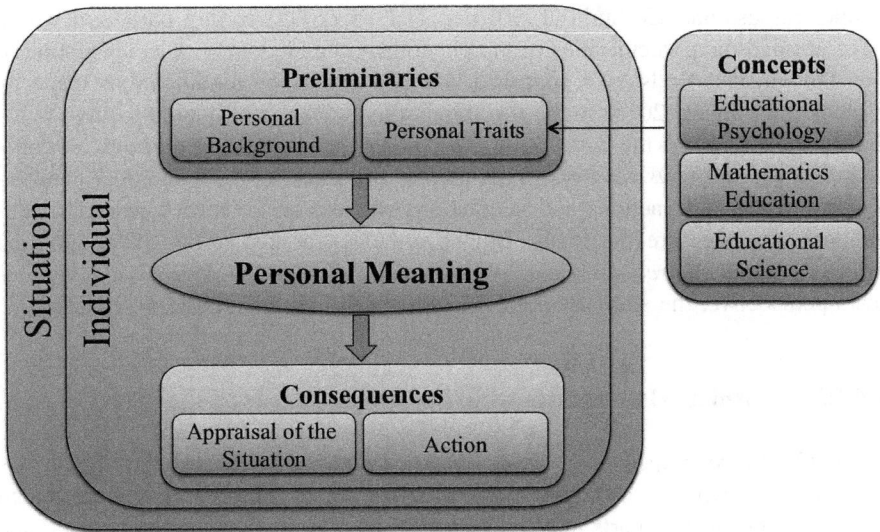

Fig. 4.1 Relational framework of personal meaning (cf. Vollstedt 2011)

The relational framework given in Fig. 4.1 shows the diagram of how the aspects described above might be interrelated to describe the construction of personal meaning. It provided the basis for the coding paradigm used by Vollstedt (2011). For each category that was developed throughout the coding process, it was attempted to fit it in this model and relate it with other relevant concepts. Thus, finally, it was possible to describe preliminaries and consequences for each core category, i.e., personal meaning, that was developed in this study (see Vollstedt 2011, 2015).

Taking a closer look at this coding paradigm, reveals that there are relations to both versions of coding paradigms provided by either Strauss and Corbin (1990) or Tiefel (2005). Vollstedt's (2011) *situation* embraces aspects from Strauss and Corbin's (1990) *context* and *intervening strategies*, whereas some aspects of the latter are also part of Vollstedt's *preliminaries*. *Consequences* are similar in both paradigms. Strauss and Corbin's *causal conditions* and *action/interaction strategies* were not found to be relevant in Vollstedt's study as they are directed towards the phenomenon, i.e., a kind of personal meaning. In Vollstedt's theory, *consequences* occur after the individual has constructed a personal meaning, so that *actions* from her framework—being part of the *consequences*—are something different than *action/interaction strategies* from Strauss and Corbin. With respect to Tiefel's (2005) aspects, on the one hand the *perspective of meaning* is similar to aspects that are described in the *preliminaries* like *personal background* and/or *personal traits*. The *perspective of structure* and the *courses of action* on the other hand relate to *situation* and *preliminaries*, and *consequences* respectively. Nevertheless, although nearly all aspects are somehow integrated in Vollstedt's (2011) coding paradigm, neither Strauss and Corbin's (1990) nor Tiefel's (2005) coding paradigm would have grasped the particularities of the phenomenon under study. It is interesting to see, though, that Vollstedt's approach is very close to the modifications made by Corbin and Strauss (2015) in the fourth edition of "Basics of qualitative research". There, they reduced the aspects of the coding paradigm to *conditions, actions-interactions*, and *consequences or outcomes*. Still, having a sociological perspective, the focus is on actions and interactions whereas in Vollstedt's research, educational processes are the focus. But nevertheless, as her coding paradigm also primarily looks at *preliminaries* and *consequences* from the context and individual's perspective, the similarities of the two approaches cannot be overlooked.

4.4.1.3 Learning Mathematics with Textbooks

Rezat (2009) developed a grounded theory on how students learn mathematics autonomously with their mathematics textbooks. Theory development is grounded in data on the specific parts that students used on their own in their textbooks, and on students' explanations of why they used these parts. He further conducted interviews with selected students in order to better understand how they proceeded when learning mathematics with their textbooks. Finally, he observed the mathematics lessons for the period of the study and took field notes (Rezat 2008).

The grounded theory comprises activities, in which students utilize their mathematics textbooks and students' utilization schemes of the textbook within these activities. Rezat (2009) finds that students refer to their mathematics textbook related to four activities:

(1) solving tasks and problems in order to get assistance from the textbook,
(2) consolidation activities in order to use the contents of the book for practicing and consolidation,
(3) acquiring mathematical knowledge that has not been a matter in class, and
(4) activities associated with interest in mathematics.

These activities clarify the causal conditions under which textbook use occurs as well as attributes of the context of the investigated phenomenon, *autonomous learning mathematics with the textbook*. In terms of activity 1, this means that the causal condition for using the textbook is that students are working on a task or a problem (that might originate from the textbook or some other source) and they need assistance for solving it. The causal condition for textbook use related to activity 2 is students' aspiration to practice and consolidate their mathematical knowledge/competencies. The inclination to acquire new mathematical knowledge or competencies is the causal condition for textbook use related to activity 3 and students' interest in mathematics motivates textbook use related to activity 4.

Although the coding paradigm of grounded theory according to Strauss and Corbin (1990) allows for a general analysis of students' actions and interactional strategies with their textbooks associated with the four activities, Rezat (2009) argues that the instrumental approach (Rabardel 2002) provides theoretical concepts and relations that grasp students' interactions with their textbook better than the general focus on actions and interactional strategies of the coding paradigm in grounded theory. Therefore, he enhances the coding paradigm by including the instrumental approach (Rabardel 2002). Instead of analyzing actions and interactional strategies he analyses students' "instrumentalization" und "instrumentation" (Rabardel 2002) of the mathematics textbook within the different learning activities. While the analysis of the instrumentalization of the mathematics textbook relates to functions that users attribute to the textbook within the activities, the analysis of instrumentation relates to the development of utilization schemes. The latter are characterized by "1. goals and anticipations; 2. rules of action, information seeking, and control; 3. operational invariants; 4. possibilities of inference" (Vergnaud 1998, p. 173). Based on this conceptualization of schemes, Rezat reconstructs different utilization schemes of students using their textbook within the different activities. For example, he finds three different utilization schemes related to consolidation activities: (1) *position-dependent practicing*; (2) *block-dependent practicing*; and (3) *salience depended practicing* (Rezat 2013). The three schemes differ in particular in terms of their operational invariants. Position-dependent practicing is based on the operational invariant that contents of the textbook that is useful for practicing can be found at a certain relative position to other contents in the textbook, e.g. tasks that are appropriate for practicing are adjacent to tasks that the teacher explicitly asked the students to work on. On the contrary, block-dependent practicing is based on the selection of a specific structural element of the textbook such as tasks, rules (in a box) or worked examples for practicing. Finally, salience-dependent practicing is based on an operational invariant that takes salient visual features of the contents as the main criteria for selection of contents from the textbook.

On the one hand, the instrumental approach and the notion of utilization schemes is included in the study as a means to increase theoretical sensitivity and to describe the cognitive aspects of students' actions and interactions with their textbooks. On the other hand, the concepts of the instrumental approach provide a language, which can be used to describe students' actions and interactions with their textbooks from a cognitive perspective as exemplified in the three utilization schemes related to students' consolidation activities with mathematics textbooks.

In the study by Rezat (2009), parts of the very general coding paradigm are substituted by a well elaborated theory. Consequently, the question has to be raised if this is actually still a grounded theory study or if a well-developed theory already existed before. However, a well-developed theory about the phenomenon under study, namely students' autonomous learning of mathematics with their textbooks, had not existed before the study. Therefore, grounded theory appears to be an adequate overall methodology of the study. In order to grasp specific aspects of the phenomenon under study in more detail, Rezat (2009) refers to existing and more general theory, which is not solely linked to the phenomenon under study. While Rabardel's (2002) theory conceptualizes human interactions with (technological) artefacts in general, Rezat (2009) develops a theory of students' learning of mathematics with their textbooks. Therefore, his approach seems to reconcile theory development and building on existing theory. While the overall goal of the study is to develop a grounded theory related to a particular phenomenon, theory development builds on more general existing theories, which seems to be a helpful approach in order to focus and describe particular elements of the developing theory. Thus, existing theory seems to be included in the grounded theory wherever it appears to be useful in the developing theory.

4.5 Concluding Remarks

In this chapter, we gave a cursory introduction to grounded theory methodology and methods. We briefly described the coding procedures, the notions of *theoretical sensitivity*, *theoretical sampling*, and *theoretical saturation* and how these components serve the main aim of grounded theory, namely to develop a theory that is empirically grounded in the data. We recommend that the (early career) researcher, who has become curious and wants to start developing grounded theory, also refers to the original sources. These describe the techniques and procedures of grounded theory in much more detail. As already pointed out at the beginning of this chapter, some of them were even written for early career researchers.

Our chapter might support the early career researcher in becoming aware of differences between the two main schools of grounded theory—grounded theory in the tradition following the foundations of Glaser or of Strauss, respectively. These differences are mainly rooted in the role of theory within grounded theory. We pointed out that the role of theory is actually an inherent epistemological issue in grounded theory methodology. We further provided examples of studies that challenge this issue by adjusting the coding paradigm according to the needs of the phenomenon under study. However, in these cases, the researcher has to justify whether the study remains a grounded theory study. We see this as just another challenge to the theoretical sensitivity of the researcher. And theoretical sensitivity is the core ability a researcher has to bring to, cultivate within, and gain from the endeavor of developing a grounded theory.

References

Biller, K. (1991). *Habe Sinn und wisse Sinn zu wecken! Sinntheoretische Grundlagen der Pädagogik [Have meaning and know how to arouse meaning! Theoretical foundations of education related to meaning]*. Hohengehren: Schneider.

Böhm, A. (2004). Theoretical coding: Text analysis in grounded theory. In U. Flick, E. von Kardorff, & I. Steinke (Eds.), *A Companion to qualitative research* (pp. 270–275). London: Sage.

Corbin, J., & Strauss, A. (2008). *Basics of qualitative research: Techniques and procedures for developing grounded theory* (3rd ed.). Thousand Oaks: Sage.

Corbin, J., & Strauss, A. (2015). *Basics of qualitative research: Techniques and procedures for developing grounded theory* (4th ed.). Newbury Park: Sage.

Gass, S. M., & Mackey, A. (2000). *Stimulated recall methodology in second language research. Second language acquisition research*. Monographs on research methodology. Mahwah: Lawrence Erlbaum.

Glaser, B. G. (1978). *Theoretical sensitivity: Advances in the methodology of grounded theory*. Mill Valley: Sociology Press.

Glaser, B. G., & Strauss, A. (1967). *The discovery of grounded theory. Strategies for qualitative research*. Chicago: Aldine.

Glaser, B. G. with the assistance of J. Holton (2004). Remodeling grounded theory [80 paragraphs]. *Forum Qualitative Sozialforschung/Forum: Qualitative Social Research, 5*(2), Art. 4. http://nbn-resolving.de/urn:nbn:de:0114-fqs040245.

Howson, A. G. (2005). "Meaning" and school mathematics. In J. Kilpatrick, C. Hoyles, & O. Skovsmose (Eds.), *Meaning in mathematics education* (pp. 17–38). New York: Springer.

Kelle, U. (2005). "Emergence" vs. "forcing" of empirical data? A crucial problem of "grounded theory" reconsidered. *Forum Qualitative Sozialforschung/Forum: Qualitative Social Research, 6*(2), Art. 27. http://nbn-resolving.de/urn:nbn:de:0114-fqs0502275.

Kilpatrick, J., Hoyles, C., & Skovsmose, O. (2005). Meanings of 'meaning of mathematics'. In J. Kilpatrick, C. Hoyles, & O. Skovsmose (Eds.), *Meaning in mathematics education* (pp. 9–16). New York: Springer.

Leung, F. K. S., Graf, K.-D., & Lopez-Real, F. J. (Eds.). (2006). *Mathematics education in different cultural traditions: A comparative study of East Asia and the West. The 13th ICMI Study*. New York: Springer.

Mey, G., & Mruck, K. (2011). Grounded-Theory-Methodologie: Entwicklung, Stand, Perspektiven [Grounded theory methodology: Development, status quo, and perspectives]. In G. Mey & K. Mruck (Eds.), *Grounded theory reader* (pp. 11–48). Wiesbaden: VS Verlag für Sozialwissenschaften.

Meyer, M. A. (2008). Unterrichtsplanung aus der Perspektive der Bildungsgangforschung [Lesson planning from the perspective of research on educational experience and learner development]. *Zeitschrift für Erziehungswissenschaft, 10* (Special issue 9), 117–137. https://doi.org/10.1007/978-3-531-91775-7_9.

Morse, J. M., Stern, P. N., Corbin, J., Bowers, B., Charmaz, K., & Clarke, A. (2009). *Developing grounded theory. The second generation*. Walnut Creek: Left Coast Press.

Rabardel, P. (2002). *People and technology: A cognitive approach to contemporary instruments*. https://halshs.archives-ouvertes.fr/file/index/docid/1020705/filename/people_and_technology.pdf.

Rezat, S. (2008). Learning mathematics with textbooks. In O. Figueras, J. L. Cortina, S. Alatorre, T. Rojano, & A. Sepúlveda (Eds.), *Proceedings of the Joint Meeting of PME 32 und PME-NA XXX* (Vol. 4, pp. 177–184). Morelia: Cinestav-UMSNH.

Rezat, S. (2009). *Das Mathematikbuch als Instrument des Schülers. Eine Studie zur Schulbuchnutzung in den Sekundarstufen* [The mathematics textbook as instrument of students. A study of textbook use at secondary level]. Wiesbaden: Vieweg + Teubner.

Rezat, S. (2013). The textbook-in-use: students' utilization schemes of mathematics textbooks related to self-regulated practicing. *ZDM Mathematics Education, 45*(5), 659–670.

Strauss, A., & Corbin, J. (1998). *Basics of qualitative research: Grounded theory procedures and techniques* (2nd ed.). Newbury Park: Sage.

Strauss, A. L. (1987). *Qualitative analysis for social scientists*. New York: Cambridge University Press.

Strauss, A. L., & Corbin, J. M. (1990). *Basics of qualitative research: Grounded theory procedures and techniques*. Thousand Oaks: Sage Publications.

Strauss, A. L., & Corbin, J. M. (1996). *Grundlagen Qualitativer Sozialforschung [Basics of qualitative social research]*. Weinheim: Beltz Psychologie Verlags Union.

Teppo, A. (2015). Grounded theory methods. In A. Bikner-Ahsbahs, C. Knipping, & N. Presmeg (Eds.), *Approaches to qualitative research in mathematics education: Examples of methodology and methods* (pp. 3–21). Dordrecht: Springer.

Tiefel, S. (2005). Kodierung nach der Grounded Theory lern- und bildungstheoretisch modifiziert: Kodierleitlinien für die Analyse biographischen Lernens [Coding in terms of Grounded theory: Modifying coding guidelines for the analysis of biographical learning within a theoretical framework of learning and education]. *Zeitschrift für qualitative Bildungs-, Beratungs- und Sozialforschung (ZBBS), 6*(1), 65–84.

Vergnaud, G. (1998). A comprehensive theory of representation for mathematics education. *Journal of Mathematical Behaviour, 17*(2), 167–181.

Vinner, S. (2007). Mathematics education: Procedures, rituals and man's search for meaning. *Journal of Mathematical Behaviour, 26*(1), 1–10. https://doi.org/10.1016/j.jmathb.2007.03.004.

Vollstedt, M. (2011). Sinnkonstruktion und Mathematiklernen in Deutschland und Hongkong. Eine rekonstruktiv-empirische Studie [Personal meaning and the learning of mathematics: A reconstructive-empirical study]. Wiesbaden: Vieweg + Teubner.

Vollstedt, M. (2015). To see the wood for the trees: The development of theory from empirical data using grounded theory. In A. Bikner-Ahsbahs, C. Knipping, & N. Presmeg (Eds.), *Doing qualitative research: Methodologies and methods in mathematics education*. Advances in mathematics education series (pp. 23–48). Heidelberg: Springer. https://doi.org/10.1007/978-94-017-9181-6_2.

Vollstedt, M., & Duchhardt, C. (in press). Assessment and structure of secondary students' personal meaning related to mathematics. In M. S. Hannula, G. C. Leder, F. Morselli, M. Vollstedt, & Q. Zhang (Eds.), *Affect in mathematics education: Fresh perspectives on motivation, engagement, and identity*. ICME-13 Monographs. Cham: Springer.

Open Access This chapter is licensed under the terms of the Creative Commons Attribution 4.0 International License (http://creativecommons.org/licenses/by/4.0/), which permits use, sharing, adaptation, distribution and reproduction in any medium or format, as long as you give appropriate credit to the original author(s) and the source, provide a link to the Creative Commons license and indicate if changes were made.

The images or other third party material in this chapter are included in the chapter's Creative Commons license, unless indicated otherwise in a credit line to the material. If material is not included in the chapter's Creative Commons license and your intended use is not permitted by statutory regulation or exceeds the permitted use, you will need to obtain permission directly from the copyright holder.

Chapter 5
Interactional Analysis: A Method for Analysing Mathematical Learning Processes in Interactions

Marcus Schütte, Rachel-Ann Friesen and Judith Jung

Abstract When looking at learning processes from an interactionist perspective, interaction between individuals is seen as central for learning. In order to understand and describe these interactions and therefore the learning processes, a method was developed in mathematics education grounded in the theory of Symbolic Interactionism and Ethnomethodology—the Interactional Analysis. In this chapter, at first the underlying theory for the Interactional Analysis is presented, before the steps of the method are explained, giving an example for each step. Findings of research using this method have been widely published, however, the method has not been described in depth in English yet. Therefore, this chapter makes a valuable contribution for enabling this method to be more accessible for an international research community, as well as helping international researchers understand the findings produced by using this method more clearly.

Keywords Methodology · Interactional analysis · Reconstructive-interpretive research · Interactionism · Qualitative research

5.1 Introduction

Three children—Mira, Franka and Emilio—are sitting on a carpet in a classroom and are working together on a task. They have just placed ten rods, which are each made up out of ten wooden beads, in one long row. After taking wooden cards with tens on them from a plastic bag, Mira says "ten divided by three"<01> and Franka asks her what "divided" means. After Mira gives Franka the example that "six

M. Schütte (✉) · R.-A. Friesen · J. Jung
Technische Universität Dresden, Dresden, Germany
e-mail: marcus.schuette@tu-dresden.de

R.-A. Friesen
e-mail: rachel-ann.friesen@tu-dresden.de

J. Jung
e-mail: judith.jung1@tu-dresden.de

© The Author(s) 2019
G. Kaiser and N. Presmeg (eds.), *Compendium for Early Career Researchers in Mathematics Education*, ICME-13 Monographs,
https://doi.org/10.1007/978-3-030-15636-7_5

divided divided by three is three"<05>, Franka and Mira have the dialogue in Table 5.1.

When examining this kind of interaction between pupils from the perspective of mathematics education research, many questions arise: What is the relevance of the material being used? What mathematical idea of division do the participating children show? In what way is mathematical learning taking place within this interaction? For finding answers to many of these kind of questions, the method of Interactional Analysis provides a useful analytical tool, however, the main focus is on the exploration of the last question in various differentiations. Depending on the specific interest of a study, this would be further specified, with the research-leading questions normally being the following: How does the topic (of division) develop between Franka and Mira? How are these two pupils negotiating this mathematical topic in the interaction? In what way are Mira and Franke able to participate in this group work? Specifically for this interaction between Mira and Franka, the Interactional Analysis allows us to describe how the two pupils negotiate the theme of division, which mathematical ideas they express and to what extent these become attuned to each other in the interaction.

Hence, the Interactional Analysis is an empirical social-scientific research method that can be used to evaluate collected data on the reality of our social experiences. It was developed within theoretical interactional approaches of the qualitative research paradigm, and in contrast to quantitative research methods serves not to review hypotheses with defined variables, but to provide a comprehensive, holistic view on social interactions and, in the interpretive approach, to generate new assumptions and further develop theories. The method is grounded in the following assumptions: Diverse realities of social experiences exist alongside each other and can only be investigated in the holistic, contextualised reconstruction of the points of view and modes of action of the actors in interactions. Concerning scientific theories, the interaction theory is based on social-constructivist, symbolic-interactionist and phenomenological theories of cognition. In this, the theoretical assumptions of Symbolic Interactionism (Blumer 1969) and Ethnomethodology (Garfinkel 1967) are particularly significant for comprehending the method of the Interactional Analysis on a basic level. The theoretical foundations of these approaches will, therefore, be presented hereafter.

According to the basic assumptions of Symbolic Interactionism, reality presents itself to every individuals as their interpretation of what is going on around them and the meaning that they ascribe to it. Symbolic Interactionism thus concentrates on the ways individuals develop, transform and potentially consolidate their ideas about reality in interactions assisted by the use of symbols. In this perspective, reality is neither set nor given per se, but rather emerges for each individual in an individual process of interpretation. Meaning here refers not to the degree of significance for the individual, but to the meanings which everyday things have for the individuals. Therefore, things or objects do not contain meaning naturally: it only develops by individuals ascribing meaning to it. These individual processes of interpretation unfold in exchanges with other individuals. Hereby, the social

Table 5.1 Transcript <9–20>

09	02:12	#	Franka	eh. dividing six is three *[holds left hand horizontally and moves right hand, which is held vertically, up and down]*
10	02:15		Mira	Yes
11	02:15		Franka	ah/that's easy
12	02:17		Mira	And ten divided by three/(4) doesn't work\ **yes it does.** Wait
13	02:25		Franka	eh now I don't understand#
14	02:27	#	Mira	Wait
15		<	Franka	Now I don't understand
16		<	Mira	Ten divided by three is three six
17	02:31		Franka	You cut the ten *[rubs her right and her left hand vertically against each other]*
18		<	Mira	Three six nine
19		<	Franka	Then five are left over. You cut#
20	02:33	#	Mira	*[Empties the wooden cards from the plastic bag onto the carpet]* so someone has to have one number more

The rules for transcription used in this chapter are presented in Sect. 5.5.3.

interaction represents the central component in the theory of Symbolic Interactionism (Blumer 1969; Keller 2012; Turner 1988).

Social interaction, like the negotiation of Mira and Franka presented above, in which meanings are collectively negotiated, can, from the perspective of Symbolic Interactionism, be seen as a constituent of learning processes. As a consequence, Symbolic Interactionism contradicts notions that mathematical objects contain meaning only inherently in their form or internal structures. Instead, a die only becomes a die when the people involved in the interaction negotiate it as such, giving it specific characteristics and naming it.

The ethnomethodological approach based on qualitative empirical research aims to empirically investigate and reconstruct the methods used by members of a society to construct social reality in their everyday lives. These methods are described by Garfinkel (1967) as "ethnomethods". Garfinkel emphasises that talking about actions, e.g. in group discussions or interviews, is totally different to the actions themselves, and that it is therefore crucial to observe everyday actions in their execution. Records of social occurrences/situations of people's everyday lives therefore form the focus of ethnomethodological analyses. Ethnomethodology is not concerned with reconstructing the motives behind actions; instead, the focus of analyses falls upon the emergence of social reality and methods of the social production of order. These methods are not necessarily considered or applied consciously by participants, but nevertheless are familiar to them because they are used routinely (Ingram 2018; Keller 2012).

Specifically, the Interactional Analysis is based on the ethnomethodological Conversational Analysis, an approach developed in the 1960s (Sacks 1998; Sacks et al. 1974). As a fundamental practical principle of the Conversational Analysis, interactional sequences are audio-recorded in real time, the recorded data is then transcribed and afterwards the transcripts are sequentially analysed. Therefore, the internal structure of the interaction, how it is developed step by step, can be investigated.

5.2 Mathematics Learning from an Interactionist Perspective

Sociological and social-constructivist approaches to the study of learning processes have gained increasing influence in recent years in the development of theories of content-related mathematical learning (Lerman 2000). This process has also expanded the understanding of mathematics itself as a social cultural technology mediated and constructed by language (Schütte 2014; Sfard 2008; Solomon 2009). Implemented at the end of the 1980s by a group of German and American researchers (Cobb and Bauersfeld 1995a), the social turn was brought into clearer focus in the field of mathematics education via diverse studies using interactionist approaches of interpretive classroom research. Grounded in the (sociological) theory of Symbolic Interactionism and Ethnomethodology, these combined sociological and social-constructivist with subject-educational theories of learning (Bauersfeld et al. 1988).

These studies were explicitly distanced from the previously dominant view that learning was merely an internal psychological phenomenon. The social turn and the inclusion of interactionist aspects of learning and teaching meant a shifting of focus from the structure of objects to the structures of learning processes, and from the individual learner to the social interactions between learners. This transformed understanding of learning led to the development of theories that see meaning, thinking, and reasoning as products of social activity (Bauersfeld et al. 1988). Based on the fundamental assumption of these approaches, i.e. that meaning is negotiated in interactions between several individuals and that social interaction is thus to be understood as constitutive of learning processes, speaking about mathematics with others is in itself to be seen as the "doing" of mathematics and the development of meaning.

According to Cobb and Bauersfeld (1995b), studies that adopt such approaches are based—unlike individualistic approaches to learning in the tradition of Piaget—on the notion of learning as a process initiated primarily through interaction, which can only be described by tracing the coordination of the mental activities of at least two individuals, as takes place, e.g., in a conversation. Thus, social interaction becomes the focus of attention in these approaches. According to the interactionist perspective, individual processes of interpretation are developed, transformed and stabilised in the exchange with other individuals: while remaining an individual process, learning is nevertheless anchored constitutively in collective activities. Interactionism assumes that an individual is only enabled to do fundamental learning steps—these are steps that do not only involve the use or reproduction of existing knowledge—within the social group and on the basis of processes of social interaction between the individuals of this group.

This means that individually learning something new is determined by collective processes which proceed the individual learning. Thus, according to Miller (1986), the exchange with others affords the individual opportunities to systematically move beyond his or her own "limited" abilities, which is only secondarily reflected in individual processes of cognitive restructuring. Older children or adults can certainly learn individually, e.g., by using literature, however, Miller (1986) locates such individualised learning in later phases of human development, meaning in moments of reflexive consolidation of those things originally learnt collectively. Early learning or the conditions for enabling learning in the pre-school period or in primary school are, nevertheless, fundamentally social in nature.

Up to the start of the 2000s, research in this area of mathematics education predominantly took place under the umbrella of interpretive classroom research. Since the most recent work of interpretive classroom research extends the focus from everyday learning of mathematics in school to encompass learning in kindergarten, nursery school and the family, the term "classroom research" thus begins to seem limiting and no longer suitable (Krummheuer 2013; Schütte 2014; Tiedemann and Brandt 2010). In the following, we therefore use the term "interpretive research" and seek to reduce the specific focus on classroom research.

5.3 Theory Development in Interpretive Research

Interpretive research represents a kind of umbrella term that refers both to the object of investigation and the methodical approach of the research. At the same time, it implies a theoretical standpoint (Cobb and Bauersfeld 1995b; Bauersfeld et al. 1988; Krummheuer and Naujok 1999). Rather than on a ratified, conceptually anchored mathematics, conceived of as an object, the focus of interpretive research is on the interpretations and interpretive ascriptions which are constantly being produced in the interactions which take place between participants in everyday processes of mathematical learning, for example in school, in the family or in nursery school. Supporters of interpretive classroom research in mathematics education originally sought to orient research more strongly towards describing and "wanting-to-understand" mathematics teaching rather than prescribing and "wanting-to-transform" (Krummheuer 2004). The intention, hereby, was a critical shift away from the hitherto conventional, approaches of classroom research focussing on Subject Matter Didactics. This shift was expressed in the principle of reconstructive research, which places the "[…] 'How' in relation to the functioning of a slice of social reality" at the heart of the investigation, and suppresses the 'What', that is relating to content (Krummheuer 2004, p. 113, translated by the authors). The switch from focusing on the "What" of social reality to looking at the "How" of the construction of this reality is foundational to interactionist approaches of interpretive research in mathematics education—although current studies often aspire to reveal potential change in the future through describing current practice in the teaching and learning of mathematics. Through "understanding" individual actions, the overarching goal of interpretive research is therefore to develop empirically grounded, content-rich local theories. In the domain mathematics education, interpretive research is seeking to develop theories concerning the conditions of possibilities for learning of individuals in diverse teaching and learning settings. Overall, the question arises what the relationship of "everyday classroom interactions in mathematics teaching", as an object of investigation, to existing or envisaged theory is? Regarding the relationship between object and theory in interpretive research, Krummheuer (2002) mentions the "unavoidability of theory construction" and draw a link to the potential for the permanent transformation of everyday teaching.

> It will be explained that as a research scientist dealing with the domain of social interaction in primary education, one is usually not in the position to cope with an a priori stock of theories, which are sufficiently developed in order to adequately understand a certain classroom situation. In such cases the researcher is facing a specific methodological problem: the necessity for constructing elements of a theory that claim to generate a theory-consistent interpretation of the selected part of reality. (p. 340)

Naujok (2000), however, limits the scope of the concept of theory, arguing that in many other fields it tends to have global, universalising connotations. Research adopting a reconstructive-interpretive approach does not make such universalising claims for its results (Krummheuer and Naujok 1999). According to Naujok (2000), the theoretical products of interpretive research are "rather to be understood as attempts to explain empirical phenomena and contextual links between them" (p. 32, translated by the authors). As cited in Kelle (1994), Merton (1968) and Blumer (1954) differentiate between two heuristic concepts in their discussion of the hierarchical structure of social-scientific theories and the heuristic significance of their leading assumptions: one has a wide reach but little empirical content and thus limited precision[1]; the other might only be applied in limited fields of social reality, but provides more precise, richer theory.[2] The hypotheses of interpretive research thus remain beholden to the respective context of the field being investigated but consequently contain empirically rich elements and are internally consistent. The goal of interpretive research is thus to formulate hypotheses which are based on empirical results and can be understood with reference to these. In further steps, such as comparative analysis, these empirically and theoretically grounded hypotheses lead towards the development of a local theory.

---

[1] See also "grand theories" (Merton 1968, p. 50ff.) and "definitive concepts" (Blumer 1954, p. 7).
[2] See also "middle range theories" (Merton 1968, p. 50ff.) and "sensitizing concepts" (Blumer 1954, p. 7).

5.4 Basic Concepts: The Negotiation of Mathematical Meaning

Mathematics teaching is understood in interactionist approaches of interpretive research as an everyday "praxis of relaying mathematical knowledge" (Bauersfeld 1985, p. 8, translated by the authors), in which an interactive negotiation of meaning takes place between participants over mathematical content. From an interactionist perspective, the individual process of learning is constituted in the social process of the negotiation of meaning. The social interaction, therefore, holds the potential to generate meanings which are new to the individual. Based on this understanding of learning and the significance of interaction in the learning of mathematics, diverse theories with rich empirical content have been developed in recent years from a foundation of "sensitizing concepts" (Blumer 1954, p. 7)—a kind of theoretical skeleton for the interaction theory of learning, which will be described below.

At the beginning of an interaction, the participants develop preliminary interpretations of the situation on the basis of their individual experiences and knowledge. Based on Thomas (1923, p. 42) and further used in pedagogical contexts by Mollenhauer (1972), these are called *definitions of the situation*. From an interactionist perspective, these individual definitions of the situation (Krummheuer 1992) develop in anticipation of possible attempts of other participants to interpret the situation and adjust to the other interpretations emerging in the interaction within the process of collective negotiations of meaning. The concept of the definition of the situation here refers neither to a product nor to a definition, but to an open-ended, permanent process of interpretative activity.

Thus, participants in the interaction attempt to attune their definitions of the situation to each other, ideally leading to the production of *taken-as-shared meaning* (Voigt 1995, p. 172), a working consensus. The term taken-as-shared meaning seeks to express that different participants' interpretations of a situation cannot ever be exactly the same but can become sufficiently aligned with each other to create an understanding between the participants concerning the objects, ideas and rules of the interaction. This understanding is assumed to be taken as shared and allows the participants to work together. The result of the participants' negotiation only is something "temporarily", an "interim", which serves as a basis for further processes of negotiation but might also be rejected or transformed as the interaction unfolds (Bauersfeld et al. 1988; Voigt 1995). The taken-as-shared meaning—*the working consensus* (Goffman 1959, p. 9)—is on the one hand socially constituted and, on the other, potentially novel for the individual if it pushes systematically beyond his or her interpretive capacities. The working consensus represents the 'stimulation potential' of individual cognitive restructuring processes. Through the possibility for collective generation of meaning that inheres in the social interaction, the interaction acquires an *orientation function* (Krummheuer 1992, p. 7, translated by the authors) for the individuals' cognitive restructuring processes. Alongside this, through the production of the working consensus, the social interaction also acquires a *convergence function* (Krummheuer 1992, p. 7, translated by the authors). In this convergence function, the taken-as-shared meanings are repeatedly negotiated in the interaction and thereby the participants' individual definitions of situations are transformed and consolidated. This allows standardized and routinized definitions of situations to develop, which the individual can reproduce in similar situations. Drawing on Goffman (1974), Bauersfeld et al. (1988) call these definitions *framings* (see also Krummheuer 1995). Meanings are repeatedly negotiated by participants in interactions in the mathematics classroom. Thus, ideally, mathematical ascriptions of meaning, which sustain beyond the situation (framings) are constructed, or the working consensuses, which are repeatedly collectively negotiated, 'converge' in individual mathematical framings. In relation to the learning-theoretical aspect discussed here, this leads us to conclude that learning is not the new construction of individual definitions of the situation, but the new construction or reconstruction of framings.

> By learning new framings, the individual unlocks a new field of social reality. It gains a new perspective on reality, allowing new aspects and characteristics of reality to be 'seen'. (Krummheuer 1992, p. 45, translation by the authors)

However, it often happens that the framings produced by young learners either among themselves or in interaction with individuals with advanced skills are not in alignment with each other (Krummheuer 1992). Teachers interpret classroom situations based on framings from their subject-specific interactional praxis in the classroom; pupils, on the other hand, interpret situations based on framings from the environments they have experienced outside of school and in their previous school career. In order to maintain the progressive mutual negotiation of content relating to a particular theme, the *differences in framing* between the participants need to be coordinated. This coordination should be done by an individual who is advanced in the subject-specific interaction. This could also be a child or the teacher in school or kindergarten. While these differences in framing can make it more difficult for the participating individuals to adjust their definitions of the situations to fit each other, they also provide the "'motor' of learning" (Schütte 2014, p. 927) since, on the interactional level, they generate a certain necessity for negotiation. This necessity, however, through the effects of other strategies engaged in by the participants, either consciously or unconsciously, can also lead to the concealment of differences in framing (Krummheuer 1992). The result of such a process of negotiation is subject to some uncertainty concerning what has actually been negotiated and in the process of reaching an agreement an "intersubjectively reached relief" can be prioritised over a collectively reached acceptance of what is seen as mathematically "correct" (Krummheuer 1992, p. 113, translated by the authors). With regard to the understanding of collective learning, it can be expected that when concealing these differences in framing no collectively, interactively taken-as-shared meaning will be produced that will systematically move beyond the individual participants' abilities. This will mean that the 'reached agreement' is not able to stimulate sustainable processes of learning via participants' subjective convictions.

Further developing the framing concept for the learning of mathematics, Schütte and Krummheuer (2017) additionally differentiate between the gaining of mathematical concepts and the development of mathematical thinking, as an introduction to a context-specific praxis of rationalisation in mathematical discourses. They differentiate analytically between the learning of mathematical content and operations and the methods of justification and explanation which build on these, although these learning forms will not appear independently of each other in practice.

After having presented the theoretical foundations of Ethnomethodology and Symbolic Interactionism and, building on this, having described the theory of interactionist approaches of interpretive classroom research with its basic terms, the procedure of the interactional analysis for reconstructing collective mathematical learning processes is described with the help of an example. Within these procedures, one can see that the terms, which have been described above, serve with the help of the interactional analysis to describe mathematical learning in collective processes of negotiation.

5.5 Interactional Analysis

For the analysis of collective processes of negotiation in the learning of mathematics, interactionist approaches of interpretive research in mathematics education make use of a method initially developed within these same approaches—the Interactional Analysis. As mentioned above, it was first deployed in the area of interpretive classroom research in mathematics education in studies by Bauersfeld et al. (1988) and has its origins in the Conversational Analysis in the field of Ethnomethodology (Eberle 1997; Sacks 1998; Sacks et al. 1974). Interactional Analysis allows research to reconstruct the ways in which negotiations of mathematical meaning are interactively constituted by individuals, become taken-as-shared meaning within the group and thus consolidate as individual learning in form of framings of individuals which can be reconstructed. Furthermore, it can help to reconstruct patterns and structures of verbal actions of the teacher and the students. In the following, a theoretical illustration of the Interactional Analysis is provided with examples which all refer to the interaction mentioned in the introduction.

Throughout the years, the first approaches to the Interactional Analysis within interpretive research have been modified several times by various researchers according to their specific research questions (Fetzer and Tiedemann 2018; Krummheuer 2015). Further detailed descriptions of the interactional analysis can be found in German (Krummheuer 2012; Schütte 2009).

The Interactional Analysis can include the following steps:

1. Setting of the interactional unit,

2. Structure of the interactional unit,
3. Displaying transcripts of selected sequences
4. General description of each sequence,
5. Detailed sequential interpretation of individual utterances,
6. Turn-by-turn analysis and
7. Summary of the interpretation.

The steps 2, 4, 5, 6 and 7 are the steps in which the analysis takes place and are therefore always included (Krummheuer and Naujok 1999), whereas the steps 1 and 3 are not about analysing but help present the interaction which is to be analysed (Schütte 2009).

However, these steps of the Interactional Analysis should not be seen as a linear sequence of steps for interpreting the interaction but rather as principles for the process of interpretation in which it is possible and even sensible to repeat several of the steps (Krummheuer and Brandt 2001; Naujok 2000). Below, the steps of the Interactional Analysis will be described individually in theory and then shown for an exemplary sequence which was partly shown in the introduction already. The detailed sequential interpretation of individual utterances, however, is only presented for the first utterance before only those interpretations are presented which are left after the turn-by-turn analysis. This is mainly done because these steps are always done alternately when interpreting a sequence and presenting the entire detailed analysis would be too extensive.

5.5.1 Setting of the Interactional Unit

At the beginning of the analysis the setting in which the lesson takes place is briefly described so that the ensuing interpretations can be understood more easily. This may include the subject, the number of students, the arrangement of the lesson and other specifics about the beginning of the scene. The term 'interactional unit' refers to an entire lesson or to a larger part of a lesson with a connecting theme.

Example: Setting of the Interactional Unit
This interactional unit takes place at the beginning of second grade in a mathematics lesson. The students are working at different stations all on the numbers 0–100. Franka, Mira and Emilio sit down on the carpet in the classroom with a tray. On the tray, there are wooden rods of ten, a paper with the description of the station and a white box with square wooden cards with a number printed on each of them. The number cards with the tens on them are in a small transparent plastic bag and the other wooden cards are in the white box.

5.5.2 Structure of the Interactional Unit

The structure of the interactional units depends on the respective research interest. It can be determined either by aspects concerning the interactional theory, e.g. the beginning and the end of a specific form of interaction, or by subject-specific or didactical subject didactic aspects, e.g. the beginning and the end of a mathematical task solving sequence. The different criteria for structuring the interactional unit can lead to varying perspectives on the material. The structure functions mainly as an overview and as a help to structure the episodes for the reader. In this paper, we will present the structure of the part of the lesson in which these three children are working on this station in order to show where the exemplary sequence is located within this interactional unit.

Example: Structure of the Interactional Unit

For this example of analysis (Table 5.2), the interactional unit is structured according to themes which emerge within the interaction of the pupils as they are working on the task given to them for this station. This includes a change of persons involved in working on this task. Therefore, the interactional unit is structured according to general aspects of mathematics teaching as there is no specific research focus for this analysis.

5.5.3 Displaying Transcript of Selected Sequence

In the next step, the transcript of the selected sequence is presented. If several sequences of an interactional unit are analysed, then the interaction and action in between these sequences can be described in short summaries. The transcripts are always done in spoken language, meaning they transcribe what the participants actually say, and normally include descriptions of the participants action as well. Depending on the research question this can be done in various degrees of detail. Furthermore, small pictures can be added to help understand what is meant by an action or to show what the pupils are doing with the material more easily. The rules for transcribing can also be modified depending on the research question. Here the rules for the transcript presented in this chapter are given:

Table 5.2 Structure of interactional unit

Lines	Description
01–09	The children take the rods of ten off the tray and start laying them down in one row on the carpet
10–53	The children distribute the wooden cards with the tens from the plastic bag amongst themselves
	Excursus 15–33: How many cards does each child receive if one fairly distributes 10 cards among 3 children?
54–75	The children place the wooden cards next to the row of rods
75–79	The children distribute the wooden cards from the white box among themselves
80–94	The children place the wooden cards next to the row of rods
95–124	The teacher comes to the group, the children finish the task and tidy up the materials. Franka and Mira receive a new task at their desks
125–170	Emilio and the teacher place the wooden cards with the tens next to the row of rods
171–201	Emilio and the teacher place the other wooden cards from the white box next to the row of rods

Rules for Transcription

Bold	spoken with emphasis
smaller	spoken quietly, whisper
[action]	action that takes place between two temporally separate sections of the transcript
(word)	word or sentence not unequivocally clear
(*unintelligible*)	word or sentence incomprehensible
/	voice inflected up
\	voice inflected down
. .. ... (4)	pauses in speech in seconds
<	The speakers (partially) talk simultaneously
#	No pause between speakers. The second speaker interrupts first speaker

Example: Displaying Transcripts of Selected Sequences

Mira, Franka and Emilio finish laying down the rods of ten in a row on the carpet. Mira suggests first taking the cards in the plastic bag and takes the plastic bag with the wooden cards out of the box (Table 5.3).

After the children distribute the cards among each other, they start working on the actual task given by the teacher and place the wooden cards next to the row of rods at the respective positions (see Sect. 5.5.2).

Table 5.3 Transcript <1–24>

01	01:47		Mira	*[Takes plastic bag with cards out of the box]* each one gets wait. Ten divided by three
02	01:56		Franka	Do you know divided/. can you do divided/
03	01:58		Mira	Yes
04	02:02		Franka	What does divided mean/
05	02:06	<	Mira	Well divided means wait six divided divided by three is three\
06		<	Emilio	*[Takes the paper with the description of the station into his hand and looks at it]* (unintelligible) look Mira I found a three (unintelligible)
07			Franka	eh/
08	02:11		Mira	Look six divided#
09	02:12	#	Franka	eh. Dividing six is three *[holds left hand horizontally and moves right hand, which is held vertically, up and down]*
10	02:15		Mira	Yes
11	02:15		Franka	ah/that's easy
12	02:17		Mira	And ten divided by three/(4) doesn't work\ **yes it does**. Wait
13	02:25		Franka	eh now I don't understand#
14	02:27	#	Mira	Wait
15		<	Franka	Now I don't understand
16		<	Mira	Ten divided by three is three six
17	02:31		Franka	You cut the ten *[rubs her right and left hand vertically against each other]*
18		<	Mira	Three six nine
19		<	Franka	Then five are left over. You cut#
20	02:33	#	Mira	*[Empties the wooden cards from the plastic bag onto the carpet]* so someone has to have one number more
21	02:41		Franka	What/**me** *[raises right hand with extended index finger]*
22	02:43		Mira	Okay then you will get one less number **there**\ *[takes the white box with the other wooden cards into her hand and puts it back down again]*
23	02:46	<	Franka	No
24		<	Emilio	*[Takes a wooden card out of the white box and puts it next to the row of rods of ten in front of the second bead of the second rod]*

5.5.4 General Description of Selected Sequence

After presenting the transcripts, a first impression of the selected sequence is given in a general description. This general description is a coarser look which has the goal of describing the intrinsic meaning in an initial ascription and of giving an overview of the text. This is directed towards a general public who might not be interested in a detailed analysis of the selected sequence but in general matters of learning and teaching.

Example: General Description of the Selected Sequence

At first, Mira voices a mathematical problem "ten divided by three" <1>. Franka then poses several questions towards Mira about "divided" which Mira first affirms and then she starts explaining the meaning of "divided" using an example <2–8>. Afterwards Franka gives an example on her own and both girls start working on the original mathematical problem collectively <9–19>. Mira arrives at a solution for the problem and expresses the need that one child has to receive one extra number card <20>. The sequence ends with Franka and Mira negotiating who will get one more card <21–23>. During the entire sequence, Emilio is mostly focused on the material and only once addresses Mira stating that he has "found a three" <6>.

5.5.5 Detailed Sequential Interpretation of Individual Utterances

After the general description of the activities in the chosen sequence, a detailed sequential interpretation of individual utterances is done in order to take into account the sequential organization of the conversation. According to Naujok (2000), the sequential analysis has to follow these principles:

1. The utterances, or if necessary even smaller units, are interpreted one after the other in the order of their occurrence. This makes it possible to reconstruct the development of the interaction, because in the analytic process of interpretation only events are referenced, to which the participants also had access in the respective moment of interaction.
2. Plausibility checks may only (and if the first principle is taken into consideration, only can) be done backwards.
3. Interpretations have to prove themselves in the course of the interaction. (p. 44, translated by the authors).

As described above, the interactional analysis is based on the theories of Symbolic Interactionism and Ethnomethodology. In the focus of ethnomethodological analyses are records of actual everyday social events or situations that are used to investigate how members of a society produce social orders in their actions. Ethnomethodology is not concerned with the reconstruction of action motives (Ingram 2018; Keller 2012). According to this, one principle, if not the decisive principle of the interactional analysis, is that researchers do not analyse why the participants do certain actions or what their intentions are in doing so, but only how participants act, how others react to these actions and how they interpret the actions of the other participants and then design their own actions accordingly. Analyses concerning which didactical considerations are guiding e.g. a teacher's actions, in order to explain his or her way of introducing a new topic, are therefore not the focus of the interactional analysis and, taking account of the theoretical foundations of the method, always eludes access by the researchers. In this respect, expressions in the analysis such as "the teacher wants to do this ..." or "the child wants to show that ..." are 'prohibited'. Based on the theoretical foundational theories, one can only analyse how the teacher carries out his or her introduction, in what form the involved children interpret these and how the mutual actions of the participants in this introduction negotiate the new mathematical topic, so that eventually something taken-as-shared can be created among all those involved. According to ethnomethodology, this no longer has to have much in common with the previously existing intention of the teacher or other participants.

In order to find alternative interpretations of individual utterances, it can be useful, following Objective Hermeneutics (Oevermann et al. 1987), to make mental context variations in order to generate additional possible interpretations in other contexts. However, the aspiration according to Oevermann et al. (1987) to, if possible, generate every possible reading seems less reasonable since this would not necessarily lead to new results but will definitely lead to an unmanageable abundance of interpretations. Therefore, the goal sequential interpretation is the maxim of preciseness corresponding to the interest of the research (Krummheuer and Brandt 2001). In particularly difficult passages, Naujok (2000) suggests to think of actions which could possibly follow an utterance to help finding further interpretations.

This detailed sequential interpretation of individual utterances, as well as the following turn-by-turn analysis following it, is normally done in analysis group settings where each of the participants receive the transcript of the sequence to be interpreted. One utterance at a time—sometimes also more or less, depending on the length of the utterances and the amount of possible interpretations—are read. The group then starts giving possible interpretations for this utterance. It is important to note, that the participants of the group do not read the entire transcript first but only read utterance by utterance in accordance to the pace of the analysis. This is done to reconstruct the sequentiality of the interaction process.

Example: Detailed Sequential Interpretation of Individual Utterances

For this example of analysis, only for the first utterance a wide variety of possible interpretations is presented in form of notes. Considering the setting of the sequence and examining possible interpretations later by using the turn-by-turn analysis, some of these interpretations are then eliminated and not given in the full interpretation of the sequence.

01	01:47		Mira	*[takes plastic bag with cards out of the box]* each one gets wait. Ten divided by three

- This might be a mathematical problem given to the children by the teacher or the work sheet.
    - There could be 10 objects which have to be distributed.
    - The word problem could include a question like "How many does each one get?"

- However, since "10:3=" is not a typical mathematical problem given in second grade, this is not likely.

• Or it might be a situation within this lesson, which is made into a mathematical problem.

- e.g., distributing real objects to the children.

Since Mira is taking cards out of a bag, she might be referring to these cards which she might later distribute equally among three children.

• If she is referring to the cards,

- it is not clear how/if she knows that there are exactly 10 cards in the bag, since she doesn't seem to count them.

Did the teacher say this when introducing the task?
Or does she know this from the context of which numbers are printed on the cards?
Or is it a guess?

• Either way, she seems to have a mental model of partitioning[3] for this division where the number of people receiving something is clear and the amount which each person will receive needs to be determined.
• By saying "each one gets" she seems to be talking to someone else.

- Mira could be talking to either one of the two children present or to both
- Or she could be saying her thoughts out loud not necessarily for the other children to hear.

• "ten divided by three"

- This is a correct formulation according to mathematical terminology.
- This supports the interpretation that she has possibly already developed an idea of this arithmetic operation of division

• "wait"

- She could be saying this to herself because she is in the process of thinking.
- She could be saying this to Emilio and/or Franka that they should give her more time.

---

[3]In partition division, the number of subsets is given and the size of each subset has to be determined.

- Through her action and utterance, Mira seems to organize this group work.
- Justice might be important to Mira, since she is trying to distribute the cards evenly between them.

5.5.6 Turn-by-Turn Analysis

By then doing a turn-by-turn analysis, the diverse alternative interpretations of the previous sequential analysis are limited following the works of Conversational Analyses and on the basis of the sequential organization of the conversation. The goal is to arrive at conclusive interpretations of consecutive actions: "The question of the turn-by-turn analysis therefore is: How other participants of the interaction react to an utterance, how do they seem to interpret the utterance, how is it developed further collectively, what is made of the situation collectively?" (Naujok 2000, p. 46, translated by the authors). The detailed sequential interpretation and the turn-by-turn analysis were interwoven and are therefore now presented in a coherent text.

Example: Turn-by-Turn Analysis

At the beginning of the presented sequence, Mira takes the plastic bag with the cards from the box and says "each one gets wait. ten divided by three" <1>. With this utterance Mira could be mathematizing a problem from the situation of trying to distribute the cards evenly. The ten may then be referring to the amount of cards which are in the plastic bag. Why she knows that there are exactly ten cards in the plastic bag, remains unclear. Since the three children are working on this station together, the divisor 3, could refer to the amount of children to which the amount of supposedly ten cards is to be distributed to evenly. The beginning of the utterance <1> "each one gets" suggests that Mira perceives the division task within the mental model of partitioning.[4] The amount of the subset to be created in this case is predefined by the three children and the question arises how many cards are in a subset.

The task "10:3=" as a division with a remainder, however, is not a typical math problem for a second grade. This supports the interpretation that the problem emerges from the situation, is developed by Mira and is not a task given by the teacher or written on the work sheet. Nevertheless, the formulation "ten divided by three" <1> is a correct formulation according to mathematical terminology. This suggests that Mira has possibly already developed an idea of this arithmetic operation of division. The attempt to distribute the ten cards to three persons is an indicator that Mira takes the previous instruction given by the teacher, to include Emilio in the group work, seriously and that she might later distribute the cards evenly so that everyone can participate in the group work equally. By saying

---

[4]The German word for partitioning is "verteilen" which is also used for distributing e.g. cards.

"wait" <1>, Mira could be addressing Franka and/or Emilio in order to gain time so that she can state this sophisticated formulation correctly.

Before Mira expresses a solution to her task, Franka says "do you know divided. can you do divided/" <2>. This seems to be a turn on Mira's utterance in <1>, however, it may also be directed towards Emilio. The sentences formulated by Franka here are rather incomplete. The reason for this could be that she is surprised or that she only vaguely knows what the term "divided" means and therefore cannot incorporate the term in a coherent meaningful statement. This uncertainty, as well as the fact that Franka does not directly solve the task ten divided by three, supports the assumption that she herself cannot calculate "divided" and may also be unable to establish a connection to the meaning of the term "divided." She may therefore be amazed that Mira seems to be capable doing so. However, the term does not seem to be completely foreign to her, as she connects it to something that one can "know" or "can do". Franka's use of "divided" may also indicate that she uses it as the term for division. For example, she might already have heard it from the teacher, as the term for "divided" in German is often used as a didactical term for the basic arithmetic operation of division in primary school everyday teaching. However, according to this interpretation she would not be using the term grammatically correct in neither statement. With "do you know divided" <2>, Franka could rather be asking for the technical term "divided" or for the meaning of "divided" in the sense of "do you know what divided means". "Can you do divided" <2>, in the sense of "you can calculate divided by", sounds more like a question about the skill of applying the division. As she asks this second question, she seems to at least associate the term "divided" with an action. Furthermore, the participle of the verb "to divide"—divided—a would always be used for the description of the action of a division.[5]

She may be asking these two questions in immediate succession because she is making the first question more precise or modify it with the second question. She might do this because she realizes that "divided" is not something that you need to know, but rather is something you have to be able to do or perform. On the other hand, she might also rephrase the first question because she realizes that for the distribution of the cards, it would be enough for Mira to simply solve the task without explaining the concept. Lastly, she might modify her first question because Mira does not react during the pause in between her utterances and Franka asks again and therefore increasingly demands an answer. This could be out of a real interest, as she may not know the answer, or it could be a kind of interrogation in the style of a teacher.

Mira reacts to Franka's questions with "yes" <3>. This short answer may indicate that she herself is still thinking of her 'task' and therefore limits her communication to the bare minimum. However, it could also be interpreted as Mira being very sure and "yes" therefore as the direct answer to one or both of the questions. Her utterance can either be interpreted as knowing what division is, i.e.,

---

[5]In English, this is a past participle. In German, she uses the "Partizip II".

knowing the concept, but possibly not being able to divide; as being able to divide, but not being able to further explain what division is—hence only the short answer; or as being able to do both.

In <4>, Franka asks again "what does divided mean/". Repeating her question with the term "means" indicates that Franka's question was not a rhetorical question before, that she does not know the answer herself, and that she has a genuine interest in the answer to the question of what is meant by the idea of "divided." Mira had answered Franka's questions of <2> with "yes" but failed to answer to the implicit request for an explanation or the naming of a result. Another interpretation could still be that Franka acts, as mentioned above, in the style of a teacher and now 'asks' Mira if she really knows what division is. Mira might now explain the term or idea of division in response to the question with a general explanation or with a concrete example, possibly with her own task (10:3).

Mira then says, "well divided means wait six divided divided by three is three" <5>. At first glance, it does not become clear what Mira is saying with this utterance. By using "well", she seems to respond to Franka's question but paraphrases Franka's "means" with another German word for "means". She interrupts her sentence with "wait", which may indicate that she is considering how she can answer the question, as she may well know what "divided" means but cannot easily explain it in words. This may also be the reason why Mira now uses a concrete example to explain "divided" to Franka. By doing so, she reacts more to the second question "can you do divided/" than to "do you know divided". She might have a framing of division which is in alignment with the concept of division generally common within the domain of mathematics, and merely miscalculates and therefore comes to the result three. She could also have simply made a slip of the tongue by saying three instead of two—for both the first or the second "three". In this case, she would then have to make a repair afterwards, meaning revise her utterance, if this incorrect wording has negative effects on the following interaction. However, she could also have a differing framing of division and refer to decomposing a number, meaning breaking up the number six into three plus three, or refer to dividing as halving. This would mean that for her dividing ten by three equals five. Franka could interpret her utterance in this way as well. A final interpretation of Mira's utterance is that "three" is not the result of her calculation but a repetition of the first "three" in order to continue calculating with it. Additionally, it is not clear why Mira uses six as the dividend as it could be by chance or a typical mathematical problem which she has already solved previously, e.g. when doubling numbers. Or six could be an intermediate result in the process of her solving the first problem—e.g. by counting by threes "three, six, nine"—and now she uses it to explain division to Franka.

While Mira speaks, Emilio picks up the description of the station and looks at it. Then he utters something incomprehensible before he says "look Mira I found a three" <6>. This statement could be interpreted as him not being able to completely follow the conversation of Mira and Franka or as him following it and now trying to participate in the conversation and possibly even trying to support his two classmates in the search for the meaning of division. He is trying to attract attention with "look", as Mira and Franka seem to be talking to each other and not to Emilio, as interpreted in <1>. Him mentioning the number three allows for various interpretations. He could be taking up Mira's "three" (<1, 6>), which indicates that he followed the conversation attentively, or he could have randomly read the number on the description of the station regardless of the previous utterances. However, he could also point out that he has found the solution to the above task 10:3. It is also possible that he has found the card with the number three and is pleased because he can arrange the number three on the row of rods—forming a type of number line, which would correspond to the actual task of the station.

Franka now seems to be responding to Mira's explanation and her "eh/" <7> can be interpreted as indicating that she cannot follow the explanation or does not understand it. Mira repeats the beginning of her mathematical example <5> "look six divided#" <8>. The "look" can be interpreted as the beginning of an explanation and thus as a direct turn on the statement of Franka. Another interpretation could be a direct reference to Emilio's utterance, which also began with "look" and thus might be a negotiation between Emilio and Mira about what is currently in the focus of interaction.

Franka interrupts Mira with the statement "eh. dividing six is three" <9>, holding her left hand horizontally and moving her right hand vertically up and down. The "eh" could be related to the fact that she does not understand why Mira mentions six as the ten was supposed to be divided previously. However, it could also be related to the solution "three", which she cannot understand or which she does not agree with. That after a brief pause, in which she is possibly trying to understand Mira's utterance, she then says "dividing six is three" could be a repetition of Mira's utterance in <5>. On the one hand, this repetition could be interpreted as a repetition within the process of trying to understand Mira or as questioning the utterance.

At this point, Franka could solve the task "dividing six" herself and come to the result three. In contrast to Mira's utterances and her own questions, Franka now uses the gerund infinitive "dividing" instead of "divided".[6] Combined with the movement of her hand, one could derive from her utterance an idea of dividing as "cutting in half/halving", which she may only be developing in this moment by trying to understand Mira's problem. With that, Franka has moved away from the original problem of distributing the cards to three children and is trying to comprehend the meaning of "divided/dividing" introduced by Mira into the interaction.

Mira answers with "yes" <10> which could, on the one hand, support the interpretation that she accidently made a mistake in <5> and actually wanted to say the solution "three" for the task "six divided by two". On the other hand, one could also interpret that Mira here confirms Franka's idea of dividing as halving.

However, since she explicitly says "divided by three" earlier, Mira seems to already differentiate the idea of dividing as halving and the idea of dividing into more than two subsets. However, at this point this does not become clear for Franka

---

[6]In German, she uses the infinitive instead of the "Partizip II".

and could lead to difficulties in understanding later on. So far, it can be observed that Mira and Franka, despite the existing possible variety of mathematical interpretations at the interactional level, have negotiated a taken-as-shared meaning with a certain fit and continue on this basis.

With the utterance "ah/that's easy" <11> , Franka supports the interpretation that her utterance in <9> was a question for Mira, with whom she was evaluating her idea of dividing, and interprets Mira's answer in <10> as a confirmation. It remains unclear what Franka calls "easy"—the concrete calculation or the general idea of division. Therefore, this utterance does not align with the interpretation of <2> and <4> that Franka acts in the style of a teacher and her questions are merely testing Mira but underlines the interpretation that it was a sincere question.

Mira returns to the actual task and says "and ten divided by three/(4) doesn't work\ **yes it does.** wait" <12>. After formulating the mathematical problem, she pauses which may indicate that she is trying to solve it in her head at the moment of speaking. By saying "doesn't work", she may indicate that she cannot find a suitable solution, and thus assumes that the task is generally not solvable. This reinforces the interpretation that Mira has developed a relatively differentiated framing of division and can distinguish between dividing into two subsets (halving) and dividing into more than two subsets, since the set ten could be easily divided into two subsets of five elements each. For other participants in the interaction, however, the utterance could possibly also be interpreted as consistent with the idea of halving. Mira could thereby say that halving in two subsets "does not work", since they are three and not two children. With the "yes it does" Mira seems to point out that she does have an idea for the solution of the tasks. However, she does not seem to have these ready at hand but has to think again and calls for time by saying "wait."

Franka reacts with "eh now I don't understand#" <13>. Against the background of her previous definition of the situation of dividing as halving, this utterance can be interpreted as an astonishment why the ten cannot be halved in exactly the same way into two subsets as the six—in the case of the ten with five elements each. But Franka could also already be confused by the phrase "ten divided by three" because in the idea of halving one only says "divided by" and does not include the divisor. She might also be wondering about how halving helps them distribute the cards among three people. Mira interrupts Franka with "wait" <14> and asks for more time. This could be interpreted in the sense of "I cannot listen to you right now or explain it to you because I am still thinking about it." However, Franka does not wait and repeats her statement again <15>. Simultaneously, Mira now starts verbalizing her calculation "ten divided by three is three six" <16>.

On the one hand, this verbalization could serve as a support for herself to help her concentrate despite the intervening remarks and therefore be directed towards herself, or it could be interpreted as an explanation for Franka. Because of the expression "is three six", no longer an idea of dividing as halving can be interpreted here, but a mental model of quotitioning or partitioning. For solving this problem, she seems to use the inverse operation here by going through the three times table or by counting by threes. This suggests that Mira already has the assumption that when one divides ten by three each subset contains at least three elements, and she now has to only determine how many remain if she distributes three cards to each child (mental model of partitioning). But it could also be part of the process of trying out, and three at this point is a random number she picked with which she now tests how many subsets of three elements can be generated from the set ten (mental model of quotitioning).

Franka responds to Mira's statement by verbally and gesturally explicating her idea of division built up to that point "you cut the ten [rubs her right and left hand vertically against each other]" <17>. This gesture together with the verb "cut" supports the interpretation that Franka has created a definition of the situation within the interaction in which dividing is understood as halving and in which there is not yet a differentiated framing of dividing by a divisor larger than two. Her solution of the problem would therefore have to be five. At this point, differences in the framing of the two girls are seen, which initially did not come to fruition—also due to imprecise verbal formulations—and enabled a taken-as-shared meaning to develop.

The next two utterances (<18> and <19>) take place simultaneously. This indicates that both are still caught in their own thoughts and cannot properly accommodate each other's utterances. Mira continues her times table with "three six nine" <18> or counts by threes and does not seem to follow Franka's incidental remark correctly. Franka, on the other hand, pursues her idea of halving visualized by the cutting "then five are left over. you cut#" <19>. The phrase "then five are left over" may here be interpreted also in the sense of an idea of subtraction or underlines the idea of sharing (which is the same word as dividing in German), e.g. with a sibling where in most cases one half is given away. With the subsequent repetition of "you cut", Franka may be emphasizing her practical idea of sharing. However, she could also be pointing out that the resulting subset of 5 must now be "cut" or divided again so that (at least) three subsets are created.

Mira interrupts Franka's explanation, as she seems to have now arrived at a solution. She empties the wooden cards from the plastic bag onto the carpet and says "so someone has to have one number more" <20>. She does not explain the process of arriving at her solution, which supports the interpretation that her previous utterances <12, 16, 18> were rather directed towards herself and not meant as an explanation for Franka. The utterance "one number more" can be interpreted as one number card more. With this, Mira has successfully distributed the ten number cards to three children with the help of a mathematical modeling and the solution of a division problem with a remainder. Whether her result is correct, she could now possibly check by practically distributing the number cards.

Franka seems surprised by the result of Franka, reacts with "what/**me**" <21> and raises her right hand with her extended index finger. In the context of the now practical distribution situation, the mathematical differences seem to take a back seat for her, which is underlined by the gesture of signaling. This can be interpreted as a clear demand for her wanting to receive the additional number card. She thus leaves the negotiation of the mathematical content concerning the idea of division and does not question Mira's solution. Thus, the veiled differences in framing remain. Another possible interpretation could be that Franka's utterance in <21> is the beginning of the attempt to introduce her idea of the solution of the problem into the interaction.

Mira responds to Franka's utterance with "okay then you will get one less number **there**" <22>. For her too, a fair distribution between the children seems to be the main focus here. She does not add an explanation of her approach to the interaction.

Franka contradicts Mira's statement with "no" <23>. At the same time, Emilio becomes active again for the first time by taking a number card out of the box and placing it on the row of rods. At this point, he ignores the distribution negotiated in the interaction because he does not take a number of the ten numbers which Mira has just successfully distributed, but one of the other cards.

5.5.7 Summary of the Interpretation

In the last step of the Interactional Analysis, the diversity of interpretations is reduced in the summary of the interpretation where the interpretations of the sequences, which can best be justified, are summarized. This summary serves as a basis for generating theory as it represents the transition between the detailed interpretations of the Interactional Analysis and the first theorisations based on these interpretations. The research question, therefore, determines under which focus the interpretations are summarised. Often in publications, only these summaries of the interpretations are given, since the detailed interpretations are very extensive and can be hard to read due to the diversity of interpretations.

The focus of this summary is on the subject-specific processes of negotiation concerning division between Mira and Franka and the differences in framing emerging within the interactions. The summary thus again focuses on the central ideas of the interactional theory—the negotiation of meaning and the construction of framings.

Example: Summary of the Interpretation

In the situation, Mira creates a mathematical model in form of a division problem which helps her distribute the cards fairly to the three children in the group ("ten divided by three" <1>). Franka reacts in astonishment and asks Mira if she can do "divided". Mira confirms this and upon a renewed inquiry from Franka for the meaning of "divided", Mira gives an example: "six divided divided by three is three" <5>. Franka, on the basis of this example, seems to develop a definition of the situation which equates dividing with halving. This is also becomes clear through her gestures. Franka then checks her hypothesis and Mira confirms it. As a result, Franka seems to be reassured in this definition of the situation. At this point in the interaction, it seems possible to reconstruct a taken-as-shared meaning between the two girls.

In the further course, however, one can see that the framings of the girls with regard to the mathematical operation of dividing/division are different. Mira seems to already have cultivated a very differentiated mathematical framing of division, and apparently understands dividing both as halving and as division by a divisor greater than two. Franka's framing, on the other hand, seems very much related to the everyday idea of sharing meaning dividing into two halves and thus seems to have developed a less differentiated framing, according to which she understands dividing exclusively as halving. Moreover, the differences in framing that occur may be intensified or not resolved by the children, because the everyday connotation of the term 'dividing' does not coincide with the technical language and thus the varying use of the term 'dividing' remains implicit for the children involved. Thus, Mira may consciously not contradict Franka, because the term 'dividing' can be interpreted appropriately with regard to the framings of both everyday language and mathematics. Having a more everyday framing, 'dividing' can be interpreted as always implying halving or splitting into two halves. However, dividing can also be understood as dividing any amount into different numbers of subsets. Thus, Franka's solution dividing ten equals five is correct when having an everyday framing of halving and leads to a contradiction only if the divisor does not equal two and a mathematical framing is used.

Mira comes back to the original division problem and first determines that it is not solvable but then has an idea and starts to calculate. At the same time, Franka expresses her lack of understanding, however, it is unclear whether this is about Mira's utterance of unsolvabilty or in the general sense about the operation of dividing. Mira frames the division as a process of halving, and therefore arrives at the result 5 for the dividend 10. The divisor 3 remains unnoticed by her.

Mira, on the other hand, still tries to solve the division problem 10:3 by counting the saying the times three table or by counting by threes "three six nine" <18>. Her idea for the solution is successful and she arrives at the conclusion that there is a remainder of one. She directly transfers this solution to the specific situation and says that one person has to get one more card. She does not deal with the differences between Franka and her and starts organizing the next step in the group work. From this moment on, Franka is no longer interested in a resolution of the differences between her framing of division and that of Mira. She accepts Mira's solution without question and the concrete distribution of the cards comes to the fore. Emilio, the third child in the group work, is also considered for distribution of the cards, but in the course of the conversation is only a listener, as Franka and Mira lead a dyadic interaction.

5.6 Conclusion

Through the Interactional Analysis, the thematic development of the interaction was analysed on the basis of the participants' negotiations of meaning. The interaction used as an example in this chapter is only short, thus opportunities for learning which may develop for the participating children can only be reconstructed to some extent. However, the potential for learning opportunities in interactions like these can be seen for both children in the negotiation on mathematical meaning. For example, Mira, as the child with the more differentiated framing, has the opportunity to not only apply her framing, but through the negotiation to reflect on her own framing and try to understand Franka's framing. Franka, on the other hand, as the child with the framing less differentiated, has the opportunity to expand her framing by negotiating a framing more functional in the domain of mathematics.

At the end of the analysis processes, a very dense description of the learning processes within the collective negotiation processes is obtained. However, how can the scope of such interpretative research finding be transferred from the status of pure case analyses to greater generalizability in the sense of developing local theories (Merton 1968). It requires the development of a "research style" (Bohnsack 2007, p. 198), which favors theoretical constructions. For this, a central element of the research style of grounded theory, the comparative analysis—"constant comparative method" (Glaser and Strauss 1967; Strauss and Corbin 1994)—can be referred to. The comparative analysis is a method of creating comparison groups which can be applied at all levels of the research process and favors theoretical constructions (see also the description of various ways of making inferences in Schütte (2009) or Krummheuer (2002) for a more specific description of abduction). It not only describes a particular step in the analysis within the research process, but serves as a specific methodical approach throughout the entire research process. At the beginning, in comparative analysis, the aim is to depict the specificity of the segment of reality. Thereafter, the specificity of the respective cases in their relation to each other is examined via a suitable theoretical selection. By means of omparesons, criticism can be rebutted from the deductive-nomological research direction that the results obtained from qualitative works are only valid for individual cases and thus of little relevance. Comparisons lift the analyses of the research beyond a status of case analyses. The systematic and continuous comparison of cases among each other during the entire research process brings dimensions that would not be valid if the cases were considered purely. Thus, by means of comparisons, an extended "conceptual space", in which one can search for solutions or generate possible theoretical elements, is created.

Accompanying this process, the results gathered in the summaries are also compared to theory. From the second scene onward, these reflections on theory of each analysis are compared with the reflections on theory of scenes which have already been analysed. These comparative analyses can reveal structural inconsistences as well as phenomena which cannot be explained by theory and in a further step will lead to an expansion or redesign of existing theory. By doing so, inconsistences of existing theory are discovered and unique phenomena are mapped out.

Appendix

Transcript in German

09	01:47		Mira	*[nimmt Plastiktüte mit Kärtchen aus der Box]* Jeder kriegt warte zehn geteilt durch drei
10	01:56		Franka	weißt du geteilt/. kannst du geteilt/
11	01:58		Mira	Ja
12	02:02		Franka	was bedeutet geteilt/
13	02:06	<	Mira	also geteilt heißt warte sechs geteilt geteilt durch drei ist drei\
14		<	Emilio	*[nimmt das Blatt mit der Stationsbeschreibung in die Hand und betrachtet es]* (unverständlich) guck mal Mira ich habe eine drei gefunden (unverständlich)
15			Franka	hä/
16	02:11		Mira	guck mal sechs geteilt#
17	02:12	#	Franka	hä. sechs teilen ist drei *[hält linke Hand waagrecht und bewegt rechte senkrecht gehaltene Hand nach oben und unten]*
18	02:15		Mira	Ja
19	02:15		Franka	ah/das ist ja einfach
20	02:17		Mira	und zehn geteilt durch drei/(4) geht nicht\ **doch**. warte
21	02:25		Franka	hä versteh ich jetzt nicht#
22	02:27	#	Mira	Warte
23		<	Franka	versteh ich jetzt nicht
24		<	Mira	zehn geteilt durch drei ist drei sechs
25	02:31		Franka	man schneidet die Zehn durch *[reibt rechte und linke Hand senkrecht aneinander]*
26		<	Mira	drei sechs neun
27		<	Franka	dann bleiben fünf übrig. man schneidet#
28	02:33	#	Mira	*[schüttet die Holzkärtchen aus der Plastiktüte auf den Teppich]* also jemand muss eine Zahl mehr haben
29	02:41		Franka	was/**ich** *[hebt rechte Hand mit gestrecktem Zeigefinger]*
30	02:43		Mira	ok dann kriegst du **da** eine Zahl weniger\ *[nimmt die weiße Box mit den weiteren Holzkärtchen in die Hand und stellt sie wieder hin]*
31	02:46	<	Franka	Nein
32		<	Emilio	*[nimmt ein Holzkärtchen aus der weißen Box und legt es an die Zehnerstangen-Kette vor die zweite Kugel der zweiten Stange]*

References

Bauersfeld, H. (1985). Ergebnisse und Probleme von Mikroanalysen mathematischen Unterrichts. In W. Dörfler, & R. Fischer (Eds.), *Empirische Untersuchungen zum Lehren und Lernen von Mathematik* (pp. 7–25). Wien: Hölder-Pichler-Tempsky.
Bauersfeld, H., Krummheuer, G., & Voigt, J. (1988). Interactional theory of learning and teaching mathematics and related microethnographical studies. In H.-G. Steiner, & A. Vermandel (Eds.), *Foundations and methodology of the discipline mathematics education* (pp. 174–188). Antwerp: University of Antwerp.
Blumer, H. (1954). What is wrong with social theory? *American Sociological Review, 19*(1), 3–10.
Blumer, H. (1969). *Symbolic interactionism*. Englewood Cliffs, NJ: Prentice-Hall.
Bohnsack, R. (2007). *Rekonstruktive Sozialforschung. Einführung in qualitative Methoden* (6th ed.). Opladen: Barbara Budrich.
Cobb, P., & Bauersfeld, H. (Eds.). (1995a). *The emergence of mathematical meaning. Interaction in classroom cultures*. Hillsdale, NJ: Lawrence Erlbaum.
Cobb, P., & Bauersfeld, H. (1995b). Introduction: The coordination of psychological and sociological perspectives in mathematics education. In H. Bauersfeld, & P. Cobb (Eds.), *The emergence of mathematical meaning. Interaction in classroom cultures* (pp. 1–16). Hillsdale, NJ: Lawrence Erlbaum.
Eberle, T. S. (1997). Ethnomethodologische Konversationsanalyse. In R. Hitzler, & A. Honer (Eds.), *Sozialwissenschaftliche Hermeneutik* (pp. 245–281). Opladen: Leske + Budrich.
Fetzer, M., & Tiedemann, K. (2018). The interplay of language and objects in the process of abstracting. In J. Moschkovich, D. Wagner, A. Bose, J. Rodrigues Mendes, M. Schütte (Eds.), *Language and communication in mathematics education* (pp. 139–155). Cham: Springer.
Garfinkel, H. (1967). *Studies in ethnomethodology*. Englewood Cliffs, NJ: Prentice-Hall.
Glaser, B., & Strauss, A. (1967). *The discovery of grounded theory. Strategies for qualitative research*. New York: Aldine.
Goffman, E. (1959). *The presentation of self in everyday life*. New York: Doubleday.
Goffman, E. (1974). *Frame analysis. An essay on the organization of experience*. Cambridge: Harvard University Press.
Ingram, J. (2018). Moving forward with ethnomethodological approaches to analysing mathematics classroom interactions. *International Journal on Mathematics Education—ZDM* (in press).
Kelle, U. (1994). *Empirisch begründete Theoriebildung. Zur Logik und Methodologie interpretativer Sozialforschung* (2nd ed.). Weinheim: Deutscher Studienverlag.
Keller, R. (2012). *Das interpretative Paradigma*. Wiesbaden: Springer VS.
Krummheuer, G. (1992). *Lernen mit Format. Elemente einer interaktionistischen Lerntheorie. Diskutiert an Beispielen mathematischen Unterrichts*. Weinheim: Deutscher Studien Verlag.
Krummheuer, G. (1995). The ethnography of argumentation. In H. Bauersfeld, & P. Cobb (Eds.), *The emergence of mathematical meaning. Interaction in classroom cultures* (pp. 229–269). Hillsdale, NJ: Lawrence Erlbaum.
Krummheuer, G. (2002). The comparative analysis in interpretive classroom research in mathematics education. In J. Novotná (Ed.), *European Research in Mathematics Education II: Proceedings of the Second Conference of the European Society for Research in Mathematics Education (CERME 2, 24–27 February 2001)* (pp. 339–346). Mariánské Lázně: Czech Republic: Charles University, Faculty of Education and ERME.
Krummheuer, G. (2004). Wie kann man Mathematikunterricht verändern? Innovation von Unterricht aus Sicht eines Ansatzes der Interpretativen Unterrichtsforschung. *Journal für Mathematik-Didaktik, 25*(2), 112–129.
Krummheuer, G. (2012). Interaktionsanalyse. In F. Heinzel (Ed.), *Methoden der Kindheitsforschung. Ein Überblick über Forschungszugänge zur kindlichen Perspektive* (2nd ed.) (pp. 234–247). Weinheim, Basel: Beltz-Juventa.

Krummheuer, G. (2013). The relationship between diagrammatic argumentation and narrative argumentation in the context of the development of mathematical thinking in the early years. *Educational Studies in Mathematics, 84*(2), 249–265.

Krummheuer, G. (2015). Methods for reconstructing processes of argumentation and participation in primary mathematics classroom interaction. In A. Bikner-Ahsbahs, C. Knipping, & N. Presmeg (Eds.), *Approaches to qualitative research in mathematics education* (pp. 51–74). Dordrecht: Springer.

Krummheuer, G., & Brandt, B. (2001). *Paraphrase und Traduktion. Partizipationstheoretische Elemente einer Interaktionstheorie des Mathematiklernens in der Grundschule*. Weinheim, Basel: Beltz Verlag.

Krummheuer, G., & Naujok, N. (1999). *Grundlagen und Beispiele Interpretativer Unterrichtsforschung*. Opladen: Leske + Budrich.

Lerman, S. (2000). The social turn in mathematics education research. In J. Boaler (Ed.), *Multiple perspectives on mathematics teaching and learning* (pp. 19–44). Westport, CT: Ablex.

Merton, R. K. (1968). *Social theory and social structure*. New York: The Free Press.

Miller, M. H. (1986). *Kollektive Lernprozesse: Studien zur Grundlegung einer soziologischen Lerntheorie*. Frankfurt, Main: Suhrkamp.

Mollenhauer, K. (1972). *Theorien zum Erziehungsprozeß*. München: Juventa.

Naujok, N. (2000). *Schülerkooperation im Rahmen von Wochenplanunterricht. Analyse von Unterrichtsausschnitten aus der Grundschule*. Weinheim: Dt. Studien-Verl.

Oevermann, U., Allert, T., Konau, E., & Krambeck, J. (1987). Structures of meaning and objective hermeneutics. In V. Meja, D. Misgeld, & N. Stehr (Eds.). *Modern German sociology. European perspectives: A series in social thought and cultural criticism* (pp. 436–447). New York: Columbia University Press.

Sacks, H. (1998). *Lectures on conversation* (3rd ed.). Malden, Ma: Blackwell.

Sacks, H., Schegloff, E. A., & Jefferson, G. (1974). A simplest systematics for the organization of turn-taking for conversation. *Language, 50,* 696–735.

Schütte, M. (2009). *Sprache und Interaktion im Mathematikunterricht der Grundschule. Zur Problematik einer Impliziten Pädagogik für schulisches Lernen im Kontext sprachlich-kultureller Pluralität*. Münster: Waxmann.

Schütte, M. (2014). Language-related learning of mathematics. A comparison of kindergarten and primary school as places of learning. *ZDM Mathematics Education, 46*(6), 923–938.

Schütte, M., & Krummheuer, G. (2017). Mathematische Diskurse im Kindesalter. In U. Kortenkamp, & A. Kuzle (Eds.), *Beiträge zum Mathematikunterricht 2017* (pp. 877–880). Münster: WTM-Verlag.

Sfard, A. (2008). *Thinking as communicating: Human development, development of discourses, and mathematizing*. Cambridge: Cambridge University Press.

Solomon, Y. (2009). *Mathematical literacy: Developing identities of inclusion*. New York: Routledge.

Strauss, A., & Corbin, J. (1994). Grounded theory methodology. In N. K. Denzin, & Y. S. Lincoln (Eds.), *Handbook of qualitative research* (pp. 273–285). Thousand Oaks: Sage.

Thomas, W. I. (1923). *The unadjusted girl: With cases and standpoint for behavior analysis*. Boston: Little, Brown, and Co.

Tiedemann, K., & Brandt, B. (2010). Parents' support in mathematical discourses. In U. Gellert, E. Jablonka, & C. Morgan (Eds.), *Proceedings of the 6th International Conference on Mathematics and Proceedings of the 6th International Conference on Mathematics Education and Society* (pp. 457–468). Berlin, Deutschland (20–25 March 2010).

Turner, J. H. (1988). *A theory of social interaction*. USA: Standford University Press.

Voigt, J. (1995). Thematic patterns of interaction and sociomathematical norms. In H. Bauersfeld, & P. Cobb (Eds.), *The emergence of mathematical meaning. Interaction in classroom cultures* (pp. 163–201). Hillsdale, NJ: Lawrence Erlbaum.

Open Access This chapter is licensed under the terms of the Creative Commons Attribution 4.0 International License (http://creativecommons.org/licenses/by/4.0/), which permits use, sharing, adaptation, distribution and reproduction in any medium or format, as long as you give appropriate credit to the original author(s) and the source, provide a link to the Creative Commons license and indicate if changes were made.

The images or other third party material in this chapter are included in the chapter's Creative Commons license, unless indicated otherwise in a credit line to the material. If material is not included in the chapter's Creative Commons license and your intended use is not permitted by statutory regulation or exceeds the permitted use, you will need to obtain permission directly from the copyright holder.

Chapter 6
Planning and Conducting Mixed Methods Studies in Mathematics Educational Research

Nils Buchholtz

Abstract In this chapter, central ideas of Mixed Methods Research are presented in which qualitative and quantitative research methods are combined or integrated. In addition to the explanation of common Mixed Methods terminology, the chapter provides an overview of the most important aspects that must be reflected in the planning and conduction of a mixed-methodological research project. On the basis of considerations on the nature of the research object and specific conditions of mathematics education research, methodological aspects of the research question, research design and data analysis are described. The chapter concludes with considerations on the challenges of Mixed Methods, as well as recommendations on the step-by-step approach to a Mixed Methods Research project.

Keywords Mixed methods research · Triangulation · Quantitative methods · Qualitative methods · Method integration · Method combination

6.1 Introduction

The number of studies using both qualitative and quantitative methods or combining qualitative and quantitative data has increased significantly in recent years in mathematics education research. As shown by meta-analyses by Hart et al. (2009) and Ross and Onwuegbuzie (2012), researchers accounted for both qualitative and quantitative methods in no less than 29 and 31% of mathematics education articles published in international journals between 1995 and 2005 and between 2002 and 2006 respectively. More and more researchers nowadays situate their studies in the Mixed Methods Research (MMR) methodology, and the use of multi-methodological approaches to data analyses is increasingly taking place against a methodological background that has been described more broadly and in more detail in recent years. Mixed Methods, the "third research paradigm", as described

---

N. Buchholtz (✉)
University of Oslo, Oslo, Norway
e-mail: n.f.buchholtz@ils.uio.no

© The Author(s) 2019
G. Kaiser and N. Presmeg (eds.), *Compendium for Early Career Researchers in Mathematics Education*, ICME-13 Monographs,
https://doi.org/10.1007/978-3-030-15636-7_6

by Johnson and Onwuegbuzie (2004, p. 22), appears to overcome the one-sided methodological thinking of both qualitative and quantitative research paradigms, despite continuing discussions about the incompatibility of qualitative and quantitative methods (Howe 1988). Therefore, Mixed Methods studies currently enjoy great popularity in the mathematics education research community. The pragmatic and innovative combination of different research perspectives promises additional insight, which might not be accessible with a single methodological research approach.

For a long time, the Mixed Methods discussion focused on the development of new, different research designs (Teddlie and Tashakkori 2009; Creswell and Plano Clark 2018; Schoonenboom and Johnson 2017) and thus on how and when qualitative and quantitative methods are 'mixed' in concrete research designs. Several extensive handbooks on Mixed Methods have been written (Creswell 2003, Tashakkori and Teddlie 1998; Creswell and Plano Clark 2018; Hesse-Biber and Johnson 2015; Kuckarts 2014) and numerous methodological and theoretical research articles have been published in the major journals of the MMR community —among them the *Journal for Mixed Methods Research* (JMMR). Meanwhile, a large number of different design types or typologies for Mixed Methods Research designs exist, so that some researchers already speak of a "design overload" (Kuckarts 2014). Exaggeratedly, researchers can just choose a Mixed Methods design suitable for their purposes and get an appropriate methodological justification and guidance for the research process immediately. This offer sounds tempting, but falls short with regard to the subject-specific methodological reflection on one's own research approach. Not to be misunderstood: choosing a suitable Mixed Methods research design is still a crucial and important issue in the research process. But this should not be the first consideration, when one is dealing with the question of the structure of a planned research project, because, as Burton (2002) notes,

> in the majority of articles in journals and books, a description is provided on 'how' the research was done but rarely is an analysis given of 'why' and more particular out of all the methods that could have been used, what influenced the researcher to choose to do the research in the manner described to do it. (p. 1)

The decisive factor when choosing a Mixed Methods research approach is, first of all, the question 'why mixed methods at all?'

Especially for an early career researcher in mathematics education, this can be a very difficult question to answer, because it is linked to the object of research and the exact research question, which may not yet be established at the beginning of the work. Nonetheless, choosing a Mixed Methods research approach should not be based on general trends, because one thing is often overlooked in the decision: researchers not only have to be methodologically well-versed in qualitative methods, but also well-versed in quantitative methods. That is not all—in addition, good methodological knowledge in the field of Mixed Methods methodology is required. The time resources that early career researchers must devote to study all these methodologies should therefore be well considered, especially if they have been funded only for a few years. However, once a researcher decides on a MMR approach and can realize it in the framework of a study, the promise of extended knowledge gain is certainly fulfilled—even if this knowledge gain may consist in the fact that the results yielded with different methods contradict each other or are not compatible at all.

This chapter provides an overview on central questions and fundamental aspects for carrying out a multi-methodological research project in mathematics education research. There is now a broad base of literature in the field of MMR, especially developed for researchers who are at the beginning of a research process (e.g., Schoonenboom and Johnson 2017). This literature also describes the key steps in the research process and how a MMR project can be carried out. This chapter cannot and should not replace the necessary consultation of this methodological literature, but it does contribute important subject-specific reflections and justifications from mathematics education research to this topic. Therefore, the chapter is an introduction to the methodological background of MMR and refers to further literature. The terminology, methodological justifications and the central features of MMR are provided. Subsequently, central steps in the implementation of a MMR project are described.

6.2 Methodological Background of Mixed Methods Research

6.2.1 What Is Mixed Methods Research?

The discussion about Mixed Methods has gained momentum since around the 1980s and is being led more and more by methodologically reflective literature. Mixed Methods draws back on the idea of triangulation as "the combination of methodologies in the study of the same phenomenon" (Denzin 1978, p. 291). Denzin distinguished between within-methods triangulation, which refers to the use of multiple quantitative or multiple qualitative approaches, which is nowadays referred to as "Multimethod Research" (Creswell 2016, p. 216ff.), and between-methods triangulation, which involves the use of both quantitative and qualitative approaches. From the latter understanding, the current conceptual understanding of MMR has finally emerged. For a more detailed overview on the historical development of the Mixed Methods movement, I recommend reading the descriptions by Johnson et al. (2007) and Maxwell (2016). However, within the Mixed Methods Research community, the term Mixed Methods is not used as uniformly as it might appear, even though more and more consensus is emerging in some areas (Mertens et al. 2016).

In their influential article *Toward a Definition of Mixed Methods Research*, Johnson et al. (2007) list no fewer than 19 distinct definitions of Mixed Methods, most of them understanding Mixed Methods as a combination of qualitative and quantitative research. Johnson et al. (2007) summarized the situation in a general definition:

> Mixed methods research is the type of research in which a researcher or team of researchers combines elements of qualitative and quantitative research approaches (e.g., use of qualitative and quantitative viewpoints, data collection, analysis, inference techniques) for the broad purposes of breadth and depth of understanding and corroboration. [...] A mixed methods study would involve mixing within a single study; a mixed method program would involve mixing within a program of research and the mixing might occur across a closely related set of studies. (p. 123)

Although this definition is cited by many authors as describing MMR, it is ultimately only one of many different definitions. The methodological discourse within the MMR community indicates that there is disagreement, especially with regard to the definition of Mixed Methods. A too high rigidity might take the risk of being exclusive from a definitional perspective (Mertens et al. 2016), and so, for example, studies that combine hermeneutic research methods with empirical methods would be excluded from this definition. Since the discussion about Mixed Methods is based in the social sciences, the definition also unconsciously reflects the social-scientific understanding of methods. Therefore, we should ask whether and to what extent this definition is applicable to the field and to the methodology of mathematics education research (see Sect. 6.3).

6.2.2 What Kind of Research Questions Does Mixed Methods Research Require?

First of all, the main feature of each MMR approach is that a Mixed Methods study essentially consists of two or more research "components" (Schoonenboom and Johnson 2017) or "strands" (Teddlie and Tashakkori 2009) from different methodological perspectives (in most cases qualitative and quantitative). Secondly, in the context of a MMR approach, the components must be related to each other; in the terminology of MMR, this means combining components with each other if the goal of the research is to mutually complement findings of each. Alternatively, it means integrating the components if the goal is the mutual validation of the research results. This combination or integration is always a function of the research question and the purpose of the study. Both components should provide insights into a superordinate (integrated) research question, which should therefore be formulated in such a way that the components can also focus on corresponding sub-questions and provide insights that can be related to the overarching question, that is, they can be integrated.

Here is a combination example from mathematical education research: In a research project, a researcher developed and carried out a teacher professional development (PD) module for the promotion of certain skills. The researcher is now interested in the results of the training. An integrated research question could therefore be "How does this intervention within mathematics teacher PD affect the attitudes and competences of teachers?" This question could be addressed quantitatively if the number of teachers that participated in the PD module is adequate. For this purpose, for example, the researcher may use a questionnaire on specific attitudes or self-efficacy before and after the module, if he or she believes that attending the module has contributed to change, such as the willingness to apply the content in forthcoming lessons. The quantitative hypothesis on the overarching question is thus: "Attending the PD module on X leads to a significant increase in positive attitudes to X and the willingness to use X in the classroom". At the same time, the question could also be addressed qualitatively, because the researcher is interested in what other effects the attendance to the PD module had, especially effects that might not have been anticipated. A qualitative partial research question can then be, for example: "Which aspects of the PD module were particularly helpful for teachers to learn X? What other impact(s) did the course have?" These questions could be addressed with in-depth interviews with some participating teachers, focusing on qualitative evaluation methods such as content analysis. When combining both findings, a broader spectrum of the PD module's impact is considered and the results complement each other. Quantitative findings may be enhanced by results from case analyzes (for example, to find out what might be the reason why some teachers, despite attending the PD module, do not show attitude changes).

How the concrete combination or integration of the results of the different components can be realized in order to answer the overarching research question of a study must be decided on a case-by-case basis and is part of the responsibility of the researcher. The challenge here is to gain additional value from the integration of the results with regard to the overarching question, namely, "produce a whole through integration that is greater than the sum of the individual qualitative and quantitative parts" (Fetters and Freshwater 2015, p. 116; see also Bryman 2007). In the MMR community, the formulation "1 + 1 = 3" is used to symbolize the challenges of generating meta-inferences from integration, meaning qualitative + quantitative = more than the individual components (Fetters and Freshwater 2015), which is, however, difficult to endure for mathematicians. Experience has shown that this step has the greatest challenges in the research process, and because of the lack of generalizability, there is also little literature on the concrete procedure. Empirical meta-studies on the quality standards of Mixed Method studies also show that integration is often absent, and that in lower-quality Mixed Method studies, qualitative and quantitative research questions are answered rather independently (Bryman 2007), without any relation between the results produced.

6.2.3 What Is the Purpose of Doing MMR? And Why Should I Choose This Methodological Approach?

As Burton (2002) points out, the purpose of the study should be clarified depending on the research question of the study. The central question of *why* one chooses a MMR approach is at the forefront of the decision for this research approach.

It should be weighed to what extent a mixed-methodical approach has advantages over a mono-methodically oriented approach. That means, a researcher should initially reflect on the specific strengths and weaknesses of qualitative research approaches and quantitative research approaches, and to what extent a MMR approach can make use of the strengths and compensate for the weaknesses. Johnson and Christensen (2017) characterize the quantitative and qualitative research paradigms briefly as follows:

> First, the quantitative research approach primarily follows the confirmatory scientific method because its focus is on hypothesis testing and theory testing. Quantitative researchers consider it to be of primary importance to state one's hypotheses and then test those hypotheses with empirical data to see if they are supported. On the other hand, qualitative research primarily follows the exploratory scientific method [...]. Qualitative research is used to describe what is seen locally and sometimes to come up with or generate new hypotheses and theories. Qualitative research is used when little is known about a topic or phenomenon and when one wants to discover or learn more about it. It is commonly used to understand people's experiences and to express their perspectives. (p. 33)

Mixed Methods researchers argue that it is important for the research process to use both exploratory and confirmatory methods. Johnson and Onwuegbuzie (2004) describe Mixed Methods in their much-cited article as the third paradigm between quantitative and qualitative research, building on the philosophy of pragmatism. The idea behind this approach is that the combination or integration of quantitative and qualitative methods or even paradigms can compensate for the weaknesses and build on the strengths of the respective research approaches (Johnson and Christensen, 2017, p. 51). Some of these specific strengths and weaknesses can be described as follows (Johnson and Onwuegbuzie 2004, p. 19):

Strengths of quantitative research:

- Testing and validating already existing theories and hypotheses
- Generalizing results using appropriate samples
- The influence of confounding variables can be controlled in experimental settings
- Providing easy-to-handle (numerical) data
- Data analysis is relatively less time-consuming (often software-supported)
- Relative independence of the results from the researcher
- Overall high credibility for decision makers
- Useful in large sample analyzes.

Weaknesses of quantitative research:

- Research categories or theories often are not culturally sensitive
- Results depend on the theoretical assumptions and are not supported by a curriculum
- Occurring phenomena are often hidden due to the hypothesis-testing procedure (confirmation bias)
- There is discussion about a replicability crisis in quantitative research (Open Science Collaboration 2015).

On the other hand, strengths and weaknesses of qualitative research can be described as follows (for instance, see Johnson and Onwuegbuzie 2004, p. 20):

Strengths of qualitative research:

- The collected data carry a subjective context of meaning of the examined persons
- Qualitative research is suitable for looking at small case numbers in depth
- Useful for describing complex phenomena or dynamic processes
- Creating a contextual context of the results, cultural sensitivity
- Generation of theories in the context of Grounded Theory
- Case studies to illustrate results.

Weaknesses of qualitative research:

- Data analysis is often very time consuming
- Often generalizability of the results is not possible
- It is difficult to verify/falsify hypotheses
- Results may be idiosyncratically affected by the researcher
- There are ongoing discussions about quality criteria.

The mutual reproach of weaknesses to the significant other methodological approach was the subject of the so-called "Paradigm Wars" (Gage 1989) within the social sciences but also in educational science research until the 1980s (Kelle and Buchholtz 2015). Since the 1990s, however, the Mixed Methods movement has increasingly and pragmatically set itself the goal of overcoming struggles between purist representatives of both research paradigms. In doing so, MMR methodology is understood as an integrative approach in which the strengths of one research method can be used to balance the weaknesses of the other research method. Johnson and Onwuegbuzie (2004) describe the strengths as well as the weaknesses of the approach as follows (p. 21):

Strengths of Mixed Methods Research:

- Simultaneous generation and testing of theory
- Possibility of answering a broader extent of research questions
- Establishing a wealth of research designs with specific strengths and weaknesses
- Provision of validation strategies through convergent research results
- Generating insights that go beyond the use of single research methods
- Added value of additional knowledge for theory and practice.

Weaknesses of Mixed Methods Research:

- Single researchers can struggle to carry out both qualitative and quantitative research at the same time; it may require a research team
- The researcher has to be firm and confident in applying multiple research methods.

If one is aware of the specific strengths (and the weaknesses) of the MMR approach, the central characteristic of methodological reflection remains the purpose or the legitimation of the study (Schoonenboom and Johnson 2017). While the overarching goal of a MMR approach is always to deepen and strengthen the study's conclusions, depending on the research question, specific reasons may be given for why it makes sense to combine or integrate different methods. Here the MMR community has already worked out methodological justifications. Among the best known is the classification by Greene et al. (1989), which is based on an analysis of Mixed Methods studies. They identify five purposes or reasons why researchers mix quantitative and qualitative methods (p. 259):

1. *Triangulation*, which means seeking for convergence, corroboration and correspondence of results from different methods, often used for validity purposes.
2. *Complementarity*, which means seeking for elaboration, enhancement, illustration or clarification of the results from one method with the results from the other method. Here the aim of the mixing is to get a more holistic understanding of the research object.
3. *Development*, which means seeking to use the results from one method to help develop or inform the other method, where development is broadly construed to include sampling and implementation, as well as measurement decisions.
4. *Initiation*, which means seeking the discovery of paradox, and contradictory findings, new perspectives of frameworks or the recasting of questions or results from one method with questions or results from the other method.
5. *Expansion*, which means seeking to extend the breadth and range of inquiry by using different methods for different inquiry components. This for example is particularly important in follow-up studies.

Meanwhile, a variety of other classifications of purposes for Mixed Methods Research exists (e.g., Bryman 2006). However, the key point in finding the purpose for using MMR methodology is to define the research question and then carefully consider what the purposes for mixing are. As Schoonenboom and Johnson (2017) state:

> One can use mixed methods to examine different aspects of a single research question, or one can use separate but related qualitative and quantitative research questions. In all cases, the mixing of methods, methodologies, and/or paradigms will help answer the research questions and make improvements over a more basic study design. Fuller and richer information will be obtained in the mixed methods study. (pp. 111–112)

6.3 Special Features of MMR in Mathematics Education

In addition to the methodological justifications for MMR approaches, mathematics education research also provides justifications that can be given on the basis of disciplinary prerequisites. On the one hand, epistemological orientations within mathematics education research play a role, but on the other hand, there is also the complexity of mathematics didactic research objects. The research objects are in the field of tension of various disciplines such as mathematics, psychology, sociology, philosophy and educational science. They focus on different actors in different educational levels, and stand in a systemic relationship between theory and practice. Since no comprehensive discussion of the nature of mathematics educational research objects can be given here—at this point, reference should be made to the detailed considerations in Ernest (1998), Schoenfeld (2016), Steinbring (1998) or Wittmann (1995)—we are content with the following broad understanding of mathematics education research objects for the purpose of methodological reflection. Mathematics educational research objects in the broadest sense refer to the teaching and learning of mathematics in social and institutionalized educational contexts, the development, structuring and implementation of teaching materials as well as the reflection and selection of educational goals.

Starting from different research questions, we can distinguish various methodological approaches in mathematics education research, which according to the idea of multiple research paradigms (Johnson 2015) reflect a variety of different traditions of mathematics education research. For example, Bishop (1992) distinguishes three distinct traditions in research on mathematics education. Firstly, there is a pedagogue or educational tradition, whose aim is to bring about direct improvements in practice, while experiment and observation are key concepts of research. Methodologically, this research tradition is located in the field of observation and improvement of teaching activities, whereby as an example, experience from expert teachers will be generalized or participatory research methods will be applied. Bishop further distinguishes the tradition of the empirical scientist, whose goal is to analyze the practice based on empirical data and to generate explanatory models. Especially in this tradition, Bishop sees a strong methodological fixation that understands mathematics education as an analytical science and uses theory to explain scientific evidence. This approach resonates with classical qualitative and quantitative empirical research methods that are used. As a third research tradition, Bishop cites the scholastic-philosopher tradition, which sees mathematics education research as a rigorously argued theoretical reflection process. The epistemological aim from this perspective is to establish a theoretically argued position on theory-driven research questions and curricular development—strongly based on mathematical insights and logical rigor. Steinbring (2011) describes this as a research paradigm in which "the scientific elaboration of mathematical knowledge is the central and crucial means practiced for steering and optimizing mathematical instruction, learning and understanding processes" (p. 46). Research methods within this tradition—such as subject-matter didactical analysis (Sträßer 2013) or the French didactical engineering (Artigue 1988), aim at making relevant mathematical structures accessible to the learner's mental development and adapting them to the requirements of teaching and learning without distorting mathematical standards (see, e.g., Kirsch 1977). Griesel (1974, p. 118) points to the logical mathematical rigor of the research approach: "The research methods of this area are identical to those of mathematics, so that outsiders have sometimes gained the impression that, here, mathematics (particularly elementary mathematics) and not mathematics education is being conducted" (as translated by Steinbring 2011, p. 45).

The argument for MMR, that the combination or integration of different research methods leads to a combination of strengths or compensation for weaknesses, can be transferred to the subject area of mathematics education research, but requires an extended understanding of research methods within the MMR methodology. The understanding of research methods in this case must be extended also to theoretically oriented subject-specific research methods. Depending on the research question, the extended understanding of methods also enables the combination or integration of empirical-social scientific research methods (quantitative/qualitative/both) and non-empirical subject-specific research methods. Within the social sciences, the term Mixed Methods is relatively limited to the exclusive combination of qualitative and quantitative design elements (Johnson et al. 2007; Johnson and Onwuegbuzie 2004; Cresswell 2016; Baur et al. 2017). However, there are also representatives within the methodological discussion of Mixed Methods who regard the rigid separation of qualitative and quantitative methods as outdated and argue pragmatically for Mixed Methods (Bazeley 2018), Mixed Methodologies (Szostak 2015; Christ 2010; Huysmans and de Bruyn 2013) or Merged Methods (Gobo 2016) as an entanglement of different methodologies of any origin. By way of example, such integration of subject-didactic and empirical methods takes place within the framework of mathematics educational design science (Prediger et al. 2015; Prediger and Zwetschler 2013; Nührenbörger et al. 2016). The research process is designed as a cyclical process based on the mathematical specification and structuring of learning content, design development (substantial learning environments), and subsequent empirically researched design experiments (Nührenbörger et al. 2016). The subject-specific methodology aims at a local theory formation based on the contextual research results (Bakker and van Eerde 2015, p. 437), which in turn can serve to further specify and structure learning content. For the sake of simplicity, the following sections deal explicitly with the combination and integration of qualitative and quantitative research methods, but in principle, the considerations can also be applied to the field of specific mathematics education research methods.

In addition, research objects in mathematics education are characterized by a high level of complexity, which is due to the interdisciplinary nature of the discipline (Wittmann 1995; Bartolini-Bussi and Bazzini 2003). Furthermore, the objects studied are characterized by different intra- or interpersonal relationships on micro (individual), meso (e.g., group, class, school) and macro level (e.g., country level or educational system). Not least, research objects are temporally involved in the dynamics of action, but also in educational and social change processes (Schoenfeld 2016; Steinbring 1998). MMR is particularly suited to the complexity of research objects in mathematics education. Taking up the complexity, it is crucial that the different research methods are either directed toward different aspects of the research object, with the aim of being able to make as far-reaching statements as possible, or that the different research methods analyze the same research object from different perspectives. The aim is then the mutual validation of the findings (Erzberger and Kelle 2003). The principle of triangulation as "taking different perspectives" (Flick et al. 2012) is particularly relevant in social science contexts and enables a more comprehensive understanding of complex research objects (Creswell and Plano Clark 2018). Further reasons for MMR in mathematics education are as follows (see Buchholtz, forthcoming):

- Researchers can focus more on the interdisciplinary nature of the research objects studied through different subject-specific methodological approaches.
- Mixed Methods Research offers the opportunity for local subject theory (Herbst and Chazan 2017; Erzberger and Kelle 2003).
- The methodological focus of different levels of education (individual and collective) helps to maximize the scope of research findings. The orientation towards both individual and collective statements then corresponds to the normative orientation of the research discipline (Schoonenboom and Johnson 2017).
- By combining hermeneutic methods with empirical methods, the uptake and updating of the understanding of historical and social processes can be targeted from a contemporary perspective.
- MMR is effective for examining and validating education, action and change processes.

Overall, by combining or integrating different research methods, a broader picture of the complexity of the research objects can be gained, since the analysis takes up different perspectives.

6.4 Choosing a Research Design

If the rationale for the choice of a MMR project is clear, then the question arises as to how the qualitative and quantitative methods are to be related to each other in the specific case. How the researcher can compose and arrange the components in the research process is then a question of the research design. According to Morse and Niehaus (2009) and Schoonenboom and Johnson (2017), we can identify three crucial aspects that influence the design of a Mixed Methods study, which I describe shortly. First, the "theoretical drive" (Morse and Niehaus 2009) of a research question indicates whether answering a research question is more qualitatively driven or quantitatively driven, or equally qualitatively and quantitatively driven. This theoretical drive can therefore determine which component of the research is dominant in the research process or if the two components are equally dominant.

Second, the timing of the components refers to how both components are dependent on each other in the context of the research process (Morse and Niehaus 2009). Usually, the simultaneity or dependency of the components can be described in two ways: whether the research design is concurrent (sometimes referred to as parallel) or sequential (Creswell and Plano Clark 2018; Morse and Niehaus 2009). In sequential research designs, the two components are conducted at different times and one component can build on the results of the other component. In concurrent research designs, both components are conducted simultaneously. Schoonenboom and Johnson (2017) explain:

> In a commonly used mixed methods notation system (Morse 1991), the components are indicated as qual and quan (or QUAL and QUAN to emphasize primacy), respectively, for qualitative and quantitative research. As discussed […], plus (+) signs refer to concurrent implementation of components […] and arrows (→) refer to sequential implementation […] of components. Note that each research tradition receives an equal number of letters (four) in its abbreviation for equity. (pp. 108–109)

This means that for example a sequential MMR design where a dominant qualitative component builds up on the results of an earlier (not so dominant) quantitative component would be labeled as "quan → QUAL", and so on. In the handbook of Creswell and Plano Clark (2018) three core-designs are described, that frame the basis of most (even more complex) MMR designs and reflect certain purposes of mixing. The sequential exploratory design (QUAL → QUAN), seeks to generalize findings of a qualitative study:

> Building from the exploratory results, the researcher conducts a development phase by designing a quantitative feature based on the qualitative results. This feature may be the generation of new variables, the design of an instrument, the development of activities for an intervention, or a digital product, such as an app or website. Finally, in the third phase the investigator quantitatively tests the new feature. The researcher then interprets how the quantitative results build on the initial qualitative results or how the quantitative results provide a clear understanding because they are grounded in the initial qualitative perspectives of participants. (p. 65)

For example, a researcher could collect qualitative interview data about teachers' perceptions on mathematical modelling and the conditions for and contexts in which they use modelling in the classroom. Taking the resulting categories as variables, the researcher could develop a quantitative survey instrument and then use it to assess the overall prevalence of these variables for a large number of teachers or for teachers in different countries. Secondly, the sequential explanatory design (QUAN → QUAL) follows a quantitative study with a qualitative study in order to explain or expand the results of the quantitative study. For example, a researcher could collect and analyze quantitative survey data from students to identify significant predictors of mathematics anxiety. Finding a surprising association between mathematics anxiety and high mathematical achievement, the researcher could conduct qualitative focus group interviews with high achieving students to explain this rather unexpected result (e.g., finding that these students feel high achievement pressure). Third, the convergent (or concurrent) design (QUAN + QUAL) seeks for the mutual complementation or validation of results (Cresswell and Plano Clark 2018):

> The basic idea is to compare the two results with the intent of obtaining a more complete understanding of a problem, to validate one set of findings with the other, or to determine if participants respond in a similar way if they check quantitative predetermined scales and if they are asked open-ended qualitative questions. The two databases are essentially combined. (p. 64)

An example of a comparison approach to the convergent design would be if a researcher videotapes mathematics teachers during teaching and subsequently conducts reflective interviews on the teaching methods used in the lesson. The researcher can analyze the video data quantitatively with a rating instrument or an observation protocol for instructional quality (this analysis could also be qualitative, depending on the methodical focus of the instrument) and can evaluate the interviews qualitatively. Subsequently the two sets of results can be used to assess in what ways the objective results about instructional quality and the teachers' views converge or diverge. Meanwhile, there is much literature on MMR designs (Cresswell and Plano Clark 2018; Teddlie and Tashakkori 2009; Greene 2007), including so-called "emergent designs" (Morse and Niehaus 2009; Brevik, forthcoming). In these designs, the different research methods are mixed situationally during the whole research process (for example, if it is not foreseeable at the beginning of the research project that additional methodological components will be required). There is a danger that because of the "design overload" (Kuckarts 2014) one can easily lose track of the various design types, especially as different authors often use different names for similar research designs. It is also criticized that design descriptions are often too rigid to describe variable and complex designs (Guest 2013). One way out here is not to understand the multitude of design typologies as binding templates for one's own research project, but as a framework for orientation in finding a research design.

The third aspect concerning the research design is the "point of interface" (Morse and Niehaus 2009) or the "point of integration" (Schoonenboom and Johnson 2017), which refers to the stage at which the researcher combines or integrates the results from both components and the actual mixing occurs. In the case of concurrent research designs, this can happen throughout all stages of the research process (Schoonenboom and Johnson 2017), but the common point at which the mixing takes place is during the analysis of the data gathered by both components or when the data is interpreted. More details about how and when mixing takes place can be found in the writings of Bazeley (2018) or Onwuegbuzie and Teddlie (2003). In case of sequential research designs it is often the case that one component informs the following component before it is conducted, which is a form of interface or integration too. Nevertheless, a Mixed Methods study is more than the sum of its parts (Bryman 2007), so even in sequential designs, an integration should take place when analyzing or interpreting the data or at least when the research results are written up.

6.5 Mixed Data Analysis: Integrating Qualitative and Quantitative Findings—Joint Displays

Once data are collected in the research process, the data analysis process begins. In the classical case, qualitatively collected data such as, for example, open-ended interviews or questionnaire responses, observations and field notes or journals are evaluated with the help of qualitative research methods. Quantitative data such as measurements based on standardized tests, rating scales or self-reports are preferably evaluated using quantitative research methods. On the one hand, this can happen in parallel, and then qualitative and quantitative results are interrelated in the interpretation of the findings (triangulation of results) in order to conclude meta-inferences. This integration requires reducing, transforming, comparing, or correlating the results (Caracelli and Greene 1993; Bazeley 2012; Onwuegbuzie and Teddlie 2003; Onwuegbuzie and Hitchcock 2015). The guiding question of this integration is: "To what extent do the quantitative and qualitative results converge or diverge?" The results should be studied according to similarities and differences, or to what extent the results of one research component can be explained using the results of the other component. Whether the different methods were used with the proviso of investigating the same research object (e.g., for validation purposes) or different aspects of the research object (for a comprehensive picture), the results of the integration may vary (Kelle and Buchholtz 2015):

> This differentiation is not a mere play of words: only methods which refer to the same phenomena can yield results which may be used for mutual validation of methods. Different results would indicate validity problems here; but if separate aspects of the investigated phenomenon or even separate phenomena were examined with different methods we would expect different (but certainly not contradictory) results. [...] [E]ach of the following four outcomes can arise (cf. Erzberger and Prein 1997 [...]):
>
> 1. qualitative and quantitative results converge,
> 2. qualitative and quantitative results relate to different objects or phenomena, but are complementary to each other and thus can be used to supplement each other,
> 3. qualitative and quantitative results are divergent or contradictory,
> 4. qualitative and quantitative results refer to unrelated phenomena.
>
> This makes clear that both types of triangulation are applicable and can make sense within a mixed methods design: triangulation as validation may lead to convergent qualitative and quantitative findings or it may result in divergent findings which point to validity problems; triangulation as investigating different aspects of the research subject may yield complementary results (if applied successfully) or it may render unrelated results (if this triangulation strategy fails). (p. 332ff.)

In a sequential analysis in the explanatory sequential design, on the other hand, the integration mostly happens when the results of the first analysis influence the second analysis with regard to certain emphases. First of all, findings must be identified in the quantitative results that require further explanation and to which the results of the qualitative study can be referred. These can be results on content-related topics, but also particularly interesting or extreme cases that will be selected as a specific sample in the following work. In the sequential analysis of the exploratory sequential design, a selection of qualitative results must be made, which are aiming for generalization. Based on these results, a contextually appropriate feature (e.g., a new instrument) is developed which is piloted and tested on a larger sample. Already in the data analysis of one research component (qual. or quan.), however, it is possible to work multi-methodically. For example, it is possible to quantify qualitative data through the use of quantitative methods or qualitize quantitative data through the application of qualitative research methods (Tashakkori and Teddlie 1998).

Schoonenboom and Johnson (2017) recommend the use of a so-called "joint display" (Guetterman et al. 2015; Cresswell and Plano Clark 2018) to facilitate the process of integration. Following Johnson and Christensen (2017), a joint display "is a matrix juxtaposing qualitative and quantitative results for cases, research questions, variables, outcomes, times, locations, or any other dimension of interest" (p. 593). The table representation condenses the results of the mixed analysis (but cannot replace it). It should be consistent with the research design or research questions and make clear where the integration of each component occurred. In any case, the joint display should therefore contain information about the results of the individual data analyses and provide the results of the integration of the qualitative and quantitative results (see Fig. 6.1).

The possibilities of designing a joint display are manifold, as described by Johnson and Christensen (2017, p. 595), including for example that rows equal cases, and columns equal time-ordered outcomes (time 1, time 2, time 3, time 4). Rows could also equal qualitative themes, while columns equal relevant

Case/Variable/ Research Question	Quantitative Outcome	Qualitative Outcome	Difference/Similarity	Integrated Statement
1	Text from QUAN results description or summary	Text from QUAL results description or summary	Results convergent	Text from integration description or summary
2	Text from QUAN results description or summary	Text from QUAL results description or summary	Results in some parts convergent	Text from integration description or summary
3	Text from QUAN results description or summary	Text from QUAL results description or summary	Results contradict each other; discrepancies	Text from integration description or summary
…	…	…	…	…

Fig. 6.1 Joint display

quantitative statistical results such as on a 5-point scale (themes-by-statistics display). Cells could also include quotes and frequency counts (Creswell 2015).

6.6 Methodological Challenges for MMR

The choice of a MMR approach should be well considered and based on requirements of the specific research question. Throughout the research process, MMR designs may present methodological difficulties and challenges on which researchers should constantly reflect.

Frequently, a comprehensive methodological justification for Mixed Methods is already missing when determining the object of the research and the research questions (for example, if different data sources in an existing research project simply arise). In this case, there is no theoretical anchoring of the research question, and a selection of methods often takes place prior to the research question. With regard to the purpose of the study, it is then not even clear whether the combination or integration of different methods is intended to achieve mutual validation or complementarity of the results. Further difficulties may also arise in the lack of coordination between the selected research method and the empirical field.

During the data collection and the data analysis, it is imperative for a MMR study to integrate the results of the different components of the study. This integration and the interpretation of the integrated results must add value to the individual interpretation of qualitative and quantitative findings. There is a danger here that a pure parallel performance of the research methods with subsequent interpretations will be undertaken. Even in sequential designs, integration is an integral part of the research process, which must be done explicitly. The mixed data analysis does not always lead to complementary or convergent findings. In the case of a targeted combination of methods with complementary perspectives on the research object, it can happen that results can be completely incoherent and that the qualitative and quantitative results cannot be correlated at all. In the method integration with the aim of mutual validation of research results, however, it is not ensured that both methods also cover the same research object, a mandatory prerequisite for mutual validation. Results can converge here, but also diverge or even contradict each other. Often it becomes clear in the course of the research process that qualitative and quantitative components cover different aspects so that only complementary results can be achieved. Especially for early career researchers, MMR projects pose great challenges in terms of resource and time management, which is why, when working in an unsecured position or on scholarships, a reduced choice of method should be considered. The central question is: 'Is there a recognizable added value of Mixed Methods compared to a reduced choice of method?'

In presenting the results, the complexity of MMR designs can lead to difficulties in accurately identifying qualitative and quantitative proportions of studies. Care should also be taken to ensure that the research question and the complete implementation of the research project are coordinated and that this is also clear from the description of the study. Bryman (2008) generally observes a "mismatch between the rationale for the combined use of qt and ql research and how it is used in practice" (p. 94). If the process of integration is described, it is aggravating that there is no clear terminology of "mixing", so that the integration processes must be described as precisely as possible. Here, the recent editions of the handbooks with their descriptions of integration processes now provide support (Cresswell and Plano Clark 2018). In the end, the presentation of methodology and results of Mixed Methods studies will be of great importance. Finally, qualitative methodological procedures and qualitative results, quantitative methodological procedures and quantitative results as well as the procedure of integration and its results will have to be described. As a result, when one or more research papers are written instead of a monograph, space problems often arise because scientific journals set limits on the length of articles. A way out may be to either publish qualitative and quantitative results in separate articles or to submit the research article to a Mixed Methods journal for specifically methodologically-based studies, as these generally offer more generous space constraints.

6.7 Summary: How to Conduct a Mixed Methods Study

This chapter provides insight into the most important aspects to consider when deciding on a MMR approach. Reference was made to the crucial aspects of planning a Mixed Methods study in mathematics education as well as to the common terminology of the Mixed Methods community. To summarize, here is a step-by-step presentation of the sequence of important questions that should be answered in the planning and implementation of MMR studies (adapted from Schreier 2015).

Step 1: What is the research object?

- Does the research object have various constituent aspects, such as actors at different levels (e.g. teachers and students, or individual and institutional conditions) or different disciplinary characteristics?
- Does the research object have a theoretical and/or practical orientation? What forms of complexity does the research object exhibit?
- What is the relationship between the object of research and mathematics?
- What are the special features of the research (e.g., videos, conceptual training programs, teaching materials)?
- Does the investigation of the research object require a constructive or analytical orientation, or both?
- Which aspects of the research object should be investigated?

Step 2: Why mixed methods? Identifying the purpose of the study

- Should the study bring together or compare different perspectives on different aspects of the research object?
- Should the study validate different perspectives on certain aspects of the research object?
- Should existing research results be extended?
- Should statements about individual cases as well as general statements be made?
- Should the research object be explored qualitatively and the results reviewed for their generalizability? Should an object-related theory be created and tested?
- Should a questionnaire study be prepared and validated? Should a hypothesis be tested using qualitative data? Should causal factors be identified to better understand the underlying mechanisms?

Step 3: What is the exact research question?

- Which integrated research question can be formulated about the research object?
- What could be a qualitative sub-question of the integrated research question?
- What could be a quantitative sub-question of the integrated research question?
- For what aspects of the research questions are qualitative or quantitative methods needed? Which methods are suitable for answering the partial research questions?
- At which points can an integration take place?
- What can/should the integration look like?

Step 4: Which research design fits the question and the purpose of the study?

- Is a sequential explanatory design QUAL $\rightarrow$ QUAN suitable?
- Is a sequential exploratory design QUAN $\rightarrow$ QUAL suitable?
- Which parallel design is suitable, integration or combination QUAL + QUAN?
- Is a complex design needed (for example, longitudinal design)? Is an intervention design needed (Cresswell 2015; Sandelowski 1996)?
- Is the Mixed Methods design developing during the entire research process?
- Is a design-based research design needed (with alternating cycles of constructive design development and analytical empirical validation)?
- What is the position of the individual components in the research design?

Step 5: How is the research design specified?

- How many components does the design have? How many components are mixed?
- What is the priority of the different components?
- How do the components relate to each other?
- What is the theoretical orientation of the research design? Are local theories used (for example, to study particular mathematical content) or is the research design completely theoretically driven (for example, by feminist theories or theories of intercultural learning)?
- At what point in the design does integration happen? Is it in the interpretation of results or across the entire research process?

Step 6: How should the mixing happen?

- Are qualitative data and/or quantitative data generated in the study?
- Are the data collected and analzyed independently or is integration already taking place at the level of data collection and analysis?
- Are qualitative data quantified? Are quantitative data qualified?
- Which sampling strategies can be used?
- To what extent do the methods used inform each other?
- Which variables/cases are the focus of mixing?

There are many different aspects to consider when choosing a MMR approach, and a Mixed Methods study is certainly less easy to plan for early career researchers than a mono-methodical study. Frequently, the way in which the results of the different methods relate to each other is not yet foreseeable at the beginning of the research project. Nonetheless, a MMR project provides unique insights into the object of research that cannot be achieved in depth with the application of single methods. By validating or complementing research results, MMR provides an in-depth knowledge of research results. The methodological discussion within the Mixed Methods community continues to develop this methodology, and interestingly enough, mathematics education has proven to be a common field of application of mixed-methodology studies. In August 2018, for example, at the third International Conference on Mixed Methods (MMIRA) in Vienna, a whole section was devoted to Mixed Methods studies in mathematics education.

References

Artigue, M. (1988). Ingénierie didactique. *Recherches en Didactique des Mathématiques, 9*(3), 281–308.
Bakker, A., & Van Eerde, H. A. A. (2015). An introduction to design-based research with an example from statistics education. In A. Bikner-Ahsbahs, C. Knipping, & N. Presmeg (Eds.), *Approaches to qualitative research in mathematics education: Examples of methodology and methods* (pp. 429–266). New York, Springer.
Bartolini-Bussi, M. G., & Bazzini, L. (2003). Research, practice and theory in didactics of mathematics: Towards dialogue between different fields. *Educational Studies in Mathematics, 54*(2–3), 203–223.
Baur, N., Kelle, U., & Kuckarts, U. (2017). Mixed Methods – Stand der Debatte und aktuelle Problemlagen. *Kölner Zeitschrift für Soziologie und Sozialpsychologie, 69*(2), 1–37.
Bazeley, P. (2012). Integrative analysis strategies for mixed data sources. *American Behavioral Scientist, 56*(6), 814–828.
Bazeley, P. (2018). *Integrating analyses in Mixed Methods Research*. Thousand Oaks, CA: SAGE.
Bishop, A. J. (1992). International perspectives on research in mathematics education. In D. A. Grouws (Ed.), *Handbook of research on mathematics teaching and learning* (pp. 710–723). New York: Macmillan.
Brevik, L. (forthcoming). *Emergent mixed methods designs*.
Bryman, A. (2006). Integrating quantitative and qualitative research: How is it done? *Qualitative Research, 6*, 97–113.

Bryman, A. (2007). Barriers to integrating quantitative and qualitative research. *Journal of Mixed Methods Research, 1*(1), 8–22.

Bryman, A. (2008). Why do researchers integrate/combine/mesh/blend/mix/merge/fuse quantitative and qualitative research? In M. M. Bergman (Ed.), *Advances in mixed methods research* (pp. 87–100). London, England: SAGE.

Buchholtz, N. (forthcoming). *Mixed methods in mathematics education.*

Burton, L. (2002). Methodology and methods in mathematics education research: where is 'the why'? In S. Goodchild & L. English (Eds.), *Researching mathematics classrooms: a critical examination of methodology* (pp. 1–10). London: Praeger.

Caracelli, V. J., & Greene, J. C. (1993). Data analysis strategies for mixed-method evaluation designs. *Educational Evaluation and Policy Analysis, 15*(2), 195–207.

Christ, T. W. (2010). Teaching mixed methods and action research: Pedagogical, practical, and evaluative considerations. In A. Tashakkori & C. Teddlie (Eds.), *Handbook of mixed methods in social & behavioral research* (2nd ed., pp. 643–676). Thousand Oaks, CA: SAGE.

Creswell, J. W. (2003). *Research design: Qualitative, quantitative, and mixed methods approaches.* Thousand Oaks: Sage.

Creswell, J. W. (2015). *A concise introduction to Mixed Methods Research.* Thousand Oaks, CA: Sage.

Creswell, J. W. (2016). Reflections on the MMIRA. The future of mixed methods task force report. *Journal of Mixed Methods Research, 10,* 215–219.

Creswell, J. W., & Plano Clark, V. (2018). *Designing and conducting mixed methods research* (3rd ed.). Thousand Oaks, CA: SAGE.

Denzin, N. K. (1978). *The research act.* Chicago, IL: Aldine. (Original work published 1970).

Ernest, P. (1998). A postmodern perspective on research in mathematics education. In A. Sierpinska & J. Kilpatrick (Eds.), *Mathematics education as a research domain: A search for identity* (pp. 71–85). Dordrecht: Kluwer Academic Publishers.

Erzberger, C., & Kelle, U. (2003). Making inferences in mixed methods: The rules of integration. In A. Tashakkori & C. Teddlie (Eds.), *Handbook of mixed methods in social and behavioral sciences* (pp. 457–488). Thousand Oaks: Sage.

Erzberger, C., & Prein, G. (1997). Triangulation: validity and empirically-based hypothesis construction. *Quality & Quantity, 31,* 141–154.

Fetters, M. D., & Freshwater, D. (2015). The 1 + 1 = 3 integration challenge. *Journal for Mixed Methods Research, 9*(2), 115–117.

Flick, U., Garms-Homolová, V., Herrmann, W. J., Kuck, J. & Röhnsch, G. (2012). "I can't prescribe something just because someone asks for it…": Using Mixed Methods in the framework of triangulation. *Journal of Mixed Methods Research, 6*(2), 97–110.

Gage, N. (1989). The paradigm wars and their aftermath: A "historical" sketch of research and teaching since 1989. *Educational Researcher, 18,* 4–10.

Gobo, G. (2016). Why "merged" methods realize a higher integration than "mixed" methods. A reply. *Qualitative Research in Organizations and Management: An International Journal, 11*(3), 199–208.

Greene, J. C. (2007). *Mixed methods in social inquiry.* San Francisco, CA: Jossey-Bass.

Greene, J. C., Caracelli, V., & Graham, W. F. (1989). Toward a conceptual framework for mixed methods evaluation designs. *Educational Evaluation and Policy Analysis, 11,* 255–274.

Griesel, H. (1974). Überlegungen zur Didaktik der Mathematik als Wissenschaft. *Zentralblatt für Didaktik der Mathematik, 6*(3), 115–119.

Guest, G. (2013). Describing mixed methods research: An alternative to typologies. *Journal of Mixed Methods Research, 7,* 141–151.

Guetterman, T. C., Creswell, J. W., & Kuckartz, U. (2015). Using joint displays and MAXQDA software to represent the results of mixed methods research. In M. McCrudden, G. Schraw, & C. W. Buckendahl (Eds.), *Use of visual displays in research and testing: coding, interpreting, and reporting data* (pp. 145–176). Charlotte, NC: Information Age Publishing.

Hart, L. C., Smith, S. Z., Swars, S. L., & Smith, M. E. (2009). An examination of research methods in mathematics education (1995–2005). *Journal of Mixed Methods Research, 3*(1), 26–41.

Herbst, P., & Chazan, D. (2017). The role of theory development in increasing the subject specificity of research on mathematics teaching. In J. Cai (Ed.), *First compendium for research in mathematics education* (pp. 102–127). Reston, VA: NCTM.

Hesse-Biber, S., & Johnson, B. (Eds.). (2015). *Oxford handbook of multimethod and mixed methods research inquiry*. Oxford, UK: Oxford University Press.

Howe, K. R. (1988). Against the quantitative-qualitative incompatability thesis, or, Dogmas die hard. *Educational Researcher, 17,* 10–16.

Huysmans, P., & De Bruyn, P. A. (2013). A mixed methods approach to combining behavioral and design research methods in information systems research. Association for Information Systems (Ed.), *ECIS 2013–Proceedings of the 21st European Conference on Information Systems* (pp. 1–12). Utrecht: AIS.

Johnson, R. B. (2015). Dialectical pluralism: A metaparadigm whose time has come. *Journal of Mixed Methods Research, 11*(2), 156–173.

Johnson, R. B., & Christensen, L. B. (2017). *Educational research: Quantitative, qualitative, and mixed approaches* (6th ed.). Thousand Oaks, CA: Sage.

Johnson, R. B., & Onwuegbuzie, A. J. (2004). Mixed methods research: A research paradigm whose time has come. *Educational Researcher, 33*(7), 14–26.

Johnson, R. B., Onwuegbuzie, A. J., & Turner, L. A. (2007). Toward a definition of mixed methods research. *Journal of Mixed Methods Research, 1*(2), 112–133.

Kelle, U., & Buchholtz, N. (2015). The combination of qualitative and quantitative research methods in mathematics education: A "Mixed Methods" study on the development of the professional knowledge of teachers. In A. Bikner-Ahsbahs, C. Knipping & N. Presmeg (Eds.), *Approaches to qualitative research in mathematics education: Examples of methodology and methods* (pp. 321–361). Dordrecht: Springer.

Kirsch, A. (1977). Aspects of simplification in mathematics teaching. In H. Athen, & H. Kunle (Eds.), *Proceedings of the Third International Congress on Mathematical Education* (pp. 98–119). Karlsruhe: University of Karlsruhe.

Kuckartz, U. (2014). *Mixed methods*. Wiesbaden: Springer.

Maxwell, J. A. (2016). Expanding the history and range of mixed methods research. *Journal of Mixed Methods Research, 10,* 12–27.

Mertens, D. M., Bazeley, P., Bowleg, L., Fielding, N., Maxwell, J., Molina-Azorin, J. F., & Niglas K. (2016). *MMIRA Task force report. The future of mixed methods: A five year projection to 2020*. Retrieved from https://mmira.wildapricot.org/resources/Documents/MMIRA%20task%20force%20report%20Jan2016%20final.pdf. (10/05/2018).

Morse, J. M. (1991). Approaches to qualitative-quantitative methodological triangulation. *Nursing Research, 40,* 120–123.

Morse, J. M., & Niehaus, L. (2009). *Mixed method design: Principles and procedures*. Walnut Creek, CA: Left Coast Press.

Nührenbörger, M., Rösken-Winter, B., Ip Fung, C., Schwarzkopf, R., & Wittmann, E. C. (2016). *Design science and its importance in the German mathematics educational discussion (ICME-13 Topical Surveys)*. Rotterdam: Springer.

Onwuegbuzie, A. J., & Hitchcock, J. (2015). Advanced mixed analysis approaches. In S. Hesse-Biber & B. Johnson (Eds.), *Oxford handbook of multimethod and mixed methods research inquiry* (pp. 275–295). New York: Oxford University Press.

Onwuegbuzie, A. J., & Teddlie, C. (2003). A framework for analyzing data in mixed methods research. In A. Tashakkori & C. Teddlie (Eds.), *Handbook of mixed methods in social and behavioral research* (pp. 351–384). Thousand Oaks, CA: Sage.

Open Science Collaboration. (2015). Estimating the reproducibility of psychological science. *Science, 349*(6251). http://science.sciencemag.org/content/349/6251/aac4716 (10/05/2018).

Prediger, S., Gravemeijer, K., & Confrey, J. (2015). Design research with a focus on learning processes. *ZDM Mathematics Education, 47*(6), 877–891.

Prediger, S., & Zwetzschler, L. (2013). Topic-specific design research with a focus on learning processes: The case of understanding algebraic equivalence in grade 8. In T. Plomp & N. Nieveen (Eds.), *Educational design research: Illustrative cases* (pp. 407–424). Enschede: SLO, Netherlands Institute for Curriculum Development.

Ross, A., & Onwuegbuzie, A. J. (2012). Prevalence of mixed methods research in mathematics education. *The Mathematics Educator, 22*(1), 84–113.

Sandelowski, M. (1996). Focus on qualitative methods: Using qualitative methods in intervention studies. *Research in Nursing & Health, 19,* 359–364.

Schoenfeld, A. H. (2016). Research in mathematics education. *Review of Research in Education, 40*(1), 497–528.

Schoonenboom, J., & Johnson, R. B. (2017). How to construct a mixed methods research design. *Kölner Zeitschrift für Soziologie und Sozialpsychologie, 69*(supplement 2), 107–131.

Schreier, M. (2015). *Mixed methods design.* Presentation held at the 12th summerschool of the Faculty of Education of the University of Hamburg. Retrieved 03–04 Sept 2015.

Steinbring, H. (1998). Mathematikdidaktik: Die Erforschung theoretischen Wissens in sozialen Kontexten des Lernens und Lehrens. *Zentralblatt für Didaktik der Mathematik, 30*(5), 161–167.

Steinbring, H. (2011). Changed views on mathematical knowledge in the course of didactical theory development: independent corpus of scientific knowledge or result of social constructions? In T. Rowland & K. Ruthven (Eds.), *Mathematical knowledge in teaching* (pp. 43–64). Heidelberg/London/New York: Springer.

Sträßer, R. (2013). Stoffdidaktik in mathematics education. In S. Lerman (Ed.), *Encyclopedia of mathematics education* (pp. 566–570). Dordrecht: Springer.

Szostak, R. (2015). Interdisciplinary and transdisciplinary multimethod and mixed methods research. In S. Hesse-Biber & R. B. Johnson (Eds.), *The Oxford handbook of multimethod and mixed methods research inquiry* (pp. 128–143). New York: Oxford University Press. http://www.oxfordhandbooks.com/abstract/10.1093/oxfordhb/9780199933624.001.0001/oxfordhb-9780199933624-e-51

Tashakkori, A., & Teddlie, C. (1998). *Mixed methodology: Combining qualitative and quantitative approaches.* Thousand Oaks, CA: SAGE.

Teddlie, C., & Tashakkori, A. (2009). *Foundations of mixed methods research: Integrating quantitative and qualitative approaches in the social and behavioral sciences.* Los Angeles, CA: Sage Publications.

Wittmann, E. C. (1995). Mathematics education as a "design science.". *Educational Studies in Mathematics, 29,* 355–374.

Open Access This chapter is licensed under the terms of the Creative Commons Attribution 4.0 International License (http://creativecommons.org/licenses/by/4.0/), which permits use, sharing, adaptation, distribution and reproduction in any medium or format, as long as you give appropriate credit to the original author(s) and the source, provide a link to the Creative Commons license and indicate if changes were made.

The images or other third party material in this chapter are included in the chapter's Creative Commons license, unless indicated otherwise in a credit line to the material. If material is not included in the chapter's Creative Commons license and your intended use is not permitted by statutory regulation or exceeds the permitted use, you will need to obtain permission directly from the copyright holder.

Chapter 7
The Research Pentagon: A Diagram with Which to Think About Research

Angelika Bikner-Ahsbahs

Abstract Early career researchers often need assistance in their research to help them focus on and systematize relevant aspects of their research. This chapter elaborates the research pentagon as a diagram for reflecting on research. Examples show how the pentagon may represent specific aspects of research, how it allows for (re-)structuring the inquiry process in research, and finally the pentagon is used as an analytic tool to visualize the specificities of the networking of two theories in an empirical case study.

Keywords Research pentagon · Diagrammatic reasoning · Abstraction in Context · Interest-dense Situations · Networking of theories

7.1 Introduction

An early career researcher in mathematics education is often not well prepared for research. Many young researchers may be prepared for practical teaching rather than for researching, others might come from other academic disciplines going through a paradigm shift (Nardi 2015) while developing a different academic identity. In addition, conducting research with early career researchers is organized and facilitated in various ways (Batanero et al. 1994; Reys and Reys 2017; Liljedahl 2018; Nardi 2015; Haser 2018), for example in graduate programs with a coherent study program or supported by individual supervisors. There are two different types of PhDs, one is built on publishing a number of papers in scientific journals and others follow the aim of writing a monograph as a dissertation thesis. The various ways in which students are involved in research, for instance by a PhD-project, a Masters program or a postdoc position, may manifest quite different needs for support und supervision. Liljedahl (2018) investigated what kind of support PhD students need for their transition from being a dependent to an independent

---

A. Bikner-Ahsbahs (✉)
University of Bremen, Bremen, Germany
e-mail: bikner@math.uni-bremen.de

researcher. These students need, besides a peer-community of inquiry, to discuss, reflect, distribute and share their experiences in research; they also need predominantly heuristic tools or examples that help them conduct their own research.

During the last decade I have explored such a heuristic tool, the research pentagon, to find out how useful it is for early career researchers in structuring their research. Originally the research pentagon was created as a diagram to represent five aspects that are necessary to consider in research (Fig. 7.1), namely, research objects, aims, questions, methods and situations (Bikner-Ahsbahs and Prediger 2010).

As is the case for all diagrams (see Peirce 1931–1958, CP 5.162 and also Hoffmann 2005, p. 123–151) the research pentagon may assist to come to new insight, in that early career researchers may first use it to represent the relations between the five research aspects in their research, and then explore the coherence of these relations, justify their suitability, revise the pentagon to improve the research frame, use it to reflect, systematize and restructure research.

In this chapter the research pentagon will be elaborated as an epistemic tool, that is a tool to think-about ("Denkzeug", Schmitz and Groninger 2012, p. 20, own translation) with which early career researchers may elaborate and reflect on their research. Firstly, I provide an understanding of research as a practice of coming to know—a so-called epistemic practice—in a community of researchers. The research pentagon will be embedded into this practice. I then describe the ingredients of the pentagon situated within this understanding of research. Relating it to research examples I substantiate the relevance and suitability of this tool as a heuristic tool for research. This account provides a first impression of what the research pentagon is about, what it allows us to do, and where its limits are. Based on further examples I outline how it may serve to improve a research design. This elaboration then allows us to shift its purpose towards an analytic tool for describing a case of networking theories.

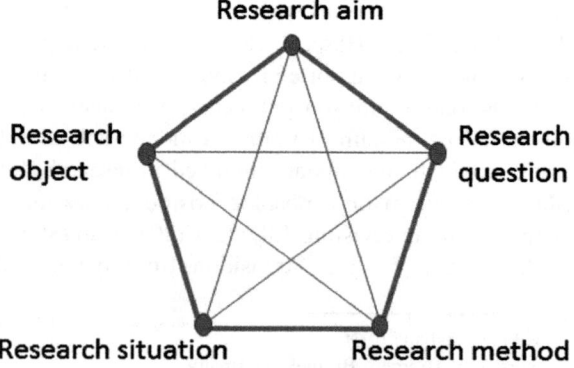

Fig. 7.1 Research pentagon describing main aspects of doing research (Bikner-Ahsbahs and Prediger 2010)

7.2 The Research Pentagon Embedded in Research as an Inquiry Practice

Knorr Cetina (2001) describes scientific practice in contrast to a rule-based practice that addresses routinized handling of ready to hand objects. The latter objects often become invisible while they are used; for example, we are not aware of how a bicycle works while riding it. Such an object is completely different from a research object. A research object is an epistemic object that draws attention by its lack of completeness. But it provides signs of how to further unfold its nature, hence, has the potential to generate meanings about itself. A researcher exploring such an object enters into a relationship with it by the epistemic practice of unfolding these meanings in a "dynamic, creative and constructive" way (Knorr Cetina 2001, p. 187). This is just how the present paper considers research, as an epistemic inquiry unfolding the research object as an epistemic object. Thus research is built on a meaning generating relationship between researcher and an epistemic object.

Interestingly, a paper by Boaler et al. (2003), written to describe research practices that are relevant for early career researchers to build, does not address these epistemic objects explicitly. Instead they describe research as practice in which knowledge is strategically used:

> Research, after all, is not knowledge. Research, whether empirical, theoretical or philosophical, is an active process of investigation, one that relies on strategic use of knowledge, in context. Because it is something people do, not just know, we turn next to examine a small but illustrative set of core practices of research: reading, formulating a research question, using data carefully to make and ground claims, moving from the particular to the general, considering mathematics, and communicating research findings. (p. 495)

All these specific practices, reading, making claims, communicating etc., are important parts of research as an epistemic practice as was defined above. But what is to be added to this description is the epistemic nature of the object under investigation, which because of its lack of completeness provides signs for its exploration, and evokes problems to be solved. For that reason the first two aspects of our research pentagon (Fig. 7.1) are the *research aim* and the *research object* (Mason and Waywood 1996). The aim comes from a problem, which indicates the kind of relevance—why a study of the specific research object is done. But a research object is rarely completely defined at the beginning. For a research study to be conducted there is a necessity to clarify the research object's nature repeatedly, based on research already done in the field, theory available, and finally, based on the results obtained. Let us consider an example Boaler et al. (2003) have used to illustrate their considerations.

The Third International Mathematics and Science Study TIMSS (Baumert and Lehmann 1997) investigated and compared students' curricular mathematical knowledge in different countries. This comparison showed that Japanese students scored much more highly on the items than students from Germany or the United States, which means the average level of curricular mathematical knowledge differed among the three countries. Here the object of research is clear, namely, students' mathematical knowledge described by an average score based on solving mathematical tasks in different mathematical domains. These TIMSS results called for a better understanding of how teaching takes place in the three countries. This *research aim* was addressed by Hiebert et al. (1999) in the follow-up TIMSS video study (see Fig. 7.2). They posed the *research question* "How is mathematics taught in the United States, Germany, and Japan?" (see Boaler et al. 2003, p. 497; Hiebert et al. 1999, p. 196), switching the epistemic object to the kinds of teaching of mathematics at grade eight in these countries. The underlying assumption is that teaching influences how students understand mathematics. In their study, Hiebert et al. (1999) identified clear differences in the national teaching scripts of the three countries, shaped by "cultural teaching patterns" (p. 200) with differences in the quality of teaching for understanding (p. 200), in the role of the teacher, in the kind of mathematics that is taught, and in the expected students' behavior. Thus after the study, the view on teaching, the research object, had changed. Hiebert et al. stated that "teaching is a cultural activity ..." (p. 196). The differences in teaching could now be understood as a consequence of the culture of schooling and "cross-cultural differences in the individual features of mathematics teaching must be understood within the cultural system of teaching of which they are part" (p. 200).

Summing up, three aspects are important to consider in research as an epistemic practice of inquiry (Fig. 7.1). The epistemic practice is related to an epistemic object, *the research object*, which is investigated to follow a *research aim* or solve a problem. This aim is partly addressed by a *research question* that directs the investigation of the research object. However, the research object may change its nature in the course of research.

Boaler et al. (2003) emphasize two further aspects that are relevant for research. Firstly, the choice of *research method* (Figs. 7.1, 7.3) must perfectly fit the research question to be answered. Indeed, only their methodical decisions of how a video study should be conducted as a large-scale comparison study between the three countries enabled Hiebert et al. to unfold the cultural characteristics of teaching; for example they had to find curricular topics related to the same grade that allowed

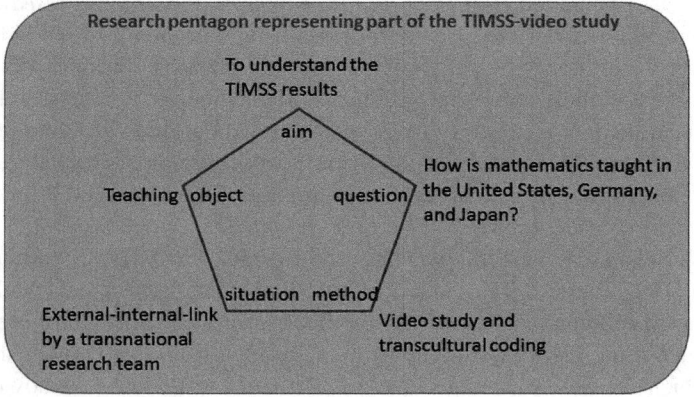

Fig. 7.2 Aspects of research of the TIMSS video study

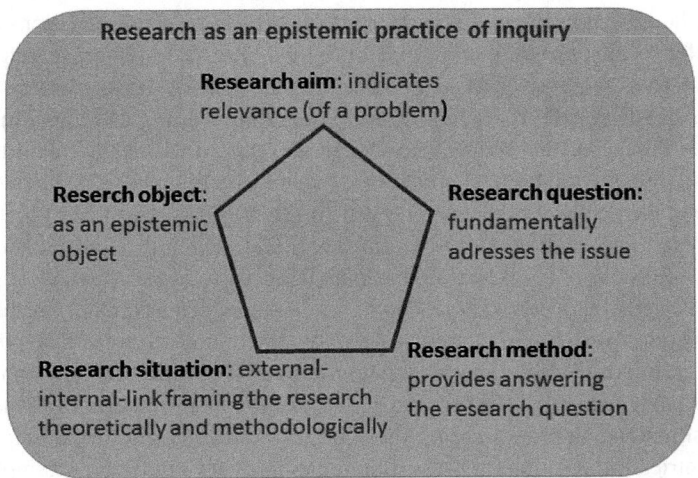

Fig. 7.3 The Research pentagon (Bikner-Ahsbahs and Prediger 2010, p. 487)

them to compare several classes and teachers in the schools along the school year. Also detailed technical decisions, such as where to put the camera, were important steps towards comparison. Secondly, researchers must become deeply familiar with the research area and the theoretical background in which the study and its methodology are embedded. The latter holds true for the theoretical as well as empirical knowledge in the specific area, which allows for framing the research in order to build a *research situation* (Fig. 7.2) for the investigations to be done. In the TIMSS video study, Hiebert and Stigler built a transnational research team with as much knowledge about the teaching in the three countries as possible, to be strategically used, for example, for identifying comparable transnational codes.

The research question normally is the driving force for conducting a successful study. So, what makes a question a good research question? Boaler et al. (2003) claim that

> One obvious characteristic is that, at their core, they [Hiebert & Stigler] get at a fundamental issue. These researchers framed and asked questions that were central to the puzzles and problems of the field in which they were working. A second characteristic of these questions is the 'fit' between question and the method. (p. 320)

The main criterion Boaler et al. stress, is digging deeply into the core concept that fundamentally solves the problem. Taken as a paradigmatic example, the research question from the TIMSS video study directly focuses on the core of solving the problem of understanding the differences of the TIMSS results from the perspective of teaching. Hiebert and colleagues unpacked the characteristics of teaching in their comparison study and revealed teaching scripts as new epistemic objects, that highlighted what could not be thought of before. As culturally determined practice, teaching scripts cannot just be transferred from one country to another; they come out of the cultural heritage of schooling in the country.

Thus, the *research method* should perfectly fit the research questions and both should refer to the *research situation* in the field (Fig. 7.3). The research situation consists of an external as well as an internal part. The *external research situation* comprises the discourse in the field to be explored by reading and attending conferences. The choice of theoretical knowledge and empirical results taken therefrom must fit not only the methodical procedure, but first and foremost it is the basis for the definition of the research object and it even comes prior to the choice of method. The *internal research situation* addresses the situation in which the study is undertaken, framed by the knowledge taken from the field. It must also fit the role of the researchers who may directly be involved in research; for example, in participatory research their role is different from that in a large scale study where objectivity is a standard to be followed, as in the TIMSS video study. It was the idea of establishing a transnational research team that enabled Hiebert and colleagues to link the external and the internal research situations, in order to bring the national knowledge about teaching from the three countries into the internal research situation of the study, for example to find comparable codes across the countries (Fig. 7.3).

In most cases, only one research study is not sufficient to fully reach the research aim or solve the problem. The reason for this is that a broad and general aim has to be broken down into answerable research questions, which may address just a specific view embedded into a narrow framework. This must not be taken as a disadvantage. On the contrary, a narrow view that at the same time still allows a general answer to be revealed (as emphasized by Boaler et al. 2003) may provide in-depth insight.

Further, with each theoretical background assumptions also enter the scene, which are not shown in the pentagon but which are equally important as a prerequisite for a coherent framework. Knowing the field helps the researcher to make good and suitable choices. Therefore, constantly re-considering the research situation while reading about the knowledge in the field, should be an ongoing activity. This activity might assist in unfolding the nature of the research object more lucidly so that research questions may also become clearer, and so that the methods may be better adapted both to the research object and to the research questions. The interrelated revision of the specific research pentagon in turn might improve the coherence of the research framework as a whole. These processes not shown in the pentagon are additionally important for communicating research finally, for example to better draw conclusion from the results and, hence, provide connectivity back to the research field.

7.3 The Research Pentagon as a Model for Practicing Research

7.3.1 *Hidden Views on Formulas*

As described in the previous section the research pentagon consists of five aspects necessary to be considered in research. In this section, I refer to a study conducted by Schou and Bikner-Ahsbahs (submitted), in order to illustrate a pathway that established the research study and is illustrated by the pentagon in Fig. 7.4.

Research often starts with a problem that gives rise to a research aim. The aim might come from a practical problem, a gap identified in research or a new situation in school as society has changed or a reform has taken place. In the example about unpacking students' hidden views on formulas, we (Schou and Bikner-Ahsbahs) started with the problem of students' difficulties when formulas are used. This problem is a practical problem as well as a problem that research has addressed in many specific but rarely general ways. For example students fail to use the right formulas in a particular context or they use the right formula in a wrong way. From there, the research aim was set up to provide explanations of the students' difficulties and to improve the teaching when formulas are involved (see aim, Fig. 7.4).

In order to solve this problem an intense literature review in the *external research situation*, the research field, had to be done to find out what was already known about the problem in the field. We found out that handling formulas are rarely addressed beyond a specific area and that there can be a variety of ways students handle formulas, for example, as a function (Malle 1993) or as an algorithm for calculating a measure (Siller and Roth 2016). This knowledge was used to prepare a lesson series on geometric formulas providing various resources for the students; from this series several kinds of data were collected (see method, Fig. 7.4).

To take into account a broad variety of views on formulas, the term *formula* had to be broadly defined. Thus, the *research object* was described as a comprehensive understanding of ways to handle formulas. But what does it mean, to understand ways to handle formulas? This understanding is shown by acting when students solve a task with all kinds of semiotic resources, inscriptions, material models, diagrams, or dynamic representations at the computer (external situation). In addition, we had to come back to where the problem is located, the classroom, where the teacher rather works with groups than with individuals (see aim, Fig. 7.4). For both reasons a socio semiotic perspective was adopted (back to external research situation, Fig. 7.4). It allowed us to include semiotic means as well as the social situation of group work in the classroom (inner/internal research situation, Fig. 7.4). This perspective then was the lens through which we captured

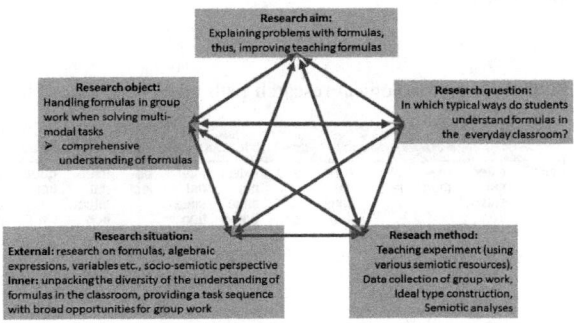

Fig. 7.4 Research pentagon of the "hidden views on formulas" (cf. Schou and Bikner-Ahsbahs, submitted)

the research object more precisely, namely, a comprehensive understanding of formulas in the classroom (research object again, Fig. 7.4). Thus, the considered situation to be researched is the internal research situation, which had to be consistent with the socio semiotic perspective we had chosen. Since we wanted to unpack the diversity of hidden views on formulas in the classroom and clearly conceptualize these hidden views, our *research question* asked for typical ways of how students understand formulas in the classroom, including the definition of the *research object*. By the *methodical* decision of building ideal types empirically (Bikner-Ahsbahs 2015), we precisely were able to answer the research question. The Ideal Types were built by identifying typical situations in the classroom in which a formula is handled in similar ways. This similarity is idealized towards the core idea of the specific understanding. We obtained an ideal type that does not depend on the situation anymore (method and inner research situation, Fig. 7.4). For example a formula may be understood as an algorithm to calculate a magnitude by inserting measures into an expression (research object, Fig. 7.4). This may of course happen in many situations.

To keep close to the original *aim* to gain knowledge for the classroom, a teaching experiment with group work was conducted and observed: the videotaped group work was analyzed for uncovering hidden views of understanding formulas (method and inner research situation, Fig. 7.4). After analyzing the data the discussion came back to the *aim* to clarify how far the *research question* could be answered and how far this answer contributed to achieve the *aim*.

Table 7.1 represents the research path described above; which is built by the five research aspects. It shows that at the beginning, single research aspects are considered one after the other going back and forth. As the work proceeds more and more aspects are considered together. A glance at Fig. 7.4 makes clear that finally all connections between the five research aspects are included in the research.

Looking back, the research object seems to have been stable throughout the research process from the beginning. But this was definitely not the case. It was the most difficult part of the study because its definition required it to be precise and at the same time to allow for generalizing our results that were to be gained just by a case study. This had consequences for all the aspects, because all five aspects are deeply intermingled and changing one aspect changes the view on others, or even involves changing others, too. This interdependence is represented by diagonals in the pentagon.

Table 7.1 Chronological research path addressing research aspects

Research path →															
aim	external situation	method	object	external situation	aim	external situation	internal situation	object	internal situation	question	question, object	method	method, internal situation	object	aim, method, internal situation	aim, question

7.3.2 Language Demands in Qualitative Calculus

With reference to her paper, Dilan Şahin-Gür (Sahin-Gür and Prediger 2018) re-interpreted her research pentagon that she had presented at a summer school. After applying it to her own research on a design-based research study on language demands in qualitative calculus, she could offer interesting comments on her experience with working with the research pentagon, specifically according to its limitations. She agreed to include a part of it in this paper in order to show her use of the pentagon in progress.

The first interesting point is the way Şahin-Gür has re-interpreted the diagram (Fig. 7.5). In our view, this is a necessary step to make the pentagon become one's own tool for research. Naming the research aim as an "overarching question" is really an interesting way to perceive this aspect since research aim and research question are often not clearly distinguished. Although in some research studies aim and question may be interchangeable, a PhD thesis is generally not meant to solve the huge problems in our field with just one study. So it is most reasonable to distinguish the two aspects in the manner Şahin-Gür has stressed them. The research object is not re-described by her, it might have been much clearer than in our study. "Remember to set your needle" means that the needle should link the inner and outside research in order to keep the research frame coherent, that means to connect and embed one's own research in the field's knowledge but also vice versa to consider the knowledge of the field within one's own research, hence, shaping the empirical setting coherently. Equally interesting is the comment about the function as well as the limits of the methods chosen. The function of the method for her is to answer the questions and fit the whole framework, including

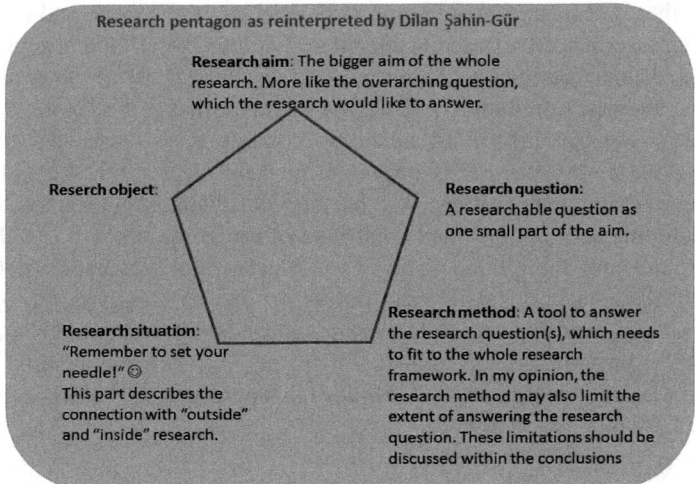

Fig. 7.5 Research pentagon re-interpreted by Dilan Şahin-Gür, from an email exchange, 19 October, 2018

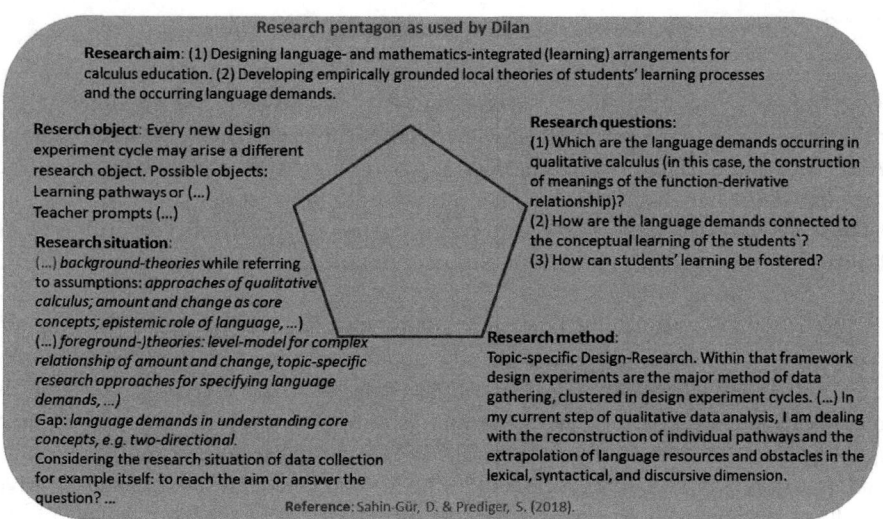

Fig. 7.6 Research pentagon related to language demands in qualitative calculus (worked out by Şahin-Gür, based on: Sahin-Gür and Prediger 2018)

methodical limitations that allow only partial answers to the research questions. Here a responsibility of researchers is addressed, namely to communicate methodical limitations.

Let us now come to the version of Şahin-Gür's individual Pentagon (Fig. 7.6) as it represents the current status of her research. The study is "Topic-specific Design-Research", which is also the research method she has chosen. This choice seems very clear. Typical for such a study is the way the research object is described; there are many research objects dependent on the cycle and the status of the development, hence they are not specified. Evenly typical for a design study are the three questions Şahin-Gür has set up: one question is about the demands, the second one addresses the link to conceptual learning, that is the learning goal, and the final one aims at identifying fostering conditions or means as tools to be designed. What seems specifically important for Şahin-Gür at this stage of research is the research situation, to think of a background theory (for example constructivism) including assumptions, and what kind of foreground theory (for the notion of background and foreground theory, see Mason and Waywood 1996) she is currently thinking of, a kind of "*level-model for complex relationship of amount and change, topic-specific research approaches for specifying language demands*".

Şahin-Gür provided some reflection on her working with this diagram, addressing the following question: How does this pentagon help me in my research process? She wrote as follows:

> (...) Only when I had filled the vertices (at least roughly), I was able to think (deeply) about the relationships between the vertices and so sharpen/refine my Pentagon. By taking a structured look at my work (now visualized in the pentagon), I have understood which vertices remain almost unchanged (e.g., the overarching research aim and methodological

framework), which become more and more defined (e.g., the research situation, in particular the foreground-theories) and that the research questions and methods of data analysis can change completely by looking at another design cycle.

(…) What the Pentagon cannot do in its present form is to illustrate the complexity of a work (its depth) and to accompany the processuality of the research process, at least not a single Pentagon. This is not to be expected when working with the Pentagon, but a powerful tool for structuring and for building consistency in your research. (Dilan Sahin-Gür, from an email exchange, 19 October, 2018, section in the original)

7.4 The Research Pentagon Illustrating a Case of Networking of Theories

In the next two sections I use the research pentagon again, but this time as an analytic tool for a case study on networking theories, in order to make visible what the networking of theories is about. The study was undertaken with two Israeli research teams led by Tommy Dreyfus and Ivy Kidron (Bikner-Ahsbahs and Kidron 2015). It will be shown that the pentagon is useful to clarify the notion of the networking of theories. Since theories are addressed, our notion of theory is explained in this section. Referring to the cultural semiotics of Lotman (1990), Radford (2008) has provided a suitable concept of theory embedded in a socio-historical and cultural view that helps to clarify what we mean by the term theory:

> More specifically, I want to suggest that a theory can be seen as a way of producing understandings and ways of action based on:
>
> - A system, P, of *basic principles*, which includes implicit views and explicit statements that delineate the frontier of what will be the universe of discourse and the adopted research perspective.
> - A *methodology*, M, which includes techniques of data collection and data-interpretation as supported by P.
> - A set, Q, of *paradigmatic research questions* (templates or schemas that generate specific questions as new interpretations arise or as the principles are deepened, expanded or modified). (p. 320, emphasis in original)

For Radford, a theory is for research and constitutes a specific language that is shared in a research community based on the set of shared principles, methodologies and paradigmatic questions that show what kind of questions are researched. The theories' principles are not questioned but can (and should) be at least partly made explicit. The methodology belongs to the theory in that it encompasses decision rules based on the principles that allow for a preference for choosing specific methods rather than others suitable for answering the paradigmatic questions. He uses the triple (P, M, Q) as a short description of theory and emphasizes its dynamic nature that develops through research revealing results R. Radford represents this developmental nature of theories by [(P, M, Q), R] (Radford 2012). I illustrate this concept of theory by the use of two examples, Abstraction in Context (AiC) and the theory of Interest Dense Situations (IDS).

7.4.1 Abstraction in Context (AiC)

The set of principles of AiC (Dreyfus et al. 2015) consists of basic assumptions, models and concepts that describe a process of constructing abstract mathematical knowledge that individuals might go through when confronted with a mathematical task or a mathematical situation. Such a process of abstraction is regarded as a human activity that takes place in a specific context. For example the activity of how to assign a value to a continued fraction (see below) takes place in a specific context including the learning arrangement, the tasks, the social situation (e.g., group work or working in pair), probably a calculator, other artifacts, the students' personal learning history, etc. Referring to the concept of vertical mathematizing by Treffers (1987), the process of abstraction consists of a vertical reorganization of previous constructs into new ones by making connections (Davydov 1972; Freudenthal 1991). It takes place in three stages of abstraction (Hershkowitz et al. 2001; Dreyfus et al. 2015):

- Stage I: there is a need for a new construct (NNC).
- Stage II: this need drives a process in which a new construct emerges. This process is described by an epistemic action model, the RBC-model (see below).
- Stage III: This new construct is consolidated (thus +C is added to the name of the epistemic action model: RBC +C-model).

The RBC-model (R stands for recognizing, B for building-with and C for constructing, these abbreviations indicate the kind of epistemic action) of stage II consists of three epistemic actions:

- **R**ecognizing previous constructs as relevant for the current task or situation.
- **B**uilding-with a previous construct with the purpose of solving a problem, making a justification, etc.
- **C**onstructing is the action that takes place when a new (to the learner) mathematical construct emerges.

These three epistemic actions are nested (Fig. 7.7), which means that constructing already includes building-with constructs and recognizing a known construct, whereas building-with also encompasses recognizing a previous construct.

The *methodology* that is used to analyze the steps shown by the students' actions when they work on a task is intimately linked to the RBC+C-model. The epistemic actions can be observed in the students' utterances and actions with artifacts,

Fig. 7.7 Illustration of the nested structure of the RBC-model

gestures used, etc. To analyze the epistemic processes, data are needed that capture them, for example, video recordings and transcriptions. The key part of a process of abstraction is the emergence of a new construct. In order to specify the new aspects of the construct clearly, an a priori analysis is conducted before the research, and after the research it is investigated how the final result differs from the prediction or confirms it, and why.

Paradigmatic questions are related to the parts of the theory, for example: How is specific knowledge constructed? How is the process of constructing knowledge determined by the context? How does the need for a new construct (NNC) impact the process? How does consolidating take place?

7.4.2 Interest-Dense Situations (IDS)

The theory of interest dense situations has been developed to identify situations in mathematics classrooms that are likely to foster *situational interest*. This kind of interest emerges dependent on the situation. It is kept for a while, but when the situation changes this kind of interest disappears normally. The question was how situational interest can be held in the mathematics classroom. Mitchell (1993) found that situational interest can be held if students become involved in an activity which is meaningful to them. In interest dense situations, this activity encompasses a process of constructing mathematical knowledge that emerges within social, mathematically oriented interactions by means of acting together in an interactive way. An IDS is a situation in which many students show interest, that is they are involved in the epistemic process of generating mathematical meaning, an activity that is meaningful to them (Bikner-Ahsbahs 2005; Bikner-Ahsbahs and Halverscheid 2014; Kidron et al. 2010).

An interest dense situation (IDS) is a situation of generating mathematical meaning as an activity of answering a mathematical question or solving a mathematical problem. Three features characterize these situations: the students

- are socially involved intensively in the activity,
- deeply participate in the epistemic process of advancing insight,
- attribute high value to the experienced mathematical activity.

Also in IDS there is an epistemic action model, the gathering-connecting-structure-seeing model (GCSt-model, G stands for gathering, C stands for connecting and St for structure seeing), which describes the process of knowledge construction by three epistemic actions; however, they need not be nested.

- **Gathering** similar mathematical meanings, ideas and signs for a mathematical situation as heuristic strategy;
- **Connecting**: relating to each other a few of the above meanings, ideas and signs as heuristic strategy;
- **Structure seeing**: Becoming aware that a specific relationship is paradigmatic for a much larger set of cases (seeing the general).

Structure seeing may lead to new knowledge but it also happens if the students already know a structure but reconstruct it in a new context. In this model knowledge is not stored anywhere. When students become involved in a social process of knowledge construction, they may re-construct a mathematical idea they have met before. Each IDS leads to structure seeing as this is the step when students experience and express advancing insight.

The main part of the methodology is ideal type construction (see Bikner-Ahsbahs 2015; see also Sect. 7.3 in this chapter) to reveal how knowledge construction typically takes place and what conditions foster or hinder it. However, this theory is open to further methodical decisions as long as they fit the principles and paradigmatic questions.

The paradigmatic questions of IDS focus on processes of knowledge construction in groups: What conditions foster or hinder such processes? For example, what can be said about semiotic tools, the role of the teacher, types of interactions and the emergence of situational interest?

7.4.3 Comparing and Contrasting the Two Theories

Before networking the two theories let us focus on their commonalities and differences. Their commonalities can be condensed in the following three principles:

- Epistemic acting reveals knowledge;
- Knowledge is constructed during involvement in solving problems, working on tasks or answering questions;
- Epistemic models are used as scientific tools to describe and investigate empirically, on the micro-level, how mathematical knowledge is produced and made accessible.

Core differences of these theories are described as follows:

- AiC regards knowledge constructing predominantly as an individual process, which may be related to a process of knowledge construction to another individual, whereas IDS regards knowledge constructing as a social process.
- Whereas the individual in AiC interacts with the given context, the social group in IDS reconstructs relevant aspects of their social semiotic environment given in the process of knowledge construction together with their knowledge construction; hence, they make explicit what they use and why.

7.4.4 A Case of Networking Between AiC and IDS

Let us now turn to a case of networking two theories. This case was first published by Kidron et al. (2010), and worked out in-depth by Bikner-Ahsbahs and Kidron

(2015). It is based on the two theories, AiC published by Hershkowitz et al. (2001) and IDS described above, published by Bikner-Ahsbahs (2005). Let us now use the research pentagon to describe this process of networking as an example.

The authors took the theories to frame the *internal research situation* of considering both theories together. The research problem they considered linked the two theories: IDS describes social situations of constructing mathematical knowledge that foster the emergence of situational interest, but the precise mechanism of how interest is fostered through the epistemic process was not clear. On the other hand, AiC allows for considering and identifying the need for a new construct in a process of constructing new knowledge that could play a fundamental role. Taking both theories into account, the *research question* was as follows: How is the need for a new construct related to the emergence of situational interest? The *research object* was twofold, the phenomenon of *the emergence of situational interest in IDS* as well as the phenomenon of *the emergence of an NNC*. Both theoretical perspectives were expected to consider the research object as a two-fold phenomenon. The aim was to clarify the role of the theories in this research in terms of their principles, methodologies and paradigmatic questions based on empirical research.

Following the commonalities of the two approaches, the first step in the networking process was to develop a task allowing for collecting data that made sense from the two perspectives. In our case, we chose a continued fraction task (see Kidron et al. 2010; Bikner-Ahsbahs and Kidron 2015). Five steps were conducted in a so-called cross-methodology involving task design, piloting the task, data preparation, data analysis and reflection on the whole process. To coordinate the two theories every step encompassed a series of five cross-over stages in the networking process; we list these and briefly illustrate them for the first step, task design. The teams decide cooperatively (e.g., about task topics), process separately (e.g., concrete developing of tasks according to each theory), exchange and working with results from the other theoretical view (e.g., the tasks from the other theory groups), rework their own results (e.g., revising their own tasks), and build consensus. Figure 7.8 shows one of the task sequences that was used for a task-based teaching interview with Tim and Matt (grade 10), Figs. 7.9 and 7.10 shows the students' written answers to task 3 and task 4, and Figs. 7.11 and 7.12 to task 5.

Before the networking of the theories is presented in more detail, the students' epistemic process is illustrated by using the two models, the RBC-model from the AiC-perspective, and the GCSt-model from the IDS-perspective.

In the first two tasks the students calculate the first three continued fractions. Addressing the task symbol by symbol, they gather *mathematical meanings* (Fig. 7.9), and then they do not build $f(3)$ by calculating but by using $f(2)$, hence they connect $f(3)$ with $f(2)$. Figure 7.10 shows that the students achieve *structure seeing* going through task 3 and task 4, shown in the answer to task 3 and task 4 translated in the caption of Fig. 7.10: The students identified and explained two patterns of how to expand the continued fractions arithmetically, adding the same amount at the bottom or on the top.

The following solving phase is described using the RBC-model, leading to a new construct which the students called "Space of places".

> **How can we interpret the continued fraction?** $1+\cfrac{2}{1+\cfrac{2}{1+\cfrac{2}{1+K}}}$
>
> 1. Construct a sequence of fractions representing the continued fraction, like this:
>
> $f(0)=1$
>
> $f(1)=1+\dfrac{2}{1}=1+2=3$
>
> $f(2)=1+\dfrac{2}{1+\dfrac{2}{1}}=1+\dfrac{2}{1+2}=1+\dfrac{2}{3}=\dfrac{5}{3}$
>
> $f(3)=1+\dfrac{2}{1+\dfrac{2}{1+\dfrac{2}{1}}}=$
>
> 2. Add 3 more terms, calculate: $f(4)$, $f(5)$, $f(6)$.
> 3. Look at the seven terms you calculated and at the way you calculated them. Can you find a pattern when passing from one term to the next one?
> 4. Explain the pattern—why does it work?
> 5. Add more terms to the sequence, using the pattern you found, until you have 20 terms in the sequence. Fill in the following table. Use a calculator to represent the fractions of the sequence as decimal fractions. Copy all the digits from the calculator pane.
> 6. Look at the sequence in the table and write a conjecture. Justify your conjecture.

Fig. 7.8 The first six of eight tasks about a continued fraction (Kidron et al. 2010, 2011, p. 2452; Bikner-Ahsbahs and Kidron 2015, p. 238)

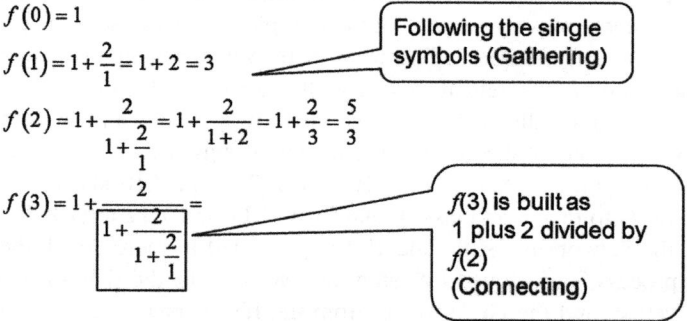

Fig. 7.9 Examples for the IDS epistemic actions gathering and connecting

Matt and Tim *recognize* in their calculation previous constructs as relevant, namely, two subsequences made of decimal fractions (Fig. 7.11). By *building-with*, they consider two alternating subsequences, an increasing and a decreasing sequence.

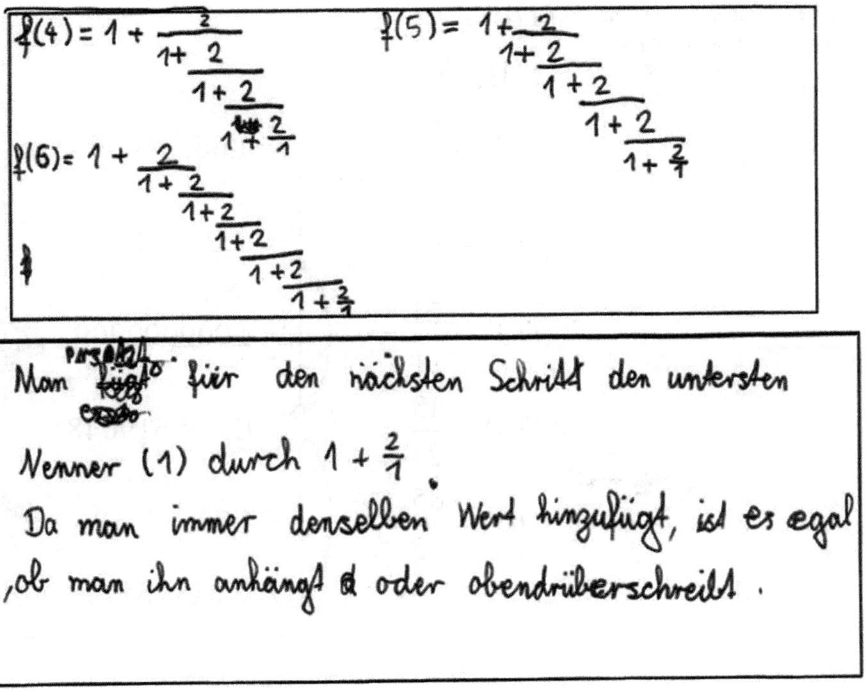

$$f(4) = 1 + \cfrac{2}{1 + \cfrac{2}{1 + \cfrac{2}{1 + \cfrac{2}{1 + \frac{2}{1}}}}}$$

$$f(5) = 1 + \cfrac{2}{1 + \cfrac{2}{1 + \cfrac{2}{1 + \cfrac{2}{1 + \frac{2}{1}}}}}$$

$$f(6) = 1 + \cfrac{2}{1 + \cfrac{2}{1 + \cfrac{2}{1 + \cfrac{2}{1 + \frac{2}{1}}}}}$$

Man setzt für den nächsten Schritt den untersten Nenner (1) durch $1 + \frac{2}{1}$.
Da man immer denselben Wert hinzufügt, ist es egal, ob man ihn anhängt oder obendrüberschreibt.

Fig. 7.10 Structure seeing is shown: "For the next step, one replaces the lowest denominator (1) by 1 + 2/1. Because one always adds the same value it does not matter whether one tacks it on or writes it on top" (translated)

Based on the calculation of $f(7)$ to $f(19)$ (Fig. 7.12) and the following eight interpretations, the students reveal a new construct, which is still a bit vague:

- There are two subsequences of values of $f(n)$.
- One increasing subsequence of numbers smaller than 2.
- One decreasing subsequence of numbers larger than 2.
- In the increasing sequence the number of decimals after the decimal comma equaling 9 grows.
- In the decreasing sequence the number of decimals after the decimal comma equaling 0 grows.
- They begin referring to a notion they call "space of places".
- With this notion they refer to the growth of the space of places.
- They conjecture it might be growing with the square root of n.

Together the students invent the notion *the space of places* for a phenomenon they observe, but at this point the meaning of it is not so clear. What is clear, though, is that this notion is used to capture the regularity in the repeating of digits after the decimal comma. Figure 7.12 illustrates that either zero or nine are repeated depending on the subsequence.

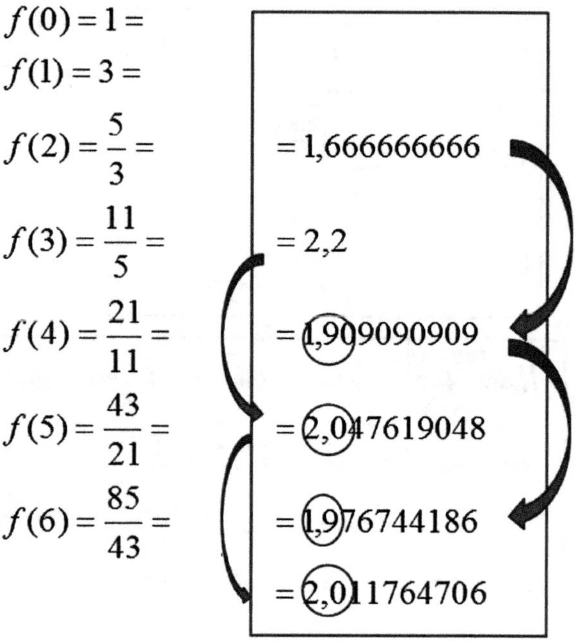

Fig. 7.11 Students' solution of task 2; arrows, rectangle and circles added by the researchers

$f(0) = 1 =$

$f(1) = 3 =$

$f(2) = \dfrac{5}{3} = \quad = 1{,}666666666$

$f(3) = \dfrac{11}{5} = \quad = 2{,}2$

$f(4) = \dfrac{21}{11} = \quad = 1{,}909090909$

$f(5) = \dfrac{43}{21} = \quad = 2{,}047619048$

$f(6) = \dfrac{85}{43} = \quad = 1{,}976744186$

$\quad\quad\quad\quad\quad\quad = 2{,}011764706$

Fig. 7.12 The written solution of Tim and Matt to task 5 using a calculator. (See Bikner-Ahsbahs and Kidron 2015, p. 240)

$f(7)$	$\dfrac{171}{85}$	$2{,}011764706$	$\dfrac{1}{85}$
$f(8)$	$\dfrac{341}{171}$	$1{,}994152047$	$\dfrac{1}{171}$
$f(9)$	$\dfrac{683}{341}$	$2{,}002932551$	
$f(10)$	$\dfrac{1365}{683}$	$1{,}998535871$	
$f(11)$	$\dfrac{2731}{1365}$	$2{,}000732601$	$7{,}32601 \cdot 10^{-4}$
$f(12)$	$\dfrac{5461}{2731}$	$1{,}999633834$	$3{,}6611 \cdot 10^{-4}$
$f(13)$	$\dfrac{10923}{5461}$	$2{,}000183117$	$1{,}8311 \cdot 10^{-4}$
$f(14)$	$\dfrac{21845}{10923}$	$1{,}999908545$	
$f(15)$	$\dfrac{43691}{21845}$	$2{,}000045777$	
$f(16)$	$\dfrac{87381}{43691}$	$1{,}999977112$	
$f(17)$	$\dfrac{174763}{87381}$	$2{,}000011444$	
$f(18)$	$\dfrac{349525}{174763}$	$1{,}999994278$	
$f(19)$	$\dfrac{699051}{349525}$	$2{,}000002861$	

7 The Research Pentagon: A Diagram with Which to Think …

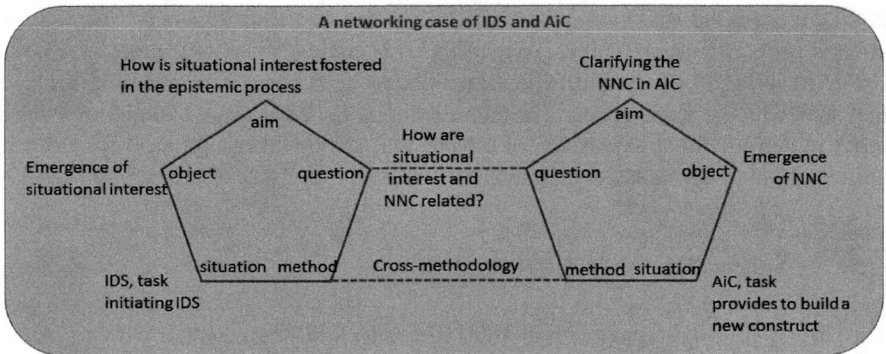

Fig. 7.13 The IDS-pentagon and the AiC-pentagon of a networking case

Let us now use the research pentagon to explore the networking of theories as described above in its two final steps.

In Fig. 7.13 two research pentagons are used to represent the research aspects for each of the two theoretical perspectives. The aspects represented by the vertices have been outlined in Sect. 7.2. Now, two theories are *coordinated* according to the research question, which links the research from the two views, and the method, which involves a *coordinated* cross-exchange along the empirical procedure (step four of the cross-methodology). This procedure is worked out in detail (see Kidron and Bikner-Ahsbahs 2015). Here I reduce the description of the networking of theories in order to present the results of this research. These results have shown that the need for a new construct (NNC) does not always appear at the beginning of the process of abstraction, but in our data mostly rather late. In the solving processes of the two students, a NNC emerged for the first time after more than half an hour:

Tim   It would be the best if we had a function equation right' (.),well if one could say exactly ‚f of x equals (…) ‚wait ‚whats that' (points at the sheet) ‚no ‚thats not a sum. (p. 247, transcription key in the appendix)

Here Tim shows a NNC for a function equation which in his view would be able to help in solving the continued fraction task. But there was a long epistemic process preceding this step. Since there was no clear NNC earlier, not even for the construct of the space of places they had built before, it was not clear what drove this process. As a driving force we identified what we called a general epistemic need (GEN). This GEN turned out to be a boundary object that could be interpreted by each of the two theory teams (Akkerman and Bakker 2013). A boundary object is an object or a concept at the boundary of two social cultures that can be understood from both cultures. From the AiC view, the GEN was a kind of individual desire to understand more about such a fraction. This GEN sometimes became more concrete, for example when one student felt the need to be more precise or to generalize. This was shown in his epistemic actions. The NNC can then be regarded as a specific GEN. It emerges when the exploration provides a collection of concrete ideas that help the students to focus on a specific construct, which they assume would help them to solve the problem. From the IDS view, such a GEN emerges as a socially shared necessity in order to proceed within a social group. This GEN could also become more specific in some situations, for example, when the students searched for an example because they needed to be more concrete in their explorations. This social situation may also result in an individual expression of a NNC that can be taken up by other students.

7.4.5 Reflecting on the Case Study

The fifth step in the cross-methodology is a reflection phase on the whole process after discussing the results.

In an epistemic process a GEN may lead to an incomplete mathematical situation from which situational interest emerges when the students enter into an epistemic situation. For example, in the task above the students identified two subsequences both of which seemed to approximate the number 2. This observation puzzled the students and they wanted to come to know how this approximation may happen depending on the length of the continued fractions. Thus, the students became deeply involved in further explorations, making sense of a kind of approximation they had not seen before. As they proceeded in sense making they showed situational interest through their involvement and sense making. According to Knorr Cetina the approximation turned into an epistemic object that the students wished to clarify. This interest pushed the epistemic process, producing a further GEN, from which emerged, in turn, incomplete situations of how the convergence to 2 can be proved. Such incompleteness called for completion again and pushed the students' investigation further.

Let us now reflect on the networking of theories, the use of theories, and methodology. In this phase the researchers clarified how the individual and social processes of constructing knowledge may be related: From the view of the social construction of knowledge this epistemic process consisted of a *flow of ideas* built upon each other and distributed among the students. Such a flow of ideas can be taken as a phase of *gathering mathematical ideas*. As a social process it provides opportunities for the individual learner to *recognize* relevant previous constructs. While within this process the students socially *connect* these constructs or ideas while working with the tasks they may *build-with* them individually. The process may lead towards *structure seeing* in which individuals *construct new knowledge* (Bikner-Ahsbahs and Kidron 2015, p. 248). This result indicates that the two theories share a boundary concept, but the result does allow for synthesizing the theories because a shift of attention is necessary when interpreting the general epistemic need from one of the two theoretical perspectives.

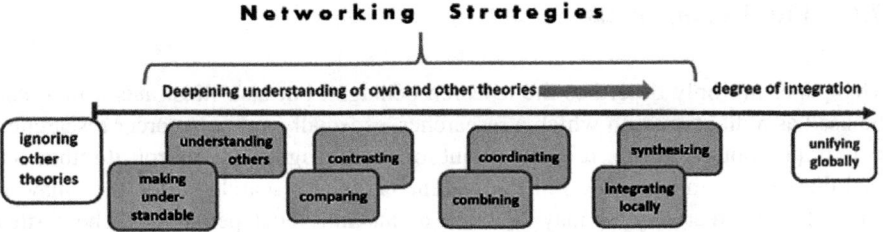

Fig. 7.14 Networking Strategies (Bikner-Ahsbahs et al. 2016, p. 34, revised version from Bikner-Ahsbahs and Prediger 2010, p. 492)

7.5 What Is Networking of Theories About?

We now step back to consider what the networking of theories is about. In this case study we wanted to use two theories to answer our research question of how the need for a new construct and situational interest are related. For that reason we related the two theories using networking strategies. These are the pairs of strategies (see Fig. 7.14), ordered according to increasing potential of integration.

The two poles in the landscape in Fig. 7.14, namely, ignoring other theories and unifying theories globally, do not belong to the networking strategies. The networking of theories consists of building relations between theories based on concrete research. In our example, we first *made* the two theories *understandable* and required the reader to *understand* the theories described by the theoretical concept developed by Radford. In the landscape of networking strategies this pair of strategies is the starting point to undertaking a networking process in order to be able to identify the specificities of the theories. We then *compared and contrasted* the theories by identifying commonalities and differences. Clarifying exactly what underlies the differences between the two theories provides an additional in-depth understanding of both theories. The third strategy encompasses *combining and coordinating*. In our case this was done in order to answer the research question "How are the need for a new construct and situational interest related?" by means of research involving a coordinated methodical procedure of exchange. The research resulted in a new concept, the general epistemic need (GEN) that allowed for a local integration in that the concept turned out to be a boundary objects that could be understood from the two perspectives. The research did not result in more than that. Synthesizing would require building a new theory in which the two theories are embedded. Such a theory would have to dissolve the difference between the individual and the social.

7.6 Final Comments

This paper not only describes the research pentagon but also illustrates how it can be used as a diagram with which a researcher, especially an early career researcher, may think-about research. It is not meant to act as a rigorous concept; it rather is a tool that allows an expression of the current status of research, which then may be worked with creatively. It may function as an individual pentagon to be further developed and restructured to support the epistemic practice of inquiry in research. At the beginning it seems useful to just focus on each aspect separately, then to relate them to each other, and finally to consider several aspect at a time. Where to begin depends on the research to be done. As shown in the networking case, the pentagon can also be used as an analytical tool making visible how the networking of theories takes place in a piece of research and what kinds of relations are built in research. The double diagram shows that the networking of theories goes beyond triangulation, in that it provides a process of boundary crossing with the potential to identify boundary objects as a link between cultures of theories. Note that the networking of theories is not an aim in itself; researchers should have good reasons why they want to follow this process. In the case study above the reason was the need to make use of the concepts, reciprocally each to each, from the other theory, because we felt that the two concepts, need and interest, could inform each other, theoretically and practically in teaching.

Acknowledgements I thank Dilan Şahin-Gür for her contribution to this chapter, Marit Hvalsøe Schou, Ivy Kidron and Tommy Dreyfus for their consent to refer to research we conducted together, and Tommy Dreyfus for reading and offering insightful feedback to this chapter.

The research on which this chapter is based was partially supported by the German-Israeli Foundation for Scientific Research and Development (GIF) under grant number 946-357.4/2006.

Appendix

An Exercise: Group Work on the Transcript of Tim and Matt
In this exercise readers who want to know about how the networking of theories is practiced may follow the instruction and use the extended transcript to obtain own experience with the networking of theories taking up the two example theories.

> **A Networking Exercise**
>
> Work in pair and decide who is taking over the view of Abstraction in Context (AiC) and who is taking over the view on Interest-Dense Situations (IDS). The research question for the networking case is: How does the need for a new construct (NNC) relate to the emergence of situational interest shown when students become involved in the task and express that something is meaningful to them. The research question for the AiC view is, how and where does the

7 The Research Pentagon: A Diagram with Which to Think ...

> NNC emerge within the process of constructing knowledge. The research question for the IDS view is, how and where is situational interest expressed during the process of knowledge construction. Go through the transcript:
>
> - *deciding cooperatively* about the part of the transcript to be analyzed,
> - *separate processing*, analyzing separately this part from each perspective addressing the emergence of the NNC on the one hand and of situational interest on the other during the process of constructing knowledge,
> - *exchange of the results and working with the results from the other view*, exchanging the analysis results and commenting on them,
> - *reworking own results*, re-analyzing the part of the transcript from the own perspective in the light of the results from the other view, and finally,
> - meet collaboratively and aim at *building consensus* about the work done.

The following discussion occurred about half an hour after the students started working on the above task about a continued fraction.

1. I: And ‚f of ‚one million'
2. T: Ohm
3. M: (sighs) F of one million
4. /T: we would have to cal- calculate now ‚whats the root of one million ‚and then round it down
5. /M: what kind of'
6. I: You- ‚you really dont need to do it accurate now now
7. /M: no ‚now we are doing it (laughs)
8. /I: (spoken simultaneously) ok.
9. M: Thousand
10. /T: (spoken simultaneously) is thousand ‚so exact thousand the set ‚of the space of places
11. I: Hmmh
12. T: So th-
13. I: And how would f of one million and one look like'
14. T: Ohm that would still be a spa- ‚that is just the set of the space of places
15. /M: so one (looks at the calculator) ‚ah never mind
16. /T: we just cant the- ‚still thousand ‚until ‚one thousand and one results
17. /M: but what we do know in any case is ‚that ohm there is a one in front of the point ‚well not for one thousand and one ‚for thou- for one-
18. /T: yes ‚for one thousand and one there is a one in front of the point ‚well no wait yes ‚a two
19. /M: thats an odd number ‚yes
20. T: Two point, ‚zero zero zero zero
21. /M: yes because its an odd ohm ‚place

22. T: Yes ,so its very close to two already
23. M: Yes
24. T: Those are about a hundred zero or something (laughs) ,and then its a different,another number
25. (.)
26. M: Yes
27. T: Yes
28. I: And how would it work then'
29. T: I would say it keeps on going like that
30. /M: its an infinite number
31. /T: and it keeps on leaning closer to zero- ,closer and closer to two ,both numbers
32. M: Yes exactly and sometime it get's
33. /T: but becomes never two there are always infinite zeros
34. /M: yes its infinite thats just it
35. /T: at the end are infinite zeros ,or infinite nines ,and then there is something.
36. /M: And then one could conjecture that
37. /T: the whol(e)-
38. /M: we can insert infinite (1:05:07.9)
39. T: When we insert infinite
40. /M: (not understandable) will always be the same
41. T: If- ,if you insert infinite ,its theoretically two
42. M: Yes on- ,yes exactly. ,then it would be two,because one
43. /T: because it has as many
44. /M: one point nine ,ey ,what was the number again' (laughs),one point nine period'
45. T: Yes
46. M: Equals two then
47. T: Yes- ,equals about two.
48. M: Equals two.
49. T: So close- ,ah ok.
50. M: So one found out that ohm- ,on(e)- one say ,our teacher told us that ohm- , one point nine period equals two.
51. I: Ok
52. /M: or wasnt it zero point nine nine
53. T: Because one ,one one ninth ,is namely ,one point nine nine nine nine nine nine nine nine ,a-nd two.,because one plus nine ninth is precisely two ,but nine , one ninth ,is zero point one one one one one
54. /M: yes but then ,do you want to do nine ninth ,that would be two
55. T: Yes
56. (.)
57. I: Ok.
58. T: Theoretically (M laughs)

59. I: Could you maybe some-how formulate the conjecture ,a little bit'
60. M: Yes ,there we write that ohm ,what we conjecture
61. T: Yes ,otherwise we just write down f of infinite equals two and expla- , explaining we do here then (points at the sheet)
62. I: Yes exactly
63. T: Right'
64. /I: afterwards we can ,you have already written so much.
65. /T: we write (speaks while writing) ,f of infinite (.) ,equals two
66. I: Hmmh
67. (..)
68. M: Ok. (laughs) That was a short exercise (laughs, looking at T)
69. I: Yes ,now that were ,yes ,a lot of conjectures ,that you have done (laughs)
70. T: So.
71. M: (grabs inside of the stack of exercises) Now comes explaining (all three laugh)
72. T: That will be more difficult (laughs)
73. I: I ,I find your last aspect now the most interesting
74. M: Yes ,that really is interesting on how-
75. T: Yes ,theoretically it keeps on leaning closer to two
76. /M: yes
77. T: When *(or "if")* you look at it closely ,it never gets two ,even if there are infinite nines ,behind it there is always ,seven three two ,whatever. ,it can be everything (.) ,the numbers behind it ,we have not looked at it ,possible that they have a pattern too ,but ,I see- ,personally I dont see anything (M laughs)
78. I: Look kinda wild ,yes.
79. T: Yes.
80. I: Now could you (.) ,explAIN it somehow ,why that somehow (bends forward to the notes of the students)
81. /M: Well we look ,lets look at the beginning again here
82. T: It would be the best if we had a function equation right' (.) ,well if one could say exactly ,f of x equals (…) ,wait ,whats that' (points at the sheet) ,no ,thats not a sum (not understandable)

Transcription Key

S(s), T	student(s), teacher
EXECT	loud voice
exect	with stressed voice
e-x-a-c-t	prolonged
exact.	dropping the voice
exact'	raising the voice
,exact	with a new onset
exact-	voice remains suspended
(.),(..)(…)	1, 2, 3 seconds pause
(….)	more than 3sec pause

(5sec)   5 seconds pause, if necessary
(gets up)   nonverbal activity, the duration of non verbal activity need not be fixed unless it is special, a pause of 2 seconds afterwards (..), interpreted (*slow*)
(exact??)   assumed utterance

References

Akkerman, S. F., & Bakker, A. (2013). Boundary crossing and boundary objects. *Review of Educational Research, 81*(2), 132–169.

Batanero, M. C., Godino, J. D., Steiner, H.-G., & Wenzelsburger, E. (1994). The training of researchers in mathematics education: Results from an international survey. *Educational Studies in Mathematics, 26*(1), 95–102.

Baumert, J., & Lehmann, R. (1997). *TIMSS-Mathematisch-naturwissenschaftlicher Unterricht im internationalen Vergleich* [Instruction in mathematics and science on an international comparison level]. Opladen: leske + Budrich.

Bikner-Ahsbahs, A. (2005). *Mathematikinteresse zwischen Subjekt und Situation. Empirisch begründete Konstruktion einer Theorie interessendichter Situationen.* [Interest in mathematics between subject and situation. Building bricks for an interest theory in mathematics education.] Hildesheim: Verlag Franzbecker.

Bikner-Ahsbahs, A. (2015). How ideal type construction can be achieved: An example. In A. Bikner-Ahsbahs, C. Knipping, & N. Presmeg (Eds.), *Approaches to qualitative methods in mathematics education—Examples of methodology and methods* (pp. 137–154). Advances in Mathematics education. New York: Springer.

Bikner-Ahsbahs, A. (2016). Networking of theories in the tradition of TME. In A. Bikner-Ahsbahs, A. Vohns, R. Bruder, O. Schmitt, & W. Dörfler (Eds.), *Theories in and of mathematics education* (pp. 33–42). ICME-13 Topical Surveys. Switzerland: SpringerOpen.

Bikner-Ahsbahs, A., & Halverscheid, S. (2014). Introduction to the theory of interest-dense situations. In A. Bikner-Ahsbahs & S. Prediger (Eds.), *Networking of theories as a research practice in mathematics education* (pp. 97–112). Advances in mathematics education series. Dordrecht: Springer.

Bikner-Ahsbahs, A., & Kidron, I. (2015). A cross-methodology for the networking of theories: The general epistemic need (GEN) as a new concept at the boundary of two theories. In A. Bikner-Ahsbahs, A., Knipping, C., & Presmeg, N. (Eds.), *Approaches to qualitative research in mathematics education: Examples of methodology and methods* (pp. 233–250). Advances in mathematics education series. Dordrecht: Springer.

Bikner-Ahsbahs, A., & Prediger, S. (2010). Networking of theories—An approach for exploiting the diversity of theoretical approaches. In B. Sriraman & L. English (Eds.), *Theories of mathematics education: Seeking new frontiers* (pp. 479–512). Advances in mathematics education series. Dordrecht: Springer.

Bikner-Ahsbahs, A., & Prediger, S. (Eds.) (2014). *Networking of theories as a research practice.* Advances in mathematics education series. New York: Springer.

Boaler, J., Ball, D. L., & Even, R. (2003). Preparing researchers for disciplined inquiry: Learning from, in, and for practice. In A. Bishop & J. Kilpatrick (Eds.), *International handbook of mathematics education* (pp. 491–521). Dordrecht: Kluwer.

Davydov, V. V. (1972/1990). *Soviet studies in mathematics education: Vol. 2. Types of generalization in instruction: Logical and psychological problems in the structuring of school curricula* (J. Kilpatrick, Ed., J. Teller, Trans.). Reston, VA: NCTM.

Dreyfus, T., Hershkowitz, R., & Schwarz, B. B. (2015). The nested epistemic actions model for abstraction in context: Theory as methodological tool and methodological tool as theory. In A. Bikner-Ahsbahs, C. Knipping, & N. Presmeg (Eds.), *Approaches to qualitative research in mathematics education: Examples of methodology and methods* (pp. 185–217). Advances in mathematics education series. Dordrecht: Springer.

Freudenthal, H. (1991). *Revisiting mathematics education: China lectures*. Dordrecht: Kluwer.

Haser, Ç. (2018). Key experiences in becoming an independent mathematics education researcher. *Canadian Journal of Science, Mathematics and Technology Education, 18*(1), 29–41.

Hershkowitz, R., Schwarz, B. B., & Dreyfus, T. (2001). Abstraction in context: Epistemic actions. *Journal for Research in Mathematics Education, 32,* 195–222.

Hiebert, J., Stigler, J. W., & Manaster, A. B. (1999). Mathematical features of lessons in the TIMSS video study. *Zentralblatt für Mathematikdidaktik (ZDM), 99*(6), 196–201.

Hoffmann, M. H. G. (2005). *Erkenntnisentwicklung. Ein semiotisch-pragmatischer Ansatz* [Recognition development. A semiotic-pragtmatic approach]. Frankfurt a.M.: V. Klostermann.

Kidron, I., & Bikner-Ahsbahs (2015). Advancing research by means of the networking of theories. In A. Bikner-Ahsbahs, C. Knipping, & N. Presmeg (Eds.), *Approaches to qualitative research in mathematics education: Examples of methodology and methods* (pp. 221–232). Advances in mathematics education series. New York: Springer.

Kidron, I., Bikner-Ahsbahs, A., Cramer, J., Dreyfus, T., & Gilboa, N. (2010). Construction of knowledge: Need and interest. In M. M. F. Pinto & T. F. Kawasaki (Eds.), *Proceedings of the 34th Conference of the International Group for the Psychology of Mathematics Education* (Vol. 3, pp. 169–176). Belo Horizonte, Brazil: PME.

Kidron, I., Bikner-Ahsbahs, A., & Dreyfus, T. (2011). How a general epistemic need leads to a need for a new construct: A case of networking two theoretical approaches. In M. Pytlak, T. Rowland, & E. Swoboda (Eds.), *Proceedings of the 7th Congress of the European Society for Research in Mathematics Education* (pp. 2451–2461). Rzeszów, Poland: University of Rzeszów.

Knorr Cetina, K. (2001). Objectual practice. In T. R. Schatzki, K. Knorr Cetina, & E. von Savigny (Eds.), *The practice turn in contemporary theory* (pp. 175–88). London and New York: Routledge.

Liljedahl, P. (2018). Mathematics education graduate students' thoughts about becoming researchers. *Canadian Journal of Science, Mathematics and Technology Education, 18*(1), 42–57.

Lotman, Y. M. (1990). *Universe of the mind. A semiotic theory of culture*. Bloomington: Indiana University Press.

Malle, G. (1993). *Didaktische Probleme der elementaren Algebra*. Braunschweig and Wiesbaden: Vieweg Verlag.

Mason, J., & Waywood, A. (1996). The role of theory in mathematics education and research. In A. J. Bishop, et al. (Eds.), *International handbook of mathematics education* (pp. 1055–1089). Dordrecht: Kluwer.

Mitchell, M. (1993). Situational interest: Its multifaceted structure in the secondary school mathematics classroom. *Journal of Educational Psychology, 85*(3), 424–436.

Nardi, E. (2015). "Not like a big gap, something we could handle": Facilitating shifts in paradigm in the supervision of mathematics graduates upon entry into mathematics education. *International Journal of Research in Undergraduate Mathematics Education, 1*(1), 135–156.

Peirce, C. S. (1931–1958). *Collected papers* (Vol. I–VIII). Cambridge: Harvard University Press.

Radford, L. (2008). Connecting theories in mathematics education: Challenges and possibilities. *Zentralblatt für Didaktik der Mathematik–The International Journal on Mathematics Education, 40*(2), 317–327.

Radford, L. (2012). *On the growth and transformation of mathematics education theories*. Paper presented at the International Colloquium The Didactics of Mathematics: Approaches and Issues. A Homage to Michèle Artigue. Université de Paris VII. May 31 to June 1, 2012. http://luisradford.ca/publications/ (14.1 pp. 1. 2018).

Reys, B., & Reys, R. (2017). Strengthening doctoral programs in mathematics education: A continuous process. *Notices of the American Mathematical Society, 64*(4), 386–389.

Sahin-Gür, D., & Prediger, S. (2018). "Growth goes down, but of what?" A case study on language demands in qualitative calculus. In E. Bergqvist, M. Österholm, C. Granberg, & L. Sumpter (Eds.), *Proceedings of the 42nd Conference of the International Group for the Psychology of Mathematics Education* (Vol. 4, pp. 99–106). Umeå: PME.

Schmitz, T. H., & Groninger, H. (2012). *Werkzeug-Denkzeug. Manuelle Intelligenz und Transmedialität Kreativer Prozesse* [Tool-tool to think with: Manual intelligence and transmediality]. Bielefeld: transcript verlag.

Schou, H. M., & Bikner-Ahsbahs, A. (submitted). *Unpacking hidden views: Seven ways to treat your formula.*

Siller, H.-S., & Roth, J. (2016). *Herausforderung Heterogenität. Grundvorstellungen als Basis- und Bezugsnorm: das Beispiel Terme* [Challenge of hetrogeneity: Basic images as fundamental reference norm: The example of algebraic expressions]. *Praxis der Mathematik in der Schule 70*, 2–8.

Treffers, A. (1987). *Three dimensions. A model of goal and theory description in mathematics instruction: The Wiskobas project.* Dordrecht: D. Reidel Publishing Company.

Open Access This chapter is licensed under the terms of the Creative Commons Attribution 4.0 International License (http://creativecommons.org/licenses/by/4.0/), which permits use, sharing, adaptation, distribution and reproduction in any medium or format, as long as you give appropriate credit to the original author(s) and the source, provide a link to the Creative Commons license and indicate if changes were made.

The images or other third party material in this chapter are included in the chapter's Creative Commons license, unless indicated otherwise in a credit line to the material. If material is not included in the chapter's Creative Commons license and your intended use is not permitted by statutory regulation or exceeds the permitted use, you will need to obtain permission directly from the copyright holder.

Chapter 8
Qualitative Text Analysis: A Systematic Approach

Udo Kuckartz

Abstract Thematic analysis, often called Qualitative Content Analysis (QCA) in Europe, is one of the most commonly used methods for analyzing qualitative data. This paper presents the basics of this systematic method of qualitative data analysis, highlights its key characteristics, and describes a typical workflow. The aim is to present the main characteristics and to give a simple example of the process so that readers can assess whether this method might be useful for their own research. Special attention is paid to the formation of categories, since all scholars agree that categories are at the heart of the method.

Keywords Qualitative data analysis · Text analysis · Qualitative methods · Qualitative content analysis · MAXQDA software

8.1 Introduction: Qualitative and Quantitative Data

Thematic analysis, often called Qualitative Content Analysis (QCA) in Europe, is one of the most commonly used methods for analyzing qualitative data (Guest et al. 2012; Kuckartz 2014; Mayring 2014, 2015; Schreier 2012). This chapter presents the basics of this systematic method of qualitative data analysis, highlights its key characteristics, and describes a typical workflow.

Working with codes and categories is a proven method in qualitative research. QCA is a method that is reliable, easy to learn, transparent, and it is a method that is easily understood by other researchers. In short, it is a method that enjoys a high level of recognition and is to be highly recommended, especially in the context of dissertations.

The aim of this paper is to present the main characteristics and to give a simple example of the process so that readers can assess whether this method might be

---

U. Kuckartz (✉)
Philipps-University Marburg, Marburg, Germany
e-mail: kuckartz@uni-marburg.de

© The Author(s) 2019
G. Kaiser and N. Presmeg (eds.), *Compendium for Early Career Researchers in Mathematics Education*, ICME-13 Monographs,
https://doi.org/10.1007/978-3-030-15636-7_8

useful for their own research. Special attention is paid to the formation of categories, since all scholars agree that categories are at the heart of the method.

Let's start with some of the basics of data analysis in empirical research: What does 'qualitative data' mean, and what do we mean by 'quantitative data'? *Quantitative data* entail numerical information that results, for example, from the collection of data from a standardized interview. In a quantitative data matrix, each row corresponds to a case, namely, an interview with a respondent. The columns of the matrix are formed by the variables. Table 8.1 therefore shows the data of four cases, here the respondents 1–4. Six variables were collected for these individuals, on a scale of 1–6, concerning how often they perform certain household activities (laundry, small repairs etc.). Typically, these kinds of data sets are available in social research in the form of a rectangular matrix, for instance as shown in Table 8.1.

A matrix like this that consists of numbers can be analyzed using statistical methods. For example, you can calculate univariate statistics such as mean values, variance, and standard deviations. You can also generate graphical displays such as box plots or bar charts. In addition, variables can be related to each other, for example by using methods of correlation and regression statistics. Another form of analysis tests groups for differences. In the above study, for example, the questions 'Are women more frequently engaged in laundry than men in the household?' and 'Are men more frequently engaged in minor repairs than women in the household?' can be calculated using an analysis of variance.

Qualitative data are far more diverse and complex than quantitative data. These data may comprise transcripts of face-to-face interviews or focus group discussions, documents, Twitter tweets, YouTube comments, or videos of the teacher-student interactions in the classroom.

In this chapter, I restrict the presentation of the QCA method to a specific type of data, namely qualitative interviews. This collective term can be used to describe very different forms of interviews, such as guideline-assisted interviews or narrative interviews on critical life events conducted in the context of biographical research. The latter can last several hours and comprise more than 30 pages as a transcription. A qualitative interview may also consist of a short online survey, like the one I conducted in preparation for my workshop at the International Congress on Mathematical Education (ICME-13).

Table 8.1 Rectangular data matrix with quantitative data

	Laundry	Small repairs	Care_sick_family	Shop_groceries	Household_cleaning	Prepares_meals
1	2	1	1	2	2	3
2	3	2	2	5	6	6
3	6	5	3	4	6	6
4	4	3	2	2	8	3
5						

Obviously, the different types of qualitative data are not as easy to analyze as the numbers in a quantitative data matrix. Numerous analytical methods have been developed in qualitative research, among them the well-proven method of qualitative content analysis.

8.2 Key Points of Qualitative Content Analysis

What are the key points of the qualitative content analysis method? Regardless of which variant of QCA is used, the focus will always be on working with categories (codes) and developing a category system (coding frame). What Berelson formulated in 1952 for quantitative content analysis still applies today, both to quantitative and qualitative content analysis:

> Content analysis stands or falls by its categories (…) since the categories contain the substance of the investigation, a content analysis can be no better than its system of categories. (Berelson 1952, p. 147)

Categories are therefore of crucial importance for effective research, not only in their role as analysis tools, but also insofar as they form the substance of the research and the building blocks of the theory the researchers want to develop. That raises the question 'What are categories?'—or more precisely, 'What are categories in the context of empirical social research?' Answering this question is by no means easy and there are at least two ways of doing so. The first way can be described as *phenomenological*: Kuckartz (2016, pp. 31–39) focuses on the use of this term in the practice of empirical social research, i.e., drawing attention to what is called a category in empirical social research. The result of this analysis is a very diverse spectrum, whereby several different types of categories can be distinguished in social science research literature (ibid., pp. 34–35):

- *Factual categories* denote actual or supposed objective circumstances such as 'length of training' or 'occupation'.
- *Thematic categories* refer to certain topics, arguments, schools of thought etc. such as 'inclusion', 'environmental justice' or 'Ukrainian conflict'.
- *Evaluative categories* are related to an evaluation scale—usually ordinal types, for example the category 'helper syndrome' with the characteristics 'not pronounced', 'somewhat pronounced' and 'pronounced'. For evaluative categories, it is the researchers who classify the data according to predefined criteria.
- *Analytical categories* are the result of intensive analysis of the data, i.e., these categories move away from the description of the data, for example by means of thematic categories.
- *Theoretical categories* are subspecies of analytical categories that refer to an existing theory, such as Ajzen's theory of planned behavior, Ainsworth's attachment theory, or Foucault's analysis of power.

- *Natural categories*, also called "in vivo codes" (Charmaz 2006, p. 56; Kuckartz 2014, p. 23), are terms used by the actors in the field.
- *Formal categories* denote formal characteristics of an analysis unit, e.g., the length of time in an interview.

The above list is not complete; there are many more types of categories and corresponding methods of coding (Saldana 2015).

A second way of answering the question 'What is a category?' can be described as conceptual and historical; this way leads us far back into the history of philosophy. The conceptual historical view of the term, originating from ancient Greece, starts with Greek philosophy more than 2000 years ago. Plato and Aristotle already dealt with categories—Aristotle even in an elaboration of the same term ("categories"). The study of categories runs through Western philosophy from Plato and Kant to Peirce and analytical philosophy. The philosophers are by no means in agreement on the concept of categories, but a discussion of the differences between the different schools would far exceed the scope of this paper; Instead, reading the mostly very extensive contributions on the terms 'category' and 'category theory' in the various lexicons of philosophy is recommended. Categories are basic concepts of cognition; they are—generally speaking—a commonality between certain things: a term, a heading, a label that designates something similar under certain aspects. Categories also play this role in content analysis, as the following quote from the Content Analysis textbook of Früh (2004) demonstrates:

> The pragmatic sense of any content analysis is ultimately to reduce complexity from a certain research-led perspective. Text sets are described in a classifying manner with regard to characteristics of theoretical interest. In this reduction of complexity, information is necessarily lost: On the one hand, information is lost due to the suppression of message characteristics that are present in the examined texts but are not of interest in connection with the present research question; on the other hand, information is lost due to the classification of the analyzed message characteristics. According to specified criteria, some of them are each considered similar to one another and assigned to a certain characteristic class or a characteristic type, which is called 'category' in the content analysis. The original differences in meaning of the message characteristics uniformly grouped in a category shall not be taken into account. (p. 42, translated by the author)

But how does qualitative content analysis arrive at its categories, the basic building blocks for forming theory? There are three principal ways to develop categories:

- Concept-driven ('deductive') development of categories; in this case the categories
  - are derived from a theory or
  - derived from the literature (the current state of research) or
  - derived from the research question (e.g. directly related to an interview guide)

- Data-driven ('inductive') development of categories; the characteristics here are
  - the step-by-step procedure,
  - the method of open coding until saturation occurs,

- the continuous organization and systematization of the formed codes, and
- the development of top-level codes and subcodes at different levels.

- Mixing a concept-driven and data-driven development of codes:
  - The starting point here is usually a coding frame with deductively formed codes and
  - the subsequent inductive coding of all data coded with a specific main category.

The terms *deductive* and *inductive* are often used for the concept-driven and data-driven approaches, respectively. However, the use of the term 'deductive' is rather problematic in this context: In scientific logic, the term 'inductive' refers to the abstract conclusion from what has been observed empirically to a general rule or a law; this has little to do with the formation of categories based on empirical data. The situation is similar with the term 'deductive': In scientific logic, the deductive conclusion is a logical consequence of its premises; the formation of categories based on the state of research, a theory, or an advanced hypothesis is very different. Categories do not necessarily emerge from a systematic literature review or from a research question. Due to its skid resistance, however, the word pair 'inductive-deductive' will probably remain in the language theorem of empirical social research or the formation of categories for a long time to come. Nevertheless, I try to avoid the terms inductive and deductive, and—like Schreier (2012, p. 84)— prefer the terms 'data-driven' and 'concept-driven' for these different approaches to the formation of categories.

The decisive action in QCA is the coding of the data, i.e. a precisely defined part of the material is selected, and a category is assigned. As shown in the following figure, this may be a passage from an interview. Here, paragraph 15 of the text was coded with the code *Simultaneousness* (Fig. 8.1).

The individuals who perform this segmentation and coding of the data are referred to as coders. In this context, we also speak of "inter- and intracoder agreement" (reliability) (Krippendorff 2012; Kuckartz 2016; Schreier 2012). In quantitative content analysis, the units to be coded are usually defined in advance and referred to as coding units. In qualitative content analysis, on the other hand,

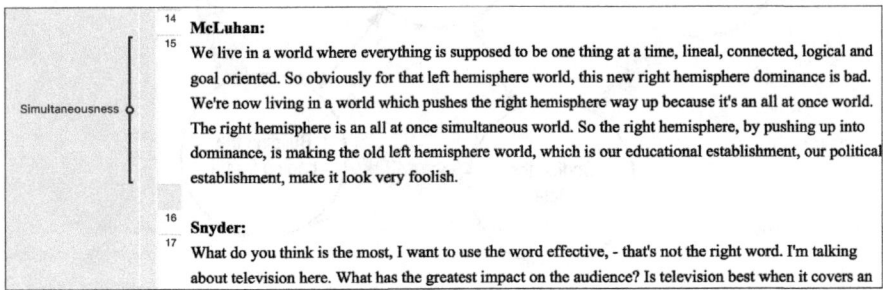

Fig. 8.1 Text passage with a coded text segment

coding units are not usually defined in advance; they are created *by* the coding process.

The general workflow of a qualitative content analysis is in Fig. 8.2. In all variants the research question plays the central role in this method: It provides the perspective for the textual work necessary at the beginning, that is, the intensive reading and study of the texts (Kuckartz 2016, p. 45). For qualitative methods, it is common for the individual analysis phases to be carried out on a circular basis. This also applies to QCA: The creation of categories and subcategories and the coding of the data can take place in several cycles. Saldana (2015) speaks of first cycle coding and second cycle coding, for example. The number of cycles is not fixed, and only in rare cases would one get by with just a single cycle.

Once all the data have been coded with the final category frame, a systematization and structuring of all the relevant data in view of the research questions at hand will have been achieved. Table 8.2 illustrates a model of such a thematic matrix. It is similar to the quantitative data matrix shown in Fig. 8.2, but instead of containing numbers, the cells of the matrix now contain text excerpts coded with the respective corresponding category.

The further analysis of the matrix can now take two directions: If you look at columns, you can examine certain topics. These forms of analysis can be described as 'category-based'. Looking at the rows, you can focus on cases (people) and carry out a 'case-oriented analysis'.

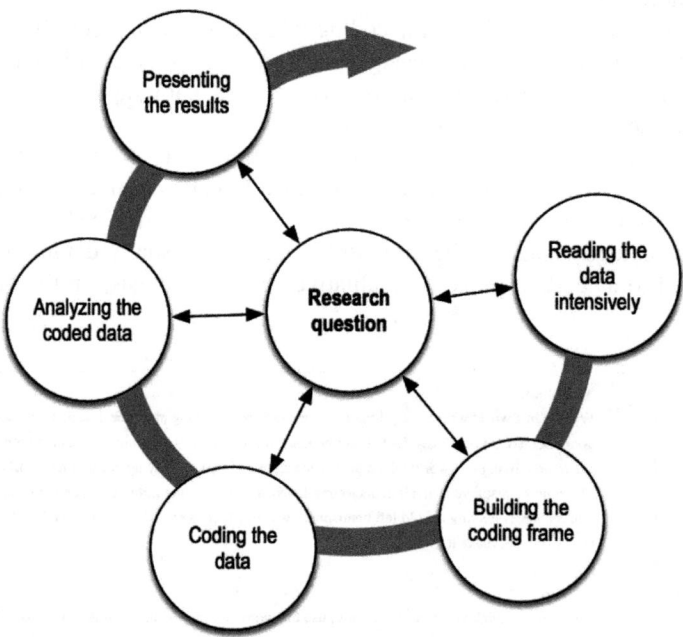

Fig. 8.2 The five phases of qualitative content analysis

Table 8.2 Typical model of a thematic matrix topics by cases

	Topic A	Topic B	Topic C	
Person 1	Person 1's text passages about Topic A	Person 1's text passages about Topic B	Person 1's text passages about Topic C	⇨ Case summary for Person 1
Person 2	Person 2's text passages about Topic A	Person 2's text passages about Topic B	Person 2's text passages about Topic C	⇨ Case summary for Person 2
Person 3	Person 3's text passages about Topic A	Person 3's text passages about Topic B	Person 3's text passages about Topic C	⇨ Case summary for Person 3
	Category-based analysis for			
	⇩	⇩	⇩	
	Topic A	Topic B	Topic C	

Category-based analyses can focus on a specific category or even consider several categories simultaneously. For example, the statements made by the research participants can be contrasted between two or across several topics. Such complex analyses can lead to very rich descriptions or to the determination of influencing factors and effects, which can then be displayed in a concept map. Case-oriented analyses allow you to identify similarities between cases, identify extreme cases, and form types. Methods of consistently comparing and contrasting cases can be used to this end. For example, if you have determined a typology, you can then visualize it as a constellation of clusters and cases.

8.3 The Analysis Process in Detail

The example used in the following is a short online survey conducted in preparation for the 'Workshop on qualitative text analysis' as part of the ICME 13. The aim of the survey was to provide an overview of the research needs of the participants and their level of knowledge. In other words, its aim was descriptive and not about the development of hypotheses or a theory. In this online interview, I asked the following five questions and asked the participants to write their responses directly below the questions. Table 8.3 contains the resulting qualitative data.

Typically, QCA consists of six steps

Step 1: Preparing the data, initiating text work
Step 2: Forming main categories corresponding to the questions asked in the interview
Step 3: Coding data with the main categories
Step 4: Compiling text passages of the main categories and forming subcategories inductively on the material; assigning text passages to subcategories
Step 5: Category-based analyses and presenting results

Table 8.3 Example of the survey questions and answers

Question #1: *Why are you planning to take part in the workshop? What goals do you have? What would you like to learn?*
I am doing a textual analysis of mathematics textbook curriculum for my dissertation work and I am interested in learning different strategies and techniques for analyzing such data
Question #2: *Are you familiar with or have you had hands-on experience with qualitative text analysis (qualitative content analysis)? Please briefly describe your experience!*
My experience thus far has been in drawing from Foucault's method of Archaeology for textual analysis which can be interpreted in many different ways. Aside from that I have little experience with qualitative text analysis
Question #3: *Do you have specific questions about the method "Qualitative Text Analysis"? Please write these questions here:*
Yes, if you are the only researcher analyzing the data—how can you make assurances about the validity and rigor of your analysis?
If you are utilizing a pre-defined framework from the literature in your coding, how appropriate is it to include your own codes in the framework and how can you describe or define this?
Question #4: *Have you had experience in working with MAXQDA (or with other QDA software)? Please briefly describe your experience!*
No prior experience
Question #5: *Please indicate your discipline (e.g. sociology, psychology, etc.) and your current status (e.g. graduate or doctoral student, researcher involved in a project, etc.)*
I am a doctoral student in mathematics education

Step 6: Reporting and documentation.

Since the purpose of the survey in this case was to get an overview of the relevant interests of the workshop participants and to tailor the workshop to their needs, the last step was omitted. There was no need for reporting and documentation.

The *first phase* consists of preparing of the data and conducting an initial read-through the responses; the analysis of this short survey did not require extensive interpretation of the responses. Since respondents used different fonts and font sizes in their e-mails, these had to be standardized first when preparing the data. In addition, the overall formatting was also adjusted to render it more uniform across responses. This would not have been absolutely necessary for the analysis, but without this preparation, later compilations of coded text passages might have looked rather chaotic.

In the *second phase* of QCA, categories are formed. When analyzing data obtained through an online survey, it is best to create a set of main categories based on the questions asked. In this analysis, the following five categories were formed for the first coding cycle:

1 Motives and goals
2 Experience with QCA

3 Specific questions about QCA
4 Experience with QDAS (Qualitative data analysis software)
5 Academic discipline.

Since the questions in the online survey were numbered, the numbers were retained for better orientation, but they could have been dispensed with without any problems.

According to the differentiation of categories laid out earlier in this paper, the categories *Motives and goals* and *Specific questions about QCA* are thematic categories. Category 5 *Academic Discipline* is a factual code. The other two categories *Experience with QCA* and *Experience with QDAS* are about the experiences with the method and with QDA software. If the researcher is interested in the extent of participants' experience, both categories are evaluative categories; alternatively, if the specific type of experience is the primary point of interest, the categories are thematic. Since the aim of this survey was to get an overview of the level of knowledge and practical experience of the respondents, an overview was sufficient; detailed knowledge of the types of experience the participants had gained was not absolutely necessary. Reading the responses also demonstrated that the respondents understood the question in this sense and that in most cases no specific details were provided. In any case, working with software like MAXQDA guarantees that you can always return to the original texts should this be useful or necessary during the course of the analysis.

In the *third phase* of the analysis, the corresponding text segments are coded with the five main categories. Figure 8.3 shows a screenshot of the software MAXQDA after this first cycle of coding was performed on the survey responses. The assignments of the codes are displayed to the left of the corresponding text sections.

In the following *fourth phase* of the analysis, the coding frame is developed further. To do this, all the text passages coded with one of the main categories are first compiled, a procedure which is also referred to as *retrieval*. Subcodes are then developed directly in the relation to this data—in other words, the creation of categories is data-driven. This process is described in the following with regard to the first main category *Motives and goals*:

The category *Motives and goals* coded the responses to the question regarding what the participants wanted to learn in the workshop. First, all text passages to which this category was assigned were compiled. Then each of these text passages was coded a second time. This was done with a procedure similar to that of open coding in Grounded Theory (Strauss and Corbin 1990). In this case, the codes were short sequences of words that described what the participants wanted to learn:

- analyze mathematics textbook curricula
- learn type-building analysis
- analyze e-portfolios and group discussions
- analyze responses to open-ended questions
- learn more about different research methods
- how to establish credibility in practice

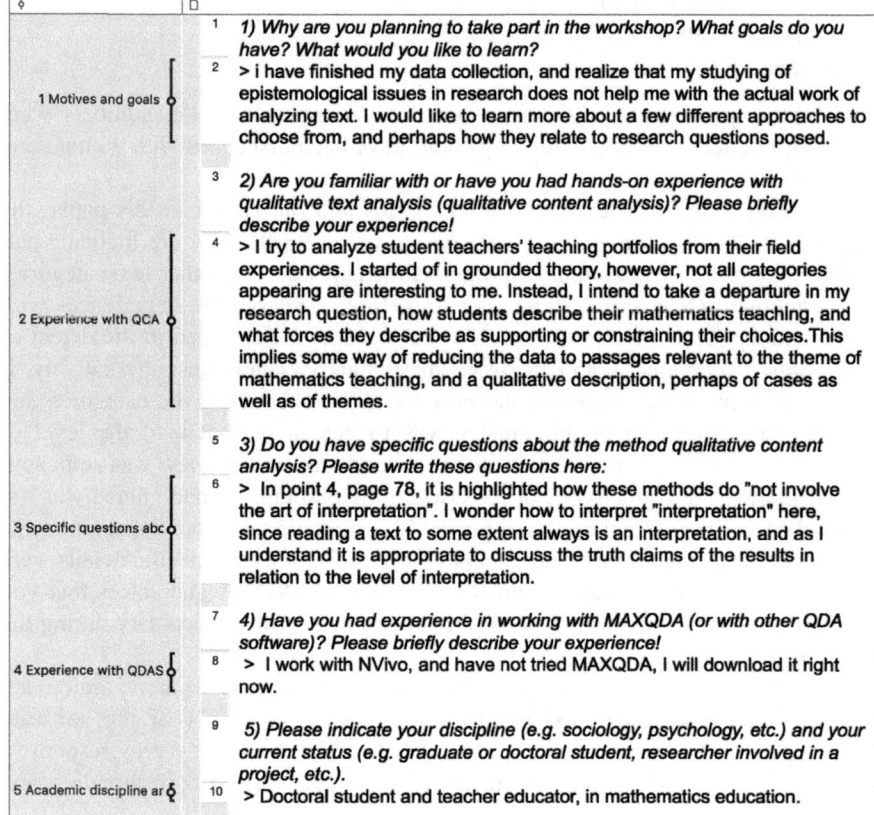

Fig. 8.3 Display of a text with code assignments after the first cycle of coding

- learn more about rigor within the process and how to ensure its validity
- the role of reliability coefficients
- insight into conducting qualitative research
- learn about the QCA method
- how to code video transcripts
- how to take the richness of data into account (not only numbers)
- analyze large numbers of open questions
- learn more about a few different approaches to choose from
- searching for a suitable method to analyze the interviews
- interesting for me to see how colleagues are working.

As part of the software MAXQDA there is a module called "Creative Coding" that allows you to visually group codes obtained through the open coding method. After arranging the open codes, seven subcategories were created for the category "Motives and Objectives", namely

- Getting an overview of qualitative research
- Getting an overview of QCA
- Learning basic techniques
- Learning about special type of analysis
- Reliability and validity
- Learning to analyze special types of data
- Interesting for me to see how colleagues are working.

Figure 8.4 shows a visual display of the category formation; the original statements are assigned to the respective category. It turns out that many participants in the workshop were mainly interested in obtaining an overview of qualitative content analysis and qualitative research in general. The graph also implicitly illustrates the differences between a quantitative and qualitative analysis of the responses: Four participants (a comparatively large proportion) wanted to learn how to analyze specific types of data, but a closer look at the details, that is, the qualitative dimension, reveals that the types of data the respondents had in mind were completely different.

Once the subcategories have been created, all the data coded with the main category *Motives and goals* must be coded a second time. This is also known as the second coding cycle. In this sample survey, all the coded text passages were included in the formation of the subcategories due to the relatively small sample. In the case of small sample sizes like this, the *Creative Coding* module automatically reassigns the subcategories. In the case of larger samples, however, category formation will usually be carried out only with a subsample and not with all the data, or the process of open coding will be performed only until the system of subcategories appears saturated and no further subcategories need to be redefined. Then, of course, the data that have not been considered up to this point must still be coded in line with the final category system.

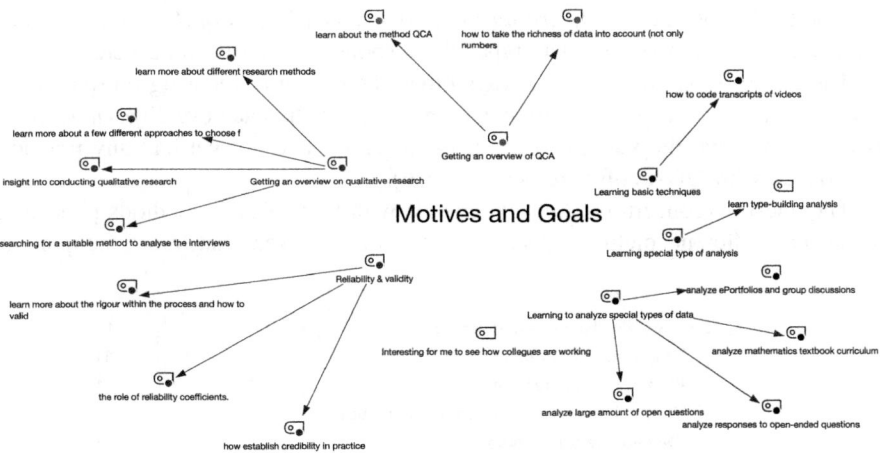

Fig. 8.4 Visualization of the motives grouped into subcategories

The two categories *Experience with QCA* and *Experience with QDAS* were used to code the text passages in which the respondents reported on their experience with the QCA method and the use of QDA software. For the purposes of preparing the workshop as described above, the analysis should address only whether participants had prior experience and how extensive this experience was. An evaluative category with the values 'yes', 'partial', 'no' was therefore defined.

For the third main category, *Specific questions about QCA*, no subcategories were formed, since the questions formulated by the participants had to be retained in their wording to answer them in the workshop. However, the questions asked were sorted by topic, and essentially identical questions were summarized.

For category 5, *Academic discipline*, subcategories were initially formed according to the disciplines mentioned by the respondents. However, it quickly transpired that almost all participants came from the field of *mathematics education* and that there were only a few individual cases from other fields such as *development psychology* or *primary school teacher* (see Fig. 8.5). These individual cases were combined into the subcategory *others* for the final category system, so that ultimately only two subcategories were formed.

After the main categories have been processed in this way—five in the case of this survey—the *fifth phase* 'Category-based analyses and presenting results' can begin. However, it should be clear that in the fourth phase of the development of the category system, an extensive amount of analytical work has already being carried out. The identification of the different motive types represents an analytical achievement in itself and is, at the same time, the foundation of the corresponding category-based analysis in phase 5. The category *Motives and goals* was of central importance in this survey. In addition to identifying the various motives, both quantitative and qualitative analyses can now be carried out. Quantitatively, we can determine how many people expressed which motives in their statement. Of course, it is quite possible for someone to have expressed several motives. In terms of a qualitative analysis, we can ask what is behind these categories in greater detail. In relation to the subcategory *Learning to analyze special types of data*, for example, we could ask which special data types the respondents had in mind here.

The category-based analysis always offers the option of focusing on qualitative and/or quantitative aspects. A frequency analysis of the category *Experience with QDAS* shows that the vast majority of participants have not yet had any practical experience with QDA software (see Fig. 8.6).

The question concerning their experience with text analysis methods presents a somewhat different picture. Quantitatively, we can see that more people are

▼ ●◎●5 Academic discipline and status	13
●◎☐Mathematics education.	11
●◎☐Primary school teacher	1
●◎☐Curriculum and instruction (mathematics)	1
●◎☐Development psychology	1

Fig. 8.5 Main category "Academic discipline and status" with subcategories

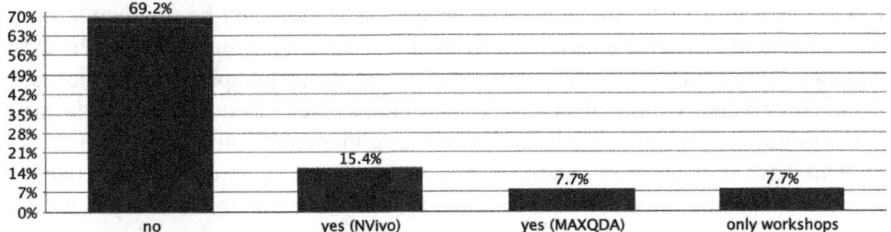

Fig. 8.6 Bar chart of the category "Experiences with QDA software"

experienced in this regard, while the more detailed qualitative view reveals that this experience mainly involved the Grounded Theory method. It is interesting to compare the two categories that deal with experience. Table 8.4 contains an excerpt from such a comparison between five people.

There are also many further possibilities regarding the analysis of interrelationships that can be carried out in this fifth phase. For example, the connection between motives and goals, and previous knowledge and experience, can be examined. In relation to the specific questions asked by respondents in the survey, one could create a cross table (or "crosstab") in which the questions asked by the experienced group are compared with the questions asked by those with no experience.

There are many other analysis options for larger studies than those presented for the small online survey. Qualitative content analysis is not a method that is always applied in the same way regardless of the data or research questions at hand. Although it is a systematic procedure, it nonetheless offers a flexibility that allows you to adapt it to the respective requirements of a project. There are other analytical possibilities in this regard, which were not mentioned in the above description. Among these, two should be highlighted in particular, namely, the possibility of paraphrasing text passages and the possibility of creating thematic summaries.

Paraphrasing passages of text can be understood in its everyday sense, namely, that researchers reformulate these text passages in their own words. This can be a very useful tool for category development. This technique is especially recommended for beginners, as it forces them to read the text line by line, interpret it to gain a thorough understanding, and then record it in their own words. It is certainly too time-consuming in most cases to edit all texts in this way but paraphrasing a

Table 8.4 Comparison table of two main categories

Documents	2 QTA-experience	4 QDA software experience
Person A	No	Yes (MAXQDA)
Person B	No	No
Person C	No	No
Person D	Grounded theory	No
Person E	Yes but video	Only workshops

selected subset of texts can sharpen your analytical view and be a valuable intermediate step in the development of a meaningful category system. Moreover, these paraphrases can then be sorted, particularly significant paraphrases can be combined, and gradually more abstract and theoretically rich categories can be formed.

In contrast to paraphrasing texts, formulating thematic summaries assumes that the texts have already been coded. In this approach, all the text passages coded in regard to a specific topic are read for each case and a thematic summary is written for each person. Usually, there is a huge gap between a category and the amount of original text assigned to it in the case of longer qualitative interviews, such as narrative interviews. On the one hand there is a relatively short code, such as 'Environmental behavior in relation to nutrition', and on the other there are numerous passages of varying length in which a respondent says something on this subject. A thematic summary summarizes all these passages as said by a certain person from the perspective of the research question. This means that the text is not repeated, but rather edited conceptually. Summaries thus create a second level between the original text and the categories and concepts. They also enable complex analyses to be carried out in which several categories are compared or the statements of different groups (women/men, different age groups, different schooling, etc.) are contrasted. This would be nigh impossible if the original quotations were always used since the amount of text would simply be too large, and it would consequently not be possible to create case overviews. A thematic summary, on the other hand, compresses what one person has said in such a way that it can easily be included in further analyses.

A third possibility the QCA method offers is the visualization of relationships between categories. Diagrams, in the form of concept maps, can be generated in which the influencing factors, effects, and relations are visualized.

Phase 6, 'Reporting and documentation', is about putting the results of your analyses on paper. The research report of a project working with the QCA method is usually divided into a descriptive and an analytical section. Depending on the method and the significance of the categories, category-based analyses will be the center of attention. The case dimension, however, which is all too often neglected, should also be taken into account in the report. It is often very valuable for the recipients of the research not only to learn something about the connections between the categories, but also something about the participants, that is, the cases that are consciously selected for such a presentation. It is particularly interesting if the cases are grouped into types and the report presents cases that are representative of these types.

The category-based presentation should be illustrated with quotes from the original material. However, you should also be aware of the danger of selective plausibility, i.e., that one mainly selects quotations that clarify the alleged connections between categories, while contradictory examples are not considered. For this reason, counterexamples should always be sought and included in the report.

Category-based analysis should not be limited to a description of the results per category but should also look at the relationships between two or more categories. In other words, you should move from the initial description to the development of a theory.

8.4 Summary and Conclusions

This chapter presents a method for the methodically controlled analysis of texts in empirical research. To conclude, therefore, the characteristics of the QCA method are concisely summarized:

- The focus of the QCA method is on the categories with which the data are coded.
- The categories of the final coding frame are described as precisely as possible and it is ensured that the coding procedure itself is reliable, i.e., that different coders concur in their coding.
- The data must be coded completely. Complete in this sense means that all passages in the texts that are relevant to the research question are coded. It does, however, make sense to leave those parts of the data uncoded, which are outside the focus of the research question.
- The codes and categories can be formed in different ways: empirically, i.e., based directly on the material, or conceptually, i.e., based on the current state of research or on a theory/hypothesis or, rather, as an implementation of the guidelines used in an interview or focus group.
- The QCA method is carried out in several phases, ranging from data preparation, category building and coding—which may run in several cycles—to analysis, report writing and presenting the results. QCA therefore means more than just coding the data. Coding is an important step in the analysis, but it is ultimately a preparation for the subsequent analytical steps.
- The actual analysis phase consists of summarizing the data, and constantly comparing and contrasting the data. The analysis techniques can be qualitative as well as quantitative. The qualitative analysis may, for example, consist of comparing the statements of certain groups (for instance according to their characteristics, e.g., socio-demographic characteristics) on certain topics. Differences and similarities are identified and summarized in a report. Quantitative analyses may, on the other hand, consist of comparing the frequency of certain categories and/or subcategories for certain groups.
- Summary tables and diagrams (e.g., concept maps) can play an important role in the analysis. A good example of a presentation in table form would be a case overview of selected research participants (or groups), in which their statements on certain topics, their judgements and variable values are displayed. An example of a concept map would be a diagram of the determined causal effects of different categories.

- Visualizations can also have a diagnostic function in QCA—similarly to imaging procedures in medicine. For example, a 'cases by categories' or 'categories by categories' display can help identify patterns in the data and indicate which categories are particularly frequently or particularly rarely associated with certain other categories.
- When analyzing texts, you should keep in mind that you are working in the field of interpretation. It can be assumed that texts or statements could be interpreted differently. Instead of adopting a constructivist 'anything goes' approach, the QCA method tries to reach a consensus—as far as this is possible—on the subjective meaning of statements and tries to define the categories formed or used by it so precisely that an intersubjective agreement can be achieved in the application of the categories.
- Group processes play an important role in this process of achieving the necessary level of agreement. Divergent assignments to categories are discussed as a team and should result in an improvement of the category definitions. Categories for which no agreement can be reached in the coding of relevant points in the data must be excluded from the analysis. Content analysis stands and falls by its categories. An analysis with the help of categories that are interpreted and applied differently in the research team, does not make sense.
- QCA does not claim to be the best method but recognizes that it has its limits (the interpretation barrier) and that its results have to face comparison with those of competing methods.

The systematic approach of QCA is multidisciplinary and can be applied in many disciplines, including mathematics education (Schwarz 2015). This method is particularly appropriate when working with clearly formulated research questions, because these questions play the central role in this method. Indeed, in every phase of the analysis there is a strong reference to the questions leading the research. One strength of QCA is that it can be used both to describe social phenomena and to develop theories or test hypotheses (Hopf 2016, pp. 155–166).

References

Berelson, B. (1952). *Content analysis in communication research*. Glencoe: Free Press.
Charmaz, K. (2006). *Constructing grounded theory*. Thousand Oaks: SAGE.
Früh, W. (2004). *Inhaltsanalyse. Theorie und Praxis* (5th ed.). Konstanz: UVK.
Guest, G., MacQueen, K. M., & Namey, E. E. (2012). *Applied thematic analysis*. Thousand Oaks: SAGE.
Hopf, C. (2016). In W. Hopf & U. Kuckartz (Eds.), *Schriften zu Methodologie und Methoden qualitativer Sozialforschung*. Wiesbaden: Springer.
Krippendorff, K. H. (2012). *Content analysis: An introduction to its methodology* (3rd ed.). Thousand Oaks: SAGE.
Kuckartz, U. (2014). *Qualitative text analysis: A guide to methods, practice and using software*. Los Angeles: SAGE.

Kuckartz, U. (2016). *Qualitative Inhaltsanalyse. Methoden, Praxis, Computerunterstützung* (3rd ed.). Weinheim: Beltz Juventa.

Mayring, P. (2014). Qualitative content analysis: Theoretical foundation, basic procedures and software solution. Klagenfurt. http://nbn-resolving.de/urn:nbn:de:0168-ssoar-395173.

Mayring, P. (2015). Qualitative content analysis: Theoretical background and procedures. In A. Bikner-Ahsbahs, C. Knipping, & N. Presmeg (Eds.), *Approaches to qualitative research in mathematics education. Examples of methodology and methods* (pp. 365–380). Dordrecht: Springer.

Saldana, J. (2015). *The coding manual for qualitative researchers* (3rd ed.). Thousand Oaks: SAGE.

Schreier, M. (2012). *Qualitative content analysis in practice*. Thousand Oaks: SAGE.

Schwarz, B. (2015). A study on professional competence of future teacher students as an example of a study using qualitative content analysis. In A. Bikner-Ahsbahs, C. Knipping, & N. Presmeg (Eds.), *Approaches to qualitative research in mathematics education. Examples of methodology and methods* (pp. 381–399). Dordrecht: Springer.

Strauss, A. L., & Corbin, J. M. (1990). *Basics of qualitative research: Grounded theory procedures and techniques*. Thousand Oaks: Sage Publications, Inc.

Open Access This chapter is licensed under the terms of the Creative Commons Attribution 4.0 International License (http://creativecommons.org/licenses/by/4.0/), which permits use, sharing, adaptation, distribution and reproduction in any medium or format, as long as you give appropriate credit to the original author(s) and the source, provide a link to the Creative Commons license and indicate if changes were made.

The images or other third party material in this chapter are included in the chapter's Creative Commons license, unless indicated otherwise in a credit line to the material. If material is not included in the chapter's Creative Commons license and your intended use is not permitted by statutory regulation or exceeds the permitted use, you will need to obtain permission directly from the copyright holder.

Chapter 9
Problematising Video as Data in Three Video-based Research Projects in Mathematics Education

Man Ching Esther Chan, Carmel Mesiti and David Clarke

Abstract In this chapter, we problematise the status of video as research data and identify ontological contingencies relevant to any research study by considering three video-based research projects in which the relationship between researcher and video material (i.e., between researcher and data) is very different. Each project (the Learner's Perspective Study, the Social Unit of Learning Project, and The International Classroom Lexicon Project) employs video material in a distinctive way, and comparison of the three studies illustrates important ontological decisions that should be addressed explicitly in educational research projects.

Keywords Video-based research · Ontology · Metaphors · Research design

9.1 Introduction

The increasing variety of theories and analytical perspectives employed to investigate educational settings, situations and issues over recent decades has created challenges for researchers to communicate their research, integrate empirical results, and make progress as a field by building upon the growing diversity of empirical research (Prediger et al. 2008). In particular, what constitute valid research findings and research evidence is of significance not only to researchers, but also to practitioners, policymakers, and other stakeholders (Schirmer et al. 2016; Simpson 2017). A major consideration regarding the validity of research

M. C. E. Chan (✉) · C. Mesiti · D. Clarke
Melbourne Graduate School of Education, The University of Melbourne,
Melbourne, VIC, Australia
e-mail: mc.chan@unimelb.edu.au

C. Mesiti
e-mail: cmesiti@unimelb.edu.au

D. Clarke
e-mail: d.clarke@unimelb.edu.au

© The Author(s) 2019
G. Kaiser and N. Presmeg (eds.), *Compendium for Early Career Researchers in Mathematics Education*, ICME-13 Monographs,
https://doi.org/10.1007/978-3-030-15636-7_9

findings and research evidence in education research is the issue of *ontology*, which is "an area of philosophy that deals with the nature of being, or what exists" (Neuman 2014, p. 94). We argue that research in education needs to pay attention to the claims that are being made about the authority of research findings and the nature of the data from which those findings have been derived. These questions are fundamentally ontological questions because they concern whether or not our research findings are drawn from and relate to phenomena that are in any sense 'real'.

As a source of research data, video occupies an unusual and possibly a unique place in mediating between the conception of actual classroom practice and our ability to theorise about the characteristics of that practice. This is because the video is a very graphic representation of that practice and should be subject to careful ontological examination before claims are made about the authority invoked for any research-based recommendations regarding those classroom practices. In this chapter, we focus on video-based research that attempts to inform the actual practice of teachers. The word *actual* invokes the notion of ontology by positing the existence of a world where things happen, a world where there are things to be studied, and a world where practices could be informed by the results of that study. This posited relationship between video-based research and the settings and situations it seeks to both study and to inform represents an ontological position implicit in most video-based research studies.

In this chapter we take three research projects as illustrative cases, each employing video. Each project had a different research design, and we examine the role of the researcher and the status of the video records in each of these projects, specifically from an ontological perspective. We have purposefully chosen these three projects because the role that video plays and the role of the researcher in each are very different. As a result, the uses made of the video material in the different research studies are distinct, where the relationship between the video material and the researcher is fundamentally different in each study. Our view is that exploring this relationship between the researcher and the video material offers insights into important ontological considerations that apply to any study involving the use of video and, we would suggest, to any study of any type, because it foregrounds fundamental issues related to the nature of data and evidence in any study and the sorts of conclusions that can be drawn. The following sections provide some background about video-based research in education and a brief overview of the three projects: (i) The Learner's Perspective Study (an international comparative study of well-taught mathematics classes in over a dozen countries); (ii) The Social Unit of Learning project (an experimental study of social interaction during collaborative problem solving in mathematics); and (iii) The International Classroom Lexicon Project (an investigation of the pedagogical vocabulary of mathematics teachers in ten countries).

9.2 Video-Based Research in Education

Video has become a popular contemporary research tool, providing a record of classroom activity rich in detail and sufficiently permanent to provide opportunities for re-analysis. In the past 50 years, learning in classroom settings became increasingly the subject of research and this interest was accompanied by the development of onsite real-time observational techniques (e.g., Amidon and Hough 1967; Beeby et al. 1979). Process-product research designs (e.g., Bourke 1984; Good and Grouws 1977) sought to identify statistically significant associations between classroom process variables (e.g., number of teacher questions) and product variables (typically measures of student achievement or attitude). Naturalistic case studies of student learning in authentic classroom settings (e.g., Clarke 2001; Cobb and Bauersfeld 1995; Erlwanger 1975) drew upon the practices of ethnographic research to understand the relationships between individuals, their practice, and their consequent learning in classroom settings.

Early attempts at on-site recording of classroom practice required the physical presence of researchers to use checklists or write field notes during their classroom observation. Both checklists and the field notes maintained by researchers involve high levels of researcher interpretation and limited opportunity for re-visiting the classroom situation being studied. This restricts the reliability of the research data and the validity of the inferences made based on such data. It was hoped that video would provide a less intrusive and more efficient means of generating detailed documentation of classroom practice, while allowing cross-validation and re-examination of the data (Hiebert et al. 2003). The affordability of video technologies and computer processing power has given rise to the increased use of video in classroom research. International comparative studies of classroom practice have been undertaken using video as a key data collection tool (e.g., Clarke et al. 2006b; Stigler and Hiebert 1999). More recently, university-based and school-based classrooms equipped with video and audio facilities have been set up around the world, such as in the USA, the Netherlands, and China (Chan et al. 2017). The three research projects chosen as illustrative cases in this chapter each employed video material in a distinctive way with a different research design.

9.3 Three Research Projects in Mathematics Education Employing Video

9.3.1 The Learner's Perspective Study (LPS)

The Learner's Perspective Study (Clarke et al. 2006b) was designed to examine the practices of eighth grade mathematics classrooms in a more integrated and comprehensive fashion than had been attempted in previous international studies. The project was originally designed to complement research studies reporting national norms of student achievement and teaching practices with an in-depth analysis of mathematics classrooms in Australia, Germany, Japan and the USA by foregrounding the learner's perspective on the practices of those classrooms. However, from its inception, research teams from other countries continued to join the LPS. The LPS project grew to accommodate 15 research teams situated in universities in Australia, China, the Czech Republic, Germany, Israel, Japan, Korea, New Zealand, Norway, the Philippines, Portugal, Singapore, South Africa, Sweden and the USA. This combination of countries gave good representation to different European and Asian educational traditions, affluent and less affluent school systems, and mono-cultural and multi-cultural societies.

Data generation in the LPS used a three-camera approach (Teacher camera, Student camera, Whole Class camera; see Fig. 9.1) that included the onsite mixing of the Teacher and Student camera images into a picture-in-picture video record (see Fig. 9.2) that was then used in post-lesson interviews with teachers and with students to stimulate participant reconstructive accounts of classroom events. These data were generated for sequences of at least ten consecutive lessons occurring in well-taught eighth grade mathematics classrooms from around the world. One of the significant and distinguishing characteristics of this study in comparison with previous research was the documentation of a sequence of lessons taught by each teacher, as opposed to single lessons (cf. Stigler and Hiebert 1999). One of the major influences on a teacher's purposeful selection of instructional strategies includes the situation of the lesson within the enfolding topic. The LPS design allowed for this consideration to be taken into account in the analysis of classroom practice.

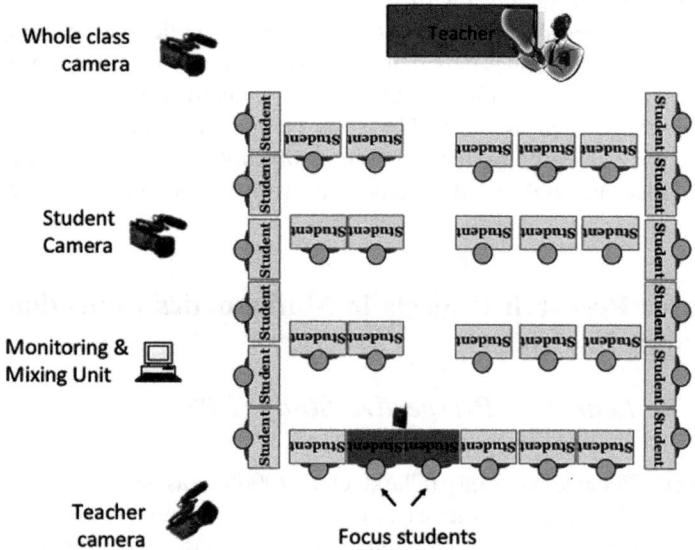

Fig. 9.1 Camera configuration in the LPS

Fig. 9.2 Picture-in-picture video display. (Image reproduced from Clarke 2006, p. 21)

The use of three video-cameras in the classroom, supplemented by post-lesson video-stimulated interviews, provided a data base sufficiently complex to support analysis of both individual learners' constructed meanings and their perspectives on classroom practice, as well as documenting behavioural norms characteristic of each class. In particular, the LPS study facilitated the comparison of quality mathematics teaching practices across a wide variety of school systems situated in different countries, by identifying similarities and differences in both teaching practice and in the associated student perceptions and behaviours in each classroom.

One of the main findings of the LPS was contesting the characterisation of national patterns of teaching as stable, distinctive lesson structures, as reported by Stigler and Hiebert (1999). Stigler and Hiebert contended that mathematics teaching in Germany, Japan and the USA could be described by a "simple, common pattern" (p. 82) referred to as a culturally-based 'lesson script'. The lesson pattern for Japan was reported as: Reviewing the previous lesson; Presenting the problem for the day; Students working individually or in groups; and Discussing solution methods (p. 79).

The LPS (Clarke et al. 2006a) documented sequences of ten lessons in the classrooms of three competent Japanese mathematics teachers (in demographically different schools in Tokyo). Each of these lessons was analysed using the categories specified by Stigler and Hiebert (1999) (see Fig. 9.3). Figure 9.4 shows the distribution of these categories across the 30 Japanese lessons recorded in the LPS.

Not one lesson matched the 'typical' sequence reported by Stigler and Hiebert (Clarke et al. 2006c). With hindsight, this is not a surprising result. Any aggregated characterisation across a phenomenon as demonstrably variable as the mathematics lesson is almost certain to produce a 'stereotype' that does not match any single instance of the aggregated phenomenon. Nonetheless, the status of the individual categories themselves was significantly enhanced by their capacity to account for almost every instance of lesson time. This result was equally true for the 30 lessons recorded in the USA and in Germany. In each case, no instance of the reported

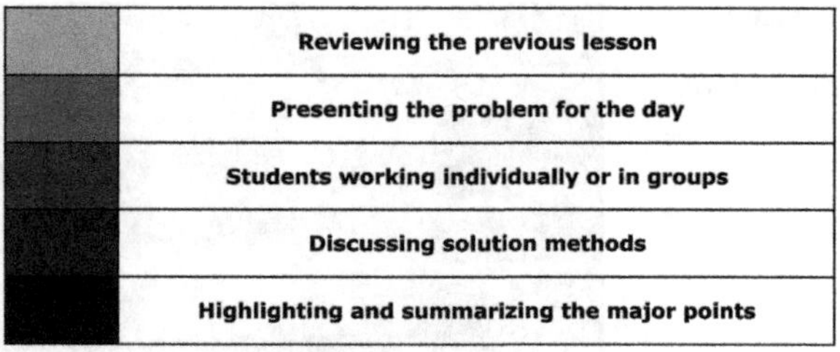

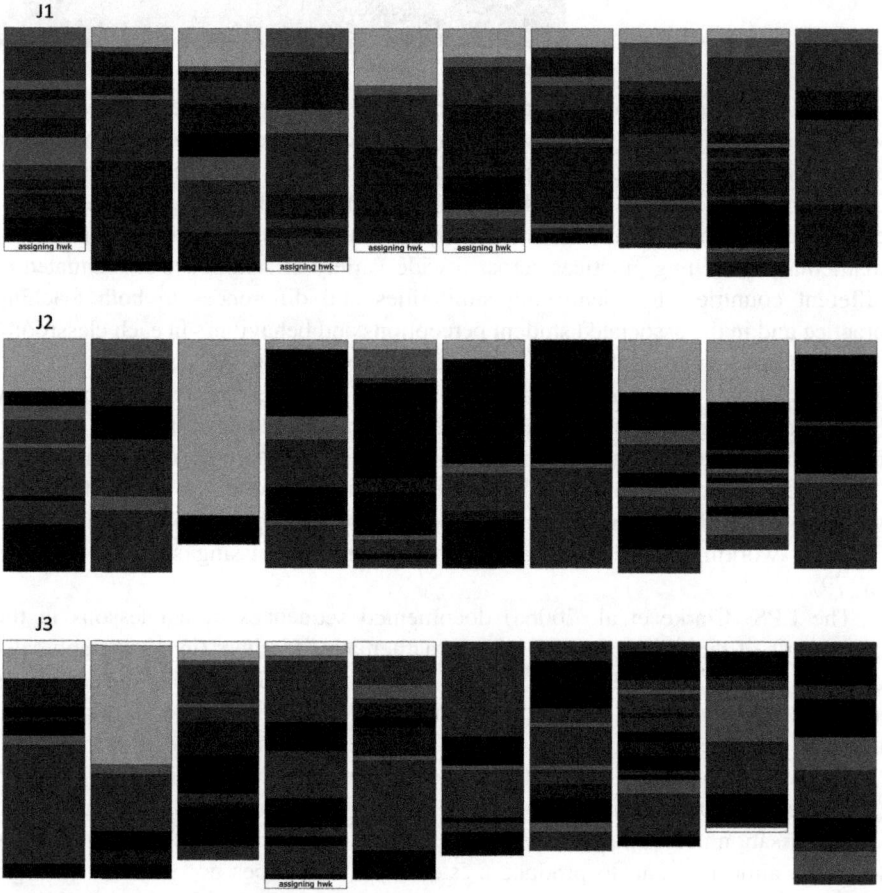

Fig. 9.3 Video coding key for the classroom activities found in the Japanese lessons. (Image reproduced from Clarke et al. 2006c, p. 38)

Fig. 9.4 Japanese lesson pattern codes as applied to LPS Japanese Schools 1, 2 and 3. (Images reproduced from Clarke et al. 2006c, pp. 38–39)

lesson script could be found in the recorded lessons. However, the constituent elements of each lesson script were sufficiently robust to accommodate almost all classroom phenomena in each of the three countries (Japan, USA and Germany). The variability in lesson structure documented in the Learner's Perspective Study by Clarke, Mesiti, Jablonka and Shimizu reflects the purposeful decision-making of competent teachers, who structure their lessons in recognition of the needs of their students, their priorities and strengths as teachers, and the situation and consequent purpose of the lesson in the instructional sequence (cf. Givvin et al. 2005, p. 341).

9.3.2 The Social Unit of Learning Project

The Science of Learning Research Classroom (SLRC) at the University of Melbourne is a 129 sq. m. teaching space that resembles a typical school classroom, but is fitted with high definition audio-visual recording equipment and physically connected to an adjacent Control Room via a one-way window (see Fig. 9.5). The development of the SLRC laboratory classroom has made possible research designs that combine a good approximation to natural social settings with the retention of some degree of researcher control over the research setting, task characteristics, and possible forms of social interaction afforded or encouraged. Such designs allow conclusions to be drawn with greater confidence about connections between interactive patterns of social negotiation and associated knowledge products (learning). The SLRC had the capability to capture classroom social interactions with a rich amount of detail using advanced video technology. The facility was purposefully designed to allow simultaneous and continuous documentation of classroom interactions using multiple cameras and microphones.

The Social Unit of Learning Project (Chan et al. 2017) used the SLRC to examine individual, dyadic, small group (four to six students) and whole class problem solving in mathematics and the associated/consequent learning. The project aimed to investigate the social aspects of learning and, particularly, those aspects for which 'the social' represents the most fundamental and useful level of explanation, modelling and instructional intervention (Chan and Clarke 2017a). Figure 9.6 shows the classroom configuration for a filming session of the project.

Fig. 9.5 Images of the science of learning research classroom (left) and the control room (right). (Images reproduced from Chan and Clarke 2019)

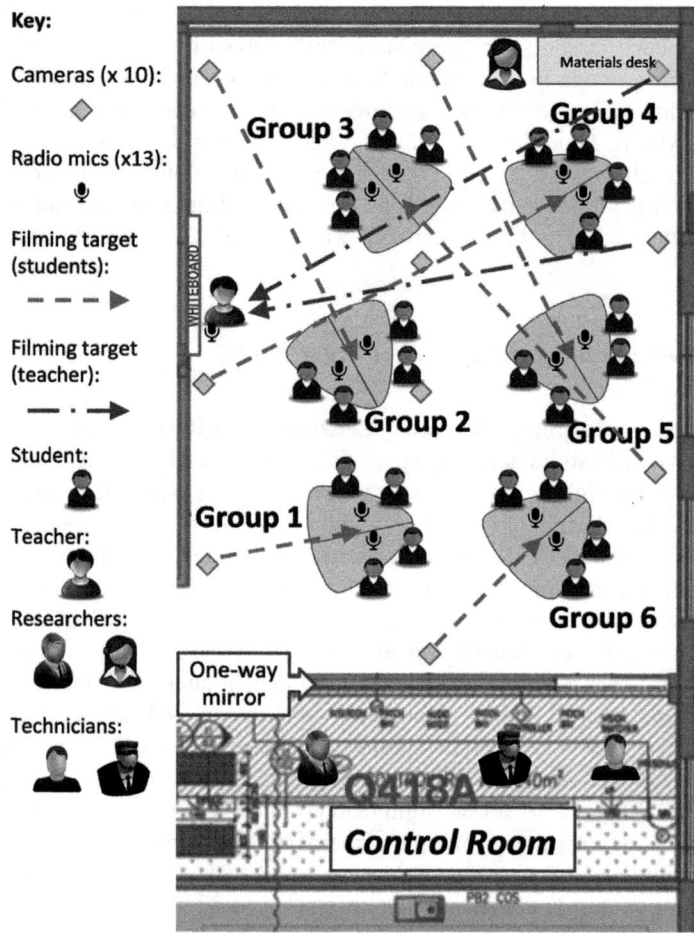

Fig. 9.6 Classroom configuration showing video camera sight lines. (Image reproduced from Chan et al. 2017, p. 46)

The Social Unit of Learning project collected multiple forms of data for analysis, including student written products and high definition video and audio recordings of every student and the teacher in the classroom. The project employed a multi-theoretic research design (Clarke et al. 2012) which afforded the examination of the complex data set from multiple perspectives by multiple researchers, as well as the reciprocal interrogation of the different theoretical perspectives through answering research questions such as the following:

1. What commonalities and differences in process and product are evident during problem solving activities undertaken by learners as members of different social units (individual, pairs, small groups and whole class groupings)?

2. Which existing theories best accommodate the documented similarities and differences in process and product and in what ways do the accounts generated by parallel analyses predicated on different theories lead to differences in instructional advocacy?

An international multi-disciplinary research team (combining education, cognitive and emotive psychology, learning analytics, and neuroscience perspectives) was recruited to develop analytical frames for coding the data, including analysis of the negotiative foci of student exchange (Chan and Clarke 2017b); sophistication in mathematical student-student exchange (Tran and Chan 2017); dialogic talk between students (Díez-Palomar 2017); student motivating desires (Tuohilampi 2018); and behavioural indicators of student engagement (Chan et al. in press), to name a few. The researchers each constructed distinct data sets according to different theoretical perspectives applied to the same set of video records and other supplementary data. The multitheoretic research design allowed the research team to juxtapose different interpretive accounts reflecting different theoretical positions in order to compare and contrast the capacity of different theories to characterise different aspects of the complex classroom setting; to examine their assumptions and implications, as well as their strengths and limitations.

9.3.3 The International Classroom Lexicon Project (The Lexicon Project)

The International Classroom Lexicon Project set out to document the professional language employed by teachers in ten countries (Australia, Chile, China, the Czech Republic, Finland, France, Germany, Japan, USA and Korea) to describe the phenomena typical of the middle school mathematics classroom. The researchers' interest in the Lexicon Project concerned the actual terms by which teachers in different countries named the objects and phenomena in their respective classrooms (Mesiti and Clarke 2017a). Documentation of the content and structure of classroom-related lexicons in ten countries revealed patterns of connection in the pedagogical terminology employed in each country. Each lexicon also articulated, in performative terms, cultural-historical differences in pedagogy, encrypted in the terms by which classroom phenomena are named and from which each community constructs its instructional practices and its theories of instruction and learning.

Each local research team contributed video material with time-stamped transcripts as well as supporting material related to one lesson of middle school mathematics. These lessons were re-packaged as "three-ups", that is, three camera angles (typically, whole class, teacher, and student videos) with a time-code and subtitles, all visible in one viewing window (see Fig. 9.7).

A stimulus package of lessons, one from each team, was constructed and distributed to each local project team (which included both researchers and experienced teachers) for project-wide use. These lessons presented a variety of classroom

Fig. 9.7 The video "three-up": three camera angles with time-code and subtitles. (Image reproduced from Mesiti and Clarke 2017b, p. 375)

settings and instructional approaches, both familiar and unfamiliar to the research team members in any particular country.

Each team began their examination of the stimulus video material with the prompt "What do you see that you can name?" The classroom videos were intended to stimulate thinking about the possible terms of the lexicon. The essential point was to record single words or short phrases that were familiar, with an agreed meaning, to at least two-thirds of middle school mathematics teachers in each participating country. Operational descriptions were developed for each of the terms (see Fig. 9.8). National surveys were subsequently developed to collect information about teachers' level of familiarity with each of the terms, and the extent to which they endorsed the descriptions, examples and non-examples provided for each term in the lexicon. The goal was to establish that the constituent terms of the lexicon were not only familiar to the teaching community whose classroom phenomena were encoded in the lexicon, but also, that their meaning was represented in a way that teachers were happy to endorse.

9.4 Ontological Grounding in Terms of Researcher Role and Status of the Video in Each Project

When discussing the use of video in classroom research, Clarke and Chan (2019) highlighted that the decision to use video has important methodological and theoretical entailments. Characterising research as a constructive and interpretive

Lexical term	Description	Examples
Assigning Homework	The teacher assigns tasks to be completed outside of the lesson typically within a specified time frame. Assigned tasks vary in nature and may include: • exercises from a textbook; • worksheets; • project work; • tasks involving computer applications; and • finishing off work that was meant to be completed in class.	For example: • Teacher writes the homework on the board and invites students to record it in their diaries. • Teacher makes a verbal statement about homework that needs to be completed. Non-example: • *Assigning work for completion during the lesson.*
Rephrasing	The teacher (or students) expresses an idea or comment in an alternative way usually for purposes of clarification. The comment or statement requiring rephrasing may be her own or a student's.	For example: • Teacher uses her tone and expression to emphasise certain words or phrases in a student's comment. Non-example: • *Repeating a statement word for word.*
Worked Example	The teacher (or student) writes out the steps involved in order to illustrate the type of solution expected to a problem or task with or without student involvement.	For example: • Teacher writes out the solution to a problem on the whiteboard, providing oral explanations and clarifications along the way. Non-example: • *Students recording their solutions at the board.*

Fig. 9.8 A sample of operational definitions developed for terms in the Australian lexicon

process, Clarke and Chan noted that video can be employed as a research tool within a variety of research paradigms. The choice of words that researchers use to describe and report on the research process and resultant accounts (e.g., *see, focus, reflect,* and *represent*) can be an indication of the implicit or explicit assumptions of the researchers about their relationship with the data and with the phenomenon of interest. Clarke and Chan identified these perspectives with the metaphors: window, lens and mirror: *Window* describes the way videos are used in a study to assist researchers to look inside the classroom (see); *lens* describes the way videos are used by researchers to focus on selected aspects of classroom activity (focus); and *mirror* describes the way videos are used to catalyse teacher and student reflection on their own practice (reflect). A further metaphor, *distorting mirror*, describes the way in which video provides a rich data source for data re-construction and re-constitution based on researchers' own values and perspectives (represent). No single project is exclusively to be identified with a single metaphor. However, the metaphors appear to be useful for distinguishing between the different ways in which video material can be used in a research study.

Clarke and Chan (2019) posit that consideration of these metaphors draws attention to some of the ontological and epistemological biases and assumptions implicit in educational research. The current chapter focuses particularly on the ontological grounding in terms of researcher role and the status of the video material, and represents the researchers' ontological options by the three metaphors (window, lens, and mirror). As will be discussed, the role of the researcher and the status of the video material in a study constitute a complex co-determining relationship. The three research projects, previously described, provide illustrative examples for the discussion.

9.4.1 The Ontological Grounding of the Three Metaphors

Each of the window, lens, and mirror metaphors corresponds to a particular ontological position in relation to the role that the video material fulfils within a study. For the window metaphor, the video material represents a reality that is assumed to exist external to the researcher. For the lens metaphor, the video material is a representation of the classroom constructed by the researcher through the orchestration of the research setting and conditions and data selection. The mirror metaphor characterises the way in which video material can be used by some researchers to catalyse reflective responses from participants as a source of data. In such studies, the video material does not serve the function of data, but rather serves as a research tool, similar to an interview protocol, test, or questionnaire, to elicit data from respondents. The use of video for such purposes in a study does not necessarily imply any particular ontological assumption, but accords ontological authority to the accounts which it is the role of the video to stimulate. Depending on the intended use of the participants' reflective responses in the study, the responses can be treated as a co-constructed reality for the participants and the researcher or a reality separate from the researcher. Each of these metaphors and associated ontological assumptions suggest different relationships between the researcher and the video material, and differences in the role that the researcher and the video material each plays within a study.

9.5 The Co-determining Nature of the Role of the Researcher and the Status of the Video Material

Rather than assuming that the researcher has full control and freedom to determine the status of the video material within a research study, we argue that the nature of the role of the researcher and the status of the video material within a study is to a certain extent co-determined. The researcher frames through the study design the purpose for which the video material is to be used in the study, which in turn determines the possible roles that the researcher can play in the study. For example, if the researcher collects video data to test a certain hypothesis, where the video is used as evidence for or evidence against a specific hypothesis, the video material is framed in a way that gives it innate veracity, appealing to its own intrinsic truth and authority to affirm or contest a proposition. Such ontological positioning has methodological entailments. If the video is accorded 'factual' status, providing access to a reality that is external to the researcher, then the researcher is obliged to minimise his or her role in distorting that reality, possibly leading to methodological adjustments.

On the other hand, if the researcher assumes the role of a 'film director' or a 'portrait photographer' and plays an active role in constructing the conditions in which the phenomenon of interest is to be recorded, then the resulting video is seen not as a window into reality but as an artefact of the research; representing a filtered and partial version of reality. The observation "all photographs are accurate; none of them is the truth", according to renowned portrait photographer Richard Avedon (Brown 2002), captures the paradoxical nature of video as research evidence. In such situations, where the researcher exercises significant control over the research setting and the manner in which it is recorded, the researcher is obliged to justify explicitly his or her decisions in constructing the research conditions and to present a theoretically coherent rationale. The status of the video material and the role of the researcher are therefore intertwined, since the form and function accorded to the video material within any research project will reflect the extent to which the researcher orchestrated both what was recorded on video and the type of analysis to which this video material was subjected.

9.6 The Role of the Researcher and the Status of the Video Material in the Three Projects

The three research projects (i.e., the LPS, the Social Unit of Learning project, and the Lexicon Project) can be contrasted in terms of the ontological grounding of their research designs and the role that the researcher and the video material each plays within the study.

In the LPS, the aim of the project was to document classroom practice in different classrooms in multiple countries. The LPS project design appealed to a naturalistic research paradigm, analogous to ethnographic approaches, in which the goal is the detailed documentation of community practices and normative activities undisturbed by the presence of the researcher. Video served as a window for researchers to see into the classrooms participating in the project (Clarke and Chan 2019). The research team acted as observers looking into these classrooms, and the video material gave access to a form of 'classroom reality' external to the research team. The classroom videos were seen as providing a factual record of that classroom reality. The many research reports (including five books), generated by LPS team members from all participating countries, addressed the challenge of describing the practices of those classrooms studied around the world and of identifying both distinctive features of each classroom but also common event types that might serve as vehicles for comparison between classrooms. "Lesson events" such as "Beginning the Lesson," "Between Desks Instruction" (what the Japanese call "Kikan-Shido"), "Student at the Front" and "Matome" (the Japanese term for summative discussion) were described and analysed in detail by Clarke et al. (2006a). Extensive investigation of Kikan-Shido in the video records of 150 lessons in 15 eighth-grade mathematics classrooms located in Australia (Melbourne), China (Hong Kong and Shanghai), Japan (Tokyo), and the USA (San Diego) led to the documentation of individual teachers' deployment of Kikan-Shido and the identification of 15 distinct purposes for which teachers in the various countries carried out Kikan-Shido in their classrooms (O'Keefe et al. 2006).

The LPS research design sought to enhance the power of in-depth case studies through comparison of classrooms in a variety of cultural settings. In designing the study, the research team had to ensure the 'cleanliness' and 'clarity' of the window (video) by minimising the possible distorting impact of their intrusion on the activities of the participants. This was achieved by allowing the teacher and students a familiarisation period of at least two to three lessons in which to become accustomed to the presence of the researchers and the video equipment in the classroom. Filming for the purpose of data generation commenced only once the teacher confirmed that the activities of the classroom approximated normality. In terms of the window metaphor, this was interpreted as indicating that normal classroom practice could be seen through the window of the video with minimal distortion and optimal clarity.

In the case of the Social Unit of Learning project, the project design can be seen as more akin to design experiments (Cobb et al. 2003), which involve "both 'engineering' particular forms of learning and systematically studying those forms of learning within the context defined by the means of supporting them" (p. 9). The main research design feature of the project was the use of the SLRC for observing and recording student-student and teacher-student interactions. The agency of the researchers in implementing the research design and in determining the data generated was acknowledged explicitly by the researchers, who reported that the research use of the SLRC facility "necessitates decisions concerning what to constrain and what to emulate within the laboratory classroom setting" (Chan and Clarke 2019). For example, the researchers determined the problem solving tasks with which the students were to engage and the social units (individual, pair, or, small group) through which the tasks were to be completed by the students. The research team exploited the control afforded by the laboratory classroom to optimise student positioning in order to generate comprehensive high-resolution audio-visual recording of student collaborative activity. Like a film director, the research team had extensive control over the video camera angle and focus, as well as over the supplementary data to be collected (e.g., student written work and pre- and post-lesson teacher interviews).

Given the extensive and detailed multimodal data generated from the laboratory classroom, the researchers had to be selective in their choice of data to be analysed, similarly to the way a camera lens works in terms of zooming in or out to adjust the focus of the analysis. The video material in the Social Unit of Learning project was accorded the status of a constructed artefact resulting from the conditions purposefully orchestrated by the researcher. Through prescribing the types of tasks being carried out by intact classes of students with their teacher and varying the social unit of the activities, the project intended to provide a greater understanding of the learning ecology (cf. Cobb et al. 2003, p. 9) of mathematics classrooms focusing on the social nature of the classroom setting. The project was designed specifically to serve the purpose of theory generation and testing through the application of a multitheoretic research design, taking advantage of the extensive data that can be generated by the laboratory classroom facility.

The principal purpose of the Lexicon Project (Mesiti and Clarke 2017b) was the construction of national lexicons representing the professional vocabulary familiar to and employed by each teacher in each country. Each such lexicon documented the actual terms by which teachers name the phenomena of the mathematics classroom. A striking feature of the Lexicon Project was the use of a stimulus package of video-recorded lessons as a key catalyst for data generation. The primary purpose of the video material was to stimulate thinking about candidate terms for the lexicon and it was these candidate terms (and not the video) that operated as data in the project. There was neither prescription nor restriction (either of content or of pedagogy) as to which lesson of middle school mathematics was recorded in each community and the researchers in each country were free to choose the school and the teacher for the recording. It was agreed, however, that capturing a variety of classroom situations and instructional approaches would facilitate the production of a diversity of candidate lexical terms. In other words, the resulting kaleidoscope of classroom situations, given the variety of international communities involved in the project, would benefit the research team in two ways:

1. The package of stimulus video material would be more extensive and therefore function more effectively as stimulus material; and
2. The initial production of lexical terms would be more likely to simulate respondent recollection or recognition of additional and related terms.

As the primary aim of the project was to record the professional vocabulary of the teaching community in each participating country, video illustrations of each term were useful, but did not serve as a condition to determine the inclusion of a term in a lexicon. Composite operational descriptions were developed for the resulting lexical items and these were subjected to a variety of local and national validation procedures. Researchers in each country sought to determine whether the lexicon was a reasonable reflection of the professional vocabulary of the community of teachers in that country.

A close parallel to the methodology employed in the Lexicon Project is what Kelly (1955) called the "projective approach" to clinical interview in which self-reflective statements were elicited from respondents using photographic images as stimulus. The role of the researcher in this case is to provide the stimulus to catalyse the interviewee's reflection and to sort and organise those reflections. The researcher can be seen as a biographer or historian who collects memories from people and organises them into a coherent narrative, constructing some aspects of the life of interviewees. However, unlike biographical or historical accounts, in the Lexicon Project, the lexicon was not structured purely by chronology, but was intended to reflect connections or associations made by the community from whose responses the lexicon was constructed.

In summary, the three research projects (i.e., the LPS, the Social Unit of Learning project, and the Lexicon Project) offer examples of different uses of video in research studies. The projects can be contrasted in terms of the ontological grounding of their research designs and the role that the researcher and the video material each plays within the study. Illustrative of the window metaphor, the classroom videos were accorded the status of factual record within the LPS, giving researchers access to a form of 'classroom reality'. The research team acted as observers looking into the classrooms through the video material to identify distinct cultural features of different classrooms. In the Social Unit of Learning project, the role that the research team played was analogous to that of a film director in the orchestration of the research condition and setting and in the data selection. As a constructed artefact, the video material served as a lens for the purpose of theory generation and testing. In the Lexicon Project, the video material was used as a probing tool for eliciting participant reflective responses. Pedagogical terms were elicited from the teaching community by consideration of the video material. It was the role of the project team to organise and structure these pedagogical terms in a way that reflected connections and meanings held by that community. As a total construction, the resulting lexicon was a structured array of locally meaningful terms that could be compared to the account of an individual's life and circumstances constructed by an experienced biographer.

The assigned role of the video in each of the three studies determined the relationship that the researchers have with the data, and the function and form of reality that the video represented.

9.7 Implications

In this chapter, we identify ontological contingencies relevant to video-based research studies through examining the relationship between researcher and video material and, by association, the role between researcher and data. Video has the seductive appeal of a surrogate reality and the video record should not be confused in a research design with the events and situations it was intended to reproduce. Explicating the role of the researcher and the status of the video material within a study and the ontological contingencies implicit in the research design can help researchers to make informed decisions in the research process, from research design and data analysis, through to reporting. An awareness of the ontological contingences relevant to video-based educational research (and any research study), allows practitioners, policymakers, and other stakeholders to read research reports in a critical way, with an understanding of the limits and the validity of the claims provided in such reports.

We have identified key issues that determine the ontological status of the video material. These issues concern the role played by the researcher as the agentic constructor of the video material, and the question of whether authority is accorded to the video material as being in some way representative of a reality that exists independently of the researcher. In projects where the researcher has actively manipulated the research setting and process of data generation, the resultant video material is less able to be treated as representative of an objective and independent reality being studied by the researcher. A complex social setting such as the classroom has idiosyncratic features that limit the generalisability of the phenomena found in any particular classroom to other classrooms. The appeal in the LPS project to the naturalistic research paradigm stands in contrast to the use of the experimental approach in the Social Unit of Learning project. In each case, the authority for extrapolating findings to other situations or other individuals is differently warranted, and it is our assertion that the warrant to extrapolate or generalise from the study of one classroom setting to another depends critically on both the role of the researcher and the status of the video material, which we have argued are co-determining. In the Lexicon Project, the video material did not have a status as data but was employed as a catalytic research tool intended to elicit useful responses from participant teachers. The research team elicits from different teaching communities detail about their perception of their world, their practices, their values, and their beliefs, and organise them into a coherent narrative to understand the connections and meanings held by different communities. These three projects each illustrates a different relationship that the research team has with the video data. It is our intention to inform the practices of video-based research in education through foregrounding these different possible ways in which video can be used in a study together with the associated ontological assumptions.

The three illustrative cases of how videos are being used in research projects offer prototypes of the relationship between researcher and video that some researchers may find relevant to their research goals. Recognition of the co-determining relationship between researcher and video, and awareness of the metaphors that may characterise the roles of the video material in a research study, make clear that variations in the researcher's role find their echo in differences in the status of the video material as data. This relationship of reciprocal dependence between the role of the researcher and the ontological status of the video material must be taken into account during the process of research design. In short, changing the status of the video material in a research study (e.g., between documented reality and constructed representation) changes the role that the researcher plays, and vice versa.

We argue that researchers, when designing a research study employing video, need to make conscious decisions regarding the role that they themselves play and that of the associated video material. Each such decision needs to attend to considerations such as the research question(s), the phenomenon of interest, and the intended generalisability of the findings. This chapter illustrates the different roles that video material can play within a study. Before deciding to employ video as a research tool in classroom research, researchers can ask the following question: Are we going to treat what is captured in the video as a representation of classroom reality, a representation of a contrived classroom situation, or a form of stimulus intended to elicit further data?

The researcher's answer to this question will determine whether the researcher decides to exert influence on the research setting, which will in turn affect how the research findings can be reported. Careful ontological examination is needed before claims and recommendations can be made about particular classroom practices. Such ontological examination places limits on the generalisability of findings drawn from video data.

We also hope that readers of research (whether researchers, practitioners, policy makers, or other stakeholders) will be led to ask themselves which metaphor is being employed in the study reported or being read, and what are the implications for the readers' interpretation of the study findings and their application of those findings to settings of significance to them. As raised by Clarke and Chan (2019), it is not our intention to privilege one metaphorical alternative over another. Each metaphor has its domain of applicability consistent with the research design for which it has been recruited. There is a need to acknowledge such recruitment as the consequence of a choice by the researcher. The complicity of readers in interpreting research reports also must be acknowledged. Through this chapter, we hope to make different ontological contingencies visible in order to inform the practice, reporting, and interpretation of video-based research in education.

References

Amidon, E. J., & Hough, J. B. (1967). *Interaction analysis: Theory, research, and application*. Reading, MA: Addison-Wesley Publishing Company.

Beeby, T., Burkhardt, H., & Fraser, R. (1979). *Systematic classroom analysis notation*. Nottingham, England: Shell Centre for Mathematics Education.

Bourke, S. F. (1984). *The teaching and learning of mathematics: National report of the second phase of the IEA Classroom Environment Study*. ACER research monograph no. 25. Hawthorn, Victoria: Australian Council for Educational Research.

Brown, J. (2002). An Avedon portrait. *The NewsHour with Jim Lehrer* [Television news coverage]. United States: Public Broadcasting Service.

Chan, M. C. E., & Clarke, D. J. (2017a). Learning research in a laboratory classroom: Complementarity and commensurability in juxtaposing multiple interpretive accounts. In T. Dooley & G. Gueudet (Eds.), *Proceedings of the Congress of European Research in Mathematics Education*, Dublin, Ireland (pp. 2713–2720).

Chan, M. C. E., & Clarke, D. J. (2017b). Structured affordances in the use of open-ended tasks to facilitate collaborative problem solving. *ZDM-The International Journal on Mathematics Education, 49*, 951–963. https://doi.org/10.1007/s11858-017-0876-2.

Chan, M. C. E., & Clarke, D. J. (2019). Video-based research in a laboratory classroom. In L. Xu, G. Aranda, W. Widjaja & D. Clarke (Eds.), *Video-based research in education: Cross-disciplinary perspectives* (pp. 107–123). New York: Routledge.

Chan, M. C. E., Clarke, D. J., & Cao, Y. (2017). The social essentials of learning: An experimental investigation of collaborative problem solving and knowledge construction in mathematics classrooms in Australia and China. *Mathematics Education Research Journal, 30*(1), 39–50. https://doi.org/10.1007/s13394-017-0209-3.

Chan, M. C. E., Ochoa, X., & Clarke, D. J. (in press). Multimodal learning analytics in a laboratory classroom. In M. Virvou, E. Alepis, G. A. Tsihrintzis, & L. C. Jain (Eds.), *Advances in learning analytics*. Cham, Switzerland: Springer.

Clarke, D. J. (Ed.). (2001). *Perspectives on practice and meaning in mathematics and science classrooms*. Dordrecht, The Netherlands: Kluwer Academic Publishers.

Clarke, D. J. (2006). The LPS research design. In D. J. Clarke, C. Keitel, & Y. Shimizu (Eds.), *Mathematics classrooms in twelve countries: The insider's perspective* (pp. 15–36). Rotterdam, The Netherlands: Sense Publishers.

Clarke, D. J., & Chan, M. C. E. (2019). The use of video in classroom research: Window, lens or mirror. In L. Xu, G. Aranda, W. Widjaja & D. Clarke (Eds.), *Video-based research in education: Cross-disciplinary perspectives* (pp. 5–18). New York: Routledge.

Clarke, D. J., Emanuelsson, J., Jablonka, E., & Mok, I. A. C. (Eds.). (2006a). *Making connections: Comparing mathematics classrooms around the world*. Rotterdam, The Netherlands: Sense Publishers.

Clarke, D. J., Keitel, C., & Shimizu, Y. (Eds.). (2006b). *Mathematics classrooms in twelve countries: The insider's perspective*. Rotterdam, The Netherlands: Sense Publishers.

Clarke, D. J., Mesiti, C., Jablonka, E., & Shimizu, Y. (2006c). Addressing the challenge of legitimate international comparisons: Lesson structure in the USA, Germany and Japan. In D. J. Clarke, J. Emanuelsson, E. Jablonka, & I. A. C. Mok (Eds.), *Making connections: Comparing mathematics classrooms around the world* (pp. 23–45). Rotterdam, The Netherlands: Sense Publishers.

Clarke, D. J., Xu, L. H., Arnold, J., Seah, L. H., Hart, C., Tytler, R., & Prain, V. (2012). Multi-theoretic approaches to understanding the science classroom. In C. Bruguière, A. Tiberghien, & P. Clément (Eds.), *E-Book Proceedings of the ESERA 2011 Biennial Conference: Part 3* (pp. 26–40). Lyon, France: European Science Education Research Association.

Cobb, P., & Bauersfeld, H. (1995). *The emergence of mathematical meaning: Interaction in classroom cultures*. Hillsdale, NJ: L. Erlbaum Associates.

Cobb, P., Confrey, J., diSessa, A., Lehrer, R., & Schauble, L. (2003). Design experiments in educational research. *Educational Researcher, 32*(1), 9–13.

Díez-Palomar, J. (2017). Analyzing dialogic talk during mathematics problem solving in small groups. In B. Kaur, W. K. Ho, T. L. Toh, & B. H. Choy (Eds.), *Proceedings of the 41st Annual Meeting of the International Group for the Psychology of Mathematics Education* (Vol. 2, pp. 281–288). Singapore: PME.

Erlwanger, S. H. (1975). Case studies of children's conceptions of mathematics. *Journal of Children's Mathematical Behaviour, 1*(3), 157–283.

Givvin, K. B., Hiebert, J., Jacobs, J. K., Hollingsworth, H., & Gallimore, R. (2005). Are there national patterns of teaching? Evidence from the TIMSS 1999 video study. *Comparative Education Review, 49*, 311–343.

Good, T. L., & Grouws, D. A. (1977). Teaching effects: A process-product study in fourth-grade mathematics classrooms. *Journal of Teacher Education, 28*(3), 49–54. https://doi.org/10.1177/002248717702800310.

Hiebert, J., Gallimore, R., Garnier, H., Givvin, K. B., Hollingsworth, H., Jacobs, J., et al. (2003). *Teaching mathematics in seven countries: Results from the TIMSS 1999 video study* (NCES 2003–013 Revised). Washington, DC: U.S. Department of Education, National Center for Education Statistics. Retrieved from http://nces.ed.gov/pubsearch/pubsinfo.asp?pubid=2003013.

Kelly, G. (1955). *The psychology of personal constructs*. New York: Norton.

Mesiti, C., & Clarke, D. (2017a). The international lexicon project: Giving a name to what we do. In R. Seah, M. Horne, J. Ocean, & C. Orellana (Eds.), *Proceedings of the Mathematical Association of Victoria annual conference, Brunswick, Australia* (pp. 31–38).

Mesiti, C., & Clarke, D. (2017b). Structure in the professional vocabulary of middle school mathematics teachers in Australia. In A. Downton, S. Livy, & J. Hall (Eds.), *Proceedings of the conference of the Mathematics Education Research Group of Australasia, Melbourne, Victoria, Australia* (pp. 373–380).

Neuman, W. L. (2014). *Social research methods: Qualitative and quantitative approaches* (7th ed.). Essex, England: Pearson Education Limited.

O'Keefe, C., Xu, L. H., & Clarke, D. J. (2006). Kikan-Shido: Between desks instruction. In D. J. Clarke, J. Emanuelsson, E. Jablonka, & I. A. C. Mok (Eds.), *Making connections: Comparing mathematics classrooms around the world* (pp. 73–106). Rotterdam, The Netherlands: Sense Publishers.

Prediger, S., Bikner-Ahsbahs, A., & Arzarello, F. (2008). Networking strategies and methods for connecting theoretical approaches: First steps towards a conceptual framework. *ZDM-The International Journal on Mathematics Education, 40*(2), 165–178. https://doi.org/10.1007/s11858-008-0086-z.

Schirmer, B. R., Lockman, A. S., & Schirmer, T. N. (2016). Identifying evidence-based educational practices: Which research designs provide findings that can influence social change? *Journal of Educational Research and Practice, 6*(1), 33–42.

Simpson, A. (2017). The misdirection of public policy: Comparing and combining standardised effect sizes. *Journal of Education Policy, 32*(4), 450–466. https://doi.org/10.1080/02680939.2017.1280183.

Stigler, J. W., & Hiebert, J. (1999). *The teaching gap: Best ideas from the world's teachers for improving education in the classroom*. New York: Free Press.

Tran, D., & Chan, M. C. E. (2017). Examining mathematical sophistications in collaborative problem solving. In B. Kaur, W. K. Ho, T. L. Toh, & B. H. Choy (Eds.), *Proceedings of the 41st Annual Meeting of the International Group for the Psychology of Mathematics Education* (Vol. 4, pp. 281–288). Singapore: PME.

Tuohilampi, L. (2018). Analyzing engagement in mathematical collaboration: What can we say with confidence? In E. Bergqvist, M. Österholm, C. Granberg, & L. Sumpter (Eds.), *Proceedings of the 42nd Annual Meeting of the International Group for the Psychology of Mathematics Education* (Vol. 1, pp. 235–242). Umeå, Sweden: PME.

Open Access This chapter is licensed under the terms of the Creative Commons Attribution 4.0 International License (http://creativecommons.org/licenses/by/4.0/), which permits use, sharing, adaptation, distribution and reproduction in any medium or format, as long as you give appropriate credit to the original author(s) and the source, provide a link to the Creative Commons license and indicate if changes were made.

The images or other third party material in this chapter are included in the chapter's Creative Commons license, unless indicated otherwise in a credit line to the material. If material is not included in the chapter's Creative Commons license and your intended use is not permitted by statutory regulation or exceeds the permitted use, you will need to obtain permission directly from the copyright holder.

Part II
Important Mathematics Educational Themes

Part II
Important Bibliometrics Educational Themes

Chapter 10
Approaching Proof in the Classroom Through the Logic of Inquiry

Ferdinando Arzarello and Carlotta Soldano

Abstract The paper analyses a basic gap, highlighted by most of the literature concerning the teaching of proofs, namely, the distance between students' argumentative and proving processes. The analysis is developed from both epistemological and cognitive standpoints: it critiques the Toulmin model of reasoning and introduces a new model, the Logic of Inquiry of Hintikka, more suitable for bridging this gap. An example of didactical activity within Dynamic Geometry Environments is sketched in order to present a concrete illustration of this approach and to show the pedagogical effectiveness of the model.

Keywords Proof · Logic of inquiry · Argumentation · Dynamic geometry environments

10.1 Introduction

In their wonderful book *Anschauliche Geometrie*, Hilbert and Cohn-Vossen (1932) wrote[1]:

> In mathematics, as in all scientific research, we find two tendencies: the tendency to abstraction—it seeks to work out (herauszuarbeiten) the *logical* points of view from the manifold material and bring this into systematic connection—and the other tendency, that

---

[1]In der Mathematik wie in aller wissenschaftlichen Forschung treffen wir zweierlei Tendenzen an: die Tendenz zur Abstraktion—sie sucht die *logischen* Gesichtspunkte aus dem vielfältigen Material herauszuarbeiten und dieses in systematischen Zusammenhang zu bringen—und die andere Tendenz, die der Anschaulichkeit, die vielmehr auf ein lebendiges Erfassen der Gegenstände und ihre *inhaltlichen* Beziehungen ausgeht.

F. Arzarello (✉)
Dipartimento di Matematica "Giuseppe Peano", Università di Torino, Turin, Italy
e-mail: ferdinando.arzarello@unito.it

C. Soldano
Dipartimento di Filosofia e Scienze dell'educazione, Università di Torino, Turin, Italy
e-mail: carlotta.soldano@unito.com

© The Author(s) 2019
G. Kaiser and N. Presmeg (eds.), *Compendium for Early Career Researchers in Mathematics Education*, ICME-13 Monographs,
https://doi.org/10.1007/978-3-030-15636-7_10

of intuitive understanding (Anschaulichkeit), which rather gets (ausgeht) the object and its *substantive* relationships from a living grasping. (p. XVII: translation of the authors).

These two aspects of mathematics are also crucial for its teaching and present a basic problem: how to suitably cultivate both aspects in the classroom? And more specifically, which roles should mathematical proofs and intuitive argumentations have in its teaching-learning activities?

This is an old controversial issue (e.g., see Fawcett 1938), and, from terminology to more *substantial* content, things appear very *mazy* in the literature. For example, in the most recent Compendium, the chapter dedicated to research on the teaching and learning of proofs (Stylianides et al. 2017), the authors report "the lack of consensus about what proof means in mathematics education research" (p. 238). However, the meaning of proof is not uniform, on the contrary there is a large consensus about the fact that an unattainable barrier seems to exist, which makes it difficult for students (and sometimes also for teachers: see *Key findings* by Stylianides et al. 2017, pp. 245–246) to grasp the formal aspects of proofs.

Teaching proofs seems to require that students (and teachers) acquire a new, not 'natural' basis for their beliefs. It is the same general notion of *formal reasoning* that creates this wall and inhibits understanding. An example is given by the following test, taken from the book by Lolli (2005), submitted to students (at secondary and university level) and also to teachers, which always gives the same results. Three syllogisms A, B, C are given one at a time (see Table 10.1) and people are asked each time to judge if they are correct or not:

Try it yourself before continuing!

A very high percentage of participants give different answers to them: generally, people judge A as correct, B as incorrect and both judgments are made at once. A lower percentage say that C is incorrect, but after some time (some after having checked with the Euler–Venn diagrams); in this case, there is also a considerable number of not-answers. However, A, B, C are instantiations of the same (incorrect) syllogism! This performance represents a typical obstacle that students must overcome in their attempt to grasp formal reasoning at a very basic level: possibly, some of the pitfalls recorded in the literature, such as the incapability of students and teachers to distinguish between proofs and invalid arguments (see Stylianides et al. 2017, pp. 242–243; Selden and Selden 2003), have a common basic cognitive root, which can be active in different (negative) ways according to the context, the representation of the situation, etc.; also the corresponding formal statements do not provide enough support for subjects' understanding. We call it the *basic gap* between (formal) proofs and (intuitive) arguments: whatever definition of proof is

Table 10.1 Examples of syllogism

A	B	C
No right-angled triangle is equilateral;	No dog is a ruminant	No S is M
Some isosceles triangles are equilateral;	Some quadrupeds are ruminants	Some P are M
Therefore, some right-angled triangles are not isosceles	Therefore, some dogs are not quadrupeds	Therefore, some S are not P

given, even the most open and inclusive, the basic gap is behind it and can make any approach to the proof in the classroom problematic. A general pedagogical consequence is that "the place of proof in typical K–12 school mathematics classroom practice [...] is marginal" (Stylianides et al. 2017, p. 251).

For this reason, we think that deepening the analysis of the basic gap is the primary goal of any study focused on the teaching/learning of proof.

In next sections we approach the basic gap from two points of view:

- cognitive: considering some pieces of research that introduce the notion of cognitive (dis-) continuity between argumentation and proof and picture the basic gap as it can arise in the classroom;
- epistemic: considering the logic of inquiry (LI) in the sense of J. Hintikka, which in a sense reverses the ways deductive concatenations are developed according to the logical rules of reasoning.

Then we illustrate an example of didactic activity, developed jointly by Arzarello and Soldano for her Ph.D. work (Soldano 2017), based on LI and aimed at reducing the basic gap in the classroom through appropriate didactic engineering within a technological environment.

The chapter concludes showing that sometimes the discontinuity thesis is based on a series of misunderstandings about what is to be assumed as proving activity. On the contrary, the two aspects (arguments and proofs) can be integrated with each other at a certain grade from both an epistemic and a cognitive point of view.

10.2 Argumentations and Proofs: Education to Rationality as a Learning Goal in Secondary School

As we observed in the introduction, the literature pertaining to the teaching and learning of proofs often highlights a tension, not to say a contrast, between the formal aspects of proofs, subject to precise logical and textual rules, on the one hand, and the more informal arguments, on the other, which on their side may correspond to creative problem solving processes and to the understanding of mathematical concepts within the classroom horizon of knowledge. The latter do not always appear easily reducible or able to be integrated coherently with the former. The concrete result of these difficulties is that, simplifying a little, we find two opposing positions on the problem of the relationship between proofs and argumentation in both epistemological and educational research.

From the epistemic side,[2] they are outlined by Hintikka (1999), to whose contributions we shall return:

---

[2]In general, we use the adjective 'epistemological' to indicate the knowledge of the methods of the sciences and of the principles according to which science constructs itself; instead we use the

> The main currently unsolved problem in the theory of argumentation concerns the function of logic in argumentation and reasoning. The traditional view simply identified logic with the theory of reasoning. This view is still being echoed in older textbooks of formal logic. In a different variant, the same view is even codified in the ordinary usage of words such as 'logic', 'deduction', 'inference', etc. For each actual occurrence of these terms in textbooks of formal logic, there are hundreds of uses of the same idioms to describe the feats of real or fictional detectives. [...]
>
> Needless to say, this traditional conception of logic and deduction has been rejected with a rare unanimity by recent theorists of human reasoning and argumentation. It is widely assumed that the truths of formal logic are mere tautologies or analytical truths without substantial content and hence incapable of sustaining any inferences leading to new and even surprising discoveries, as the detections of sleuths like Sherlock Holmes or Nero Wolfe were supposed to lead. (p. 25)

From the educational side, we also find two possible approaches. Some studies illustrate a substantial didactical discontinuity between argumentations and proofs, highlighting a jump between the two (which we have called the *basic gap*). Some scholars highlight a form of *cognitive* discontinuity between them; others highlight an *epistemic* discontinuity between the respective statuses of knowledge; often the two forms of discontinuity are both stressed in the same research. In any case, all of them say that it is very difficult to find an effective way of teaching and learning of proofs in the classroom. As examples, see the research studies touched upon in their chapter in the Compendium by Stylianides et al. (2017), and others, like those of Balacheff (1987), Duval (1991), and Thompson et al. (2012). However, in the panorama of the didactic research on proof, we also find opposite positions. The studies by Boero et al. (1996), Garuti et al. (1996, 1998), Mariotti (2006), Pedemonte (2007), Baccaglini-Frank and Mariotti (2010) and others (see for example the discussion and the related bibliography in the papers by Boero et al. 2010; Guala and Boero 2017) highlight the possibility of forms of cognitive continuity between the construction of a conjecture and the construction of the proof, which they call *cognitive unity*:

> During a problem-solving process, an argumentation activity is usually developed to produce a conjecture. The hypothesis of cognitive unity is that in some cases this argumentation can be used by the student in the construction of proof by organising in a logical chain some of the previously produced arguments. (Pedemonte 2007, p. 24)

The studies mentioned above show that proof is more 'accessible' to students if an argumentation activity is developed for the construction of a conjecture and, conversely, the construction of proof is more difficult if such a cognitive unity is not achieved.

---

adjective 'epistemic' to indicate the programs of scientific investigation, and the related theories, pursued and implemented by different schools and authors. In other words, 'epistemological' refers to the subject who studies epistemic matters, whereas 'epistemic' merely refers to knowledge, justification and belief. The distinction between 'ontics' and 'ontology' is proper to the Continental philosophy (contrasted with the Analytical one); the difference was discussed by Heidegger (1927): ontic is what makes something what it is; while ontological refers to one's own first-person, subjective, phenomenological experience of being.

Other research shows that the Dynamic Geometry Environments, DGE, (e.g. Cabri Géomètre, Geogebra, Sketchpad, etc.) can support forms of cognitive continuity, at least in the case of elementary geometry (Arzarello et al. 2012: see the discussion about abductions in the final section).

In any case, the pedagogical problem of how to teach/learn proof at school is still open, provided that it is a teaching goal in the school (e.g. it is so in the Italian Licei[3]). It requires the taking of a position with respect to the previous dilemmas (be they epistemic, cognitive, or both) on the value of the logical deductions with respect to argumentations.

10.3 The Theoretical Basis of Our Proposal

In the chapter we continually use the terms argumentation and proof. Clarifying their meaning and mutual relationships for learning purposes is among the objectives of this contribution. To orient the reader, we give now two definitions and will discuss the reasons why we have chosen this formulation.

Following Toulmin (1958, 1974), Toulmin et al. (1984), we use the term argumentation (or reasoning) to refer to a text made of one or more concatenated argumentative steps. An argumentative step is identifiable through the presence of a Fact, a Claim and a Warrant that justifies the validity (possibly with a certain degree of probability) of the Claim, because of the Fact (Fig. 10.1).

The Warrant can explicitly or implicitly refer to a set of knowledge, principles, etc. possibly organized in the system (Backing) on which the Warrant is based. Sometimes in the argumentation there are exceptions (Rebuttal) according to which the Claim does not follow from the data under the Warrant. Figure 10.2 exemplifies this situation.

For the notion of proof, we instead refer to Rav (1999): "Proofs are the mathematician's way to *display the mathematical machinery* for solving problems and to *justify* that a proposed solution to a problem is indeed a solution" (p. 13).

It should be noted that often in the literature and in the practice of teaching some people tend to identify proofs with derivations (purely syntactic objects); but a proof is never reducible to this specific aspect only (see Rav 1999, p. 12 and the comments on the so called DTP model, definition-theorem-proof, by Thurston 1994).

To deepen the analysis on the theme continuity-discontinuity between arguments and proofs we refer to two theoretical models. First of all, we consider Toulmin's

---

[3]The Italian curriculum identifies five main learning areas, one of which is the logical-argumentative one. Its main competencies are described as follows: "Knowing how to support one's own thesis and how to listen and critically evaluate the arguments of others. Acquiring the habit of reasoning with logical rigor, of identifying problems and their possible solutions. Being able to read and to critically interpret the contents of different forms of communication."

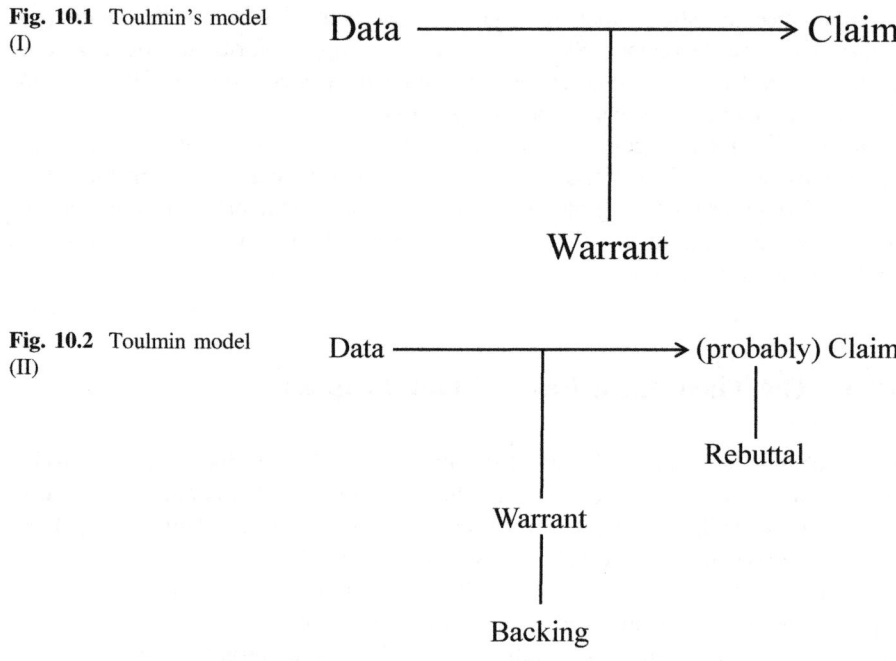

Fig. 10.1 Toulmin's model (I)

Fig. 10.2 Toulmin model (II)

model, sketched above, since it is widely used in mathematics education research (for example, by Boero et al. 1996, 2010; Boero 2011, and by Knipping and Reid 2015). Its critical analysis from an epistemic point of view led us to consider another model: the Logic of Inquiry by Hintikka (logician). For space reasons, we cannot introduce a third important model, which is due to an adaptation (Boero and Planas 2014; Guala and Boero 2017) of the construct of rationality by Habermas (we invite readers with an interest in the discursive practices related to proofs to consult these references).

10.3.1 The Model of Stephen E. Toulmin

We have already introduced the Toulmin model for our definition of argumentation. He calls his model "substantial" and "practical" in opposition to the "analytical" and "theoretical" character of the syllogism, which for him fully represents logical deduction.

For Toulmin, an argumentation makes sense only if it is contextualized: the English scholar typically thinks of it as a discourse that takes place between two people, in disagreement about the proposed statement; in this way, one of them disputes the Claim, and the other, who made the initial affirmation, tries to justify it by giving increasing Warrants with their Backings. The model is inspired by legal practice and this is the reason why Toulmin calls it jurisprudential (Toulmin 1958, pp. 41–43): in fact, the five components of the arguments assume their full meaning in a debate that takes place in a courtroom during the discussion of a specific legal case. The goal is to convince the adversary, not the search/explanation of the truth, which is instead the goal of scientific argument, in particular in mathematics. The full meaning of the Toulmin model is therefore constituted by the intertwining of the two components:

(a) the structure (Claim-Fact-Warrant-Backing-Rebuttal)
(b) the context in which the argument takes place.

The structure of part (a) makes sense only if modeled by the dynamic process of part (b) and its elements are seen according to this perspective (Zarębski 2009).

Unfortunately, most of the literature that uses Toulmin's model in mathematical education somewhat neglects the analysis of the relationships between the two components (a) and (b). This is not by chance. A first reason is that the jurisprudential model is quite different from that of scientific investigation, mathematics in particular: the distinction between Warrant and Backing is important in the jurisprudential model but it does not appear to fit so well with the mathematical field. Toulmin (1975) illustrated "how the sort of backing called for by our arguments varies from one field of argument to another" (p. 97). For example, the three different warrants 'A whale will be a mammal', 'A Bermudan will be a Briton', 'A Saudi Arab will be a Muslim' rely on different backings: the first warrant is supported by referring it to a taxonomic classification system, the second by referring to the rules governing the nationality of British colonies (at the time when Toulmin wrote), and the third to the statistics recording the distribution of religious faiths among people of different nationalities. The relative backings therefore refer to texts of Zoology, to the English laws in effect in a certain year, to statistical data collected following certain protocols.

A second reason is that the model in all the exemplifications refers exclusively to the forms of syllogistic reasoning as an example of analytical reasoning: this is a very serious limitation of its use in the analysis of mathematical reasoning, which, as it is known, cannot be reduced to syllogisms alone (Börger et al. 1997). This has important consequences for the structure of mathematical and scientific arguments in general, as we now illustrate with an example.

It is well known that in mathematics we have many sentences like "for all x, there exists a y such that...". ($\forall\exists$-form). A typical example is the continuity of a function at a point. Let's consider the function $f(x) = x^2$ and suppose we want to show that it is continuous in $x_0 = 1$. To show this to her/his students, a teacher can imagine two opponents, the first (C) supporting the truth of the statement, and the antagonist (A) denying it.[4] The scenario shows students that it is impossible for A to be right: in fact even if A chooses a very small ε, say $\varepsilon = 0.001$, C can

---

[4]It is something similar to the spirit of the jurisprudential model, even if this aspect curiously does not appear in the mathematical education texts that refer to this model.

consequently find an appropriate δ, say $\delta = 0.0001$, which satisfies the required inequality.

Of course, we can ask what the Warrant of this argumentation is, which consists of a process of generalization from the generic example given by the pair $(\varepsilon_0, \delta_0)$, where ε_0, δ_0 are the data, to the General Warrant that supports the Claim, possibly basing the warrant on some definitions and Analysis theorems (Backing). However, the crucial step in this dynamic reasoning consists in grasping and possibly making explicit in the discourse the functional dependence of δ on ε, as a result of the interactions between C and A. Toulmin's model does not seem able to explain these functional aspects, even if it can explain other aspects of the argument, such as the transition from a generic example to a general statement, its relationship with the theory that underpins the argument itself, etc.

Our conjecture is that the great idea of the jurisprudential method is like a good wine put into an inadequate barrel, that is into the ancient syllogistic scheme, to which every relational and functional aspect was extraneous. This is precisely the great step taken by modern logic thanks above all to Frege, as explained in his *Begriffshrift* (*Ideography* 1879). It is instructive to quote Frege on the new method, since he clearly indicates the relevance of a functional approach to what he defines as "a linguistic formula for pure thought, modelled on that of arithmetic", that is, for the new language of mathematical logic:

> If in an expression [...] a simple or compound sign has one or more occurrences and if we consider that sign as substitutable in all or some of these occurrences by something else (but everywhere by the same thing), then we call that part that remains invariant in the expression a function, and the substitutable part is the argument of the function[5]. (p. 16: translation by the authors)

The Toulmin model highlights an essential characteristic of scientific arguments, namely their dynamical and dialogical characteristics, but it is not suitable to capture the modern development of scientific investigation in its entirety, as it does not allow for the consideration of the functional dependence between variables and parameters, which are so frequent in mathematical discourses and constitute the fundamental objective of the modern scientific method.

Therefore, in order that the characteristics proposed in part (b) of the Toulmin model be valid for scientific investigation and in particular for mathematics, it is necessary to expand the structural part of its model by entering more dynamically and deeply into the fundamental part of its relationship (Fact-Claim-Warrant).

This was done in a substantial way by Hintikka with his Logic of Inquiry (LI), which follows a path of epistemic continuity between arguments and proofs. We introduce LI briefly in the next section, postponing some further comments on it until the final discussion.

---

[5]Wenn in einem Ausdrucke [...] ein einfaches oder zusammengesetztes Zeichen an einer oder an mehren Stellen vorkommt, und wir denken es an allen oder einigen dieser Stellen durch Anderes, überall aber durch Dasselbe ersetzbar, so nennen wir den hierbei unveränderlich erscheinenden Theil des Ausdruckes Function, den ersetzbaren ihr Argument.

10.3.2 The Logic of Inquiry by Jaako Hintikka

Here we come back to the theme of epistemic tension existing between argumentation and proof in order to deepen the analysis of this complex relationship, the clarification of which is crucial for setting up a correct teaching program in mathematics, in particular for mathematical proofs. In this section we introduce the model of argumentation that results from Hintikka's Logic of Inquiry (LI).

Hintikka was a Finnish philosopher and a professor of logic in Helsinki, Stanford and Boston. He introduced the LI to overcome the static approach to reasoning represented by the usual mathematical logic, and thus his approach was in tune with Toulmin's dynamic model. However, he developed critical positions with respect to the English linguist (Hintikka 1999, p. 9ff.). Since his work is not as well known, we briefly summarize his model and its relationships with that of Toulmin. For this purpose, we refer to his many publications in which he exhibits LI and which are the result of more than thirty years of research done by himself and by his school. We draw particular attention to the following works: the volumes by Hintikka in 1998 and 1999; and two chapters in volumes in 1997, pp. 13–33; and by Hintikka and Sandu (1997, pp. 415–466).

To enter into the merit of the interweaving of logical deductions and arguments, we follow Hintikka in the analysis of a very well-known type of reasoning-argumentation, that is, the so-called 'deductive method' of Sherlock Holmes. As Hintikka himself mentions, Sherlock Holmes is the character who best embodies the characteristics of the lucid thinker: in fact, he makes the deductive method the basis of his investigations.

The method of Holmes is admirably exemplified in the story, *Silver Blaze*, which Hintikka (1999, p. 31) takes as a typical example of logical reasoning, in particular in the "curious incident of the dog in the night". The famous racing horse Silver Blaze is stolen from the stable in the middle of the night and the next morning his coach is found dead in the heathland, having been brutally murdered. Many suspects emerge but no one knows what really happened. Here is the conversation that takes place between Inspector Gregory and Sherlock Holmes:

> Isp. Gregory: Is there any other point to which you would wish to draw my attention?
>
> S. H.: To the curious incident of the dog in the night-time.
>
> Isp. Greogory: The dog did nothing in the night-time.
>
> S. H.: That was the curious episode.

According to Hintikka, the brilliant deductions of the English detective can be rewritten as a succession of questions and answers. To explain this, in fact, he rewrites the dialogue in this form, in which Sherlock Holmes is in fact asking three questions to witnesses or to Inspector Gregory, who answer accordingly (*inquiring* process):

> a. Was there a watchdog in the stables when the horse disappeared?
> Yes, we have been told that there was.

b. Did the dog bark when the horse was stolen?

No, no one woke up, not even the stable-boys in the loft ("That was the curious incident").

c. Who is it that a trained watchdog does not bark at in the middle of the night?

His owner, the stable-master, of course. Hence it was the stable-master himself who stole the horse... Elementary, my dear Watson.

The answers given to questions are known or observed facts that help Holmes unravel the mystery of the horse's disappearance.

Holmes' way of reasoning is based on what Hintikka calls the interrogative model, to which we shall return. Holmes' deductive arguments are a transposition of the inquiring process into a *deductive* one, namely into the following logical chain (Fig. 10.3):

1. There was a watchdog in the stable at night
2. The dog did not bark when the horse was stolen
3. A trained watchdog doesn't bark only at its owner
4. Hence the thief was the owner.

However, the deductive transposition alone does not fully capture the sense of Sherlock Holmes' reasoning, which revolves around the "curious incident of the dog that did not bark". The dog that did not bark is the element of novelty in the argument (which for this reason arouses the astonished comment of the inspector): this move, consisting of the introduction of a new individual in an argument, differentiates the reasoning of Holmes from standard deductive reasoning, where every deductive move is made starting from the individuals explicitly or implicitly presented in the premises.[6]

In fact, LI is an example of epistemic logic,[7] which allows for the rendering of both processes (inquiring and deductive) in a unitary frame.

Beyond the technical aspects, to which we shall come in the final Discussion, there are three which are the most fundamental and deeply intertwined characteristics that characterize the LI model:

i. the dialectic between questions and answers;
ii. the deep link with game theory;
iii. the functional interpretation of connectives and quantifiers.

We have seen (i) in the example of S.H. (questions a, b, c): "asking a question and receiving an answer (that is, an interrogative move) is radically different from a step in a logical deduction (logical inference move)." (Hintikka 1999, p. x). For (ii),

---

[6]For example, the existential instantiation is a move that does not add a substantially new element, insofar the statement $\exists x A(x)$ is replaced by the statement $A(b)$, where b is a new individual term, which precisely serves as a generic individual for the statement $A(x)$. Term b is implicitly present in preamble $\exists x A(x)$. We further enter into this issue in the final Discussion.

[7]See: https://plato.stanford.edu/entries/logic-epistemic/.

Fig. 10.3 The reasoning of Sherlock Holmes

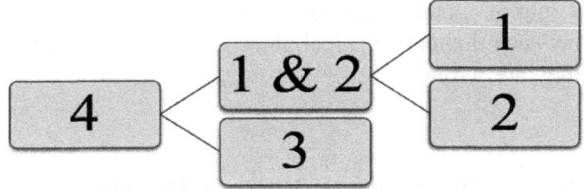

fHintikka explains the complexity of LI through the fundamental distinction between two types of "rules" that govern it, as in a chess game (pp. 2–3):

definitory rules (framing the deductive steps);
strategic principles (generating the inquiry steps).

It is through an appropriate combination of the two that the "game of logic", as Hintikka calls it, can be developed: they are like the two sides of the same coin and the issue of game is more than a metaphor. On the one hand, the canonical version of game theory has a specific logical sense in that it extends the framework of deductive logic to a wider coherent theoretical context. On the other hand, its model interpreted according to the LI captures the dynamics of a rational theory of discovery, so it is relevant in teaching and learning mathematics as well as in research.

For (iii), it is exactly the interpretation through game theory that the functional interpretation of mathematical sentences (illustrated above with the *xy* statement about continuity) acquires its full sense. Commenting on the way Weierstrass explains the concept of limit, Hintikka explains this point in the same words used by Stewart (1992, pp. 105–108):

> A function $f(x)$ approaches a limit L as x approaches a value a if, given any positive number ε, the difference $f(x) - L$ is less than ε whenever $x - a$ is less than some number δ depending on ε. It's like a game: 'You tell me how close you want $f(x)$ to be to L; then I'll tell you how close x has to be to a.' Player Epsilon says how near he pleases; then Delta is free to seek his own pleasure. If Delta always has a winning strategy, then $f(x)$ tends to the limit L. (Stewart 1992, pp. 105–106)

Hintikka accepts Stewart's interpretation, except for his use of the expression "as a game"; in his opinion this explanation is not a metaphor but the real way to interpret mathematical statements based on game theory: the description by Stewart is exactly a *semantic game*, that is a game-theoretical way to explain a mathematical property through an inquiry process.

The LI framework allows us to deal more precisely than Toulmin does with the epistemic relationship between argumentations and classical logical deductions: consequently, we can define a consistent and coherent program for teaching and learning proof in the classroom.

Compared with the Toulmin model (upon which Hintikka comments in this sense), a substantial difference in the inquiry process is that the aim of reasoning in the Hintikka model is *to seek the truth* and not *to convince the opponent*, as in the

Toulmin model. The focus of the former is in investigating the relationships between the mathematical objects, the latter's aim is to convince the opponents that they are wrong.

10.4 Educating to Rationality Through an Inquiring-Game Activity

Hintikka's LI model allows the inquiry and the deductive processes to be deeply intertwined through a game-theoretical approach. With this in mind we designed a didactical project with the aim of developing students' argumentation and proof competences, both as specific mathematical competences and as transversal educational competences within a cognitive and epistemic continuity frame.

The project, developed jointly by Arzarello and Soldano in Soldano's (2017) Ph. D. dissertation, proposes a learning trajectory that aims to develop the rationality of the students in accordance with that which is required by the Italian curriculum for Licei, mentioned at the beginning of this chapter (see footnote 3). Unfortunately, it is beyond the scope of this chapter to make a complete exposition of the project and so we limit ourselves to some of its essential aspects to show the didactic consequences of the theoretical framework illustrated above.

Grade 9 students with basic knowledge of elementary geometry were invited to play games which trigger the dynamics within DGEs described by Hintikka, to establish the truth of formulas of the type $\forall x \, \exists y \, S[x,y]$.[8] Remember that in the semantic game associated with this formula the falsifier chooses a value x_0 for x, while the verifier is asked to find a value y_0 for such that $S[x_0, y_0]$ is true. If a winning strategy for the verifier exists, the statement is true. In our game-activities the falsifier, through his/her move, is supposed to drag a dynamic object so that the figure does not show a certain geometric property, while the verifier through his/her move should drag the dynamic object so that the figure shows the property.

Of course, when transposing a theorem into a game, a minimum level of ingenuity is needed to build a situation that is interesting for the pupils. For example, to discover the theorem: "If the median and the angle bisector drawn from the same vertex of a triangle coincide, then the triangle is isosceles", in a dynamic triangle ABC (vertices built as free points)[9] a segment CD and a line b are robustly constructed[10] as median and angle bisector from the vertex C using appropriate GeoGebra tools.

---

[8]Many elementary geometry theorems do not go beyond the complexity of this formula. It is our project to rewrite the theorems in the first book of Euclid's Elements, according to the canons of the LI inside a DGE.

[9]This game was created by an Italian teacher taking inspiration from another game shown by the authors in a conference.

[10]See below the explanation about robust and soft constructions.

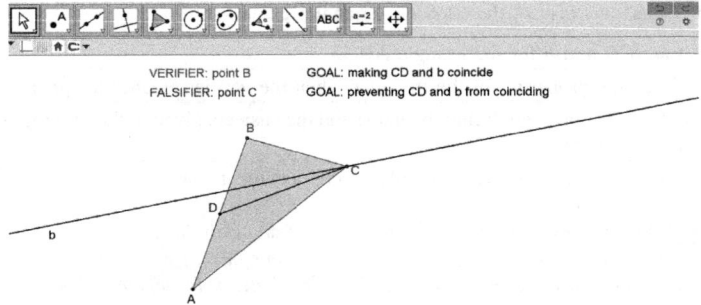

Fig. 10.4 The 'isosceles triangle' game (Link to the game: https://www.geogebra.org/m/amgmh3mf)

Table 10.2 Rules of the 'isosceles triangle' game

Within your pair, establish one **verifier** who moves the point **B** and one **falsifier** who moves the point **C**. Each match is made by two moves and the first one is always made by the falsifier.

The **goal** of the **verifier** is to make segment **CD** and line **b coincide**, while the **goal** of the **falsifier** is to **prevent the verifier from reaching his/her goal**.
The winner of the match is the player who reaches the goal at the end of the verifier's move.

After each match go backward with the GeoGebra arrows to reseat the initial configuration. Play some matches and mark an X in the following table corresponding to the winner of each match.

	Verifier	Falsifier
Match 1		
Match 2		
Match 3		
...		

Exchange your roles and play again

	Verifier	Falsifier
Match 1		
Match 2		
Match 3		
...		

The verifier's goal is to make the segment CD coincide with the line b by moving point B (see Fig. 10.4) while the falsifier's goal is preventing the verifier from reaching the goal by moving the point C.

Table 10.2 contains the rules of the game as they were given to the students. Following the rules of the game, the verifier and the falsifier play a semantic game on the following statement: 'For all positions of point C there exists a position of point B such that the segment CD and the line b coincide'.

Table 10.3 Worksheet task of the 'isosceles triangle' game

(1)	What are CD and b for the triangle ABC?
(2)	Which are the properties of the triangles when the verifier reaches his goal?
(3)	From the facts observed during the game and the answers given to the previous questions formulate a geometric conjecture
(4)	Using the given connectives, formulate truth statements based on the game. Write as many as you can. List of connectives: ...since...; if... then...; ...if and only if...; every time that... then...; ...if...; When...it happens that...; In order that... it is necessary that...; In order that... it is *sufficient that*...
(5)	Link the discovered statements that have the same meaning

From a theoretical point of view the verifier can always win the game by transforming any configuration produced by the falsifier into an isosceles triangle (or a degenerate case).

While playing, students do not know the geometric theorem on which the game is based: the guiding questions contained in the worksheet task (see Table 10.3) are meant to shift students' attention from the game to the geometric properties of the game.

To answer the first two questions, students have to discover that CD is a median, b an angles bisector and that the triangles produced by the verifier are isosceles triangles. The third question requires students to link the observed and discovered facts so to produce a geometric conjecture. The fourth question provides the students with the mathematical terms for transforming their conjecture in a more strictly logical way. Finally, the last question is meant to focus students' attention on the equivalence of the mathematical statements that are produced.

It is important to remember that each verifier's move produces an example of triangle in which the median and the angle bisector drawn from vertex C coincide, namely an example of an isosceles triangle, while each falsifier's move produces a non-example of it. Thus, the game's dynamics push students to create logical links between the discovered facts, supporting the transition from inquiring to deductive processes. It should be noted that these logical links refer to the facts observed while accomplishing certain actions in GeoGebra, and not to an axiomatic theory (as happens in standard mathematics): they can help students in their reflections on the relationship between the objects involved in a theorem, catching its meaning and its universal truth.

10.5 Discussion

In this section we discuss the meaning of our proposal, expounding some aspects of its theoretical framework and commenting further on its didactical significance.

The paper has focused on the issue of didactical and epistemological continuity between argumentations and proofs in mathematics learning and is based on two theoretical frameworks, designed by Toulmin and Hintikka respectively.

The Toulmin model has been useful for defining the structure of an argumentation but is inadequate for fully grasping the nature of mathematical statements, for two reasons:

(i) the misleading frame of the jurisprudential context by which it is inspired;
(ii) the limits of syllogistic reasoning, to which Toulmin reduces his analysis, which are structurally incapable of grasping the relational aspects of mathematical properties, in particular its functional features.

The LI model of Hintikka was the theoretical basis on which to overcome such difficulties. To illustrate it, we used the example of Sherlock Holmes' reasoning in *Silver Blaze*. The episode, according to Hintikka, is paradigmatic to show the philosophy behind the so-called inquiry-based approach to mathematics and science (Harlen 2013):

> This idea [of the Logic of Inquiry] is as old as Socrates, and hence older than most of our familiar epistemology and logic. It is the idea of knowledge-seeking by questioning or, more accurately, of all rational knowledge-seeking as implicit or explicit questioning. I am using the phrase 'inquiry as inquiry' to express the idea. For what my leading idea is precisely an assimilation of all rational inquiry in the generic sense of searching for information or knowledge to inquiry in the etymological sense, that is, to a process of querying, or interrogation. (Hintikka 1999, p. ix)

The model of Hintikka offers the following advantages with respect to that of Toulmin:

i. the context: scientific investigation against legal inquiry;
ii. modern logic with respect to syllogistic logic;
iii. a compact dynamic corpus (logic of the investigation/logic of game theory), in which there is a deep dialectic between definitory and strategic rules, which allows the building of new knowledge.

The most important difference is (iii), which deeply distinguishes the two methods. In short, the Toulmin model does not capture in the structural part the innovative aspects theorized in the meta-model, and this makes it incapable of catching the essence of the logic of scientific investigation in its core (it must be said to be true that this it is not Toulmin's goal; he was more interested in everyday argumentation in general).

A relevant aspect of LI is that it makes the functional interpretation of statements natural through its interpretation within the frame of games, ruled by the dialectics between the strategic principles (which guide the inquiry processes) and the definitive rules (upon which the deductive steps are founded). The functional interpretation based on the notion of strategy has consequences for the semantic arrangement of the model, as we have mentioned, and also reveals the deep links with the questioning method of research as a succession of question-answers, as in the Silver Blaze questions. It appears that the statements that structure the argumentations depend on the class of answers that the researcher is able to receive in the course of his research; for this purpose, a purely deductive logic is inadequate:

> Most philosophers have apparently assumed that for a scientific inquirer all the rock-bottom answers must be thought of as particular propositions. This assumption has led to the inductivist and to the hypothetico-deductive models of science. In reality, it is nevertheless totally unrealistic, as is illustrated among other things by the possibility of putting questions to nature in the form of experiments. An answer to an experimental question is typically a functional dependence between two variables, which can only be expressed in terms of dependent quantifiers, and hence not a particular proposition. (Hintikka 1999, p. xi)

As a consequence of this approach, Hintikka can show an epistemic unity between argumentations and proofs by introducing a new definition of mathematical truth based on the notion of strategies in game theory: a strategy is a rule that tells a player what to do in every imaginable situation that could arise in any hand of the game. To ascertain the truth of a statement S, a semantic game is defined between two players, who assume alternatively the role of verifier and falsifier. In each phase of the game, speaking intuitively, the verifier tries to show that the statement considered at that moment is true and the falsifier tries to prove that it is false. It is shown that every semantic game ends after a finite number of moves, with one player winning and the other losing. S is true if there is a winning strategy for the initial verifier (Hintikka and Kulas 1983).

In this way, LI 'reverses', so to say, the standard definition of truth, given by Tarski (1933) and used in all textbooks of logic. In fact, Tarski's definition starts from the condition of truth of the simplest (atomic) sentences and proceeds recursively to the complex ones: for example, to say if A&B is true one refers to the truth of A and B. The definition in LI is in the opposite direction: it starts with complex sentences and goes inside them, according to a top-down procedure, which is in accordance with the functional method previously sketched out.

Hintikka's results in the field of logic are the basis of our project, in which elementary geometry theorems are introduced through DGE inquiring-game activities. The aim is to promote learning practices in which inquiring and deductive processes are deeply intertwined with each other. In fact, while playing, students' inquiring processes are guided by strategic choices triggered by typical, maybe implicit, questions that players ask themselves before making a new move: "What can I do in this situation? What is best to do?" To answer these questions, they have to reflect on both the moves that have been made previously and the possible moves that can be made. They activate what is known in the literature as *anticipatory thinking* (Harel 2001) and *backward reasoning* (Gómez Chacón 1992; Shachter and Heckerman 1987). Moreover, while answering the questions contained in the worksheet task, students' processes of inquiry are integrated with their deductive ones through the activation of definitory rules.

The previously described Inquiring-Game activity shows that LI can give a solid theoretical basis for setting up didactic projects in which students are introduced to argumentation and proof in an integrated way: in such a way, it can provide also their epistemic unity.

Fig. 10.5 Non-prototypical configuration of isosceles triangle

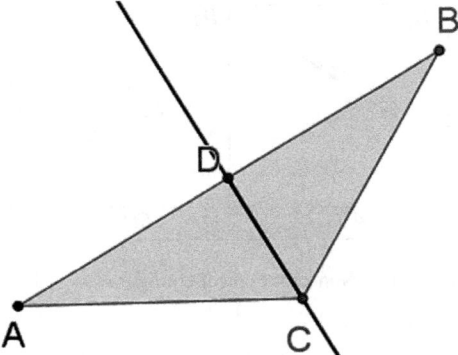

In this regard, LI also constitutes an appropriate epistemic framework for so-called experimental mathematics,[11] which has become increasingly important in mathematics education because of classroom activities with computers (or more generally with technological devices).

Let us now comment on how the game-activities can influence the processes of student discovery and justification.

The first important thing to note concerns the enlargement of students' *personal example space*, which is the "set of mathematical objects and construction techniques that a learner has access to as examples of a concept while working on a given task" (Sinclair et al. 2011). The desire to win the game competition drives students to broaden the exploration of the configurations that can be produced with the game, experiencing different examples of the geometric concepts and properties on which the activity is based. By playing, students create not only prototypical configurations of the geometric concept or property, but also non-prototypical and degenerate configurations. In this way, they extend their personal example space. In the problem about the isosceles triangle we observed students struggling with non-prototypical configurations of isosceles triangle such as the case of 'upside-down' isosceles triangles, namely triangles with vertex downside and base upside as shown in Fig. 10.5.

By moving the vertexes, the students make sense of non-prototypical configurations by transforming them into prototypical ones. This investigation is particular

---

[11] Borwein and Kevin (2009) describe the main features of mathematics in this way:
- Gaining insight and intuition.
- Discovering new patterns and relationships.
- Using graphical displays to suggest underlying mathematical principles.
- Testing and especially falsifying conjectures.
- Exploring a possible result to see if it is worth formal proof.
- Suggesting approaches for formal proof.
- Replacing lengthy hand derivations with computer-based derivations.
- Confirming analytically derived results.

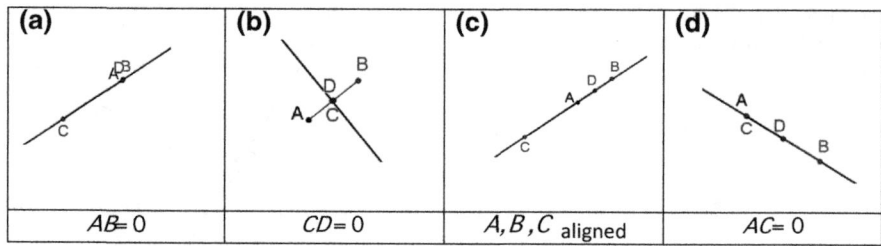

Fig. 10.6 Non-prototypical configuration of isosceles triangle

useful for developing what de Finetti (2015) called the "mathematical way of seeing":

> It is especially useful to reflect on examples, to learn and reflect on different examples and to modify them or to build new ones, and, in this way, to be able to better understand and discover what we need to see to overcome a problem. (p. 299, translation by the authors)

During the game phase, students produce degenerate configurations, such as those showed in Fig. 10.6 a, b, c, d. These configurations are a typical product of the competition created by the game: to cause difficulties for the verifier, the falsifier creates configurations in which the verifier can win only by producing degenerate cases. Here there can be perceived a subtle, yet relevant, difference between our model and the jurisprudential one. On one side, the game environment pushes the falsifier to make trouble for the verifier by creating non-prototypical configurations, in which the verifier can win only by producing degenerate cases: this has some similarity with a courtroom dispute between the defence attorney and the prosecutor in a trial and could seem coherent with the Toulmin model.

However, due to the second part of the task (illustrated in Table 10.3), the degenerate cases assume a completely different meaning from the cavils of a lawyer in a trial. In fact, we observed that students propose these configurations again while answering the questions in Table 10.3, and discuss their relationship with the isosceles triangles: some students conceive them as counterexamples that falsify the discovered property, some others conceive them as limit cases, to which it is possible to transform the isosceles triangle. In other words, students start playing the reflective-game (Soldano and Arzarello 2016) in which comparative skill level is insignificant but rather the aim is to discover whether or not the verifier can always win, and, if so, that the geometric properties are still preserved.

The discussion of these configurations moves the attention from the figural to the conceptual aspects of the geometric figures (Fischbein 1993), activating students' critical thinking (Abrami et al. 2015; Toulmin et al. 1984). We can therefore observe empirical evidence for a reduction of the basic gap in these discussions.

The example above shows another interesting aspect of our didactical design: we have just discussed that it is the game environment that promotes the introduction of new elements in students' discussion, namely the degenerate triangles. In a sense, they are similar to the curious incident of the dog that did not bark in the Silver

Blaze episode. It is an unexpected element introduced in the discourse: C.S. Peirce studied such forms of reasoning and called them *abductions*. They are typical non-analytical forms of reasoning. Peirce gave different definitions of abduction, some of which are particularly fruitful for mathematical education. One is the so-called *syllogistic abduction* (Peirce 1960), according to which a *Case* is drawn from a *Rule* and a *Result*. There is a well-known example from Peirce about beans: All the beans from this bag are white (*Rule*), These beans are white (*Result*), hence: These beans are probably from this bag (*Case*). Polya (1971) called it heuristic syllogism. Such an abduction is different from a *Deduction* that would have the form: the *Result* is drawn from the *Rule* and the *Case*, and it is obviously different from an *Induction*, which has the form: from a *Case* and many *Results* a *Rule* is drawn. Other forms of abductions are discussed by Magnani (2001, pp. 17–18). According to Peirce, an abduction is "the only logical operation which introduces any new ideas" (Peirce 1960) and is essential for every human inquiry, because it is intertwined both with perception and with the general process of invention. In geometry, typically there are theorems that can be proved by considering only the configurations of the objects actually mentioned in the statement of the theorem. In other cases, instead, it is necessary to introduce new objects that are not mentioned in the statement, performing auxiliary constructions.[12] These distinctions are based on the relevance that Peirce gives to the so-called iconic-diagramatic reasoning or model-based reasoning; therefore, it can be extended to any type of reasoning (on this point see Dörfler 2016). Hence a game approach (particularly within DGS environments) can trigger the production of abductive reasoning, which constitutes again an important aspect of cognitive continuity:

> Abductions can be produced within DGS environments, and can bridge the gap between perceptual facts and their theoretical transposition through supporting a *structural cognitive unity* [...] between the explorative and the proving phase, provided there is a suitable didactic design. (Arzarello et al. 2012, p. 113)

A last remark concerns students' validation and refutation processes. Inside DGE, students validate or refute their conjecture exploiting the dragging test guided by "descending control" (Arzarello et al. 1998, 2002), namely they move dragable or semi-dragable points in order to see whether the geometric configuration keeps the conjectured invariant property. This dragging modality follows what we call the "logic of yes" and leads students to empirically test their conjecture. Within game activities we also observed the activation of another type of logic, the "logic of not" (Arzarello and Sabena 2011), which guides students in the indirect validation of a conjecture, by observing empirically the impossibility of refuting it.[13] This logic is triggered by the verifier/falsifier dynamics (Soldano et al. 2018). In fact, the falsifier, in order to establish if there is a possibility for her/him to win,

---

[12]Peirce called the two types of proof *theoretical* and *corollarial*.

[13]In fact, if there is no counterexample to a statement, the statement is valid: this way of thinking can be in its turn an example of backward reasoning.

generally acts in the following way: he produces a configuration which, provided there is the possibility of winning, would happen with that configuration (it is generally a configuration that forces the verifier to produce a degenerate case); when the falsifier realizes that the verifier wins even in this particular case, this situation leads him/her to establish that the verifier can win in any case. This type of strategy is also activated by students for establishing the truth of the conjectured theorem on which the game is based. This form of backward reasoning is not so spontaneous within a purely deductive framework: it is the game environment which promotes it.

The LI has allowed us to develop a mathematics teaching program that can extend its theoretical epistemic unity/ continuity also to the cognitive and didactic dimensions, in a substantially unitary framework, in order to afford the teaching of proof in the classroom.

There are still many open problems which have emerged from our research, which warrant further study that we intend to develop in the future. Here we list those that seem to us particularly important:

- the transposition of the theorems of elementary geometry and of the elementary analysis within the LI model, using our gamification approach;
- the in-depth study of the links between backward reasoning in game theory and the model described by the LI;
- the analysis of the relationships between the LI and the Lakatos model on conjectures-refutations.

Acknowledgements We wish to thank the teacher Gaetano Di Caprio and the professor Cristina Sabena for their fruitful collaboration in the design of the 'isosceles-triangle' activity.

References

Abrami, P. C., Bernard, R. M., Borokhovski, E., Waddington, D. I., Wade, C. A., & Persson, T. (2015). Strategies for teaching students to think critically: A meta-analysis. *Review of Educational Research, 85*(2), 275–314. https://doi.org/10.3102/0034654314551063.

Arzarello, F., & Sabena, C. (2011). Semiotic and theoretic control in argumentation and proof activities. *Educational Studies in Mathematics, 77*(2), 189–206.

Arzarello, F., Micheletti, C., Olivero, F., Robutti, O., & Paola, D. (1998). A model for analysing the transition to formal proofs in geometry. In A. Olivier & K. Newstead (Eds.), *Proceedings of the 22nd Conference of the International Group for the Psychology of Mathematics Education* (Vol. 2, pp. 24–31). Bellville, ZA: Kwik Kopy Printing.

Arzarello, F., Olivero, F., Paola, D., & Robutti, O. (2002). A cognitive analysis of dragging practises in Cabri environments. *ZDM—The International Journal on Mathematics Education, 34*(3), 66–72.

Arzarello, F., Bartolini Bussi, M. G.M., Leung, A., Mariotti, M.A., & Stevenson, I. (2012). Experimental approaches to theoretical thinking: Artefacts and proofs. In G. Hanna & G. de Villiers (Eds.), *Proof and proving in mathematics education* (Vol. 15, pp. 97–146). New ICMI studies series. New York: Springer.

Baccaglini-Frank, A., & Mariotti, M. A. (2010). Generating conjectures in dynamic geometry: The maintaining dragging model. *International Journal of Computers for Mathematical Learning, 15*(3), 225–253.

Balacheff, N. (1987). Processus de preuve et situations de validation. *Educational Studies in Mathematics, 18*(2), 147–176. https://doi.org/10.1007/BF00314724.

Boero, P. (2011). Argumentation and proof: Discussing a "successful" classroom discussion. In M. Pytlak, T. Rowland, & E. Swoboda (Eds.), *Proceedings of 7th Congress of the European Society for Research in Mathematics Education* (pp. 120–130). Rszéskow, PL: ERME.

Boero, P., & Planas, N. (2014). Habermas' construct of rational behavior in mathematics education: New advances and research questions. In *Proceedings of the 38th Conference of the International Group for the Psychology of Mathematics Education and the 36th Conference of the North American Chapter of the Psychology of Mathematics Education* (Vol. 1, pp. 205–235). Vancouver, CND: PME.

Boero, P., Garuti, R., Lemut, E., & Mariotti, M. A. (1996). Challenging the traditional school approach to theorems: A hypothesis about the cognitive unity of theorems. In L. Puig, & A. Gutierrez (Eds.), *Proceedings of the 20th Conference of the International Group for the Psychology of Mathematics Education* (Vol. 2, pp. 113–120). Valencia, ES: Encuademaciones Artesanas.

Boero, P., Douek, N., Morselli, F., & Pedemonte, B. (2010). Argumentation and proof: A contribution to theoretical perspectives and their classroom implementation. In M. M. F Pinto & T. F Kawasaki (Eds.), *Proceedings of the 34th Conference of the International Group for the Psychology of Mathematics Education* (Vol. 1, pp. 179–204). Belo Horizonte, BR.

Börger, E., Grädel, E., & Gurevich, Y. (1997). *The classical decision problem.* Universitext. Berlin: Springer.

Borwein, J. M., & Devlin, K. (2009). *The computer as crucible: An introduction to experimental mathematics.* Wellesley, MA: A K Peters.

de Finetti, B. (2015). Saper vedere in matematica. In G. Anichini, L. Giacardi, & E. Luciano (curatori). *Bruno de Finetti e l'insegnamento della Matematica dalla Realtà, nella realtà, per la Realtà.* Bollettino UMI, Sez A. dicembre 2015. 299–408. New Edition of: Saper vedere in matematica. Loescher (1967).

Dörfler, W. (2016). Signs and their use: Peirce and Wittgenstein. In A. Bikner-Ahsbahs, A. Vohns, R. Bruder, O. Schmitt, & W. Dörfler (Eds.), *Theories in and of mathematics education.* ICME-13 topical surveys. Cham: Springer. https://doi.org/10.1007/978-3-319-42589-4_4.

Duval, R. (1991). Structure du raisonnement deductif et apprentissage de la demonstration. *Educational Studies in Mathematics, 22*(3), 233–261.

Fawcett, H. P. (1938). *The nature of proof (1938 Yearbook of the National Council of Teachers of Mathematics).* New York, NY: Bureau of Publications, Teachers College, Columbia University.

Fischbein, E. (1993). The theory of figural concepts. *Educational Studies in Mathematics, 24*(2), 139–162.

Frege, G. (1879). *Begriffschrift: eine der Arithmetischen nachgebildete Formelsprache des reinen Denkens.* Halle a/S: L. Nebert Verlag.

Garuti, R., Boero, P., Lemut, E., & Mariotti, M. A. (1996). Challenging the traditional school approach to theorems. In *Proceedings of the 20th International Group for the Psychology of Mathematics Education* (Vol. 2, pp. 113–120). Valencia, ES: Encuademaciones Artesanas.

Garuti, R., Boero, P., & Lemut, E. (1998). Cognitive unity of theorems and difficulty of proof. In *Proceedings of the 22nd Conference of the International Group for the Psychology of Mathematics Education* (Vol. 2, pp. 345–352). Bellville, ZA: Kwik Kopy Printing.

Gómez Chacón, I. M. (1992). Desarrollo de diversos juegos de estrategia para su utilización en el aula. *Epsilon: Revista de la Sociedad Andaluza de Educación Matemática "Thales", 22,* 77–88.

Guala, E., & Boero, P. (2017). Cultural analysis of mathematical content in teacher education: the case of elementary arithmetic theorems. *Educational Studies in Mathematics, 96*(2), 207–227. https://doi.org/10.1007/s10649-017-9767-2.

Harel, G. (2001). The development of mathematical induction as a proof scheme: A model for DNR-based instruction. In S. Campbell & R. Zazkis (Eds.), *The learning and teaching of number theory: Research in cognition and instruction* (pp. 185–212). Dordrecht, NL: Kluwer Academic Publishers.

Harlen, W. (2013). Inquiry-based learning in science and mathematics. *Review of Science, Mathematics and ICT Education, 7*(2), 9–33.

Heidegger, M. (1927). *Sein und Zeit*. Halle: M. Niemeyer. Trans. By Macquarrie, J., & Robinson, E. (1962). *Being and time*. New York: Harper & Row.

Hilbert, D., & Cohn-Vossen, S. (1932). *Anschauliche Geometrie*. Berlin: Springer. (English translation: Geometry and the imagination. New York: Chelsea, 1952). 2nd ed. Berlin, 1996.

Hintikka, J. (1997). The place of C.S. Peirce in the history of logical theory. In J. Brunning & P. Forster (Eds.), *The rule of reason, the philosophy of Charles Sanders Peirce* (pp. 13–33). Toronto: University of Toronto Press.

Hintikka, J. (1998). *The principles of mathematics revisited*. Cambridge: Cambridge University Press.

Hintikka, J. (1999). *Inquiry as inquiry: A logic of scientific discovery*. Dordrecht: Springer.

Hintikka, J., & Kulas, J. (1983). *The game of language: Studies in game-theoretical semantics and its applications*. Dordrecht: D. Reidel.

Hintikka, J., & Sandu, G. (1997). Game theoretical semantics. In van Benthem & Ter Meulen (Eds.), *Handbook of logic and language* (pp. 361–410). Amsterdam: Elsevier.

Knipping, C., & Reid, D. (2015). Reconstructing argumentation structures: A perspective on proving processes in secondary mathematics classroom interactions. In A. Bikner-Ahsbahs, P. Knipping, & N. Presmeg (Eds.), *Approaches to qualitative research in mathematics education* (pp. 75–101). Advances in mathematics education. Dordrecht, NL: Springer.

Lolli, G. (2005). *QED: Fenomenologia della dimostrazione*. Torino: Boringhieri.

Magnani, L. (2001). *Abduction, reason, and science: Processes of discovery and explanation*. Dordrecht, The Netherlands: Kluwer.

Mariotti, M. A. (2006). Proof and proving in mathematics education. In A. Gutiérrez & P. Boero (Eds.), *Handbook of research on the PME: Past, present and future* (pp. 173–204). Rotterdam, NL: Sense.

Pedemonte, B. (2007). How can the relationship between argumentation and proof be analysed? *Educational Studies in Mathematics, 66*, 23–41.

Peirce, C. S. (1960). *Collected papers of Charles Sanders Peirce* (CP, Vol. I–VI). In C. Hartshorne & P. Weiss (Eds.), Cambridge, MA: The Belknap Press of Harvard University Press.

Polya, G. (1971). *How to solve it: A new aspect of mathematical method*. Princeton, NJ: Princeton University Press.

Rav, Y. (1999). Why do we prove theorems? *Philosophia Mathematica, 7*, 5–41.

Selden, A., & Selden, J. (2003). Validations of proofs written as texts: Can undergraduates tell whether an argument proves a theorem? *Journal for Research in Mathematics Education, 36*(1), 4–36.

Shachter, R. D., & Heckerman, D. (1987). Thinking backward for knowledge acquisition. *AI Magazine, 8*(3), 55–61.

Sinclair, N., Watson, A., Zazkis, R., & Mason, J. (2011). The structuring of personal example spaces. *The Journal of Mathematical Behavior, 30*(4), 291–303.

Soldano, C. (2017). *Learning with the logic of inquiry. A game-approach within DGE to improve geometric thinking*. Unpublished doctoral dissertation, University of Turin.

Soldano, C., & Arzarello, F. (2016). Learning with touchscreen devices: Game strategies to improve geometric thinking. In K. Larkin & N. Calder (Eds.), *Mathematics Education Research Journal, 28*(1), 9–30.

Soldano, C., Luz, Y., Arzarello, F., & Yerushalmy, M. (2018). Technology-based inquiry in geometry: Semantic games through the lens of variation. *Educational studies in mathematics*. https://doi.org/10.1007/s10649-018-9841-4.

Stewart, I. (1992). *The problems of mathematics* (New ed.). New York: Oxford University Press.

Stylianides, G. J., Stylianides, A. J., & Weber, K. (2017). Research on the teaching and learning of proof: Taking stock and moving forward. In J. Cai (Ed.), *Compendium for research in mathematics education*. National Council of Teachers of Mathematics: Reston, VA.

Tarski, A. (1933). *The concept of truth in the languages of the deductive sciences* (Polish), Prace Towarzystwa Naukowego Warszawskiego, Wydział III Nauk Matematyczno-Fizycznych 34, Warsaw; reprinted in Zygmunt 1995 (pp. 13–172); expanded English translation in Tarski 1983 [1956] (pp. 152–278).

Thompson, D. R., Senk, S. L., & Johnson, G. J. (2012). Opportunities to learn reasoning and proof in high school mathematics textbooks. *Journal for Research in Mathematics Education, 43*, 253–295.

Thurston, W. (1994). On proof and progress in mathematics. *Bulletin of the American Mathematical Society, 30*(2), 161–177.

Toulmin, S. E. (1958). *The uses of argument*. Cambridge, UK: Cambridge University Press.

Toulmin, S. E. (1974). Rationality and scientific discovery. *Boston Studies in the Philosophy of Science, 20*, 387–406.

Toulmin, S. E. (1975). *Gli usi dell'argomentazione*. Torino, IT: Rosemberg & Sellier (traduzione di Toulmin 1958).

Toulmin, S. E., Rieke, R., & Janik, A. (1984). *An introduction to reasoning*. New York: Macmillan.

Zarębski, T. (2009). Toulmin's model of argument and the "logic" of scientific discovery. *Studies in Logic, Grammar and Rhetoric, 16*(29), 267–283.

Open Access This chapter is licensed under the terms of the Creative Commons Attribution 4.0 International License (http://creativecommons.org/licenses/by/4.0/), which permits use, sharing, adaptation, distribution and reproduction in any medium or format, as long as you give appropriate credit to the original author(s) and the source, provide a link to the Creative Commons license and indicate if changes were made.

The images or other third party material in this chapter are included in the chapter's Creative Commons license, unless indicated otherwise in a credit line to the material. If material is not included in the chapter's Creative Commons license and your intended use is not permitted by statutory regulation or exceeds the permitted use, you will need to obtain permission directly from the copyright holder.

Chapter 11
A Friendly Introduction to "Knowledge in Pieces": Modeling Types of Knowledge and Their Roles in Learning

Andrea A. diSessa

Abstract Knowledge in Pieces (KiP) is an epistemological perspective that has had significant success in explaining learning phenomena in science education, notably the phenomenon of students' prior conceptions and their roles in emerging competence. KiP is much less used in mathematics. However, I conjecture that the reasons for relative disuse mostly concern *historical differences in traditions rather than in-principle distinctions in the ways mathematics and science are learned*. This chapter aims to explain KiP in a relatively non-technical way to mathematics educators. I explain the general principles and distinguishing characteristics of KiP. I use a range of examples, including from mathematics, to show how KiP works in practice and what one might expect to gain from using it. My hope is to encourage and help guide a greater use of KiP in mathematics education.

Keywords Knowledge in pieces · Conceptual change · Complex systems

11.1 Introduction

11.1.1 Overview

Knowledge in Pieces (KiP) names a broad theoretical and empirical framework aimed at understanding knowledge and learning. It sits within the field of "conceptual change" (Vosniadou 2013), which studies learning that is especially difficult. While KiP began in physics education—in particular to provide a deeper

---

Some parts of this chapter are based on text in diSessa, A. A. (2017), "Knowledge in Pieces: An evolving framework for understanding knowing and learning," in T. G. Amin and O. Levrini (Eds.), *Converging perspectives on conceptual change: Mapping an emerging paradigm in the learning sciences,* Routledge. Used by kind permission of Taylor and Francis/Routledge.

A. A. diSessa (✉)
University of California, Berkeley, CA, USA
e-mail: disessa@berkeley.edu

© The Author(s) 2019
G. Kaiser and N. Presmeg (eds.), *Compendium for Early Career Researchers in Mathematics Education*, ICME-13 Monographs,
https://doi.org/10.1007/978-3-030-15636-7_11

understanding of the phenomenon of "prior conceptions" (misleadingly labeled as "misconceptions"; Smith et al. 1993)—it has since engaged other areas, such as mathematics, chemistry, ecology, computer science, and even views of race and racism (Philip 2011).

I aim to produce a relatively non-technical introduction to KiP that can be understood by those who are not experts in the field of conceptual change, KiP's "home discipline." I emphasize breadth and "big ideas" over depth, while still pointing in the direction of KiP's distinctive fine structure and technical precision. A longer but still general introduction to KiP for those who want to pursue these ideas more deeply is diSessa et al. (2016).

Before beginning discussion in earnest, I would like to make two points about my strategy of exposition. First, the initial examples I give will be from physics, KiP's "home turf." I beg the (mathematical) reader's indulgence in doing so, but it allows me to select some of the best and most accessible examples of KiP analyses, where its core features are transparent, and where some competitive advantages over contrasting points of view are easiest to see. These examples are at the high-school level, so I do not expect them to be too much of a conceptual challenge. Mathematical examples will follow in Sects. 11.3 and 11.4. Second, with respect to mathematical examples, there are, of course, perspectives in the mathematics literature that bear on the same topics. While I will mention some of these (see comments and references in Sects. 11.3 and 11.4), careful comparative analysis is too complex for the scope of this paper. Readers who already know the relevant perspectives from mathematics education, of course, should be prepared to elaborate their own comparisons and conclusions.[1]

KiP is essentially epistemological: It aims to develop a modern theory of knowledge and learning capable of comprehending both short-term phenomena—learning in bits and pieces (hence the name, Knowledge in Pieces)—and long-term phenomena, such as conceptual change, "theory change," and so on. It aims to build a solid two-way bridge between, on the one hand, theory, and, on the other hand, data concerning learning and intellectual performance. "Two-way" implicates that (a) the theory is strongly constrained by and built out of observation, but also that (b) the theory can "project" directly onto what learners actually do as they think and learn, giving general meaning to their actions. KiP is, thus, a reaction against theories that are a priori, very high level, and consequentially are difficult to apply to the messiness of real-world learning.

KiP shares important features with two major progenitors. The first is Piagetian and neo-Piagetian developmental psychology, epitomized in mathematics education by Les Steffe, Ernst von Glasersfeld, Robbie Case, and many others. The core

---

[1]While I provide specific hints later for more detailed comparisons on a per-topic basis, probably the most effective single hint I can provide for reader-developed comparisons is to consider (a) whether work on the same topic identifies intuitive pre-cursor ideas in detail (few do), including their productive as well as problematic nature, and (b) whether data analysis includes extensive examination and explanation of students' in-process thinking, in addition to long-term comparisons. The presentation of distinctive KiP themes, just below, elaborates these points.

unifying feature of KiP with this work is constructivism, the focus on how long-term change emerges from existing mental structure. The second progenitor is cognitive modeling, such as in the work of John Anderson (e.g., his work on intelligent tutoring of geometry), or Kurt vanLehn (e.g., his work on students' "buggy" arithmetic strategies). The relevant common feature with KiP in the case of cognitive modeling is accountability to real-time data. A key distinctive feature of KiP, however, is its attempt to combine *both* long-term and short-term perspectives on learning. Piagetian psychology, in my view, was never very good at articulating what the details of students' real-time thinking have to do with long-term changes. In complementary manner, I judge that cognitive modeling has not done well comprehending difficult changes that may take years to accomplish.

I now introduce a set of interlocking themes that characterize KiP as a framework. These will be elaborated in the context of examples of learning phenomena to illustrate their meaning in concrete cases and their importance.

***Complex systems* approach**—KiP views knowledge, in general, as a complex system of many *types* of knowledge elements, often having many particular *exemplars* of each type. Two contrasting types of knowledge are illustrated in the next main section.

Learning is viewed as a transformation of one complex system into another, perhaps with many common elements across the change, but with different organization. For example, students' *intuitive knowledge* (see the definition directly below) is fluid and often unstable, but *mature concepts* must achieve more stability through a broader and more "crystalline" organization, even if many of the same elements remain in the system. The pre-instructional "conceptual ecology" of students must usually be understood with great particularity—essentially "intuition by intuition"—in order to comprehend learning; general properties go only so far. A number of such particular intuitions will be identified in examples.

I use the terms "intuitive" and "intuition" here loosely and informally to describe students' commonsense, everyday "prior conceptions." However, consistent with the larger program, I will introduce a technical model of a very particular class of such ideas that has proven important in KiP studies.

***A modeling approach*—**The learning sciences are still far from knowing exactly how learning works. It is more productive to recognize this fact explicitly and to keep track of how our ideas fail as well as how they succeed. Concomitantly, KiP builds models, typically models of different types of knowledge, not a singular and complete "theory of knowledge and learning," and the limits of those models are as important (e.g., in determining next steps) as demonstrated successes.

***Continuous improvement*—**A concomitant of the modeling approach is a constant focus on improving existing models, and, sometimes, developing new models. In fact, the central models of KiP have had an extended history of extensions and improvements (diSessa et al. 2016). It is a positive sign that the core of existing models has remained in tact, while details have been filled in and extensions have been produced to account for new phenomena.

I call the themes above "macro" because they are characteristic of the larger program, and they are best seen in the sweep of the KiP program as a whole. In contrast, the "micro" themes, below, can be relatively easily illustrated in many different contexts, which will be seen in the example work presented below.

A multi-scaled approach—I already briefly called out the commitment to both short-term and long-term scales of learning and performance phenomena, a *temporally multi-scaled approach*. Most conceptual change research, and, indeed, a lot of educational research, is limited to before-and-after studies, and there is almost no accountability to process data, to change as it occurs in moments of thinking.

A systems orientation also entails a second dimensional scale. Complex systems are built from "smaller" elements, and indeed, system change is likely best understood at the level of transformation and re-organization of system constituents. So, for example, the battery of "little" ideas, intuitions, which constitute "prior conceptions," can be selected from, refined, and integrated in order to produce normative complex systems, normative concepts. Since normative concepts are viewed as systems, their properties as such—both pieces and wholes—are empirically tracked. I describe a focus on both elements and system-level properties as *structurally multi-scaled*.

Richness and productivity—This theme is not so much a built-in assumption of KiP, but it is one of the most powerful and consistent empirical results. Naïve knowledge is, in general, rich and escapes simple characterizations (e.g., as isolated "misconceptions," simple false beliefs). Furthermore, learning very often—or always—involves recruiting many "old" elements into new configurations to produce normative understanding. This is the essence of KiP as a strongly constructivist framework, and it is one of its most distinctive properties in comparison to many competitor frameworks for understanding knowing, learning, and conceptual change. diSessa (2017) systematically describes differences compared to some contrasting theories of conceptual change. In my reading, assuming richness and productivity of naïve knowledge is comparatively rare, but certainly not unheard of, in mathematics, just as it is in science.

Diversity—An immediate consequence of the existence of rich, small-scaled knowledge is that there are many dimensions of potential difference among learners. Each learner may have a different subset of the whole pool of "little" intuitions, and might treat common elements rather differently. KiP may be unique among modern theories of conceptual change in its capacity to handle diversity across learners.

Contextuality—"Little" ideas often appear in some contexts, and not others. Furthermore, as they change to become incorporated into normative systems of knowledge, the contexts in which they operate may change. So, understanding *how knowledge depends on context* is core to KiP, while it is marginally important or invisible in competing theories. This focus binds KiP with situative approaches to learning ("situated cognition"). See Brown et al. (1989) for an early exposition, and continuing work by such authors as Jean Lave and Jim Greeno.

11.1.2 Empirical Methods

KiP is not doctrinaire about methods, and many different ones have been used.

Two modes of work are, however, more distinctive. First, KiP has *the development and continuous improvement of theory* (models) at its core. We in the community articulate limits of current models, encourage the refinement of old models and the development of new ones, when necessary.

Theory development, in turn, usually requires the richest data sources possible in order to synthesize and achieve the fullest possible accountability to the details of process. This is opposed to data that is quickly filtered and reduced to a priori codes or categories. In practice, *microgenetic* or *micro-analytic* study of rich data sources of students thinking (e.g., in clinical interviews) or learning (full-on corpora of individual or classroom learning) have been systematically used in KiP not only to validate, but also to generate new theory. See Parnafes and diSessa (2013) and the methodology section of diSessa et al. (2016). This kind of data collection and analysis is strongly synergistic with design-based research (diSessa and Cobb 2004), and iterative design and implementation of curricula—along with rich real-world tracking of data in concert with more cloistered and careful "break-out" studies of individuals—have been common.

I now proceed to concretize and exemplify the generalizations above with respect both to theory development and empirical work. I will boldface themes from the above list, as they are relevant. As mentioned, I start with examples having to do with physics, but then proceed to mathematics.

11.2 Two Models: Illustrative Data and Analysis

In this section I sketch the two best-developed and best-known KiP models of knowledge types. As such, the section illustrates KiP as a **modeling approach**. While both models are both **temporally** and **structurally multi-scaled**, the first model, p-prims, emphasizes smaller scales in time and structure. The second, coordination classes gives more prominence to larger scales.

11.2.1 Intuitive Knowledge

P-prims are elements of intuitive knowledge that constitute people's "sense of mechanism," their sense of which happenings are obvious, which are plausible, which are implausible, and how one can explain or refute real or imagined possibilities. Example p-prims are (roughly described): increased effort begets greater results; the world is full of competing influences for which the greater "gets its way," even if accidental or natural "balance" sometimes exists; the shape of a situation determines the shape of action within it (e.g., orbits around square planets are recognizably square). Comparable ideas in mathematics are that "multiplication makes numbers bigger" (untrue for multipliers less than one); a default assumption that a change in a given quantity generally implies a similar change in a related quantity (more implies more; less implies less, whereas, in fact, "denting" a shape may decrease area but increase circumference); and "negative numbers cannot apply to the real world" (what could a negative cow mean?). In the rest of this section, I will discuss physics examples only.

We must develop a new model for this kind of knowledge because, empirically, it violates presumptions of standard knowledge types, such as beliefs or principles. First, classifying p-prims as true or false (as one may do for beliefs or principles) is a category error. P-prims *work*—prescribe verifiable outcomes—in typical situations of use, but always fail in other circumstances. Indeed, when they will even be brought to mind is a delicate consequence of context (**contextuality**, both internal: "frame of mind"; or external: the particular sensory presentation of the phenomenon). So, for example, it is inappropriate to say that a person "believes" a p-prim, as if it would always be brought to mind when relevant, and as if it would always be used in preference to other ways of thinking (e.g., other p-prims, or even learned concepts). Furthermore, students simply cannot consider and reject p-prims (a commonly prescribed learning strategy for dealing with "misconceptions"). Impediments to explicit consideration are severe: There is no common lexicon for p-prims, and people may not even be aware that they have such ideas. Furthermore, "rejection" does not make sense for ideas that usually work, nor for ideas that may have very productive futures in learning (see upcoming examples).

Example data and analysis: J, a subject in an extended interview study (diSessa 1996), was asked to explain what happens when you toss a ball into the air. J responded fluently with a completely normative response: After leaving your hand, there is only one force in the situation, gravity, which slows the ball down, eventually to reverse its motion and bring it back down.

Then the interviewer asked a seemingly innocuous question, "What happens at the peak of the toss?" Rather than responding directly, J began to reformulate her model of the toss. She added another force, air resistance, which is changing, "gets stronger and stronger [as if to anticipate an impending balance and overcoming; see continuing commentary] to the point where when [sic] it stops." But then, she introduced yet another force, an upward one, which is equal to gravity, "in equilibrium for a second" at the top, before yielding to gravity. Starting anew, she provided a source for the upward force: It comes from your hand, and it "can only last so long against air and against gravity." In steps, she further decided that it's just gravity that is opposing the upward force, not air resistance, and gradually she reformulated the whole toss as a competition where the upward force initially overbalances gravity, reaching an equilibrium at the top, and then gravity takes over.

The key to understanding these events is that the interviewer "tempted" J to apply intuitive ideas of balancing and overcoming; he asked about the peak because the change of direction there looks like overcoming, one influence is getting weaker, or another is getting stronger. J "took the bait" and reformulated her ideas to include conflicting influences: The downward influence is gravity, but she struggled a bit to find another one, first trying air resistance, getting "stronger and stronger," but then introducing an upward force that is changing, getting weaker and weaker. This is a striking example of **contextuality**: J changed her model entirely after focusing attention on a particular part of the toss that suggested balancing. However, more surprises were to come.

Over the next four sessions, the interviewer continually returned to the tossed ball, providing increasingly direct criticism. "But you said the upward force is gone at the peak of the toss, and also that it balances gravity there. How can it both be zero and also balance gravity?" Over the last two sessions, the interviewer broke clinical neutrality and provided a computer-based instructional sequence on how force affects motion, including the physicist's one-force model of the toss. At the end of the instructional sequence, J was asked again to describe what happens in the toss. Mirroring her initial interview but with greater precision and care, she gave a pitch-perfect physics explanation. But, when asked to avoid an incidental part of her explanation (energy conservation), J reverted to her two-force model. So, we know that J exhibits not only surprising **contextuality** in terms of what explanation of a toss she would give, but that contextuality, itself, seems strongly persistent, a core part of her conceptual system.

After the completion of interviewing sessions, J reflected that she knew that it would appear to others that she described the toss in two different ways, and the "balancing" one might be judged wrong. But she felt both were really the same explanation.

Salient points: The dominant description of intuitive physics in the 1990s was that it constituted a coherent theory (see diSessa 2014, for a review and references), and the two-force explanation of the toss was a perfect example. External agents (the hand) supply a force that overcomes gravity, but is eventually balanced by it, and finally overcome. The KiP view, however, is that the "theory" only appears in particular situations (e.g., when overcoming is salient). Indeed, J did not seem to have the theory to start, but constructed it gradually, over a few minutes. **Contextuality** is missing from the then "conventional" view; "theories" comparable to Newton's laws don't come and go depending on what you emphasize in a visual scene. J's case is particularly dramatic since she never relinquished her intuitive ideas, even while she improved her normative ones. Instead, situation-specific saliences continued to cue one or the other "theory" of the toss. The long-term stability of an instability (the shift between two models of a toss) shows an attention to **multiple temporal scales** that is unusual in conceptual change studies but critical to understanding J's frame of mind. What happened in a moment each time it happened (shifting attention and corresponding shift in model of the toss), nonetheless continued to happen regularly over months of interviewing. Such critical phenomena test the limits of observational and analytical methods. For example, before and after tests are very unlikely even to observe the phenomenon. Attributing "misconceptions" categorically to a subject—"J has the non-normative dual force model of a toss"—fails to enfold this essentially **multi-scaled** and highly contextual analysis of J.

Another subject in the same study, K, started by asserting the two-force model of the toss. However, this subject reacted to similar re-directions of her attention concerning her explanation by completely reformulating her description to the normative model. She then observed that she had changed her mind and explained the reasons for doing so. The two-force model was then gone from the remainder of her interviews.

Ironically, a standard assessment employing first responses would classify J as normative, and K as "maintaining the naïve theory." Rather, K was a very different individual who could autonomously correct and stabilize her own understanding. J, in contrast, alternated one- and two-force explanations, and didn't really feel they were different. KiP methodologies did not assume simple characterization of either student's state of mind (**richness**), and they could also therefore better document and understand their differences (**diversity**). Neither J nor K would be well characterized by their initial responses. J, and not K, was deeply committed to a balancing view of many aspects of physics, even if both found balancing salient and significant in some cases.

Some lessons learned: The knowledge state of individuals is complex, and assessments cannot presume first responses will coherently differentiate them. The assumption of coherence in students' understanding is plainly suspect; J consistently maintained both the correct view and the "misconception," even in the face of direct instruction. The interviewer, knowing that fragile knowledge elements like p-prims are important, primed one (balancing, at the peak), and saw its dramatic influence. P-prims explain a lot about the differences and similarities between J and K (both used balancing, but J had a much greater commitment to it), but not everything. In continuing study (diSessa et al. 2002), we discovered that J showed an unusual and often counterproductive view of the nature of physics knowledge, which K did not. Modesty is the best policy: The complex conceptual ecology of students needs continuing work (**continuous improvement**).

One lesson learned here is that p-prims behave very differently than normative concepts. In terms that might be familiar to mathematics education researchers, p-prims provide a highly articulated version (specific elements whose use and contextuality can be examined across many circumstances) of a student's "concept image" (Tall and Vinner 1981). We need a different model to understand substantial, articulate and context-stable ideas, something roughly akin to "concept definition," but something that, in my view, uses KiP to better approach the cognitive and learning roots of expertise.

11.2.2 Scientific Concepts

Coordination classes constitute a model aimed at capturing central properties of expert concepts.

According to the coordination class model, the core function of concepts is to read out particular concept-relevant information reliably across a wide range of circumstances, unlike the slip-sliding activation of p-prims. Figure 11.1 explains.

Figure 11.2 shows the primary difficulty in creating a coherent concept. All possible paths from world (or imagined world) to concept attributes must result in the same determination. This is called *alignment*, and it is a property of the whole system, not of any part of it.

A physics example of lack of alignment is that students will sometimes determine forces by using intuitive inferences ("An object is moving; there must be a force on it."), and sometimes by "formal methods" ("An object is moving at a constant speed; according to Newton's third law, there is no net force on it."). A mathematical example is that students may deny that an equator on a sphere with three points marked on it is a triangle, even if they have agreed that any part of a great circle is a "straight line," and that a triangle is any three connected straight line segments.

Coordination classes are large and complex systems. This is structurally unlike p-prims, which are "small," simple, and relatively independent from one another. Alignment poses a strict constraint on all possible noticings (e.g., noticing F_1 or F_2 in Fig. 11.2) and all possible inferences (e.g., I_1 and I_2): All paths should lead to the same determination. That is, there is a *global* constraint on all the pieces of a coordination class, which makes the model essentially **multi-scaled**. In this case, multi-scaled refers to the **structure** of the knowledge system—pieces and the whole system—rather than to its **temporal** properties, which were emphasized with J.

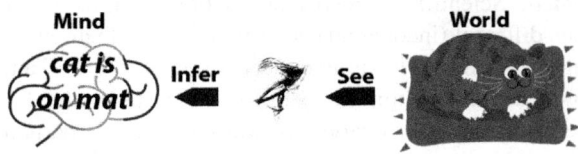

Fig. 11.1 Coordination classes allow reading out information relevant to concepts, here illustrated by "location," from the world. The readout happens in two stages. (1) "See" or "notice" involves extracting *any* concept-relevant information: "The cat is *above* the mat," and "The cat is *touching* the mat." (2) "Infer" draws conclusions specifically about the relevant information (location) using what has been seen: "The cat is *on* the mat."

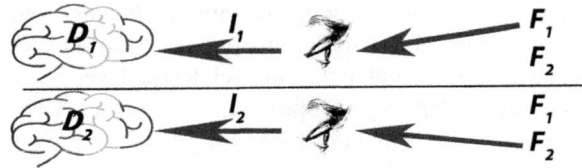

Fig. 11.2 In situations where multiple features (F_1, F_2) are available, different choices of what to observe may lead to different inferences (I_1, I_2) and potentially contradictory determinations (D_1, D_2) of the "same" information

I will not belabor a full taxonomy of parts of coordination classes, but, because it is relevant to an example from mathematics (Sect. 3.1), I note that a coordination class needs to include *relevance*, in addition to *noticings* and *inferences*. Relevance means that a coordination class needs to "know" when a concept applies and when information about it *must* be available. If you are asked about slope, there *must* be some available information about "rise" and "run," and it behooves one to attend to that information.

Dufresne et al. (2005) provided an accessible example of core coordination class phenomena. They showed two groups of university students, engineering and social science majors, various simulated motions of a ball rolling along a track that dipped down, but ended at its original height. They asked which motion looked most realistic. Subjects saw the motions in two contexts: one that showed only the focal ball, and another that also showed a simultaneous and constant ball motion in a parallel, non-dipping path. The social scientists' judgments of the realism of the focal motion remained nearly the same from the one- to two-ball situation. But, the engineers showed a dramatic shift, from preferring the correct motion to preferring another motion that literally no one initially believed to be realistic. In the two-ball case, engineers performed much worse than social scientists!

Using clinical interviews, the researchers confirmed that the engineers were looking at ("noticing") different things in the different situations. Relative motion became salient with two balls, changing the aspects of the focal motion that were attended to. In the two-ball presentation, a kind of balancing, "coming out even" dominated their inferences about realism. The very same motion that they had resoundingly rejected as least natural became viewed as most realistic.

Lessons learned: Scientific concepts are liable to shifts of attention during learning, and thus different (incoherent) determinations of their attributes. This is an easily documentable feature of learning concepts such as "force," and there is every reason (and some documentation) to believe this is also true for mathematical concepts. So, people must learn a variety of ways to construe particular concepts in various contexts, ways that are differentially salient in various conditions, yet all determinations must "align." Again, this local/global coherence principle shows KiP's attention to **multiple scales of conceptual structure**.

It is only mildly surprising that the "culprit" inference here is a kind of balancing, as implicated in J's case. So, once again, a relatively small-scaled element, similar to balancing p-prims, plays a critical role. Balancing is a core intuitive idea, but it also becomes a powerful principle in scientific understanding (**productivity**). Changes in kinetic and potential energy do always *balance out*. In this case, engineering students have elevated the importance and salience of balancing compared to social scientists, but have not yet learned very well what exactly balances out, and when balancing is appropriate (relevance). Certain p-prims are thus learned to be powerful, but they have not yet taken their proper place in understanding physics. Incidentally, this analysis also accounts for a very surprising difference (**diversity**) between different classes of students—engineers and social scientists.

P-prims and coordination classes are nicely complementary models. Within coordination class theory, p-prims turn out to account for certain problems (mainly in terms of inappropriate inferences), but they also can lie on good trajectories of learning, in constructing the overall system. Balancing is a superb physical idea, but naïve versions of balancing need to be developed precisely and not overgeneralized. Linearity is a comparable idea in mathematics. It is a wonderful and powerful idea, but it does not work, for example, for functions in general. $\sin(a + b)$ is not $\sin(a) + \sin(b)$. As balancing and linearity develop, they both need to be properly coordinated with checks and other ways of thinking.

11.3 Examples in Mathematics

This section displays some mathematical examples. The field of KiP analyses in mathematics is less rich than for physics, and overall trends are less well scouted out. But, to give a sense of what KiP looks like in mathematics and to encourage further such work is a primary goal of this article.

11.3.1 The Law of Large Numbers

Joseph Wagner (2006) used the main ideas of coordination class theory to study the learning of the statistical "law of large numbers": The distribution of average values in larger samples of random events hews more closely to the expected value (long-term average) than for smaller samples. In complementary manner, smaller samples show a greater dispersion; a greater proportion of their averages will be far from the expected value. So, if one uses a sample of 1000 coin tosses, one is nearly assured that the sample will have an average close to 50% heads and 50% tails. A sample of 10 tosses can easily lead to averages of, say, 70% heads and 30% tails. In the extreme case, a single toss, one is guaranteed of "averages" that are as far as possible from the long-term average: one always gets 100% heads, or 100% tails.

Wagner discovered that students often showed canonical coordination class difficulties during learning. Many had exceedingly long trajectories of learning, corresponding to learning in different contexts of use of the law of large numbers. In more technical detail, thinking in different contexts typically involves different knowledge (different noticings and different inferences), which may need to be acquired separately for different contexts. Furthermore, reasoning about the law in each context must *align* in terms of "conceptual output" (e.g., what is the relevant expected value) across all contexts. In short, **contextuality** is a dramatic problem for the law of large numbers, and systematic integrity (a **large-scale structural property**—in fact, the central-most large-scale property of coordination classes) is hard won in view of the **richness** of intuitive perspectives that may be adopted local to particular contexts (**small-scale structure**; think p-prims).

I present an abbreviated description one of Wagner's case studies to illustrate. Similar to the case of J, this is a fairly extreme case, but one in which characteristic phenomena of coordination class theory are easy to see. In particular, we shall see that learning across a wide range of situations appears necessary. The law of large numbers might not even appear to the learner as relevant to some situations, or it might be applied in a non-aligned way, owing to intuitive particulars of the situations. I sketch the subject's learning according to diSessa (2004), although a fuller analysis on most points and a more extensive empirical analysis appear in Wagner (2006).

The subject, called M ("Maria" in Wagner 2006), was a college freshman taking her first course in statistics. Wagner interviewed her on multiple occasions throughout the term (methodologically similar to J's study), and used a variety of near isomorphic questions involving the law of large numbers. The questions asked whether a small or large sample would be more likely to produce an average within particular bands of values, bands that include the expected value, or bands that are near or far from it. Would you choose a small or large sample if you wanted to get an average percentage of heads in coin tosses between 60% and 80% of the tosses? The law of large numbers says you would want a smaller number of tosses; in contrast, a very large number of tosses is almost certain to come out near 50% heads.

We pick up M's saga after she learned, with some difficulty, to apply the law of large numbers to coin tosses. Just after an extensive discussion of the coin situation, the interviewer (Jo) showed M a game "spinner," where a spun arrow points to one of 10 equal angular segments. Seven of the segments are blue, and three are green. Jo proceeded to ask M whether one would want a greater or lesser number of spins if one wanted to get an average of blues between 40 and 60% of the time.

M: OK. ... Land on blue? ... Well, 70% of the // of that circle is blue. Yeah. Seventy percent of it is blue, so, for it to land between 40 and 60% on blue, then, I would say there really is no difference. [She means it doesn't make a difference whether one does few or a lot of spins.]

Jo: Why?

M: Because if 70% of the // the circle, or, yeah, the spinner is blue, so ... it's most likely going to land in a blue area, regardless of how many times I spin it. It kinda really doesn't matter. It's not like the coins...

M is saying that she does not see the spinner situation as one in which the law of large number applies. The coordination class issue of *relevance* defines one of her problems. The larger data corpus suggests that a significant part of the problem is that M does not see that the concept of expected value applies to the spinner. She knows that in one spin, 70% of the time you will get blue, and 30% of the time you will get green. She reasons pretty well about "chances" for individual spins. But she simply does not believe that the long-term average, the expected percentage of blues or greens, exists. She "sees" chances, but does not infer from them a long-term average, nor even appear to know that a long-term average exists in this case.

Jo showed M a computer simulation of the spinner situation and proposed to do an experiment of plotting the result (histogram) of many samples of a certain number of spins. Would the percentages of blue pile up around any value, the way coin tosses always pile up around 50%? M was reluctant to make any prediction at all. But she very hesitantly suggested that the results might pile up around 70%. When the simulation was run, M was evidently surprised. "It *does* peak [pile up] around 70!!"

Here, we are at a disadvantage because we know much less about the relevant p-prims (or similar knowledge elements) that are controlling M's judgments, unlike the fact that, for J, the interviewer suspected balancing might provoke a different way of thinking about the toss, or that Dufresne et al. found that "balancing out" also sometimes controlled engineers' judgments about the realism of depicted motions of rolling balls. A good coordination class analysis demands a better analysis than the data here allow. However, a hint was offered earlier in the conversation when Jo pressed M to explain how the spinner differed from coins. M reported, "The difference, uh, between the coins and this [spinner] is that, in every toss, in the coin, I know that there's a ... 50% chance of getting a head, 50% chance of getting a tail." But with a spinner, "It's just not the same." Although M cannot put her finger on the difference, it seems plausible that she sees the 50–50 split of a coin flip to be *inherent in the coin*, "in every toss...," while the spinner arrow, per se, does not visibly (to her) have 70–30 in its very nature. An alternative or contributing factor involves the well-known fact concerning fractions that students seem conceptually competent first with simple ones, like ½. But, again, there is not enough data to distinguish possibilities.

Independent of the reason, the big picture relevant to coordination classes is that M simply does not see the spinner as essentially similar to coins. The *relevance* part of her developing coordination class is the most obvious problem. In particular, she doesn't naturally see an expected value as relevant to (nor determinable for) spinners. This case has a happy ending because the empirical (computer simulation) result was enough to convince M that expected value existed in the spinner case, and she began to reason more normatively about Jo's questions. To summarize, there was a conceptual **contextuality** that prevented using the same pattern of reasoning, the law of large numbers, in different situations. M needed to learn that expected value existed for spinners, and that it related to the "chances" concerning a single case in the same way as for coins: The long-term expected average is the same as the "chances" for a single case.

The final case of contextuality I report (there are many others!) concerns the average height of samples of men, corresponding to men in the U.S. registering for the military draft at small or large post offices. If the average height in the U.S. is 5 ft 9 inches, would a small or large post office (small or large sample) be more likely to find an average height for one day of more than 6 feet? At first, M had no idea how to answer the question. Pressed, she offered an uncertain reference to larger sets of numbers having smaller averages. The law of large numbers was, again, invisible to her in this context.

Jo improvised yet another context. Would you rather take a big or small sample of men at a university in order to find the average height? M was quick and confident in her answer. A larger sample would be "more representative,"[2] "more accurate." Arguably, the sampling context evoked a memory or intuition that larger samples are "better." Having made the connection to this intuition, M applied it relatively fluently to the post office problem.

The reason "representativeness" and "accuracy" were cued in the university sampling situation and not previously might not be clear. But M did not mention these intuitive ideas in any previous problems, and, once cued, she took those ideas productively into new contexts. The combination of **contextuality** and **productivity**, shown here, is highly distinctive of KiP analyses. Some intuitions, even if they are not usually evoked, can be useful if, somehow, they are brought to the learner's attention.

The next example is among the first applications of KiP to mathematics (a decade earlier than Wagner's work), and the final one is among the latest (a decade later than Wagner).

11.3.2 Understanding Fractions

Jack Smith (1995) did an investigation of student understanding of rational numbers and their representation as fractions according to broad KiP principles. He began by critiquing earlier work as (a) using a priori analysis of dimensions of mathematical competence, and also (b) systematically assessing competence according to success on tests. Instead, he proposed to look at competence directly in the specific strategies students use to solve a variety of problems. In particular, he did an exhaustive analysis of strategies used by students during clinical interviews on a set of fractions problems that was carefully chosen to display core ideas in both routine and novel circumstances. Smith looked most carefully at the strategies used by students who could be classified as "masters" of the subject matter. So, his intent was to describe the nature of achievable, high-level competence by looking directly at the details of students' performance.

The results were surprising in ways that typify KiP work. Masters used a remarkable range of strategies adapted rather precisely to particulars of the problems posed. While they did occasionally use the general methods that they had been taught (methods like converting to common denominators or converting to decimals), general methods appeared almost exclusively when none of their other

---

[2]Kahneman and Tversky (1972) provide a now-canonical treatment of statistical "misconceptions," including representativeness. However, their theoretical frame is very different from KiP. **Productivity**, in particular, is missing, unlike the cited role of representativeness in M's learning. These authors maintain that, to learn, intuitions must be excluded, and formal rules must be followed without question. Pratt and Noss (2002) provide a KiP-friendly treatment of statistical intuitions.

methods worked. A careful look at textbooks suggested that it was unlikely that many, if any, of the particular strategies had been instructed. Student mastery seems to transcend success in learning what is instructed.

In net, observable expertise is: (a) "fragmented" (**contextual**) in that it is highly adapted to problem particulars; (b) **rich**, composed of a wide variety of strategies; and (c) significantly based on invention, rather than instruction. The latter two points suggest **productivity**, the use of rich intuitive, self-developed ideas, and that richness is maintained into expertise, in contrast to what conventional instruction seems to assume.

One can summarize Smith's orientation so as to highlight typical KiP strategies, which contrast with those of other approaches:

- avoiding a priori or "rational" views of competence in favor of directly empirical approaches: Look at what students do and say about what they do.
- couching analysis in terms of knowledge systems (**a complex systems approach**) of elements and relations among them (e.g., particular strategies were often, but not always, defended by students by reference to more general, instructed ways of thinking).
- discovering that the best student understanding, not just intuitive precursors, is rich (many elements), diverse, and involves a lot of highly particular and contextually adapted ideas (**contextuality**). Thus it is in some ways more similar to pre-instructional ideas than might be expected.

Smith did not use the models (p-prims, etc.) that later became the recognizable core of KiP. But, still, the distinctiveness of a KiP orientation proved productive. I believe this is an important lesson, that, independent of technical models and details, KiP's general principles and orientations can provide key insights into learning that are not available in other perspectives. Newcomers to KiP might do well to start their work at this level, and move to more technical levels when those details come to seem sensible, and when and if the value of technicalities becomes palpable.

11.3.3 Conceptual and Procedural Knowledge in Strategy Innovation

The relationship of procedural to conceptual knowledge is a long-standing, important topic in mathematics education. There is a general agreement that one should strike a balance between these modes. However, at a more intimate level, the detailed relations should be important. What conceptual knowledge is important, when, and how? It is known that students can (e.g., Kamii 2000) and do (e.g., Smith's work, above) spontaneously innovate procedures. How might conceptual knowledge be important to innovation, specifically what knowledge is important, and what is the nature and origin of those resources?

Mariana Levin (2012, 2018) studied strategy innovation in early algebra. Her study involved a student who started with an instructed guess-and-check method of solving problems like: "The length of a rectangle is six more than three times the width. If the perimeter is 148 ft., find the length and width." Over repeated problem solving, this student moved iteratively, without direct instruction, from guess-and-check to a categorically different method: a fluent algorithmic method that mathematicians would identify as linear interpolation/extrapolation. One of the interesting features of the development was that intuitive "co-variation schemes," more similar to calculus (related rates) than anything instructed in school, rooted his development (**productivity**). Indeed, his development could be traced through six distinct levels of co-variation schemes, progressively moving from qualitative (the "more implies more" intuition, but in a circumstance where it is productive), toward more quantitatively precise, general, and "mathematical-looking" principles.

In order to optimally track and generalize this student's progress, Levin extended the coordination class model to what she calls a "strategy system" model, demonstrating the generative and evolving nature of KiP (**continuous improvement**). Her model maintained a focus on perceptual categories ("seeing" in Fig. 11.1), and inferential relations (e.g., co-variation schemes). But there were also theoretical innovations: Typically more than one coordination class is involved in strategy systems. General conceptions (inferences) specifically supported procedural actions in particular ways.

In addition to the core co-variational idea, a cluster of intuitive categories, such as "controller," "result," "target," and "error" played strongly into the student's development. All in all, Levin's study showed the surprising power of intuitive roots—ones that may never be invoked in school—and provided a systematic framework for understanding their use in the development of procedural/conceptual systems.

11.3.4 Other Examples

In addition to what was presented above, I recommend a few other examples of KiP work that will be helpful for mathematics education researchers with different specialties in order to understand the KiP perspective. Andrew Izsák has developed an extensive body of work using KiP to think about learning concerning, for example, area (Izsák 2005), and early algebra (Izsák 2000). Similarly Adi Adiredja (2014) treated the concept of limit from a KiP perspective. Adiredja's analysis is important in the narrative of this article in that it takes steps to comprehend learning of the topic, limits, at a fine grain-size, including the productivity and not just learning difficulties that emerge from prior intuitive ideas. The work may be profitably contrasted with that of Sierpinska (1990) and Tall and Vinner (1981) on similar topics.

11.4 Cross-Cutting Themes

In this final section, I identify KiP's position and potential contributions to two large-scale themes in the study of learning in mathematics and science.

11.4.1 Continuity or Discontinuity in Learning

I believe that one of the central-most and still unsettled issues in learning concerns whether one views learning as a continuous process or a discontinuous one. In particular, how do we interpret persistent learning problems that appear to afflict students for extended periods of time? In science education, so-called "misconceptions" or "intuitive theories" views treat intuitive ideas as both entrenched and unproductive. They are assumed to be unhelpful—blocking, in fact—because they are simply wrong (Smith et al. 1993). In mathematics education, one also finds a lot of discussion about misconceptions (e.g., concerning graphing, Leinhardt et al. 1990) and also about the essentially problematic nature of "intuitive rules" such as "more implies more" (Stavy and Tirosh 2000). But, more often than in science, researchers implicate discontinuities of form, rather than just content. For example, Sierpinska (1990) talks about basic "epistemological obstacles," large-scale changes in "ways of knowing." Vinner (1997) talks about "pseudo-concepts" as bedeviling learners, and some interpretations of the distinction between process and object conceptualizations in mathematics (Sfard 1991) put process forms as inferior to conceptions that are at the level of objects (not necessarily Sfard's contention). Or, the transition from process to object modes of thinking is always intrinsically difficult. Tall (2002) emphasizes the existence of discontinuities possibly due to deep-seated brain processes ("the limbic brain;" sensory-motor thinking). Along similar lines (as anticipated in footnote 2), Kahneman and Tversky's view of difficulties in learning about chance and statistics relies on so-called "dual process" theories of mind. (See Glöckner and Witteman 2010, for a review and critical assessment.) Instinctive (intuitive) thinking must be *replaced* with a categorically different kind of thinking based on a conscious and explicit rule following.

On the reverse side, mathematics education researchers sometimes have supported the productivity of intuitive ideas (e.g., Fischbein 1987), and, most particularly, constructivist researchers have pursued important lines of continuity between naïve and expert ideas (Moss and Case 1999, is, in my view, an exceptional example from a large literature). However, very few studies approach the detail and security of documentation of elements, systems of knowledge, and processes of transformation of the best KiP analyses.

The issues are too complex and unresolved for a discussion here, but KiP offers a view and accomplishments to support a more continuous view of learning and to critique discontinuous views. For example, both experts and learners use intuitive ideas, even if their knowledge is different at larger scales of organization. Gradual organization and building of a new system need not have any essential discontinuities: There may not be any chasm separating the beginning from the end of a long journey. It is just that, before and after, things may look quite different. A core difficulty in learning might simply involve (a) a mismatch between our instructional expectation concerning how long learning should take and the realities of the transformation, and (b) a lack of understanding of the details of relevant processes. KiP offers unusual but tractable and detailed models of small-scale, intuitive knowledge that can support its incorporation into expertise, and methodologies capable of discovering and carefully describing particular elements. These issues are treated in more detail in Gueudet et al. (2016).

11.4.2 Understanding Representations

To conclude, I wish to mention two KiP-styled studies concerning the general nature of representational competence—central to mathematical competence—and the roles of intuitive resources in learning about representations.

Bruce Sherin (2001) undertook a detailed study of how students use and learn with different representational systems (algebra vs. computer programs) in physics. One of Sherin's key findings was that p-prim-like knowledge mediates between real-world structure ("causality") and representational templates. For example, the idea of "the more X, the more Y" (e.g., more acceleration means greater force) translates into the representational form "$Y = kX$" (e.g., $F = ma$). Sherin's work will be most interesting to mathematics education researchers interested in how representations become meaningful in thinking about real-world situations (modeling), how such situations bootstrap understanding of mathematical structure, and the detailed role that intuitive knowledge plays in these processes. This work builds on similar earlier work by Vergnaud (1983), but in distinctly KiP directions.

Finally, diSessa et al. (1991) studied young students' naïve resources for thinking about representations. In contrast to misconceptions-styled work, we uncovered very substantial expertise concerning representations. However, the expertise was different than what is normally expected in school. It had more to do with the generative aspects of representation (e.g., design and judgments of adequacy) and less to do with the details of instructed representations. This repository of intuitive competence is essentially ignored in school instruction, an insight shared with a few (e.g., Kamii 2000), but not many, mathematics education researchers

References

Adiredja, A. (2014). *Leveraging students' intuitive knowledge about the formal definition of a limit (Unpublished doctoral dissertation)*. Berkeley, CA: University of California.

Brown, J. S., Collins, A., & Duguid, P. (1989). Situated cognition and the culture of learning. *Educational Researcher, 18*(1), 32–42.

diSessa, A. A. (1996). What do "just plain folk" know about physics? In D. R. Olson & N. Torrance (Eds.), *The handbook of education and human development: New models of learning, teaching, and schooling* (pp. 709–730). Oxford, UK: Blackwell Publishers Ltd.

diSessa, A.A. (2004). Contextuality and coordination in conceptual change. In E. Redish & M. Vicentini (Eds.), *Proceedings of the International School of Physics "Enrico Fermi": Research on Physics Education* (pp. 137–156). Amsterdam: ISO Press/Italian Physics Society.

diSessa, A. A. (2014). A history of conceptual change research: Threads and fault lines. In K. Sawyer (Ed.), *Cambridge handbook of the learning sciences* (2nd ed., pp. 88–108). Cambridge, UK: Cambridge University Press.

diSessa, A. A. (2017). Conceptual change in a microcosm: Comparative analysis of a learning event. *Human Development, 60*(1), 1–37.

diSessa, A. A., & Cobb, P. (2004). Ontological innovation and the role of theory in design experiments. *Journal of the Learning Sciences, 13*(1), 77–103.

diSessa, A. A., Elby, A., & Hammer, D. (2002). J's epistemological stance and strategies. In G. Sinatra & P. Pintrich (Eds.), *Intentional conceptual change* (pp. 237–290). Mahwah, NJ: Lawrence Erlbaum Associates.

diSessa, A. A., Hammer, D., Sherin, B., & Kolpakowski, T. (1991). Inventing graphing: Meta-representational expertise in children. *Journal of Mathematical Behavior, 10*(2), 117–160.

diSessa, A.A., Sherin, B., & Levin, M. (2016). Knowledge analysis: An introduction. In A. diSessa, M. Levin, & N. Brown (Eds.), *Knowledge and interaction: A synthetic agenda for the learning sciences* (pp. 30–71). New York, NY: Routledge.

Dufresne, R., Mestre, J., Thaden-Koch, T., Gerace, W., & Leonard, W. (2005). When transfer fails: Effect of knowledge, expectations and observations on transfer in physics. In J. Mestre (Ed.), *Transfer of learning from a modern multidisciplinary perspective* (pp. 155–215). Greenwich, CT: Information Age Publishing.

Fischbein, E. (1987). *Intuition in science and mathematics: An educational approach*. Dortrecht, Netherlands: Kluwer Academic.

Glöckner, A., & Witteman, C. (2010). Beyond dual-process models: A categorisation of processes underlying intuitive judgement and decision making. *Thinking & Reasoning, 16*(1), 1–25.

Gueudet, G., Bosch, M., diSessa, A., Kwon, O. N., & Verschaffel, L. (2016). Transitions in mathematics education. In G. Kaiser (Ed.), *ICME-13 topical surveys*. Springer International: Switzerland.

Izsák, A. (2000). Inscribing the winch: Mechanisms by which students develop knowledge structures for representing the physical world with algebra. *Journal of the Learning Sciences, 9*(1), 31–74.

Izsák, A. (2005). "You have to count the squares": Applying knowledge in pieces to learning rectangular area. *Journal of the Learning Sciences, 14*(3), 361–403.

Kahneman, D., & Tversky, A. (1972). Subjective probability: A judgment of representativeness. *Cognitive Psychology, 3*, 430–454.

Kamii, C., & Housman, L. (2000). *Young children reinvent arithmetic* (2nd ed.). New York, NY: Teachers College Press.

Leinhardt, G., Zaslavsky, O., & Stein, M. K. (1990). Functions, graphs, and graphing: Tasks, learning, and teaching. *Review of Educational Research, 60*(1), 1–64.

Levin (Campbell), M. E. (2012). *Modeling the co-development of strategic and conceptual knowledge during mathematical problem solving* (Unpublished doctoral dissertation). Berkeley, CA: University of California.

Levin, M. (2018). Conceptual and procedural knowledge during strategy construction: A complex knowledge systems perspective. *Cognition and Instruction, 36*(3), 247–278.

Moss, J., & Case, R. (1999). Developing children's understanding of the rational numbers: A new model and an experimental curriculum. *Journal for Research in Mathematics Education, 30*(2), 122–147.

Parnafes, O., & diSessa, A. A. (2013). Microgenetic learning analysis: A methodology for studying knowledge in transition. *Human Development, 56*(5), 5–37.

Philip, T. (2011). A "Knowledge in Pieces" approach to studying ideological change in teachers' reasoning about race, racism and racial justice. *Cognition and Instruction, 11*(3), 297–329.
Pratt, D., & Noss, R. (2002). The microevolution of mathematical knowledge: The case of randomness. *The Journal of the Learning Sciences, 11*(4), 453–488.
Sfard, A. (1991). On the dual nature of mathematical conceptions: Reflections on processes and objects as different sides of the same coin. *Educational Studies in Mathematics, 22*(1), 1–36.
Sierpinska, A. (1990). Some remarks on understanding in mathematics. *For the Learning of Mathematics, 10*(3), 24–36.
Sherin, B. (2001). A comparison of programming languages and algebraic notation as expressive languages for physics. *International Journal of Computers for Mathematical Learning, 6*(1), 1–61.
Smith, J. P. (1995). Competent reasoning with rational numbers. *Cognition and Instruction, 13*(1), 3–50.
Smith, J. P., diSessa, A. A., & Roschelle, J. (1993). Misconceptions reconceived: A constructivist analysis of knowledge in transition. *Journal of the Learning Sciences, 3*(2), 115–163.
Stavy, R., & Tirosh, D. (2000). *How students (mis-)understand science and mathematics.* New York, NY: Teachers College Press.
Tall, D. (2002). Continuities and discontinuities in long-term learning schemas. In D. Tall & M. Thomas (Eds.), *Intelligence, learning and understanding: A tribute to Richard Skemp* (pp. 151–177). Flaxton QLD, Australia: Post Pressed.
Tall, D., & Vinner, S. (1981). Concept image and concept definition in mathematics with particular reference to limits and continuity. *Educational Studies in Mathematics, 12*(2), 151–169.
Vergnaud, G. (1983). Multiplicative structures. In R. Lesh & M. Landau (Eds.), *Acquisition of mathematics concepts and processes* (pp. 127–174). New York, NY: Academic Press.
Vinner, S. (1997). The pseudo-conceptual and the pseudo-analytical thought processes in mathematics learning. *Educational Studies in Mathematics, 34*(2), 97–129.
Vosniadou, S. (Ed.). (2013). *International handbook of research on conceptual change* (2nd ed.). New York, NY: Routledge.
Wagner, J. (2006). Transfer in pieces. *Cognition and Instruction, 24*(1), 1–71.

Open Access This chapter is licensed under the terms of the Creative Commons Attribution 4.0 International License (http://creativecommons.org/licenses/by/4.0/), which permits use, sharing, adaptation, distribution and reproduction in any medium or format, as long as you give appropriate credit to the original author(s) and the source, provide a link to the Creative Commons license and indicate if changes were made.

The images or other third party material in this chapter are included in the chapter's Creative Commons license, unless indicated otherwise in a credit line to the material. If material is not included in the chapter's Creative Commons license and your intended use is not permitted by statutory regulation or exceeds the permitted use, you will need to obtain permission directly from the copyright holder.

Chapter 12
Task Design Frameworks in Mathematics Education Research: An Example of a Domain-Specific Frame for Algebra Learning with Technological Tools

Carolyn Kieran

Abstract Theorizing about task design is a fairly recent area of attention within the educational research community, emerging in the late 1960s and continuing with growing interest to the present day. To reflect the evolution in task design theorization, this chapter focuses first on historical aspects and highlights the main theorizing initiatives of the past half-century. The second part offers a conceptualization of current theoretical frameworks and principles for task design within mathematics education research—a conceptualization that distinguishes among the three levels of grand, intermediate, and domain-specific frames. The third part of the chapter elaborates on the notion of domain-specific frames by presenting an example of the design features underpinning a study on the CAS-supported co-emergence of technique and theory within the activity of algebraic factorization and describes how the classroom implementation of the proving phase of the designed task-sequence was supported by the instructional practice of the teacher and by the role played by the technology as a tool to spark thinking.

Keywords Task design · Theoretical frameworks for task design · Domain-specific frames · Task design in algebra education · Design as intention · Design as implementation · Digital artifacts as tools for thinking · Instructional practice within the activity of proving

---

The historical overview in this paper is drawn partially from my contribution to a chapter (Kieran et al. 2015) in the Springer publication, *Task Design in Mathematics Education* (Watson and Ohtani 2015), and the domain-specific example is based on our team's past research and was featured briefly in Kieran (2017).

C. Kieran (✉)
Département de Mathématiques, Université du Québec à Montréal, 201 avenue du Président-Kennedy, local PK-5151, Montréal, QC H2X 3Y7, Canada
e-mail: kieran.carolyn@uqam.ca

© The Author(s) 2019
G. Kaiser and N. Presmeg (eds.), *Compendium for Early Career Researchers in Mathematics Education*, ICME-13 Monographs,
https://doi.org/10.1007/978-3-030-15636-7_12

12.1 Introduction

The field of mathematics education could be said to have been involved in design ever since its beginnings. However, as Erich Wittmann (1995) remarked, in a paper titled *Mathematics Education as a Design Science*, the design of teaching units was never a focus of the mathematics education research community until the mid-1970s. Michèle Artigue (2009) too has argued that "didactical design has always played an important role in the field of mathematics education, but it has not always been a major theme of theoretical interest in the community" (p. 7). The movement toward theoretically-based design research from the 1960s onward has benefitted largely from the emergence of an international research community in mathematics education, as well as from contributions from the disciplines of mathematics and psychology (Kilpatrick 1992).

To illustrate these influences and their evolution within the community, this chapter is divided as follows. The first section (Sect. 12.2) provides a brief historical overview of theorizing initiatives with respect to task design in our field over the past half-century. The second section (Sect. 12.3) presents a conceptualization of current frameworks for task design in mathematics education and describes the characteristics of the design principles offered by these frames—a conceptualization that distinguishes among the three levels of grand, intermediate, and domain-specific frames. The third section (Sect. 12.4) offers an example of a domain-specific frame developed to guide our research team's investigations into the learning of algebraic techniques and theory in an environment involving computing technology.

12.2 Brief History of the Emergence of Design-Related Theoretical Work from the 1960s Onward

In 1969, the first International Congress on Mathematical Education (ICME) took place in Lyon. A round table at that congress set the stage for the formation in 1976 of what was to quickly become the largest association of mathematics education researchers in the world, the International Group for the Psychology of Mathematics Education (PME). The emergence of this community was accompanied by the creation of several research journals, as well as research institutes in many countries. The late 1960 and 1970s thus signalled a huge surge and interest in research in mathematics education, leading to theorizing initiatives related to design.

12.2.1 Influences from Psychology

This surge in research in mathematics education had to rely almost exclusively in its early days on psychology as a source of theory (Johnson 1980). Piaget's (1971) cognitively-oriented, genetic epistemology was one of the main examples of psychological frames adopted by the emerging mathematics education research community in its studies on the learning of mathematics. However, it was psychologists who had an interest in education who would initiate some of the early theorizing efforts related specifically to design. For example, in 1965 Robert Gagné published *The Conditions of Learning*. Based on models from behaviourist psychology, Gagné's (1965) nine conditions of learning were viewed as principles for instructional design. In parallel with the instructional design approach being developed by Gagné and others, advances in design considerations were stimulated by the theorizing of the cognitive scientist and Nobel laureate, Herbert Simon (1969), in his book, *The Sciences of the Artificial*. Robert Glaser (1976) in his *Components of a Psychology of Instruction: Toward a Science of Design* distinguished between the descriptive nature of theories of learning and the prescriptive nature of theories of instruction. In integrating design considerations into instructional research, he argued that the structure of the subject-matter discipline may not be the most useful for facilitating the learning of less expert individuals—a point of view that was questioned somewhat by researchers in mathematics education. Thus, mathematics education researchers would need to develop during the years to come their own scientific approaches to designing environments for the learning of mathematics and to generating frameworks for task design in particular.

12.2.2 Early Design Initiatives of the Mathematics Education Research Community

During the 1970s, the focus within the emerging mathematics education research community was on the learning of mathematics and the development of models of that learning. For example, the paper that the mathematician Hans Freudenthal presented at PME3 in 1979 (one of the 24 research reports presented in 1979 at the recently formed PME) dealt with the growth of reflective thinking in learners (Freudenthal 1979). That paper sowed the seeds for a mathematical-psychological approach to task design—an approach that was to develop during the late 1980s and 1990s into the instructional theory specific to mathematics education known as Realistic Mathematics Education.

In contrast to the majority of the 1979 PME3 papers oriented toward learning, the paper by Alan Bell (1979) touched more directly upon issues related to design. While he too focused on learning, it was done through the lens of different teaching approaches with various curriculum units that had been designed for the South Nottinghamshire project. In Bell's paper, which was a forerunner of the early ways of thinking about design within the mathematics education research community, design considerations were seen more from the perspective of particular teaching methods than as approaches to the design of tasks per se.

The 1980s brought some evolution in this regard with, for example, the work of Wittmann. In his 1984 *Educational Studies in Mathematics* paper (a modified version of his opening address at the 14th annual meeting of German mathematics educators in 1981), titled *Teaching units as the integrating core of mathematics education*, Wittmann (1984) argued for tasks displaying the following characteristics: the objectives, the materials, the mathematical problems arising from the context of the unit, and the mostly mathematical, sometimes psychological, background of the unit. He suggested that a teaching unit is not an elaborated plan for a series of lessons; rather it is an idea for a teaching approach that leaves open various ways of realizing the unit.

During the years 1985–1988, one of the PME working groups focused on establishing principles for the design of teaching. In 1988, a collection of papers from this working group was put together by the Shell Centre under the title *The Design of Teaching—Papers from a PME Working Group*, and subsequently published in a special issue of *Educational Studies in Mathematics* in 1993. In his editorial for the special issue, Bell (1993) emphasized that the principles of teaching practice should be in harmonious integration with the principles that are incorporated into the design of teaching materials—a characteristic that would continue to be important in task design within the community over the decades to come.

The 1980s in France ushered in the development of *didactical engineering* (Artigue 1992)—a theory-based approach to conducting research that had didactical design at its heart. However, as noted by Artigue (2009), the original designs tended to go through a certain mutation in practice, leading her to remark that "the relationships between theory and practice as regards didactical design are not under theoretical control" (p. 12). This awareness pointed to one of the inherent limitations in theorizing about task design in isolation from considerations regarding instructional practice.

12.2.3 The 1990s and Early 2000s: Development of Design Experiments

The term *design experiment* came into prominence in the 1990s with the psychologist Ann Brown's (1992) publication on educational design. Several factors had fallen into place, including the maturing of the mathematics education research community over a 20-year period and an evolving desire to be able to study within one's research not just learning or not just teaching (Lesh 2002). Design experiments aimed at taking into account the entire learning picture. As Cobb et al. (2003) pointed out: "Design experiments ideally result in greater understanding of a learning ecology. ... Elements of a learning ecology typically include the tasks or problems that students are asked to solve, the kinds of discourse that are encouraged, the norms of participation that are established, the tools and related material means provided, and the practical means by which classroom teachers can orchestrate relations among these elements" (p. 9). Within this conception of design experiments, the task or task-sequence is but one of a larger set of design considerations involving the entire learning ecology.[1]

12.2.4 From Early 2000 Onward

Theorizing related to design in mathematics education research developed considerably during the 2000s (Kelly et al. 2008). Contributing to this development was the recommendation put forward by Cobb et al. (2003):

> General philosophical orientations to educational matters—such as constructivism—are important to educational practice, but they often fail to provide detailed guidance in organizing instruction. The critical question that must be asked is whether the theory informs prospective design and, if so, in precisely what way? Rather than grand theories of learning that may be difficult to project into particular circumstances, design experiments tend to emphasize an intermediate theoretical scope. (pp. 10–11)

Cobb et al. also argued that design experiments are conducted to develop theories, not merely to tune empirically 'what works': "a design theory explains why designs work and suggests how they may be adapted to new circumstances" (p. 9).

In addition to the evolution in theoretical perspectives on design during these years, the term *task design* came to be more clearly present in discussions of research related to design. For example, at the 2005 PME conference, a research forum was dedicated to task design for the first time and had as its stated theme, "The significance of task design in mathematics education" (Ainley and Pratt 2005). At ICME-11 in 2008 the scientific program committee initiated the idea of having a Topic Study Group (TSG) on task design: "Research and development in task design and analysis". The excitement generated regarding this research area was such that a similar TSG was put on the program for ICME-12 in 2012, as well as for ICME-13 in 2016 and for ICME-14 in 2020. This interest was further illustrated by the holding of the 2013 ICMI Study-22 Conference on the same theme.

12.2.5 A Key Issue

In closing this section on the historical overview of the emergence of theorizing research related to design activity, I want to draw attention to an issue that is central to the complex role of theory as both a resource for and a product of design

---

[1]The term *task* (or *task-sequence*, which could take an entire lesson, or more) is characterized in the ICMI Study-22 Discussion Document as "anything that a teacher uses to demonstrate mathematics, to pursue interactively with students, or to ask students to do something ... also anything that students decide to do for themselves in a particular situation" (Watson et al. 2013, p. 10).

research. It involves the terms *design as intention* and *design as implementation*. In a paper on design tools in didactical research, Ruthven et al. (2009) expanded upon the distinction between *design as intention* and *design as implementation* (Collins et al. 2004). *Design as implementation* focuses attention on the process by which a designed sequence is integrated into the classroom environment and subsequently is progressively refined, whereas *design as intention* addresses specifically the initial formulation of the design. While many studies address both, the distinction can be useful for understanding certain nuanced differences between one study and another. Ruthven et al. (2009) state that design as intention emphasizes the "original design and the clarity and coherence of the intentions it expresses" (p. 329). The provision for this clarity and coherence is generally achieved by the use of theoretical frames that are already well developed.

In contrast to the front-end importance given to theory-based design tools by Ruthven et al. (2009), Gravemeijer and Cobb (2006) put the focus more toward the *development* of theory and its role as a product of the design research. In their design-experiment studies, the initial theoretical base for the study, and its accompanying instructional plan, undergo successive refinements by means of the implementation process. The description of the entire process constitutes the development of the theory. Because of the centrality of the implementation process in the development of the resulting theory, such studies are characterized as *design as implementation* studies, even though they also have a strong initial theoretical base. The complexity of the dialectical role played by theory in such research warns, however, against equating, on the one hand, design as intention and theory as a resource or, on the other hand, design as implementation and theory as a product.

Put another way, theories are both a resource and a product. As a resource, they provide theoretical tools and principles to support the design of a teaching sequence (e.g., Ruthven et al. 2009) and, as a product of design research, theories inform us about both the processes of learning and the means that have been shown to support that learning (Cobb et al. 2003). In practice, most design experiments combine both orientations: the design is based on a conceptual framework and upon theoretical propositions, while the successive iterations of implementation and retrospective analysis contribute to further theory building that is central to the research.

12.3 A Conceptualization of Current Theoretical Frameworks and Principles for Task Design in Mathematics Education Research

12.3.1 Introduction

The historical look at the early research efforts related to theorizing about task design hinted at a mix of task and instructional considerations. However, the extent to which instructional aspects are factored into task design is but one of the ways in which design frameworks can vary. Frameworks can also differ according to the manner in which they draw upon cognitive, sociological, sociocultural, discursive, or other theories. In addition, frameworks are distinguishable according to their relation to various task genres, that is, whether the tasks are geared toward (i) the development of mathematical knowledge (such as concepts, procedures, representations), (ii) the development of the processes of mathematical reasoning (such as conjecturing, generalizing, proving, as well as fostering creativity, argumentation, and critical thinking), (iii) the development of modelling and problem-solving activity, (iv) the assessment of mathematical knowledge, processes, and problem solving, and so on.

As well, some frameworks may be more suited to the design of specific tasks; others to the design of lesson flow; still others to the design of sequences involving the integration of particular artefacts. Because several considerations enter into an overall design—considerations that include the specific genre of the task, its instructional support, the classroom milieu, the tools being used, and so on—each part of the design might call for different theoretical underpinnings. Thus, the resulting design can involve a *networking* of various theoretical frames and principles (Prediger et al. 2008).

A more holistic way of thinking about frames is elaborated immediately below. It involves conceptualizing them in terms of three different levels, that is, grand frames, intermediate level frames, and domain-specific frames—all of these levels of frames together constituting the theoretical base for the design of a given study.

12.3.2 Grand Theoretical Frames

Mathematics education research has tended in large measure to adopt such grand theoretical perspectives as the cognitive-psychological, the constructivist, the socio-constructivist, and the sociocultural. However, as pointed out by Lerman et al. (2002), these are but four from the vast array of theoretical fields, in addition to those from educational psychology and/or mathematics, that have back-grounded mathematics education research. In line with Cobb (2007), who argued that such grand theories need to be adapted and interpreted in order to serve the needs of design research, and the fact that these grand theories have already been well described in the literature, I now address the less well-documented levels of intermediate and domain-specific design frames.

12.3.3 Intermediate Level Frames

Intermediate level frames have a more specialized focus than the grand theories and, as such, have the property that they can contribute in a more refined way to the design of particular curricular areas. In brief, intermediate level frames are located between the grand theories and the more local, domain-specific frames, the latter of which will be seen to deal with distinct mathematical concepts, procedures, or processes of mathematical reasoning. The multitude of intermediate level frames that are being applied to design research in mathematics education include, for example, Realistic Mathematics Education theory (Treffers 1987), the Theory of Didactical Situations (Brousseau 1997), the Anthropological Theory of the Didactic (Chevallard 1999), Lesson Study (Lewis 2002), Variation Theory (Runesson 2005), Conceptual Change Theory (van Dooren et al. 2013), and so on.

In general, intermediate level frames can be characterized by explicit principles/heuristics/tools that can be applied to the design of tasks and task-sequences. Because these frames tend to be highly developed, they are often used in *design as intention* approaches. In addition, intermediate level frames can also be characterized according to whether their roots are primarily theoretical or whether they are based to a large extent on deep craft knowledge. An example of the former is the Theory of Didactical Situations and the latter, Lesson Study.

The Theory of Didactical Situations (TDS) (Brousseau 1997, 1998), an intermediate level theory that draws upon the grand theory of Piagetian cognitive development, can be characterized by its framing within a deep *a priori* analysis of the underlying mathematics of the topic to be learned, integrating the epistemology of the discipline, and supported by cognitive hypotheses related to the learning of the given topic. According to Ruthven et al. (2009), one of the central design tools provided by TDS is the *adidactical situation*, which mediates the development of students' mathematical knowledge through independent problem solving. The term *adidactical* within TDS refers specifically to that part of the activity "between the moment the student accepts the problem as if it were her own and the moment when she produces her answer, [a time when] the teacher refrains from interfering and suggesting the knowledge that she wants to see appear" (Brousseau 1997, p. 30). A *situation* includes both the task and the environment that is designed to provide for the adidactical activity of the student. According to the TDS frame, the adidactical situation tool furnishes guidelines as to: "the problem to be posed, the conditions under which it is to be solved, and the expected progression toward a strategy that is both valid and efficient" (Ruthven et al. 2009, p. 331). In addition to the adidactical situation tool, TDS-based design is also informed by a second design heuristic, that of the *didactical variables* tool. This supplementary design tool allows for choices regarding particular aspects of the main task and how it is to be carried out. Although certain modifications are made to those aspects of the task that are found to improve the learning potential of the situation (i.e., that students are more likely to learn what is intended), the initial design of the task is absolutely central to the TDS-framed *design as intention* process.

Lesson Study, an intermediate level frame typically associated with Japanese education (see, e.g., Fernandez and Yoshida 2004; Fujii 2015; Jacobs and Morita 2002), is a culturally-situated, collaborative, approach to design situated within the grand theory of socioculturalism and one where teachers with their deep, craft-based knowledge are pivotal to the process. It is a frame devoted as much to *design as intention* as it is to *design as implementation*. Lesson Study consists of the following phases: (1) collaboratively planning a research lesson; (2) seeing the research lesson in action; (3) discussing the research lesson; and optionally (4) revising the lesson; (5) teaching the new version of the lesson; and (6) sharing reflections on the new version of the lesson. Three design principles constitute the Lesson Study frame: (i) *kyozaikenkyu*, (ii) *structured problem solving,* and (iii) *task evaluation.* Kyozaikenkyu means literally "instructional materials research" and focuses on the detailed planning of the research lesson. The second principle, that of *structured problem solving*, involves, according to Stigler and Hiebert (1999), a single task and the following four specific phases: (i) teacher presenting the problem (*donyu*, 5–10 min), (ii) students working at solving the problem without the teacher's help (*jiriki-kaiketsu*, 10–20 min), (iii) comparing and discussing solution approaches (*neriage*, 10–20 min), and (iv) summing up by the teacher (*matome*, 5 min). After the research lesson has been observed by other teachers, school administrators, and sometimes an outside expert, it is then discussed and evaluated in relation to its overall goals. This process of lesson evaluation, and in particular *task evaluation*, is considered a third design principle. The post-lesson discussion focuses to a large extent on the effects of the initial task design with respect to student thinking and learning. The teacher's thought-out key questioning receives much attention. Another of the main aspects discussed is whether the anticipated student solutions were in fact evoked by the task and its accompanying manipulative materials, or whether improvements in specific parts of the task design are warranted.

12.3.4 Domain-Specific Frames

In contrast to intermediate level frames whose characterizations do not specify any particular mathematical reasoning process or any particular mathematical content area, domain-specific frames for the design of tasks or task-sequences do specify particular reasoning processes (e.g., conjecturing, arguing, proving) or particular content (e.g., geometry, integer numbers, numerical concepts, algebraic techniques) or particular tools (e.g., computers, calculators, tablets; for further exposition of various task-design frames related directly to the integration of tools, see Leung and Bolite-Frant 2015). Task-design-research studies involving domain-specific frames typically draw upon past research findings in a given area, in addition to being situated within certain intermediate level, and more general grand-level, frameworks. As such, domain-specific frames for task design research tend to be more eclectic than their intermediate level counterparts.

Note that some researchers use the term "local theories" or "local frames" for what I am referring to here as domain-specific frames. In general, research designed with domain-specific frames can have the characteristics of both *design as intention* and *design as implementation* studies with their attention to, on the one hand, the theoretical underpinnings of the design of the tasks and the proposed instructional supports, and, on the other hand, the aim of further developing the theoretical domain-specific frame by means of the implementation process. Examples of studies on the use and development of domain-specific frames include, for instance, Prusak et al.'s (2013) research involving a domain-specific frame for fostering mathematical argumentation within geometric problem solving, Komatsu and Tsujiyama's (2013) frame for proof problems with diagrams, and Stephan and Akyuz's (2012, 2013) frame for the learning of integer concepts and operations. With the aim of elaborating further on the nature of domain-specific frames, I offer an example drawn from our team's research on algebra learning with technological tools.

12.4 A Domain-Specific Frame for the CAS-Supported Co-emergence of Technique and Theory within the Activity of Algebraic Factorization

In our past research on the use of CAS[2] technology in algebra learning, we[3] have carried out several studies with classes of Grade 10 students (16-year-olds), with each study involving multiple sets of CAS-supported task-sequences. In the paper by Kieran and Drijvers (2006), we reported on the classroom implementation of two of these task-sequences (see also Hitt and Kieran 2009), one of which is the focus of this section and which is herein presented with a detailed description of the domain-specific frame that underpinned its design.

12.4.1 The Theoretical Underpinnings of the Design Study

One of the two specific task-sequences described in the Kieran and Drijvers (2006) paper involved an elaboration of the factoring task of $x^n - 1$, a task inspired by the earlier work of Mounier and Aldon (1996).

The design of the $x^n - 1$ task-sequence, as was the case with the design of all of our algebra task-sequences, was situated within and drew upon aspects of the following intermediate level and domain-specific level frameworks, the entire combination of these specific frameworks constituting the domain-specific frame for our design study:

---

[2] A Computer Algebra System (CAS) is a software program that facilitates symbolic mathematics. The core functionality of a CAS is manipulation of mathematical expressions in symbolic form.

[3] Team members: C. Kieran, A. Boileau, D. Tanguay, and J. Guzmán†; also including at various times: F. Hitt, P. Drijvers, L. Saldanha, M. Artigue, A. Solares, and A. I. Sacristán. Website: profmath.uqam.ca/~APTE/TachesA.html

- The *intermediate level* frameworks of:
  - The Anthropological Theory of the Didactic (ATD) (Chevallard 1999) with its *Task-Technique-Theory* (TTT) tool,
  - The Instrumental Approach to Tool Use with its dual Vygotskian and Piagetian roots (Artigue 2002; Vérillon and Rabardel 1995),
  - Pólya's (1945/1957) mathematical problem-solving frame (especially the phase of "looking back", i.e., reflecting), and
  - Didactical Engineering (Artigue 1992), the design-based frame with an emphasis on *a priori* mathematical and epistemological analyses for shaping not only the design of individual tasks but also their ordering;
- The *domain-specific* frames resulting from prior research involving:
  - Algebraic activity (Kieran 1992, 2007)—in particular, Kieran's (2004) domain-specific model for conceptualizing such activity in terms of its generational, transformational, and global/meta-level aspects,
  - Mathematical reasoning processes developed by means of teacher-student and student-student social interaction within collective classroom discussion (e.g., Herbel-Eisenmann and Cirillo 2009), and
  - Tool-based activity with CAS technology for symbol manipulation in algebra (e.g., Artigue 1997; Lagrange 2002).

While all of these frameworks were included in various ways and to various extents within the design of the task-sequence and how it was projected to unfold, space constraints do not allow for specifying exactly where and how each frame was instantiated. But it can be noted, more generally, that in line with the ATD framework, which is an integral part of the Instrumental Approach to Tool Use frame and where the TTT tool is well characterized (see Artigue 2002), our focus was on the interplay between the technical and the conceptual, that is, on the techniques and theories that students develop while using technological tools and in social interaction. Crucial to the notion that conceptual understanding can co-emerge with technique, and in line with the Kieran (2004) model of algebraic activity, the transformational aspects of algebra (involving factoring, expanding, etc.) need to be linked—especially during their early phases of learning—to the global/meta-level activity of algebra (involving, e.g., noticing structure, generalizing, analyzing relationships, predicting, justifying, proving). As Lagrange (2003) has argued: "Technique plays an epistemic role by contributing to an understanding of the objects that it handles, particularly during its elaboration. It also serves as an object for conceptual reflection when compared with other techniques and when discussed with regard to consistency" (p. 271).

Emanating from the above frameworks that underpinned our research, the crafting of the multiple task-sequences involved the following five *design principles*:

- Integrate a dialectic between technical and theoretical activity within a predominantly exploratory, inquiry-based approach;
- Integrate the CAS as an epistemic motor for developing students' theoretical thinking and as a tool for generating and testing conjectures;

- Interweave paper-and-pencil work with CAS activity with the aim of coordinating the technical and theoretical aspects of the mathematics;
- Include questions of a reflective nature where students write about how they are interpreting the content they are working on and eventually talk about and explain their ways of thinking;
- Integrate questions that call upon processes such as pattern seeking, looking for different ways of structuring a given expression, conjecturing, predicting, testing conjectures, and justifying.

The design of the particular task-sequence related to the factoring of $x^n - 1$, because of its strong focus on generalization, also drew upon additional domain-specific frames related to the process of generalizing (e.g., Cañadas et al. 2007; Mason 1996)—frames that shaped the following *three-phase sequence* for the individual tasks we designed:

1. Seeing patterns in factors and moving toward a generalization;
2. Refining a generalization—with conjecturing and reconciling; and
3. Proving a generalization.

The first phase, which involved CAS as well as paper and pencil, linked students' past experience with factoring to the generalization that they would be working towards regarding the factoring of $x^n - 1$. The beginning group of tasks was oriented towards noticing a particular regularity in the factored examples of the $x^n - 1$ family of polynomials for positive integral values of n and then justifying the form of these products. As is illustrated by the sample questions provided in Fig. 12.1, the tasks aimed at promoting an awareness of the presence of the factor $(x - 1)$ in the given factored forms of the expressions $x^2 - 1$, $x^3 - 1$, and $x^4 - 1$. To promote *generalization* of the form $x^n - 1 = (x - 1)(x^{n-1} + x^{n-2} + \cdots + x + 1)$, students were then to be asked to judge the validity of the equality presented in Question 6 of Fig. 12.1. After students began to conjecture a general rule for the factorization of the $x^n - 1$ family, they were to be requested to reflect on how they

---

1. Perform the indicated operations: $(x - 1)(x + 1)$; $(x - 1)(x^2 + x + 1)$.
2. Without doing any algebraic manipulation, anticipate the result of the following product
   $(x-1)\left(x^3 + x^2 + x + 1\right) =$
3. Verify the above result using paper and pencil, and then using the calculator.
4. What do the following three expressions have in common? And, also, how do they differ?
   $(x - 1)(x + 1)$, $(x - 1)(x^2 + x + 1)$, and $(x-1)\left(x^3 + x^2 + x + 1\right)$.
5. How do you explain the fact that when you multiply: i) the two binomials above, ii) the binomial with the trinomial above, and iii) the binomial with the quadrinomial above, you always obtain a binomial as the product?
6. Is your explanation valid for the following equality:
   $(x - 1)(x^{134} + x^{133} + x^{132} + \ldots + x^2 + x + 1) = x^{135} - 1$? Explain.

Fig. 12.1 Some of the initial tasks from the first phase of the $x^n - 1$ task-sequence

might express this conjecture by means of symbolic notation, using the symbol n for the exponent, rather than specific integers.

The next phase of the task-sequence involved students' *confronting* the paper-and-pencil factorizations that they produced for x^n-1, for integer values of n from 2 to 6 (and then from 7 to 13), with the completely factored forms produced by the CAS, and in *reconciling* these two factorizations (see Fig. 12.2).

An important aspect of this phase of the task-sequence involved reflecting on and *forming conjectures* (see Fig. 12.3) on the relations between particular expressions of the x^n-1 family and their completely factored forms.

The third phase of the task-sequence (see Fig. 12.4) focused on students' *proving* one of the conjectures that they had generated during the previous phase of the task-sequence.

In this activity each line of the table below must be filled in completely (all three cells), one row at a time. Start from the top row (the cells of the three columns) and work your way down. If, for a given row, the results in the left and middle columns differ, reconcile the two by using algebraic manipulations in the right hand column.		
Factorization using paper and pencil	Result produced by the FACTOR command	Calculation to reconcile the two, if necessary
$x^2 - 1 =$		
$x^3 - 1 =$		
$x^4 - 1 =$		
$x^5 - 1 =$		
$x^6 - 1 =$		

Fig. 12.2 One of the factorization tasks from the second phase of the $x^n - 1$ task-sequence

Conjecture, in general, for what numbers n will the factorization of $x^n - 1$:
(i) contain exactly two factors?
(ii) contain more than two factors?
(iii) include $(x+1)$ as a factor?
Please explain.

Fig. 12.3 A conjecturing task from the second phase of the $x^n - 1$ task-sequence where students examine more closely the nature of the factors produced by the CAS

Prove that $(x+1)$ is always a factor of $x^n - 1$ for even values of n.

Fig. 12.4 The proving task from the third phase of the $x^n - 1$ task-sequence

The nature of the students' reflections related to the proving task was to be revealed by having some of them present and explain their proofs at the board, and by encouraging classroom discussion, query, and reaction to the presented proofs. This and other *instructional practice principles*, which were fully described in the accompanying teacher guide that we designed, included the following:

- Allow enough time for students to grapple with and think through the given tasks (both individually and group-wise) before initiating collective discussion of this work;
- Have students present and explain their work at the board;
- Support students in presenting their work and in having them justify their thinking;
- Encourage classroom discussion, query, and reaction to work presented at the board; and
- Elicit students' thinking during collective discussions and encourage them to share their ideas, questions, and conjectures, rather than accepting quick and easy answers or rapidly giving them the answers.

Up to this point, the study could be characterized as primarily one of *design as intention*, with its rigorous attention to the initial formulation of the design by means of existing theoretical bases and their design principles, as well as the setting of instructional practice principles. However, we were also interested in the further development of theory by means of the implementation of the design study—the development of theory being a principal characteristic of *design as implementation* studies. We wanted to document the process by which the designed sequence was integrated into the classroom environment and focus on aspects that appeared to be especially crucial to the growth of learning. While the entire description of the design study constitutes its theoretical role, it is important that a design theory explain why designs work. In our case, the designed task-sequence—and the design study as a whole—was found to work especially well, not only because of the nature of the tasks in the sequence itself, but also because of two additional factors: the instructional practice of the participating teacher and the role played by the computing technology as a tool for thinking. An extract drawn from the process of classroom implementation, which encapsulates this dual aspect, now follows. It centers on the proving task presented above in Fig. 12.4.

12.4.2 The Implementation of the Design Study

The intermediate and domain-specific theoretical frames underpinning the study, in particular, the Task-Technique-Theory tool of the ATD framework, guided the analysis of the implementation process and allowed for the identification of students' going back-and-forth between theoretical thinking and technical growth (see Kieran and Drijvers 2006). However, the students' progress could not be completely accounted for without developing complementary theoretical explanations while analyzing the implementation process—theoretical explanations involving both the teacher and the technology.

After students had completed the first two phases of the $x^n - 1$ task-sequence, they were faced with the proving segment: "Prove that $(x+1)$ is always a factor of $x^n - 1$ for even values of n." It is noted that none of the students had had any prior experience with proving in algebra. They worked on this part of the task-sequence, mostly within small groups, for about 15 min. Several of the students were using their CAS calculators; others were just talking about how they might approach the task and occasionally jotting down notes on paper. During that time, the teacher (T) circulated and was heard to offer the following remark to a group of students—a remark that was in fact addressed to the whole class (see Kieran and Guzmán 2010, pp. 131–132):

T: See if you can prove this and not just state it, as some people have done so far (picking up one student's worksheet and reading it to the class): 'When n is greater than or equal to 2, $(x + 1)$ is a factor because.' Let's see if we can go a little bit beyond that. Can you write down what you come up with…. Yeah, but you need more than just examples. … You need to get something written down. … Look, you need to think in order to answer this. This is the only hint I'm giving you, you need to think about where the $(x + 1)$ comes from.

With the teacher's encouragement, the students began to move forward in the proving task. When he sensed that the majority of them had arrived at some form of a proof, he opened up a whole-class discussion, oriented around various students' sharing their work:

T: Ok, guys. Quite a lot of you got quite close in doing this. What I want you to do, and I've asked a couple of people who've done it in completely different ways, to see if they can put forward their explanation. I want you to be quiet, listen to their explanation, then we'll discuss it once they've got it done, once they've completed their little spiel, ok.

He invited selected students to come to the board, one at a time. The first "proof" by Paul revolved around the idea of 'difference of squares':

Paul: Ok. So, my theory is that whenever $x^n - 1$ has an even value for n, if it's greater or equal to 2, that, one of the factors of that would be $x^2 - 1$, and since $x^2 - 1$ is always a factor of one of those, a factor of $x^2 - 1$ is $(x + 1)$, so then $(x + 1)$ is always a factor.
Student2: Could you say it again? [other students react all at once, making many comments]
Student3: Why don't you write it on the board?
T: Guys! Give him a chance.
Paul: You want me to write? [addressing the teacher]
T: Write down what you want to write down.
Student4: Can you talk at the same time?

Paul proceeded to write down at the board what he had just stated orally. The teacher then asked: "Is everyone willing to accept his explanation?" While many seemed to agree with what Paul had proposed, a few voiced disagreement. One student, Dan, argued that, for example, $x^{12} - 1$ did not have to be approached as a difference of squares; it could be factored in another way so as to end up with a factor that was a sum of cubes, $x^3 + 1$, which would in turn yield $(x + 1)(x^2 - x + 1)$. However, Paul insisted that, just because $x^{12} - 1$ could be factored in a different way, this did not contradict his original claim. After further class discussion, the teacher pointed out that, for Paul's proof to be complete, there needed to be a theoretical link connecting the two main lines of the proof (i.e., the $x^n - 1$ line and the $x^2 - 1$ line): "Yes, we know we will get there eventually, but how do we know that we will eventually get there without doing all the actual factoring?" Paul's proof had a 'gap' in it.

The second approach to the proving problem was put forward by Janet. Janet's proof, which she and her partner Alexandra had together generated, was based on their earlier work on reconciling CAS factors with their paper-and-pencil factoring (for the tasks shown in Fig. 12.2). They had noticed that for even ns, the number of terms in the second factor was always even. Janet argued, as she presented the proof at the board using $x^8 - 1$ as an example, that it would work for any even n:

Janet: When n is an even number
T: Write it on the board, show it on the board.
Janet: [she writes "$x^8 - 1$" and below it: $(x - 1)(x^7 + x^6 + x^5 + x^4 + x^3 + x^2 + x + 1)$]
T: Ok, listen 'cause this is interesting [addressed to the rest of the class], it's a completely different way of looking at it, to what most of you guys did. Ok, so explain it, Janet.
Janet: When n is an even number [she points to the 8 in the $x^8 - 1$ that she has written], the number of terms in this bracket is even, which means they can be grouped and a factor is always $(x + 1)$.
T: Can you show that?
Janet: [she groups the second factor as follows,
$x^6(x + 1) + x^4(x + 1) + x^2(x + 1) + 1(x + 1)$]
T: Thanks Janet. Do we understand what she put out there?

Shortly after Janet had finished explaining her proof, the issue of Paul's proof came up once more. When Paul had presented his proof to the class, the implicit underlying argument was that when one begins with $x^n - 1$ where n is an even integer, and if one continually takes the even exponent and treats the binomial as a difference of squares, then one eventually arrives at $x^2 - 1$. To provoke the students, the teacher offered the following counter-example: "Just out of interest, what would happen if this was $x^{14} - 1$? [he wrote $(x^{14} - 1)$ under the $(x^n - 1)$], to which a student easily responded: "$(x^7 - 1)$ times $(x^7 + 1)$." The teacher wrote at the board $(x^{14} - 1) = (x^7 - 1)(x^7 + 1)$ and then wondered aloud: "Where does that leave your proof, Paul?" However, rather than leaving the class stymied, this question provided an opening for another student who had been conjecturing something new, based on his trial explorations with the CAS calculator:

Andrew: See, when it's a prime number, then the first part here is $x + 1$ as a factor. … From, like $x^5 + 1$ you get, $x^4 - x^3 + x^2 - x + 1$, like when you factor it on the calculator, that's what you get.
T: Ok.
Andrew: $x + 1$ times $x^4 - x^3 + x^2 - x + 1$.
T: Say it again Andrew [he is ready to write down Andrew's verbalizings at the board]
Andrew: When you factor $x^{10} - 1$ on the calculator, you get $(x - 1)$ times $(x + 1)$ times $(x^4 + x^3 + x^2 + x + 1)$ times $(x^4 - x^3 + x^2 - x + 1)$.
T: Yeah [while completing the writing of Andrew's factorization at the board]. So, just go back a bit. That was these two together [tracing an arc joining $(x - 1)$ and $(x^4 + x^3 + x^2 + x + 1)$] to give you the $x^5 - 1$.
Andrew: Yeah, and the next two would be $(x + 1)$ and $(x^4 - x^3 + x^2 - x + 1)$.
T: So you're going into something that we haven't looked at in this class. You're setting up another hypothesis. What is your hypothesis?
Andrew: Well, that's what I was trying to get at. … If the division by 2 gives an odd number, then it goes $(x + 1)$.
T: So you're saying that, for the second hypothesis, something like this [he writes down $(x^5 + 1) = (x + 1)(x^4 - x^3 + x^2 - x + 1)$]. And you're saying that's true for all odd numbers?
Andrew: That's what I think.
T: So if we could prove this, then we've got it.

When Andrew had been working earlier on the second phase of the $x^n - 1$ task-sequence, which had involved the reconciling of his paper-and-pencil factorings with the CAS factorings, the $x^{10} - 1$ example had presented a surprise. He had first factored it with pencil and paper as $(x^5 + 1)(x^5 - 1)$, and then refactored the $(x^5 - 1)$ according to the newly-learned general rule for $x^n - 1$, but had left the $(x^5 + 1)$ factor as is. But the CAS produced as its factored form for $x^{10} - 1$: $(x - 1)(x + 1)(x^4 + x^3 + x^2 + x + 1)(x^4 - x^3 + x^2 - x + 1)$. Andrew noticed this additional factoring by the CAS, that is, that $x^5 + 1 = (x + 1)(x^4 - x^3 + x^2 - x + 1)$. He then remembered something similar from the previous task-sequence on the sum of cubes (done the week prior) and involving the factoring of $x^3 + 1$. At the same moment that he noticed the $x^5 + 1$ phenomenon, he mentioned to his desk-mate: "Isn't that how it works for the sum of cubes?" So, he then began to conjecture and test the more general rule: $x^n + 1 = (x + 1)(x^{n-1} - x^{n-2} + \ldots - x + 1)$, when n is odd. Andrew, in presenting this emerging conjecture to the class, insisted that, even though "it does not seem to work for even ns, it is true for all odd numbers n, and $x + 1$ would always be a factor of it." While Andrew never did come up with a generic proof for $x^n + 1$ for odd ns, as had Janet for $x^n - 1$ for even ns, his new conjecture provided a basis for handling the counter-example of $x^{14} - 1$. In sum, Andrew's activity with the CAS was quite remarkable in that not only did he notice the pattern in the factoring of $x^5 + 1$, but also that he spontaneously connected it with what he remembered about the factoring of $x^3 + 1$, and that all of this led to generating a novel conjecture that he was able to test with his CAS calculator.

12.4.3 Theorizing Resulting from the Implementation of the Proving Phase of the Design Study

The proving phase of the design study—and so too the previous phases of the study in the same classroom—is noteworthy for at least two aspects. As has been illustrated, the roles played by the teacher and by the computing technology in the emergence and evolution of students' learning were striking. The teacher was one who worked very hard at encouraging his students to reflect, at giving them time to do so, at listening closely to their reflections, and at having them share their reflections with the rest of the class. His predisposition to such practice was related to the importance he ascribed to students' learning to think for themselves. One of the signs of this didactical stance on mathematical learning was the way in which he presented counter-examples to challenge students' thinking rather than immediately correcting them or giving the right answer. He aimed at having students develop their mathematical reasoning and critical thinking.

As the case of this teacher suggests, not only can listening to students support the development of students' thinking, it can also lead to new awarenesses and professional growth in the teacher. He mentioned on several occasions during the post-lesson interview how struck he was by the quality of the mathematical contributions of his students, contributions such as those by Janet and Andrew, which had evoked new mathematical insights within him, as well as within the students of his class. He was clearly a teacher who could learn from his students.

His disposition toward student reflection and student learning of mathematics, as well as his attitude with respect to his own learning, supported each other in a mutually intertwining manner. This is of interest from a theoretical perspective. It suggests firstly that the integration of novel materials and resources that have been designed to spur mathematical learning is more likely to be successful when the teachers who are doing the integrating are able to see that these resources are having a positive effect on their students' learning. Secondly, the novel materials and resources have a greater likelihood of producing this positive effect on student learning when the teacher doing the integrating engages in teaching practices that encourage student reflection and mathematical reasoning.

The second noteworthy aspect concerns the role of the CAS technology in the students' learning. To clarify, while the CAS technology was not initially created by its programming designers for pedagogical purposes but rather as a tool for doing mathematics, its integration into learning environments has been shown to lead students to explore their own novel conjectures and to allow for generating, testing, and improving conjectures. Ample evidence of this facet of CAS technology use was observed in Andrew's activity within our own design study.

It would be hard to envisage him even *noticing* the phenomenon regarding the factorization of $x^5 + 1$, much less being able to formulate and test effectively his newly formed conjecture about the factors of $x^n + 1$ for odd ns in a pencil-and-paper environment. The role of the CAS calculator was crucial at this moment, and reminds us of a point made by Mason (2010): "Learning has taken place when people discern details, recognize relationships, and perceive properties not previously discerned through attending in fresh or distinct ways, and when they have fresh possibilities for action from which to choose" (p. 24). The CAS offered Andrew and the other students the "fresh possibilities for action" and allowed for the "discernment of details and the recognition of relationships."

But the CAS technology also played an important role for the teacher and for his practice. The teacher remarked at the completion of the $x^n - 1$ task-sequence that the presence of the technology changes the nature of the questions that can be asked of students, and thus the kind of mathematical reflection they engage in. While the tasks themselves were, according to the teacher, a crucial component of the students' learning and pushed them beyond what is normally asked of them in their mathematics program, it must be added that the actual design of the tasks was set up in such a way as to work hand-in-hand with the affordances of the technology. In fact, the first two phases of the $x^n - 1$ task-sequence, which were foundational to the proving part of the activity, could not have been managed without the CAS. The teacher added that the interaction with the CAS calculators actually "made the students think more about the algebraic processes that they knew how to do, in particular, to think about the way in which they understood this material—basically the meta-cognition kind of idea of thinking about the process you're going through yourself. That's something we don't do enough of in mathematics." Before the unfolding of the design study in his own classroom, he never imagined the impact of this technology on his students' mathematical learning, and thus on his own learning of what his students could accomplish. In his reflecting on his students' reflections, his vision of what his students could learn mathematically had changed, as well as his awareness of the role within the learning process that CAS technology can play when situated within the context of suitably demanding task-sequences.

12.5 Concluding Remarks

In this chapter, I have examined the design process and task design from the standpoint of the frameworks and principles that are reflective of the historical development of design-oriented theorizing research in mathematics education. The particular perspective that was used was that of grand, intermediate, and domain-specific levels of frames—a perspective illustrating the ways in which frames and task design are related. An example was provided of a domain-specific frame for a design study focusing on the processes of conjecturing, generalizing, and proving within the algebraic content area of factoring technique and involving the CAS calculator tool. This example embodied the two dimensions of (i) *design as intention*, with its description of the initial formulation of the design that was underpinned by specific frameworks and principles, and (ii) *design as implementation* with its description of the process by which the designed sequence was integrated into the classroom environment—a process that specified the tasks, the kinds of classroom discussion that were encouraged, the tools that were provided, and the practical means by which the teacher orchestrated relations among these elements. While the entire description of the initial formulation and implementation of the design study constitutes the development of the theoretical role played by such studies, specific theoretical products resulting from this design study included the following:

- the emergence of students' theoretical notions within the further growth of their technical knowledge in algebra,
- the nature of the teacher's classroom practice, which fostered the co-emergence of algebraic theory and technique,
- the students' capacity to notice theory-inducing phenomena in the outputs provided by the CAS technology tool, and
- the quality of the teacher's reflections on his students' learning that were provoked by the designed task-with-technology environment and which in turn constituted a form of professional development for him.

In sum, the domain-specific frame that was used for the design study, and its further elaboration that was the result of the study, is one that theorized the co-emergence of algebraic conceptual and technical knowledge in a technology-supported, task-based classroom environment that constituted learning for both students and teacher. Its success depended to a great extent upon the specific instructional practice of the participating teacher, as well as the affordances of the CAS technology as a tool to spur thinking. To conclude, the frame is one that can serve as a basis for further design research in the recursive process of domain-specific-frame-development in the particular content area of algebra.

References

Ainley, J., & Pratt, D. (2005). The significance of task design in mathematics education: Examples from proportional reasoning. In H. L. Chick & J. L. Vincent (Eds.), *Proceedings of the 29th conference of the international group for the psychology of mathematics education* (Vol. 1, pp. 103–108). Melbourne: PME.

Artigue, M. (1992). Didactical engineering. In R. Douady & A. Mercier (Eds.), *Recherches en Didactique des Mathématiques, Selected papers* (pp. 41–70). Grenoble: La Pensée Sauvage.

Artigue, M. (1997). Le Logiciel 'Derive' comme révélateur de phénomènes didactiques liés à l'utilisation d'environnements informatiques pour l'apprentissage [Derive software, a revealer of didactical phenomena related to the use of computer learning environments]. *Educational Studies in Mathematics, 33,* 133–169.

Artigue, M. (2002). Learning mathematics in a CAS environment: The genesis of a reflection about instrumentation and the dialectics between technical and conceptual work. *International Journal of Computers for Mathematical Learning, 7,* 245–274.

Artigue, M. (2009). Didactical design in mathematics education. In C. Winslow (Ed.), *Nordic research in mathematics education: Proceedings from NORMA08 in Copenhagen* (pp. 7–16). Rotterdam: Sense Publishers.
Bell, A. W. (1979). Research on teaching methods in secondary mathematics. In D. Tall (Ed.), *Proceedings of the third conference of the international group for the psychology of mathematics education* (pp. 4–12). Warwick: PME.
Bell, A. (1993). Guest editorial. *Educational Studies in Mathematics, 24,* 1–4.
Brousseau, G. (1997). *Theory of didactical situations in mathematics* (N. Balacheff, M. Cooper, R. Sutherland, & V. Warfield, Eds. & Trans.). Dordrecht: Kluwer Academic.
Brousseau, G. (1998). *Théorie des situations didactiques* [Theory of didactical situations] (N. Balacheff, M. Cooper, R. Sutherland, & V. Warfield, Eds.). Grenoble: La Pensée Sauvage.
Brown, A. L. (1992). Design experiments: Theoretical and methodological challenges in creating complex interventions in classroom settings. *Journal of the Learning Sciences, 2*(2), 141–178.
Cañadas, M. C., Deulofeu, J., Figueiras, L., Reid, D. A., & Yevdokimov, O. (2007). The conjecturing process: Perspectives in theory and implications in practice. *Journal of Teaching and Learning, 5*(1), 55–72.
Chevallard, Y. (1999). L'analyse des pratiques enseignantes en théorie anthropologique du didactique [The analysis of teaching practice in the anthropological theory of the didactic]. *Recherches en Didactique des Mathématiques, 19,* 221–266.
Cobb, P. (2007). Putting philosophy to work: Coping with multiple theoretical perspectives. In F. K. Lester Jr. (Ed.), *Second handbook of research on mathematics teaching and learning* (pp. 3–67). Charlotte: Information Age.
Cobb, P., Confrey, J., diSessa, A., Lehrer, R., & Schauble, L. (2003). Design experiments in educational research. *Educational Researcher, 32*(1), 9–13.
Collins, A., Joseph, D., & Bielaczyc, K. (2004). Design research: Theoretical and methodological issues. *Journal of the Learning Sciences, 13,* 15–42.
Fernandez, C., & Yoshida, M. (2004). *Lesson study: A Japanese approach to improving mathematics teaching and learning.* Mahwah: Lawrence Erlbaum Associates.
Freudenthal, H. (1979). How does reflective thinking develop? In D. Tall (Ed.), *Proceedings of the third conference of the international group for the psychology of mathematics education* (pp. 92–107). Warwick: PME.
Fujii, T. (2015). The critical role of task design in Lesson Study. In A. Watson & M. Ohtani (Eds.), *Task design in mathematics education: An ICMI Study 22* (pp. 273–286). New York: Springer.
Gagné, R. M. (1965). *The conditions of learning.* New York: Holt, Rinehart & Winston.
Glaser, R. (1976). Components of a psychology of instruction: Toward a science of design. *Review of Educational Research, 46*(1), 1–24.
Gravemeijer, K., & Cobb, P. (2006). Design research from a learning design perspective. In J. van den Akker, K. Gravemeijer, S. McKenney, & N. Nieveen (Eds.), *Educational design research* (pp. 45–85). http://www.fisme.science.uu.nl/publicaties/literatuur/EducationalDesignResearch.pdf.
Herbel-Eisenmann, B., & Cirillo, M. (Eds.). (2009). *Promoting purposeful discourse. Teacher research in mathematics classrooms.* Reston: National Council of Teachers of Mathematics.
Hitt, F., & Kieran, C. (2009). Constructing knowledge via a peer interaction in a CAS environment with tasks designed from a Task-Technique-Theory perspective. *International Journal of Computers for Mathematical Learning, 14,* 121–152.
Jacobs, J. K., & Morita, E. (2002). Japanese and American teachers' evaluations of videotaped mathematics lessons. *Journal for Research in Mathematics Education, 33,* 154–175.
Johnson, D. C. (1980). The research process. In R. J. Shumway (Ed.), *Research in mathematics education* (pp. 29–46). Reston: National Council of Teachers of Mathematics.
Kelly, A. E., Lesh, R. A., & Baek, J. Y. (Eds.). (2008). *Handbook of design research methods in education.* London: Routledge.
Kieran, C. (1992). The learning and teaching of school algebra. In D. A. Grouws (Ed.), *Handbook of research on mathematics teaching and learning* (pp. 390–419). New York: Macmillan.

Kieran, C. (2004). The core of algebra: Reflection on its main activities. In K. Stacey, H. Chick, & M. Kendal (Eds.), *The future of the teaching and learning of algebra: The 12th ICMI Study* (pp. 21–33). Dordrecht: Kluwer Academic Publishers.

Kieran, C. (2007). Learning and teaching algebra at the middle school through college levels: Building meaning for symbols and their manipulation. In F. K. Lester Jr. (Ed.), *Second handbook of research on mathematics teaching and learning* (pp. 707–762). Greenwich: Information Age.

Kieran, C. (2017). Task design in mathematics education: Frameworks and exemplars. In S. Oesterle, D. Allan, & J. Holm (Eds.), *Proceedings of the 2016 annual meeting of the Canadian mathematics education study group* (pp. 45–66). Kingston: CMESG.

Kieran, C., & Drijvers, P. (2006). The co-emergence of machine techniques, paper-and-pencil techniques, and theoretical reflection: A study of CAS use in secondary school algebra. *International Journal of Computers for Mathematical Learning, 11*, 205–263.

Kieran, C., & Guzmán, J. (2010). Role of task and technology in provoking teacher change: A case of proofs and proving in high school algebra. In R. Leikin & R. Zazkis (Eds.), *Learning through teaching mathematics: Development of teachers' knowledge and expertise in practice* (pp. 127–152). New York: Springer.

Kieran, C., Doorman, M., & Ohtani, M. (2015). Frameworks and principles for task design. In A. Watson & M. Ohtani (Eds.), *Task design in mathematics education: An ICMI Study 22* (pp. 19–81). New York: Springer.

Kilpatrick, J. (1992). A history of research in mathematics education. In D. A. Grouws (Ed.), *Handbook of research on mathematics teaching and learning* (pp. 3–38). New York: Macmillan.

Komatsu, K., & Tsujiyama, Y. (2013). Principles of task design to foster proofs and refutations in mathematical learning: Proof problem with diagram. In C. Margolinas (Ed.), *Task design in mathematics education: Proceedings of ICMI Study 22* (pp. 471–480). https://hal.archives-ouvertes.fr/hal-00834054.

Lagrange, J.-B. (2002). Étudier les mathématiques avec les calculatrices symboliques. Quelle place pour les techniques? [Studying mathematics with symbolic calculators. What place is there for techniques?] In D. Guin & L. Trouche (Eds), *Calculatrices symboliques. Transformer un outil en un instrument du travail mathématique: un problème didactique* (pp. 151–185). Grenoble: La Pensée Sauvage.

Lagrange, J.-B. (2003). Learning techniques and concepts using CAS: A practical and theoretical reflection. In J. T. Fey (Ed.), *Computer algebra systems in secondary school mathematics education* (pp. 269–283). Reston: National Council of Teachers of Mathematics.

Lerman, S., Xu, G., & Tsatsaroni, A. (2002). Developing theories of mathematics education research: The ESM story. *Educational Studies in Mathematics, 51*, 23–40.

Lesh, R. A. (2002). Research design in mathematics education: Focusing on design experiments. In L. English (Ed.), *Handbook of international research in mathematics education* (pp. 27–50). Hillsdale: Lawrence Erlbaum Associates.

Leung, A., & Bolite-Frant, J. (2015). Designing mathematics tasks: The role of tools. In A. Watson & M. Ohtani (Eds.), *Task design in mathematics education: An ICMI Study 22* (pp. 191–225). New York: Springer.

Lewis, C. (2002). *Lesson study: A handbook of teacher-led instructional change*. Philadelphia: Research for Better Schools.

Mason, J. (1996). Expressing generality and roots of algebra. In N. Bednarz, C. Kieran, & L. F. Lee (Eds.), *Approaches to algebra: Perspectives for research and teaching* (pp. 85–86). Dordrecht: Kluwer Academic.

Mason, J. (2010). Attention and intention in learning about teaching through teaching. In R. Leikin & R. Zazkis (Eds.), *Learning through teaching mathematics: Development of teachers' knowledge and expertise in practice* (pp. 23–47). New York: Springer.

Mounier, G., & Aldon, G. (1996). A problem story: factorisations of x^n-1. *International DERIVE Journal, 3*, 51–61.

Piaget, J. (1971). *Genetic epistemology*. New York: W. W. Norton.

Pólya, G. (1945/1957). *How to solve it: A new aspect of mathematical method*. Princeton: Princeton University Press.
Prediger, S., Bikner-Ahsbahs, A., & Arzarello, F. (2008). Networking strategies and methods for connecting theoretical approaches: First steps towards a conceptual framework. *ZDM: The International Journal on Mathematics Education, 40*, 165–178.
Prusak, N., Hershkowitz, R., & Schwarz, B. B. (2013). Conceptual learning in a principled design problem solving environment. *Research in Mathematics Education, 15*(3), 266–285. https://doi.org/10.1080/14794802.2013.836379.
Runesson, U. (2005). Beyond discourse and interaction. Variation: A critical aspect for teaching and learning mathematics. *The Cambridge Journal of Education, 35*(1), 69–87.
Ruthven, K., Laborde, C., Leach, J., & Tiberghien, A. (2009). Design tools in didactical research: Instrumenting the epistemological and the cognitive aspects of the design of teaching sequences. *Educational Researcher, 38*, 329–342.
Simon, H. A. (1969). *The sciences of the artificial*. Cambridge: MIT Press.
Stephan, M., & Akyuz, D. (2012). A proposed instructional theory for integer addition and subtraction. *Journal for Research in Mathematics Education, 43*, 428–464.
Stephan, M., & Akyuz, D. (2013). An instructional design collaborative in one middle school. In C. Margolinas (Ed.), *Task design in mathematics education: Proceedings of ICMI Study 22* (pp. 509–518). https://hal.archives-ouvertes.fr/hal-00834054.
Stigler, J. W., & Hiebert, J. (1999). *The teaching gap*. New York: Free Press.
Treffers, A. (1987). *Three dimensions: A model of goal and theory description in mathematics instruction - The Wiskobas Project*. Dordrecht: D. Reidel.
Van Dooren, W., Vamvakoussi, X., & Verschaffel, L. (2013). Mind the gap—Task design principles to achieve conceptual change in rational number understanding. In C. Margolinas (Ed.), *Task design in mathematics education: Proceedings of ICMI Study 22* (pp. 519–527). https://hal.archives-ouvertes.fr/hal-00834054.
Vérillon, P., & Rabardel, P. (1995). Cognition and artifacts: A contribution to the study of thought in relation to instrumented activity. *European Journal of Psychology of Education, 10*, 77–103.
Watson, A., et al. (2013). Introduction. In C. Margolinas (Ed.), *Task design in mathematics education: Proceedings of ICMI Study 22* (pp. 7–13). https://hal.archives-ouvertes.fr/hal-00834054.
Watson, A., & Ohtani, M. (Eds.). (2015). *Task design in mathematics education: An ICMI Study 22*. New York: Springer.
Wittmann, E. (1984). Teaching units as the integrating core of mathematics education. *Educational Studies in Mathematics, 15*, 25–36.
Wittmann, E. Ch. (1995). Mathematics education as a 'design science'. *Educational Studies in Mathematics, 29*, 355–374.

Open Access This chapter is licensed under the terms of the Creative Commons Attribution 4.0 International License (http://creativecommons.org/licenses/by/4.0/), which permits use, sharing, adaptation, distribution and reproduction in any medium or format, as long as you give appropriate credit to the original author(s) and the source, provide a link to the Creative Commons license and indicate if changes were made.

The images or other third party material in this chapter are included in the chapter's Creative Commons license, unless indicated otherwise in a credit line to the material. If material is not included in the chapter's Creative Commons license and your intended use is not permitted by statutory regulation or exceeds the permitted use, you will need to obtain permission directly from the copyright holder.

Chapter 13
Gender and Mathematics Education: An Overview

Gilah C. Leder

Abstract Key findings and theoretical trends that have shaped research on gender and mathematics education are described in context. A brief historical note precedes the overview of the foundational work conducted in the 1970s. The assimilationist and deficit models that framed the early intervention programs designed to promote females' participation and learning of mathematics are discussed, as are the subsequent challenges and reassessments provided by broader feminist perspectives. The interactive influence on mathematics learning of relevant personal and contextual variables and the move towards more complex models of equity embedded in broader social justice concerns are highlighted. Given its enabling role in educational and career pursuits, and that gender equity concerns will thus remain a significant item on the research agenda of (mathematics) educators in many countries, guidelines for future work are offered.

Keywords Mathematics · Performance · Participation · Feminist perspectives · Gender · Sex

13.1 Introduction

Historically, males were thought to be more suited than females to studying mathematics and being engaged in related areas. According to Mackinnon (1990): "There are perhaps only three or four women until the nineteenth century who have left behind a name in mathematics. Women were lucky to receive any education at all" (p. 347).

G. C. Leder (✉)
Monash University, Melbourne, VIC, Australia
e-mail: gilah.leder@monash.edu

G. C. Leder
La Trobe University, Melbourne, VIC, Australia
e-mail: g.leder@latrobe.edu.au

Reviews of research on gender and mathematics learning typically begin with findings from the 1970s. Yet history should not be ignored. It is useful to refer, briefly, to several females now celebrated or remembered for their mathematical prowess in earlier times.

13.1.1 A Brief Historical Note

Emilie du Châtelet (1706–1749), Maria Agnesi (1718–1799), Sophie Germain (1776–1830), Mary Somerville (1780–1872), and Ada Lovelace (1815–1852) are among those who lived during the eighteenth and nineteenth centuries and whose contributions to mathematics are still considered noteworthy (see for example Lewis 2017; Osen 1974). While the quality and focus of their mathematical endeavours varied, a common thread is evident in accounts of their lives: a firm determination to pursue mathematics, an environment that lauded education, and at pivotal times, constructive support for their work from a critical family member or friend. Mary Somerville, for example, came from a home where the education of sons was considered more important than that of a daughter. In her case an important advisor made a difference: the Scotsman William Wallace, editor of the mathematical journal, the Gentleman's Diary. Early widowhood gave Somerville the financial security to pursue her mathematical studies. Subsequently a supportive second husband enabled her to develop her mathematical interests more intensively (see Patterson 1974 for more information).

Other earlier but more mundane examples of females' successful participation in mathematical pursuits can be gleaned from an English publication, the Ladies' Diary or Women's Almanack, launched in 1704. Three years later the editor began adding mathematical questions to its contents. This strategy continued until the final issue in 1840, when, co-incidentally or not, the Ladies' Diary merged with the above mentioned Gentleman's Diary.

Thanks to the decision by successive editors to reward early and elegant solutions with a copy of the following year's diary, and a listing of the names of those who proposed and answered the questions (Leybourn's Index 1817), confirmation of females' mathematical contributions to the Diary can be traced. Reflecting on the quite remarkable history of this publication, Perl (1979) argued that the "existence of the Ladies' Diary ... indicates that stereotypes about the inability of women to understand and enjoy mathematics were less strongly believed in the 18th century than they are today" (p. 36). From careful inspection of the writings of Leybourn (1817), and other sources, it can be inferred that many of the female contributors to the mathematical section of the Ladies Diary' were the wives, daughters or other close relatives of men engaged in mathematical pursuits (see e.g., Costa 2000; Leder 1980; Perl 1979). Decades ago, it appears, given an appropriate milieu and academic and personal support, there were females who were willing and capable of engaging in mathematical pursuits.

13.2 More Recent Times

Research and community interests in gender differences in achievement and participation in mathematics grew rapidly in the 1970s. Recognition of the critical filter role played by mathematics in educational and career options has ensured that stake holders, researchers, practitioners, and policy makers continue to have an interest in this issue.

Key findings and theoretical trends that have shaped research on gender and mathematics education are considered in the remainder of this chapter. Early trends, evidenced in the 1970s, are considered first, followed by brief overviews of dominant trends and developments in successive decades.

13.2.1 The 1970s—The Work Begins

The seminal research of Fennema and her colleagues in the 1970s (e.g., Fennema and Sherman 1976, 1977) can be considered as an important catalyst for substantive and scholarly investigations on gender issues in mathematics education. Evidence of the extensive, and enduring, impact of this work can be inferred from multiple sources. These include Walberg and Haertel's (1992) finding that the Fennema and Sherman (1977) article was among the most commonly cited work in the Social Sciences Citation Index for the period 1966–1988. More recently, in September 2014, it was reported in the Journal for Research in Mathematics Education [JRME] that Fennema and Sherman's (1976) article had been its most frequently accessed article over the previous three years.[1] More broadly, Lubienski and Bowen (2000) examined 48 major educational research journals accessible on the ERIC data base and published between 1982 and 1998, and found that, of the equity groupings used to categorize the content of relevant articles, gender and mathematics issues received the most attention.

From the mid 1970s onwards, the documentation of gender differences in participation and performance in mathematics, and explorations of apparent positive and negative contributing factors, were important foci of those concerned with gender and mathematics. Factors likely to be implicated were identified, and intervention strategies were initiated and evaluated. As summarised by Fennema (1974), sex differences in boys' and girls' mathematics achievement were rarely found before or in the early grades of elementary school. In the upper elementary and early high school grades differences were sometimes reported. When significant differences were found they tended to be in the boys' favour on higher-level cognitive tasks but in the girls' favour when lower-level cognitive tasks were being measured. "Is there 'sexism' in mathematics education?" Fennema (1974) asked

---

[1]Information retrieved September 2014 from http://www.jstor.org.ezproxy.lib.monash.edu.au/action/showMostAccessedArticles?journalCode=jresematheduc.

rhetorically. "If mathematics educators believe that there is a sex difference in learning mathematics ... and have not attempted to help girls achieve at a similar level to boys, then this question must be answered in the affirmative" (p. 137).

Assumptions that gender differences in mathematics learning were, at least in part, the result of social structures, inadequate educational opportunities, and biased instructional methods and materials shaped much of the work undertaken. Traditional quantitative research methods usually informed the experimental work devised. The removal of school and curriculum barriers, and possibly the resocialization of females, were assumed to serve as fruitful pathways for achieving gender equity. Male (white and Western) norms of performance, standards, participation levels, and methods of work were typically accepted uncritically as the optimum goal for all students. If these were not attained, females were considered deficient, or to use a theme from Kaiser and Rogers (1985), they were perceived as a problem in mathematics, and were to be encouraged and helped to assimilate. This notion, of supporting females to reach standards and achievement equivalent to those of males, was consistent with the tenets of liberal feminism.

13.2.2 A Terminological Interlude

The mix of the terms "sex differences" and "gender differences" in the above paragraphs is not fortuitous. In early work, researchers invariably used the term sex differences when referring to differences in mathematics performance or participation between males and females. In recognition that such differences were not necessarily biologically based, the term gender began to be used as an indicator that differences found were unlikely to be attributable to biology alone. Increasingly the use of gender, rather than sex, differences in mathematics began to appear in scholarly publications. Not all agreed with this putative distinction.

> Experts and lay people alike are well aware that the words they use reflect and shape how we think. What words should we use when discussing differences in achievement tests scores for boys and girls? Those who advocate the use of "gender" for differences that are psychosocial in origin and "sex" for differences that are biological in origin are implicitly assuming that these are two separable influences, an approach that is consistent with behavioural genetics which assigns separate numerical estimates to each type of influence. (Halpern 2002, p. 89)

The sex/gender conceptual distinction, and attendant terminology, has continued to attract attention, more frequently beyond rather than within mathematics education. Reflecting on years of research in studies in education and in psychology, Damarin (2008) concluded:

> the psychological literature on women, gender, and mathematics has two distinct strands, the first continuing a tradition of probing and documenting sex-based differences in various aspects of mathematical performance and the second investigating how knowledge of group differences affects judgment and thus experience of individuals. (p. 108)

This distinction is reflected in documents published under the auspices of the American Psychological Association [APA], including the *APA Dictionary of Psychology* (2015a). There gender and sex are respectively defined as follows:

> Gender (n): the condition of being male, female, or neuter. In a human context, the distinction between gender and SEX reflects the usage of these terms: Sex usually refers to the biological aspects of maleness or femaleness, whereas gender implies the psychological, behavioral, social, and cultural aspects of being male or female (i.e., masculinity or femininity). (APA 2015b, p. 2)

and

> Sex (n): the traits that distinguish between males and females. Sex refers especially to physical and biological traits, whereas GENDER refers especially to social or cultural traits, *although the distinction between the two terms is not regularly observed*. (APA 2015b, pp. 5–6, emphasis added)

The binary construction of sexuality is itself progressively being examined and found wanting is some quarters, inside and beyond the educational research community. Notably, beginning in 2017 the American Educational Research Association [AERA] has been collecting demographic data from its membership via a more extensive range of sex and gender self-identifiers:

Which best describes your gender identity?

Female/Woman

Male/Man

Transgender Female/Transgender Woman

Transgender Male/Transgender Man

Another gender identity (please specify): _____ (AERA 2018)

How, or whether, such new categorizations will impinge on future research in gender/sex differences in mathematics learning remains to be seen.

13.3 The 1980s—The Field Matures and Diversifies

Throughout the 1980s assimilationist and deficit model approaches continued to mould and underpin many of the intervention initiatives aimed at achieving gender equity in mathematics learning outcomes. Data on males' and females' participation and performance in mathematics subjects and tests continued to be reported in scholarly publications. Attempts to identify underlying sources and causes often accompanied such reports. Personal and environmental factors as well as previously unchallenged government policies began to be examined. Researchers concerned with gender differences and mathematics learning were acknowledged as significant contributors to the broader field of research on affect and mathematics learning.

As argued by McLeod (1992), the "important area of research on beliefs comes mainly out of the work on gender differences in mathematics education" (p. 580).

Undoubtedly influenced by work developed in the broader research community, new and searching issues were raised. The themes fuelled by the work of Gilligan (1982) and Belenky et al. (1986), as well as other feminist critiques of the sciences and of the Western notions of knowledge proved particularly powerful. Provocative questions, which also served as pointers to new research directions, began to be raised more forcefully. No longer was it uncritically accepted that subjects such as mathematics and science should be taught, valued, and assessed in ways that seemingly favoured males. No longer was it simply assumed that learning styles, materials and conditions that advantaged males should uniquely be supported. That young women should strive to emulate males' ambitions, goals, and values was no longer taken for granted. These perspectives intensified during the 1980s and served as powerful catalysts for attempts to make the curriculum and instructional strategies less alienating for females.

To summarise, the more critical attempts to question earlier and historically accepted explanations for gender differences in mathematics learning began to affect the framing and delivery of interventions aimed at combating inequities. Efforts were made not only to make females more central to mathematics but also to review and expand the curriculum to incorporate the needs and interests of a broader range of students. More broadly, Leder (2001) reflected:

> The assumptions of liberal feminism that discrimination and inequalities faced by females were the result of social practices and outdated laws were no longer deemed sufficient or necessary explanations. Instead, emphasis began to be placed on the pervasive power structures imposed by males for males.... Some researchers...wished to settle for nothing less than making fundamental changes to society. Advocates of this approach, often classed as radical feminists, considered that the long-term impact of traditional power relations between men and women could only be redressed through such means. (vol.1, p. 48)

The assumptions embedded in the "women as central to mathematics" phase were not without their dangers. The focus of some intervention programs on women with exceptional and rare mathematical talents ultimately proved problematic. Some of the portrayals, it seemed, simply confirmed how difficult it was for an "ordinary" (female) student to become an "extraordinary" mathematician. Reinforced were the hardships that needed to be endured, the challenges to be overcome, and the price to be paid by females for success in mathematics. Programs which valued and nourished qualities and characteristics presumed to be exclusively or primarily female might give the impression, directly or indirectly, that such qualities were essential to females. That females who did not possess or aim for them might feel excluded and devalued was unintended and a consequence to be avoided. The essentialism inherent in some programs risked perpetuating traditional gender stereotypes rather than redressing gender inequities. Nevertheless, there was widespread recognition that previously unchallenged assumptions, traditions, and cultural exclusivity needed to be examined and possibly redefined. Snyder's (2008) claim that responses "to the 'category of women' debates of the late 1980s and early 1990s, that began with a critique of the second wave contention that women share something in common as woman: a common gender identity and set of experiences" (p. 183), captured the thrust of yet another phase, variously addressed in the literature and often labelled as the third wave of feminism.

The meta-analysis published by Hyde et al. (1990) serves as one useful indicator of performance statistics on gender differences in mathematics recorded by the end of the 1980s. Their sample comprised 100 studies of gender differences in mathematics performance. These studies were published between 1963 and 1988, yielded 254 independent effect sizes, and collectively represented test data of more than three million students. Core information on which their data were based and basic conclusions they drew can be summarised as follows:

- Gender differences in mathematics performance in samples of the general population were negligible ($d = -0.05$) and favoured females; averaged over all studies the difference in mathematics performance was a little larger but still small ($d = 0.20$) and in favour of males.
- Girls did slightly better than boys in computation.
- In elementary and middle school there were no gender differences in problem solving, but in high school and in college, differences on this component favoured males.
- Gender differences in favour of males "grew larger with increasingly selective samples and were largest for highly selected samples and samples of highly precocious persons" (Hyde et al. 1990, p. 139).
- The effect size of the gender difference declined over the years – from $d = 0.31$ for studies published in or before 1973 to $d = 0.14$ for studies in or after 1974.

Pointing to the different performance patterns, the authors argued that general statements about gender differences in mathematics performance masked the complexity of the performance pattern and could thus be misleading. Furthermore, "where gender differences do exist, they are in critical areas" (Hyde et al. 1990, p. 151). Schools, they further argued, should implement programs and procedures to improve the teaching of mathematics, "such as internalized belief systems about mathematics, external factors such as sex discrimination in education and in employment … and the mathematics curriculum at the pre-college level" (p. 151).

A detailed overview of intervention programs developed and produced in the 1980s is clearly beyond the scope of this chapter. Fennema et al. (1980) intervention compendium, with its reprints of (then) relevant research articles, as well as detailed materials for student, teacher, counsellor, and parent workshops still serves as an informative source some 40 years after its publication. Many of the programs developed and adopted in the 1980s and beyond can be traced to this comprehensive resource, although this is typically unacknowledged.

It seems judicious to conclude this section with a quote from Leder et al. (1996, p. 966) with which they began their overview of intervention programs as follows:

On December 6, 1989,

At the Ecole polytechnique de Montréal,

A young man entered an engineering classroom.
He ordered women to stand on one side,
men on the other side.
He shot the women.
Then he walked through the school
and shot some other women.

"In this tragic incident", they added, "13 female students and one female staff member were killed. The perpetrator believed that women had usurped his rightful place in engineering and in society" (Leder et al. 1996, pp. 966 and 979). The massacre, it became known, was the shooter's lone fight against feminism and what he regarded as women unfairly taking up positions in traditionally male fields.

13.4 The 1990s—Consolidation and New Directions

Reviews of research about mathematics and gender published in the first half of the 1990s (e.g., Leder 1992; Fennema and Hart 1994) indicated that the trends in performance differences in mathematics between males and females reported two decades earlier were still apparent. Possible explanations for these persistent findings shadowed those considered in earlier research and comprised both environmental variables, including school-, teacher-, peer group-, and parent-related variables, as well as the impact of the wider society. The influence of learner-related cognitive variables and internal belief variables also continued to attract considerable research activity. When gender differences were found, Leder (1992) concluded, they are typically small compared to the much larger within-group variations. "Collectively the body of research available to date suggests that there are small, subtle, interactive, and cumulative links between gender differences in selected internal belief variables and gender differences in mathematics learning" (p. 616). Implied in this summary is a warning against conducting research, or interpreting its findings, with a simplistic focus on the impact of gender per se, without a recognition of the interactive influence of relevant personal and contextual variables.

According to Fennema and Hart (1994), while feminist perspectives were increasingly recognized by those working outside mathematics education, research on mathematics and gender, as gleaned from the contents of JRME, had remained largely untouched by this broader body of work. At the same time they argued presciently, "we think that feminist perspectives can contribute to mathematics education research in the kind of research questions that are explored, whose questions are asked, whose voices are heard, and the research methods employed" (p. 653). Looking at the wider field of mathematics education research reported beyond JRME, Leder et al. (1996) noted "the growing feminist literature on the gendering of mathematics" (p. 945) that added to the pool of work embedded within the traditional research paradigms.

Throughout the 1990s different theoretical models were invoked to support mathematics and gender focussed research. The interactions between gender, learner-related, and contextual variables such as socio-economic status, cultural and ethnic affiliations, continued to be explored, not only using the more traditional quantitative approaches but increasingly also drawing on alternate methodologies that foregrounded social constructivist perspectives. A considerable body of work at that time drew, directly or indirectly, on the expectancy-value theory of achievement motivation and often also on the model of academic choice. This has continued until the present. The model of academic choice was expounded in some detail in the early 1980s by Eccles et al. (1983). Factors likely to enhance, or reduce, students' performance in mathematics and continued engagement with the subject were examined. At the same time, different research paradigms were considered. Damarin's (2000) evocative explanation why some students choose options other than mathematics is worth noting:

> Mathematics teachers and researchers have observed that mathematics is unique among school subjects in that, for many students, failure in mathematics is not an occasion of embarrassment; these students (often with the support of parents, peers, and sometimes guidance counselors and other teachers) refer to the inability to do mathematics with a certain pride. Thus, from leading journals of public intellectual discussion, from the analyses of sociologists of science, from the work of (genetic) scientists themselves, from the pages of daily papers, and from practices of students and adults within the walls of our schools, there emerges and coalesces a discourse of mathematics ability as marking a form of deviance and the mathematically able as a category marked by the signs of this deviance. (p. 78)

Given the reality of the social climate in which they functioned, Damarin among others drawing on sociological perspectives, emphasized that it could not simply be assumed that all students, whether male or female, would necessarily aim for intensive study or proficiency in mathematics and feel diminished if they focussed their attention and efforts elsewhere.

Increasingly, a subtle but gradual shift in the focus on equity broadened. Social justice issues became more prominent. New avenues for research in mathematics education were generated by concerns raised about disadvantages, in the home and in the labour force, faced by females from a working class background, from certain ethnic groups, or those whose dominant language differed from that spoken in their country of residence. To quote Burton (2003), "since earlier publications on gender and mathematics education ... there has been a shift in focus on equity to a more inclusive perspective that embraces social justice as a contested area in mathematics education" (p. xv). For many researchers the term equity could no longer simplistically be considered a virtual synonym for gender; gender was more constructively linked to, or within, a complex set of variables. More complex research designs and varied research methods were needed, with advocates of a social constructionist approach often placing strong reliance on qualitative methods. By the early years of the 21st century, Gutiérrez (2013) argued: "Sociocultural theories, once seen as on the fringe of a mainly cognitive field, now take their place squarely within mainstream mathematics education journals" (p. 38).

13.5 Contemporary Times: The 21st Century

Drawing on 25 years of research on gender and mathematics education Leder (2001) wrote:

> Gender equity concerns have represented a significant item on the research agenda of (mathematics) educators in many countries - in highly technological societies as well as developing nations. International comparisons, formal and informal, have highlighted the roles of class and culture. For a given society, the status of mathematics in the lives of females is invariably linked to their status in that society. Male norms, and acceptance of difference without value judgments, have been more likely to be challenged in countries with active and long standing concerns about equity issues. Collectively, the body of work on gender and mathematics education reflects an increasing diversity in the inquiry methods used to examine and unpack critical factors. More radical feminist perspectives are being adopted, females are less frequently considered as a homogeneous group, and scholarly evaluations of interventions are becoming more prevalent (vol. 1, pp. 48–49).

As expected, themes and directions tracked in previous decades have also dominated in more recent research. Gender is often included among the variables whose impact on learning mathematics is being explored, but now frequently not to the exclusion of other moderators. As noted by Morgan (2014), within the field of mathematics education, too, many are seeking "to go beyond a focus only on conventional educational outcomes as indicators of success or failure, seeing identity, social recognition and participation as equally important dimensions of social justice" (p. 124).

In their account of the rich and ongoing journey leading from Mathematics and Education to Mathematics Education, Furinghetti et al. (2013) pointed to the variety of research perspectives, fields as diverse as psychology, sociology, cultural studies, and political studies, on which researchers have drawn to explore issues in mathematics education. The different lenses used by those adding to research on mathematics and gender make summarising the ongoing pool of studies a daunting task. Careful scrutiny is needed to decide whether a researcher's personal beliefs and theoretical orientation might have influenced, directly or indirectly, the scope of the study undertaken, the modes of data gathering used, and the interpretation of the findings obtained.

Now, more than four decades since gender differences in mathematics performance were highlighted and spawned intensive and extensive investigations, are gender differences in mathematics achievement still being reported? Data pertaining to achievement data are examined first. Inevitably only a small sample from the large pool of relevant information is cited.

13.5.1 Achievement

According to the Organisation for Economic Co-operation and Development [OECD] (2009) there are at least three core reasons for studying gender differences in mathematics achievement: "(i) to understand the source of any inequalities; (ii) to improve average performance; and (iii) to improve our understanding of how students learn" (p. 8).

The meta-analysis reported by Lindberg et al. (2010) not only contains useful summative data but also serves as a ready comparison with the work published 20 years earlier (Hyde et al. 1990) and referred to earlier in the chapter. The sample in the Lindberg et al. (2010) meta-analysis comprised 242 studies of gender differences in mathematics performance. These studies were published between 1990 and 2007 and represented test data of 1,286,350 people. Collectively their data revealed the following:

- The gender difference weighted over all studies was small ($d = 0.05$).
- Examination of data by problem type and content, by sample characteristics including ability, nationality, ethnicity, and age yielded few statistically significant differences in performance, with selectivity (in terms of achievement level) and age being the exception.
- In high school, small gender differences in complex problem solving were found in favour of boys.
- There was no apparent trend over time, between 1990 and 2007, of a decrease in any gender differences reported.

Overall, Lindberg et al. (2010) concluded that their data "provide strong evidence of gender similarities in mathematics performance … the existence and magnitude of gender differences in performance varies as a function of many factors … gender can be conceptualized as one of many predictors of mathematics performance" (p. 1133). Socioeconomic status, parents' occupation, and the quality of schooling were among other variables likely to influence performance outcomes.

Although the existence and extent of gender differences in mathematics learning remains a contested issue, the persistence of small gender differences in favour of males continues to be reported in data derived from large scale studies. For example, Else-Quest et al. (2010) used a meta-analysis of the Programme for International Student Assessment [PISA] and Trends in International Mathematics and Science Study [TIMSS] data to examine the occurrence of gender differences in mathematics performance on these large scale international tests. They invoked the gender stratification hypothesis (that is, societal stratification and inequality of opportunity based on gender) as an explanation for the continuing gender gap in mathematics achievement reported in some, but not in other, countries. They concluded that cross-national variability found in the gender gap "can be explained by important national characteristics reflecting the status and welfare of women … (and) the magnitude of gender differences in math also depends, in part, upon the quality of the assessment of mathematics achievement" (Else-Quest et al. 2010,

p. 125). Perhaps a caveat should be introduced here. While useful for reviewing a large body of literature focussed on a common concern, the acknowledged preference for publication of studies with statistically significant findings may bias the outcome of a meta-analysis.

Given the emphasis on large scale data as a resource for the identification, or rejection, of gender differences in performance it is useful to inspect these data in more detail. Leder and Forgasz (2018) are not alone in illustrating how the content of a test or task can influence apparent gender differences in performance. Considering group data for TIMSS 2015 they pointed to provocative nuanced differences which emerge when the data are reported by content domain. At the grade 4 level, boys performed better than girls on *number* items in 21 countries (see Martin et al. 2016) while the mean score for girls was higher than for boys in seven countries. For *geometric shapes and measures*, the mean score for boys was higher than for girls in 14 countries but higher for girls than for boys in nine countries. For *data display*, girls outperformed boys in 13 countries, and boys did better than girls in two countries. Inconsistencies in gender differences in performance by content domain were also found for students in eighth grade. No mean difference in the performance of girls and boys was found in 26 of the 39 countries in which the eighth grade mathematics survey was administered. The mean score for girls was higher in seven countries, and higher for boys in six countries. In *number*, on average, boys did better than girls in 17 countries, while girls did better than boys in four countries. In contrast, on *algebra* domain items, girls did better than boys in 21 countries, and boys did not outperform girls in any countries. Girls also did better than boys on *geometry* items in eight countries compared with two countries where boys outperformed girls on items in this domain. For *data and chance*, boys outperformed girls in six countries, and girls outperformed boys in seven countries.

Group findings for PISA also show an interesting pattern. Again a nuanced appraisal of mathematics assessment data provides constructive insights. In OECD (2014), data are presented *inter alia* in terms of the four content subscales: *change and relationships*, *space and shape*, *quantity*, and *uncertainty and data*. Mean differences in the scores of boys and girls across the OECD countries, it was reported, ranged from 15 points in favour of boys on the *space and shape* scale to a difference of nine points in favour of males on the *uncertainty and data* subscale. Within country group differences varied considerably, however. In the *quantity* subscale, for example, differences ranged from 31 points in favour of boys to 19 points in favour of girls. Such varying patterns of gender differences across the performance of large groups of students on the different scales "highlight the difficulties in designing educational policies that promote gender equity" (OECD 2009, p. 22).

Large scale surveys such as PISA and TIMSS undeniably provide much contextual and moderating information beyond (mean) students' scores on test items. This includes information about the students' home, school, and broader learning environment and measures of students' attitudes, beliefs, and longer term aspirations. Yet, as noted by Leder and Forgasz (2018), carefully contextualized presentations of the vast sets of data generated by these large surveys are often simplified in discussions of national and international performance data. External influences, local expertise, and individual teacher or pupil preferences, participants' social class and the accompanying associated advantages or disadvantages may influence test results. These factors are often minimized or ignored when the outcomes of tests are reported or interpreted by stakeholders or in the popular media. Group differences in mathematics achievement may be simplistically attributed to gender rather than a combination of factors, some more influential than gender per se. Perhaps, not coincidentally, in their exploration in nine countries of the general public's views about mathematics Forgasz et al. (2014) reported that many of the respondents, whose views were sought through advertising on the popular media site *Facebook,* indicated that they believed that studying mathematics was important for all students, irrespective of their gender. However, among those who held gender-stereotyped views, more considered that boys were better than girls at mathematics, science, and computing and that being a scientist or working with computers was more suitable for males than for females. Perceptions that mathematics is a male domain seemingly linger and persist among sections of the general public. According to Hill et al. (2010), some of those who explicitly reject agreement with gender and mathematics and science stereotypes might nevertheless hold such beliefs at an unconscious level. Fictional depictions of school mathematics in books aimed at young adults may further perpetuate rather than challenge gender bias (Darragh 2018).

In contrast to the test measures considered in some detail so far, Voyer and Voyer (2014) compared males' and females' academic performance using the measure of teacher-assigned marks. Their analysis drew on 369 samples yielding 502 effect sizes. For the overall sample of effect sizes, females were found to have a small but significant advantage. Course content, nationality, racial and gender composition, but not year of publication, were significant moderators of effect sizes. The largest effects were in language courses; the smallest in mathematics and science courses. The study by Voyer and Voyer (2014) is another challenging reminder that how achievement is measured can influence apparent gender differences in performance.

In summary: after four decades of consistent, persistent, and often insightful research on gender and mathematics there seems to be at best limited consensus on the size and direction of gender differences in mathematics performance. Might the tendency for statistically significant results to be accepted for publication while non-significant findings are rejected (as discussed by, e.g., Howard et al. 2009) perhaps influence this summation? That there is great variation in the explanations put forward to account for any gender differences found is widely acknowledged.

13.5.2 Participation

Mathematics is considered to be a critical component of the school curriculum, an enabling discipline for STEM-based studies [science, mathematics, engineering and technology], and an important gateway to adult life and occupational opportunities: "Being able to read, understand and respond appropriately to numerical and mathematical information are skills that are essential for full social and economic participation" (OECD 2013, p. 98). Much is written in policy documents and more broadly about the need for the population at large to be equipped with adequate quantitative skills. "There is a global perception that a workforce with a substantial proportion educated in Mathematics, Engineering and Science (MES) is essential to future prosperity" (Marginson et al. 2013, p. 6). At the same time concerns are expressed that the pool of students intending to continue with mathematical studies once they are no longer compulsory appears to be stable or, in the most advanced mathematics courses, to be decreasing (AMSI 2017). Not surprisingly, there are between-country differences in the proportions of students studying non-compulsory mathematics courses at the secondary and tertiary levels (Van Langen and Dekkers 2005), though differences in educational program structures make it difficult to quantify these precisely.

As indicated at the beginning of the chapter, research conducted in the 1970s was partly driven by data on gender differences in participation in post compulsory mathematics courses. Lower female participation in higher level mathematics courses internationally was publicized by early researchers (including, for example, Schildkamp-Kündiger 1982) and continues to be documented (AMSI 2017; OECD 2009; Leder 2015; Lubienski and Ganley 2017; Reilly et al. 2017; Stoet and Geary 2018; Wang and Degol 2017; Wilson and Mack 2014). Particularly disturbing is the trend for females to be under-represented in school level enrolments in the most challenging mathematics subjects and, at tertiary level, the relatively small numbers enrolled in masters and Ph.D. courses. In Australia, for example, the number of masters and Ph.D. graduates has increased slightly, largely due to an increase in number of female graduates. Nevertheless, male graduates at this level still outnumber female graduates three to one (AMSI 2017). As well, females remain in the minority in Engineering and other STEM-related fields (e.g., AMSI 2017; Hill et al. 2010; OECD 2006). Stoet and Geary (2018) maintain that the number of females who continue with, and graduate in STEM studies falls well short of the number that could take that path: "there is a loss of female STEM capacity between secondary and tertiary education" (p. 590).

Over the years, a range of strategies to encourage students to persist with mathematics studies has been advocated. These include, but are certainly not limited to, the following: improving problem solving strategies, curriculum adjustments, single-sex classes, and better pre- and in-service preparation for teachers. That such programs may be particularly beneficial to females is often added strategically. Approaches advocated or adopted in different countries to improve the participation and achievement of students in mathematics and science are variously described at some length, for example, in reports by Marginson et al. (2013) and UNESCO (2017). A promising current, comprehensive Australian initiative, CHOOSEMATHS which is aimed at increasing the participation in mathematics of all students and especially for girls and young women, is certainly worth noting. Importantly not only students and teachers, but also parents are targeted through different aspects of the program. The scope of the longitudinal project is described as follows:

> Since 2015 we have been leading the national implementation of key classroom and pipeline strategies to transform Australia's mathematical capability. With maths essential to a growing number of jobs, it is critical we foster understanding of the value and impact of maths and equip students to embrace these opportunities now and into the future. Working across four key components, the project is addressing pipeline challenges through Schools Outreach, Careers Awareness, CHOOSEMATHS Awards and the Women in Maths Network. (ChooseMaths n.d.).

Many of the perspectives and (inevitably) theoretical and value-driven programs and interventions invoked to explain or combat persistent patterns in gender differences in participation in mathematics and related areas mirror those directed at performance differences. The models proposed typically contain a range of interacting factors, both intra-personal and environmental. Included among the latter are the school culture, social mores, and the values and expectations of peers, parents, and teachers. A contemporary snapshot of workplace environments based on American data is disconcerting. Information, gathered from adults, aged 18 years and over, and who were working in STEM related areas and careers was inspected by gender, race, and ethnicity. Focussing on gender, Funk and Parker (2018) reported as follows:

> ... the workplace is a different, sometimes more hostile environment than the one their male coworkers experience. Discrimination and sexual harassment are seen as more frequent, and gender is perceived as more of an impediment than an advantage to career success. Three groups of women in STEM jobs stand out as more likely to see workplace inequities: women employed in STEM settings where men outnumber women, women working in computer jobs, ... and women in STEM who hold postgraduate degrees. (p. 6)

They further noted that diversity in the STEM workforce varied quite dramatically and depended on the type and level of occupation. The pervasiveness of females' lower participation than males' in mathematics and other STEM subjects at different levels of education, and acknowledged contributing factors, are also revisited and reviewed in the UNESCO (2017) report.

In summary: As mentioned earlier, gender differences in participation in mathematics in favour of males emerge when the studying of mathematics is optional, and are more pronounced in advanced mathematics subjects. The imbalance increases at higher levels of education and is also evident in gender differences in participation in STEM fields, and again particularly at the more advanced career levels.

13.6 Future Directions

National policies for promoting STEM, it is often claimed, are "generally conceived in human capital terms. Emphasis on the 'pipeline' of school and tertiary STEM education is frequently motivated by issues concerning the STEM labour force argued instrumental to economic growth and well being" (Marginson et al. 2013, p. 94). To this is added the need to address "the gender challenge, ... a deepening issue across all STEM disciplines, (which) is critical to ensure skill supply can meet industry need into the future" (AMSI 2017, p. 6). Given these assumed priorities, taken from Australian publications but also voiced elsewhere, and the ambivalent and at times contradictory findings reported to date and reflected in this chapter, work on gender and education will continue to be an important part of the research agenda in mathematics education. From the material presented so far it is clear that relevant data and research on gender and mathematics were gleaned from a staggering range of sources embedded in a variety of disciplines (many indirectly rather than directly linked to mathematics education), and interrogated using multiple methods and procedures. What research is worth doing and reporting? Where should new research efforts be directed to ensure that the field will continue to advance and develop? According to Howard et al. (2009):

> Scientific progress is made by trusting the bulk of current knowledge in the form of implicit assumptions in our research efforts. For example, we trust that ... subjects will truthfully report their behavior, and that the theoretical variables of interest are reflected in the specific operational definitions employed. ... The corpus of scientific knowledge changes and improves as new evidence supports or alters our beliefs. (p. 117)

Replications and small extensions of earlier work have featured heavily in the annals of educational research and, undoubtedly, will continue to play an important role in future research on gender and mathematics. Replication studies fall into one of two categories: an exact replication of an original study or research involving conceptual replication, for example by exploring from a different perspective the contexts in which the original results were obtained (Cai et al. 2018). Given the unpredictability of human behaviour, the difficulty of random assignment of "treatments" or experiences, and the limitations imposed by practical constraints, exact replication of a previous study is extremely difficult, if not impossible. What criteria should underpin the conduct and reporting of new research? What about studies in which no statistically significant findings are found? When should journal editors be encouraged to publish these? Recently Star (2018) provided a number of benchmarks in the context of replication studies. With some adjustment these requirements clearly have relevance more widely:

> An outstanding replication study article: 1. Makes a convincing case that the study topic of the replication is of great importance to the field, 2. Makes a convincing case that the field will learn something significant from the replication that is not already known, and 3. Convincingly shows that there is reason to believe that the results of the original study may be flawed. (p. 99)

Adhering to the core issues embedded in these principles in planning and executing new research could yield the productive and constructive new insights needed to achieve equitable outcomes in mathematics education for all.

References

American Educational Research Association [AERA]. (2018). AERA expands gender category options for member. http://www.aera.net/Newsroom/AERA-Highlights-E-newsletter/AERA-Highlights-April-2016/AERA-Expands-Gender-Category-Options-for-Member.

American Psychological Association [APA]. (2015a). APA dictionary of psychology (2nd ed.). Washington, DC: Author. https://www.apa.org/pi/lgbt/resources/sexuality-definitions.pdf.

American Psychological Association. (2015b). Definitions related to sexual orientation and gender diversity in APA Documents (pp. 5–6). Washington, DC: Author. http://204.14.132.173/pi/lgbt/resources/sexuality-definitions.pdf.

AMSI. (2017). Discipline profile of the mathematical sciences. Melbourne, Australia: AMSI.

Belenky, M. F., Clinchy, B. M., Goldberger, N. R., & Tarule, J. M. (1986). *Women's ways of knowing: The development of self, voice, and mind*. New York: Basic Books.

Burton, L. (2003). Introduction. In L. Burton (Ed.), *Which way social justice in mathematics education?* (pp. xv–xxiii). Westport, Connecticut: Praeger.

Cai, J., Morris, A., Hohensee, C., Hwang, S., Robison, V., & Hiebert, J. (2018). *Journal for Research in Mathematics Education, 49*(1), 2–8.

ChooseMath. (n.d.). Changing the face of mathematics. https://choosemaths.org.au/.

Costa, S. A. (2000). The Ladies' Diary: Society, gender and mathematics in England, 1704-1754. (Unpublished doctoral dissertation). Ithaca, NY: Cornell University.

Damarin, S. (2008). Thinking feminism and mathematics together. *Signs, 34*(1), 101–123.

Damarin, S. K. (2000). The mathematically able as a marked category. *Gender and Education, 12*(1), 69–85.

Darragh, L. (2018). Loving and loathing: Portrayals of school mathematics in young adult fiction. *Journal for Research in Mathematics Education, 49*(2), 178–209.

Eccles, J. S., Adler, T. F., Futterman, R., Goff, S. B., Kaczala, C. M., Meece, J. L., et al. (1983). Expectancies, values, and academic behaviors. In J. T. Spence (Ed.), *Achievement and achievement motivation* (pp. 75–146). San Fransisco, CA: W. H. Freeman.

Else-Quest, N. M., Hyde, J. S., & Linn, M. C. (2010). Cross-national patterns of gender differences in mathematics: A meta-analysis. *Psychological Bulletin, 136*, 103–127.

Fennema, E. (1974). Mathematics learning and the sexes: A review. *Journal for Research in Mathematics Education, 5*(3), 126–139.

Fennema, E., & Hart, L. E. (1994). Gender and the JRME. *Journal for Research in Mathematics Education, 25*(6), 648–659.

Fennema, E., & Sherman, J. A. (1976). Fennema-Sherman mathematics attitude scales: Instruments designed to measure attitudes toward the learning of mathematics by females and males. *Journal for Research in Mathematics Education, 7*, 324–326.

Fennema, E., & Sherman, J. (1977). Sex-related differences in mathematics achievement, spatial visualization and affective factors. *American Educational Research Journal, 14*, 51–71.

Fennema, E., Becker, A. D., Wolleat, P. L., & Pedro, J. D. (1980). *Multiplying options and subtracting bias*. Cambridge, Mass: Educational Development Corporation.

Forgasz, H., Leder, G., & Tan, H. (2014). Public views on the gendering of mathematics and related careers: International comparisons. *Educational Studies in Mathematics, 87*(3), 369–388.

Funk, C., & Parker, K. (2018). Women and men in STEM often at odds over workplace equity. Pew Research Center. http://www.pewsocialtrends.org/2018/01/09/women-and-men-in-stem-often-at-odds-over-workplace-equity/.
Furinghetti, F., Matos, J. M., & Menghini, M. (2013). From mathematics and education, to mathematics education. In M. A. (Ken) Clements et al. (Eds.), *Third International Handbook of Mathematics Education* (pp. 273–302). New York: Springer. https://doi.org/10.1007/978-1-4614-4684-2_9.
Gilligan, C. (1982). *In a different voice: Psychological theory and women's development*. Cambridge, MA: Harvard University Press.
Gutiérrez, R. (2013). The socio-political turn in mathematics education. *Journal for Research in Mathematics Education, 44*(1), 37–68.
Halpern, D. F. (2002). Using test data to inform educational policies. *Issues in Education. Contributions, 8*(1), 87–93.
Hill, C., Corbett, C., & St. Rose, A. (2010). Why so few? Women in science, technology, engineering, and mathematics. Washington, DC: AAUW. http://www.aauw.org/learn/research/upload/whysofew.pdf.
Howard, G. S., Hill, T. L., Maxwell, S. E., Baptista, T. M., Farias, M. H., Coelho, C., et al. (2009). *Review of General Psychology, 13*(2), 146–166.
Hyde, J. S., Fennema, E., & Lamon, S. J. (1990). Gender differences in mathematics performance: A meta-analysis. *Psychological Bulletin, 107*(2), 139–155. http://dx.doi.org/10.1037/0033-2909.107.2.139.
Kaiser, G., & Rogers, P. (1985). Introduction: Equity in mathematics education. In P. Rogers & G. Kaiser (Eds.), *Equity in mathematics education* (pp. 1–10). London: Falmer Press.
Leder, G., & Forgasz, H. (2018). Measuring who counts: Gender and mathematics assessment. *ZDM Mathematics Education, 50*(4), 687–697. https://doi.org/10.1007/s11858-018-0939-z.
Leder, G. C. (1980). The Ladies' Diary: Women and mathematics. In *Proceedings of the Tenth Annual ANZHES Conference* (pp. 1–16). Newcastle, Australia.
Leder, G. C. (1992). Mathematics and gender: Changing perspectives. In D. A. Grouws (Ed.), *Handbook of research in mathematics teaching and learning* (pp. 597–622). New York: Macmillan.
Leder, G. C. (2001). Pathways in mathematics towards equity: A 25 year journey. In M. van den Heuvel-Panhuizen (Ed.), *Proceedings of the 25th Conference of the International Group for the Psychology of Mathematics Education* (Vol. 1, pp. 41–54). Utrecht, The Netherlands: Freudenthal Institute, Faculty of Mathematics and Computer Science, Utrecht University.
Leder, G. C. (Chair). (2015). Gender and mathematics education revisited. In S. Cho (Ed.), *Proceedings of the 12th International Congress on Mathematical Education* (pp. 145–170). Cham: Springer. https://doi.org/10.1007/978-3-319-12688-3_12.
Leder, G. C., Forgasz, H. J., & Solar, C. (1996). Research and intervention programs in mathematics education: A gendered issue. In A. Bishop, K. Clements, C. Keitel, J. Kilpatrick, & C. Laborde (Eds.), *International handbook of mathematics education, Part 2* (pp. 945–985). Dordrecht, The Netherlands: Kluwer Academic Publishers.
Lewis, J. J. (2017). Women in mathematics history. https://www.thoughtco.com/women-in-mathematics-history-3530363.
Leybourn, T. (1817). The mathematical questions proposed in the Ladies' Diary, and their original answers, together with some new solutions, from its commencement in the year 1704 to 1816. (In four volumes.). London: Mawson.
Lindberg, S. M., Hyde, J. S., Petersen, J. L., & Linn, M. C. (2010). New trends in gender and mathematics performance: A meta-analysis. *Psychological Bulletin, 136*(6), 1123–1135.
Lubienski, S. T., & Bowen, A. (2000). Who's counting? A survey of mathematics education research 1982-1998. *Journal for Research in Mathematics Education, 31*, 626–633.
Lubienski, S. T., & Ganley, C. M. (2017). Research on gender and mathematics. In J. Cai (Ed.), *Compendium for research in mathematics education* (pp. 649–666). Reston, VA: National Council of Teachers of Mathematics.

Mackinnon, N. (1990). Sophie Germain: or was Gauss a feminist? *Mathematical Gazette, 74*(470), 346–351. https://doi.org/10.2307/3618130.

Marginson, S., Tytler, R., Freeman, B., & Roberts, K. (2013). STEM: Country comparisons. Report for the Australian Council of Learned Academies. www.acola.org.au.

Martin, M. O., Mullis, I. V. S., Foy, P., & Hooper, M. (2016). TIMSS 2015 international results in science. Retrieved from Boston College, TIMSS & PIRLS International Study Center Website. http://timssandpirls.bc.edu/timss2015/international-results/.

McLeod, D. B. (1992). Research on affect in mathematics education: A reconceptualization. In D. A. Grouws (Ed.), *Handbook of research in mathematics teaching and learning* (pp. 597–622). New York: MacMillan.

Morgan, C. (2014). Social theory in mathematics education: Guest editorial. *Educational Studies in Mathematics, 87*, 123–128.

OECD. (2006). Women in scientific careers: Unleashing the potential. Paris: OECD Publishing. https://doi.org/10.1787/9789264025387-en.

OECD. (2009). Equally prepared for life? How 15-year-old boys and girls perform in school. Paris: OECD Publishing. https://www.oecd.org/pisa/pisaproducts/42843625.pdf.

OECD. (2013). OECD skills outlook 2013: First results from the Survey of Adult Skills. http://dx.doi.org/10.1787/9789264204256-en.

OECD. (2014). *PISA 2012 results: What students know and can do—Student performance in mathematics, reading and science* (Vol. I, Rev. ed.). Paris, Pisa: OECD Publishing. http://dx.doi.org/10.1787/9789264201118-en.

Osen, L. (1974). *Women in mathematics*. Cambridge, Mass: MIT Press.

Patterson, E. C. (1974). The case of Mary Somerville: An aspect of nineteenth century science. *Proceedings of the American Philosophical Society, 118*, 269–275.

Perl, T. (1979). The Ladies' Diary or Woman's Almanack, 1704-1841. *Historia Mathematics, 6*, 36–53.

Reilly, D., Neumann, D. L., Andrews, G. (2017). Investigating gender differences in mathematics and science: Results from the 2011 trends in mathematics and science survey. *Research in Science Education*. https://doi.org/10.1007/s11165-017-9630-6.

Schildkamp-Kündiger, E. (Ed.). (1982). International review on gender and mathematics. Columbus: ERIC Clearinghouse for Science, Mathematics and Environmental Education. [ERIC Document No. 222326].

Snyder, R. C. (2008). What is third-wave feminism? A new directions essay. *Signs: Journal of Women in Culture and Society, 34*(1), 175–196.

Star, J. R. (2018). When and why replication studies should be published: Guidelines for mathematics education journals. *Journal for Research in Mathematics Education, 49*(1), 98–103.

Stoet, G., & Geary, D. C. (2018). The gender-equality paradox in science, technology, engineering, and mathematics education. *Psychological Science, 2018, 29*(4), 581–593.

UNESCO. (2017). Cracking the code: Girls' and women's education in science, technology, engineering and mathematics. Paris: Author.

Van Langen, A., & Dekkers, H. (2005). Cross-national differences in participating in tertiary science, technology, engineering and mathematics education. *Comparative Education, 41*(3), 329–350. https://doi.org/10.1080/03050060500211708.

Voyer, D., & Voyer, S. D. (2014). Gender differences in scholastic achievement: A meta-analysis. *Psychological Bulletin, 2014*(4), 1174–1204.

Walberg, H. J., & Haertel, G. D. (1992). Educational psychology's first century. *Journal of Educational Psychology, 84*, 6–19.

Wang, M. T., & Degol, J. L. (2017). Gender gap in science, technology, engineering, and mathematics (STEM): Current knowledge, implications for practice, policy, and future directions. *Educational Psychology Review, 29*(1), 119–140. https://doi.org/10.1007/s10648-015-9355.

Wilson, R., & Mack, J. (2014). Declines in high school mathematics and science participation: Evidence of students' and future teachers' disengagement with maths. *International Journal of Innovation in Science and Mathematics Education, 22*(7), 35–48, 2014.

Open Access This chapter is licensed under the terms of the Creative Commons Attribution 4.0 International License (http://creativecommons.org/licenses/by/4.0/), which permits use, sharing, adaptation, distribution and reproduction in any medium or format, as long as you give appropriate credit to the original author(s) and the source, provide a link to the Creative Commons license and indicate if changes were made.

The images or other third party material in this chapter are included in the chapter's Creative Commons license, unless indicated otherwise in a credit line to the material. If material is not included in the chapter's Creative Commons license and your intended use is not permitted by statutory regulation or exceeds the permitted use, you will need to obtain permission directly from the copyright holder.

Chapter 14
Theoretical Aspects of Doing Research in Mathematics Education: An Argument for Coherence

Stephen Lerman

Abstract One of the hardest tasks for new researchers, actually all researchers throughout their careers, is what theory to use to inform their work, and how to work with theory. In this chapter I try to set out what theory is for, in research, and what are the challenges for theory choices. I indicate that we are in a period of proliferation of theories, one from which there is no going back, if indeed there was ever a time without such choices being faced. I look on this proliferation as positive for our work, not a hindrance to progress, as some in our field believe. I am not aiming for an encyclopaedic approach, a full list of all theories and how they might inform research. Were I to attempt such a task new theories would have emerged before the chapter appears in print. I try to explain how that happens, in this chapter. Instead I take a position in relation to theory, a position that informs the writing of the whole chapter; I look for coherence of theoretical work, as it informs research.

Keywords Theory · Research · Proliferation · Coherence

14.1 Introduction

In this chapter I focus on recruitment of, and working with, theories in mathematics education research in a time of proliferation of theories. The task of reading about theoretical perspectives on learning, on teaching, on community, on communication, on mathematics, and so on is a demanding one. The growth of theories over the recent decades makes the task much more difficult. I will discuss why this proliferation exists and suggest it might be a good thing, though there are many people in the field who do not agree.

The task for research students is to make some choices regarding these theories, and which theory or theories will be the ones to be worked with in their research. Some will argue that the research questions drive that choice, and it does not matter

S. Lerman (✉)
London South Bank University, London, UK
e-mail: lermans@lsbu.ac.uk

© The Author(s) 2019
G. Kaiser and N. Presmeg (eds.), *Compendium for Early Career Researchers in Mathematics Education*, ICME-13 Monographs,
https://doi.org/10.1007/978-3-030-15636-7_14

which theories are taken up as long as they can provide answers to the research questions. Still others will argue for the recruitment of a range of theories, each of which will offer a different perspective or outcome of the research and all of which are valid. I will present some thoughts on these and other challenges in recruiting and working with theory.

This chapter is not, however, an encyclopedia of research theories, nor of research methods. I take a position in relation to theories and that is one of seeking coherence. There are many good textbooks that provide information across the educational field (e.g., Cohen et al. 2018). There is also the Encyclopedia of Mathematics Education for specifically mathematics educational material, including very detailed information on theories (Lerman 2014a).

A successful research study at doctoral level can be achieved by working with one established theory and drawing on the body of work that appears in the literature for operationalization of that theory, for identification of research questions, for appropriate research methods and for analysis of data. Coherence across these four central elements of research and of writing a thesis is essential. A good doctoral study can be achieved by recruiting more than one theory but again I will argue for coherence. Some theories contradict others. If you are going to use more than one they should work together and you will need to do some work to show that they do, and how they do. I will discuss and exemplify these points too.

I like to think that research in mathematics education develops our thinking as a community and pushes forward our understanding of the processes of teaching and learning mathematics. I like to hope that we have good effects on practice in teaching and learning mathematics too. I have to admit, however, that it is not easy to see how one can judge progress in any way that convinces, even in one sociocultural context, let alone more widely. I will leave that sceptical concern aside though, for the purposes of this chapter. Those discussions are for elsewhere.

14.2 Theory Proliferation

Education, as one of the social sciences, is a special kind of field, what Bernstein, the sociologist of education, called a 'region' (see, e.g., Bernstein 2000). Unlike, say, the field of psychology, or the field of science, it draws both on theory and on practice. It is similar to medicine in that sense. In mathematics education we have a face towards intellectual fields such as psychology, anthropology, philosophy, sociology, semiotics and so on. Each and all of these fields have something to say to education, something we can draw from in thinking about and researching teaching and learning. In addition, we have another face, towards practice. Research questions generally arise from practice and should, ultimately, have something to say to and about practice.

A further important and significant feature of educational research is that, according to Bernstein, it exhibits a 'horizontal knowledge structure'. Science, in contrast, exhibits a 'vertical knowledge structure', because, as theories and knowledge grow, they replace previous theories and knowledge. Phlogiston theory was replaced by the discovery of oxygen; the notion of the earth as the centre of the universe was replaced by the sun as the centre of our immediate universe; the theory of relativity replaced Newtonian mechanics, and so on. Of course this is somewhat simplified. Sometimes theories are subsumed into newer ones; competing theories can remain for a long time until technology reaches a stage where suitable critical experiments can be carried out to resolve which is deemed correct. The history and philosophy of science is full of such events and disputes. Kuhn (1978) argues that old 'normals' are replaced by the new 'normals', but proceed in this way through conflicts, initially at the periphery, but eventually at the centre.

However, Bernstein is arguing that the new 'normal' today, at the meta-level, which Kuhn presents as a linear process of theory development, is on the contrary proliferation, a multiplicity of perspectives and languages. Horizontal knowledge structures, according to Bernstein, develop in two ways: with the creation of new theories or languages/discourses; and within existing theories or languages/discourses. This is typical of the social sciences, but also, strangely, of mathematics itself, though another important distinction, which will not be developed here, is that of the strength of a grammar; that is to say, how precise in meaning are the terms used. Mathematics has a strong grammar; the difference between a ring and a field are very precise, for example. Social science, and education in particular, has a very weak grammar. If we were to discuss what 'understanding' means and how we identify it in learning we might talk for days without reaching consensus. New fields, or better, sub-fields of mathematics develop, string theory for example, but do not replace other sub-fields. As the sub-field develops the language (theorems etc.) becomes so specific that mathematicians in other sub-fields can hardly understand each other.

In mathematics education, as new theories develop, they sit alongside existing ones. We might have expected that behaviourism, a psychological theory that dominated educational thinking until the early part of the 20th century would, perhaps, have been replaced in education, either by Piagetian or by Vygotskian theories, as both thinkers were opposed to behaviourism, considering it to be a theory very limited in its relevance to human cognitive development at least, but that did not happen. Behaviourism still has its proponents and is still researched. It appears in classrooms as behaviour modification techniques (gold stars for good behaviour for example), and in therapy for the treatment of specific phobias, such as fear of spiders.

Vygotsky's writings became known in education outside of the Soviet Union only in the 1960s and 1970s. Vygotsky was critical, in quite fundamental ways, of Piaget's ideas but, once again, these two theories sit alongside each other, giving competing accounts, stories, of how children learn and what is the role of teaching. Neither replaces the other. I shall have more to say about Piaget and Vygotsky later in this chapter. A quite recent development has been the introduction of biosocial theories (de Freitas 2017), offering new perspectives on learners and learning.

This account of knowledge structures and theory development by Bernstein is at least one way of accounting for the proliferation of theories. As well as behaviourism, Piagetian and Vygotskian/sociocultural theories, in mathematics education research we can point to enactivism, socio-political theories, critical theory, post-structuralism and postmodernism, and work informed by Levinas, Kant, and Aristotle. This list is by no means exhaustive. Karmiloff-Smith and Inhelder (1974) wrote a paper entitled 'If you want to get ahead get a theory' to capture the phenomenon of research students, or more experienced researchers, thinking that if they can find a theory new to the field they may be assured of success in their thesis and career. In fact it is usually the case that new theories do provide new insights and new ideas for researching the teaching and learning of mathematics and its wider context. It is certainly not just a strategy for carving out a career path.

Historically, in terms of the mathematics education research community, psychology was the main knowledge domain on which researchers drew. Hence the name of the leading research group, the International Group for the Psychology of Mathematics Education, known as PME. It was founded in 1976 and has met annually ever since. In 2005 the constitution was changed to give equal credit to research drawing on other perspectives, though I think it fair to say that psychology remains the leading theoretical field. The proliferation of theories has been matched by an increasing range of journals and conferences on mathematics education, supporting the opportunity for new ideas and theories. The series of conferences called Mathematics, Education and Society (MES) that began in Nottingham in 1998 and will hold its 10th meeting in 2019, focuses on political, sociological and other perspectives, and was established to enable researchers who were not working with psychological theories to have a forum for writing, meeting and networking. As I write this chapter, the 6th International Conference on Ethnomathematics is being held in Colombia. These are just some of the examples.

I have not yet mentioned Mathematics as one of the theoretical fields that impact significantly on our research. It is obvious of course. Mathematics education research is essentially about mathematics just as art education research is about art. But we cannot just say 'mathematics' without thinking about the range of ways we need to think about it and what part that plays in our research. Mathematics is about problem-solving; mathematics is a body of certain knowledge; mathematical thinking is a way of seeing the world, a lens through which to see circles in wheels etc.; mathematics is a powerful tool in formatting society, including its inequalities; traditional mathematics teaching does violence to children; inquiry/reform mathematics is the panacea; children from disadvantaged backgrounds do no better in reform mathematics classrooms than in traditional ones. These are just some of the competing views that surround our research in relation to mathematics and about which researchers often have to take a position. It is quite legitimate of course to choose to work with the status quo, the existing mathematics curriculum, if the research is in schools or Universities, without feeling required to take a position on what mathematics is. Studies of workplace or street mathematics will engage directly and necessarily with what mathematics is, or perhaps better expressed as what it is for. Research on what might be the best environment for students to learn mathematics, and that includes pre-service or in-service teachers, will need to take into account the range of ways that the subject can be perceived.

We should not leave the way we perceive the field of mathematics as it might/ should impact on mathematics education research without referring to Hans Freudenthal's most important work. His 'psychology' of mathematics learning, and he was one of the founders of PME, he called didactical phenomenology. He saw learning as a tour of discovery and teaching as guiding that discovery. He argued that students learn mathematics best by reinventing it, recognising that the discoveries of school students would be new to them but not to the world of mathematics. He argued that all students taught in the way he described ought to be able to succeed in learning mathematics.

I see our task as a research sub-field to seek an explanation of how socially, culturally and historically located knowledge, in our case knowledge of mathematics, becomes the knowledge of the individual in that society at that time. An equally important question is why, for so many children from disadvantaged backgrounds, in many countries around the world, that knowledge does not become theirs; they are excluded. The nature of the knowledge, whether of science, history or art, must play a significant role in conceptualising teaching and learning and therefore research. Mathematics presents unique challenges of course. Consider some of the features of mathematics: proof and proving; certainty of results, abstract objects to be handled and manipulated; success in the subject highly valued across the world, taken as an indicator of intellectual ability more generally; a climate of bewilderment for most people, including parents of children studying the subject; the list can go on. The teacher of mathematics, similar but also different to teachers of other subjects, most similar to science teachers, together with textbooks where they are used, is the arbiter of what is correct and what is not. In a class discussion of even and odd numbers a child might claim that one is even because it can be split into two halves. We might all agree that the proposal is delightful and creative, but outside the definition of even and odd. Somehow the teacher has to correct the knowledge whilst retaining the climate of supporting children's thinking and imagination. A much deeper analysis of this kind of challenge and dilemma for teachers can be found in the extensive work of Deborah Ball and her colleagues (see, e.g., Ball 1993).

14.3 Incommensurability and 'Home-Grown' Theories

There have been, and continue to be, some in our community who consider this proliferation to be damaging as we find it increasingly hard to speak to each other across languages/discourses, an incommensurability of meanings, and this limits the work we can do, but especially the chance that our work might affect positively what goes on in school mathematics (e.g., Goldin 2003). First, this proliferation is typical in thought in the 21st century: it should not be surprising therefore that we see the same in mathematics education research. Since the 'Pandora's box' has been opened, in this sense, how can it be closed again? Which theory would be the one agreed and accepted by everyone? We could even ask which intellectual field, psychology, sociology, political theory for example, would provide the best research context? I think that sociology, with its ability to explain the appearance of multiple theories and their relationship to each other, has been a vital feature in mathematics education research since it entered the field in the 1990s. But I am not alone in arguing that we gain enormously from the research in mathematics education just because of the range of theories and we would lose far more than we might gain by attempting to narrow that range. Lather (2006), for example, argues that the call for simplification aligns with the neo-positivist response, called by Hodkinson (2004) the 'new orthodoxy', to anxieties raised by postmodernism. Lather says:

> Against this new orthodoxy, I have endorsed a 'disjunctive affirmation' of multiple ways of going about educational research in terms of finding our way into a less comfortable social science full of stuck places and difficult philosophical issues of truth, interpretation and responsibility. Neither reconciliation nor paradigm war, this is about thinking difference differently, a reappropriation of contradictory available scripts to create alternative practices of research as a site of being and becoming. (p. 52)

Just as the well known visual version of incommensurability below (Fig. 14.1) means you can see only one image at a time, the faces or the vase, but you can see both successively, so too I can 'speak' both the languages of sociocultural theory and radical constructivism, which are argued to be incommensurable (Lerman 1996).

The issue for researchers in mathematics education is how competing theories are chosen, worked with, and why, in the search for justifiable answers to research questions. Theories, as discourses, offer worldviews. They are much more than a framing for research methods. As I will discuss below, working with worldviews that differ in fundamental ways can lead to incoherence, an attempt to see both the vase and the faces at the same time. An argument can be made for layers of interpretations of research findings, each layer drawn from a different theoretical

Fig. 14.1 Face vase optical illusion

framework. Nevertheless, researchers working with opposing theories will need to work very hard to make sense of their analysis to avoid a kind of stalemate of opposing accounts that cannot be brought together usefully.

There have also been some who regret that all our theories have been drawn from outside mathematics education research and we lack 'home-grown' theories (Kilpatrick 1981). Silver and Herbst (2007) claimed that this has long been the goal of some pioneers in our field such as H. G. Steiner, though their approach is along the lines of the new orthodoxy critiqued by Lather. They write:

> The development of a grand theory of mathematics education could be useful in providing warrants for our field's identity and intellectual autonomy within apparently broader fields such as education, psychology, or mathematics. In that sense, a grand theory could be helpful to organize the field, imposing something like a grand translational or relational scheme that allows a large number of people to see phenomena and constructs in places where others only see people, words, and things. A grand theory of the field of mathematics education could seek to spell out what is singular (if anything) of mathematics education as an institutional field or perhaps seek to spell out connections with other fields that may not be so immediately related and that establish the field as one among many contributors to an academic discipline. (p. 60)

In contrast, Sriraman and English (2010) argue the following:

> We however do not agree with the claims of Silver and Herbst for the following reason. In Sriraman and English (2005) we put forth an argument on the difficulty of abstracting universal invariants about what humans do in different mathematical contexts, which in turn, are embedded within different social and cultural settings; this suggests that it is a futile enterprise to formulate grand theories. At this point in time such a grand theory does not appear evident, and indeed, we question whether we should have such a theory. (p. 17)

Bernstein uses the term 'recontextualisation' to refer to the process of taking a discourse developed in one context and moving it to another. It is a process at the heart of education. For example, Piaget's psychological studies have been recontextualised as principles of learning. He was not an educator, though he followed closely how his work was reinterpreted and selected for school classrooms. Elements of research produced in the mathematics education research community are selected and recontextualised for teacher education courses and texts and for school classrooms. Bernstein (1990) wrote:

> The recontextualising rules regulate not only selection, sequence, pace, and relations with other subjects, but also the theory of instruction from which the transmission rules are derived. (p. 185)

That selection is not a neutral process. Selection always takes place driven by principles at the more local level, and ideology at a macro-level. In many countries most people engaged in research in mathematics education are also teacher educators. The choice of what is presented as pedagogic principles are backed up by a selection from research. In turn, what gets selected by student teachers as they progress into schools is again a recontextualisation (Ensor 2001).

Similarly, researchers recontextualise theories when they are brought into our field, and in this sense they become 'home-grown'. That is an essential part of the process of working with theory. Laying out Hegelian principles of judgement in the literature review requires an elaboration by the researcher of how those principles, developed by Hegel in a certain cultural-historical context and for certain purposes, can be useful in mathematics education research; Hegel's ideas are recontextualised for new purposes in a new context (Davis 2001). Perhaps 'home-recontextualised' is a better characterisation than 'home-grown', if rather more clumsy.

14.4 Working with Theoretical Frameworks, and Paradigms

I want to elaborate a little further here what it might mean to 'use' a theory. To the best of my knowledge Bakhtin never wrote about educational research and for sure not about mathematics education research. Those who take up the ideas of Bakhtin for their research are in fact doing the work of seeing relevance in what he wrote about discourse, communication and meaning, for classrooms, or teaching or whatever. It is therefore more appropriate to think in terms of working with, harnessing, or, as I have written above, recruiting theoretical ideas from elsewhere to guide thinking about the research problem(s). That necessitates work to justify the selection of particular theories or ideas to help frame and interpret the research problem in ways that can then be researched. If I see my goal as researching why children from disadvantaged backgrounds in England do worse in mathematics than other children I would need to seek for a theory that can engage with the problem. I would argue (remember, this is not a neutral chapter; it is written from my position) that radical constructivism cannot help me. But sociologists of education such as Basil Bernstein, Michael Apple, and Pierre Bourdieu can, because they have theorised how and why the phenomenon of schooling reproducing disadvantage (and advantage) occurs. Now my job is to recruit key ideas from one of those sociologists for my particular study.

This is a most important stage in research and one that has to be done properly. By this I mean that the research student has to read deeply and widely in the work of their chosen theorist(s). It is no good cherry picking a few ideas from someone else's research in place of doing the reading and learning the language oneself. The 'gate-keepers' in the community (examiners, journal editors and reviewers, grant committees) will see through this strategy. The languages of these theorists are very specific; that's why they have something useful and powerful to offer. Whether it be Halliday's systemic functional analysis; Bernstein's pedagogic device and recontextualisation rules; Piaget's concepts of accommodation, assimilation and reflective abstraction; the Marxist notion of ascent from abstract to concrete; or Vygotsky's stages of conceptual development, to be able to recruit the ideas to help frame the research requires serious engagement and hard work.

So how does one go about 'choosing' a theory? I think two issues come to the fore here. One is recognising which field I am in when I think about the research problems I am posing. Dowling and Brown (2010) describe this stage in research well. They ask is this question best addressed within psychology, or sociology or anthropology or some other field? Once I recognise that, I can narrow down the authors that I need to read and hence the scope of the literature. They call this identifying the theoretical field. When one chooses the setting within which the research will be carried out, namely, textbooks; school classrooms; workplace training or whatever, that is called the empirical field, and research is about the conversation between the two.

The second issue is what I'd call a personal/philosophical one. Assuming I have done the work required to understand the language and ideas of theorists, I may find the ideas of one appealing to me more than another. This may be about finding inspiration in one author more than others, my own history of ideas, experiences and feelings, or particular sympathy for the author.

Having identified the research questions, almost always the starting point for research anyway, there is a temptation to choose a theory or theories according to what will work. Statistical testing of data is often thought to be a matter of applying a test and if it does not produce the result you want, try another test. Of course this does a disservice to statistics but my point is that 'what works' seems to assume a particular outcome and the researcher wants to make sure that he/she will find that result emerging from their study. A justification for theory choice, and also research methods on the basis of 'what works' doesn't work, at least for me. I am not referring to research methods here. I will say more below, but what methods I choose to gather data to help me find what will constitute answers to my research questions is a later process, and can be put under the heading of 'what works' in some sense. To return to my proposed research topic above, statistical techniques may well work for me in identifying factors that lead to the strong connection between social class and achievement. Or I might find that sitting in a range of classrooms observing how knowledge is distributed (another term from Bernstein's sociology of education) might work better. My criticism of justification of theory in terms of 'what works' is that it carries a whole set of intended principles and outcomes from the research that are not spelt out in advance.

In summary, we could say that our job is putting theories to work in research. As I have suggested above, this could be a single elaborated theory. The French term *bricolage* taken from the notion of building construction, encourages the idea of working with multiple theories and constructing a framework out of them that will then be worked upon in order to frame the research. Prediger et al. (2008, p. 8) suggest the idea of networking of theories, offering the following diagram (Fig. 14.2) to set out how that might work.

In my view one needs to worry about working with contradictory theories. Multiple theories are to be recommended, I feel, as long as there is coherence between them. Within my position on theories, I would say that working with sociocultural theory at a macro-level of a classroom of school students but then turning to constructivist theories to work at the individual level (see Lerman 2013) is to be entering into a clash of competing theories. I develop this position below.

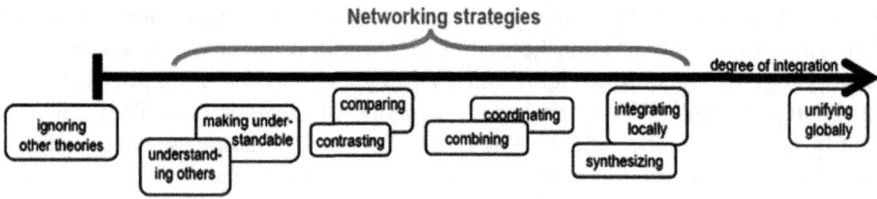

Fig. 14.2 A landscape of strategies for connecting theoretical approaches

14.5 Methodology

This chapter is not about methodology or methods. Other chapters will address these areas of research. I must, however, discuss the relationship between theories and methodology, as they are relevant to this chapter.

Let's be clear. Methodology is about the philosophy of research, strongly related to issues of truth. Where truth is to be found in social science research, and particularly in mathematics education research, our concern in this book, is the work of methodology. Is truth to be found in large numbers and statistical techniques of significance, such as in randomised tests? Is it to be found in deep studies of the life of classrooms? These are the kinds of questions to be considered and once again, like the choices faced in relation to theories, the choice of methodology is philosophical and to some degree personal/philosophical. A strong adherence to a scientific approach will pull one to the large-scale randomised studies and statistical techniques and positivism. It may be that a strong conviction that trying as far as is possible to enter into the life of the people and situations to be providing the data through ethnography, phenomenology, perhaps drawing on narrative methods, is required to answer the research questions.

Regarding the proliferation of theories, a phenomenon in education in general, not just in mathematics education research, Patti Lather (2006) has proposed a classification of methodologies in terms of paradigms, with a split coming with the appearance of post-structural and postmodern theories (Table 14.1).

I think this is very useful in that it makes clear the philosophical commitment of methodological choices.

Once again, 'methods' involve a different set of choices. A statistical analysis may well reveal important trends that would best be further investigated by ethnographic means. Statistical techniques may add a level of confirmation for connections that have appeared in ethnographic studies, or are suggested by theoretical orientations.

Table 14.1 Part of paradigm chart (Lather 2006, p. 37)

Predict	Understand	Emancipate	Break	Deconstruct	Next?
Positivist	Interpretive	Critical		Poststructural	Neo-positivism

14.5.1 *A Coherent Framework for Research*

My goal to this point has been to set out the task of selection and working with theory or theories. I indicated that working with more than one theory requires the work of ensuring that there is coherence between those theories and how they will be recruited for research, though I made it clear that this is my view, and not held by all in the research community. Those working with or within complexity theory would completely disagree. Relevant sections of the Encyclopedia of Mathematics Education would lead readers to those ideas and research and researchers who work in that area.

In this section I look at what I see as a very common incoherence in research in our field, namely, a false distinction between cognition and social-cultural context. Put another way, constructivism, the individual construction of knowledge, or individual sense-making, provides the theoretical framing for studying cognition, whilst one must also take into account the social context, sometimes called sociocultural context. But the latter does not help with the former. It helps the researcher to discuss society and schooling within it but does not help with studying individual students' learning.

Researchers are attempting a blend of constructivism, derived from Piagetian theory, and sociocultural theory, devised by Vygotsky. At first glance that seems to make sense as a research programme. However, a deeper study of the work of these two great thinkers reveals that both were cognitive scientists, though firstly with a different understanding of the origins of cognition, and secondly that there are fundamental differences between the two sets of ideas. Vygotsky would be turning in his grave with the knowledge that some researchers in child development did not see that studying cognitive development through a cultural- historical lens was his whole life's work. His work too was cognitive science.

To take the first point, and I am focusing here specifically on the danger of incoherence in working with both theories of child development, both Piaget and Vygotsky were concerned with how children develop, addressing directly what I set out above as one of the two key tasks as a research sub-field, to account for how socially, culturally and historically located knowledge becomes the knowledge of the individual in that society at that time. They began their investigations of that task from two different directions. Piaget's background in biology led him to look to adaptation of the individual species. Children learn something new when a new experience causes a disequilibrium with existing knowledge, leading the child to assimilate that new knowledge into their existing mental make-up or accommodate to the new knowledge by a mental reorganisation. Vygotsky's background in philosophy and the arts, working at the time of the Russian revolution, and with his experience of the role of language in cognition, saw cognitive development as occurring as a result of immersion in a sociocultural setting. For Piaget, then, cognition comes about within the mind of the individual. For Vygotsky, meaning is first on the social plane, in the sociocultural context, and only subsequently on the individual plane. Researching learning from a Piagetian point of view starts and ends with the individual. Researching learning from a Vygotskian point of view starts with the social and then moves to the individual.

The second point, the fundamental differences between the theories, results from the first. For Piaget biological, mental development, maturation, leads learning. For Vygotsky learning leads to mental development. For Piaget language succeeds cognition and serves to organise it. For Vygotsky language precedes development, it pre-exists the individual and the individual internalises language and meaning. For Vygotsky, teaching and learning have to be taken together since one does not happen without the other. For Piaget, the teacher's actions are just one of the ways that the individual can experience disequilibrium. For Piaget learning begins in the concrete and moves to the abstract. For Vygotsky, learning involves the ascent from the abstract to the concrete.

My concern is to take these differences as an example of how one can slip into working with contradictory theories that can lead to incoherence. Bruner has addressed the same concern in a much more developed and eloquent way than I have here. In 1996, on the centenary of the birth of both Piaget and Vygotsky, at the Growing Mind conference, Bruner said the following in a keynote address:

> So should we try to combine Piaget and Vygotsky into a common system in the hope of explaining both extremes of this astonishing human variability? I think that would be naïve. The justifiable pedagogical optimism of cultural revolutionaries is not just the sunny side of the equally justified stoicism of principled pedagogical "realism". The two perspectives grow from different world views that generate different pedagogical strategies, different research paradigms, perhaps even different epistemologies, at least for a while. Better each go their own way. Let the Dionysian partisan activists specialize in finding leverages of change—e.g. how collaborative learning environments empower learners, what scaffolding helps learners over what seemed before to be 'innate' constraints. But also let the Apollonian realists explore 'natural' constraints and seek out the regularities they impose on development, wherever found in whatever culture. (Bruner 1996, online)

If one looks for learning in the individual's construction the origins of meaning being in the social-cultural-historical cannot be taken into the account. Conversely, if one looks for learning in social-cultural-historical processes, through analyses in the ZPD, or in Activity Theory, studies of individual students' construction of knowledge won't suffice.

14.6 An Example of Coherence

As will be clear from the earlier sections of this chapter I find the work of the sociologist of education Basil Bernstein extremely important and useful in my understanding of educational processes. I could say the same for Pierre Bourdieu, or Michael Apple, or a number of other sociologists of education, though through historical circumstances I have worked with Bernstein's sociological theories (e.g., Morgan et al. 2002; Lerman 2014b) and with Vygotsky's (e.g., Lerman 2001; Meira and Lerman 2009). I have to ask the question: is Bernstein's work coherent with Vygotsky's?

We can answer this in the positive. What they have in common is that both were Marxist theorists, both worked with the following idea:

> It is not the consciousness of men that determines their being but, on the contrary, their social being that determines their consciousness. (Marx 1859, pp. 328–329)

Taking this theoretical argument either sociologically or cognitively, the task of the researcher is to set out indicators of how one would identify the social being determining consciousness, and carry out suitable research to reveal whether the theory is borne out. I will show two examples of research designed to confirm or otherwise the theories of Bernstein and of Vygotsky elaborating, from their theoretical positions, this statement of Marx.

For Bernstein, language and meanings can be classified into context dependent and context independent, reflecting what he calls restricted and elaborated codes respectively. When children begin school they will have acquired one of these two codes depending on social class (a concept relevant in Britain still, though harder to identify in recent decades), the former associated with the working class, the latter with the middle class. Schooling is concerned with context independent meanings and so children entering school with that orientation to meaning will be immediately at an advantage. In this way, schooling reproduces social inequality. It should be made clear, though, that this is not a deficit model, merely a contingent outcome of a particular home life and education.

The study reported is of eight-year olds being interviewed over their classification of pictures of food items. The social class of each of the children was identified before the study (Holland 1981). The children were asked to group the foods in whichever way they wished. The two strategies were everyday ones, such as 'these I like, these I don't like' and by organisational criteria such as 'these are vegetables, these are fruit' and so on. She concluded as follows:

> Our results showed that the children in our sample did differ in the way in which they contextualised the pictures of food items which were used—some emphasized their own experience with such items, and others stressed general properties of the items. These differences emerged most clearly in their own first and last groupings, when the basic orientation informed their organization of the entire set of food items, and were clearly related to social class position. Those children who used chiefly a context independent orientation to meaning were middle class, and those who focussed their contextualizations in terms of their practical experience of food and were thus oriented towards context dependent meaning, were working class. (p. 16)

Vygotsky, taking the same Marxist notion, argued that, in the opportunity arising from the Russian revolution in which education was a vital element of the new social organisation for the freed peasants, it should be possible to observe changes in meanings of everyday objects for people, just as in the food pictures. In place of research requiring a longitudinal change to observe the development of higher thinking, as he called it, Vygotsky and his student and colleague Luria designed a study of members of collective farms, *kolhoz*, which included peasants who had not had any schooling, peasants who had become involved in organising the community, and children who were attending school. In that way they were approximating a longitudinal study of the process of intellectual development and change. The three groups were presented with three everyday objects, an axe, a hammer and a piece of wood. They, too, were asked to group the objects. In this case the everyday, context dependent response was that they all belong together since hammer and saw are useless without wood to work on, and the context independent response of a division into tools, the saw and hammer, and object to be worked on, the wood. The first two groups, the peasants involved in the community and those not involved, employed the context dependent meanings. The schooled children employed the context independent meaning. Vygotsky and Luria concluded as follows:

> Our investigations, which were conducted under unique and non-replicable conditions involving a transition to collectivized forms of labour and cultural revolution, showed that, as the basic forms of activity change, as literacy is mastered, and a new stage of social and historical practice is reached, major shifts occur in human mental activity… A basic feature of the shifts we observed is that the role of direct graphic-functional experience was radically altered in the transition to collectivized labor and new forms of social relations and with the mastery of rudiments of theoretical knowledge. (Luria 1976, pp. 161–162)

In contrast to what I see as a confusion of constructivist and sociocultural theories which have many elements of fundamental difference and indeed contradictions, I have presented briefly how the two intellectual fields of sociology, specifically Bernstein's sociology of education, and psychology, specifically Vygotsky's can be seen to be coherent. I am not claiming that coherence can be achieved only when two theoretical accounts both draw from the same fundamental inspiration. I am arguing that researchers, in their doctoral studies or in other research, need to do the work necessary to show how theories articulate together, and that they do not carry hidden contradictions. It has been intentional, of course, that the example of contradictory theories and the example of coherent theories overlap. I have been interested in these ideas for more than 30 years.

14.7 Concluding Remarks

In this chapter I have discussed the role of theory or theories in research in mathematics education, as a sub-field of educational research. I have set particular features of research in mathematics education within the explanatory framework provided by Basil Bernstein: its face to practice and at the same time its face to theory; and its horizontal knowledge structure leading to multiple competing discourses existing and developing separately alongside each other. I have tried to do this in general terms but also not to hide my own orientation, that of coherence where the researcher draws from more than one theory.

As one of the gatekeepers I have referred to, those who select students for research grants, examine doctoral students, review articles for journals, interview for positions and promotions, or select research projects for funding, I do not demand or expect any particular theory or theories to be worked with. If the researcher has done her/his job well in working with theory or theories, whatever they be, I will be happy. I do expect a position to be taken in relation to working with theory or theories, with a rationale, as I have tried to do in this chapter.

These concluding remarks are not just a brief repeat of the themes in the chapter. In reading/examining a thesis I expect a researcher to reflect, at the end, on the theoretical position taken and its fruitfulness for the research. That reflection may mean proposing developments of the theory, or it may not. But that reflection, as mine here, is an important final step, not to be neglected.

References

Ball, D. L. (1993). With an eye on the mathematical horizon: Dilemmas of teaching elementary school mathematics. *Elementary School Journal, 93*, 373–397.

Bernstein, B. (1990). *The structuring of pedagogic discourse: Class, codes and control* (Vol. 4). London: Routledge.

Bernstein, B. (2000). *Pedagogy, symbolic control and identity: Theory, research, critique.* Maryland: Rowman & Littlefield.

Bruner, J. (1996). Celebrating divergence: Piaget and Vygotsky. https://people.ucsc.edu/~gwells/Files/Courses_Folder/.../Bruner_Piaget-Vygotsky.pdf

Cohen, L., Manion, L., & Morrison, K. (2018). *Research methods in education* (7th ed.). Abingdon, Oxon: Routledge

Davis, Z. (2001). Measure for measure: Evaluative judgement in school mathematics pedagogic texts. *Pythagoras, 56,* 2–11.

de Freitas, E. (2017). Biosocial becomings: Rethinking the biopolitics of mathematics education research. In A. Chronaki (Ed.), *Proceedings of the Ninth International Mathematics Education and Society Conference.* Greece, Volos: University of Thessaly Press.

Dowling, P., & Brown, A. (2010). *Doing research/reading research: Re-interrogating education.* Abingdon, Oxon.: Routledge.

Ensor, P. (2001). From pre-service mathematics teacher education to beginning teaching: A study in recontextualising. *Journal for Research in Mathematics Education, 32,* 296–320.

Goldin, G.A. (2003). Developing complex understandings: On the relation of mathematics education research to mathematics. In R. Even, & D. Loewenberg Ball (Eds.), *Special Issue. Educational Studies in Mathematics, 54,* (2–3), 171–202.

Hodkinson, P. (2004). Research as a form of work: Expertise, community and methodological objectivity. *British Educational Research Journal, 30*(1), 9–26.

Holland, J. (1981). Social class and changes in orientation to meaning. *Sociology, 15*(1), 1–18.

Karmiloff-Smith, A., & Inhelder, B. (1974). If you want to get ahead, get a theory. *Cognition 3*(3), 195–212.

Kilpatrick, J. (1981). The reasonable ineffectiveness of research in mathematics education. *For the Learning of Mathematics, 2*(2), 22–29.

Kuhn, T. (1978). *The structure of scientific revolutions.* Chicago: Chicago University Press.

Lather, P. (2006). Paradigm proliferation as a good thing to think with: Teaching research in education as a wild profusion. *International Journal of Qualitative Studies in Education, 19*(1), 35–57.

Lerman, S. (1996). Intersubjectivity in mathematics learning: A challenge to the radical constructivist paradigm? *Journal for Research in Mathematics Education, 27*(2), 133–150.

Lerman, S. (2000). The social turn in mathematics education research. In J. Boaler (Ed.), *Perspectives on teaching and learning* (pp. 19–44). Westport, CT: Ablex.

Lerman, S. (2001). Accounting for accounts of learning mathematics: Reading the ZPD in videos and transcripts. In D. Clarke (Ed.), *Perspectives on practice and meaning in mathematics and science classrooms* (pp. 53–74). Dordrecht: Kluwer.

Lerman, S. (2013). Technology, mathematics and activity theory. *The International Journal for Technology in Mathematics Education, 20*(1), 39–42.

Lerman, S. (Ed.). (2014a). *Encyclopedia of mathematics education*. Dordrecht: Springer.

Lerman, S. (2014b). Mapping the effects of policy on mathematics teacher education. *Educational Studies in Mathematics, 87*(2), 187–201.

Luria, A. R. (1976). *Cognitive development: Its social and cultural foundations*. Cambridge MA: Harvard University Press.

Marx, K. (1859). A preface to contribution to the critique of political economy. *Marx and Engels selected works* (pp. 361–365). London: Lawrence and Wishart.

Meira, L., & Lerman, S. (2009). Zones of proximal development as fields for communication and dialogue. In C. Lightfoot, & M. C. D. P. Lyra (Eds.), *Challenges and strategies for studying human development in cultural contexts* (pp. 199–219). Rome: Firera Publishing.

Morgan, C., Tsatsaroni, A., & Lerman, S. (2002). Mathematics teachers' positions and practices in discourses of assessment. *British Journal of Sociology of Education, 23*(3), 443–459.

Prediger, S., Bikner-Ahsbahs, A., & Arzarello, F. (2008). How can networking strategies for connecting theoretical approaches help to develop theories in mathematics education? *First Reflections. ZDM, 40*(2), 165–178.

Silver, E. A., & Herbst, P. (2007). Theory in mathematics education scholarship. In F. K. Lester (Ed.), *Second handbook of research on mathematics teaching and learning* (pp. 39–67). Charlotte, NC: Information Age Publishing and Reston, VA: National Council of Teachers of Mathematics.

Sriraman, B., & English, L. (2005). Theories of mathematics education: A global survey of theoretical frameworks/trends in mathematics education research. *Zentralblatt für Didaktik der Mathematik, 37*(6), 450–456.

Sriraman, B., & English, L. (2010). Surveying theories and philosophies of mathematics education. In B. Sriraman, & L. English (Eds.), *Theories of mathematics education* (pp. 7–32). Berlin: Springer.

Open Access This chapter is licensed under the terms of the Creative Commons Attribution 4.0 International License (http://creativecommons.org/licenses/by/4.0/), which permits use, sharing, adaptation, distribution and reproduction in any medium or format, as long as you give appropriate credit to the original author(s) and the source, provide a link to the Creative Commons license and indicate if changes were made.

The images or other third party material in this chapter are included in the chapter's Creative Commons license, unless indicated otherwise in a credit line to the material. If material is not included in the chapter's Creative Commons license and your intended use is not permitted by statutory regulation or exceeds the permitted use, you will need to obtain permission directly from the copyright holder.

Chapter 15
The Professional Development of Mathematics Teachers

Björn Schwarz and Gabriele Kaiser

Abstract The chapter offers an overview of different approaches to the professional development of mathematics teachers. Starting point is the expert-novice-approach establishing both a distinction between experts and novices as well as an attempt to characterise expertise. The question of how to conceptualise professional competence of mathematics teachers is subsequently deepened by a detailed description of related prominent theoretical and empirical approaches followed by a discussion of central empirical results. The chapter closes with a short summary of recent research emphases especially taking into account the various discussions on teachers' professional development at ICME-13.

Keywords Professional development · Expert-novice-approach · Mathematics teachers' professional competence · Mathematics teachers' knowledge

15.1 Introduction

Professional development of teachers is currently seen as a central influential factor for the efficiency of school education, which has been shown by empirical results identifying relations between teachers' professional knowledge and students' achievement (e.g., Blömeke and Delaney 2012). However, reflections on the professional development of mathematics teachers put two different perspectives in the foreground, namely, the development of a teacher from a novice to an expert, and conceptualizations and assessments of teachers' professional competence and its development. Naturally, both perspectives overlap in manifold ways and cannot be separated in a strict way.

B. Schwarz (✉)
University of Vechta, Vechta, Germany
e-mail: bjoern.schwarz@uni-vechta.de

G. Kaiser
University of Hamburg, Hamburg, Germany
e-mail: gabriele.kaiser@uni-hamburg.de

The focus of this paper is set at a general level, as differences between teacher education systems at least across countries, often also within countries, are significant (cf. Blömeke and Kaiser 2012 with an approach to cross-nationally identify profiles of teacher education). Overall, the paper aims to offer an overview on important trends within the professional development of mathematics teachers and related discussions. However, the aim is not an entire and detailed description of the aspects mentioned. To use a metaphor, the paper unfolds a map of some central areas concerning the landscape of teachers' professional development. This might help the reader to identify the area in which she or he is interested, and to find the beginning of paths to an in-depth-analysis in this area.

In the following we use as departure point for the description, the currently most influential approach for the professional development of teachers, namely the expert-novice-approach. Its importance also follows from its inherent combination of two central aspects of expertise: an also intuitively plausible distinction between experts and novices for describing various degrees of experience in a field of profession and a theoretical sound foundation of characteristics of expertise. Especially the latter allows several opportunities for operationalising expertise and led to many empirical studies in the last two decades based on this theoretical approach.

15.2 The Expert-Novice Approach

Discussions about teachers' expertise can be characterised to a large extent by the fundamental distinction between experts and novices, an approach strongly influenced by Berliner (2004). Even though this distinction seems to be self-evident as especially older discussions often focused only on experts as humans who are exceptional in their domain. Against this background the cognitive processes or structures, conditions under which these humans exceptionally perform, or the way in which they practice are analysed (Chi 2011). In contrast to this absolute approach, subsequently the relative approach was introduced building up on the distinction between experts and novices (Chi 2011).

Independently from the chosen approach, a central problem is the identification of expert teachers. As there is no consensus on this question across various studies, this leads to different criteria for what makes a teacher an expert teacher. Examples of characteristics used in such identification are their years of teaching experience, their educational background, their academic performance during their education, or estimation or recommendation by peers or administrators (Li and Kaiser 2011). Furthermore also the particular researcher's beliefs about what characterizes an expert or what constitutes a 'good' performance in the classroom, influences the particular identification of expert teachers (Schoenfeld 2011).

Coming back to the distinction between the absolute and the relative approach reveals several advantages of the relative approach. Thus, in a relative approach an expert is not regarded as an exceptional individual but as someone who is just more advanced in terms of the various measurements of expertise (e.g., degrees, professional assessment, years of experience). Conceptualizing an expert this way allows the assumption that a novice can become an expert, i.e., expertise in the relative approach can be defined by the teachers' knowledge in contrast to innate capability in the absolute approach (Chi 2011).

Concerning the distinctions between experts and novices, it is obvious that a simple distinction only between experts and novices might be too imprecise for several reasons. Instead, a more precise distinction with intermediate levels seems to be an appropriate way to describe the professional development of a mathematics teacher. Following different theoretical backgrounds leads to different distinctions, both with regard to the number of stages, as well as with regard to the description of each particular stage. Before introducing his own model, Berliner (2004) for example distinguished the following theoretical approaches and their related stage-models:

- Studies of Psychomotor Learning: A novice stage, an intermediate stage and a stage with high levels of performance are distinguished. The focus strongly lies on psychomotor skills, whereas, for example, mistakes are characteristic of the novice stage, and the development of automaticity characterizes the intermediate stage. Accordingly, this approach is not an adequate attempt to describe the professional development in cognitive skills.
- Cognitive Psychology: Also from this perspective, several stages can be distinguished. The stages differ with regard to changing agency, that is, a progression in the stages comes along with a decreasing proportion of support and an increase of self-controlled learning processes. The model seems to be adequate for describing the development of learning in areas of individual performances (e.g., chess) but is less helpful for areas with a stronger social influence on behaviour. Hence, it is less adequate for describing the learning processes of teachers.
- Model of Domain Learning: The focus of this model is the development when attempting to learn a discipline such as mathematics. It again differentiates between three stages, a stage of acclimation to the appropriate discipline, a stage of competence, and a stage of proficiency or expertise (Alexander 1997). The stages, though, follow the process of learning a subject beginning with fragmentary knowledge and ending with integrated knowledge. Because teachers, as part of their professional development, also have to learn topics of several subjects, the model is helpful for describing the development of teachers' expertise with regard to subject matter knowledge. In contrast, it is less helpful for describing the development of pedagogical skills.

All that these models have in common is that they are at most partly suitable for describing the professional development of teachers. Therefore, Berliner (2004) introduced his fundamental five-stage theory, which was developed with reference to Dreyfus and Dreyfus (1986) as a central heuristic theory. The model is based on studies comparing teachers in different phases of their professional development.

Thus, in contrast to the models described above, it was explicitly developed for analysing teachers' professional development. In addition, it offers a rough orientation suggesting how much time a teacher normally takes to reach each particular stage. The five stages can be summarised briefly as follows (Berliner 2004, pp. 205–208):

- Novice stage: This first stage is the stage of student teachers and first-year teachers. "At this stage, the commonplaces of an environment must be discriminated, the elements of the tasks to be performed need to be labeled and learned, and the novice must be given a set of context free rules" (p. 205). Normally the novice is quite inflexible and follows given rules.
- Advanced beginner: This stage is normally reached by second- and third-year teachers. "This is when experience can become melded with verbal knowledge, where episodic and case knowledge is built up. Without meaningful past episodes and cases to relate the experience of the present to, individuals are unsure of themselves; they do not know what to do or what not to do. Through case knowledge, similarities across contexts can be recognized." (p. 206). In particular, this stage has been reached when the acquisition of practical knowledge starts, which will continue during the following stages. This aspect is especially important as "it is practical knowledge, not theories or textbooks, that is the proximal guide for a good deal of a teacher's classroom behaviour" (p. 206).
- Stage of competence: Although not every advanced beginner reaches this stage, the regular case is that teachers come up to this stage in their third to fifth year or later. Teachers in this stage "make conscious choices about what they are going to do. They set priorities and decide on plans. They have rational goals and choose sensible means for reaching the ends that they have in mind. […] While enacting their skills, they can determine what is and what is not important. From their experience, they know what to attend to and what to ignore" (p. 207).
- Proficient stage: This stage is the first stage that is not regularly reached by many teachers, but instead is reached by only a small number after about five years. "This is the stage at which intuition or know-how becomes prominent" (p. 207). Due to their experience "at some higher level of pattern recognition, the similarities between disparate events are understood" (p. 207). Proficient teachers can use this understanding of similarities to predict possible problems and counteract the problems in advance.
- Expert stage: This stage is the highest level, reached by only a few teachers. It is harder to discriminate this stage from the proficient stage than to discriminate the other stages from each other. "Experts have both an intuitive grasp of the situation and seem to sense in nonanalytic and nondeliberative ways the appropriate response to be made. They show fluid performance" (p. 207). The behaviour of expert teachers corresponds with Schön's (1983) discussion of the practitioner's knowledge-in-action and Polya's (1954) considerations of the role of tacit knowledge in the process of problem solving.

However, independent of the concrete research attempt and the concrete distinction between experts and novices, there are some core ideas of expertise, which can be identified across these research approaches. Central aspects of these core ideas are a broad and substantial subject-related knowledge together with deep representations of the taught mathematics topics and better strategies in problem-solving processes. Concerning the teaching process, experts show a higher flexibility and the use of automatisms for recurrent teaching activities. A very important aspect of teachers' expertise furthermore is a fast, holistic and accurate perception of classroom situations together with a categorial interpretation of these situations using categories for pattern identification, based on their knowledge and previous experiences. This category-led interpretation thereby allows teachers to make fast and meaningful decisions for the further process of instruction, to recognize and anticipate problems, and to react sensibly (see, e.g., Chi 2011; Kaiser and Li 2011; Berliner 2001, 2004).

Finally, this combination of both a widely accepted core of expertise and different attempts to characterize expertise in particular, leads to the question of how to conceptualize professional competence, which is dealt with in the next section.

15.3 Conceptualisation and Assessment of Mathematics Teachers' Professional Competence

Along with various approaches to expertise as described in the last section there are also different conceptualisations of professional competence of mathematics teachers, both from a theoretical as well as from an empirical perspective. In the following, prominent concepts are described mainly in the order in which they were developed.

The central starting point for the more recent discussions concerning teachers' professional competence is the famous paper by Shulman (1986) in which he distinguished several areas of teacher knowledge. In a first step, he differentiated between general pedagogical knowledge and content knowledge. With regard to the teaching of mathematics, especially the subsequent distinction between several categories of content knowledge is of special interest. In this regard Shulman (1986) distinguished the following categories:

- Subject matter content knowledge: This area covers the body of knowledge of the domain, in this context mathematics, but also covers aspects "going beyond knowledge of the facts or concepts of a domain" (p. 9). The latter means that also knowledge about the structure of the particular subject is necessary for a teacher. "The teacher needs not only understand that something is so; the teacher must further understand *why* it is so […]. Moreover, we expect the teacher to understand why a given topic is particularly central to a discipline whereas another may be somewhat peripheral" (p. 9).

- Pedagogical content knowledge: Shulman described this area as "subject matter knowledge *for teaching*" (p. 9). It covers knowledge about the typical representations of topics to be taught as well as knowledge about typical students' preconceptions when learning a topic. As these preconceptions also can be misconceptions, this area further includes knowledge about how to deal with those misconceptions.
- Curricular knowledge: This category focuses the area of knowledge about the whole field of curriculum in a wider sense. "The curriculum is represented by the full range of programs designed for the teaching of particular subjects and topics at a given level, the variety of instructional materials available in relation to those programs, and the set of characteristics that serve as both the indications and contraindications for the use of particular curriculum or program materials in particular circumstances" (p. 10). The teacher needs to know about this curriculum to choose the parts of it that are relevant for teaching. In addition, she or he should know when teaching a class in a certain grade about the curriculum of the preceding and following grades and about the curriculum in other subjects at the same grade.

Although regarded as a milestone and still often referred to in recent studies, Shulman's position was also criticized from different perspectives. Amongst others, it was emphasised that Shulman's distinction implies a certain image of the taught subject (Meredith 1995). With regard to teaching mathematics, Meredith specifies "that the concept of pedagogical content knowledge [...] is perfectly adequate if subject knowledge is seen as absolute, incontestable, unidimensional and static. On the other hand, teachers who conceive of subject knowledge as multidimensional, dynamic and generated through problem solving may require and develop very different knowledge for teaching" (p. 184).

Fennema and Franke (1992) formulated a critique from another perspective, demanding a more precise consideration of interaction processes between students and teachers. They claimed that "teachers' use of their knowledge must change as the context in which they work changes" (p. 162), as for example the students change during the process of teaching and learning. Therefore, they further developed the model by Shulman by integrating the "interactive and dynamic nature" (p. 162) of teacher knowledge and set "each component in context" (p. 162). The resulting model is illustrated in Fig. 15.1.

Fennema and Franke (1992) explained their model as follows: "The center triangle of our model indicates the teachers' knowledge and beliefs in context or as situated. The context is the structure that defines the components of knowledge and beliefs that come into play. Within a given context, teachers' knowledge of content interacts with knowledge of pedagogy and students' cognitions and combines with beliefs to create a unique set of knowledge that drives classroom behaviour" (p. 162).

Another prominent critical position taken against Shulman's approach considered the description of the various areas of content knowledge as not sufficiently precise, for example with regard to an operationalisation. One approach to fill this

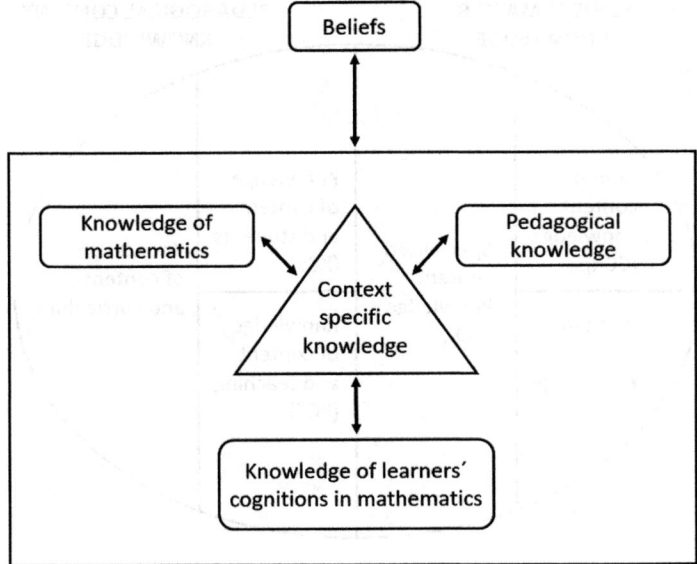

Fig. 15.1 Teachers' knowledge developing in context (Fennema and Franke 1992, p. 162)

gap was the attempt by researchers of the University of Michigan within the "Mathematics Teaching and Learning to Teach Project" and the "Learning Mathematics for Teaching Project" (Ball et al. 2008). The theoretical focal point of the projects was the concept of "mathematical knowledge for teaching" understood by the group as "mathematical knowledge needed to carry out the work of teaching mathematics" (p. 395). The construct consists of several domains, which can be assigned to subject matter knowledge and pedagogical content knowledge according to Fig. 15.2.

The domains can be summarised as follows:

- Common content knowledge: This is "the mathematical knowledge and skill used in settings other than teaching" (Ball et al. 2008, p. 399) and is reasoned by the fact that teachers of course also need to have knowledge about mathematics itself.
- Specialized content knowledge: This "is the mathematical knowledge and skill unique to teaching" (p. 400) and therefore furthermore "mathematical knowledge not typically needed for purposes other than teaching" (p. 400). This domain for example covers the identification of patterns in mathematical errors.
- Knowledge of content and students: This "is knowledge that combines knowing about students and knowing about mathematics" (p. 401). This for example contains the knowledge about what students are likely do with an assigned task or what might confuse students. Another example of this domain is knowledge about students' conceptions or misconceptions about certain topics. This domain therefore is related to the "interaction between specific mathematical understanding and familiarity with students and their mathematical thinking" (p. 401).

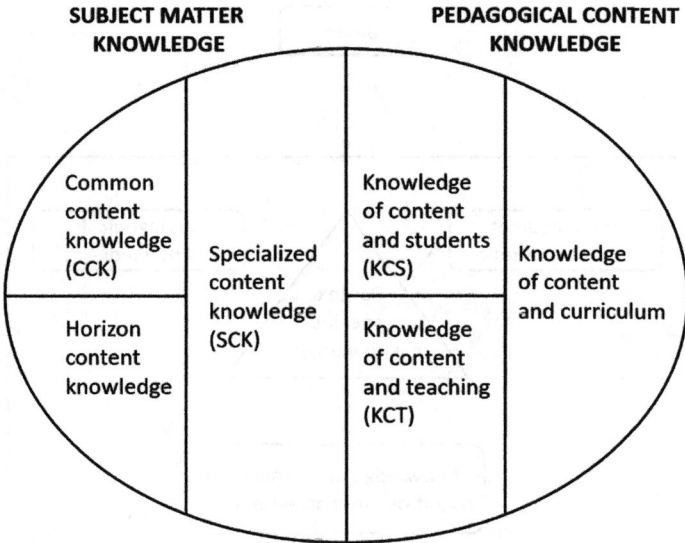

Fig. 15.2 Domains of mathematical knowledge for teaching (Ball et al. 2008, p. 403)

- Knowledge of content and teaching: This domain "combines knowing about teaching and knowing about mathematics" (p. 401). Examples of this domain are the choice of an order according to which examples are taught, or the evaluation of different representations with regard to their instructional advantages or disadvantages. The domain is therefore related to "interaction between specific mathematical understanding and an understanding of pedagogical issues that affect student learning" (p. 401).
- The curricular knowledge is taken from Shulman's distinction and "provisionally placed [...] within pedagogical content knowledge" (p. 403) according to later publications of researchers of Shulman's group. Ball et al. (2008) left it open whether it is a part of knowledge of content and teaching or a new domain, or whether it runs across the domains.
- Similarly, the domain "horizon knowledge" is provisionally included, meaning "an awareness of how mathematical topics are related over the span of mathematics included in the curriculum" (p. 403). Like the preceding domain, this one also could ran across the other domains.

The last two points especially illustrate one difficulty of the approach, namely how to distinguish between domains, which are quite close to each other. Another aspect is that beliefs are not taken into consideration within the model. However, a central achievement of this approach is that it not only developed a theoretical conception of mathematical knowledge for teaching but also developed instruments to measure it with multiple-choice-items (see also, e.g., Hill et al. 2004). Moreover, the ability of the project to identify a relation between mathematical knowledge and student achievement (Hill et al. 2005) is of special importance.

Another project aiming at both conceptual development and empirical research, is the German COACTIV project (Baumert and Kunter 2013). Its theoretical framework also has roots in approaches to teachers' professional knowledge and integrates the concept of professional competence (Weinert 2001). The developed "nonhierarchical model of professional competence is a generic structural model that needs to be specified for the context of teaching" (Baumert and Kunter 2013, p. 28). The result is displayed in Fig. 15.3 and shows that COACTIV "distinguish between four *aspects* of competence (knowledge, beliefs, motivation, and self-regulation), each of which comprises more specific *domains* derived from the available research literature. These domains are further differentiated into *facets*, which are operationalized by concrete indicators" (p. 28).

With regard to the subject-related domains, from a theoretical perspective COACTIV divided mathematical knowledge into four parts, which distinguish from academic mathematical knowledge over advanced and basic perspectives on school mathematics to everyday knowledge. From an empirical perspective, content knowledge was regarded as "teachers' understanding of the mathematical concepts underlying the content taught in middle school" (Baumert and Kunter 2013, p. 34). Content knowledge was in addition described "as a necessary condition for the development of [...] PCK" (p. 33). The construct of pedagogical content

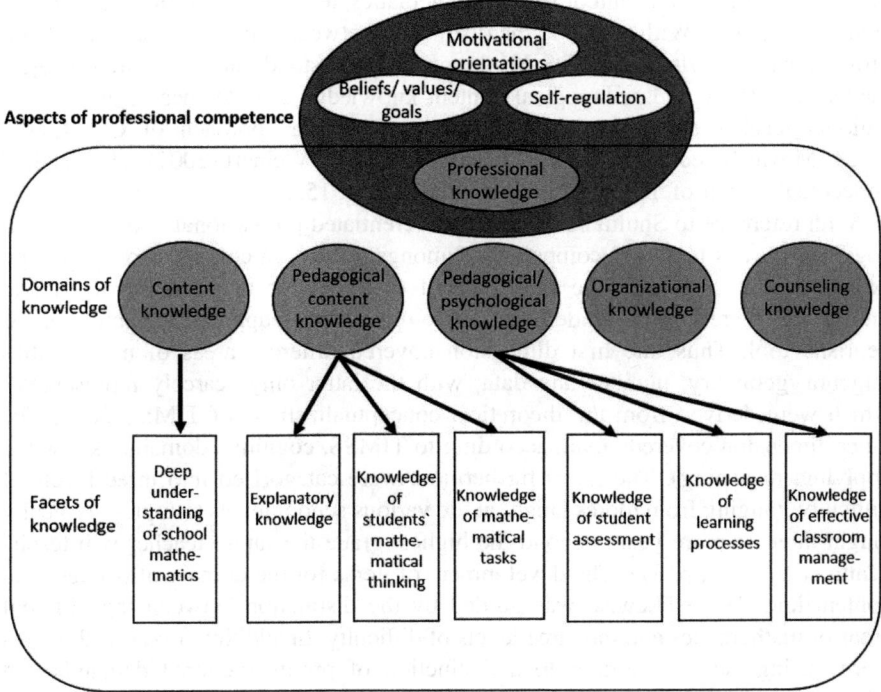

Fig. 15.3 The COACTIV model of professional competence, with the aspect of professional knowledge specified for the context of teaching (Baumert and Kunter 2013, p. 29)

knowledge is therefore theoretically and empirically distinguished from content knowledge and contains three dimensions, as follows:

- "Knowledge of the didactic and diagnostic potential of tasks, their cognitive demands and the prior knowledge they implicitly require, their effective orchestration in the classroom, and the long-term sequencing of learning content in the curriculum
- Knowledge of student cognitions (misconceptions, typical errors, strategies) and ways of assessing student knowledge and comprehension processes
- Knowledge of explanations and multiple representations" (Baumert and Kunter 2013, p. 33).

Similarly to the Michigan-group, COACTIV also could identify as a central result empirical relations especially between teachers' pedagogical content knowledge and students' achievement (Baumert et al. 2010).

Another study aiming at both theoretical development and empirical research, is the TEDS-M study (Blömeke et al. 2014; Döhrmann et al. 2012, 2018), which consisted of two sub-studies, one for primary teachers and one for secondary teachers. In contrast to the other studies described above, TEDS-M particularly was designed as an international comparative study, including 23,000 participants from 17 countries. "Its aim was to understand how national policies and institutional practices influence the outcomes of mathematics teacher education" (Döhrmann et al. 2018, p. 65). With regard to the distinction between different parts of teachers' professional knowledge, TEDS-M therefore understood and measured subject matter knowledge and pedagogical content knowledge as outcomes of the various national teacher education systems. Similarly to the approach of COACTIV, TEDS-M was based on the concept of competence by Weinert (2001). The detailed conceptual model of TEDS-M is illustrated in Fig. 15.4.

With reference to Shulman, TEDS-M differentiated professional knowledge as a cognitive part of teachers' competence, amongst others, in content knowledge and pedagogical knowledge. The development of items for the domain of content knowledge thereby was guided by a two-dimensional approach functioning as heuristic tool. Thus, the first dimension covered different areas of mathematics (algebra, geometry, number and data, with the latter only scarcely represented), which were derived from the theoretical conceptualizations of TIMSS 2007. The other dimension covered, again according to TIMSS, cognitive domains (knowing, applying, reasoning). The items furthermore were categorised into three levels of difficulty, ranging from topics taught at the various school levels to topics "typically taught three or more years beyond the highest grade the future teacher will teach" (Tatto et al. 2008, p. 37). The development of items for the domain of pedagogical content knowledge likewise was guided by the distinction between the different areas of mathematics and the three levels of difficulty. In addition, two sub-domains were distinguished according to a distinction of pre-instructional demands and demands during teaching, in detail "(a) *curricular knowledge and knowledge of planning for mathematics teaching and learning* and (b) *knowledge of enacting mathematics for teaching and learning.*" (Döhrmann et al. 2018, p. 73).

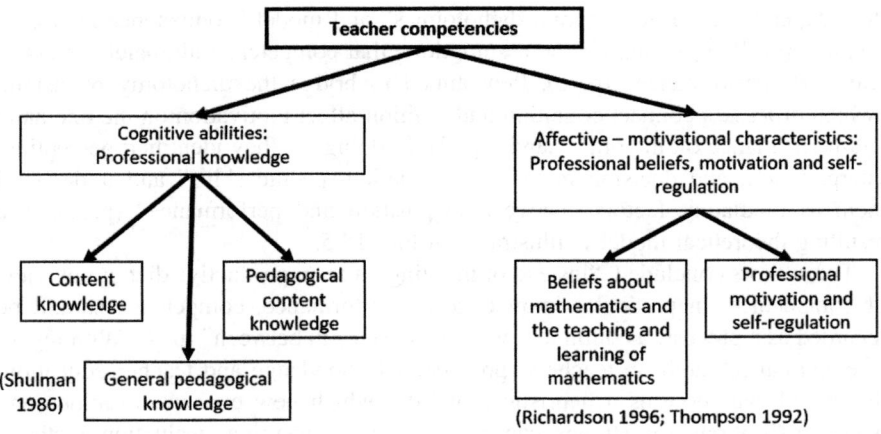

Fig. 15.4 Conceptual model of teachers' professional competencies (Döhrmann et al. 2012, p. 327)

Along with the ongoing development of empirical research on teachers' professional competence, again new theoretical concepts were introduced. A recent approach of conceptualising mathematic teachers' knowledge aimed at bridging the gap between school mathematics and academic mathematics by introducing the concept of "school-related content knowledge" which could be empirically separated from academic content knowledge and pedagogical content knowledge (Dreher et al. 2018). Generally, this knowledge was understood "as a special kind of mathematical CK [content knowledge] for teaching secondary mathematics." (Dreher et al. 2018, p. 329). Conceptually, three facets of school-related content knowledge were derived from corresponding theoretical perspectives on the relationship between school and academic mathematics: "(1) knowledge about the curricular structure and its legitimation in the sense of (meta-)mathematical reasons as well as knowledge about the interrelations between school mathematics and academics mathematics in (2) top-down and in (3) bottom-up directions" (p. 330).

Another recent important milestone with regard to both theoretical and empirical perspectives on teachers' competence was the conceptualisation of teachers' competence as a continuum (Blömeke et al. 2015a). The conceptual starting point was the question of how to overcome dichotomous ways of understanding competence. Amongst others, from a conceptual position these dichotomies were formed by the distinction between an analytic and a holistic position, with each position also implying consequences on the methodological level. Following the analytic position, "competence is analytically divided into several cognitive and affective-motivational traits" (p. 3). In contrast, the holistic position "focuses on the "real-life" part [...] and thus on observed behavior in context. Competence itself, then, is assumed to involve a multitude of cognitive abilities and affect-motivation *states* that are ever changing throughout the duration of the performance" (p. 4). Against this background, the idea of Blömeke et al. (2015a)—following the title of their paper—was to go "beyond dichotomies" and model "competence as a continuum" (p. 7). Agreeing on the assumption "that competence ultimately refers to real-world-performance" (p. 6), they aimed to bridge the dichotomy by asking "which *processes* connect cognition and volition-affect-motivation on the one hand and performance on the other hand" (p. 7). In doing so, they identified perception, interpretation, and decision making as "situation-specific skills" and understood them as mediating factors "between disposition and performance" (p. 7). The resulting theoretical model is illustrated in Fig. 15.5.

The authors concluded, "instead of insisting on an unproductive dichotomy view of competence, in particular knowledge *or* performance, competence should be regarded as a process, a continuum with many steps in between" (p. 7). With regard to empirical research on teachers' professional knowledge and teacher education, the model can serve as a heuristic tool from which new conceptualisations and operationalisations for studies can be derived. Concerning evaluation methods Blömeke et al. (2015a) stated: "Besides multiple-choice and constructed-response items or performance assessments in real life or laboratories, they suggested video-based assessments using representative job situations so that the perception of real-life, that is unstructured situations, can be included" (p. 9).

An example of such a study using video-vignettes to ensure a more situated item format, is the TEDS-FU-study, a follow up study to the TEDS-M-study. The sample of TEDS-FU consisted of German mathematics teachers in the fourth year of their professional practice. As all participants formerly also participated in TEDS-M, TEDS-FU is a longitudinal study examining mathematics teachers' development from the end of their teacher education into the first years of teaching profession. Its theoretical framework referred to the idea of competence as a continuum, as sketched above, with a special emphasis on the PID-model. Additionally, TEDS-FU also used the concept of expertise together with the distinction between experts and novices as a theoretical starting point. Therefore, the

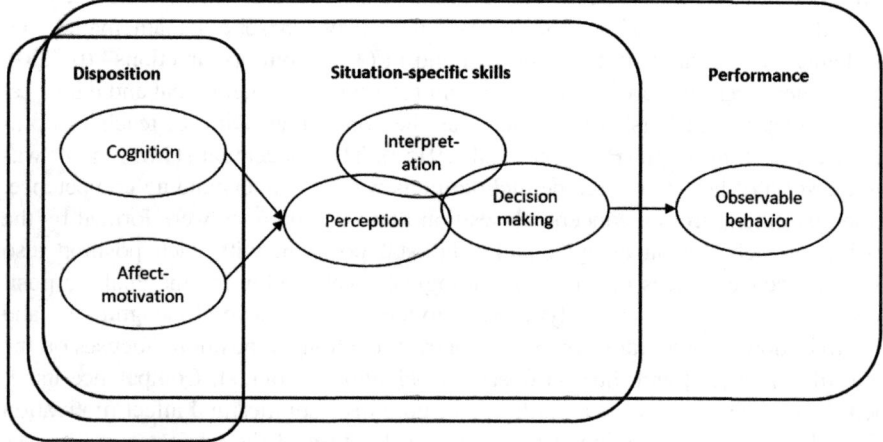

Fig. 15.5 Modelling competence as a continuum (Blömeke et al. 2015a, p. 7)

idea of a more advanced perception of classroom events and the idea of a more integrated knowledge as characteristics of experts' knowledge also functioned as reference for the item development (Kaiser et al. 2015). Selected central results of TEDS-FU are summarised in the following section. A detailed comparison of the cognitive approach in TEDS-M and the situated approach of TEDS-FU together with summarised results of both studies can be found in Kaiser et al. (2017).

Video-based assessment instruments were also used in the COACTIV-video study, a follow-up study to COACTIV. The study aimed at measuring "situated reaction competency". Therefore, teachers were shown videos of classroom situations which stopped at an educationally decisive moment. Using open answer items the teachers should then describe how they would continue within the respective situation (Bruckmaier et al. 2016). Another example for a study using video-based assessments is the v-ACT study, which combined video-based items with other formats such as items based on photos. The theoretical framework of the study thereby distinguished between reflective competence (i.e., abilities concerning pre- and post-instructional phases), action-related competence (i.e., abilities for the phases of instruction itself) and basic knowledge (Knievel et al. 2015).

15.4 Empirical Results Concerning Teachers' Professional Development

Teachers' professional development focuses empirically on two phases, namely, the development during the phase of teacher education and the development within teaching practice. Empirical results from both phases are discussed in the following.

The first kind of studies focused on the growth of knowledge during teacher education. Here, once again it has to be taken into account that there are several very different ways of becoming a teacher, sometimes already within a country and certainly across different countries. Despite this variation, there is empirical evidence of the efficiency of teacher education. Especially, the international comparative study on teacher education Mathematics Teaching in the 21st Century (MT21) (Schmidt et al. 2011) revealed in a quasi longitudinal design that future teachers' achievements in tests on pedagogical content knowledge, content knowledge and general pedagogical knowledge are related to the number of opportunities to learn to which the future teachers could attend. The international comparative study on the efficiency of teacher education, the TEDS-M study, showed remarkable differences referring to the professional knowledge of future teachers at the end of their study, among the participating 16 countries, with the East Asian future teachers outperforming the other groups by far (Blömeke et al., 2014). Furthermore König et al. (2018), in a comparison of German future teachers in the bachelor and the master phase of their university studies, showed that master students performed better in both pedagogical content knowledge as well as general pedagogical knowledge. Moreover, this result was confirmed for future teachers with different subject specializations, namely for mathematics, German and English.

The second kind of studies on the question of how teachers' knowledge develops sets the focus on the first years of professional experience in school and its influence on teachers' competence development. With regard to this question, Blömeke et al. (2015b) showed for German primary teachers within the framework of TEDS-FU that after about three and a half years in school the teachers' general pedagogical knowledge increased, while mathematical pedagogical content knowledge remained approximately stable and mathematical knowledge decreased slightly. The study reported in addition, that the ranking order of teachers' achievements between the end of their teacher education and their first years of teaching practice remained unchanged concerning mathematical content knowledge, and showed significant changes concerning mathematics pedagogical content knowledge and pedagogical knowledge. Moreover, with regard to their beliefs when teachers started positions in schools, the so-called "practical shock" could not be confirmed, as "none of the facets changed towards more traditional directions" (Blömeke et al. 2015b, p. 300). In contrast "the primary teachers' beliefs about the nature of mathematics even changed significantly towards a more process-oriented direction" (p. 300.). Furthermore, the environment in which the teachers worked had an influence on their professional development. Again based on TEDS-FU, for German teachers in the fourth year of their profession, Blömeke and Klein (2013) revealed similar relations between the teachers' teaching quality and the school environment they experienced. In summary, these researchers amongst others "point out that the extent of teacher support depended on the quality of the school management and was, in turn, an important predictor of the teaching quality" (Blömeke and Klein 2013, p. 1043). Finally, looking on the distinction between declarative knowledge and practical skills, again an influence of professional experience can be identified. König et al. (2015) found for German middle school mathematics teachers that general pedagogical knowledge can be predicted by the grades gained at the end of teacher education, whereas teachers' competence to interpret classroom situations was associated with their amount of time spent on teaching relative to their overall working time. (A broader discussion on the current state of empirical results on teacher's competencies can be found in Kaiser and König, under review).

15.5 Summary and Concluding Remarks

Teacher education and the professional development of mathematics teachers has been an important topic in the last decades and especially at ICME-13. In the Topic Study Group (TSG) on "Knowledge in/ for Teaching Mathematics" (at Primary Level as topic of TSG 45 and at Secondary Level in TSG 46) the increasing broadness of the ongoing debate on theoretical focal points, as well as differing or complementing empirical approaches were discussed. Overall—in line with the development of empirical studies on teachers' professional knowledge, which goes from Shulmans' distinction towards more situated approaches (see above)—also the debate in the two TSGs set a strong focus on aspects of teachers' actual activities in the classroom. Important topics of this discussion, amongst others, covered challenges in empirically analysing context-orientated knowledge and the consequences of an ever-growing number of theoretical approaches towards mathematics teachers' professional knowledge (Maher et al. 2017; Even et al. 2017).

A second important strand of discussion about professional development of mathematics teachers during ICME-13 focused on the actual education of mathematics teachers, which was tackled in four TSGs at ICME-13.

For example, concerning the pre-service education of primary mathematics teachers a clear relation to aspects of professional knowledge, such as content knowledge and knowledge for teaching, became obvious. Besides this, a second focus was on the assessment of future teachers' competences in teacher education and classroom experiences in teacher education. Furthermore, similarly to considerations in TEDS-FU and the understanding of teachers' competence as a continuum (Blömeke et al. 2015a), aspects of noticing were included (Hino et al. 2017; and in more detail, Stylianides and Hino 2018). The particular TSG about pre-service education of secondary mathematics teachers discussed similar topics to a large extent. Furthermore, a focus was placed on technology and tools used within teacher education, and in relation to concepts of competence, questions about professional identities of future mathematics teachers were discussed (Strutchens et al. 2017a; and in more detail Strutchens et al. 2017b).

Summarising the discussions within the TSG on primary teachers' in-service education, strong emphasis on the situated requirements a teacher has to face and the complexity of mathematics teaching can be identified. Besides considering the requirements of direct in situ teaching activities, aspects of working in school in a broader context was a focus, for example working with new curricula, the use of new technologies for teaching, and aspects of inclusion. With regard to these challenges, the TSG discussed approaches for educating practicing teachers. Again of course, conceptualisations of teachers' knowledge played a central role, as well as empirical studies on in-service teacher education and an analysis of various policies of in-service teacher education and primary teachers' professional development (Takashashi et al. 2017). This combination of practice, research and policies in discussions also took place in the parallel TSG on secondary teachers. Here, again amongst others, the distinction between knowledge, beliefs and practice was stressed and several programs were discussed. Furthermore the use of several technologies, especially as interaction tools, played a central role (Adler et al. 2017).

In this chapter we aimed to summarise central issues concerning teachers' professional development. It became obvious, that even though the prominent distinction of areas of teachers' professional knowledge by Shulman (1986) is still widely received, the debate went on, accumulating a variety of new conceptions. One motor for this rapid development of theories surely was the remarkably growing number of large-scale empirical studies on teacher education, teacher competence and the development of teachers, such as TEDS-M, COACTIV, the studies of the Michigan-Group or TEDS-FU. All these studies developed their own conceptual frameworks and by this process helped to further elaborate on the theoretical considerations concerning mathematics teachers' competence and its development. However the variety of ongoing discussions, as summarised in Sect. 15.5 with regard to ICME-13, showed that there is still a huge amount of work to do and of discussions to have. This finally leads us back to the intention of the chapter to serve as a map, which may provide individually interesting areas. The ongoing discussions and the related ICME-13 materials may serve as a guidepost to show how to find a path in order to provide greater depth in the discussions. In this spirit: Bon voyage!

References

Adler, J., Yang, Y., Borko, H., Krainer, K., & Patahuddin, S. (2017). Topic Study Group No. 50: In-service education, and professional development of secondary mathematics teachers. In G. Kaiser (Ed.), *Proceedings of the 13th International Congress on Mathematical Education—ICME-13* (pp. 609–612). Cham: Springer.

Alexander, P. A. (1997). Mapping the multidimensional nature of domain learning: The interplay of cognitive, motivational, and strategic forces. In M. L. Maehr & P. R. Pintrich (Eds.), *Advances in motivation and achievement* (Vol. 10, pp. 213–250). Greenwich, CT: JAI.

Ball, D. L., Thames, M. H., & Phelps, G. (2008). Content knowledge for teaching. What makes it special. *Journal of Teacher Education, 59*(5), 389–407.

Baumert, J., & Kunter, M. (2013). The COACTIV model of teachers' professional competence. In M. Kunter, J. Baumert, W. Blum, U. Klusmann, S. Krauss, & M. Neubrand (Eds.), *Cognitive activation in the mathematics classrooms and professional competence of teachers* (pp. 25–48). New York, NY: Springer.

Baumert, J., Kunter, M., Blum, W., Brunner, M., Voss, T., Jordan, A., et al. (2010). Teachers' mathematical knowledge, cognitive activation in the classroom, and student progress. *American Educational Research Journal, 47*(1), 133–180.

Berliner, D. C. (2001). Learning about and learning from expert teachers. *International Journal of Educational Research, 35*(5), 463–482.

Berliner, D. C. (2004). Describing the behavior and documenting the accomplishments of expert teachers. *Bulletin of Science, Technology & Society, 24*(3), 200–212.

Blömeke, S., & Delaney, S. (2012). Assessment of teacher knowledge across countries: a review of the state of research. *ZDM Mathematics Education, 44*(3), 223–247.

Blömeke, S., Gustafsson, J., & Shavelson, R. J. (2015a). Beyond dichotomies—Competence viewed as a continuum. *Zeitschrift für Psychologie, 223*(1), 3–13.

Blömeke, S., Hoth, J., Döhrmann, M., Busse, A., Kaiser, G., & König, J. (2015b). Teacher change during induction: Development of beginning primary teachers' knowledge, beliefs and performance. *International Journal of Science and Mathematics Education, 13*(2), 287–308.

Blömeke, S., Hsieh, F.-J., Kaiser, G., & Schmidt, W. H. (Eds.). (2014). *International perspectives on teacher knowledge, beliefs and opportunities to learn. TEDS-M results.* Dordrecht: Springer.

Blömeke, S., & Kaiser, G. (2012). Homogeneity or heterogeneity? Profiles of opportunities to learn in primary teacher education and their relationship to cultural context and outcomes. *ZDM Mathematics Education, 44*(3), 249–264.

Blömeke, S., & Klein, P. (2013). When is a school environment perceived as supportive by beginning mathematics teachers?—Effects of leadership, trust, autonomy and appraisal on teaching quality. *International Journal of Science and Mathematics Education, 11*(4), 1029–1048.

Bruckmaier, G., Krauss, S., Blum, W., & Leiss, D. (2016). Measuring mathematics teachers' professional competence by using video clips (COACTIV video). *ZDM Mathematics Education, 48*(1–2), 111–124.

Chi, M. T. H. (2011). Theoretical perspectives, methodological approaches, and trends in the study of expertise. In Y. Li & G. Kaiser (Eds.), *Expertise in mathematics instruction* (pp. 17–40). New York: Springer.

Döhrmann, M., Kaiser, G., & Blömeke, S. (2018). The conception of mathematics knowledge for teaching from an international perspective. The case of the TEDS-M Study. In Y. Li, & R. Huang (Eds.), *How Chinese acquire and improve mathematics knowledge for teaching* (pp. 57–81). Rotterdam: Sense.

Döhrmann, M., Kaiser, G., & Blömeke, S. (2012). The conceptualisation of mathematics competencies in the international teacher education study TEDS-M. *ZDM Mathematics Education, 44*(3), 325–340.

Dreher, A., Lindmeier, A., Heinze, A., & Niemand, C. (2018). What kind of content knowledge do secondary mathematics teachers need? *Journal für Mathematik-Didaktik, 39*(2), 319–341.

Dreyfus, H. L., & Dreyfus, S. E. (1986). *Mind over machine*. New York: Free Press.

Even, R., Yang, X., Buchholtz, N., Charalambous, C., & Rowland, T. (2017). Topic Study Group No. 46: Knowledge in/for Teaching Mathematics at the Secondary Level. In G. Kaiser (Ed.), *Proceedings of the 13th International Congress on Mathematical Education—ICME-13* (pp. 589–592). Cham: Springer.

Fennema, E., & Franke, L. M. (1992). Teachers' knowledge and its impact. In D. A. Grouws (Ed.), *Handbook of research on mathematics teaching and learning* (pp. 147–164). Reston, VA: National Council of Teachers of Mathematics.

Hill, H. C., Rowan, B., & Ball, D. L. (2005). Effects of teachers' mathematical knowledge for teaching on student achievement. *American Educational Research Journal, 42*(2), 371–406.

Hill, H. C., Schilling, S. G., & Ball, D. L. (2004). Developing measures of teachers' mathematics knowledge for teaching. *The Elementary School Journal, 105*(1), 11–30.

Hino, K., Stylianides, G. J., Eilerts, K., Lajoie, C., & Pugalee, D. (2017). Topic Study Group No. 47: Pre-service Mathematics Education of Primary Teachers. In G. Kaiser (Ed.), *Proceedings of the 13th International Congress on Mathematical Education—ICME-13* (pp. 593–597). Cham: Springer.

Kaiser, G., Blömeke, S., König, J., Busse, A., Döhrmann, M., & Hoth, J. (2017). Professional competencies of (prospective) mathematics teacher—Cognitive versus situated approaches. *Educational Studies in Mathematics, 94*(2), 161–182, 183–184.

Kaiser, G., Busse, A., Hoth, J., König, J., & Blömeke, S. (2015). About the complexities of video-based assessments: Theoretical and methodological approaches to overcoming short-comings of research on teachers' competence. *International Journal of Science and Mathematics Education, 13*(2), 369–387.

Kaiser, G., & Li, Y. (2011). Reflections and Future Prospects. In Y. Li & G. Kaiser (Eds.), *Expertise in mathematics instruction* (pp. 343–353). New York: Springer.

Kaiser, G., & König, J. (under review). Competence measurement in (mathematics) teacher education and beyond—Implications for policy. *Journal for Higher Education Policy*.

Knievel, I., Lindmeier, A. M., & Heinze, A. (2015). Beyond knowledge: Measuring primary teachers' subject-specific competences in and for teaching mathematics with items based on video vignettes. *International Journal of Science and Mathematics Education, 13*(2), 309–329.

König, J., Blömeke, S., & Kaiser, G. (2015). Early career mathematics teachers' general pedagogical knowledge and skills: Do teacher education, teaching experience, and working conditions make a difference? *International Journal of Science and Mathematics Education, 13*(2), 331–350.

König, J., Doll, J., Buchholtz, N., Förster, S., Kaspar, K., Rühl, A.-M., et al. (2018). Pädagogisches Wissen versus fachdidaktisches Wissen?-Struktur des professionellen Wissens bei angehenden Deutsch-, Englisch- und Mathematiklehrkräften im Studium. *Zeitschrift für Erziehungswissenschaften, 21*(3), 1–38.

Li, Y., & Kaiser, G. (2011). Expertise in mathematics instruction: Advancing research and practice from an international perspective. In Y. Li & G. Kaiser (Eds.), *Expertise in mathematics instruction* (pp. 3–16). New York: Springer.

Maher, C. A., Sullivan, P., Gasteiger, H., & Lee, S. J. (2017). Topic Study Group No. 45: Knowledge in/for Teaching Mathematics at Primary Level. In G. Kaiser (Ed.), *Proceedings of the 13th International Congress on Mathematical Education—ICME-13* (pp. 585–587). Cham: Springer.

Meredith, A. (1995). Terry's learning: Some limitations of Shulman's pedagogical content knowledge. *Cambridge journal of education, 25*(2), 175–187.

Polya, G. (1954). *How to solve it*. Princeton, NJ: Princeton University Press.

Schmidt, W. H., Blömeke, S., & Tatto, M. T. (2011). *Teacher education matters. A study of middle school mathematics teacher preparation in six countries*. New York: Teachers College Press, Columbia University.

Schoenfeld, A. H. (2011). Reflections on teacher expertise. In Y. Li & G. Kaiser (Eds.), *Expertise in mathematics instruction* (pp. 327–341). New York: Springer.

Schön, D. (1983). *The reflective practitioner*. New York: Basic Books.

Shulman, L. S. (1986). Those who understand: Knowledge growth in teaching. *Educational Researcher, 15*(2), 4–14.

Strutchens, M., Huang, R., Losano, L., Potari, D., & Schwarz, B. (2017a). Topic Study Group No. 48: Pre-service Mathematics Education of Secondary Teachers. In G. Kaiser (Ed.), *Proceedings of the 13th International Congress on Mathematical Education—ICME-13* (pp. 599–603). Cham: Springer.

Strutchens, M., Huang, R., Losano, L., Potari, D., da Ponte, J. P., de Costa Trindade Cyrino, M. C., & Zbiek, R. M. (2017b). *The mathematics education of prospective secondary teachers around the world*. Cham: Springer.

Stylianides, G. J., & Hino, K. (Eds.). (2018). *Research advances in the mathematical education of pre-service elementary teachers*. Cham: Springer.

Takahashi, A., Varas, L., Fujii, T., Ramatlapana, K., & Selter, C. (2017). Topic Study Group No. 49: In-service education and professional development of primary mathematics teachers. In G. Kaiser (Ed.), *Proceedings of the 13th International Congress on Mathematical Education—ICME-13* (pp. 605–608). Cham: Springer.

Tatto, M. T., Schwille, J., Senk, S., Ingvarson, L., Peck, R., & Rowley, G. (2008). *Teacher Education and Development Study in Mathematics (TEDS-M): Policy, Practice, and Readiness to Teach Primary and Secondary Mathematics. Conceptual framework*. East Lansing, MI: Teacher Education and Development International Study Center, College of Education, Michigan State University.

Weinert, F. E. (2001). Concept of competence: A conceptual clarification. In D. S. Rychen & L. H. Salganik (Eds.), *Defining and selecting key competencies* (pp. 45–65). Seattle, WA: Hogrefe & Huber.

Open Access This chapter is licensed under the terms of the Creative Commons Attribution 4.0 International License (http://creativecommons.org/licenses/by/4.0/), which permits use, sharing, adaptation, distribution and reproduction in any medium or format, as long as you give appropriate credit to the original author(s) and the source, provide a link to the Creative Commons license and indicate if changes were made.

The images or other third party material in this chapter are included in the chapter's Creative Commons license, unless indicated otherwise in a credit line to the material. If material is not included in the chapter's Creative Commons license and your intended use is not permitted by statutory regulation or exceeds the permitted use, you will need to obtain permission directly from the copyright holder.

Part III
Academic Writing and Academic Publishing: Academic Writing

Part III
Academic Writing and Academic
Publishing: Academic Writing

Chapter 16
Pleasures, Power, and Pitfalls of Writing up Mathematics Education Research

Norma Presmeg and Jeremy Kilpatrick

Abstract Research in mathematics education consists of both doing a study and reporting its thesis and conclusions. Communicating one's research clearly and adequately is at least as important as conducting it proficiently. At ICME-13, we each conducted a workshop on academic writing in which we drew upon our experiences as writers and editors to acquaint novice researchers with potential benefits and costs of reporting in our field. In this chapter, we present some of the points made in our workshops. We look at the nature of research in our field, the elements of a research report, its structure, the importance of choosing an appropriate publication outlet, and some pitfalls of academic writing. The chapter ends by reprinting a satirical editorial that underlines some of the ways in which a research report can go wrong.

Keywords Academic writing · Nature of mathematics education research · Elements of a report · Appropriate publication outlet · Pleasures, power and pitfalls of writing up research

16.1 Why Publish?

Once you have completed an investigation on some topic of mathematics education —research that may have taken several years of your life—you may find yourself under pressure to disseminate the results of your hard work in a published paper (or more than one). Why is this process important, and what are some of the potential pitfalls in this type of academic writing? This chapter explores answers to both of those questions.

N. Presmeg (✉)
Mathematics Department, Illinois State University, Normal, IL, USA
e-mail: npresmeg@msn.com

J. Kilpatrick
University of Georgia, Athens, GA, USA
e-mail: jkilpat@uga.edu

© The Author(s) 2019
G. Kaiser and N. Presmeg (eds.), *Compendium for Early Career Researchers in Mathematics Education*, ICME-13 Monographs,
https://doi.org/10.1007/978-3-030-15636-7_16

One issue that is relevant to the publication of research reports is the nature of the word *academic* as it appears in "academic writing." The meaning of this word resonates with a concern through the decades (Sowder 1990; Teppo 1998) that research in mathematics education has not been particularly fruitful in its implementation in mathematics classrooms. Is "academic" writing irrelevant in the field? Dorier (2008) pointed out that there are two contrasting meanings of the word: One of these is "related to education and scholarship," and the other is "not related to a real or practical situation and therefore irrelevant" (p. 40). These concerns go to the very heart of why we do research in mathematics education. If the goal of research is to improve the teaching and learning of mathematics in some way, then it is important that our writing be academic in the scholarly sense, with the relevance of our work in the lives of mathematics teachers and learners on full display.

Do these concerns imply that development of theory in our field is less important than practical relevance and implementation? On the contrary, we regard theory as a collection of lenses through which the complex phenomena of mathematics education may be observed. Theory permeates all aspects of the research process, from the initial choices of questions to be addressed, through suitable methods of data collection and analysis, to the conclusions reached as a result of the research, and future directions that the research might take.

Thus, in a sense, theory is the *glue* that holds the study together and guarantees its integratedness, as well as defining its boundaries and limitations. Without these aspects, the relevance of research could be severely compromised. Academic writing concerning research can be both scholarly *and* empirically significant. Some of these issues are developed further in the following sections.

16.2 Quality Criteria

Dissemination is a vital element of the scientific research process. In this section, we address some aspects of research that have been considered essential in shaping what counts as good quality in mathematics education research. Although the following lists are historical—in the sense that they were compiled several decades ago and thus may be considered part of the history of our field—they are timeless because they outline elements of an ongoing scientific endeavor. After a general introduction to the research itself in this section, in the sections that follow we put forward some possible structures and essential elements in writing about research.

16.2.1 *What Is Research in Mathematics Education?*

Mathematics education research is a relatively young field in comparison with the millennia of *mathematics* research: the two fields are related but distinct (Kilpatrick 2008; Presmeg 2014). In the 1990s there were strong efforts to identify what makes mathematics education research distinctive, what its components are, and how we can identify *quality* in this field (Sierpinska and Kilpatrick 1998). These are still significant questions, especially for the necessary dissemination of one's research through publication. There are different types of research, and quality criteria are of necessity specific to these types. Nevertheless, basic foundational components can be identified. Some types of research used in education generally were already identified by Jaeger in 1988:

- Historical methods
- Philosophical inquiry methods
- Ethnographic research
- Case study methods
- Survey research methods
- Comparative experimental methods
- Quasi-experimental methods.

These types are still current in mathematics education research. A trend that started in the decade of the 2000s, however, is to use a mixed methods design, which acknowledges the different purposes of quantitative and qualitative research and that these types of research may complement each other in order to give a fuller picture of some phenomenon.

What, then, is research in mathematics education specifically? In a discussion group at the 13 Annual Meeting of the *International Group for the Psychology of Mathematics Education* in Paris in 1989, Kath Hart proposed that the nature of educational research is *disciplined enquiry*, repeating (and 'briticizing') the term introduced by Lee Cronbach and Patrick Suppes (1969; see also Kilpatrick 1992). Research in education entails the following essential components:

1. There is a problem.
2. There is evidence/data.
3. The work can be replicated.
4. The work is reported.
5. There is a theory (Hart 1993, p. 411).

The importance of publication may be inferred from this list. Criteria for judging the quality of mathematics education research were formulated already in these early years of our field. One such report identified the following characteristics: relevance, validity, objectivity, originality, rigor and precision, predictability, reproducibility, and relatedness (Kilpatrick and Sierpinska 1993). Another identified elements that are not unlike these, in different terms: worthwhileness, goodness of fit, competence, openness (awareness of researcher biases, and full reporting tempered by ethics), credibility (grounded in data, with evidence), and intangible qualities such as lucidity, conciseness, and originality (Lester and Cooney 1994; see also Lester and Lambdin 1993).

In unpacking some of these terms, essential elements that relate to writing up research may be highlighted. *Worthwhileness* indicates that an author should make the significance of the study clear. Why was it important to address this particular question? What does this study add to what was already known from previous research? The author should thus take into account the prior state of the field, as reflected in relevant literature. *Goodness of fit* relates to the suitability of choices regarding theory, the broad umbrella of methodology, and specific methods of data collection and analysis within this methodology. The relative merits and purposes of quantitative and qualitative methodologies have been debated through the decades (e.g., Lester 2007), and it is now recognized that a combination of methodologies is possible and may exploit the benefits of each, in what has come to known as "mixed methods" (e.g., Keller and Buchholtz 2015). Examples of methodology and methods, with appropriate theories, are presented in books such as that by Bikner-Ahsbahs et al. (2015), in which theoretical chapters are paired with empirical chapters that illustrate the implementation of theories and methods in particular studies. All aspects of the research need to hang together in an integrated whole.

Competence, openness, and credibility are characteristics of the researcher, as manifested in the writer's awareness of the need to be open to his or her biases, and to provide evidence for each claim made as a result of the empirical work. The sensitivity of the researcher to ethical issues is also relevant here: There may be ethical reasons *not* to report some aspects of the research (e.g., inadvertent data gathered without permission). Further, conflict of interests may be a source of bias that may detract from the *validity* and *objectivity* of the conclusions. In providing evidence for claims made, there are three possible sources of evidence, namely, the data themselves, evidence from trustworthy literature, and logical argument, which relates to the *rationality* and *lucidity* of the writing. However, beliefs and values of the researcher are inevitably implicated in this process:

> How researchers go about convincing others of the claims they make and how they defend their claims on ethical and practical grounds are, only in part, matters of marshaling adequate contextualized evidence embedded in sets of beliefs and theories. Indeed, convincing others is also a matter of persuading them to accept the values the researcher holds about the objects and phenomena being studied as well as about the very purpose of research itself. (Lester and Wiliam 2000, p. 136)

From the foregoing lists, for the purposes of academic writing in order to disseminate the results of empirical research, some further essential elements may be inferred. The following section addresses aspects that editors and reviewers may look for in deciding what will be published in mathematics education journals.[1]

---

[1]We note here that both authors have served not only as reviewers but also as editors for research journals in our field. Norma has been associated with *Educational Studies in Mathematics* in various capacities (reviewer, associate editor, advisory editor) since the early 1990s, serving as Editor-in-Chief from 2009 to 2013; Jeremy edited the *Journal for Research in Mathematics Education* from 1982 to 1988, editing the Research Commentary section from 2004 to 2008.

16.2.2 What Are the Essential Elements in a Research Report in Our Field?

Nuts-and-bolts matters to be taken into account by prospective authors include the following:

- Select an issue on which the report will center; even if the research study addressed several issues, the report needs a focus.
- Decide on a publication venue (e.g., journal) and become acquainted with its style, formatting, and referencing, making sure that these are appropriate for your study.
- Think through the structure of the paper, and write a first draft according to the resulting outline (see the next section for a possible outline of a structure).
- Supply evidence or justification for every statement. Justification may be presented in one of the three ways: by referring to relevant literature, by evidence from data, or by logical argument.
- Be sure the manuscript is checked for fluency and accuracy in language (including citations and the reference list) *before* it is submitted.

After you have produced the first draft of your manuscript, put it aside for several days and then return to it prepared to make revisions. Find some colleagues willing to read the revised draft and provide suggestions for revision. Revise the manuscript in light of your colleagues' suggestions. Proofread the manuscript and submit it to the journal. Respond to the feedback you receive. The following are components of a well-structured research paper:

- There is a well-written abstract, describing the area of the research, its design, extent, and the main results.
- The introduction provides a succinct but interesting background to the main issues.
- The issues addressed emerge unambiguously from the introduction. Research questions may be presented towards the end of the introduction, or after the next component. Meanings of key terms are clarified.
- There is a succinct, scholarly review of relevant literature (international in nature, using original papers if possible) leading to a clear conceptual framework. The unique contribution to knowledge in the field of the study should be clear.
- Details are provided for the empirical design, for the sample of participants, and of how the design was implemented. Are the data representative? Were there various stages in the research?
- There is a summary of actual data obtained, and a detailed report of how the analysis of the data was carried out.
- Finally, there is discussion of the implications and limitations of the research, and of possible directions for carrying the line of research forward in the future. The discussion should make clear how the conclusions of the report address the main issues.

16.2.3 One Possible Structure for a Report on Empirical Research

The foregoing points may be distilled in the following effective structure,[2] which could be used for a thesis or a research report (and see also the similar structure presented in Fig. 20.8 in Chap. 20 of this volume).

1. Introduction: Describe a real problem.
   2. Situate the problem in theory, with reference to relevant literature.
      3. Methodology: Provide a broad description and a rationale for choices made.
      4. Give an explicit description of the methods of data collection.
      5. Describe how the data analysis was carried out and the results of the analysis.
   6. Relate the results back to the theory and literature.
7. Provide conclusions: Include self-critique, and suggestions for future research.

This structure includes a zooming-in feature: Points 1 and 7 are quite general in nature, progressively becoming more specific and detailed as the internal aspects of this particular study are described in Points 3, 4, and 5. The results in Point 6 are related back to the literature and theory in Point 2. Finally, the conclusions outline what has been accomplished in addressing the problem with which the research started in the first place.

This structure resonates well with an outline put forward by Brown and Dowling (1998), in which a theoretical field (in the "theoretical domain") and an empirical field (in the "empirical domain") sandwich the central phases of the research, zooming in with increasing specializing and localizing, respectively, to the details of the research study, which are supplied in the middle of the report.

16.2.4 An Example of a Mission Statement of a Research Journal

In deciding on a suitable venue for publication, it is important to take into the account the purpose and nature of various journals. The following is the original and current mission statement of *Educational Studies in Mathematics* (ESM), which is published in every issue of this journal:

> ESM presents new ideas and developments which are considered to be of major importance to those working in the field of mathematics education. It seeks to reflect both the variety of research concerns within the field and the range of methods used to study them. It deals

---

[2]We are grateful to Alan Bishop for providing this structure; he has been a valuable mentor to both of us.

with didactical, methodological and pedagogical subjects rather than with specific programs for teaching mathematics. All papers are strictly refereed and the emphasis is on high-level articles which are of more than local or national interest.

Different journals have different aims and reasons for their existence, as the following section illustrates. Thus *choice of journal* is an important concern that should be taken into account at the outset.

16.3 An Activity That Illustrates Why Choice of Journal Is Important

Because unpublished writing is protected, in one workshop preceding ICME-13 we reviewed a *published* paper from a respected journal, *For the Learning of Mathematics* (*FLM*), using the criteria from another respected journal that has a different purpose and focus, the *Journal for Research in Mathematics Education* (*JRME*). The paper from *FLM* is a delightful account by Jenny Houssart in 2001, titled "Rival Classroom Discourses and Inquiry Mathematics: 'The Whisperers.'" Jenny served in the role of classroom helper, observing while sitting at the back of a mathematics classroom (of a "bottom set" of pupils) in a British primary school, during a year of participation research in which she was engaged. She had not intended to concentrate on "the whisperers"—her observation of the events reported in the paper was serendipitous. Thus she did not record the boys' words verbatim, e.g., using a tape recorder. Her research interest was in "inquiry classrooms" and the culture of inquiry. The following is an anecdote from the paper:

> A class of nine- and ten-year old children were working on fractions of shapes. Two worksheets were given out and the children were asked to look first at the one starting with a rectangle. This caused some confusion as one sheet started with a circle and one with a square. In response to this the teacher asked, 'Do you know what a rectangle is?' He pointed to the sheet in question and one of the children said, 'But it's a square.' The teacher looked again at the sheet, admitted that it was a square, and apologised for calling it a rectangle. As the teacher started to explain the sheet, one of the children sighed slightly and said in a whisper, 'Well, anyway, it is a rectangle'. (Houssart 2001, p. 2)

The following are some details of the research and events reported in the paper:

> *Data sources:* The words of four boys whispering at the back of the room; interviews and discussions with the teacher; documents such as lesson plans and pupils' work.
> *Methodology:* Qualitative: participant observation once a week for an entire school year.
> *Authors of literature invoked and cited in the paper:* Bauersfeld, Brissenden, Cobb and Yackel, Pimm, Richards.

The paper does not start with an abstract. In the activity of critiquing this paper, we used basic questions considered useful for authors and reviewers associated with *JRME*, for the purpose of deciding whether Houssart's paper was suitable for publication in *JRME*. These questions were as follows:

- Does the research deepen our understanding of important issues? Does it have the potential to lead the field in new directions?
- Do the research questions pertain to issues of significant theoretical or practical concern? Are they well-grounded in theory or in prior research?
- Is there an appropriate match between the research questions and the methods and analyses employed?
- Does the conduct of the study include the effective application of appropriate data collection, analysis, and interpretation techniques?
- Are the claims and conclusions in the manuscript justified, and do they logically follow from the data or information presented?
- Is the writing clear, lucid, and well-organized?

Many of the current journals in mathematics education (including *JRME*) present four alternative choices for reviewers' recommendations to the editor after they have critiqued a manuscript:

- Accept the manuscript for publication as it is;
- Suggest minor revisions, after which the manuscript is *likely* to be accepted (although not always) after review by the editor and possibly one or more other reviewers;
- Suggest major revisions, after which a new reviewing cycle will be carried out, and the manuscript may or may not be accepted;
- Reject the manuscript.

In practice the first of these alternatives is rarely used; in most cases authors can be helped to strengthen their writing by some form of revision, either major or minor in nature. A decision of minor revisions implies that the write-up is basically sound, requiring only superficial changes. Major revisions might entail a complete restructuring of the manuscript, perhaps with a request for additional information. The difference between a decision of major revisions and one of rejection is that in the former case the editor believes that the researcher has the materials from the research to bring the manuscript into a publishable form; while in the latter case the editor believes that no amount of re-writing will remedy elements that are missing or unsuitable. Thus elements from the research itself, and the nature of the write-up, are both entailed in decisions about whether a manuscript should be published.

In the case of workshop participants' critique of "The Whisperers" both the nature of the research, and the academic aspects of the write-up, were taken into account in discussion of the manuscript. If it had been only the writing that needed changes (e.g., adding an abstract, bringing in more relevant literature, etc.), then clearly the decision could be *major revisions needed*—or as some participants suggested initially, even *minor revisions*. However, in this case there were issues with the research itself, as addressed by some of the six categories of *JRME* questions. Let us consider these points in turn:

- Yes. The research does deepen our understanding by raising significant issues regarding the teacher's beliefs about the abilities of the whisperers; this paper does have the potential to lead the field in different directions;
- No. There were no *research questions* formulated by the researcher at the outset, concerning the whisperers;
- Thus it was not appropriate to ask for a match between research questions and the methods and analyses employed; the observations were serendipitous;
- No. The data presented were anecdotal, without formal audio or video recording; thus it could not be considered that there were "techniques of effective and appropriate data collection, analysis, and interpretation";
- Yes and no. Some of the claims and conclusions in the manuscript appeared to be justified and to follow logically from the information presented; however, the informal nature of the boys' words that were overheard, might be considered a negative aspect if the study is taken to be an example of formal research;
- Yes. The writing is clear, lucid, and well-organized, within the parameters of the nature of the study.

Thus, despite the significance of the issues highlighted, it is apparent that no amount of re-writing would bring the manuscript into a form that would be acceptable for publication in *JRME*. The unanimous final decision resulting from the review by the workshop participants was that this paper should be rejected for *JRME*. An appropriate response to the author of the manuscript was that she "should consider resubmission of the manuscript to a different journal [not *JRME*], such as *For the Learning of Mathematics*." It was acknowledged that *FLM*'s purpose was a wider, more exploratory one than that of a stringent research journal such as *JRME*. Both purposes are important for the furthering of the field of mathematics education. The merits of Houssart's observations in her paper were acknowledged to be important for mathematics education, in that the teacher of 'the whisperers' considered these four boys to be less able mathematically, yet their whispered comments often manifested insight and ability. The message is clear: Choice of the correct journal for a manuscript is a significant issue.

16.4 Pitfalls

There are many pitfalls in academic writing into which unprepared writers can fall. For example, they may omit relevant information, assuming that because they are familiar with the issue under investigation or the conditions under which the data were gathered, the reader will be too. Another problem commonly faced by novices arises from an attempt to squeeze a dissertation's worth of research into a single journal article, thereby confusing the reader by raising too many issues and providing too much information. The scope of the report should be clear at the outset, and if it raises more than two or three main issues, the writer should consider writing more than one article. Sometimes writers forget either that they are telling a story—and therefore the parts need to fit together—or that they are also reporting research—and therefore the claims they make need to be supported with evidence. By the time they reach the conclusion section, they also may have forgotten the rationale they gave for the study and the research questions they posed at the outset, thereby leaving the reader dissatisfied.

We end with a deeply ironic piece written as an editorial for the *JRME* more than three decades ago (Kilpatrick 1985) and reprinted by permission of the National Council of Teachers of Mathematics. The editorial raises a number of pitfalls that are unfortunately all too common in academic writing in our field.

16.5 Editorial Sarcasm

Irony is a powerful literary device that may take various forms, several of which are present in this piece:

> *antiphrasis*—broad use of words that convey a meaning opposite to what is intended;
> *epitrope*—ironical permission to act in a certain way;
> *paralipsis*—phrases that reveal some aspect despite a proposal not to do so. (Joseph 2005, p. 138)

The following editorial gives some ironic hints about why we consider the reporting of scientific research to be a significant issue worthy of time and care. It seems to have arisen because the editor lost patience after receiving too many submissions of unpublishable manuscripts.

> Editors and reviewers are reputed to be busy people, but that is a fiction. The *JRME* editors and reviewers lead dreary lives of unremitting sloth. If you plan to submit a manuscript to the *JRME,* here are several easy ways that you can bring stimulation and challenge to some idle minds.First, do not bother to read the journal itself and pay no attention to what the *Publication Manual of the American Psychological Association* (Third Edition) has to say about preparing a manuscript. Be a free spirit. Try to convey the impression that you are not a person to be bothered with petty details of style and format.Second, see if you can give your manuscript the portentous tone of a dissertation or project report. Start with the title; it should be as long as possible. Mention every variable you studied, along with the names of the instruments you used. If the title still seems too short, try adding "A Report of a Study Designed in an Attempt to Investigate Various Factors That Might Be Associated With...." If that is not enough, add the name of the institution and the city where you did the study. Either omit the abstract altogether (you're a busy person, right?) or, better, stretch it out to at least 250 words so that you can allude to results that are not included in the body of the report, thereby providing the reviewers with more of a challenge. In setting up tables and figures, just remember that they should not be easily interpreted on their own. Verbatim copies of computer printouts usually make wonderful tables. If a table seems too stark, you can add a dozen or so cryptic footnotes. Most tables should be discussed entry-by-entry in the text, but the virtuoso writer will include at least one table or figure that is not cited anywhere.
>
> Third, do not let the organization be obvious. Avoid headings or subheadings that might reveal too much. Use *Introduction* at the beginning and put *Results* somewhere in the middle, if you wish, but report the results all the way to the end, as they occur to you. Aim at a stream-of-consciousness effect. If you want to give the purpose of the study, follow

Agatha Christie's style and tell your secret at the end. You can, however, give the manuscript a nice absurdist touch by omitting any statement of purpose.

Finally, do not let anyone else read your manuscript before you submit it. After all, who are you writing for if not yourself? Proofreading the manuscript carefully and letting colleagues look it over might suggest that you were eager to have it published. If you follow the simple suggestions above, you will not need to worry about publication. And you can know the satisfaction of having given some extra work to the editors and reviewers.

References

Bikner-Ahsbahs, A., Knipping, C., & Presmeg, N. (Eds.). (2015). *Approaches to qualitative research in mathematics education: Examples of methodology and methods.* Dordrecht: Springer.

Brown, A., & Dowling, P. (1998). *Doing research/ reading research: A mode of interrogation for education.* New York: Falmer Press.

Cronbach, L. J., & Suppes, P. (Eds.). (1969). *Research for tomorrow's schools: Disciplined inquiry for education (Report of the Committee on Educational Research of the National Academy of Education).* New York: Macmillan.

Dorier, J.-L. (2008). Reaction to J. Kilpatrick's plenary talk, 'The development of mathematics education as an academic field'. In M. Menghini, F. Furinghetti, L. Giacardi, & F. Arzarello (Eds.), *The First Century of the International Commission on Mathematical Instruction (1908–2008): Reflecting and shaping the world of mathematics education* (pp. 40–46). Rome: Istituto della Enciclopedia Italiana.

Hart, K. M. (1993). Basic criteria for research in mathematics education. In A. Sierpinska & J. Kilpatrick (Eds.), *Mathematics education as a research domain: A search for identity* (pp. 409–413). Dordrecht: Kluwer.

Houssart, J. (2001). Rival classroom discourses and inquiry mathematics: "The whisperers." *For the Learning of Mathematics, 21*(3), 2–8.

Jaeger, R. M. (Ed.). (1988). *Complementary methods for research in education.* Washington, DC: American Educational Research Association.

Joseph, M. (2005). *Shakespeare's use of the arts of language.* Philadelphia: Paul Dry Books.

Keller, U., & Buchholtz, N. (2015). The combination of qualitative and quantitative research methods in mathematics education: A "mixed methods" study on the development of the professional knowledge of teachers. In A. Bikner-Ahsbahs, C. Knipping, & N. Presmeg, (Eds.). *Approaches to qualitative research in mathematics education: Examples of methodology and methods* (pp. 321–361). Dordrecht: Springer.

Kilpatrick, J. (1985). Editorial. *Journal for Research in Mathematics Education, 16*(3), 162.

Kilpatrick, J. (1992). A history of research in mathematics education. In D. Grouws (Ed.), *Handbook of research on mathematics teaching and learning* (pp. 3–38.). New York: Macmillan.

Kilpatrick, J. (2008). The development of mathematics education as an academic field. In M. Menghini, F. Furinghetti, L. Giacardi, & F. Arzarello (Eds.), *The first century of the International Commission on Mathematical Instruction (1908–2008): Reflecting and shaping the world of mathematics education* (pp. 25–39.). Rome: Istituto della Enciclopedia Italiana.

Kilpatrick, J., & Sierpinska, A. (1993). Criteria for judging the quality of mathematics education research. In G. Nissen & M. Blomhøj (Eds.), *Criteria for scientific quality and relevance in the didactics of mathematics.* Danish Research Council for the Humanities. Roskilde: Stougaard Jensen.

Lester, F. (Ed.) (2007). *Second handbook of research on mathematics teaching and learning.* vol. 1 and 2. Charlotte: Information Age Publishing.

Lester, F., & Cooney, T. (1994). Criteria for judging the quality of mathematics education research. In Discussion Group Report, 16th Annual Meeting of the North American Chapter of the International Group for the Psychology of Mathematics Education. November 5–8, 1994, *Baton Rouge*, Louisiana, USA.

Lester, F., & Lambdin, D. V. (1993). The ship of Theseus and other metaphors for thinking about what we value in mathematics education research. In A. Sierpinska & J. Kilpatrick (Eds.), *Mathematics education as a research domain: A search for identity* (pp. 415–425.). Dordrecht: Kluwer.

Lester, F., & Wiliam, D. (2000). The evidential basis for knowledge claims in mathematics education research. *Journal for Research in Mathematics Education, 31*(2), 132–137.

Presmeg, N. (2014). Mathematics at the center of distinct fields: A response to Michael and Ted. In M. N. Fried & T. Dreyfus (Eds.), *Mathematics and mathematics education: Searching for common ground* (pp. 45–53). Dordrecht: Springer. https://doi.org/10.1007/978-94-007-7473-5_4.

Sierpinska, A., & Kilpatrick, J. (Eds.). (1998). *Mathematics education as a research domain: A search for identity*. Dordrecht: Kluwer.

Sowder, J. T. (Ed.). (1990). *Research agenda for mathematics education: Setting a research agenda*. Washington, DC: Erlbaum.

Teppo, A. R. (Ed.). (1998). *Qualitative research methods in mathematics education (Journal for Research in Mathematics Education Monograph Series, No. 9)*. Reston: National Council of Teachers of Mathematics.

Open Access This chapter is licensed under the terms of the Creative Commons Attribution 4.0 International License (http://creativecommons.org/licenses/by/4.0/), which permits use, sharing, adaptation, distribution and reproduction in any medium or format, as long as you give appropriate credit to the original author(s) and the source, provide a link to the Creative Commons license and indicate if changes were made.

The images or other third party material in this chapter are included in the chapter's Creative Commons license, unless indicated otherwise in a credit line to the material. If material is not included in the chapter's Creative Commons license and your intended use is not permitted by statutory regulation or exceeds the permitted use, you will need to obtain permission directly from the copyright holder.

Chapter 17
Scholarly Writing

Helen J. Forgasz

Abstract In this chapter, the basic elements associated with scholarly writing in English are presented. In some sections, exercises (with answers) are provided. With respect to writing theses as well as scholarly journal papers and book chapters, the abstract and the literature review are the main sections focused on in this chapter.

Keywords Abstract · Literature review · APA referencing style · Grammar · Tense and voice · Clarity of writing · Support for writing

17.1 Introduction

The structure of many scholarly pieces of writing (e.g., thesis, conference paper, journal paper) is similar. Reports of empirical studies should include all of the following:

- An introduction, including the rationale for the study (the 'why' the study is needed), and an outline of the context and setting (e.g., country, level of schooling, etc.) of the study.
- The aims/objectives of the study and the research questions.
- A literature review—a synthesis of what is already known in fields pertinent to the study.
- A clear description of the research design and the research approaches adopted.
- The results and findings of the research undertaken.
- A discussion of the findings and how they compare with relevant previous research.
- Conclusions that can be drawn, directions for further research, and implications of the results as they may apply to pertinent contexts or settings.

H. J. Forgasz (✉)
Monash University, Melbourne, VIC, Australia
e-mail: Helen.Forgasz@monash.edu

© The Author(s) 2019
G. Kaiser and N. Presmeg (eds.), *Compendium for Early Career Researchers in Mathematics Education*, ICME-13 Monographs,
https://doi.org/10.1007/978-3-030-15636-7_17

Scholarly books and book chapters usually contain the same structural elements, but there is greater flexibility. Some of the differences in the structure of the writing for a thesis, journal paper, conference paper, book, and book chapter include the following:

- target audience;
- word or character or page limits;
- amount of detail required;
- content focus;
- writing style;
- formatting and referencing styles.

In this chapter, the focus is on some of the common elements for any form of scholarly writing. In general, trustworthiness is critical, that is, the reader must trust what has been written; the written language must be clear and grammatically correct; and expectations for length and formatting must be met.

17.2 Aspects of Scholarly Writing

Three elements critical for most scholarly writing are examined first: the abstract; the literature review; and referencing style (in-text and in reference lists), with a focus on the American Psychological Association [APA][1] publication style.

17.2.1 Writing an Abstract

An abstract is a short summary of the research reported. Well written abstracts are informative, entice the reader to want to learn more about the research reported, and include the following basic components:

1. A statement of the research problem/focus—what is the problem? What "gap" is your research filling or why are your replicating a study, and what is new in the study?
2. Methods/procedure/approach—what you did to get your results (e.g., interviewed 17 12-year old students, surveyed 750 grade 10 students).
3. Results/findings—report the results, highlighting the critical findings (i.e., what you learnt from your research).
4. Conclusion/implications: Describe the main implications of your findings, especially in light of the research questions or problem that you identified.

---

[1]Editorial note: The book in which this chapter appears uses a modified ('lean') version of APA style, which is also the Springer in-house style. Except where the author is specifically referring to APA style (6th edition of the APA Manual), the chapter conforms to the Springer in-house style.

5. The word limit of an abstract can vary; whatever the allowance, you must adhere to it. The number of key words, if requested, should be supplied.

> **Exercise 1**
> Here is an abstract from an article published in a highly ranked journal (*Educational Studies in Mathematics* [ESM]), authored by Jiang et al. (2014, p. 27). ESM has a requirement that the abstract be 150–250 words.
>
> **For this abstract, can you identify the elements of the well-written abstract described above?**
>
> *This study examined 361 Chinese and 345 Singaporean sixth-grade students' performance and problem-solving strategies for solving 14 problems about speed. By focusing on students from two distinct high-performing countries in East Asia, we provide a useful perspective on the differences that exist in the preparation and problem-solving strategies of these groups of students. The strategy analysis indicates that the Chinese sample used algebraic strategies more frequently and more successfully than the Singaporean sample, although the Chinese sample used a limited variety of strategies. The Singaporean sample's use of model-drawing produced a performance advantage on one problem by converting multiplication/division of fractions into multiplication/division of whole numbers. Several suggestions regarding teaching and learning of mathematical problem solving, algebra, and problems about speed and its related concepts of ratio and proportion are made.*
>
> Solution to Exercise 1
> *This study examined 361 Chinese and 345 Singaporean sixth-grade students' performance and problem-solving strategies for solving 14 problems about speed. By focusing on students from two distinct high-performing countries in East Asia, we provide a useful perspective on the differences that exist in the preparation and problem-solving strategies of these groups of students. The strategy analysis indicates that the Chinese sample used algebraic strategies more frequently and more successfully than the Singaporean sample, although the Chinese sample used a limited variety of strategies. The Singaporean sample's use of model-drawing produced a performance advantage on one problem by converting multiplication/division of fractions into multiplication/division of whole numbers. Several suggestions regarding teaching and learning of mathematical problem solving, algebra, and problems about speed and its related concepts of ratio and propor--tion are made.*
> In Green: Point 1   In Purple: Point 2   In Blue: Point 3   In Red: Point 4
>
> Point 5 has not been met; the abstract has fewer than 150 words.
>
> [Sometimes editors do not fuss as much over fewer words, particularly if the elements of an abstract are present, as they do if the abstract is too long.]

17.2.2 Writing a Literature Review

A literature review is needed to demonstrate appropriate knowledge of previous research in the relevant field/s in which your research is situated. The research to be reported may have been designed to address a gap in the literature, to repeat previous research in a new context or setting or to confirm earlier findings, or it may be that an alternative methodological approach has been adopted to verify or to challenge previous results. Whichever the case, your literature review should provide the needed evidence to justify the research undertaken.

The sources you cite in your literature review should be reputable. Refereed research reported in scholarly academic journal papers, professional journals (when relevant), book chapters, and books are the most appropriate sources; official reports (e.g., PISA reports, OECD reports, and government sources) can also be included. Information from websites and the popular media should be included sparingly only if the sources are dependable; these references need to be appropriately cited in the reference list.

When you are ready to commence the literature review, you should keep your research question/s in mind; the literature review must be relevant to the topic/s at hand. Using headings or dot points, a draft structure for the literature review (for your own use) should be outlined. As you read the literature, you should keep good records including full citations and summaries of the content, that is, an annotated bibliography of your sources; there are various software packages that can assist in the task (e.g., EndNote). You will then be in a good position to commence synthesising what you have read under the headings you have developed.

It is expected that the structure of the literature review will be described in the opening section. When writing the literature review, you should keep the following points in mind:

- The literature review must be a synthesis of what you have read. You should not write summaries of one research study after the other; a critical synthesis is expected.
- Do not selectively "cherry pick" findings from research studies that support your arguments and omit findings that do not; conflicting findings should be included and evaluated. It is important that you point out the shortcomings of particular studies (e.g., methodological issues) and/or the gaps in what is known.
- Include an overall summary of each section of the literature review, taking into account the weight of evidence.
- Whenever possible, use primary sources. Secondary sources can be used if there is some difficulty in accessing the original writing. If authors have critiqued or summarised previous research (e.g., literature surveys in particular fields), such secondary sources can be invaluable and must be acknowledged appropriately.
- If a direct quotation is used, make sure that it is accurately reproduced; in the citation, the page number must be included.
- Avoid too many direct quotations and avoid very long quotations. Instead, you can paraphrase the text of interest, but it must be accurate. Paraphrasing

demonstrates that you understand the literature. Never omit the citation when paraphrasing; this constitutes plagiarism (the most heinous crime in academia).
- Do not use direct quotations as substitutes for text; relevant comments or words should introduce or accompany the direct quotations you use.
- Know how to cite references accurately, both in-text and in the reference list. APA (or slight variations of it) is a common referencing style used in the field of education.
- If you are citing or quoting from trustworthy web-based documents, you must cite the sources appropriately; if using the APA style, you may need to consult the latest APA manual; the method for citing web-based sources has changed over the years.

Why Use References?

The main purposes for using references include the following:

- to provide evidential support and/or develop the points you are trying to make in the text;
- to demonstrate your breadth of reading and knowledge of the topics discussed;
- to establish your trustworthiness as an author;
- to enable readers to trace citations to the original source if they are interested in doing so;
- to give due credit for the previous research of the authors of the cited work; in so doing, plagiarism is avoided.

As well as appropriate coverage of earlier research in the field, there are other important issues to consider when writing a literature review. In the next sections, various aspects of appropriate writing and grammatically correct writing are examined.

Writing Style for the Literature Review

Writing style is important to ensure that what is written is appropriate and does not convey inaccuracies.

Consider the two sentences below. Both are less than adequate. Why?

1. Girls outperform boys at high school.
2. Data reveal that for many years girls have outperformed boys at the secondary school level overall; for example, from 1990–1999, females' mean university ranking scores were found to be 15 points higher than males' (XX, date).

Sentence 1 demonstrates unsubstantiated opinion. Sentence 2 provides a cautious, supported, but quite limited view of the field.

Here is an example of how the writing associated with the two sentences might have been shaped to provide evidence for the claims made:

There is extensive research evidence that girls outperform boys overall at the end of high school in (e.g., country X)... Author A (date), for example, has reported that... Other reports on performance at the end of schooling (Author B, date; government document; date) in (same country) reveal that this pattern has persisted over a number of years (date range).... In several other studies, similar findings have been reported (e.g., Author C, date; Author D, date; etc.] in (same country) and elsewhere in the world, although the same pattern is not universal (e.g., in country Y, Author E, date). At other grade levels in (country X), however, girls are also generally found to outperform boys in schooling overall (e.g., Author E, date; Author F, date). Yet, when performance within mathematics is considered in (country X), the gender difference is frequently found to be in the opposite direction, that is, boys generally outperform girls at all grade levels (e.g., multiple citations) ... This gender difference favouring boys is also commonly found internationally (e.g., PISA report). In summary, it would appear that....

Direct Quotations (in APA Style) in the Literature Review

The formatting associated with direct quotations varies according to the number of words being quoted. The APA citation style also varies.

1. If the quotation has fewer than 40 words, include the quotation in the text. Double quotations marks should be used around the direct quotation ("...."). The citation can take the following forms:

   - "...." followed by (Author, date, p. xx) OR
   - Author (date) noted that "...." (p. xx) or Author (date, p. xx) noted that "....".

2. For direct quotations of 40 words or more, use a new line, indented from the margins and do not use quotation marks. The citation can take the following forms. An example is shown in the box below:

> Forgasz, Tan, Leder, and McLeod (2017) presented arguments in favour of using Facebook advertising to recruit survey participants, claiming that:
>
> > ... depending on funding availability and desired sample sizes, Facebook advertising has much potential as a viable recruitment method to extend conventional methods of data collection in educational research studies, particularly if faced with difficult to access participants, the need to supplement low response rates, and budget limitations in obtaining national or international data. (p. 12)
>
> [Note that the page number appears after the full stop.]
>
> Alternatively, the page number for the same quote could have been provided as follows:
>
> > Forgasz, Tan, Leder, and McLeod (2017, p. 12)....

APA Referencing Style

The APA [American Psychological Association] citation style is commonly used in mathematics education research; sometimes slight modifications are required (e.g., the Springer in-house style used in this book and in some Springer journals, such as *ZDM Mathematics Education*). I have recommended to all my doctoral (and masters) students that in their dissertations they use APA style. As well as citation guidelines, formatting guidelines are provided in the APA manual (e.g., for data tables, etc.). In this chapter, the focus is only on APA referencing styles (in-text and reference list).

At the time of writing, the APA manual (6th ed.) is the most accurate source to consult regarding the APA referencing style (see the APA style homepage: http://www.apastyle.org/). There is also a vast array of online resources to assist. Examples include:

- APA style blog: http://blog.apastyle.org/apastyle/.
- http://www.library.kent.edu/files/APACheatSheet.pdf.
- http://library.calu.edu/citation/apa (also includes other style guides)
- https://guides.lib.monash.edu/citing-referencing/apa https://library.unimelb.edu.au/recite/apa.

Try Exercise 2 below to see how well you know the APA referencing style (the answers are provided). If you have any difficulties with the items, or cannot understand the solution, you should consult the APA manual or the various online resources.

Exercise 2

There are APA referencing style errors, some in-text, others in the reference list, in what follows. Identify the errors and provide the corrections.

According to Smith (2005), the best approaches to teaching mathematics include…. Williams (2009) conducted a study based on Smith's work, and found that… *Worth et al* (2010) present an alternative perspective, claiming that…

Reference list

Smith, P. R. (2005). Mathematics teaching. In: Boyd, G., & Gordon, K. (Eds.), *Good teaching, 46–70*. Glasgow: School Book press.

Worth, A., Hammer, J., Lyle, J M, and Corbin, A. (2010). What's new in mathematics education? *Mathematics Learning Journal*, 41(7), pp. 6–20.

Williams, M. (2009). *A New Approach to Teaching Mathematics*. Melbourne, Australia: Bridges Press.

Answers to Exercise 2

In text:

- Smith (2005) ✓
- Williams (2009) ✓
- Smith's work ✓

Written this way means that reference is being made to the same Smith (2005) reference. Because it is cited again in the same paragraph, omitting the date is allowed. Using "Smith's (2005) work" would also be correct.

- Worth et al. (2010) X

If this is NOT the first time that the reference is cited in the text, it should have been written as "Worth et al. (2010)". Italics should not have been used, and a full stop was needed for "et al." If this is the first time the reference is being cited, it should have been written as "Worth, Hammer, Lyle, and Corbin (2010)".

In the reference list, each entry has one or more errors. Also, the list itself is out of alphabetical order; the Williams reference should have come before the Worth et al. reference. The corrections for each reference are shown below:

Smith, P. R. (2005). Mathematics teaching. In G. Boyd & K. Gordon (Eds.), *Good teaching* (pp. 46–70). Glasgow, Scotland: School Book Press.

Williams, M. (2009). *A new approach to teaching mathematics*. Melbourne, Australia: Bridges Press.

Worth, A., Hammer, J., Lyle, J. M., & Corbin, A. (2010). What's new in mathematics education? *Mathematics Learning Journal, 41*(7), 6–20.

Additional Resources Related to the Writing of Literature Reviews

There are many resources online that you can use to assist in the writing of the literature review. Here are a few:

University of Toronto: http://advice.writing.utoronto.ca/types-of-writing/literature-review/

Cornell University: http://guides.library.cornell.edu/ilrlitreview

Monash University: https://guides.lib.monash.edu/researching-for-your-literature-review/home

In summary, a well referenced literature review demonstrates the writer's integrity and skill as a responsible and knowledgeable participant in the scholarly enterprise. As noted earlier, it is also important to use clearly written and grammatically correct language in all scholarly writing. In the next sections, other relevant issues are explored.

Table 17.1 Examples of author prominent and information prominent sentences

Author prominent	Brie (1988)* showed that the moon is made out of cheese	The moon's cheesy composition was established by Brie (1988)	According to Brie (1988), the moon is made of cheese	Brie's (1988) perspective on the moon's composition is that it is made of cheese
Information prominent	In previous research it has been established that the moon is of cheese (Brie 1988)	It has been shown that the moon is made of cheese (Brie 1988)	It has been argued that the moon is made of cheese (Brie 1988)	The moon may be made of cheese (Brie 1988), but in later research the moon was found to have a composition similar to Earth (Rock 1989)

17.3 Clear and Grammatically Correct Writing

There are two ways to refer to the research of others: author-prominent and information-prominent citations. The focus of author-prominent citations is on the work of the author. For information-prominent citations the focus is on the information, with the author/s acknowledged as the source of that information. The examples in Table 17.1 have been drawn from *Writing about the ideas of others* (n.d.); some sentences have been modified slightly. The authors and content are fictitious and are only meant to illustrate the two types of citations.

Here is an exercise for you to think about.

> **Exercise 3**
> Supervisors and reviewers sometimes read statements written in the same style as the following: "The moon is made of cheese (Brie 1988)." What is wrong with the statement?
>
> **Answer to Exercise 3**
>
> As written, the sentence reads as a statement of fact, a fact that is inaccurate. Using the information from Table 17.1, it can be seen that the work of another (fictitious) researcher, Rock (1989), challenged Brie's (1988) finding.
>
> Care needs to be taken when writing a literature review not to make generalised statements of fact that can be easily challenged. [There is a similar example, "Girls outperform boys at high school", that was discussed earlier in the chapter.]

Although each sentence in Table 1 is grammatically correct, some of the sentences could be considered preferable to others with respect to how the information is conveyed. In the next section, the different ways of paraphrasing the words of others are examined.

17.3.1 Different Ways of Paraphrasing Others' Words

Look at the following two sentences. While superficially they appear to convey the same information, there are variations in the meanings conveyed.

1. Byron (2007) has expressed concern that university students are not taught presentation skills using electronic technology and this disadvantages them in their business and professional careers.
2. There is concern that university students are not taught presentation skills using electronic technology and this disadvantages them in their business and professional careers (Byron 2007).

Sentence 1 is author-centred and, in my view, is the better one in this context. Here Byron's (2007) view is shared with the reader. The second is information-centred but could be interpreted as a statement of fact that the reader may know is contestable. Sentence 2 could have been improved by using "(e.g., Byron 2007)" possibly accompanied by other citations. A slight modification such as "Researchers have expressed concern that.... (e.g., Byron 2007)" would also improve the sentence.

To avoid the possibility of writing a statement that might be interpreted as fact, there are certain verbs that can be used when constructing the sentence, for example, "X (date) claimed/maintained/proposed/considered/found/suggested/argued that...".

The exercise below includes a pair of paragraphs for you to consider.

Exercise 4
Which paragraph is the better one? Why?

1. Inclusion is the fairest and most productive approach to educating children with special needs (Smith 1999; Tollington 2000). The visually impaired achieve high levels of social interaction and intellectual development in mainstream schools (Johnstone 2001).
2. Smith (1999), writing about schooling in Victoria, Australia, argued that inclusion is the fairest and most productive approach to educating children with special needs (see also Tollington 2000). In a study of 10 young adolescent students with visual impairment, Johnstone (2001) found that all participants achieved high levels of intellectual development for their

year level and that they also reported improved wellbeing in social interaction.

Suggested answer to Exercise 4

In my view, paragraph 2 is written more convincingly. Evidence and context are provided, and no sentences are written to suggest that the claims represent fact. In paragraph 1, although references are provided, the message conveyed by the content is that the claims are factual.

17.3.2 Tense and Voice to Use in Scholarly Writing

For the literature review, there is inconsistency among researchers whether to use the present tense or the past tense. In the APA (2010) guidelines it is recommended that the past tense be used "to express an action or a condition that occurred at a specific time in the past, as when discussing another researcher's work and when reporting your results" (p. 78). Whichever tense is used, consistency is paramount. In line with APA (2010) guidelines, my preference has always been to use the past tense. In my view, every research study cited in a literature review was published before what is now being written. That is, the research reported in the articles and the claims made by the authors are from the past. However, when writing up the research approaches adopted in a study and the results/findings from the study, the past tense must be used. After all, the work that you are reporting has been completed.

It would appear that there is now general consensus that the *voice* used in scholarly writing—*active* (emphasising the performer) or *passive* (emphasising the product of the action)—should be dependent on what is being emphasised. Even researchers in science who have traditionally written in the passive voice are now encouraged to use active voice when appropriate (e.g., Biomedical Editor 2015). Active rather than passive voice is the preferred style advocated in the 6th edition of the APA publication manual (APA 2010), although "passive voice is acceptable in expository writing when you want to focus on the object... of the action rather than on the actor" (APA 2010, p. 77).

Relevant writing advice on the use of active or passive voice can be found on various websites. Examples include:

- The University of Toronto: http://advice.writing.utoronto.ca/revising/passive-voice/
- Purdue online writing lab: https://owl.purdue.edu/owl/general_writing/academic_writing/active_and_passive_voice/active_and_passive_voice.html
- American journal experts: https://www.aje.com/en/arc/writing-with-active-or-passive-voice/

17.3.3 Issues of English Grammar

The English language can be grammatically challenging. It is important in scholarly writing that the English language used is of a high standard. How English is spoken and how it is written can be very different. Even people for whom English is their first language can have difficulties in writing good, clear, grammatically correct, English.

Long sentences, with many phrases, can be confusing for a reader. Short, sharp sentences are often preferable. Remember that a sentence must contain a verb.

In what follows, common grammatical errors are discussed. Many books are available and many websites can be accessed for more comprehensive overviews of the rules of English grammar. A few recommended websites include the following:

Strunk, W. Jr., & White, E. B. (2000). *The elements of style* (4th Ed.). Allyn & Bacon. [Retrieved from http://www.jlakes.org/ch/web/The-elements-of-style.pdf]

The Oxford dictionary website: https://en.oxforddictionaries.com/grammar/grammar-tips
OWL Purdue online writing lab: https://owl.english.purdue.edu/owl/section/1/5/

Some common errors that I have encountered with students' writing or when reviewing include:

- Subject-verb disagreements. There are many situations in which this error can be found. It is important to be able to identify the subject and the verb in a sentence and make sure that they are in agreement, that is, either both are singular or both in plural. Two incorrect and correct sentence pairs are shown below:

Incorrect: Each of Mary's answers are wrong.
Correct: Each of Mary's answers is wrong.
Incorrect: The majority of students believe what lecturers say.
Correct: The majority of students believes what lecturers say.

Further examples, with explanations for the types of errors being made, can be found at http://bethune.yorku.ca/writing/s_v/
- Omitted or incorrect use of apostrophes. Often apostrophes are omitted when they should be included, for example, "…the students voices…" should be written "…the students' voices…". In other cases the apostrophe is wrongly placed, for example, "Johns' classmates…" should be written "John's classmates…"
- Incorrect use of "there/their/they're", "which/that", "who/whom", "fewer/less", "affect/effect", etc.
- Missing or incorrect punctuation including, for example, missing commas, and misuse of colons and semi-colons.
- Confusing "i.e.," and "e.g.,".
"i.e.," means "that is" and "e.g.," means "for example".
Both abbreviations should be used only in parentheses; "that is" and "for example" should be used in-text.

- Anthropomorphisms, defined as "[T]he attribution of human characteristics or behaviour to a god, animal, or object" (English Oxford living dictionaries, n. d.). The use of anthropomorphisms has become widespread, and authors seem unaware that human characteristics are being conferred upon chapters, text, manuscripts/papers/articles etc. Unfortunately, when there is a word limit (e.g., for abstracts) sentences with anthropomorphisms are often used, resulting in reduced word usage (e.g., avoiding the anthropomorphism found in the opening sentence of the abstract in Exercise 1 above would have increased the number of words in the abstract).

Examples such as the following illustrate the incorrect use of anthropomorphisms in academic writing:

This chapter summarises the literature in the field.
As written, the author has given the "chapter" the capability of doing something that only humans can do. This sentence is better written as, "In this chapter, the literature in the field is summarised".

The study found that students enjoy algebra more than trigonometry.
Better versions of this sentence would be, "The researchers found that…" or "In the study, it was found that…".

Although technically incorrect, I agree that some anthropomorphisms are acceptable in academic writing, particularly when it would be clumsy to convey the intended messages. Here is an example:

The data/findings/results/responses reveal/indicate that....

Avoiding anthropomorphisms can be challenging. The Walden University (Writing Center) website, https://academicguides.waldenu.edu/writingcenter/apa/other/anthropomorphism, is an excellent resource. Appropriate and inappropriate uses of anthropomorphisms in writing, consistent with APA style guidelines, are illustrated.

Resources

Here is a selection of other web resources where you will learn about the most common grammatical errors in the English language and how to avoid them:

Oxford Royale Academy: https://www.oxford-royale.co.uk/articles/15-common-grammar-gripes-avoid.html
Authority Pub: https://authority.pub/common-grammar-mistakes/
Your Dictionary: http://grammar.yourdictionary.com/grammar-rules-and-tips/5-most-common.html
Grammar Monster: http://www.grammar-monster.com/common_grammar_errors.htm

In the final exercise below, your task is to identify the grammatical and/or APA referencing style errors and fix them.

Exercise 5
Identify the Grammatical and/or APA Referencing Style Errors (and Others) in Each of the Following in-Text Statements.

1. Coyle measured childrens levels of hostility before and after exposure to violent videogames (2012, p. 15).
2. Neither group showed any significant difference (Frame and Bills 2010).
3. One study (Jones 2015) explored elementary teacher's use of manipulatives.
4. In three separate studies, Lefty (2004a, 2004b, 2004c) found that rats had higher levels of stress hormone after exposure to bright light.
5. Badger (2013) found that there was "no significant difference between the treatment group and the control group".
6. 12 students improved and twelve students did not improve.
7. There were less mathematical errors made by students in Class A than in Class B.
8. The mathematical content areas examined included; algebra, geometry, and statistics.
9. Each of the following students - James, John, Sally, and Jane – were absent on the day of testing.

Answers to Exercise 5

1. Coyle (2012) measured children's levels of hostility before and after exposure to violent videogames.
2. No statistically significant difference was found by group (Frame & Bills, 2010).
3. Jones (2015) explored elementary teachers' use of manipulatives.
4. In three separate studies, Lefty (2004a, 2004b, 2004c) found that rats had higher levels of stress hormone after exposure to bright light.
5. Badger (2013) found that there was "no significant difference between the treatment group and the control group" (p. xx).
6. Twelve students improved and 12 students did not improve.
7. There were fewer mathematical errors made by students in Class A than in Class B.
8. The mathematical content areas examined included: algebra, geometry, and statistics.
9. Each of the following students—James, John, Sally, and Jane—was absent on the day of testing.

17.4 Support for Your Writing Efforts

When writing your masters or doctoral dissertation, you should receive regular feedback from your supervisor(s) and/or supervising panel members. Before submitting your writing for comment and critique, you should proof-read and edit the work as best you can. Sloppy writing draws attention away from focusing on the contents of the writing. Examiners and reviewers get very irritated when grammatical, spelling, and/or referencing errors are found in the abstract or in the first few pages of a manuscript/dissertation.

Whatever type of scholarly writing you are doing, at an appropriate time, you should do the following:

- Ask a colleague or mentor to read your work. Ask for constructive feedback, and then act on the feedback (if relevant) before submitting.
- Native English speakers, as well as those for whom English is not their first language, must have the final version of the article/dissertation proof-read for grammatical and various typographical errors, including spelling and punctuation. Authors (and supervisors) can become so familiar with the writing that they are no longer alert to errors. Someone who is less familiar with the writing can often spot overlooked mistakes.

Following submission of the manuscript, journal article, or conference paper, reviewers will provide feedback. If you are requested to make changes, do so in a timely manner and with humility. If something asked for is inappropriate, you should explain to the editor why you have decided not to make the particular change. Sometimes reviewers appear to have read a 'different' article from the one you wrote and submitted. Some have argued that the outcomes of reviewing processes for journal articles or conference papers can be a 'lottery'. Chin up! Smile! Things could be worse. Even experienced, widely published 'experts' are rejected from journals and conference presentations!

Dissertation examiners are usually carefully selected for their expertise, and most theses will pass, even if some changes are needed. Occasionally errors are made in the choice of an examiner, and a report comes in that is not what was expected. Your supervisors will provide appropriate advice on what you need to do and/or how to respond. In most cases, reviewers for journal articles are also selected with care. Nevertheless, there are times when a reviewer's comments may be inappropriate, irrelevant, or unfair; at times a review may seem to be about an article different from the one written. At times like these, you should seek the advice of an experienced colleague on how to proceed. There are various responses possible depending on the nature of the review. At times, it may be appropriate to write to the journal editor; at other times, the criticisms can be addressed when documenting the changes that have been made in response to reviewers.

17.5 Final Words

It needs to be recognised that good scholarly writing is a challenge. Whether a novice or a more experienced researcher, care and attention are needed to write well. Poor writing—content or writing style—is not acceptable. Help should be sought in editing and proof-reading before submission of the final version of the writing. Expect, and do not be put off, by constructive criticism; most supervisors, reviewers, and examiners are critiquing your work with the aim of providing advice that will improve it further. Work hard at your writing; persistence and diligence pay off.

References

American Psychological Association [APA]. (2010). Publication manual (6th ed.). Washington, DC: Author.
Biomedical Editor. (2015). *Clear science writing: Active voice or passive voice?* http://www.biomedicaleditor.com/active-voice.html.
English Oxford living dictionaries. (n.d.). https://en.oxforddictionaries.com/definition/anthropomorphism.
Jiang, C., Hwang, S., & Cai, J. (2014). Chinese and Singaporean sixth-grade students' strategies for solving problems about speed. *Educational Studies in Mathematics, 87*(1), 27–50.
Writing about the ideas of others. (n.d.). Retrieved from http://artsonline.monash.edu.au/apw/files/2013/03/writing-about-the-ideas-of-others.pdf.

Open Access This chapter is licensed under the terms of the Creative Commons Attribution 4.0 International License (http://creativecommons.org/licenses/by/4.0/), which permits use, sharing, adaptation, distribution and reproduction in any medium or format, as long as you give appropriate credit to the original author(s) and the source, provide a link to the Creative Commons license and indicate if changes were made.

The images or other third party material in this chapter are included in the chapter's Creative Commons license, unless indicated otherwise in a credit line to the material. If material is not included in the chapter's Creative Commons license and your intended use is not permitted by statutory regulation or exceeds the permitted use, you will need to obtain permission directly from the copyright holder.

Part IV
Academic Writing and Academic Publishing: Description of Major Journals in Mathematics Education

Chapter 18
Educational Studies in Mathematics: Shaping the Field

Merrilyn Goos

Abstract This chapter provides a description of the distinctive features of *Educational Studies in Mathematics*, a major journal in mathematics education, together with information and advice on manuscript submission, reviewing processes, and editorial decision making. Key aspects of the journal's history are also highlighted to draw attention to its role in developing editorial policies and processes that are now common in all major mathematics education journals. Although the journal's content and procedures have evolved significantly since its founding in 1968, its unique ethos has remained unchanged and is characterised by an emphasis on high-level articles of international significance, encouragement of manuscript submissions from a wide range of countries, an inclusive orientation to research content and methods, and consistency in editorial approach and standards.

Keywords Journals in mathematics education · Educational Studies in Mathematics · Academic publishing · Manuscript submission and review · Editorial decisions

18.1 Introduction

In this chapter I describe the distinctive characteristics of *Educational Studies in Mathematics (ESM)*, one of the first international journals in mathematics education founded in 1968, and outline issues to bear in mind when submitting manuscripts to this journal. The journal's evolution reflects not only the development of mathematics education as a field of research, but also the formalisation of editorial procedures and policies that are now common in all major mathematics education research journals. In the next section of the chapter I provide a brief historical overview of the journal's development. I then discuss the distinctive features of *ESM* in the context of deciding on which journal to target as an outlet for your

M. Goos (✉)
University of Limerick, Limerick, Ireland
e-mail: merrilyn.goos@ul.ie

research. Next I describe the manuscript submission and review processes, and offer advice on interpreting editorial decisions, responding to reviewers, and preparing revisions. Finally, I outline the role of special issues and the emergence of editorial policies for their management. The overarching aim of the chapter is to open the 'black box' of journal publishing so as to reveal the workings of one of the leading journals in mathematics education.

18.2 Some History

Readers interested in *ESM*'s history are encouraged to consult the paper by Hanna and Sidoli (2002), which celebrated the publication of Volume 50. In that paper the authors noted that *ESM* was born out of the International Commission on Mathematical Instruction (ICMI), with ICMI President Hans Freudenthal its founding Editor. The first issue, published in 1968, began with Freudenthal's address at a 1967 ICMI Colloquium titled "Why to teach mathematics so as to be useful". In the journal's early days Freudenthal exercised significant autonomy: for example, although he appointed an Editorial Board, its role was unclear in terms of influencing journal content since "papers were selected at Freudenthal's discretion" (p. 126). However, the beginnings of *ESM*'s editorial policies can be observed in Freudenthal's interest in publishing articles "by authors from as many different countries as possible" (p. 127). This international flavour remains a feature of *ESM*.

ESM's second Editor, Alan Bishop, succeeded Freudenthal in 1978. During his tenure Bishop introduced the practice of having every manuscript reviewed by at least two members of the Editorial Board. This approach created a distinct style for the journal and laid the foundation for consistency and continuity of standards that has underpinned the work of the *ESM* Editorial Board over subsequent years. Bishop was also responsible for writing the first statement of editorial policy that articulated the journal's aims and scope:

> *Educational Studies in Mathematics* presents new ideas and developments which are considered to be of major importance to those working in the field of mathematics education. It seeks to reflect both the variety of research concerns within this field and the range of methods used to study them. It deals with didactical, methodological and pedagogical subjects rather than with specific programmes for teaching mathematics. All papers are strictly refereed and the emphasis is on high-level articles which are of more than local importance.

This editorial statement communicated Bishop's desire to make *ESM* both academically rigorous and inclusive, in terms of research aims and methodologies. A version of Bishop's statement of aims and scope still appears, in almost exactly the same form, on the journal's website (https://www.springer.com/education+%26+language/mathematics+education/journal/10649).

Willibald Dörfler took on the role of *ESM* Editor-in-Chief in 1990, for the first time with the support of two additional editors due to increases in the journal workload. Under his editorship the Editorial Board was expanded "to represent as broad as possible a range in terms of location, culture, nationality, and theoretical orientation" (Hanna and Sidoli 2002, p. 130). Dörfler also formalised and documented the manuscript review process, although most reviews were still done by members of the Editorial Board. He was the first *ESM* Editor to communicate quality criteria for publishable papers, which he described in an invited symposium talk as follows:

> (1) the rationale for the research should be explicitly formulated and explained; (2) the background philosophy should be stated and recognisable; (3) the research results should be presented and separated from their interpretation; and (4) the relevance of the research to mathematics education should be made clear. (Dörfler 1993, cited in Hanna and Sidoli 2002, p. 131)

It was not until Kenneth Ruthven took over as Editor-in-Chief in 1996 that these criteria became part of the journal's editorial policy, and since then they have been published in the form of "Advice to Prospective Authors" at the beginning of every Volume of *ESM*. While successive Editors-in-Chief have introduced additional measures to manage the journal, its distinctive ethos has remained unchanged and is characterised by an emphasis on high-level articles of international significance, encouragement of manuscript submissions from a wide range of countries, an inclusive orientation to research content and methods, and a consistent editorial approach achieved through relatively stable membership of the Editorial Board and selection of Associate Editors and Editor-in-Chief from amongs its members.

18.3 Selecting a Target Journal: Why Choose *ESM*?

Decisions about which journal to target as a publication outlet for your research can be guided by three questions: (1) Is the journal a good fit for your research? (2) What is the standing of the journal? (3) What practical issues should be taken into account? Each of these questions is addressed in what follows, in the context of *ESM*'s distinctive features and publication format.

18.3.1 Goodness of Fit

A first 'rule of thumb' for evaluating whether a journal is a good fit for your research involves looking at the journal's statement of aims and scope. One of the key requirements of papers published in *ESM* is that they should be of more than local importance. This means that, although the data for a study may have been collected in a specific context, the research questions and findings need to be framed so that they are relevant and accessible to audiences beyond this context. The role of theory is crucial in demonstrating such relevance, since a strong theoretical framework allows readers to reinterpret the findings of a study in light of their local circumstances.

A second, related, consideration is the journal's intended audience. *ESM* has always sought to engage with an international audience: an indicator of its success in achieving this goal comes from an analysis of visits to the journal website by geographic region. For the last few years the largest reader groups have been in the Asia-Pacific region, Europe and North America, with smaller but still significant numbers accessing the website from Africa, the Middle East, and Latin America. The author of a publishable manuscript will be sensitive to this broad and diverse audience, and will avoid making assumptions about what readers know of the local educational context and the language used to describe this context. Another measure of the journal's international reach is the large number of countries of origin of authors of submitted manuscripts, usually exceeding 50 different countries each year. The number of countries from which authors of accepted manuscripts come is around 20 per year. Although the source of most of these articles tends to be countries in which English is the dominant language, in recent years *ESM* has published articles from many other countries, such as Chile, China, Colombia, Indonesia, Japan, Kenya, Lebanon, Peru, and Turkey.

18.3.2 Journal Standing

Beginning researchers are often curious as to how to evaluate a journal's quality and academic standing. While the rejection rate can give an indication of how easy or difficult it might be to have a manuscript accepted for publication, it can also be an artefact of the very large number of manuscript submissions received by high-quality journals (more than 300 per year for *ESM*) combined with the fixed number of journal issues per year that limits the number of articles that can be published. Other indications of journal standing can be derived from three sources: (1) knowledge of the academic reputations of the journal Editors and Editorial Board members, (2) the journal's record of publishing ground breaking research, and (3) journal impact data and ranking studies. Information on the first of these indicators can be obtained from a journal's website: Are the editorial team and Editorial Board members leaders in their fields? Do they represent a range of theoretical and methodological perspectives? Knowledge related to the second indicator can result from familiarity with your own research field: Which landmark studies inform your own research, and in which journals were they published?

Information on journal impact and ranking can come from either quantitative sources, such as citation-based metrics, or qualitative sources, such as surveys that seek expert assessments of journal quality. Although citation-based measures such as journal impact factors and similar indices are widely used by universities to evaluate the work of academics for promotion and tenure, these metrics have shortcomings that suggest they should be used with caution. For example, one problem with the three major journal ranking systems—the Web of Science's Impact Factor, Scopus's SCImago Journal Rank, and Google Scholar Metrics' *h5-index*—is that citations for each are only tracked within their own databases.

For mathematics education, this practice excludes many important journals. (See Nivens and Otten 2017, for a discussion of journal metrics).

Expert peer assessment provides an alternative methodology for judging journal quality, although a difficulty here is possible lack of consistency amongst peer assessors in deciding what is meant by 'quality'. In addition, surveys seeking such assessments rarely achieve wide international coverage, which might raise questions about the influence of academic cultures in different countries on journal rankings obtained via these methods. Williams and Leatham (2017) addressed these problems in a recent study that compared rankings of mathematics education research journals from citation-based and opinion-based (i.e., peer assessment) methods. There was substantial agreement between the rankings yielded by both these approaches, which identified the *Journal for Research in Mathematics Education* and *Educational Studies in Mathematics* as "the two most cited and respected journals in our field by a substantial margin" (p. 389). Their study also found that many other mathematics education journals are regarded as being of at least medium to high quality. A further valuable finding of their study was a list of factors that had influenced survey respondents providing their journal quality rankings. The top three factors judged as "Very Influential" were the high quality of most of the articles published, the quality of the peer-review process, and the high reputation of the journal amongst colleagues and experts. With regard to peer review, high-quality journals used reviewers who provided "rigorous and constructive" feedback, and had editorial teams that "worked closely with authors to improve the articles, both with respect to shepherding authors through the revision process and through quality editing in preparing the final version for print" (p. 388).

18.3.3 Practical Issues

Prospective authors are usually interested in finding out about such practical matters as article length limitations and the time taken for manuscripts to be reviewed and then published if accepted. *Educational Studies in Mathematics* has a longstanding preference for articles no longer than 8000 words, including references and estimation of an equivalent word allowance for the space taken up by any Tables and Figures. This results in finished articles usually no longer than 20 pages when published. As most revisions make a manuscript longer, accepted manuscripts often end up being somewhat longer than 8000 words.

The time period from submission to publication depends on a number of factors, including the journal's publication schedule. *ESM* publishes three Volumes per year, each comprising three issues, and so there are nine journal issues produced each year. Every journal issue contains six to eight articles, resulting in around 70 articles being published per year in numbered journal Volumes and Issues. However, all articles are published *Online First* on the journal's website within days of being accepted, and they have the status of published articles even before they are allocated to a journal issue. The time from submission to publication also depends critically on the speed of reviewing and the number of review cycles before the handling editor makes a final disposition. These matters are discussed in the next section, which describes the manuscript submission and review procedures.

18.4 *ESM*'s Manuscript Submission and Review Processes

Like most international journals, *ESM* uses an online manuscript submission platform that allows its editors to manage the review process and communication of decisions to authors. Figure 18.1 gives an overview of the manuscript submission and review process. However, this is a simplified representation that shows only the first round of reviewing, when in practice several review iterations are usually carried out.

18.4.1 Technical Check

The most important technical check of manuscripts, carried out before they are screened by the Editor-in-Chief, involves submitting each manuscript to text similarity screening software that checks journal submissions against the thousands of published articles in the software database. The output is a similarity report, communicating the percentage overlap between the manuscript submission and previously published sources. The report also identifies these sources, which allows the Editor-in-Chief to investigate the nature and extent of the overlap and determine what action should be taken. Journal publishers and editors adhere to a publishing ethics policy that sets out ethical principles including guidelines on originality, copyright, approval by all co-authors, and assurance that the work has not been

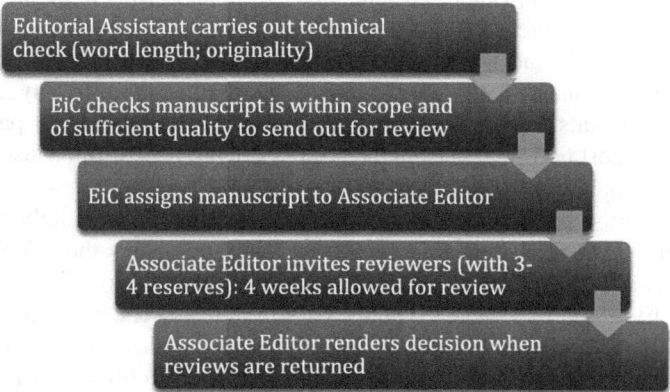

Fig. 18.1 Manuscript submission and review workflow

previously published and is not under consideration for publication elsewhere. There are also guidelines for editors on handling suspected plagiarism and redundant publication.

Plagiarism involves presentation of the work of others as though it were one's own, while redundant publication refers to the practice of splitting a study into several parts and publishing the parts in different journals without adequate cross referencing or permission. Sometimes these practices are unintentional, resulting from lack of knowledge or differences in cultural background in relation to behaviours concerning copying. The Editor-in-Chief needs to exercise careful judgment in dealing with such cases. Prospective authors are advised to consult information on "Ethical Responsibilities of Authors" in the "Instructions for Authors" found on the journal website (https://www.springer.com/education+%26+language/mathematics+education/journal/10649).

18.4.2 Screening of Manuscripts

Following the technical check of submitted manuscripts, the Editor-in-Chief screens manuscripts to decide whether they should be sent out for review. I ask myself two questions when making this decision:

1. Is the manuscript within the journal's scope? That is, does it report on an "educational study in mathematics"?
2. Is the manuscript of sufficient quality to warrant sending it out for review?

When answering the first question, I think about whether the manuscript has a clear educational focus, deals in some way with mathematics, and could be regarded as a 'study'. In my view, the latter requirement permits inclusion of not only empirical studies but also theoretical and philosophical papers and critical reviews of mathematics education research literature that yield new insights with potential to advance knowledge in our field. (See recently published articles by Simon 2017, and Darragh 2016, as examples of theoretical and review studies respectively.) Manuscripts that I consider to be out of scope, and thus reject without review, typically fall into one of the following categories:

(i) The manuscript is about mathematics and not mathematics education.
(ii) The manuscript reports on a study that primarily draws on and contributes to the literature in educational psychology, with mathematics learning as the research context.
(iii) The manuscript reports on the psychometric properties of a new instrument, in the context of mathematics education but without contributing new knowledge to our field.
(iv) The manuscript reports on an evaluation of a new teaching approach or course, typically at university level in service teaching of mathematics, with limited theoretical support and inadequate data (e.g., student satisfaction surveys and examination marks).

When answering the second screening question, concerning manuscript quality, I turn to the journal's review criteria (shown in Fig. 18.2) to help me decide whether to send the manuscript out for review. If the manuscript has obvious flaws that even a major revision could not remedy, I provide the author with a brief review and submit a "reject without review" decision.

18.4.3 Reviews and Decisions

I allocate each screened manuscripts to one of ESM's editorial team, comprising myself as Editor-in-Chief and seven Associate Editors. This handling editor then acts autonomously in managing the review process and making editorial decisions. Each manuscript is sent to three reviewers, usually two from the Editorial Board and one external reviewer, who have relevant expertise in the field of research addressed by the study. Research journals are finding it increasingly difficult to secure reviewers because of the escalating volume of manuscript submissions from around the world, and the huge rate of growth in scientific publishing—estimated to result in the doubling of scientific output every nine years (Van Noorden 2014). *ESM* editors will therefore select up to six 'reserve' reviewers in case invitations to review are declined by their first choice candidates. Once reviewers accept an invitation they are given four weeks to submit their review.

As well as responding to the questions displayed in Fig. 18.2, reviewers write a comprehensive scholarly critique of manuscripts assigned to them, and make a recommendation to the handling editor regarding the suitability of the manuscript for publication in *ESM*. Once all the reviews of a manuscript have been submitted, the handling editor must weigh up the comments and recommendations against his or her own assessment of the manuscript, and select a decision from amongst the following options, to indicate that the manuscript is:

---

1. Is this article clearly an educational study in mathematics?

2. Does it make an original contribution to mathematics education?

3. Are the aims of the article made clear, and are they formulated sufficiently early in the article?

4. Are the aims of the article fulfilled?

5. If applicable, are the aims, hypotheses and methodology of the research, reported in the article, clear and reasonable?

6. Does the article provide a well founded and cogently argued analysis?

7. Do the conclusions follow from the data and/or the argument?

8. Does the article take appropriate account of previous work?

9. Is it accessible and interesting to an international readership?

Fig. 18.2 ESM review criteria

(a) acceptable for publication in its present form;
(b) acceptable for publication with minor revisions;
(c) worthy of reconsideration after major revision;
(d) not acceptable for publication but a different article based on the same research can be resubmitted;
(e) not acceptable for publication.

It is rare for a manuscript to be accepted after the first round of reviews (option a). After the initial review only 7% of manuscripts are judged to be acceptable for publication pending *minor revisions* (option b), with roughly one-third receiving a *major revision* decision (option c) and the same proportion a *revise/resubmit* decision (option d). Just under one-quarter of manuscripts sent out for review are rejected as being *unacceptable for publication* at this stage (option e). If you receive a *minor revision* decision then your revised manuscript will be assessed and further shepherded by the handling editor without further external review. A *major revision* decision indicates that your revised manuscript will undergo another round of external review. A *revise/resubmit* decision is rendered if, in the handling editor's opinion, the authors need to do some more substantial work involving either a new literature review, collection of new data, or a different analysis of the existing data. Manuscripts re-written after receiving this decision are treated as fresh submissions, with a new manuscript number, and are usually assigned to a different handling editor from the one who managed the original version.

When dealing with a manuscript that has undergone major revisions, the handling editor would normally choose the same reviewers who assessed the original manuscript—but this is not always the case. For example, if there was an unforeseen mismatch between the reviewer's and author's theoretical stances then it is not likely to be productive to send the revised manuscript to this same reviewer. Even if the handling editor does want to invite the same reviewers, this is not always possible if one or more reviewers is unavailable or too busy to accept the invitation. A decision then needs to be made as to whether to work with fewer than three of the original reviewers or to invite a fresh reviewer to assess the revised manuscript. Both alternatives have their disadvantages. An outcome to be avoided, if possible, is initiating multiple rounds of reviewing that bring a succession of new reviewers into the process, since this approach often produces conflicting advice to the author that makes it difficult for him or her to maintain the coherence of the revised manuscript. Multiple rounds of major revision, even involving the same reviewers, can also signal that the manuscript is not yet ready for publication if there is little improvement between each version. In this case it is often more productive to reject the manuscript and encourage the author to take the time to develop the work further before seeking to have it published.

18.4.4 Interpreting Editors' Decisions and Responding to Reviews

As well as indicating the review outcome (from the options listed above), the handling editor writes a letter to the author explaining the reasons for the decision. If the decision involves revision (options b, c, or d above) then the handling editor will identify the essential improvements that must be made to the manuscript and where possible refer to points made by the individual reviewers, whose full reviews are also made available to the author. A sample decision letter requesting major revisions, and edited to preserve the author's anonymity, is shown in Fig. 18.3.

When submitting your revised manuscript you will be asked to include a letter explaining how you have responded to the reviews and the editor's advice. Here it is important to explain in step-by-step fashion the changes you have made to the manuscript or the reasons why you may have decided not to take into account some recommendations. This can be done either by making a table that summarises the

---

Perhaps the most important point for revision is the need to articulate a clear research aim, which might also be elaborated via explicit research questions. Both reviewers found it difficult to identify your research goals—you mention aims or purposes in several places but these are introduced too late, and referred to in an inconsistent manner throughout the manuscript. Also, a research aim should involve more than describing or discussing something. The research aim should then link logically to your literature review, theoretical framework, and research design—in particular, it's important for readers to see that your data collection and analysis methods are capable of producing evidence to address your research questions. In the current version of the manuscript, these connections are not clear at all.

Unfolding from this advice are several other points that need attention, and are identified by the reviewers. For example, the methodology section is very brief and gives too little information on what data were collected, why, and how, and no information at all as to how the data were analysed. Both reviewers found it difficult to interpret Table 2 (as did I)—What does "xxxx" mean, and how were these numbers arrived at?

The findings do give glimpses of some very interesting outcomes of your work, but at present the study is framed mainly as a pedagogical project rather than a research project. A revised version of the manuscript will need to offer a deeper and better organized theoretical discussion of the affordances of XXXX, which then informs the analysis of your data. This is a substantial undertaking, but I hope you will rise to the challenge.

Fig. 18.3 Sample *ESM* editor's decision letter requesting major revisions

editor's and each reviewer's comments and shows your specific responses, or by copying the text of the reviews and inserting your responses to the point they make. The handling editor will find it helpful if you indicate the page and line numbers where you have made changes to the manuscript. The most unhelpful kind of response is simply to write that you have addressed all the reviewers' comments—be specific about how and where you have done so.

18.4.5 Why Manuscripts are Rejected

The most common reasons for rejecting manuscripts after one or more rounds of review are displayed in Fig. 18.4. It should be clear that they align closely with the review criteria shown in Fig. 18.2.

The most important criterion for acceptance is the requirement that the manuscript make an original and significant contribution to advancing knowledge in mathematicw education. It is surprising how often authors fail to make this contribution explicit. There are three places in the manuscript where you should consider identifying your contribution to knowledge. The first is in the Introduction section where you state the problem you are investigating and argue for its significance. The second place is in the Literature Review section, where you identify key works, their contribution to the field, and then the *gap* and *need* that your study addresses. (Just because there is a gap in the literature does not mean that it needs to be filled.) The third place to reinforce your contribution to knowledge is in the Discussion section, where you connect your findings to the literature you reviewed earlier in the manuscript.

18.4.6 Writing in English

A manuscript is never rejected solely because the English language and expression is insufficiently fluent and clear, although reviewers and editors do take these

Does not make an original andn significant contribution to advancing knowledge in mathematics education.
Not accessible to an international readership.
Lack of explicit theoretical framework.
Literature review does not take sufficient account of previous research.
Inadequate rationale for and/or description of methodology.
Analysis is inappropriate or unconvincing.
Insufficient evidence to support claims.

Fig. 18.4 Most common reasons for rejecting ESM manuscripts after review

features into account. There is no formal provision or special procedure for handling manuscripts submitted to *ESM* by authors who do not have English as their first language. However, if a manuscript presents innovative ideas and results and there is potential for making an original contribution to knowledge, but the language is not yet of the quality necessary for publication, there are several steps that can be taken, described below.

(1) When assigning manuscripts to one of *ESM*'s Associate Editors I try, where possible, to align their language expertise with the dominant language of the corresponding author. If I am the handling editor of such a manuscript I do the same when selecting reviewers.
(2) I am more willing to support several rounds of major revisions to help the author produce a publishable article, whereas only one or at most two major revisions would be the norm for other manuscripts.
(3) Along with the Associate Editors, I spend many hours on language editing of the penultimate version of each manuscript that I handle from an author who does not have English as their first or dominant language. My aim is not only to achieve an acceptable standard of academic English but also to preserve some of the distinctive linguistic features of the author's first language (lexical choices, syntactic structures, etc.). I want *ESM* readers to 'hear' the traces of the author's first language, in keeping with the journal's commitment to being genuinely international.

Around 40% of articles *published* in *ESM* come from countries where English is not the dominant language, but the proportion of *submitted* manuscripts with authors from a non-English language background is substantially higher. Some caution is needed in looking for causes of manuscript rejection in these cases—language is certainly not the only reason, nor even the main reason. Many authors struggle to frame and communicate their research so that it is relevant and accessible to an international audience, and this can be a consequence of differences in the significance of research questions across cultural contexts. Thus language diversity is part of a bigger global challenge in understanding culturally inflected ways of framing and communicating research (Bartolini Bussi and Martignone 2013; Geiger and Straesser 2015; Meaney 2013).

18.5 Special Issues

In addition to the regular publication schedule described in Sect. 18.3.3, *ESM* has published special issues almost since its inception. For example, Frendenthal dedicated several special issues to presentations given at major conferences, including the first meeting of the International Group for the Psychology of Mathematics Education. Throughout his tenure as Editor, Bishop published several special issues devoted to a single topic, with a guest editor who introduced the issue with an editorial. Dörfler formalised this feature in the editorial introducing Volume 25 as a special issue dedicated to the life and scientific work of Freudenthal, the journal's founder. According to Hanna and Sidoli (2002), "the goal of the special issues was not to offer a comprehensive overview or a systematic exposition of the state of the art, but rather to present examples of current research methods and various critical and theoretical approaches" (p. 147). Today, as in the past, guest editors seek out innovative and challenging work, including research that might not yet be well known to the international mathematics education community. The titles, guest editors, and publication dates of *ESM* special issues published since 2014 are shown in Table 18.1.

There is now a formal procedure for prospective guest editors to propose a special issue of *ESM*. Proposals for special issues may be emailed to the Editor-in-Chief at any time, but no more than one special issue will be published in each Volume of the journal. Special issues will normally have two or three guest editors, with an editorial that introduces the topic and the papers, and a concluding commentary on the papers written by an expert on the chosen topic. The length of a special issue should be about the same as a regular issue of *ESM*—between 120 and 140 pages, comprising six to eight papers.

Special issue proposals should include the following:

1. A title for the special issue that clearly and succinctly conveys its focus.
2. The names, affiliations, and email addresses of the guest editors.
3. Evidence of the guest editors' previous editorial experience and familiarity with the scope and standards of *ESM* (e.g., journal editing, membership of editorial boards, relevant publications).
4. A convincing rationale for the special issue.

Table 18.1 *ESM* special issues published since 2014

Volume and date	Title	Guest editors
Volume 85(3) March 2014	Representing mathematics with digital media: Working across theoretical and contextual boundaries	Jean-Baptiste Lagrange and Chronis Kynigos
Volume 86(2) June 2014	Characterising and developing vocational mathematical knowledge	Arthur Bakker and Gail FitzSimons
Volume 87(2) October 2014	Social theory and research in mathematics education	Candia Morgan and Clive Kanes
Volume 88(3) March 2015	Statistical reasoning: Learning to reason from samples	Dani Ben-Zvi, Arthur Bakker, and Katie Makar
Volume 91(3) March 2016	Communicational perspectives on learning and teaching mathematics	Michal Tabach and Talli Nachlieli
Volume 92(3) July 2016	Mathematics education and contemporary theory	Tony Brown, Yvette Solomon, and Julian Williams
Volume 96(2) October 2017	Research-based interventions in the area of proof	Gabriel Stylianides and Andreas Stylianides

5. A description of, and justification for, the approach to be taken for soliciting manuscripts. This may take the form of a list of abstracts and authors for invited contributions, an open call for extended abstracts from which prospective contributions would be selected, or some other approach that would arguably deliver a high quality set of manuscripts. Whatever approach is taken, the guest editors should make it clear that submission of a manuscript does not guarantee its publication in the special issue.
6. A timeline for publication that includes:
   - a date for submission of extended abstracts, if an open call is made;
   - a date for acceptance or rejection of extended abstracts, if an open call is made;
   - a date for submission of first drafts of manuscripts to the guest editors;
   - a date for completion of an internal review process (about 2 months later);
   - a date for revisions to be submitted for the *ESM* reviewing process (about 6 weeks later);
   - a date for completion of reviewing and acceptance or rejection decisions (about 6 months later);
   - a possible publication date.

Special issue proposals are reviewed by the *ESM* Advisory Editors, comprising all the past Editors-in-Chief, with comments also invited from the Associate Editors. Guest editors may be asked to revise proposals based on this feedback. When a special issue proposal is accepted, one of the *ESM* editors is assigned as a shadow editor to advise the guest editors on journal editorial procedures and standards.

18.6 A Final Word

A journal is much more than a collection of articles. It reflects the development of new ideas, interests, and theories in the field it serves, and provides a vehicle for dissemination and debate within a research community over time. When you submit a manuscript to *ESM*, you are seeking to join this international community and contribute to its debates, history, and knowledge building activities. For an early career researcher in mathematics education, this is surely an exciting prospect!

References

Bartolini Bussi, M., & Martignone, F. (2013). Cultural issues in the communication of research on mathematics education. *For the Learning of Mathematics, 33*(1), 2–7.

Darragh, L. (2016). Identity research in mathematics education. *Educational Studies in Mathematics, 93,* 19–33.

Geiger, V., & Straesser, R. (2015). The challenge of publication for English non-dominant-language authors in mathematics education. *For the Learning of Mathematics, 35*(3), 35–41.

Hanna, G., & Sidoli, N. (2002). The story of ESM. *Educational Studies in Mathematics, 50,* 123–156.

Meaney, T. (2013). The privileging of English in mathematics education research, just a necessary evil? In M. Berger, K. Brodie, V. Frith, & K. le Roux (Eds.), *Proceedings of the Seventh International Mathematics Education and Society Conference* (Vol. 1, pp. 65–84). Cape Town: MES.

Nivens, R., & Otten, S. (2017). Assessing journal quality in mathematics education. *Journal for Research in Mathematics Education, 48,* 348–368.

Simon, M. (2017). Explicating mathematical concept and mathematical conception as theoretical constructs for mathematics education research. *Educational Studies in Mathematics, 94,* 117–137.

Van Noorden, R. (2014). Global scientific output doubles every nine years. Retrieved September 6, 2018, from http://blogs.nature.com/news/2014/05/global-scientific-output-doubles-every-nine-years.html.

Williams, S., & Leatham, K. (2017). Journal quality in mathematics education. *Journal for Research in Mathematics Education, 48,* 369–396.

Open Access This chapter is licensed under the terms of the Creative Commons Attribution 4.0 International License (http://creativecommons.org/licenses/by/4.0/), which permits use, sharing, adaptation, distribution and reproduction in any medium or format, as long as you give appropriate credit to the original author(s) and the source, provide a link to the Creative Commons license and indicate if changes were made.

The images or other third party material in this chapter are included in the chapter's Creative Commons license, unless indicated otherwise in a credit line to the material. If material is not included in the chapter's Creative Commons license and your intended use is not permitted by statutory regulation or exceeds the permitted use, you will need to obtain permission directly from the copyright holder.

Chapter 19
For the Learning of Mathematics: An Introduction to the Journal and the Writing Within It

Richard Barwell and David A. Reid

Abstract This chapter provides an overview of the journal *For the Learning of Mathematics* (FLM) from the point of view of its current editor and his immediate predecessor. It begins with a brief description of the nature of genres, especially in academic writing and more specifically in mathematics education. The aims of the journal and how these are situated in its history are described. The particular genres of writing in FLM are then illustrated with examples. The technicalities of submitting articles to FLM are outlined.

Keywords For the Learning of Mathematics · Genre · Academic writing · Mathematics education journals

19.1 Introduction

What is distinctive about the journal *For the Learning of Mathematics* (FLM)? As editors of the journal (past and present), we both believe the writing in FLM to be distinctive, in the sense of having unique style and purpose amongst journals in our field, but how so? And why? In this overview of FLM, we take a genre perspective, with which we first discuss academic publishing in mathematics education in general, and then discuss the particular nature of FLM. We write as current editor (DAR) and previous editor (RB), and we have both been associated with FLM for many years as board members, reviewers and associate editors, prior to our editorial terms.

In research on academic writing and academic literacy, the concept of genre is widely used to examine and understand differences in the organisation, style and

---

R. Barwell
University of Ottawa, Ottawa, Canada
e-mail: richard.barwell@uottawa.ca

D. A. Reid (✉)
University of Bremen, Bremen, Germany
e-mail: dreid@uni-bremen.de

purpose of different kinds of text (see, for example, Swales 1990). This notion is therefore a useful way to understand similarities and differences in the kinds of writing that appear in academic journals in mathematics education. We begin with a brief description of the nature of genres, especially in academic writing and more specifically in mathematics education. We then describe the aims of FLM, and situate these aims in its history. Turning to examples of articles published in FLM over the years, we discuss some of the genres of writing found in FLM and qualities that make articles appropriate for the journal. Finally, we outline the technicalities of submitting articles to FLM.

19.2 Genre

In linguistics the term genre refers, roughly, to recognizable textual forms or structures. Everyday examples of textual genres include recipes, instruction manuals, crosswords, or food labels. There are many perspectives on genre and many approaches to genre analysis, ranging from formalist perspectives, in which genres are defined entirely by their structural features, to social perspectives that understand genres as culturally situated activities. As a starting point for this chapter, we recognize that genres have both recognizable textual features and communicative functions. For example, recipes generally include a sequence of often numbered instructions (a textual feature) and are designed to guide readers through a process to produce some kind of dish, such as a cake.

Swales (e.g., 1990) has conducted significant research on genres of academic text. His treatment of genre develops our basic definition. We summarise some key ideas, and illustrate them with reference to the common mathematics classroom genre of word problems, since this genre is familiar to all mathematics educators. We then apply these ideas to academic journal writing.

Swales underlines the relationship between genres and what he calls discourse communities. That is, genres are *recognizable* to groups of people who interact around some common activity or purpose (see Swales 1990, p. 58). A word problem is instantly recognizable to any mathematics teacher, as well as to their students. Word problems have a common structure (Gerofsky 1996), and a particular purpose: to rehearse the application of some previously taught aspect of school mathematics to a situation described in the problem. Both the structure and the purpose are recognizable to people who work regularly with word problems.

The recognizable nature of genres within a discourse community is linked to a broader cultural function of genres: they are a link between past and present (Swales 1990, p. 45). Genres are 'handed down' from one generation to the next, providing stability within cultures over time and, thus, contributing to the maintenance of cultures. Word problems, for example, have existed for thousands of years and their persistence contributes to the maintenance of some aspects of the culture of mathematics teaching down the ages.

Finally, in this cultural function, genres embody ideological perspectives (Bakhtin 1986; Hanks 1987). Word problems, for example, are not only a method for organizing the application of mathematical techniques; they represent a particular set of assumptions about what it means to do and learn mathematics, assumptions about the situations depicted in the word problem, and assumptions about the students doing the word problem (Barwell 2018).

Applying these ideas to academic journals in mathematics education, we can quickly identify some common genres of text:

- Empirical research report
- Theoretical paper
- Book review
- Response or reaction to a previously published article
- Editorial

Many journals in mathematics education do not publish much outside this set of genres. The features of these genres can be deduced from examining multiple examples (see Table 19.1 for a summary). An empirical research report, for example, commonly includes the following:

- an introduction stating the problem
- a review of relevant literature
- a theoretical framework
- an account of research design and methods of data collection and analysis
- results
- discussion and conclusions
- references

Table 19.1 Summary of common components and functions of widely used genres of text appearing in mathematics education journals

Genre	Common principal structural components	Function
Empirical research report	Literature review, theoretical framework, research design and methods, results, discussion and conclusions	To report results of research
Theoretical paper	Review of theoretical literature, presentation of new theoretical proposition, illustration of theoretical proposition	To propose new theories or theoretical developments
Book review	Summary of a book, discussion of merits and contribution of book	To discuss new book-length contributions to the field
Response or reaction to a previously published article	Summary of selected points from previously published article, discussion or critique of these points	To contribute to academic debate
Editorial	Comments on a specific topic of relevance to readers	To orient readers to topics of interest in the journal

These components have important functions. Indeed, a key part of academic socialization in mathematics education is about using and understanding these components (the structure is similar for other texts, including doctoral theses or PME papers). The structure serves to organize the various components of a research report in a way that, to a well-socialized member of the academic community of mathematics education, is recognizable and hence easy to navigate, interpret and, significantly, evaluate. While there has been evolution over time, these basic features are well established and can be seen in papers published in the last 40 years. These genres of academic writing therefore pass on and maintain a particular culture of academic writing—a culture that is, by the way, relatively specific to mathematics education. Research reports in journals of chemistry, mathematics, or even applied linguistics all look a bit different from research reports in mathematics education journals. Moreover, these genres embed various ideological commitments, such as the assumption that the learning and teaching of mathematics can be understood through work that can be presented in the generic form of a research report. This assumption entails various deeper beliefs about learning and teaching mathematics as amenable to some kind of scientific, empirical process. Such texts also construct readers in a particular way—as being, for example, familiar with theory and research methodology, and the often complex technical language that might go with them.

Later in this chapter, we discuss the distinctive nature of article genres published in FLM. First, though, we need to provide some context.

19.3 Historical Context

In 1968 Hans Freudenthal launched a new journal, *Educational Studies in Mathematics* (ESM), devoted to research in mathematics education. He did so over objections from the secretary of the International Mathematics Union, who wondered if "there is a market for two international journals of that kind" (Furinghetti and Giacardi 2010, p. 33). The only other international journal in the field at that time was *L'Enseignement Mathématique*, first published in 1899, and the official organ of ICMI since ICMI's foundation (as the International Commission on the Teaching of Mathematics) in 1908. The field of mathematics education was clearly ready to support more journals, as ESM was joined in 1969 by *Zentralblatt für Didaktik der Mathematik* (ZDM), founded by Hans Georg Steiner and Heinz Kunle, and in 1970 by the NCTM's *The Journal for Research in Mathematics Education* (JRME). About a decade later Robert Davis's *Journal of Children's Mathematical Behavior* (JMB) joined the field, and shortly thereafter (in 1980) the first issue of *Recherches en didactique des mathématiques* (RDM) appeared. This was the context in which David Wheeler founded FLM, hoping that it would be different from the existing offerings. In the first issue in July 1980, he wrote as follows:

> My hope that this journal may grow into one that learns along with its writers and its readers is my justification for introducing a new journal into a crowded field. "Print, print, and still more print. Who needs it?", as several people have said to me, using other words. The dangers are worth risking, I think. A new journal makes no demands by itself: only people do that, on themselves or on others. And although life, including the life of classrooms, will no doubt go on much the same with or without *For the Learning of Mathematics*, well-chosen words *can* trigger awarenesses and stimulate reflections and give experience to those sensitive to them. If any who are reading this sigh at the prospect of yet more to read, I'd say they have missed the point. I want to do something to serve the interests of those who have to learn mathematics. I hope some who share that desire may find *For the Learning of Mathematics* a journal which it is in their own interest to read. (1980a, p. 2)

The title David Wheeler chose for his new journal reflected his desire to "do something to serve the interests of those who have to learn mathematics." In his editorial in the third issue of FLM he discussed the meaning of the title:

> Being "for" the learning of mathematics in the sense of this journal's title means more than generalised approval. It means making an important issue out of the learning of mathematics, not taking it for granted, not remaining content with being ignorant about it. It means being aware and becoming aware of difficulties to study and to resolve. It means putting into circulation ideas and techniques that will eventually benefit those who want to learn mathematics. (1981, p. 2)

FLM is a journal *for* the learning, and the learners, of mathematics, rather than being *of* behavior or *for* didactics, research or teaching. The title echoes that of Gattegno's (1963) collection of articles, *For the Teaching of Mathematics* but with a very intentional shift in focus, from teaching and teachers to learning and learners. While most journals in mathematics education include the learning of mathematics as part of their scope (as an aspect of their focus on didactics, research or teaching), the title of FLM indicates a particular concern, not just with learning as a general category, but with the individual experience of learning mathematics.

19.4 Aims of FLM

The aims of FLM are stated on the inside front cover of each issue, and they have remained unchanged since the first issue appeared:

> The journal aims to stimulate reflection on mathematics education at all levels, and promote study of its practices and its theories: to generate productive discussion; to encourage enquiry and research; to promote criticism and evaluation of ideas and procedures current in the field. It is intended for the mathematics educator who is aware that the learning and teaching of mathematics are complex enterprises about which much remains to be revealed and understood.

A few keywords stand out (at least in the minds of the editors): "stimulate reflection", "productive discussion", "encourage enquiry", "promote criticism". All of these suggest an opening out, rather than a drawing together of the discourse.

What is sought are not answers, but new questions. There is more focus on what "remains to be revealed and understood" than on what is known and established.

Given these aims, the empirical research report is not a genre of writing that is often found in FLM. Research reports are often focused on reporting results, and unless those results are surprising enough to stimulate further reflection and inquiry, a research report is unlikely to fit the aims of FLM. Even a research report that does stimulate discussion might stimulate the same discussion more effectively if written in another way.

The aims of FLM were chosen by David Wheeler, and subsequent editors have been strongly guided by them. To understand FLM it is useful to return to David Wheeler's thinking about the journal, as reflected in his editorials in its first issues. In issue 1(1) David Wheeler wrote:

> An editor may want to ease into existence a journal with certain concerns, a certain style or tone, a certain level of discourse. (The inside front and back covers of this issue tell you something about what this editor has in mind. The contents of the issue tell you some more). (1980a, p. 2)

Over the years the "style and tone" of FLM, reflected already in its first issue, have been maintained, even as they have evolved. They reflect, perhaps, an FLM style of academic writing, which we hope in this article to describe.

As noted above, the inside front cover states the aims of the journal. The inside back cover offers "Suggestions to Writers" including a definition of "mathematics education":

> "Mathematics education" should be interpreted to mean the whole field of human ideas and activities that affect, or could affect, the learning of mathematics. Articles about mathematics or about psychology, for example, are welcomed provided their content bears on the learning of mathematics: directly, or indirectly through offering a significant perspective to teachers of mathematics. The journal has space for articles which attempt to bring together ideas from several sources and show their relation to the theories or practices of mathematics education. It is a place where ideas may be tried out and presented for discussion.

This paragraph has evolved somewhat over the years, but its key point, that FLM, as an international journal of mathematics education, is open not only to articles that mathematics educators write, but also to articles that mathematics educators might want to read. The contents of that first issue reflect this idea, since it includes a graphic and commentary by the artist Josef Albers, reprinted from *Despite Straight Lines* (Bucher, 1977) a posthumous analysis of Albers' graphic constructions. Presumably this was selected by David Wheeler as an example of the kind of thing he wanted FLM to include. The next two issues include mathematical poems from the anthology *Against Infinity* (Robson and Wimp 1980), as well as an essay by Dick Tahta (1981) discussing the relation between mathematics and poetry, inspired by the anthology. Of course, there are also articles by mathematics educators about geometry, multiplication tables, word problems, and so on.

FLM aims to "generate productive discussion" and one sign of this is the inclusion of articles and communications that continue a discussion begun in a previous article. This genre of writing was encouraged by David Wheeler from the beginning. He wrote in the second issue:

> I would like to see perhaps one fourth of the pages of each issue given over to correspondence and comments arising out of the articles that appear in the journal. Whether that measure of open discussion is achievable, I don't know. I cannot think of any journal which manages so much, but perhaps the others haven't tried. (1980b, p. 2)

It is rare that FLM manages to fill a fourth of its pages with such contributions, but it has happened. And perhaps more importantly, FLM is still trying. This means that the genre of comment finds a place in its pages. Comments need not only be inspired by articles that appear in the journal. FLM does not publish book reviews,[1] but it does publish articles that are inspired by reading a particular book (like Dick Tahta's essay mentioned above).

19.5 Genres of FLM Articles

We have already mentioned commentaries on prior publications and poems as genres published in FLM. These are not the genres most often represented in its pages, however. Most FLM articles could be called essays, but other important genres include narratives and dialogues.

19.5.1 Essay

The word 'essay' comes from 'essayer' and an essay is a trying or testing of an idea. It can take many forms, but importantly, it should be *about something*. This can be a critical take on a common assumption, a reinterpretation of a well-known phenomenon, a questioning of theoretical assumptions, interrogation of a surprising event, reflection on the nature of learning, or many other topics. Whatever it is about, that idea should be tested, argued, questioned and interpreted in multiple ways. It should be put on trial.

In *Reification as the birth of metaphor*, in issue **14**(1), Anna Sfard (1994) puts the concept of 'understanding' on trial. She begins with an interesting quote, states the topic of her essay in one sentence, and then relates a brief anecdote that sets the stage. She clearly says what she plans to do:

> I soon discovered that, as far as the issue of understanding is concerned, current developments in the psychology of mathematics go hand-in-hand with some of the most significant recent advances in linguistics and in philosophy. [...] In this paper I will show how the idea of reification—the basic notion of the conceptual framework on which I have been working for quite a long time now—combines with the new general theories of

---

[1] Almost every rule of FLM has an exception. The exception to this rule appeared in issue **5**(1).

understanding. I hope to make it clear that the theory of reification is perfectly in tune with the latest philosophical and linguistic developments. (p. 44)

She spends some pages describing "the latest philosophical and linguistic developments", which is fine as we know how this will be relevant. She brings in some empirical results, but always in the service of her quest to explore 'understanding'. The quotes from the mathematicians she interviewed illustrate and elaborate the points she is making and are connected to the theory she has already introduced and other concepts as they become relevant. In the last page and a half she brings it together, showing, and illustrating with her data, how the theory of reification connects with the embodied metaphors of Lakoff and Johnson.

19.5.2 Narrative

A narrative tells a story. It should have a beginning, middle and end, and characters we care about. And like an essay it should be *about something*. David Reid's favourite example of this genre is *Norman*, by Jennifer MacPherson (1987), in issue 7(2).

It says right away what it is about: "the conceptual gulf that may exist between cultures [...] which may allow a teacher to [...] pursue goals that are conceptually incompatible with those of her students" (p. 24). That is a topic that should interest us all. And then the story starts. The stage is set. The context is described in no more detail than we need.

The writing is engaging. More academic articles should have a paragraph, on the first page, that begins "The guinea pigs did not flourish". In the next paragraph we meet the main character, Norman. He is building a sled out of Lego. Then the story takes a surprising turn, and the writing becomes more detailed, giving us the 'data' we will need for the later 'analysis'.

The narrative part of the essay is now over, and the discussion continues, ranging over topics such as language, gender, the relationships between humans and non-human animals, mathematical competencies, cultural relevance, and the goals of education. All this in less than 2500 words, without any (explicit) references.

19.5.3 Dialogue

The closing article in the FLM special issue on ethnomathematics[2] by Marcia Ascher and Ubiratan D'Ambrosio (1994) is a dialogue. In this case they worked from a recording of an actual conversation, but dialogues can also be constructed from exchanges of emails, for example, or out of whole cloth. The aim remains, however to reflect the thinking of two (or more) distinct individuals on an issue or

---

[2]FLM does not publish special issues. This is one of the exceptions.

topic. Dialogues have a deceptively simple structure: two or more authors have named turns, so that each writes in their own voice and with their own ideas. Unlike other forms of co-authorship, in dialogues different points of view are explicitly set against each other and explored, often without coming to any concluding consensus. This genre has appeared through FLM's history, starting with the first issue, in which the founding editor, David Wheeler, discusses the film "The Foundations of Geometry" with its creator, Caleb Gattegno (Gattegno and Wheeler 1980).

19.5.4 Comment

We have already referred to Wheeler's desire that the pages of FLM should include comments on previously published articles and such comments have regularly appeared, usually in a section of shorter pieces collectively labelled "Communications". Comments are a bit like the letters to the editor that appear in newspapers: the main requirement for a comment is that it is prompted by a previously (and usually recently) published article, which is mentioned in the first line. Comments may offer critique, or seek to extend or refute the ideas in the original article. Or not—comments may simply report interesting reflections prompted by the original article, but that may be considered tangential to its original theme.

19.5.5 Other

Taxonomists in biology know that it is vital not only to characterize the prototype of a species, but also to explore its variations, to map out the extent to which members of a species can look and behave differently but still interact is ways that marks them as parts of a whole. The genres of essay, narrative and dialogue are prototypical genres of FLM articles, but FLM articles can take on many forms while still being part of the FLM 'conversation'. For example, issue **34**(1) includes what could be called a 'graphic article' akin to graphic novels in which drawings are used to tell a story. Issue **37**(3) includes a work of fiction, a short story relating a mathematical exploration, while an article in issue **29**(2) includes a fictional Socratic dialogue featuring Xanthippe, the wife of Socrates, and a slave girl named Menousa, that the authors wrote, by their own admission, "for fun" (Mason and Watson 2009). We leave it to readers to explore the pages of FLM to identify the many other minor and sometimes quirky genres.

19.5.6 Some Comments on These Genres

The genres we have described make FLM what it is and reflect its aims and values. While each of the genres is distinctive, there are some commonalities. They are rather looser than some commonly used genres in mathematics education journals. While there is structure, authors have quite a bit of scope to shape the writing (although within strict word limits). Another common feature, often implicit, is the place of authors' voices. Dialogues explicitly feature the voices of the authors, as do comments, but voice is also a feature of the main essay-form articles. The engaging opening of FLM articles is also a way to give the sense of a writing author, using first-person verb forms: "I argue" rather than "It is argued". The presence of authors' voices is related to the what might be called the *ideology*, or perhaps better the *ethos* of FLM, as reflected in the nature of the genres of article it includes, and which make it the distinctive journal that it is. FLM can be understood in terms of conversation: articles speak to each other and contribute to longer conversations that have developed in the pages of the journal over the years. Why 'conversation'? Because conversation reflects the view that that academic thinking is a collective activity, that ideas arise in response to other ideas, and that learning mathematics is a "complex enterprise" about which it is difficult to say anything with any finality. As Lesley Lee (2014) wrote in issue **34**(1): "The conversation is not for those who feel they have all the answers but for those who are searching and willing to contribute their understandings and questions to the ongoing inquiry" (p. 6). Conversations do not end; there is always more to be said.

This spirit of conversational enquiry is embodied in the genres of FLM, and perhaps stands in contrast to some of the genres that do not appear in its pages. Research reports, for example, are designed to, well, report: they provide a self-contained account of a piece of research and, as such, do not invite a response. Of course, many journals sometimes include responses to research reports, and we don't claim that FLM has a monopoly on conversational style. But we do claim that FLM is a rare example of a mathematics education journal that is organized around an ethos of conversation.

For the rest of this chapter, we provide some information about the submission and review process.

19.6 The Submission Process

FLM does not use any management software to handle the submission process. Submissions are sent electronically to editor@flm-journal.org, or, if that is impossible, printed submissions can be sent by post (email the editor for the address). There are no formatting requirements for initial submissions. Articles should generally be within the range of 2500–5000 words. Longer articles are rarely accepted, and are then published in two or more parts. Short communications (for example, comments on already-published articles) should generally contain fewer than 2000 words.

Contributions may be submitted in English or French. The English may be US, British, or some other self-consistent variant. FLM is an international journal and welcomes submissions from all parts of the world. The editors recognize that the languages of publication give an advantage to authors who are native speakers of French and English. Encouragement and support is given to authors who are not writing in their first language.

Authors are strongly advised to read the "Suggestions to Writers" found on the inside back cover of each issue, and on the website flm-journal.org. The last line of these suggestions reads "Current house style may be inferred from the articles in **38** (1) and later issues." This should be taken as an invitation to become familiar with recent articles, but there is no expectation that initial submissions conform perfectly to our house style. Accepted manuscripts are carefully edited by the editor prior to publication.

If submissions are submitted blind, then they are reviewed blind; otherwise reviewers know the identities of authors. In other words, authors may choose to have a blind review or not, according to what they submit. Similarly, reviewers may choose to identify themselves in their reviews, and if they do not then blind reviews are sent to authors.

For the Learning of Mathematics is edited by the Editor and two Associate Editors, supported by an Advisory Board of about two dozen mathematics educators, all of whom have previously published in FLM. The first stage of our review process is an internal reading by the editors and members of the Advisory Board. This first stage is usually quick and is intended to sort out submissions that are not well suited to FLM from those that are. Many submissions are rejected at this first stage, usually because they are research reports, teaching activities, or mathematical results that are better published elsewhere. If an issue, problem or observation in such a submission could form the focus of an essay or narrative, authors are may be encouraged to submit a new piece of writing in a more suitable genre. Suitable submissions may receive feedback as to revisions that should be done prior to external review, to allow that review to be more productive. Suitable submissions are sent to two or more external reviewers, who are experts in the field, and familiar with the journal, its style and aims. It is normal that the external review leads to several cycles of revisions before manuscripts can be published, although an indication of provisional acceptance is often made early in this process.

The review process requires at least two months and usually rather longer. Shorter communications may be handled more quickly. FLM is published three times a year, in March, July and November, and the process of editing, typesetting and printing each issue takes about four months, so articles accepted in March appear in July.

19.7 Some Advice

A feature of the different genres of articles that appear in FLM is that they often have engaging openings. Most readers are reading out of interest, not obligation, and so it is important that the beginning of an article be interesting. This is especially important because a common strategy for deciding if an article is worth reading, reading the abstract, involves a trip to the web site, as the abstracts of articles appear only there. Instead, the title of an FLM article and the first few paragraphs must engage the reader's attention.

There are almost as many ways to engage the reader as there are FLM articles. Some start with a provocative quote. Some start with an interesting bit of transcript or a narrative of something interesting that happened in a classroom. Some start by asking a question. We encourage you to pick an issue at random and to look through it for an article that piques your interest, on a topic that is not a research focus of yours. Look at the beginning. How did the authors engage your attention?

Once readers are interested, their interest has to be maintained. Not every paragraph has to be as fascinating as the first one, but it is important not to try the readers' patience too much. One thing to avoid is 'academic throat clearing'.[3] This is the listing of other researchers who consider your topic worth discussing, definitions of terms you will later use a few times, and so on. For some reason, academic writing often includes such material towards the beginning, before finally getting to the point some paragraphs (or pages) later. One feedback we often give authors is along the lines of 'delete everything on pages 2–5'. As with giving a speech, do your throat clearing in private, and then start talking when you are ready.

For the reader, it is helpful to know what an article is about quite quickly and without making much of an effort. It is tempting to spring a surprise, to bring something unexpected in at the end, but the danger is that no one reads to the end, and so no one is surprised. As editors, we read many articles out of obligation, not out of interest, so we stick it out to the end, and sometimes find ourselves pleasantly surprised. If that happens then the advice is always to at least hint strongly at the surprise early on.

So, we've said something about the kind of writing that appears in FLM. If you have questions, we urge you to read the journal: back issues are available without subscription at flm-journal.org. If you have an idea for a contribution, you can contact the editor to discuss it at editor@flm-journal.org.

To conclude, we return to the words of the founding editor. In an editorial in the last issue he edited, **17**(2) David Wheeler (1997) expressed his gratitude to:

> authors with something germane, intriguing, and substantive to say—something that provokes thought and brings a fresh point of view—and who write in ways that take account of their readers, speaking plainly and putting their cards on the table. (p. 2)

This sums up our advice to prospective authors: have something thought provoking to say, and say it as clearly as you can.

---

[3]This phrase has been used by FLM editors for some time. We learned it from Laurinda Brown who learned it from Dick Tahta. We assume David Wheeler was familiar with the concept, and probably also with the phrase, which pops up from time to time in critiques of academic writing.

References

Ascher, M., & D'Ambrosio, U. (1994). Ethnomathematics: A dialogue. *For the Learning of Mathematics, 14*(2), 36–43.
Bakhtin, M. M. (1986). *Speech genres and other late essays* (C. Emerson & M. Holquist, Eds., W. McGee, Trans.). Austin, TX: University of Texas Press.
Barwell, R. (2018). Word problems as social texts. In K. Yasakuwa, A. Rogers, K. Jackson, & B. V. Street (Eds.), *Numeracy as social practice: Global and local perspectives* (pp. 101–120). Abingdon, UK: Routledge.
Bucher, F. (1977). *Josef Albers: Despite straight lines: An analysis of his graphic constructions*. Cambridge, MA: MIT Press.
Furinghetti, F., & Giacardi, L. (2010). People, events, and documents of ICMI's first century. *Actes d'Història de la Ciència i de la Tècnica, Nova Època, 3*(2), 11–50.
Gattegno, C. (1963). *For the teaching of mathematics* (Vol. 1). Reading, UK: Education Explorers.
Gattegno, C., & Wheeler, D. (1980). The foundations of geometry. *For the Learning of Mathematics, 1*(1), 10–16.
Gerofsky, S. (1996). A linguistic and narrative view of word problems in mathematics education. *For the Learning of Mathematics, 16*(2), 36–45.
Hanks, W. F. (1987). Discourse genres in a theory of practice. *American Ethnologist, 14*(4), 668–692.
Lee, L. (2014). The FLM conversation. *For the Learning of Mathematics, 34*(1), 6–7.
Macpherson, J. (1987). Norman. *For the Learning of Mathematics, 7*(2), 24–26.
Mason, J., & Watson, A. (2009). The Menousa. *For the Learning of Mathematics, 29*(2), 33–38.
Robson, E., & Wimp, J. (1980). *Against infinity: An anthology of contemporary mathematical poetry*. Parker Ford, PA: Primary Press.
Sfard, A. (1994). Reification as the birth of metaphor. *For the Learning of Mathematics, 14*(1), 44–55.
Swales, J. M. (1990). *Genre analysis: English in academic and research settings*. Cambridge, UK: Cambridge University Press.
Tahta, D. (1981). On poetry and mathematics. *For the Learning of Mathematics, 1*(3), 43–47.
Wheeler, D. (1980a). Editorial. *For the Learning of Mathematics, 1*(1), 2.
Wheeler, D. (1980b). Editorial. *For the Learning of Mathematics, 1*(2), 2.
Wheeler, D. (1981). Editorial. *For the Learning of Mathematics, 1*(3), 2.
Wheeler, D. (1997). Editorial. *For the Learning of Mathematics, 17*(2), 2.

Open Access This chapter is licensed under the terms of the Creative Commons Attribution 4.0 International License (http://creativecommons.org/licenses/by/4.0/), which permits use, sharing, adaptation, distribution and reproduction in any medium or format, as long as you give appropriate credit to the original author(s) and the source, provide a link to the Creative Commons license and indicate if changes were made.

The images or other third party material in this chapter are included in the chapter's Creative Commons license, unless indicated otherwise in a credit line to the material. If material is not included in the chapter's Creative Commons license and your intended use is not permitted by statutory regulation or exceeds the permitted use, you will need to obtain permission directly from the copyright holder.

Chapter 20
The International Journal of Science and Mathematics Education: A Beginner's Guide to Writing for Publication

Peter Liljedahl

Abstract Three hundred manuscripts on mathematics education are submitted for review to the International Journal of Science and Mathematics Education (IJSME) every year. The vast majority of these are rejected. In many cases, manuscripts that are being rejected are based on good research on interesting topics, but are being rejected because the author has failed to articulate his or her work in ways that reviewers and editors find appealing. This chapter looks closely at what constitutes a good paper and offers guidance for early researchers on how to write for publication in IJSME.

Keywords Mathematics education · IJSME · Good writing · Publication

20.1 Introduction

Since 2015 IJSME has received well over 1000 submissions from authors in the field of mathematics education. The vast majority of these are rejected, with most years IJSME having rejection rates upwards of 80%. Although there are many reasons why a manuscript may be rejected, the three most common are poor research, uninteresting results, and poor writing. Poor research refers to manuscripts reporting on results that were gathered through a methodology that either does not look deeply enough into a phenomenon of interest, is missing a theoretical framework to analyze the data, uses an inappropriate or ineffective theoretical framework, ignores prior work on the topic, or is unethical or disrespectful of its participants. If the manuscript is constructed on a foundation of rich data and the issue was only theoretical in nature, then a new manuscript involving complete re-analysis may be possible. Otherwise, very little can be done to salvage poor research into publishable content.

P. Liljedahl (✉)
Simon Fraser University, Burnaby, Canada
e-mail: liljedahl@sfu.ca

Manuscripts that are deemed to be uninteresting tend to either answer questions that are uninteresting to the field or produce results that are redundant with research already published in the field. The first of these, uninteresting questions, are most often the result of too much specificity. Redundant research results can either be the result of looking at a known phenomenon from a slightly different perspective or using an existing research method in a slightly different context. This is not to say that such research should not be done, but rather that if all that is accomplished from doing such research is to confirm prior results then not much has been added to the knowledge of the field. Such research is rarely salvageable as it is most likely built on a data set that does not have the depth or breadth to produce more interesting results.

The third reason why manuscripts are rejected is where, in my opinion, the real tragedy lies. These are manuscripts that result from solid methodologies designed on interesting research questions and built on a foundation of rich data. What is preventing these manuscripts from being published is poor writing. In this chapter I look closely at this phenomenon and offer some basic tips for beginning researchers to think about how to write up their research for publication.

20.2 About IJSME

The International Journal of Science and Mathematics Education (IJSME) was founded in 2003 by Taiwan's Ministry of Science and Technology with the mandate to provide a venue for authors from non-English speaking countries to publish peer reviewed articles on a variety of topics in both science and mathematics education. This mandate is being realized with submissions from 60 different countries in the last four years (see Fig. 20.1) and publications from 46 countries in that same time period (see Fig. 20.2).

The founding editor-in-chief of the journal was Fou-Lai Lin from the National Taiwan Normal University. The current editor-in-chief is Huann-shyang Lin, National Sun Yat-sen University, Taiwan. In 2011 IJSME sought, and was granted, admission to the Social Science Citation Impact Factor. Since then, IJSME has seen a rapid growth in the number of submissions to the journal (see Fig. 20.3) and along with it, a growth in the rejection rate (see Fig. 20.4). Despite the increase in rejection rate of IJSME, the rapid increase in the number of submissions has required an increase in the absolute number of papers being accepted each year, and as a result a need to publish more articles per year.

Since entering the Thompson Reuters Index in 2011 IJSME has seen an overall increase in its impact factor year over year (see Fig. 20.5). The exception to this being 2017 where the increase in the number of articles published lowered the impact factor. Along with the increase in impact factor IJSME has enjoyed a rapid growth in the number of article downloads per year with 2018 projecting 140,000 downloads (see Fig. 20.6).

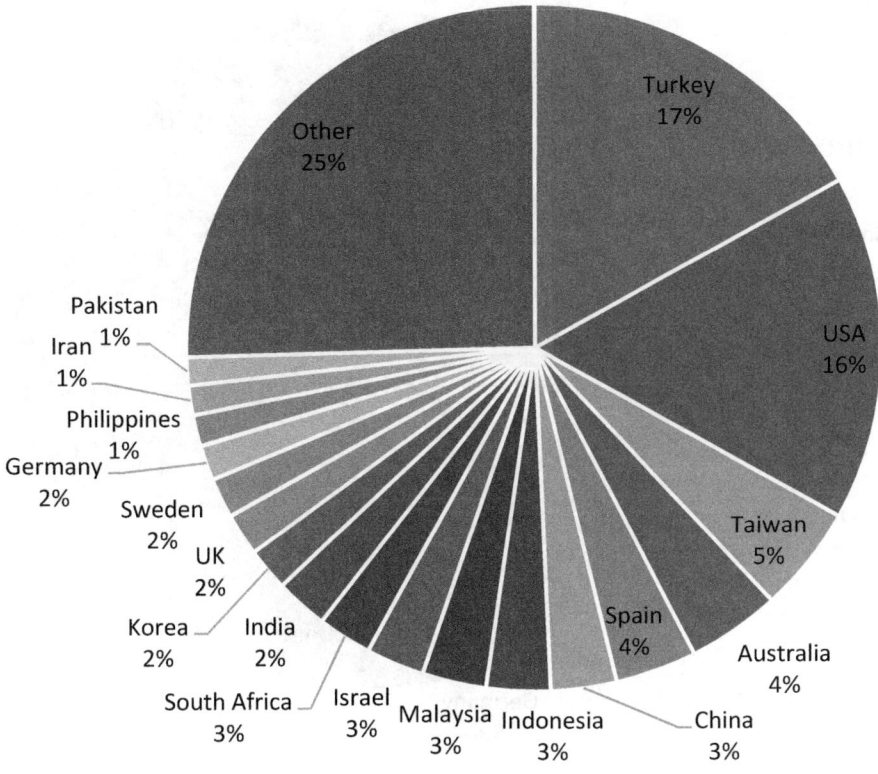

Fig. 20.1 Submissions by country since 2015 (n = 2194)

In addition to publishing eight regular issues a year, IJSME has also published a special issue each year since 2010 (except 2012), on the following topics:

2017: STEM for the Future and the Future of STEM
2016: Metacognition for Science and Mathematics Learning in Technology-Infused Learning Environments
2015: Video-Based Research on Teacher Expertise
2014: Neuroscience Perspectives for Science and Mathematics Learning in Technology-Enhanced Learning Environments
2013: International Perspectives on Mathematics and Science Teacher Education for the Future
2011: Enhancing the Participation, Engagement and Achievement of Young People in Science and Mathematics Education
2010: First Cycle of Pisa (2000–2006)—International Perspectives on Successes and Challenges: Research and Policy Directions

IJSME strives to focus these special issues on emerging, or recently emerged, trends in science and mathematics education as evidenced by the number of citations

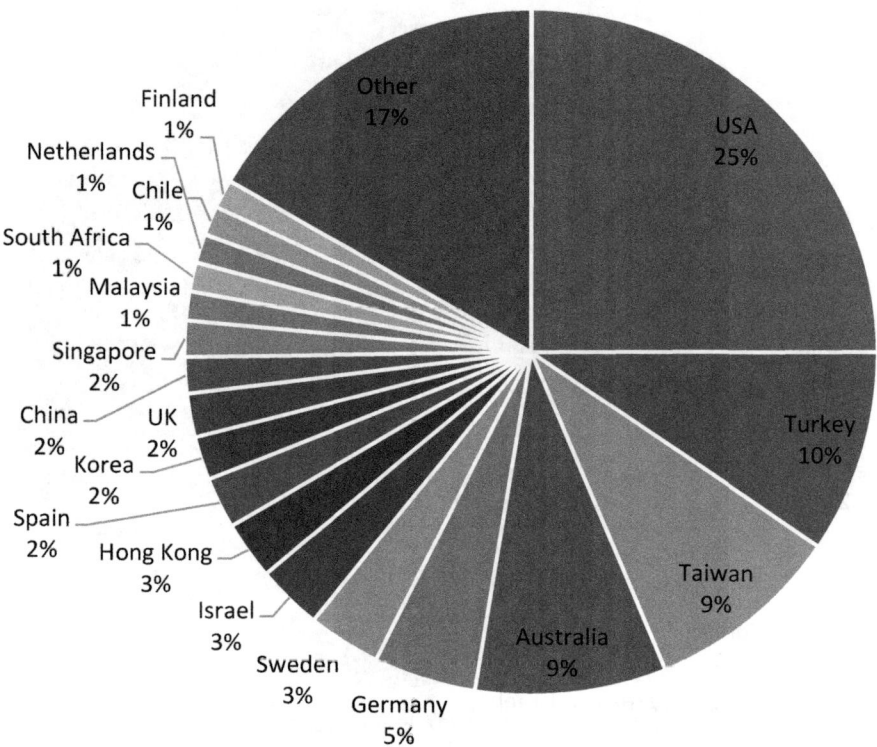

Fig. 20.2 Acceptance by country since 2015 (n = 293)

each garner. In fact, the special issues from 2013, 2014, and 2015 contains some of the most cited articles in IJSME history and speak to the currency of the content.

20.3 The Emergence of Patterns

As a senior editor of IJSME since 2013 I have overseen over 600 manuscripts, sending them out for review and making final decisions when the reviews come back. In this capacity I have read well over 2000 reviews. Through my interactions with these 600 manuscripts and 2000 reviews, patterns have emerged. First to emerge were patterns of what makes a poor manuscript—a manuscript that reviewers are likely to reject and why. These patterns were the basis of my aforementioned three reasons for a manuscript being rejected—poor research, uninteresting results, and poor writing. More slow to emerge, and more difficult to discern, were patterns for what made a manuscript good. The reason for this is that while there are three main ways for a manuscript to be deemed poor, there are many different ways for a manuscript to be considered good.

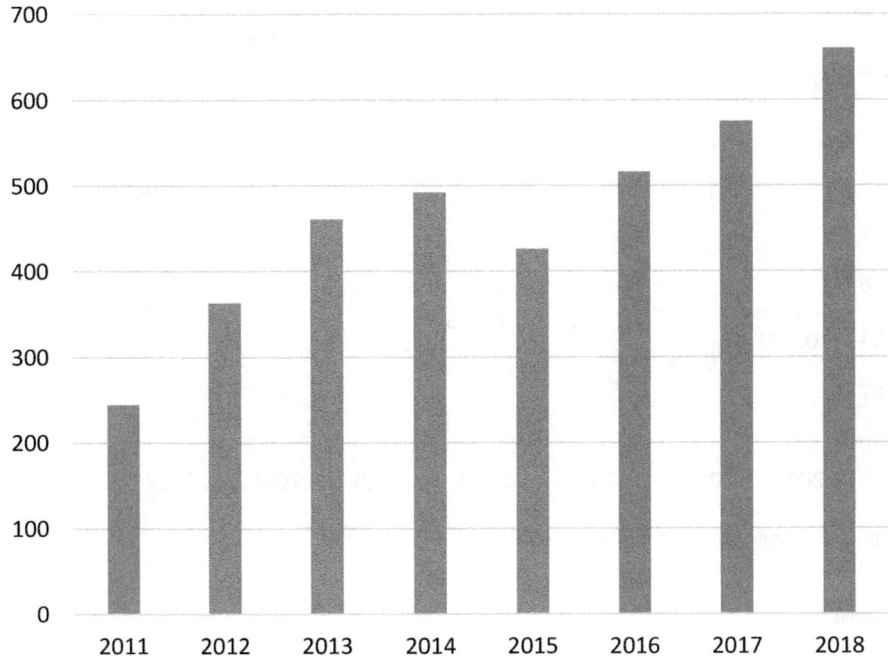

Fig. 20.3 Total submissions per year since 2011

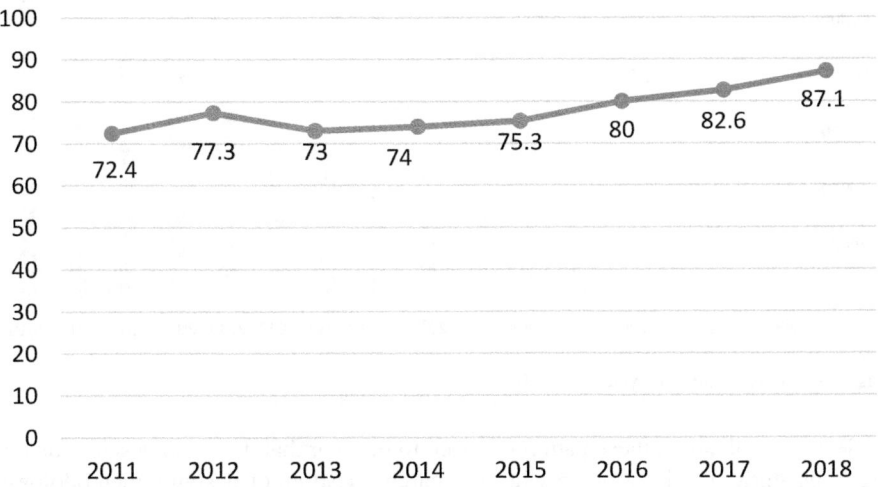

Fig. 20.4 Rejection rate per year since 2011

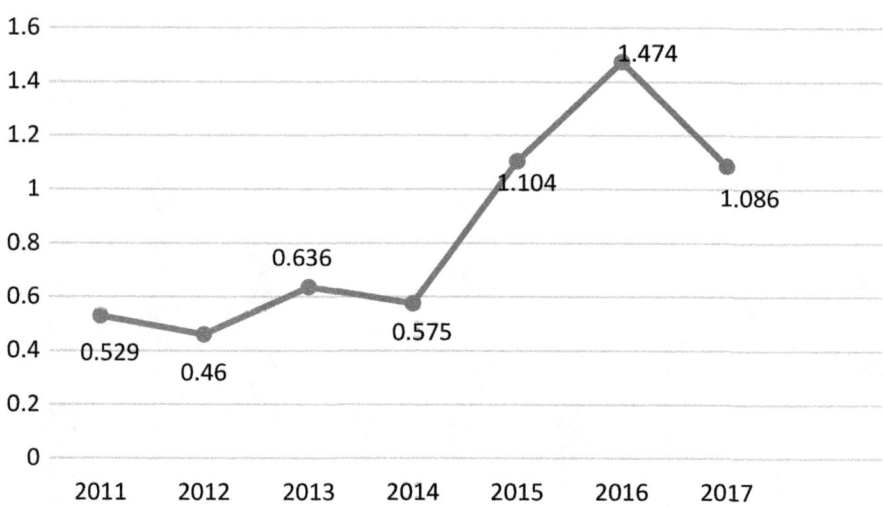

Fig. 20.5 Impact factor per year since 2011

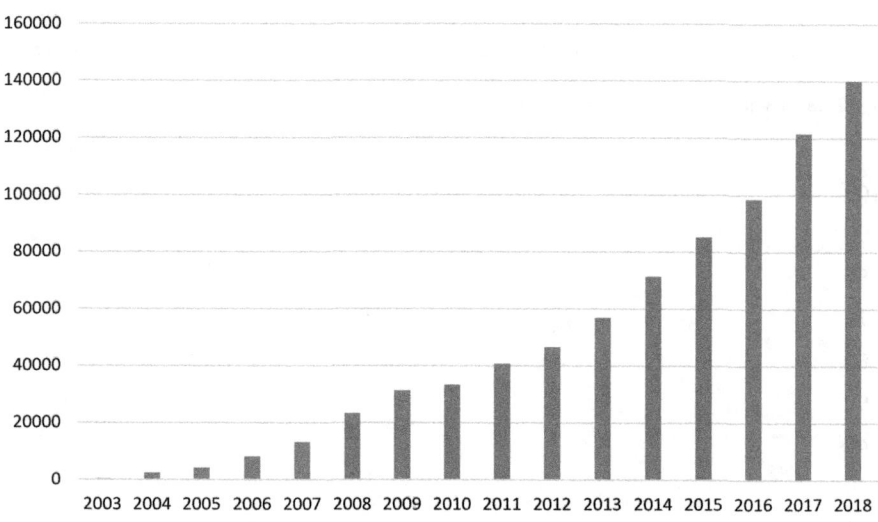

Fig. 20.6 Downloads per year since 2011

Before I talk about these patterns, I want to be clear that this is not a scientifically rigorous study. I did not begin with a research question, or design a methodology, or engage in prior literature. The question as to what makes a good manuscript emerged naturally out of my many and varied interactions with manuscripts over the years, and the patterns were reified in my work of trying to guide my graduate students in their writing of conference papers, journal articles, and their theses. Having said that, there was a method to the emergence of the framework that I present below. First and foremost, this method has been guided by noticing others' writing and how reviewers respond to that writing. At the same time, I was also noticing my own writing and how this was being informed by others' writing and how reviewers responded to it.

20.4 Structure for a Good Paper

What emerged from this lived experience was the observation that an article[1] is a story. And like a story it has a discernable beginning, middle, and end. And as with stories, there are many ways to write an article. There can be foreshadowing, detours into related events, and reflections on past events. There is a development of tension and eventual resolution, and there is a deliberate effort to bring the reader into the complexity of the plot and themes through threads that are engaging and inviting. And there are considerations of voice and audience. How these elements are structured determines how well a story is told and how well it is received. The same is true of an article.

Good papers are a telling of the research that is being presented. The authors of such papers have found an engaging and inviting way to gradually pull the reader into the complexity and nuance of the research while building the tension that the research question will resolve, all the while using voice and consideration of audience as they guide the reader from the introduction to the conclusion. Although there are many ways to do this, all good papers have these elements. What follows is a reification of one way for an author to tell the story of their research.

Before I share this, however, it is important to recognize that this is but one way. What follows is not to be thought of as a panacea of how to write for publication. It is not to be used as a checklist for reviewing manuscripts, or as a criterion for soliciting manuscripts. This is a place to start, a way to write for publication that may help a beginning researcher to think more clearly about the story he or she is trying to tell.

In what follows I move through the various elements of a paper, from the title to the conclusion with discussion and elaboration of each element and how it can be structured so as to tell the story effectively. Whenever possible I provide examples–both good and bad–to illustrate some of the more nuanced aspects that I discuss. What I do not do, however, is discuss how to perform good research. I do not discuss how to pick literature, how to select an appropriate methodology or how to choose a theoretical framework. What I am trying to do is to help future authors turn good research into a good manuscript and, in so doing, I make the assumption that good research has already been done.

---

[1] Throughout this chapter I very deliberately refer to something that is submitted for review as a manuscript. Anything that has been published I refer to either as an article, paper, or chapter.

20.4.1 Title and Abstract

Our ability to search for relevant research has changed drastically in the last few decades. Fifty years ago we used a variety of indexes available in university libraries. Every few years journals published an index of every paper published in that journal for some period of time—1 year, 5 years, 10 years, etc. There was also an annual index of all PhD theses written. These indexes were most often organized by title, but sometimes also by topic—as articulated in the title. Searching through these indexes involved the reading of many titles and, as such, what the title was became vital. Over time, some of these indexes began to include abstracts, which provided much more detail, but were more tedious to read and searching became a two part process–first by title and then by abstract. In this era both the title and the abstract were vital for providing access to what the research contained.

Now, in 2018, search engines such as Google Scholar, Scopus, Web of Science, ERIC, etc. are able to search the entire text of a document, returning a focused list of relevant papers, chapters, and reports. This list, as in the past, is still comprised of titles and abstracts, but because these no longer serve as the only gateway into the research the role of the title has changed. Whereas a title previously needed to include every dimension of the research, these dimensions can now be searched for directly, allowing titles to be more concisely focused on the object of study rather than on how the study was done. For example, *The Elusive Slope* (Lingefjärd and Farahani 2018) identifies the object of study (slope) and implies that it may be about student difficulty around this concept. However, which students and which context are opaque. Fifty years ago, the title of this article might have been something like *Upper Secondary Students Difficulties with Interpreting Distance-Time Graphs and ECG Graphs*. Although an extreme case, the point is that there is no longer a need to include every dimension of the research in the title. So, while *Tool Use and the Development of the Function Concept: From Repeated Calculations to Functional Thinking* (Doorman et al. 2012) is now an appropriate title, 50 years ago the title may have been something more like *Secondary School Students Development of the Concept of Function in a Technology-Intensive Setting*.

This is not to say that anything goes with a title. The title should still be on point, and should still reveal some specific details about the content of the article (slope, functions, etc.). However, keep in mind that the more detailed the title, the more narrow the potential interest in the paper. So, whereas someone might be interested in *Learning to Think Spatially: What do Students 'See' in Numeracy Test Items?* (Diezmann and Lowrie 2012) because they have an interest in spatial thinking, posing the title as *Year 3 Students' Spatial Thinking on Items 1 and 22 of the 2008 Australian NAPLAN Test*, has narrowed that potential interest to a very specific subset of topics in spatial reasoning. Of course, this is an exaggerated extreme of how overly specific a title can be, but it does highlight many of the errors I often see in how a title has been selected.

First, the title specifies the country within which this research has been done. All research is done somewhere. Unless the research is an international comparison, there is no need to specify the country—it unnecessarily narrows the scope of potential interest in the manuscript. The same is true of the age group of the participants and the instruments used to gather the data. In short, the title should not include anything from the methodology (except possibly the theoretical framework —if well known). If the research cannot say something that transcends the country in which it is done, or who the participants are, or the instrument used, then it is likely not of interest to an international audience. The aforementioned fictional title on year 3 students' performance on a NAPLAN test sounds as if it is better suited as a national or regional report than as a journal paper in an international research journal—irrespective of what the content is.

When thinking about how to craft an abstract, a different set of parameters needs to be considered. The most common error I see with abstracts is that they are written for an audience who has read the paper. This is the wrong audience. The abstract is read, if at all, prior to reading the paper—and sometimes instead of reading the paper. The reader is not yet aware of the technical terminology that is carefully developed within the manuscript as the author educates the reader. As such, the abstract needs to be written using lay terminology and taken-as-shared concepts that can stand on their own without the weight of 40 pages of text to make sense of it. Further to this point, an abstract should not contain any references. Not only does this imply that specific knowledge is needed, it creates a space where a reference is indicated without an accompanying reference list.

This principle also extends to the considerations of how much of the results to reveal. The results of research, as presented in a journal paper, require the full weight of past literature, theory, and analysis to make sense of. Thus, to think that a specific result can be sensibly understood in an abstract is absurd. For example, whereas *"results indicate that students' dispositions towards mathematics improved"* is a reasonable statement in an abstract, a statement such as *"there was a general shift away from instrumentalist and Platonist views of mathematics"* relies too much on the specific terminology introduced later in the manuscript.

20.4.2 Introduction

What brings a reader to a specific article varies from a search engine result, to browsing a journal, to following a thread of references from a different article, to a random occurrence—none of which guarantees that the reader has an a priori interest in the article. Thus, the purpose of the introduction is not so much to introduce the reader to the *phenomenon of interest* but rather to inform them why the phenomenon of interest is, in fact, interesting.

The primary way to do this is, first and foremost, to write a manuscript about an interesting and important topic. This point cannot be overstated. The number of manuscripts that are rejected because the topic is either uninteresting or redundant is staggering. Reviewers and editors at IJSME tend to be quick to point out if a manuscript, irrespective of how technically well it is written, does not significantly contribute to the knowledge of the field. However, an interesting and important topic, although necessary, is far from sufficient. The author must also tell the reader why they should care about this topic. That is, it is not the reader's job to determine if the research presented in a manuscript is either interesting or important—it is the job of the author.

Although not universal, an effective way to do this is to first identify the phenomenon from literature, data, a personal experience, or a taken-as-shared experience—*some students have the goal to learn while other students have the goal to get good grades*. Once the phenomenon has been introduced the author needs to then argue for why this is an important phenomenon for the field of mathematics education in general—*we don't know enough about how these varying goals affect student behavior in the mathematics classroom*—or mathematics education research in particular—*this calls into question the assumption that in a didactic contract the teacher and the students have a common goal*.

Regardless, this structure segues perfectly into a general and lay statement of the research question—*in what follows I explore these varying goals and the impact they have on student learning behavior*. In doing so, the author has successfully narrowed the phenomenon of interest down to a research question. As with the abstract, however, the statement of the research question needs to be accessible to a reader who has not yet learned the nuances that the literature review and discussion of theory has yet to present. As such, overly technical language should be avoided.

20.4.3 Literature Review

The most common misconception that I see in rejected manuscripts is that the purpose of the literature review is to showcase that you have read prior and related research on your phenomenon of interest. The result of this misconception is a parade of summaries of past literature, sometimes (but not always) using some organizational heuristic such as time or demographic. Although it is important that the author be aware of the related research, this is not the purpose of a literature review.

I find it best to think of a literature review as the place where the author is going to continue to narrow their phenomenon of interest down to their precise research question. Thus, the literature review is not a random walk through the literature, but a guided tour of the literature, constructed in such a way so as to direct the reader's attention and interest towards the research question.[2] If done well, when the

---

[2] I write this chapter as though a paper has a single research question. This is for convenience sake and is not a recommendation to authors. Papers often have multiple research questions.

research question is posed the reader will say, "*of course that is the research question*".

Consider the analogy of giving a tour of your city to a visitor from out of town. This tour can either be a drive through your city pointing out every major landmark or it can be a carefully selected tour wherein you point out the historical and cultural relevance of selected landmarks so as to try to imprint on your guest what it is that makes your city unique and interesting. Too many literature reviews are the former type of tour. It is uninteresting and uninformative, and it is especially boring for the visitor who has already been to your city many times and has visited these landmarks many times over. In many instances the reader of a paper is aware of much of the research being cited. He or she does not need to be introduced to it again. What is needed is to see how you are positioning and vectoring this literature to reveal the gaps or hidden corners that your research is hoping to respectively fill or illuminate.

Thus, the most natural place for the research question to appear is at the end of the literature review. Not only does this complete the tour by providing the last bit of narrowing from the phenomenon of interest, it also creates a natural segue to the methodology section. Unlike the general and lay posing of your research question in the introduction, however, the reader now has the technical language and terminology along with the nuanced understanding of the field to understand the articulation of the research question in its full complexity and subtlety. As mentioned, such a research question should clearly articulate how the results to follow will either fill a gap or illuminate a dark corner in the research literature. This can be done in a number of different ways, from applying existing theories to a new context, to looking at a phenomenon of interest through a new lens.

Regardless, the research question should be posed in such a way that it cannot be answered with a yes or no response. For example, the research question *Does cognitively guided instruction improve students' learning experiences?* hints at a complex and rich research project with intricate methodologies and deep data analysis, all of which are overshadowed by the drive to answer the question. A better research question may have been, *In what ways does cognitively guided instruction affect students' learning experiences?*

Aside from this important focusing of the phenomenon of interest to a research question, the literature review also serves to introduce the reader to the technical vocabulary and terminology that will be used to discuss the analysis and results. In this regard, the literature review should also introduce the reader to the theoretical or analytic framework that will be used in the forthcoming analysis of the data. However, the fact that a subset of the literature being presented will be the theoretical framework does not necessarily need to be revealed at this time. It can be, but that reveal can also be made within the methodology section. For now, the theory can just be another stop on the guided tour through the literature.

20.4.4 Methodology

There was a time when the primary role of the methodology section was to provide the details so that the research could be recreated by another researcher. In many ways this is still true. However, the methodology section has also come to serve an additional and, although implicit, important purpose—to help readers see how the results of the research can explain a phenomenon within their own setting. This is not to say that the job of the methodology is to make the results generalizable to any context or to say that it is the author's job to identify the specific contexts to which the results can generalize to. Rather, it is the job of the author to identify the details of the contexts within which the research was done so that readers can perform this alignment themselves.

To these ends, the methodology needs to include the necessary information of where the research was performed, who the participants are, how the data were gathered, what the data are, and how the data were analyzed. The first two of these (where and who) need to have enough contextual detail for the reader to understand the demographic that this research is relevant to, without being so detailed that anonymity is compromised. How the data were gathered, should include detailed descriptions of the interview questions used or the survey instruments administered. It should also include a narrative of how and why these questions or instruments were constructed or selected.

There are three common errors made by authors on this last point—the first of which is to talk about their data gathering instruments as if the reader already knows what they are. Providing four and five letter acronyms does not help. Neither does placing the entirety of the instrument in the appendix. The author should be articulate about what the instrument is and how and why it was chosen within the body of the methodology section. This is not to say that an entire questionnaire should be inserted, but rather a sampling of the types of questions participants were asked to answer should be provided.

The second error is to introduce an instrument or method that has not been previously encountered in the literature review. If the literature review is vectored towards the research question as discussed above, then the methods used in the research will have already been encountered. As such, the appearance of an, as of yet undiscussed, method is a strong indicator of a poorly structured literature review.

The third mistake is that authors forget to discuss what the data are. To be clear, detailed descriptions of the methods of collecting data do not necessarily result in a clear understanding of what constitutes the data for the research to be presented. This is especially true when a research paper draws on only a subset of data from a broader research project.

The methodology should conclude with a clear articulation of how the aforementioned data were analyzed. This is where the author will identify (or re-identify) the theoretical or analytical framework that will be used as a lens to make sense of the data. The importance of this cannot be understated. The number one reason that a manuscript is rejected is for the lack of a well-articulated or explicitly used theoretical or analytical framework. That is, whereas a complete absence of a framework is seen as intolerable by reviewers and editors, to state that a framework exists but then not use it in the analysis is no better. The same is true of introducing a framework with no prior grounding or discussion in the literature.

Further to this point, a lack of a theoretical or analytic framework can very rarely be compensated for by the trivial use of thematic analysis, constant comparative method, or grounded theory. In most cases, such methods are used where an abundance of literature and theory exists and could have been used to analyze the data in robust and rigorous ways. This is rarely tolerated, and only when the author acknowledges the existence of relevant literature and theory and has a well-articulated argument for why these are inappropriate for the purposes of answering the research question.

Having said that, depending on the level of detail provided in the literature review, the methodology section may require a more detailed exposition of what the framework is and how it will be used to analyze the data. Further, select the theoretical or analytic frameworks carefully. I often see authors using very elaborate and complex frameworks to see things that are obviously at on the surface of the data. The complexity of the framework should match, to some degree, the depth of the analysis and allow the author to see and discuss results that are not apparent without the framework.

20.4.5 Results and Discussion

Whereas in quantitative papers the results are often presented separately from discussion, in qualitative papers this is much less the case. The reason for this is that while quantitative results can be presented in the form of tables and graphs prior to discussion, qualitative results need to be discussed in order to situate them. This is not to say that qualitative results and discussion cannot be separated, but rather that it is difficult to present results without naturally sliding into the discussion. Having said that, there are some things to keep in mind when structuring the presentation and discussion of results.

First, the discussion of results is the best place to demonstrate how the theoretical or analytical framework is being explicitly used to analyze the data. Be transparent about this. From a reviewer's or editor's perspective there is no difference between not using a framework and using one in opaque ways. Second, use the structure of the framework to organize the discussion. Manuscripts are often rejected because the discussion is a dizzying and confusing walk through the results. The analogy of a guided tour is as relevant to the literature review as it is to the presentation and discussion of results. Often a framework comes with explicit visuals, tables, or headings that can be used to organize the discussion so as to guide the reader towards the conclusions. Without this, the conclusions risk being seemingly random outcomes of the research.

Further to this point, the detail around the results and analysis should be at a level so as to allow the reader to participate in the analysis and arrive at the conclusions with the author. Too often authors provide either too little or too much detail. Whereas too little detail leaves the reader having to take the word of the author that the analysis led to the conclusions, too much details bores the reader and often overshoots the conclusion—both of which will likely run afoul in the review process.

At the same time, the author needs to keep in mind that there is a difference between doing research and writing research. Whereas doing research happens in time, time is often a poor organizer of the results and discussion. The presentation of results and discussion should focus much more on the *logical* portion of chronological than the *chrono* part. As part of this, the author should take care to think ahead to how the discussion is going to contribute to the answering of the research question.

With respect to tables and graphs, authors need to be mindful of why and how they are using them. There are two main uses of tables and graphs in a research paper—to summarize results and to organize results. The first of these is often used early on in the section to present all, or a portion, of the results in a clear and concise way. This clarity is obfuscated if the tables or graphs are not well labelled and the conciseness is compromised if the author presents the table or graph and then proceeds to painstakingly narrate every entry. This is not to say that individual pieces of the table or graph cannot be discussed or elaborated on to give depth of meaning. But efforts should be made to allow the tables and graphs to speak for themselves.

The second way in which tables and graphs are used is to summarize results that have been presented and discussed. In this use, tables and graphs often come near the end of the section as they pull together the discussion that has preceded them. In this use, elaborations of tables and graphs should be used only for the purpose of directing the reader to intricacies in the organization and not to the substance of the graph or table.

20.4.6 Conclusion

Whereas the beginning of a paper is focused on narrowing the scope of the research from the phenomenon of interest, through the use of literature, down to the research question, the conclusion reverses this process as it moves the research from the specificity of the results and discussion back towards the phenomenon of interest. As such, and although it is seen as one section of a journal article, the conclusion actually serves four purposes—the first two of which are to answer the research question and to present any other results from the research. As mentioned in the previous section, the answering of the research question begins already during the discussion of results. This is a delicate formulation and care should be taken in

Fig. 20.7 Mapping the discussion onto the conclusion

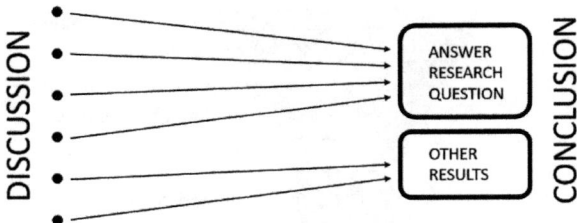

doing it well. The analog of a functions that maps the discussion onto the conclusion becomes a useful structure for thinking about this (see Fig. 20.7).

In such a mapping there are important rules to pay attention to. The first is that there exists no part of the discussion that is not present in the conclusion. That is, everything that is discussed about the results must either contribute to answering the research question or be mentioned as part of other results emerging from the research. The second rule is that no one discussion point should answer the whole of the research question. Not only does this make the conclusion redundant, but it also calls into question either the appropriateness of the research question or the depth of the methodology and theoretical or analytical framework used in answering the research question. A final rule is that there should be many more discussion points that contribute to answering the research question than do not. Otherwise it signals a mismatch between the research question and the methodology.

The third purpose of the conclusions is to speak back to the literature presented throughout the paper and talk about the ways in which the results of the research confirm, refute, extend, or nuance the existing literature. This is the primary way in which the author can validate to the reader that the research was, indeed, interesting. This speaking back to the literature is also how the research results are lifted from the specificity of the context and reach out to touch on more general areas of mathematics education.

The final purpose of the conclusion is to speak back to the phenomenon of interest and comment on how the research results contributed in some way to resolving or understanding that phenomenon. Whereas the research question sits at the bottom of the funnel that has been narrowed and refined by the literature review, the phenomenon of interest sits at the top of this same funnel. As such, the answer to the research question, which the research is fundamentally about, does not illuminate the whole of the phenomenon of interest. But it does illuminate part of it. The conclusion should end with some statements about this.

20.5 Final Words

Pulling all of these thoughts together, we can think of a reader's experience with an article as having an hour glass shape (see Fig. 20.8, and see also the structure presented in Chap. 16 of this volume, in Sect. 16.2.3). The paper starts out broadly

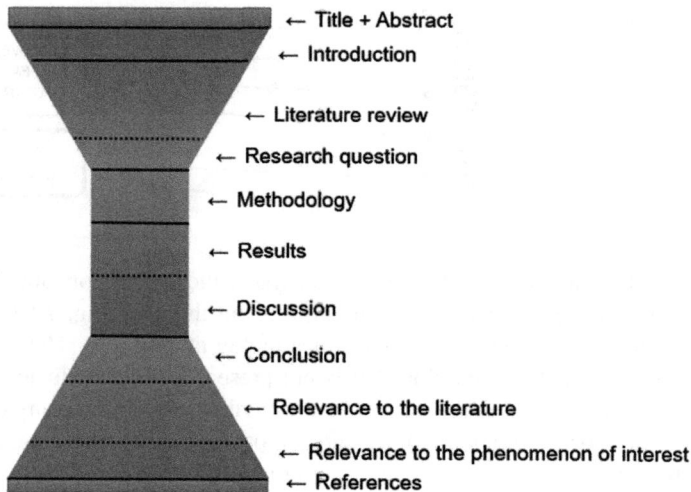

Fig. 20.8 The structure of a paper

with an engaging title that invites a wide range of interests. Through the introduction and literature review the article is narrowed towards the research question, which finishes the funneling of the interest down to a very precise statement that will define the research work to come. The methodology, results, and discussion define this middle part of the hour glass remaining within the precise boundaries defined by the research question and the methodology. As the reader enters the conclusion the article starts to broaden out again, first by answering the research question and then by speaking back to the literature and the phenomenon of interest that initiated the research to begin with.

Of course, the visual in Fig. 20.8 is completely disproportionate in scale to the time spent within various phases of the research as well as within the various parts of an article. But the image creates a certain symmetry between the way an article should begin and end and provides a useful metaphor for authors to think about how to write up their research.

This same framework is not only relevant to the writing of a 30–40 page journal paper, however. This is the same structure I use with my graduate students when they are outlining and writing their theses. It is also a relevant framework for writing shorter articles, such as conference papers.

As mentioned in the introductory sections of this chapter, absent from the aforementioned discussion is any treatment of how an author should think about selecting his or her theoretical or analytic framework, as well as how to select a commensurate research methodology, both of which are important aspects of the doing the research and should be treated with great care and anticipation. Although this chapter begins at the point where the research has been done and the writing up of the research for publication is about to begin, there are other aspects of the writing for publication in IJSME that I have not mentioned, one of which is the technical requirements of IJSME.

IJSME has some technical requirements for authors to follow when submitting manuscripts. Although there is not a template to follow authors are expected to follow a style guide which specifies page limits, heading levels, font size, margins, spacing, and referencing style. Authors need to pay close attention to these parameters when writing and submitting a manuscript. Ignoring such requirement may, at worst, be grounds for rejection and, at best, annoy the editor and reviewers.

A specific part of these parameters to pay attention to is what is referred to as the meta-data. These are the details that you are asked to enter into fields during the submission process and include your name, affiliation, title of the paper, and the abstract. The meta-data are used, along with your manuscript, to produce the document that is seen by the editor and sent to the reviewers, and has important implications for how your manuscript is tracked within the digital submission and review system as well as how it is blindeded for review. Again, careful attention to these requirements is needed.

Also absent from the above discussion about different parts of an article is any mention of references. IJSME has specific criteria for how referencing is to be done and how the reference list is to be organized. The APA format forms the basis of this criterion, but careful attention to the slight variations of this format that IJSME uses is needed. Thus, cutting and pasting references from one paper to another will not work unless careful editing follows.

Finally, I want to go back to how the paper began by stating, once again, that what I have offered here is a set of guidelines for authors looking for advice on how to write for publication in IJSME. These guidelines have emerged, as stated, from looking at hundreds of submissions and thousands of reviews. These guidelines are neither inflexible nor criteria. They are a starting point, a place for a beginning researcher to begin to think about how to output a good research publication.

References

Diezmann, C. M., & Lowrie, T. (2012). Learning to think spatially: What do students "see" in numeracy test items? *International Journal of Science and Mathematics Education, 10*(6), 1469–1490.

Doorman, M., Drijvers, P., Gravemeijer, K., Boon, P., & Reed, H. (2012). Tool use and the development of the function concept: From repeated calculations to functional thinking. *International Journal of Science and Mathematics Education, 10*(6), 1243–1267.

Lingefjärd, T., & Farahani, D. (2018). The elusive slope. *International Journal of Science and Mathematics Education, 16*(6), 1187–1206.

Open Access This chapter is licensed under the terms of the Creative Commons Attribution 4.0 International License (http://creativecommons.org/licenses/by/4.0/), which permits use, sharing, adaptation, distribution and reproduction in any medium or format, as long as you give appropriate credit to the original author(s) and the source, provide a link to the Creative Commons license and indicate if changes were made.

The images or other third party material in this chapter are included in the chapter's Creative Commons license, unless indicated otherwise in a credit line to the material. If material is not included in the chapter's Creative Commons license and your intended use is not permitted by statutory regulation or exceeds the permitted use, you will need to obtain permission directly from the copyright holder.

Chapter 21
Journal for Research in Mathematics Education: Practical Guides for Promoting and Disseminating Significant Research in Mathematics Education

Jinfa Cai, Stephen Hwang and Victoria Robison

Abstract Research journals play significant roles in the advancement of academic fields of inquiry. This chapter starts with a brief description of the *Journal for Research in Mathematics Education*. Most importantly, this chapter provides practical guides to promoting and disseminating significant research in mathematics education. The guides provided in this chapter will be helpful and insightful for those who are interested in publishing in the *Journal for Research in Mathematics Education*.

Keywords Journal for Research in Mathematics Education · Mathematics education · Significant research · Research dissemination

21.1 Introduction

As the official research journal of the National Council of Teachers of Mathematics (NCTM), the *Journal for Research in Mathematics Education* (*JRME*) is unique in the sense that it is sponsored by an organization of mathematics teachers. For nearly 50 years, it has been a premier research journal in the field of mathematics education devoted to the interests of mathematics teachers and education researchers at all levels. When *JRME* was first established in 1970, its stated purpose was to "provide a means for more systematic and comprehensive reporting of research"

J. Cai (✉) · S. Hwang · V. Robison
University of Delaware, Newark, USA
e-mail: jcai@udel.edu

S. Hwang
e-mail: hwangste@udel.edu

V. Robison
e-mail: vrobison@udel.edu

(Johnson 1970, p. 5), and, in particular, to disseminate research dealing with significant problems in mathematics education.

In service to this mission and to NCTM's broad goal of enhancing the mathematics education of all students, *JRME* has been a high-profile venue in which to publish papers that systematically and comprehensively report research that will ultimately have an impact on educational practice in mathematics classrooms. Increasing the impact of mathematics education research on practice has been a longstanding conundrum for the field (Battista et al. 2007; Bazzini 1991; Heck et al. 2012; Heid et al. 2006; Herbel-Eisenmann et al. 2016; Kieran et al. 2012; Malara and Zan 2002; Ruthven 2002; Silver and Lunsford 2017). The editors of *JRME* have maintained a consistent focus over the years on this issue (see, e.g., Cai et al. 2017a; Langrall 2014; Silver 2003).

In this chapter, we discuss *JRME*'s influential role in the field as well as the kinds of manuscripts that it publishes. In providing a brief overview of how the editorial team processes manuscripts, from initial submission to final publication, we hope to illuminate what characteristics make a manuscript likely to be published in *JRME* and to have an impact on the field. Our goal is that this chapter will provide readers with insightful and useful information for preparing manuscripts to be published in *JRME*.

21.2 A Journal of Record in Mathematics Education

JRME has consistently been rated as one of the top journals in the field of mathematics education, both in the United States and internationally (Dreyfus 2006; Holbrook et al. 2009; Nivens and Otten 2017; Toerner and Arzarello 2012; Williams and Leatham 2017). Indeed, *JRME* serves as a journal of record for the field, archiving reports of the highest quality studies in mathematics education.

Papers published in *JRME* have become some of the most influential in the field. The 20 most cited papers that have appeared in *JRME* had collectively been cited well over 20,000 times by June 28, 2018, with the top 10 having been cited a total of over 13,000 times (see Table 21.1). These and other papers published by *JRME* have led mathematics education research in new directions, provided widely used tools for mathematics education researchers, and informed policy decisions in the United States and abroad.

Since its inception, *JRME* has reflected the evolving patterns and trends of research in the field. In their review of papers published in *JRME* and *Educational Studies in Mathematics* (*ESM*) over the last 5 decades, Inglis and Foster (2018) investigated patterns in content, theories, and methods characterizing studies published in these journals over the years. Inglis and Foster observed that, after experiencing a peak in the 1970s, the number of studies with experimental designs declined consistently. They also noted the shift from the constructivism-dominated studies of the 1980s to studies increasingly driven by sociocultural theories in both *JRME* and *ESM*. With this shift came an apparent change in the methods used to

Table 21.1 The 20 most cited papers published in JRME

Title	Author(s)	Citations
Sociomathematical Norms, Argumentation, and Autonomy in Mathematics	Yackel and Cobb (1996)	2,129
Reconstructing Mathematics Pedagogy from a Constructivist Perspective	Simon (1995)	1,590
Unpacking Pedagogical Content Knowledge: Conceptualizing and Measuring Teachers' Topic-Specific Knowledge of Students	Hill, Ball, and Schilling (2008)	1,511
The Nature, Effects, and Relief of Mathematics Anxiety	Hembree (1990)	1,503
Fennema-Sherman Mathematics Attitudes Scales: Instruments Designed to Measure Attitudes Toward the Learning of Mathematics by Females and Males	Fennema and Sherman (1976)	1,488
Duality, Ambiguity, and Flexibility: A "Proceptual" View of Simple Arithmetic	Grey (1994)	1,210
The Acquisition of Addition and Subtraction Concepts in Grades One Through Three	Carpenter and Moser (1984)	1,208
A Longitudinal Study of Learning to Use Children's Thinking in Mathematics Instructions	Fennema, Carpenter, Franke, Levi, Jacobs, and Empson (1996)	1,068
Mathematical Tasks and Student Cognition: Classroom-Based Factors That Support and Inhibit High-Level Mathematical Thinking and Reasoning	Henningsen and Stein (1997)	1,040
An Exploration of the Mathematics Self-Efficacy/Mathematics Performance Correspondence	Hackett and Betz (1989)	951
A Constructivist Alternative to the Representational View of Mind in Mathematics Education	Cobb (1992)	905
Task-Related Verbal Interaction and Mathematics Learning in Small Groups	Webb (1991)	874
Explorations of Students' Mathematical Beliefs and Behavior	Schoenfeld (1989)	860
Prospective Elementary and Secondary Teachers' Understanding of Division	Ball (1990)	828
Metacognition, Cognition Monitoring, and Mathematical Performance	Garofolo and Lester (1985)	801
Open and Closed Mathematics: Student Experiences and Understandings	Boaler (1998)	771
Number Sense as Situated Knowing in a Conceptual Domain	Greeno (1991)	748
Making Sense of Graphs: Critical Factors Influencing Comprehension and Instructional Implications	Friel, Curcio, and Bright (2001)	722

(continued)

Table 21.1 (continued)

Title	Author(s)	Citations
Sex-Related Differences in Mathematics Achievement and Related Factors: A Further Study	Fennema and Sherman (1978)	721
A Meta-Analysis of the Relationship Between Anxiety Toward Mathematics and Achievement in Mathematics	Ma (1999)	720

investigate research goals, with more studies focusing on classroom discourse observations rather than on individual student interviews. In addition, they observed that research focused on teaching and learning environments has seen a particularly strong increase in representation among papers published in *JRME*, especially research on teacher knowledge and beliefs and curriculum and reform as well as novel assessment development.

21.3 What *JRME* Publishes

JRME is a forum for the highest caliber of disciplined inquiry into the teaching and learning of mathematics. The journal's editors welcome submissions from researchers all around the world and seek to publish high-quality manuscripts that will contribute significant knowledge to the field of mathematics education. Papers published in *JRME* include Research Reports and Brief Reports as well as Research Commentaries and Book Reviews. Because of space limitations, this chapter focuses on Research Reports and Brief Reports.

The vast majority of the papers published in *JRME* are Research Reports. Research Reports aim to move the field of mathematics education forward and include, but are not limited to, the following: various genres and designs of empirical research; philosophical, methodological, and historical studies in mathematics education; and literature reviews, syntheses, and theoretical analyses of research in mathematics education.

Brief Reports of research are appropriate when a fuller report is available elsewhere or when a more comprehensive follow-up study is planned. Topics for Brief Reports vary. For example, a Brief Report of a novel first study on some topic might stress the rationale, hypotheses, and plans for further work. Alternatively, a Brief Report might provide an executive summary of a large study. A Brief Report of a replication or extension of a previously reported study might contrast the results of the two studies, referring to the earlier study for methodological details. Finally, a Brief Report of a monograph or other lengthy nonjournal publication might summarize the key findings and implications or might highlight an unusual observation or methodological approach.

Whether intended to be a Research Report or a Brief Report, for an author's work to be published in *JRME*, it must exhibit qualities that characterize well-conceived and well-reported research studies. The following section addresses guidelines for preparing high-quality manuscripts.

21.4 Guidelines for Preparing High-Quality Manuscripts

High-quality manuscripts submitted to *JRME* share a number of key characteristics. The document *Characteristics of High Quality Manuscripts*, available on the *JRME* web page as well as in the Appendix, provides detailed information about these characteristics, which include aspects of the study's purpose, rationale, and contribution; the literature review, theoretical framework, and research questions; the terminology, writing, and mathematical accuracy; and, for manuscripts that report empirical research findings, the research methods, study design, and results and implications. Past *JRME* editors have also provided guidance on what makes a strong manuscript (see, e.g., Blume et al. 2010; Heid 2010; Heid and Blume 2011). Of central importance is that the manuscript should make a significant contribution to the scholarly dialogue in mathematics education research.

An essential component of any strong manuscript includes a clearly communicated purpose for the study and research questions. Authors should seek to establish why the general area of study is important and how their particular study contributes important new information to the field of mathematics education (Blume et al. 2010; Cai et al. 2019). A recent analysis of peer reviews of manuscripts receiving *JRME* decisions in 2017 showed that *JRME* reviewers look for authors to make a strong, explicit case for the significance of their research questions (Cai et al. 2019). In fact, 55% of the reviews for manuscripts that were rejected by *JRME* in 2017 raised concerns about the research questions (e.g., lack of a clear motivation or connection to a theoretical framework).

Thus, authors preparing manuscripts for submission to *JRME* should make the case that addressing their research questions about some aspect of the teaching and learning of mathematics will offer new insights to mathematics education that extend beyond what has been reported in prior studies. The study may also move the field beyond current methods, instruments, or theories (Heid 2010). Authors are encouraged to focus on understanding a phenomenon deeply rather than investigating any particular classroom, student, lesson, or content. This guidance, however, should not be interpreted as discouraging the submission of reports of replication studies. As we discuss below, *JRME* welcomes such reports. As is the case for all submissions to *JRME*, manuscripts reporting findings from replication studies must include a compelling argument for carrying out and publishing the work being reported (see Cai et al. 2018; Schoenfeld 2018; Star 2018).

Another important aspect of any strong manuscript submitted to *JRME* is its literature review and the inclusion of a theoretical framework. Rather than simply listing or summarizing existing studies, authors should aim to synthesize the findings of existing studies in a way that provides a basis for performing the study reported in the manuscript. Authors should include important work that supports and grounds the research, such as current research in mathematics education, foundational research that is the basis for the study, and potentially research outside of mathematics education as appropriate. In addition, the literature review connects to and supports the manuscript's theoretical framework, which guides the study. Authors should pay special attention to situating their study in the existing research to highlight the significance of their study. The research questions or hypotheses should be explicitly stated and should be guided by the theoretical framework. For manuscripts that report empirical findings, the theoretical framework should be reflected in the study design, data collection and analysis, and interpretation of the findings, and the research questions should be addressed by the collected data.

Manuscripts that report empirical research findings should also include clearly described research methods and a sound research design. Key elements of the research methodology should be defined, such as how and why the study subjects were selected as well as their number and background information, timelines and procedures for data collection, how each variable was measured, how the research instruments were developed, details of the procedures used to analyze the collected data, and so on. Including examples of instruments, instructional approaches, and observation or interview protocols is encouraged. Moreover, authors should strive to convince readers that the research design and methods are appropriate for answering the study's research questions by providing the validity and reliability data for the instruments, using appropriate statistical procedures, addressing potential threats to validity or reliability of the data, addressing discrepancies in the data, and so on. Finally, all claims about the findings and their implications should be supported by the data.

Whether reporting empirical or theoretical work, manuscripts should include appropriate and clearly defined terminology, coherent writing, and accurate mathematical terminology and content. International authors for whom English is a second language are encouraged to seek editing by a native English speaker. Ideas should be carefully developed, with transitions provided to help the reader understand what will be addressed from one section to the next. It is very important to have a clear chain of argumentation in the manuscript, from well-specified research questions, to a comprehensive literature review that situates the study and demonstrates how it will answer the research questions, to a theoretical framework that guides the study design, to the selection of research methods and data analysis, and to presenting the results and discussing the findings in a way that highlights the contribution of the study.

It should be indicated that because of the varying nature of studies, some of the above characteristics of high-quality manuscripts might warrant more emphasis than others. For example, the Institute of Education Sciences and the National Science Foundation (2013) promote six categories of research that serve as guidelines for individuals preparing grant proposals: foundational, early stage or exploratory, design and development, efficacy, effectiveness, and scale up. The categories can be grouped primarily by what they aim to contribute, with foundational and early-stage or exploratory research aiming to contribute to fundamental knowledge on teaching and learning; design and development research aiming to develop interventions that target specific learning goals; and efficacy, effectiveness, and scale-up research aiming to generate evidence of the impact of interventions. Because, for example, the parameters, characteristics, and scope of an exploratory study differ from those of a scale-up study, different characteristics of high-quality manuscripts might be more relevant to one than the other.

The current *JRME* editorial team began a series of editorials in March of 2019 that examine some guiding principles for conducting and disseminating research that has an impact on practice. This series of editorials discusses issues related to identifying and selecting significant research questions, framing a study, choices of methodology within and outside of mathematics education, and crafting a research report. Readers are encouraged to seek out these free access editorials for useful perspectives on conducting research.

21.5 Preparing a Manuscript for *JRME*

Manuscripts prepared for submission to *JRME* should generally follow the style guidelines laid out in the latest edition of the *Publication Manual of the American Psychological Association*, currently in its sixth edition (American Psychological Association 2010). The maximum length for Research Reports is 12,000 words and the maximum length for Brief Reports is 4,000 words. Word counts for both types of manuscripts exclude references, tables, figures, and appendices. Copies of source materials that are needed to evaluate a Brief Report should be included. Crespo and Cai (in press) have described academic writing as communicating with reviewers. They have provided some strategies for anticipating skeptical reviews when researchers prepare their manuscripts for publication.

21.6 Dissertations

Manuscripts based on doctoral dissertations form a notable category of submissions to *JRME*. They often represent emerging and promising work but also suffer from the difficulties of translating from the goals of a dissertation and its usual format and organization to the tighter, more focused approach of a research paper in an academic journal. Authors who intend to submit a manuscript based on their dissertation would be well advised to consult "From Dissertation to Publication in *JRME*" by Thanheiser et al. (2012). This paper provides useful guidance on transitioning from a dissertation to a research journal submission, gleaned from the authors' reflections on their own experiences publishing work from their dissertations in *JRME*. They begin by suggesting that authors of dissertations read and review for *JRME* to become familiar with the types of papers that it publishes and the language used in them. A primary challenge of reporting dissertation work within the format of a standard research paper is narrowing the focus to a limited number of key findings. Thanheiser et al. (2012) recommend that authors submitting dissertation work spend ample time determining which ideas they want to focus on and how they will communicate those ideas to readers who may not be thoroughly familiar with the particular topic under study.

In addition to its primary goal of disseminating high-quality research, *JRME* is dedicated to building capacity in the field by treating the review process as an educative experience. Thus, the editor may provide additional feedback on promising manuscripts that appear to be derived from an author's dissertation work but which are not yet in a form that is suitable for consideration for publication as a scholarly research paper. Therefore, authors are encouraged to indicate in their cover letter whether their submission is based on a dissertation.

21.7 Peer Review and Publishing in *JRME*

21.7.1 Peer Review Process

Although the *JRME* editor is responsible for all aspects of the journal, all decisions are collaborative processes among the editorial team members (Fig. 21.1). When a manuscript is submitted to the *JRME* Online Submission System, the staff checks

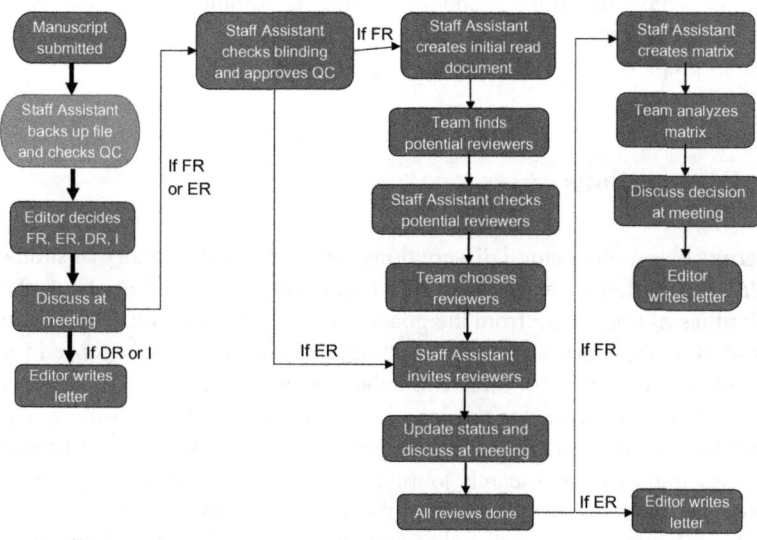

Fig. 21.1 *JRME* manuscript processing flowchart

that it meets technical requirements (e.g., blinding, formatting) and that the manuscript topic falls within the journal's domain of interest in mathematics education research. The editor reads the manuscript, discusses it with the editorial team, and categorizes it in one of four categories:

Inappropriate (I): Manuscripts pertaining to topics that do not fit the purposes of *JRME* (e.g., the presentation of a mathematical proof) are considered inappropriate for the journal and are returned to the author without further consideration.

Desk Reject (DR): Manuscripts for which the quality of the research does not meet the standards of *JRME* or manuscripts that do not meet the journal's technical or stylistic requirements (e.g., a verbatim chapter of a thesis) are desk rejected and returned to the author without undergoing external review. Typically, these reports have serious flaws or the work does not move the field of research in mathematics education forward in significant ways.

Editorial Review (ER): Manuscripts designated for editorial review show promise but are unlikely to be accepted for publication in their current form. As part of the educative mission of *JRME*, manuscripts from dissertation work often receive an editorial review rather than a desk reject. For an editorial review, a single member of the *JRME* Editorial Panel is chosen to evaluate the manuscript and provide feedback.

Full Review (FR): Manuscripts designated for full review are typically sent to three to five reviewers. Typically, one reviewer is a member of the *JRME* Editorial Panel and the other reviewers are selected for their expertise relative to various aspects of the manuscript.

JRME reviews serve both an educative and an evaluative purpose (Silver 2003; Williams 2008). For manuscripts given an editorial or full review, the reviews are meant to help authors think carefully and deeply about their work, and they "inform the editor's decision not as 'votes' but as sources of insight and perspective" (Heid and Zbiek 2009, p. 474). Thus, the editor synthesizes the points raised in the reviews along with input from the editorial team and makes a collaborative decision that is informed, but not determined, by the various viewpoints:

- **Accept** the manuscript for publication in *JRME*, often pending revisions;
- **Revise and Resubmit**, which is a rejection with encouragement to the author(s) to revise the manuscript substantially and resubmit it for a new round of evaluation by reviewers; or
- **Reject** the manuscript.

Finally, the editor drafts a decision letter to communicate the decision to the author, including suggestions for a revision or an indication of the reasons for a rejection.

21.7.2 Strengthening Manuscripts Through the Revision Process

Authors receiving a Revise and Resubmit (R&R) decision have up to a year from the date of the decision to make substantial revisions to the manuscript and resubmit it for a further round of peer review. However, authors are encouraged to do so within 4 or 5 months to ensure that returning reviewers are secured. Resubmissions are again sent for a round of evaluation by reviewers, some of whom reviewed the original submission and the rest of whom are new to the manuscript. When the reviewers' evaluations have been received, the editor again provides one of three decisions as before.

Although an R&R decision can be disheartening, it may in fact represent an encouraging outcome (Louie et al. in press). As Martin and Miller noted in 2014, the acceptance rate for revised manuscripts that are resubmitted after receiving an initial R&R decision is significantly higher than the overall acceptance rate for manuscripts submitted to *JRME*. For example, in 2017, the acceptance rate for manuscripts resubmitted after an R&R decision was about four times the overall acceptance rate. This is because manuscripts that receive an R&R generally report significant research that has the potential to make a strong contribution to the field and add to the literature. However, they often require further elaboration or development of particular aspects of the manuscript. A resubmitted manuscript that has been revised, taking into careful consideration the feedback from the reviewers and the editor, is much more likely to fare well in the second round of peer reviews than the original submission.

Common concerns that often result in an R&R decision include (a) issues with the literature review or theoretical framework, (b) issues with the methods, (c) claims that go beyond the data provided, and (d) a lack of coherence among the different parts of the manuscript. In some manuscripts, the literature review or theoretical framework is not appropriate or there is a disconnect between the framework and the design of the study or the data analysis. The theoretical framework may not be described clearly enough to situate the study and highlight the significance of the work. Another concern arises when manuscripts leave important aspects of the research methods unclear or incompletely described. In such cases, the reviewers will often call for more information on coding, data analysis, instruments, subjects, and so on. A third common concern arises when manuscripts include claims that are not clearly supported by the data that have been presented. This can, for example, take the form of overinterpreting the findings or making overly expansive statements about implications. Finally, some manuscripts suffer from an overall lack of coherence. The various components of a research article must hang together logically and fit together into a coherent storyline or narrative. The literature review and theoretical framework should situate the study and justify the research questions. The methods used to investigate the research questions must make sense with respect to the theoretical framework. The presentation and discussion of the results should, again, be clearly connected to the literature reviewed and the study's theoretical framework.

In their letters, *JRME* editors aim to provide detailed summaries of the major issues of the manuscript and to provide specific suggestions for how to address the reviewers' concerns. Authors are encouraged to discuss their revision plan and any issues that are unclear to them with the editor. With this approach, it is the editorial team's hope that authors will regard the editor as a partner in undertaking the revision process rather than as a mere evaluator. As part of the revision process, authors must submit a response letter that details the ways in which they addressed all of the concerns raised by the editor and the reviewers. When, as sometimes happens, reviewers raise conflicting issues, the editor will provide a suggestion to the authors. In their response letter, authors must carefully elaborate on and justify how they chose to handle any conflicting issues raised by the reviewers. In the event that authors disagree with one of the suggestions or concerns raised by the editor or a reviewer, it is strongly recommended that they carefully explain why they did not address the suggestion or concern. Though not a requirement, it is recommended that authors discuss such conflicting issues with the editor before submitting a revised manuscript.

21.7.3 What to Expect After a Manuscript Is Accepted

A manuscript that has been accepted for publication in *JRME* is typically accepted pending revisions. Even after a manuscript is accepted for publication, there is often room for additional clarification and refinement that would strengthen the reporting of the research. The editorial team typically provides detailed feedback to authors in the decision letter. The editor specifies the remaining issues that must be addressed before the manuscript can be published. Authors are strongly encouraged to communicate with the editor to discuss their plan for revisions. Communication between the author(s) and the editor in this way is extremely worthwhile and helps to ensure the timely publication of accepted articles. It can also help authors to clarify any questions or issues arising during the revision process.

Once the editorial team receives the revised manuscript, they begin copyediting it for APA formatting, references, citations, and quote accuracy as well as reviewing it for internal consistency and clarity. This process often involves multiple rounds of communication with the author(s) until all issues are resolved. When all issues are resolved, the team sends the manuscript to NCTM's copyediting team to be set in page proofs. Two rounds of page proofs ensue.

The first round of page proofs is sent to both the author(s) and the *JRME* editorial team. Authors review the proof of their article and send corrections to the editorial team, who then forward them to NCTM. Substantial changes to content are not appropriate at this time. The final round of page proofs is sent to the editorial team only. This serves as the final round of editing before the issue in which the manuscript is to appear is sent for printing.

21.8 Looking to the Future

Research journals play significant roles in the advancement of academic fields of inquiry. At the same time, journal publication is usually a passive process. That is, the journal editorial team receives whatever authors choose to submit and then conducts a rigorous peer review process that informs a publication decision. However, from time to time, *JRME* has attempted to look to the future of mathematics education research by actively calling the community's attention to topics of special significance through the publication of editorials and issues focused on those topics. For example, in a recent series of editorials, Editor Jinfa Cai and his team have highlighted the conundrum of increasing the impact of research on educational practice (Cai et al. 2017b). They described an alternative vision of a world in which tightly woven, sustainable partnerships between teachers and researchers would make steady progress to solve significant problems of practice (Cai et al. 2017a). Moreover, they proposed alternative pathways for research that would enable such partnerships to address teachers' pressing problems through innovative uses of data and technology, artifacts to store and share professional knowledge, and radical changes in institutional structures and incentives for both researchers and practitioners (Cai et al. 2019). The aim of these editorials was to stimulate discussion and to encourage those in the field of mathematics education to look to the horizon of what might be possible.

Another example of *JRME*'s effort to both deepen and push forward the conversation in the field took the form of a 2013 *JRME* special issue on equity that highlighted the increasing importance (and relevance to mathematics education) of sociopolitical issues in an increasingly globalized world (D'Ambrosio et al. 2013). The special issue's 10+ articles "all illustrate that mathematics education is always social and political" (D'Ambrosio et al. 2013, p. 6) and call upon the reader to explore issues of identity and power as they relate to ensuring that all students have the opportunity to experience high-quality mathematics education.

Early in 2018, through a fortunate confluence of manuscript submissions, *JRME* was able to publish a number of replication studies. Once again taking the opportunity to engage the mathematics education research community in an important conversation about moving the field forward, the editorial team raised questions about the long-standing but largely unaddressed calls for more replication research (Cai et al. 2018). Sir Ronald Fisher, the father of modern educational statistics, considered replication to be one of the fundamental building blocks of experimental research design (Fisher 1935). Collins (1985) referred to replication as "the Supreme Court of the scientific system" (p. 19) in which prior findings can be tested for validity or explored to find the conditions under which they do or do not hold true. As far back as 1970, Nathanial Smith referred to replication studies as "a neglected aspect of psychological research" (p. 970). This has been true both in the larger field of psychology (Makel and Plucker 2006; Makel et al. 2012) and in mathematics education. Indeed, although replication is a key aspect of knowledge building in many fields of research, its place in mathematics education research journals has never been prominent. The editorial team saw this as an opportune moment to advance the conversation around replication, proposing that conceptual replications might be the key to making replication a more powerful tool in mathematics education (Cai et al. 2018).

When NCTM decided to establish *JRME*, it was with the conviction that research was essential to improving mathematics education. As Julius Hlavaty, the NCTM president at the time, remarked in 1970,

> It has become increasingly clearer to the responsible leaders of the Council and to its large and talented subset of people interested in research that the time has passed for occasional and sporadic concern in this area. We must—and will—strive mightily through the JOURNAL FOR RESEARCH IN MATHEMATICS EDUCATION to give the teacher in the classroom, the administrator and curriculum consultant at the planning level, and even the man in the street, the information, guidance, and help that research can provide. (p. 7)

Through its nearly 50-year existence, *JRME* has therefore served the mathematics education research community as a journal of record, a forum for scholarly discussion and debate, and, on occasion, a platform from which to call the field forward to new and exciting developments. The current *JRME* editorial team and ones to come continue the commitment of all those that have preceded them to disseminate significant research that will ultimately promote high-quality mathematics education for all students.

Appendix

Characteristics of a High Quality Manuscript

The *Journal for Research in Mathematics Education* seeks high quality manuscripts that contribute knowledge to the field of mathematics education. For an author's work to be publishable, it needs to exhibit qualities that characterize well-conceived and well-reported research studies.

The following information illustrates characteristics of strong manuscripts that have been submitted to *JRME*. This advice for potential authors is intended to be illustrative rather than exhaustive and pertains primarily to reports of empirical studies and theoretical articles; it does not necessarily reflect what would be appropriate for research commentaries or book reviews.

Inclusion of Appropriate Purpose and Rationale

- Describe a clear purpose for the study.
- Establish why the general area of study is important and how this particular study can contribute important information to the field. (One should not conduct a study simply because no such study has ever been done.)
- If examining a second context for an existing study, explain why the second study is useful. (This is not intended to suggest that replication studies are not appropriate.)

Clear Research Questions

- State research questions or research hypotheses explicitly and clearly in the manuscript. (The reader should not have to guess what the research questions were.)

  Clear research questions are guided by the theoretical framework and are addressed by the data collected and analysis performed on that data.

An Informative Literature Review

- Provide a basis for doing the study that is reported.
- Synthesize studies, creating more than a listing or summary of existing studies.
- Include credible sources (e.g., peer-reviewed journal articles) rather than drawing exclusively on project reports and unpublished works. Address results of previous research along with pertinent policy documents.
- Cite from a source accurately and reflect what was published in the original source.
- Include pertinent international research literature rather than limiting the review to that of a single country.
- Cite a variety of pertinent studies, not just your own work or that of your colleagues and collaborators.
- Include important works that support and ground the research such as current research in mathematics education; foundational research that is the basis for the study; and potentially works outside of mathematics education as appropriate.

A Coherent Theoretical Framework

- The study is guided by a theoretical framework that influences the study's design; its instrumentation, data collection, and data analysis; and the interpretation of its findings.
- The literature review connects to and supports the theoretical framework.
- Make it clear to the reader how the theoretical framework influenced decisions about the design and conduct of the study.

Clearly Described Research Methods*

Include key elements of research methodology such as:

- From what population the subjects were drawn, how and why they were selected, and how many were included;
- Information on the instructors and their backgrounds;
- When and how often the subjects were interviewed or tested;
- How many classrooms were included in the study;
- How each variable was measured;
- How research instruments were adapted or developed;
- Examples of items from research instruments;
- Descriptions of instructional approaches;
- Examples from instructional materials;

- Protocols used for classroom observation or interviews; and
- Details of the procedures used to analyze qualitative data.

Sound Research Design and Methods*

Employ research design and methods appropriate for answering the study's research questions:

- Give validity and reliability data for the instruments used;
- Use appropriate statistical procedures and meet their assumptions; and
- Use instruments appropriate to the study's subjects to measure outcome variables.
- Address threats to trustworthiness.
- Describe discrepant events.
- Use member checking when appropriate.

Claims about Results and Implications that are Supported by Data*

- Provide supporting data for each claim that is made.
- Do not draw conclusions or suggest implications that inappropriately extend beyond what is reasonable based on the data.
- Interpret and contextualize the study's results.

Contribution to the Field of Mathematics Education

- The study examines some aspect of the teaching and learning of mathematics and offers new results or new insights to mathematics education that extend beyond what has been reported in prior studies.
- The study moves the field beyond current methods, instruments, and/or theories.
- Focus goals on understanding a phenomenon deeply rather than investigating any particular classroom, student, lesson, or content.

Clearly Explained and Appropriately Used Terms

- Clearly define terms that are likely not to be understood by many readers (e.g., educational terminology unique to a particular country or region).
- If using familiar terms in nonstandard ways, provide explanations for doing so.
- When using terms that have several possible interpretations, clearly identify which interpretation is intended.
- Avoid using terms interchangeably that have different meanings (e.g., proof, reasoning, argumentation, and justification).
- Do not treat multidimensional entities as if they were one-dimensional (e.g., "reform curricula" are not a singular entity and "reform" involves changes in curriculum, pedagogy, and assessment, not just in curriculum)

High Quality Writing

- Provide helpful transitions so the manuscript flows well from one section to another.
- Develop ideas rather than listing collections of thoughts in paragraph form.

- Ask colleagues or employ editors to correct errors in grammar, spelling, and sentence structure.

Mathematical Accuracy

- Use mathematical terms correctly in conceptualizing their research.
- Use correct mathematics content in instructional materials, interview protocols, and written instruments.

* These items may not be applicable to manuscripts that primarily address theoretical issues.

References

American Psychological Association. (2010). *Publication manual of the American Psychological Association* (6th ed.). Washington, DC: Author.

Battista, M. T., Fey, J. T., King, K. D., Larson, M., Reed, J., Smith, M. S., et al. (2007). Connecting researching and practice at NCTM. *Journal for Research in Mathematics Education, 48*(2), 108–114.

Bazzini, L. (1991). Curriculum development as a meeting point for research and practice. *Zentralblatt für Didaktik der Mathematik, 4,* 128–131.

Blume, G. W., Heid, M. K., & Zbiek, R. M. (2010). Editorial: What is the purpose of publishing papers in a mathematics education research journal? *Journal for Research in Mathematics Education, 41*(3), 210–211.

Cai, J., Morris, A., Hohensee, C., Hwang, S., Robison, V., & Hiebert, J. (2017a). A future vision of mathematics education research: Blurring the boundaries of research and practice to address teachers' problems. *Journal for Research in Mathematics Education, 48*(5), 466–473. https://doi.org/10.5951/jresematheduc.48.5.0466.

Cai, J., Morris, A., Hwang, S., Hohensee, C., Robison, V., & Hiebert, J. (2017b). Improving the impact of educational research. *Journal for Research in Mathematics Education, 48*(1), 2–6. https://doi.org/10.5951/jresematheduc.48.1.0002.

Cai, J., Morris, A., Hohensee, C., Hwang, S., Robison, V., & Hiebert, J. (2018). The role of replication studies in educational research. *Journal for Research in Mathematics Education, 49*(1), 2–8. https://doi.org/10.5951/jresematheduc.49.1.0002.

Cai, J., Morris, A., Hohensee, C., Hwang, S., Robison, V., & Hiebert, J. (2019). Research pathways that connect research and practice. *Journal for Research in Mathematics Education, 50*(1), 2–10. https://doi.org/10.5951/jresematheduc.50.1.0002.

Cai, J., Morris, A., Hohensee, C., Hwang, S., Robison, V., Cirillo, M., et al. (2019). Posing significant research questions. *Journal for Research in Mathematics Education, 50*(2), 114–120. https://www.jstor.org/stable/10.5951/jresematheduc.50.2.0114.

Collins, H. M. (1985). *Changing order: Replication and induction in scientific practice.* London, UK: Sage.

Crespo, S., & Cai, J. (in press). Writing as communicating with reviewers: Strategies for anticipating and addressing insightful and skeptical reviews. In K. Leatham (Ed.), *Designing, conducting, and publishing quality research in mathematics education.* New York, NY: Springer.

D'Ambrosio, B., Frankenstein, M., Gutiérrez, R., Kastberg, S., Martin, D. B., Moschkovich, J., et al. (2013). Introduction to the *JRME* Equity Special Issue. *Journal for Research in Mathematics Education, 44*(1), 510.

Dreyfus, T. (2006). Linking theories in mathematics education. In A. Simpson (Ed.), *Retirement as process and concept: A festschrift for Eddie Gray and David Tall* (pp. 77–82). Durham, UK: Durham University.

Fisher, R. A. (1935). *The design of experiments*. Edinburgh, UK: Oliver & Boyd.

Heck, D. J., Tarr, J. E., Hollebrands, K. F., Walker, E. N., Berry, R. Q., III, Baltzley, P. C., et al. (2012). Reporting research for practitioners: Proposed guidelines. *Journal for Research in Mathematics Education, 43*(2), 126–143.

Heid, M. K. (2010). Editorial: The task of research manuscripts—Advancing the field of mathematics education. *Journal for Research in Mathematics Education, 41*(5), 434–437.

Heid, M. K., & Blume, G. W. (2011). Strengthening manuscript submissions. *Journal for Research in Mathematics Education, 42*(2), 106–108.

Heid, M. K., Larson, M., Fey, J. T., Strutchens, M. E., Middleton, J. A., Gutstein, E., et al. (2006). The challenge of linking research and practice. *Journal for Research in Mathematics Education, 37*(2), 76–86.

Heid, M. K., & Zbiek, R. M. (2009). Editorial: Manuscript review as scholarly work. *Journal for Research in Mathematics Education, 40*(5), 474–476.

Herbel-Eisenmann, B., Sinclair, N., Chval, K. B., Clements, D. H., Civil, M., Pape, S. J., et al. (2016). Positioning mathematics education researchers to influence storylines. *Journal for Research in Mathematics Education, 47*(2), 102–117.

Hlavaty, J. H. (1970). Message from Julius H. Hlavaty, President, NCTM. *Journal for Research in Mathematics Education, 1*(1), 7–8.

Holbrook, A., Bourke, S., Fairbairn, H., Preston, G., Cantwell, R., & Scevak, J. (2009). *Publishing in academic journals in education [CD]*. Melbourne, Australia: Professional Resources Services.

Inglis, M., & Foster, C. (2018). Five decades of mathematics education research. *Journal for Research in Mathematics Education, 49*(4), 462–500.

Institute of Education Sciences & National Science Foundation. (2013). *Common guidelines for education research and development*. Washington, DC: Author.

Johnson, D. C. (1970). Editorial comment. *Journal for Research in Mathematics Education, 1*(1), 5–6.

Kieran, C., Krainer, K., & Shaughnessy, J. M. (2012). Linking research to practice: Teachers as key stakeholders in mathematics education research. In M. A. K. Clements, A. Bishop, C. Keitel-Kreidt, J. Kilpatrick, & F. K.-S. Leung (Eds.), *Third international handbook of mathematics education* (pp. 361–392). New York, NY: Springer.

Langrall, C. W. (2014). The state of the journal. *Journal for Research in Mathematics Education, 45*(1), 2–4.

Louie, N., Reinholz, D., & Shah, N. (in press). Getting published: Perspectives from early-career scholars. In K. Leatham (Ed.), *Designing, conducting, and publishing quality research in mathematics education*. New York, NY: Springer.

Makel, M. C., & Plucker, J. A. (2006). Facts are more important than novelty: Replication in the education sciences. *Educational Researcher, 43*(6), 304–316.

Makel, M. C., Plucker, J. A., & Hegarty, B. (2012). Replications in psychology research: How often do they really occur? *Perspectives on Psychological Science, 7*(6), 537–542. https://doi.org/10.1177/1745691612460688.

Malara, N. A., & Zan, R. (2002). The problematic relationship between theory and practice. In L. English (Ed.), *Handbook of international research in mathematics education* (pp. 553–580). Mahwah, NJ: Lawrence Erlbaum Associates.

Martin, T. S., & Miller, A. L. (2014). I received a "Revise and Resubmit" decision: Now what? *Journal for Research in Mathematics Education, 45*(3), 286–287.

Nivens, R. A., & Otten, S. (2017). Assessing journal quality in mathematics education. *Journal for Research in Mathematics Education, 48*(4), 348–368.

Ruthven, K. (2002). Linking researching with teaching: Towards a synergy of scholarly and craft knowledge. In L. D. English (Ed.), *Handbook of international research in mathematics education* (pp. 581–598). Mahwah, NJ: Lawrence Erlbaum Associates.

Schoenfeld, A. H. (2018). On replications. *Journal for Research in Mathematics Education, 49*(1), 91–97. https://doi.org/10.5951/jresematheduc.49.1.0091.

Silver, E. A. (2003). Border crossing: Relating research and practice in mathematics education. *Journal for Research in Mathematics Education, 34*(3), 182–184.

Silver, E. A., & Lunsford, C. (2017). Linking research and practice in mathematics education: Perspectives and pathways. In J. Cai (Ed.), *Compendium for research in mathematics education* (pp. 28–47). Reston, VA: National Council of Teachers of Mathematics.

Smith, N. C. (1970). Replication studies: A neglected aspect of psychological research. *American Psychologist, 25*(10), 970–975. https://doi.org/10.1037/h0029774.

Star, J. R. (2018). When and why replication studies should be published: Guidelines for mathematics education journals. *Journal for Research in Mathematics Education, 49*(1), 98–103. https://doi.org/10.5951/jresematheduc.49.1.0098.

Thanheiser, E., Ellis, A., & Herbel-Eisenmann, B. (2012). From dissertation to publication in JRME. *Journal for Research in Mathematics Education, 43*(2), 144–158.

Toerner, G., & Arzarello, F. (2012, December). Grading mathematics education research journals. *Newsletter of the European Mathematical Society, 86*, 52–54.

Williams, S. (2008). Editorial: A view on reviewing. *Journal for Research in Mathematics Education, 39*(3), 218–219.

Williams, S. R., & Leatham, K. R. (2017). Journal quality in mathematics education. *Journal for Research in Mathematics Education, 48*(4), 369–396.

Open Access This chapter is licensed under the terms of the Creative Commons Attribution 4.0 International License (http://creativecommons.org/licenses/by/4.0/), which permits use, sharing, adaptation, distribution and reproduction in any medium or format, as long as you give appropriate credit to the original author(s) and the source, provide a link to the Creative Commons license and indicate if changes were made.

The images or other third party material in this chapter are included in the chapter's Creative Commons license, unless indicated otherwise in a credit line to the material. If material is not included in the chapter's Creative Commons license and your intended use is not permitted by statutory regulation or exceeds the permitted use, you will need to obtain permission directly from the copyright holder.

Chapter 22
The Journal of Mathematical Behavior

Carolyn A. Maher, Elizabeth Uptegrove and Louise C. Wilkinson

Abstract *The Journal of Mathematical Behavior* solicits original research on the learning and teaching of mathematics, from young children to adults, with a focus on how mathematical ideas are developed in learners under certain conditions that support learning. We are interested especially in basic research that aims to clarify, in detail and depth, how mathematics is learned.

Keywords Mathematics · Learning · Teaching · Research

22.1 Introduction

The Journal of Mathematical Behavior (JMB) has continued to serve as a leading journal in the field for almost half a century. It was founded by the late Robert B. Davis in 1971 as the *Journal of Children's Mathematical Behavior*. The first issue of the journal that was available for the research community was Volume 1, issue number 3, September 1975. This volume includes the following statement: "The Madison Project is one of the federally-funded 'New Math' projects. It is concerned both with practical assistance to schools and teachers, and also with theoretical questions in the areas of the nature of learning, the selection of appropriate curricula, and the creation of effective learning environments." In autumn 1980, Volume 3 became the first issue of *The Journal of Mathematical Behavior*, with the expanded focus on mathematics learning, teaching, assessment and policy.

C. A. Maher (✉) · E. Uptegrove
Rutgers University, New Brunswick, NJ, USA
e-mail: carolyn.maher@gse.rutgers.edu

E. Uptegrove
e-mail: uptegrovee@felician.edu

L. C. Wilkinson
Syracuse University, Syracuse, NY, USA
e-mail: lwilkin@syr.edu

© The Author(s) 2019
G. Kaiser and N. Presmeg (eds.), *Compendium for Early Career Researchers in Mathematics Education*, ICME-13 Monographs,
https://doi.org/10.1007/978-3-030-15636-7_22

Robert B. Davis' view in establishing the journal was to introduce new perspectives about learning mathematics with ideas drawn from cognitive science, to reshape, and make more rigorous, the ways that we investigate and conceptualize how mathematics can be learned. His book *Learning mathematics: The cognitive science approach to mathematics education* (Davis 1984) summarized this new perspective. Many influential papers were published at this time in a range of research journals, illustrating the cognitive science approach for studying mathematics learning.

The original mission of *The Journal of Mathematical Behavior* is reflected in current work. *The Journal of Mathematical Behavior* continues to seek to stimulate investigation and discussion of important questions about how people learn mathematics, reason mathematically, solve mathematical problems and use mathematics in their daily lives. As noted on the Journal's web site, "*The Journal of Mathematical Behavior* solicits original research on the learning and teaching of mathematics. We are interested especially in basic research that aims to clarify, in detail and depth, how mathematical ideas develop in learners." We welcome papers that "develop detailed, fundamental understanding of how people, in realistic settings, build, retain, communicate, apply and understand important mathematical ideas."

A *distinguishing feature* of JMB is that we focus on qualitative analyses that provide detail in how mathematical ideas and ways of reasoning are built by learners, supported, if applicable, with appropriate quantitative (statistical) data analysis.

22.2 Scope

As described on the JMB website, "Our intended audience includes researchers who concentrate on the learning of mathematics and science, psychologists, mathematicians, cognitive scientists, teachers, teacher educators, curriculum developers, parents, administrators, and policy makers." For example, recent findings have highlighted the importance of research on newly-developing aspects of mathematics learning, teaching, and assessment such as the complexity of learning mathematics and the attention to be paid to issues for English language learners (EL students) and learners with specific learning challenges.

The editors encourage submission of reports of basic studies that might indicate a range of possibilities not commonly recognized. Such studies might do the following: clarify potential obstacles to student understanding of mathematics; describe and analyze relevant efforts to improve curriculum or pedagogy in mathematics, at any level, from early childhood through adulthood; offer analyses of appropriate goals for mathematics curricula for diverse student populations; and critically discuss what might be changed in curricula or in learning experiences. In addition to more formal studies, the editors welcome dialogue, discussion, and debate. We encourage authors to submit short papers that continue, extend, modify, or challenge work that has appeared in JMB.

22.3 Guide for Authors

Instructions for preparing a paper for submission are available on the Elsevier website https://www.journals.elsevier.com/the-journal-of-mathematical-behavior.

From that site, authors can download the *Understanding the Publishing Process* document or the *Author Information Pack* or read the *Guide for Authors* online. Also refer to the *Authors' Update* web page https://www.elsevier.com/connect/authors-update for up-to-date information of interest to authors, reviewers, and readers.

To submit a manuscript, log on to EVISE for *The Journal of Mathematical Behavior* at https://www.evise.com/profile/#/MATBEH/login.

Follow the instructions for creating an account if you do not already have one. Submit a manuscript by selecting the *My Author Tasks* tab and then clicking on the blue button for *Start New Submission*. Enter information under the four categories (*Enter manuscript information*, *Upload files*, *Provide additional information*, and *Review and submit*).

Authors should note the following common misunderstandings relating to submitting manuscripts to JMB.

- The EVISE system requires that you submit only a blinded version of the manuscript. Please do not submit an unblinded manuscript.
- There is no limit on the length of a submission.
- Page numbers are not required, but they are very helpful to reviewers and editors.
- This Journal does not accept manuscripts focusing on strictly statistical analyses. We accept manuscripts with statistical analyses that supplement and support qualitative research.
- Manuscripts submitted to this journal that include summaries of results must also include supporting data.
- The Journal does not accept manuscripts describing lesson plans, unless they are in the context of student learning.
- Papers on strictly mathematical topics (e.g., proofs of theorems) are not suitable for this journal.
- Due dates for submissions of revised manuscripts are set automatically by system default. If you need more time to revise a manuscript, send a request to the editor handling your manuscript. Such requests are usually granted.
- If any parts of the decision letter are not clear, ask the editor handling your manuscript for clarification.

22.4 Language Editing Services

Editing, proofreading, and translation services are available to authors whose first language is not English. These services are available through the WebShop at https://webshop.elsevier.com/.

22.5 Special Issues

In order to address particular areas of mathematics learning that require multiple perspectives and contributions, we invite proposals for *Special Issues*. Over the years, *Special Issues* involved a variety of topics related to learning and teaching particular areas of mathematics, elementary through tertiary.

Special Issues, either stand-alone or as Special Issue Sections, consist of original papers focused on a particular topic; these collections have made important contributions to the field. Table 22.1 gives the range of Special Issue topics that have been published in this journal.

Table 22.1 Special issues of the journal of mathematical behavior

Year and Vol.	Special issue/Link	Editors
2018	Learning through activity	Martin Simon, Maria Blanton
2018	International teaching and learning of mathematics	Peter Sullivan, Louise C. Wilkinson
2018	The roles of examples in proving and learning to prove	Orit Zaslavsky, Eric Knuth, Amy Ellis
2017, 46	Preparing and implementing successful mathematics coaches and teacher leaders	Aimee Ellington, Joy Whitenack, Christine Trinter
	https://www.sciencedirect.com/journal/the-journal-of-mathematical-behavior/vol/46/suppl/C	
2016, 41	The many colors of math: Engaging students through collaboration and agency	Jo Boaler
	https://www.sciencedirect.com/journal/the-journal-of-mathematical-behavior/vol/41/suppl/C	
2015, 40A	The language of learning mathematics	Louise Wilkinson
	https://www.sciencedirect.com/journal/the-journal-of-mathematical-behavior/vol/40/part/PA	
2013, 32.4	The teaching abstract algebra for understanding project: designing and scaling up a curriculum innovation	Sean Larsen, Estrella Johnson, Keith Weber
	https://www.sciencedirect.com/journal/the-journal-of-mathematical-behavior/vol/32/issue/4	
2007, 26.3	An inquiry oriented approach to differential equations	Chris L. Rasmussen
	https://www.sciencedirect.com/journal/the-journal-of-mathematical-behavior/vol/26/issue/3	

(continued)

Table 22.1 (continued)

Year and Vol.	Special issue/Link	Editors
2005, 24.3	Mathematical problem solving: What we know and where we are going	Jinfa Cai, Joanna Mamona-Downs, Keith Weber
	https://www.sciencedirect.com/journal/the-journal-of-mathematical-behavior/vol/24/issue/3	
2003, 22.3	Fractions, ratio and proportional reasoning, Part B	Gary E. Davis
	https://www.sciencedirect.com/journal/the-journal-of-mathematical-behavior/vol/22/issue/3	
2003, 22.2	Fractions, ratio and proportional reasoning, Part A	Gary E. Davis
	https://www.sciencedirect.com/journal/the-journal-of-mathematical-behavior/vol/22/issue/2	
1998, 17.2	Representations and the psychology of mathematics education, Part II	Gerald A. Goldin, Claude Janvier
	https://www.sciencedirect.com/journal/the-journal-of-mathematical-behavior/vol/17/issue/2	
1998, 17.1	Representations and the psychology of mathematics education, Part I	Gerald A. Goldin, Claude Janvier
	https://www.sciencedirect.com/journal/the-journal-of-mathematical-behavior/vol/17/issue/1	
1997, 16.3	An investigation into students' understanding of abstract algebra (binary operations, groups, and subgroups) and the use of abstract structures (through cosets, normality, and quotient groups)	Ed Dubinsky
	https://www.sciencedirect.com/journal/the-journal-of-mathematical-behavior/vol/16/issue/3	
1994, 13.1	What mathematics should children learn?	Robert B. Davis
	https://www.sciencedirect.com/journal/the-journal-of-mathematical-behavior/vol/13/issue/1	

22.5.1 Proposals for Special Issues

The editors encourage new proposals. Special Issues (about 12–15 papers) or Special Sections (about 8–10 papers) should appear in fewer than half the issues that make up the Journal each year. Given the number of suggestions received, the editors have to be quite selective in accepting ideas and topics that will make an important, timely and high-quality contribution to the field. To optimize the appropriate timing of publication, the editors welcome suggestions at an early stage in their development. In some cases, initial contact may be made with any of the editors for exploratory discussions, and these may lead to a proposal by the prospective guest editors. Alternatively, guest editors may also proceed directly to submitting a proposal. The following list gives the information needed in a proposal for a Special Issue. All proposals are reviewed by the journal editors in consultation with the Publisher.

22.5.1.1 Basic Information

- Provisional title
- Names, titles, affiliations and contact information (including email information) of all the proposed guest editors
- Short title of the Special Issue (maximum 23 characters including spaces).

22.5.1.2 Overview

- Proposed topic, with outline scope and structure
- Academic rationale (contribution of the issue to the development of the field, etc.)
- Any special circumstances (conference, major research project, festschrift, etc.)
- Special Issue rationale.

22.5.1.3 Possible Contributors

- Number of expected papers to be published in this Special Issue
- If known, a list of the potential authors plus topics; if not known, the steps to be used to identify such a list.

22.5.1.4 Process for Reviewing Papers

- Stages of submission, review and decision
- Mode of submission and review
- Role of any workshops, meetings, etc.
- Brief information about the editorial and related experience of the guest editors.

22.5.1.5 Schedule

- The date the first submission is expected
- The date by which all papers should be submitted
- The delivery date by which all manuscripts should be fully reviewed and final decisions made on all manuscripts
- Expected date of submission to the publishers.

22.6 Reviewing for *the Journal of Mathematical Behavior*

If you register for the Evise system in order to submit a manuscript, you are automatically placed in the system to be considered as a reviewer. Potential reviewers should specify areas of interest (e.g. *algebra, preservice teacher preparation, language of mathematics*). Alternately, those interested in reviewing manuscripts can get in touch with one of the editors.

Reviewer guidelines can be found at https://www.elsevier.com/reviewers/how-to-review.

Brief guidelines are as follows:

- You should agree to do a review only if the manuscript fits with your area of expertise, there is no conflict of interest, and you will be able to complete the review within the required time frame.
- The manuscript should be treated as confidential.
- Verify that the methods section describes a sound methodology and that the conclusions are consistent with the data.
- Reviews should be courteous and constructive. Personal details about the reviewer, including name, should not be included.
- The recommendation will be reject, accept, major revisions, or minor revisions. All recommendations should be supported by specific details about the manuscript.

22.7 Summary Statistics on Utilization

From July 2017 through June 2018, there were 193 manuscripts submitted to the Journal, with 71 manuscripts accepted, a rate of about 37%.

Table 22.2 gives information about most-downloaded articles.

Table 22.3 gives information on most-cited manuscripts.

22.8 Editorial Team

In conclusion, *The Journal of Mathematical Behavior* offers researchers and scholars an unparalleled opportunity to share knowledge and to invite colleagues to join in discussion about the significant issues of mathematical learning, teaching, and assessment. We encourage potential authors to search the published articles in the journal for colleagues whose interests and work align with their own; this, in turn can lead to collaborations that enhance the efforts that each individually may make.

Carolyn A. Maher, Editor
  carolyn.maher@gse.rutgers.edu
Timothy Fukawa-Connelly
  tug27597@temple.edu
Steven Greenstein
  greensteins@mail.montclair.edu
Louise C. Wilkinson
  lwilkin@syr.edu
Elizabeth Uptegrove
  uptegrovee@felician.edu
Rina Zazkis
  zazkis@sfu.ca

Table 22.2 Articles most-downloaded from JMB

Title	Date	Authors
Learning mathematics through algorithmic and creative reasoning	December 2014	Bert Jonsson, Mathias Norqvist, Yvonne Liljekvist, Johan Lithner
Knowledge of nonlocal mathematics for teaching	March 2018	Nicholas H. Wasserman
Mathematics teachers' attention to potential classroom situations of argumentation	March 2018	Michal Ayalon, Rina Hershkowitz
Secondary mathematics teachers' instrumental integration in technology-rich geometry classrooms	March 2018	Karen Hollebrands, Samet Okumuş
Reflective abstraction in computational thinking	September 2017	Ibrahim Cetin, Ed Dubinsky
Playing number board games supports 5-year-old children's early mathematical development	September 2016	Jessica Elofsson, Stefan Gustafson, Joakim Samuelsson, Ulf Träff
Designing mathematics classes to promote equity and engagement	March 2016	Jo Boaler
Discovering and addressing errors during mathematics problem-solving—A productive struggle?	June 2016	Carina Granberg
The many colors of algebra: The impact of equity focused teaching upon student learning and engagement	March 2016	Jo Boaler, Tesha Sengupta-Irving
An operational definition of learning	September 2010	Guershon Harel, Boris Koichu

(continued)

Table 22.2 (continued)

Title	Date	Authors
From language as a resource to sources of meaning in multilingual mathematics classrooms	June 2018	Richard Barwell
Prerequisite algebra skills and associated misconceptions of middle grade students: A review	September 2013	Sarah B. Bush, Karen S. Karp
Are indirect proofs less convincing? A study of students' comparative assessments	March 2018	Stacy Ann Brown
Students' conceptualisations of multiplication as repeated addition or equal groups in relation to multi-digit and decimal numbers	December 2017	Kerstin Larsson, Kerstin Pettersson, Paul Andrews
Academic literacy in mathematics for English Learners	December 2015	Judit N. Moschkovich
The language of learning mathematics: A multimodal perspective	December 2015	Kay L. O'Halloran
Educative experiences in a games context: Supporting emerging reasoning in elementary school mathematics	June 2018	P. Janelle McFeetors, Kylie Palfy
Habits of mind: An organizing principle for mathematics curricula	December 1996	Al Cuoco, E. Paul Goldenberg, June Mark
Eye color and the practice of statistics in Grade 6: Comparing two groups	March 2018	Jane Watson, Lyn English
Students' epistemological frames and their interpretation of lectures in advanced mathematics	March 2018	Victoria Krupnik, Timothy Fukawa-Connelly, Keith Weber
Using contextualized tasks to engage students in meaningful and worthwhile mathematics learning	January 2018	Doug Clarke, Anne Roche
Effectively coaching middle school teachers: A case for teacher and student learning	June 2017	Aimee Ellington, Joy Whitenack, David Edwards
Evaluation of three interventions teaching area measurement as spatial structuring to young children	June 2018	Douglas H. Clements, Julie Sarama, Douglas W. Van Dine, Jeffrey E. Barrett, Craig J. Cullen, Aaron Hudyma, Ron Dolgin, Amanda L. Cullen, Cheryl L. Eames
Undergraduates' images of the root concept in $\mathbb{R}$ and in $\mathbb{C}$	March 2018	Igor' Kontorovich
How mathematicians assign points to student proofs	March 2018	David Miller, Nicole Infante, Keith Weber

Table 22.3 Most-cited manuscripts from JMB

Title	Date	Authors
Developing mathematical competence: From the intended to the enacted curriculum	March 2014	Jesper Boesen, Ola Helenius, Ewa Bergqvist, Tomas Bergqvist, Johan Lithner, Torulf Palm, Björn Palmberg
The fractional knowledge and algebraic reasoning of students with the first multiplicative concept	September 2013	Amy J. Hackenberg
Learning trajectories in teacher education: Supporting teachers' understandings of students' mathematical thinking	June 2013	P. Holt Wilson, Gemma F. Mojica, Jere Confrey
The language of learning mathematics: A multimodal perspective	January 2015	Kay L. O'Halloran
A local instructional theory for the guided reinvention of the group and isomorphism concepts	December 2013	Sean P. Larsen
Learning mathematics through algorithmic and creative reasoning	December 2014	Bert Jonsson, Mathias Norqvist, Yvonne Liljekvist, Johan Lithner
Examining novice teacher leaders' facilitation of mathematics professional development	March 2014	Hilda Borko, Karen Koellner, Jennifer Jacobs
The role of problem representation and feature knowledge in algebraic equation-solving	September 2013	Julie L. Booth, Jodi L. Davenport
High school students' understanding of the function concept	March 2013	Ed Dubinsky, Robin T. Wilson
Equation structure and the meaning of the equal sign: The impact of task selection in eliciting elementary students' understandings	June 2013	Ana C. Stephens, Eric J. Knuth, Maria L. Blanton, Isil Isler, Angela Murphy Gardiner, Tim Marum
Young children's recognition of quantitative relations in mathematically unspecified settings	September 2013	Jake A. McMullen, Minna M. Hannula-Sormunen, Erno Lehtinen
Covariational reasoning and invariance among coordinate systems	September 2013	Kevin C. Moore, Teo Paoletti, Stacy Musgrave
A framework for characterizing student understanding of Riemann sums and definite integrals	March 2014	Vicki Sealey
Prerequisite algebra skills and associated misconceptions of middle grade students: A review	September 2013	Sarah B. Bush, Karen S. Karp
Impacting positively on students' mathematical problem solving beliefs: An instructional intervention of short duration	March 2014	Andreas J. Stylianides, Gabriel J. Stylianides
The negative sign and exponential expressions: Unveiling students' persistent errors and misconceptions	March 2013	Richard Cangelosi, Silvia Madrid, Sandra Cooper, Jo Olson, Beverly Hartter

(continued)

Table 22.3 (continued)

Title	Date	Authors
ICT-supported problem solving and collaborative creative reasoning: Exploring linear functions using dynamic mathematics software	March 2015	Carina Granberg, Jan Olsson
Academic literacy in mathematics for English Learners	January 2015	Judit N. Moschkovich
A formative assessment of students' algebraic variable misconceptions	March 2014	Joan Lucariello, Michele T. Tine, Colleen M. Ganley
Learning angles through movement: Critical actions for developing understanding in an embodied activity	December 2014	Carmen Petrick Smith, Barbara King, Jennifer Hoyte
About the concept of angle in elementary school: Misconceptions and teaching sequences	March 2013	Claude Devichi, Valérie Munier
A model of students' combinatorial thinking	June 2013	Elise Lockwood
A local instructional theory for the guided reinvention of the quotient group concept	December 2013	Sean Larsen, Elise Lockwood
A power meaning of multiplication: Three eighth graders' solutions of Cartesian product problems	September 2013	Erik S. Tillema
Knowledge shifts and knowledge agents in the classroom	March 2014	Michal Tabach, Rina Hershkowitz, Chris Rasmussen, Tommy Dreyfus

Reference

Davis, R. B. (1984). *Learning mathematics: The cognitive science approach to mathematics education*. Norwood, New Jersey: Greenwood Publishing Group.

Open Access This chapter is licensed under the terms of the Creative Commons Attribution 4.0 International License (http://creativecommons.org/licenses/by/4.0/), which permits use, sharing, adaptation, distribution and reproduction in any medium or format, as long as you give appropriate credit to the original author(s) and the source, provide a link to the Creative Commons license and indicate if changes were made.

The images or other third party material in this chapter are included in the chapter's Creative Commons license, unless indicated otherwise in a credit line to the material. If material is not included in the chapter's Creative Commons license and your intended use is not permitted by statutory regulation or exceeds the permitted use, you will need to obtain permission directly from the copyright holder.

Chapter 23
Publishing in the *Journal of Mathematics Teacher Education*

Despina Potari

Abstract This chapter has the aim of supporting early career researchers who want to publish a paper in the *Journal of Mathematics Teacher Education* (*JMTE*) by providing them with information about the scope of the journal, its impact on the field, the papers published, the reviewing process and the required quality. It ends by providing some advice on issues that an early career researcher needs to consider if he or she decides to submit a paper to *JMTE*.

Keywords Quality of research · Reviewing process · *Journal of Mathematics Teacher Education*

23.1 Introduction

JMTE is one of the mathematics education journals published by Springer. It was founded by Professor Tom Cooney in 1998 as a journal specializing in mathematics teacher education research and practice. Although the life of the journal is rather short, *JMTE* has been established among the top journals in mathematics education (Williams and Leatham 2017).

Cooney (1998), in his first editorial, considered *JMTE* as a professional setting for mathematics teacher educators to communicate their work both at the research and practice levels:

> The establishment of the *Journal of Mathematics Teacher Education* (*JMTE*) provides us with a forum singularly devoted to our work in teacher education. Indeed, we now have more reason than ever to integrate our study of teacher education with our practice of teacher education. We have much to learn. (p. 1)

Theory-practice relations, diversity of ideas and perspectives, acknowledgment of the complexity of mathematics teaching and mathematics teacher education as

D. Potari (✉)
National and Kapodistrian University of Athens, Athens, Greece
e-mail: dpotari@math.uoa.gr

well as theorization and critical analysis have been important goals of *JMTE* throughout its 20 years' journey.

I have contributed to *JMTE* since its establishment in different roles, including those of author, reviewer, member of the editorial board, associate editor, and as editor in chief, and so I have participated in this journey. In this chapter I provide some information about the journal and share some of my experiences, especially related to the reviewing process, which may be helpful to an early career researcher who has done research related to mathematics teachers and mathematics teacher education, and who wants to publish it in *JMTE*.

The chapter is structured in six sections, after the introduction 23.1. Section 23.2 concerns the scope of the journal. Section 23.3 provides information about the acceptance rate and the impact of *JMTE* in the international research community. Section 23.4 presents the results from a short survey of the content, theoretical perspectives and methodologies of the papers published in 2017. Section 23.5 discusses the process from the submission until the publication of a paper, focusing mainly on the procedure itself. Section 23.6 discusses the reviewing and decision making process, focusing mainly on issues of quality. Section 23.7 concludes with some guidelines for early career researchers focusing on main issues to consider when they prepare a manuscript for *JMTE*.

23.2 The Scope of the Journal

In the homepage of the journal the scope of the journal is presented, which I cite below:

> The *Journal of Mathematics Teacher Education* (*JMTE*) is devoted to research into the education of mathematics teachers and development of teaching that promotes students' successful learning of mathematics. *JMTE* focuses on all stages of professional development of mathematics teachers and teacher educators and serves as a forum for considering institutional, societal and cultural influences that impact on teachers' learning, and ultimately that of their students. Critical analyses of particular programmes, development initiatives, technology, assessment, teaching diverse populations and policy matters, as these topics relate to the main focuses of the journal, are welcome. (*JMTE* homepage)

This scope was determined by the founding editor and has been clarified by subsequent editors and editorial teams. In her editorial, Jaworski (2005) addressed the close links among mathematics teacher education, mathematics teaching and students learning that studies in *JMTE* have reported:

> It allows the linking of theory in the learning of mathematics to the learning of teachers of mathematics, and considerations of how teachers learn related to the learning of their pupils. Increasingly it allows us to address the learning of teacher educators and its relation to the learning of teachers. (p. 1).

Although students' learning is an ultimate goal of mathematics teacher education and mathematics teaching, a study on students' learning per se is not in the scope of *JMTE*.

Education of mathematics teachers includes both initial teacher education and also professional development initiatives. However, its scope goes beyond programs, tasks, or approaches used for the education of prospective and practicing mathematics teachers. Chapman (2011), in her first editorial as editor in chief, pointed out that it also involves the study of the mathematics teacher focusing on her beliefs, knowledge, identity and teaching practice. Nevertheless, the ways that the emphasis on the mathematics teacher informs mathematics teaching and in particular mathematics teacher education needs to be considered by the authors of *JMTE*. A current emphasis on mathematics teacher educators in the field of mathematics education is also reflected in the published papers in *JMTE* and in the current special issue published in issue 5 of volume 21. The relation between mathematics teachers, mathematics teacher educators, mathematics teaching and mathematics teacher education is very complex and cannot be studied through cause-effect approaches. *JMTE* acknowledges the importance of addressing this relation by considering contextual dimensions that play an important role in understanding this complexity.

Diversity is also promoted in relation to theoretical perspectives, methods and content areas. A sense of this diversity is provided in Sect. 23.4 through the analysis of the papers published in 2017. Submitted manuscripts need to have a clear focus on mathematics teacher education and not to teacher education in general. Also, the authors need to be able to justify the importance of mathematics in their study.

Summarizing, a paper to be published in *JMTE* should focus on approaches in mathematics teacher education (initial and professional development), on the main participants in mathematics teacher education (mathematics teachers and mathematics teacher educators) or on classroom teaching with the mathematics teacher being the centre of attention. Large-scale or small-scale studies, studies adopting different theoretical perspectives (ranging from cognitive to socio-cultural and socio-political) and methods (quantitative and qualitative) are welcome in the journal.

23.3 Acceptance Rate and Impact

Six issues per year are published in *JMTE* (before 2005 four issues were published) with an average of 24 papers published per year. Up to today (September 2018) 2035 manuscripts have been submitted to the journal and 395 research papers have been accepted and published (in regular issues and in online first) while 9 papers have been published in the section on mathematics teachers around the world, and 15 in the section on reader commentary—mainly book reviews. The acceptance rate has varied through the years but on the average is about 20%.

The impact that a journal has in the field is measured by the number of the citations of papers published in this journal. The impact factor (IF) gives an indication of the quality of a journal in relation to its citations. However, *JMTE* is not indexed in the Social Science Citation Index (SSCI) data base so IF is not available. Williams and Leatham (2017) found that *JMTE* is fifth in the order of the ten most cited journals in mathematics education, and through a survey based on experts' opinions they ranked it as fifth in the order of high quality journals of mathematics education. In the site of *JMTE* some journal metrics can be found. In 2017, 89,816 downloads of papers were counted; different impact factors have been calculated in different ways (the impact factor by CiteScore 2016 is 1.14, by SNIP-2016 is 1,317, by SJR-2016 is 1,041 and the h5 Index-22016 is 21); and in 2017, 80% of the authors said that they would be likely to publish again in this journal.

23.4 Papers Published in *JMTE*

Cooney (2000) raised the question about the character of *JMTE* in the year 2010, and in future years 2020 or even 2050. He foresaw possible changes in the research on and practice of mathematics teacher education, due to the extended use of technology as well as the differences of current reforms in relation to ones targeted in the nineties. Nevertheless, he expected that mathematics teachers' learning and mathematics teacher educators' struggles would be central topics in *JMTE*. To do a systematic survey in order to explore the development of the journal is beyond the scope of this chapter, but I discuss below the papers published in *JMTE* in 2017 in terms of their focus, the participants, the research methodology and the adopted theoretical perspectives. This analysis may offer insights to young researchers on the diversity of the mathematics teacher education research reported in this journal. A classification of the papers is presented in the systemic network in Fig. 23.1. Teacher resources such as beliefs, knowledge, and identity, teacher education programs and their impact on prospective teacher development, teacher noticing of students' mathematical thinking are research areas indicating that *JMTE* fullifils the expectations of its founder as it focuses on the mathematics teacher and on the struggles of mathematics teacher educators to support (prospective and practicing) teachers' learning. Papers also focus on classroom teaching and its development as well as on mathematics teacher collaboration. The role of technology in mathematics teacher education research is mainly seen through the use of video in promoting teacher noticing or through the use of dynamic geometry software (DGS) in classroom teaching.

Concerning the participants, most of the studies focus on prospective primary school teachers while teacher educators have become the focus of attention in some studies. In the papers published in 2017 we see also the multiplicity of theoretical perspectives and methodological approaches that the scope of the journal underlines. However, cognitive perspectives and qualitative research methods are most commonly adopted. Although this short survey does not give an overall picture of the papers published in *JMTE*, to some extent they fit in with the current research on mathematics teacher education research reported in other review studies (Strutchens et al. 2016).

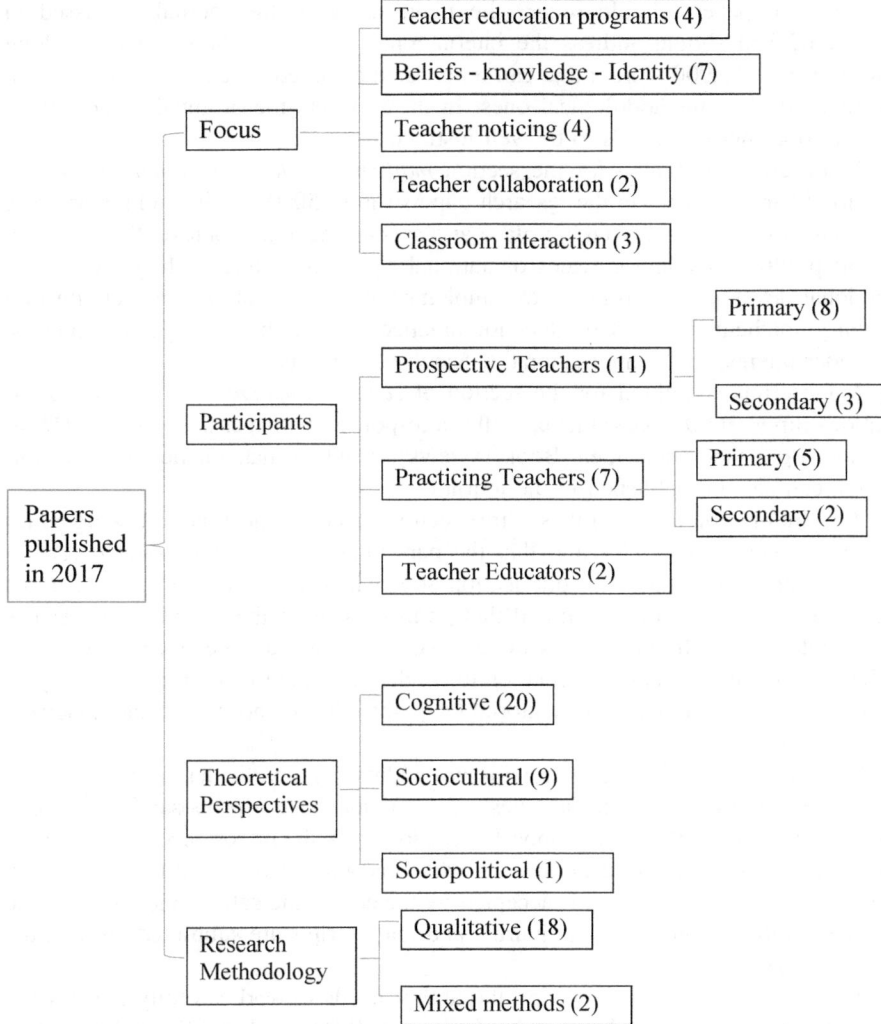

Fig. 23.1 Papers published in *JMTE* in 2017

23.5 From Submission to Publication

23.5.1 Submission of a Manuscript

Manuscripts submitted to *JMTE* can fall into one of three sections: research papers, mathematics teacher education around the world, and reader commentary. In the manuscript submission, authors should state clearly the section for which their paper will be considered.

Research papers should reflect the main scope of the journal discussed in Sect. 23.2 and should address the international audience. These are rather long papers (up to 10,000 words) that can report studies based on empirical data or can be theoretical or methodological ones. In these papers the originality and contribution to knowledge needs to be well justified.

Manuscripts submitted for the section *mathematics teacher education around the world* are shorter than the research papers (up to 5000 words) and report more than just a research study taking place at a specific national context. They need to report programmes and/or issues of national significance (e.g., a large scale professional development program, the implementation of a national curriculum in a country, mathematics teacher education practices around the country) that could be of wider interest to the international research community.

Manuscripts submitted for the section of *reader commentary* are short contributions (up to 3000 words) that can offer a response to a paper published in *JMTE*, or develop a theoretical idea. Book reviews related to mathematics teacher education can also be published in the journal.

Any submission in one of these three sections needs to meet the following ethics criteria, ensuring the following: that the paper has not been published before or been under consideration for publication somewhere else; that all the co-authors have approved the publication; and that permission from the copyright owner has been obtained for figures, tables or text passages that have been published elsewhere. Following the ethics in relation to conducting the research is increasingly an issue for the journal, which the editorial team, the editorial board, and the reviewers take into account.

The journal publishes also special issues addressing a particular research area. In this case, researchers (acting as guest editors) can make a proposal for a special issue to the chief editor. The proposal needs to justify the importance of this area of research and provide solid arguments why this will be of interest to the *JMTE* audience. When the proposal is accepted by the editor, the call for the special issue appears in the homepage of the journal and manuscripts are submitted through the editorial manager.

Before submitting a manuscript, the author needs to read carefully the instructions for authors provided in the homepage of *JMTE*, and to follow them while preparing the manuscript. The submission is made online through the editorial manager of *JMTE*. The author selects on the homepage of the journal the hyperlink 'Submit online' and follows the instructions on how and what materials need to be uploaded. The author can track the status of his/her submission through the system.

23.5.2 The Reviewing Process

When the manuscript is submitted, the editor in chief is informed through the system about the new submission. The editor reads the paper and checks if it is in the scope of the journal and then either sends it to reviewers or assigns it to one of the associate editors who will manage the reviewing process. Manuscripts that are not in the scope of the journal are rejected by the editors without sending them out for review. Reviewers can be members of the editorial board or researchers around the word that are registered in the editorial manager. The editor can also add a new reviewer into the system. Searching for reviewers can be done through the editorial manager by using specific keywords (e.g., name, country, university, research area). Three reviewers are usually invited by the editors on the basis of their expertise in the area of research reported in the paper. Sometimes, the reviewer does not accept the invitation so a new reviewer is invited. This cycle may be repeated several times. The reviewers are given 35 days to submit their reviews. On the basis of the three reviews and of her own reading, the editor decides if the paper will be (a) accepted for publication without further changes, (b) accepted for publication if minor revisions will be undertaken by the author, (c) reconsidered for sending for a second round of reviews after major revisions, or (d) rejected. The time needed for the author to get an initial response for his or her submission is approximately four months. While in the case of minor revisions the revised version is reviewed by the editor, the case of major revisions requires a new reviewing cycle. Usually, some of the reviewers used in the first round are invited for the second round and some new ones are added. Nevertheless, there are a few cases in which the reviewers who accept the invitation had not reviewed the paper before. However, the reviews from the first round and the decision letter of the editor, together with the initial and revised submissions, are made available to the reviewers of the second round.

Usually, after this cycle of review the paper is either accepted (with or without minor revisions) or rejected, while there are a few exceptional cases where a new reviewing cycle can start. If the manuscript requires minor revisions, the revised paper (in most cases) is reviewed only by the editor and no other reviewers are invited. To get acceptance after two reviewing cycles takes more than one year.

23.5.3 Publication

When the paper is accepted by the editor it goes to the publishing office. The authors receive the proofs of their papers, which they need to check. In this process they mainly have to accept some editorial changes that have been made in the paper, provide some clarifications that the publisher asks for, or make some final minor changes (mainly typographical) in the text. The time from the acceptance to publishing is rather short—it takes about 10 days for the paper to be published online first. The time needed for the paper to be published in a regular issue depends on the number of papers accepted in the journal at this period of time.

23.6 Deciding on the Quality of a Submission

The quality of a study and of a paper has always been an issue of concern in the research community. Quality is usually discussed in doctoral programs, mainly in the context of courses on research methodology. Public discussion on this issue takes place in journal papers and book chapters. Kilpatrick (1993) argued for quality criteria such as relevance, validity, objectivity, originality, rigour and precision, predictability, reproducibility and relatedness. These criteria were elaborated by other researchers in their attempts to communicate the nature of research in mathematics education (Schoenfeld 2000). However, these criteria have been challenged as they have been considered rather rigid. For example, Simon (2004) considered quality in relation to the strength of arguments of the researcher.

Quality criteria in *JMTE* are not defined explicitly in the homepage, but actually quality is evaluated through the expertise of the members of the editorial board, the reviewers and the editors. Quality improvement of a submitted manuscript is made through the interaction among the author, the reviewers and the editor. A professional learning community is established with a goal of reviewing and developing further the quality of the paper, where the author is a member of this community. The author's (professional?) learning takes place through the revision process while attempting to recognize/appreciate the reviewers' different perspectives and address their comments. The reviewers and the editor are learning in the process of reviewing the paper but also from reading the other reviewers' reviews, which become available to all reviewers who have access in the editorial manager. Although there are cases in which reviewers may have different opinions about the quality of a manuscript, in most cases there is an agreement about the strengths and the weaknesses of the submission.

In Table 23.1, through some illustrative examples, I present issues of quality raised often by reviewers. The examples have been modified or in some cases have been developed by me for ethical reasons of anonymity.

The study's contribution to knowledge is a main issue that reviewers address. The authors need to make explicit what their study adds to what we already know on the research area that their study addresses. For example, the contribution could be related to important empirical findings or to new methodological and theoretical perspectives to study a phenomenon. The clarity of the article is another issue that is very often addressed by the reviewers. Clarity may be related to the following: the focus and the research questions; the coherence between research questions, theoretical framework, design of the study and findings; the justification of claims; and the use of language. Comments about theoretical perspectives are mainly related to the definitions of theoretical constructs used in the study and to the way that these perspectives are operationalized in data analysis and presentation of results. Methodological issues addressed by the reviewers often refer to the need for more contextual information and for detailed description of the data analysis process. Addressing the quality of the submission is often challenging even for experienced reviewers. There are cases where a manuscript may have clear research

Table 23.1 Quality issues often addressed by reviewers

Issues of quality	Examples
Contribution to knowledge	"It is not clear what we might generalize from this study. You discuss about a sequence of tasks but what are the key features of the task sequence that may develop new knowledge to the field about how to support prospective teachers?"
Clarity of research questions	"I left the section wondering what exactly is your purpose for the study. I wanted a clearly stated research goal"
Theoretical framing	"The theoretical grounding is conducted in a very shallow way. What do these particularly cited authors actually say, and how does the theory referred to implement and ground the reported research?" "The concept of identity is a fragile and elusive concept that needs to be clearly defined and theoretically elaborated and then to be used in a consistent manner" "There are important constructs not defined, used in a sort of naive meaning: for example, authors discuss attitudes' change in the result section but they don't give any explicit definition of the construct"
The context of the study	"Practices differ so much across the world that for an international journal the context seems important"
The justification of claims	"Your claims do not seem to be grounded in empirical evidence"
The analytical process	"More care is needed in making connections between the methods and the findings. But more fundamentally, although this looks like an interesting exercise in quantitative data analysis, I am seriously unconvinced that the findings could be generalised beyond the surprisingly small set of participants in this study" "I think that the article would benefit from a more coherent and specific explanation of how exactly the analysis was carried out at this phase"
The discussion of the findings	"The results are too descriptive and do not give a better insight into teachers' practices in problem solving. That is the reason the conclusions of the study do not contribute any further to the well-known importance of teachers' mastery in problem solving" "There are too many new ideas in the conclusions that are not addressed in the results"
Coherence of the article	"There is not a clear focus in the article since in different parts of the manuscript the reader could spot different research focus statements" "Make sure that the research question and conclusion align. It seems that additional questions were addressed that are not included in the current question"

goals, explicit theoretical framework, appropriate methodology, well-structured results, but a weak contribution to the field. The question 'so what?' cannot be easily answered in the research community. Niss (2018) invites researchers to reconsider issues of quality beyond the "ideal-typical mathematics education research article" that meets a number of quality criteria:

> … more than ever we must analyse and discuss quality, but in the same way as we should not endorse only one understanding and version of democracy, like the one found in, say, Switzerland, in the USA, or in Denmark, we should not allow too narrow and rigid paradigms to jeopardise our discussions or our field of research. (p. 48)

In summary, deciding on the quality of a submission is related not only to the policy of this journal. Rather, it is a decision the reviewers and editors take in the process of participating in the mathematics education research community. Searching for the quality constitutes a professional learning experience for authors, reviewers and editors, characterized by considering perspectives outside their own and inquiring into their research practice collectively.

23.7 Advice to Early Career Researchers and Concluding Remarks

In this section, I attempt to give some advice that may seem helpful to an early career researcher who would like to submit a manuscript to *JMTE*, on the basis of my experience with the process of publishing a paper in *JMTE* from different positions (author, reviewer, editor).

- The manuscript needs to fit in with the scope of the journal, to be suitable for one of the three sections (research article, mathematics education around the world, commentary article) and to comply with the word limits.
- The high quality of the paper is the main requirement for a paper to be published in *JMTE*. This criterion means that it should have interesting and important research questions, clarity and coherence, explicit theoretical and methodological framework, solid empirical evidence of the claims, and make a contribution to the field.
- If the submission is rejected because it is not in the scope of *JMTE*, then the authors need to select carefully another journal that is appropriate in relation to the content of the manuscript and its perspective.
- In case the rejection relates to the quality of the submission, then the authors need to read carefully the comments of the reviewers and the editor and see if the suggested changes can be made for a future resubmission to *JMTE* or to another journal. Revise and resubmit is not a possible decision up to now for *JMTE*, so the editor may suggest informally to the authors that they rewrite most parts of the article and submit it again to *JMTE*. Otherwise, the editor would suggest that the authors send the revised article to another journal.
- In case of major revisions, the authors need to think carefully in which directions the revision will go. The decision letter and the suggestions of the editor would help the authors to recognize these directions and through reviewers' comments to decide on how to deal with them. It is important for the author to distinguish the significant from the minor changes that need to be undertaken.
- The first reaction of the authors to the editor's and reviewers' comments is usually emotional. The authors have done much work in conducting the study and reporting on it. Thus, it is quite common to feel frustrated when weaknesses of their work are addressed. Overcoming these feelings is important for starting the revision. Considering the perspectives of others is the first step for improving the article.

Revising the article is not only responding to the editor's and reviewers' comments. Reflecting on the received feedback, the authors develop better understanding of their study, identifying strengths and weaknesses. On this basis, the authors take decisions on how they will structure the revision of the article.

The authors also need to pay attention to language and editing issues. Communicating their work is also important. For example, following the APA style consistently throughout the paper, avoiding typographical mistakes, getting help with the language from a native English person, will improve the clarity of the article and make easier the communication of the authors' ideas. In addition to APA guidelines, *JMTE* has also some specific style aspects in relation to expressions that need to be used. For example, the use of "teacher education" instead of "teacher training", "prospective teachers" instead of "pre-service teachers", "practicing teachers" instead of "in-service teachers" are some of the main expressions.

Regardless of the outcome of the reviewing process, the feedback that the authors get helps them to develop their research further, beyond the specific submission. Through the whole process the authors communicate with other colleagues who have worked on similar research areas and they open their work to the international research community.

Overall, *JMTE* is a high quality mathematics education journal, with a strong impact on the field of mathematics education and in particular on the area of mathematics teacher education. It accepts different types of papers with a diversity of research foci, theoretical and methodological perspectives. The editorial team, the board and the body of reviewers registered in the editorial manager have long experience in the area of mathematics teacher education and so they can provide rich feedback to authors whose studies fall in this area. Therefore, *JMTE* is a journal appropriate for an early career researcher whose research focuses on mathematics teacher education, on mathematics teacher resources, or on mathematics teaching with a particular focus on the mathematics teacher.

References

Chapman, O. (2011). The field of research in mathematics teacher education. *Journal of Mathematics Teacher Education, 14*, 247–249.
Cooney, T. J. (1998). Hospitality and homage. *Journal of Mathematics Teacher Education, 1*, 1–2.
Cooney, T. J. (2000). The millennium and mathematics teacher education. *Journal of Mathematics Teacher Education, 3*, 1–20.
Jaworski, B. (2005). New beginnings and recurring themes. *Journal of Mathematics Teacher Education, 8*, 1–3.
Kilpatrick, J. (1993). Beyond face value: Assessing research in mathematics education. In G. Nissen & M. Blomboj (Eds.), *Criteria for scientific quality and relevance in the didactics of mathematics* (pp. 15–34). Roskilde: Danish Research Council for the Humanities.
Niss, M. (2018). The very multi-faceted nature of mathematics education research. In E. Bergvist, M. Osterholm, C. Granberg & L. Sumpter (Eds.). *Proceedings of the 42nd Conference of the International Group for the Psychology of Mathematics Education* (Vol. 1, pp. 35–50). Umeå, Sweden: PME.

Simon, M. (2004). Raising issues of quality in mathematics education research. *Journal for Research in Mathematics Education, 35,* 157–163.

Schoenfeld, A. H. (2000). *Purposes and methods of research in mathematics education* (pp. 641–649). June/July: Notices of the AMS.

Strutchens, M., Huang, R., Losano, L., Potari, D., Ponte, J. P. D., Cyrino, M. C. D. C. T., et al. (2016). *The mathematics education of prospective secondary teachers around the world.* Cham, Switzerland: Springer Open.

Williams, S. R., & Leatham, K. R. (2017). Journal quality in mathematics education. *Journal for Research in Mathematics Education, 48,* 369–396.

Open Access This chapter is licensed under the terms of the Creative Commons Attribution 4.0 International License (http://creativecommons.org/licenses/by/4.0/), which permits use, sharing, adaptation, distribution and reproduction in any medium or format, as long as you give appropriate credit to the original author(s) and the source, provide a link to the Creative Commons license and indicate if changes were made.

The images or other third party material in this chapter are included in the chapter's Creative Commons license, unless indicated otherwise in a credit line to the material. If material is not included in the chapter's Creative Commons license and your intended use is not permitted by statutory regulation or exceeds the permitted use, you will need to obtain permission directly from the copyright holder.

Chapter 24
Towards Article Acceptance: Avoiding Common Pitfalls in Submissions to *Mathematical Thinking and Learning*

Lyn D. English

Abstract This chapter examines core aspects of quality publishing in mathematics education journals, with a particular focus on the journal, *Mathematical Thinking and Learning: An International Journal* ([*MTL*] https://www.tandfonline.com/loi/hmtl20). Following an introduction to *MTL*, I provide recommendations for writing and submitting a research journal article, from both a general perspective and from that of *MTL*. I give consideration to core components of a journal article and offer suggestions for maximising one's chances of final publication acceptance. Next, I examine journal reviewing processes from the perspectives of a journal editor, an author, and reviewer. *MTL* serves to illustrate key points in the reviewing processes.

Keywords Publishing journal articles · *Mathematical Thinking and learning*

24.1 Overview of *Mathematical Thinking and Learning*

The first issue of *Mathematical Thinking and Learning* (*MTL*) was published in 1999 by Lawrence Erlbaum Associates, Inc., Publishers (Mahwah, New Jersey, USA). I remain the journal's founding editor. There are three associate editors and a book review editor. In 2007, beginning with Volume 9, Taylor & Francis took over the publishing of the journal on the retirement of Larry Erlbaum and the cessation of Lawrence Erlbaum Assoc. as a publishing company. *MTL* publishes four issues per year, with all articles having undergone rigorous peer review based on initial editor screening and anonymous review by at least three reviewers. Volume 21 commenced in 2019. The journal's Impact Factor Score for 2017 is 1.393, with a journal ranking of 112/238 (Education & Educational Research). In addition to research reports, *MTL* publishes Short Reports and book reviews. Special issues are also produced from time to time, with no more than one such issue per year. Authors who are interested in undertaking a special issue on a timely research area

L. D. English (✉)
Queensland University of Technology, Brisbane, Australia
e-mail: l.english@qut.edu.au

are encouraged to make contact. The most recent special issue (volume 20, issue 1) comprised articles that explored computational thinking and mathematics learning.

As the title implies, *MTL* publishes scholarly articles that primarily address mathematical thinking, reasoning, and learning. Articles can draw upon a number of theoretical domains including the various fields of psychology, sociology, philosophy, anthropology, and information technology. In addition to receiving articles that report on research studies conducted, the journal invites articles that present theoretical and philosophical analyses of pertinent issues. Specifically, *MTL* seeks articles that address one or more of the following:

- Interdisciplinary studies on mathematical learning, reasoning or thinking, and their developments at all ages;
- Technological advances and their impact on mathematical thinking and learning;
- Studies that explore the diverse processes of mathematical reasoning;
- New insights into how mathematical understandings develop across the life span, including significant transitional periods;
- Changing perspectives on the nature of mathematics and their impact on mathematical thinking and learning in both formal and informal contexts;
- Studies that explore the internationalization of mathematics education, together with other cross-cultural studies of mathematical thinking and learning; and
- Studies of innovative instructional practices that foster mathematical learning, thinking, and development.

24.2 Choosing a Potential Research Journal

The scope of articles that a journal publishes should be one of the first aspects a potential author should check. As *MTL* editor, I receive several submissions that do not meet the aims and scope of articles published in *MTL*. In these cases, I have to reject the paper outright and sometimes suggest an alternative journal such as one in the field of educational psychology. When scoping a journal for a potential submission, it is important to note the range of articles and reports it publishes. In addition to regular research articles, several mathematics education journals including *MTL* publish special issues, book reviews, and shorter research reports. *Short Reports* for *MTL* might report on larger, more comprehensive studies that might be documented elsewhere in non-journal format (e.g., doctoral dissertations). Short Reports might also address introductory or pilot studies, with proposals included for further research. Theoretical pieces that address significant and timely issues on mathematical thinking and learning could likewise form a Short Report. Such reports typically comprise around 15 manuscript pages. Other types of submissions considered by *MTL*, although rarely received, include an occasional *discourse section* comprising timely dialogue among researchers on significant issues pertaining to mathematical thinking and learning. *Letters to the editor* and more extensive *critical commentaries* on published articles are welcomed. These should comprise critical, timely, and responsible comment on issues of significance to mathematical thinking and learning.

Once the aims and scope of a particular journal have been checked, it is worth reading a range of articles published in the journal to obtain a sense of their nature. Prior to writing an intended article for submission, a journal's style guidelines should be studied. These include features such as the nature of section headings, the line spacing, font type, referencing format, table and figure requirements, and word/page length. It is easy for a journal editor to gauge whether an author has studied these guidelines, especially if several key points have not been followed. Editors will often return a submission prior to sending for external review if these guidelines are not adhered to, in particular, if a journal's page or word limits are exceeded (if this criterion applies). For *MTL*, authors are to follow the style guidelines described in the current edition of the *Publication Manual of the American Psychological Association* (6th edn. 2013, [APA]). Taylor & Francis advises authors to consult Merriam-Webster's Collegiate Dictionary (11th ed.) for spelling.

In the remaining Sections I give consideration to some key issues that potential authors for *MTL* should keep in mind. For example, sometimes an *MTL* submission suffers from a number of weaknesses that need to be addressed before it can be sent for external review. These include a limited or outdated literature background, a lack of a theoretical or conceptual framework, poor expression, and other scholarly attributes a submission should display. Ensuring that a submitted paper adheres to the requirements of a scholarly research publication can be difficult, especially when there are limited resources that can assist a beginning researcher. A few valuable resources include the *American Educational Research Association* (AERA 2006), the *Journal for Research in Mathematics Education* (JRME 2015), and the *Publication Manual of the American Psychological Association* (APA 6th edn. 2013). The *APA* is a foundational reference that applies to many journals.

24.3 Creating an Appropriate Title and Abstract

Article titles and abstracts provide a window into a study and thus need to be clear, concise, and accurately represent its contents, both for the reader and for electronic indexing purposes (Saracho 2013). Overly long titles are not recommended, as they can detract from the overall appeal of the article and can also be misleading for indexing (APA 6th edn. 2013). When I receive submissions to *MTL*, I find very long titles off-putting; likewise, some submissions have titles that would be more appropriate for a professional journal than a research journal.

Writing abstracts is not a simple matter and can take considerably longer than anticipated. Abstracts should convey within 150–250 words (depending on the journal) the study's purpose, methodology, key findings, and conclusions or implications. As Saracho (2013) emphasises, an abstract should provide a "complete but concise description of the study" as well as incorporate key words that can be used for indexing and data bases (p. 48). The advice of Bol and Hacker (2014) is worth citing here:

> A poorly written abstract creates a poor first impression that could set a negative tone for the remainder of the manuscript. Do not lose your audience in the first few words. One sure way to do this is to write an abstract that omits important details of one or more components of your research so that there is no easy way for the reader to judge your research as worth reading. (p. 41)

Reviewers who devote substantial time to a submission need to be "captured" by an article's abstract and be motivated to read the paper. As can be seen in the excerpt below, this reviewer had to alert the author to the importance of detailing clearly and concisely the key components of a study.

> The abstract is currently written in vague language that does not communicate a summary of findings, assertions, or implications very clearly or precisely. Since many readers only look at the abstract, it is essential that it be written in a way that clearly communicates key details about the study. In a revision, it would be useful to clearly state 1-2 key findings, 1-2 central assertions about how/why the findings happened, and 1-2 conclusions or implications about what these findings mean for scholarship and for practice.

1. Setting the Scene: The Many Facets of the Literature Review

Literature reviews fulfil many roles. Importantly, they should highlight the existing gaps in the topic area and how the reported study is targeting these missing aspects and thus is advancing the field. Literature reviews need to go beyond simply reporting; rather, the existing literature requires critical analysis to identify areas that remain under-researched and in need of attention. One of the more frequent concerns of *MTL* reviewers is the author's failure to indicate the significance of the problem being investigated and how the study is advancing the field. This concern is compounded by articles that do not convey a clear statement of the problem, with the result that reviewers are uncertain of exactly what is being studied. A submission without a clear problem statement and/or a limited review of the literature is unlikely to receive favourable reviews. A poor literature review might be characterized by brevity, omission of important studies in the field and/or inappropriate/irrelevant studies, dated literature that does not convey the current state of play, literature that is confined to just one nation (for international journals), and a literature review that does not highlight the importance of the topic of investigation. As can be seen in the following example of one reviewer's feedback, the authors did not argue adequately the case for their study (words have been omitted to avoid any possible identification):

> The authors need to provide more background on the value and importance of X activities as established in the mathematics research literature and field. Why is this approach so critical to developing students' mathematical knowledge and skills, and that of their teachers? The authors need more description of the current research in order to build the argument for their study.... Why is it so important to determine how Y abilities develop? What impact does this development have on teaching and learning in mathematics? In what ways has the current research on X activities informed the field and what areas remain to be

investigated? The authors provide brief treatment of this topic on p x, but more depth is needed. It is not clear why the study purpose, Z, is critical to enhancing the current mathematics knowledge base.

Literature reviews also provide the basis for a study's theoretical or conceptual framework. This framework is important in potentially advancing the field, guiding the research questions or hypotheses, the subsequent conduct of the study, and the data collected and analysis performed. The framework further guides the discussion of results, which in turn, might reveal extensions or modifications to the framework. Submissions that lack such a conceptual or theoretical framing are likely to have reduced impact, with reviewer requests to address this omission. It is also worth mentioning that if parts of a study, such as key components of the theoretical framework, have been reported in another research outlet, the unique contributions of the new, submitted article must be clearly indicated. In addition, readers should not be expected to search for authors' publications for required information; a submission should stand alone. Reviewers might source the author's other articles that have emanated from the same study and question how the new submission differs from previously published works, if this has not been made clear in the submitted article. On the other hand, reviewers might choose to locate an author's cited publications out of interest in the research. It is thus important that all references are correctly cited. Considerable time is lost and frustration experienced by reviewers and readers when a reference is listed incorrectly.

Many of the foregoing points regarding a literature review apply also to articles that present theoretical and philosophical analyses of pertinent issues. Such articles can be difficult as they need to present timely, well-argued ideas that flow logically and cohesively. The concepts need to be not only well grounded in the literature but also significantly advance the field. *MTL* does not receive many articles of this type. Unfortunately, to judge by those that have been submitted, they are not often accepted for publication primarily because they might not extend existing work, might not offer new insights into, say, a vexing issue or an emerging topic of importance, draw on a limited range of research, and might lack coherence. Articles that suffer from one or more of these weaknesses can of course, be substantially revised and resubmitted for further review. In essence, theoretical and philosophical articles need to stimulate the interested reader with thought-provoking ideas, which might prompt possible further exploration and application to existing research.

24.4 Explaining and Justifying the Design and Methodology

For articles that report on research studies undertaken, the research design and methodology need to contain sufficient detail and be appropriate for answering the research questions. With many journals having strict length limits, giving adequate attention to design and methodology can be difficult. Nevertheless, required information generally includes the nature, number, and background of the participants, the population from which they were drawn, and how they were chosen for study. Describing the instruments developed or sourced, how they were administered, their appropriateness for addressing the research questions, their reliability for yielding the required data, and samples of items (or the entire instrument) should be included in the methodology, where appropriate. When authors omit aspects or all of this information, it is difficult for readers to determine the validity of the results and any subsequent claims made. For experimental studies, control of variables is essential if causal inferences are to be made. As Bol and Hacker (2014) point out, reviewers will look for potential confounding factors and possible competing hypotheses. For both experimental and qualitative studies, any methodological limitations should be noted in the discussion section or in a separate section towards the end of an article.

Another important methodological component, with respect to studies that report on treatments or classroom interventions, is that sufficient detail should be provided so that their key features can be determined and applied in interpreting the results (AERA 2006). The types of approaches adopted, examples of instructional materials or treatments implemented, and the duration and frequency of implementation or administration should also be indicated. The nature of the intervention should be guided/supported by the theoretical framework, which enables the reader to see how the study emanated from its conceptual foundation/s. It is not uncommon for an author to advocate a particular perspective (e.g., constructivism) but then describe a study that does not reflect its core philosophy or ideas. Reviewers invariably question this failing, as can be seen in a sample review below (some words have been omitted to avoid any author/reviewer identification):

> The authors start Sect. 24.3 by claiming that they "employed a teaching experiment approach (Cobb and Steffe 1983; Simon 1990) to explore the potential …. Neither of the references named in this sentence were included in the reference section, nor did the paper do a thorough job of explaining the purpose and process of a teaching experiment. In readings I did myself to re- familiarize myself with the teaching experiment methodology, I found that what the authors did does not fit this methodology and there isn't a match between the authors' goals and the goals of a teaching experiment.

Articles that omit or have inadequate information on how a study's data were obtained and analysed, including justification for the data analysis methods used, will be questioned by a reviewer. As emphasized by AERA (2006), data analysis procedures should be:

> precisely and transparently described from the beginning of the study through presentation of the outcomes. Reporting should make clear how the analysis procedures address the research question or problem and lead to the outcomes reported. The relevance of the analysis procedures to the problem formulation should be made clear (p. 37).

24.5 Results

In reporting the results of data analysis, it is important to keep in mind the research questions being investigated. It should be made clear how the analysis addresses the research questions and leads to the outcomes (AERA 2006; Bol and Hacker 2014). As expressed succinctly by Bol and Hacker (2014), "The whole point of the research can be lost if the analyses are improperly and inadequately conducted and do not clearly provide the answers to the research questions" (p. 43).

It is not uncommon for a submitted *MTL* article to overlook the questions posed and to report on results that address other issues. One approach to avoiding this problem is to organize the results according to each research question, that is, revisit each question in turn (assuming there is more than one question). Only those results that actually answer the questions should be included. If other relevant findings emerge from the data analysis, they could be incorporated within the discussion and cited as unanticipated outcomes. Such results could serve as one area for further research.

Ensuring that all claims and conclusions made are supported by the data is especially important (AERA 2006) and is an aspect that can be easily overlooked even by experienced researchers. Making claims or generalisations that are not supported by evidence will be picked up by reviewers, as is frequently the case with *MTL* submissions. The reader needs to be able to trust the claims made. A number of approaches to providing such a warrant are cited by AERA (2006), including triangulation of data, having data coded by other researchers, and a critical examination of how the researchers' pre-existing perspectives or beliefs might have impacted on the data collection and analysis. Triangulation is frequently used in mathematics education research, such as including examples of specific participant responses from classroom or group discussions to support quantitative data. If, for example, a claim is made that students were engaging in metacognitive activity, then specific, concrete examples of students' actions in this regard can further support the claim from the reported data.

In documenting data outcomes, it is recommended that tables should be used only when they clarify or summarise outcomes involving multiple data points (Saracho 2013). The APA (6th edn. 2013) provides examples of appropriate table layouts. It is generally recommended that the fewer tables the better, as too many tables can detract from a paper and extend its length, especially for those journals that have a strict page limit. While tables should be readily interpreted, the messages they convey need to be summarised in the associated text. One of the problems with several of the manuscripts submitted to *MTL* is their overuse of tables and figures. Furthermore, sometimes these tables and figures, especially figures, can be so dense and have such small font size, that they are barely legible and more importantly, will not reproduce well in the printed journal issue. The use of colour is also problematic for printed issues of journals (but not the online format), as colour is costly for the publisher (and the author). If authors require colour then they will have to cover the costs. Problems can arise when colour is essential for some graphs or other figures where it is used as a distinguishing feature. In this instance, the use of shading or other such effects will need to serve as a substitute.

24.6 Developing an In-Depth and Insightful Discussion

There are a number of approaches to the discussion section but typically these include a summary of the outcomes, together with an "interpretive commentary" (AERA 2006, p. 38) providing a more in-depth understanding of the claims made. Such a commentary would indicate how each research question was addressed, offer possible reasons for how and why particular outcomes occurred, the context/s in which the outcomes took place, how they support or challenge existing theory and previous research results, and possible alternative interpretations. Importantly, the discussion should indicate how the outcomes and conclusions drawn from the study connect to and support (or perhaps challenge) the study's theoretical framework. Implications that follow from the study might refer to theoretical, practical, or methodological considerations (AERA 2006), but importantly, any claims and recommendations made in the discussion section must be backed up by data from the study (Bol and Hacker 2014; Robinson et al. 2013). An interesting recommendation by Robinson et al. (2013) is that authors should limit their discussion and conclusions to their study's data and not offer recommendations regarding educational practice or educational policy. Such a recommendation was proposed to maintain a "separation between evidence and opinion concerning the legitimate warrants of empirical research" (p. 291). Although educational implications from mathematics education studies are valuable and indeed usually expected, maintaining a clear distinction between evidence and opinion is nevertheless essential.

One of the drawbacks I frequently see in submissions to *MTL* is a failure to revisit the study's conceptual framework in light of the findings. Limited reference, if at all, to existing research in discussing the study outcomes is also present in some submissions. It is important that researchers indicate how their study has extended current work in the field, thus advancing the existing knowledge base. One of the more common reasons for a reviewer to reject a paper is that it does not make a significant contribution to the field, rather, it simply reinforces well-established research; the reviewer thus comes away questioning why the study did not progress beyond this point. Although studies that duplicate the findings of earlier research can still make a contribution, the nature of any such contribution should be well argued with implications for further studies clearly indicated, such as how a task or context variation might generate new insights.

24.7 Acknowledging Limitations and Drawing Conclusions

The inclusion of a concluding section is not always followed in mathematics education journal articles but can provide a valuable summation statement. Conclusions are normally brief and succinct, with Saracho (2013) recommending that they include a clear statement on the key outcomes and justification for their significance with reference to related studies, and a few core conclusions from the study results. Recommendations for future research are sometimes included in this section. Acknowledging the limitations of a study is an aspect that can also be overlooked by authors. Suggestions for reducing these limitations should be indicated, such as the need for a larger sample or interviewing participants to obtain greater insights into their thinking.

24.8 Checking References, Structure, and Readability

As for each journal, the *MTL* website contains instructions for authors (https://www.tandfonline.com/action/authorSubmission?show=instructions&journalCode=hmtl20). *MTL* follows the APA (6th edn. 2013) guidelines in overall layout including how references should be cited. Common mistakes made by authors who fail to check the *MTL* guidelines include using non-blinded submissions (reviewers become concerned when this is the case), numbered instead of non-numbered section headings, single instead of double line spacing, inappropriate referencing, and the inclusion of figures and tables within the body of the paper (*MTL* does accept these as separate files). Checking that all references cited within the text also appear in the reference list and vice versa is important. Although authors are usually aware of this standard requirement, it is easy to miss some references.

Appendices are valuable for including important information that can be distracting or difficult to incorporate within the text, such as questionnaires and tests administered, or excerpts from these. The APA (6th edn. 2013) guidelines provide detailed instructions on the inclusion of appendices together with other supplementary materials, which might be included in the electronic version of an article.

On completion of an article, undertaking a review of its overall structure and readability is essential. In structuring an *MTL* submission, it is recommended that the following order be adhered to: title page, abstract, text, quotations, acknowledgments, references, appendices, footnotes, tables and figures. It is paramount that an article reads well and flows smoothly. A submission should be cohesive, address the required components, and be free of typographical errors and awkward expression. This last aspect can be difficult when English is not an author's primary language; in this case, some editorial assistance will need to be sought prior to submission. One of the many obstacles to achieving journal publication is to submit a paper that is not 'reader-friendly'. Undertaking a review of a journal article is time consuming for busy scholars; trying to interpret an article for meaning, prior to undertaking a review of its contents, adds an extra layer of unwelcome work.

24.9 Being Aware of the Review Processes for *MTL*

Manuscript review processes vary across mathematics education journals. For *MTL*, all submissions are rigorously reviewed by three reviewers, occasionally four if needed. As noted on the journal website:

> Taylor & Francis is committed to peer-review integrity and upholding the highest standards of review. Once your paper has been assessed for suitability by the editor, it will then be double blind peer-reviewed by expert referees. (https://www.tandfonline.com/action/authorSubmission?journalCode=hmtl20&page=instructions)

The *Author Services* section of Taylor & Francis provides an outline of "What to expect during peer review." Within a week or less on receipt of a new submission (submitted via *Editorial Manager,* http://www.edmgr.com/mtl/default.aspx), my editorial assistant and I commence the review process. As *MTL* editor, I reject outright those submissions that are unsuitable for the journal and should be submitted to a more appropriate outlet. Other submissions might meet the journal's aims and scope but suffer from one or more problematic issues, as addressed in this chapter. In these instances, I provide feedback to the author on some of these issues and indicate that the submission cannot be sent for external review as it stands. For submissions that appear borderline or problematic, I might seek the advice of the associate editors. For all other submissions, I identify up to a dozen scholars to invite as potential reviewers, in the hope of securing three. These reviewers are chosen from the Editorial Board as well as from external sources, such as authors whose work has been cited. Many scholars refuse to review for various reasons, while some will never review for the journal. It is not uncommon for over half of potential reviewers to decline, which makes the task of securing reviewers extra difficult. Although disappointing, such a decline rate is understandable given that undertaking insightful and helpful reviews of a journal article is time consuming; there has also been a substantial increase in mathematics education journals in the past decade, all seeking reviewers.

Reviewers are allowed up to six weeks to complete their review, which appears to be a considerably longer period than permitted by many other journals. Even then, we have to chase late reviews and often need to send at least two reminders. Together with reviewers who agree to review but then never submit a review, these delays in reviewer feedback naturally cause problems for both the editor and author.

In submitting their review, reviewers are to make one of four recommendations: accept, accept with revisions, revise and resubmit, and reject. It is rare for a final editorial decision to be a complete acceptance on an article's first submission; most submissions are to be revised, sometimes substantially, and then resubmitted for further review. Authors receive a letter from me usually within two weeks of my receipt of reviews, where I summarise the key points raised by the reviewers. Authors are advised to submit their revised paper within a six-weeks window but are permitted extra time if needed. To enable us to keep track of all submitted articles and to enable a resubmission on the Editorial Manager system, we request that authors inform us of their intention to revise, or their wish to withdraw their submission. For the former, we then send a standard letter from the Editorial Manager system to notify authors that they can revise and resubmit their paper. If authors do not inform us of their intention to revise and resubmit, the Editorial Manager system will not enable a revised paper to be submitted.

For resubmitted *MTL* manuscripts, we try to include at least one of the original reviewers. This is not always possible, however, as some reviewers decline or are reviewing another *MTL* submission. For manuscripts that are borderline between reject outright, and revise and resubmit, it might be necessary to seek three new reviewers, depending on the nature of the original reviewer feedback. For example, a reviewer who provided limited commentary on the original submission would probably not be more forthcoming on a resubmission. The difficult aspect of revising and resubmitting a paper is that there is no guarantee that a revised version will be accepted. As both an author and editor I appreciate this difficulty, and to reject a paper after revision is not a decision I enjoy conveying to an author. I know what it is like being in such a situation as an author. When a submission has to be revised and resubmitted, it is not uncommon for two or more revisions to be requested.

New reviewers for a resubmitted *MTL* paper have access to the previous reviews when considering the revisions an author has made. An author should respond to reviewers' feedback in a detailed and easy-to-follow manner; this is essential for both the reviewer and editor. Authors who simply indicate that a reviewer's points were addressed on pages x, y, and z, or were not followed up because the author considered the reviewer to have different or inappropriate viewpoints, do not do their revised paper justice. On the other hand, sometimes a reviewer might suggest a change that the author does not deem suitable for the paper. It is acceptable to indicate why the change was not made (e.g., some suggested research that does not align with the direction of the submission). Bol and Hacker's (2014) words of advice are worth citing here:

> You not only need to make nearly all of the revisions suggested but describe the revisions made and how they were responsive to the reviewers. Your chances of acceptance in the next round greatly decrease if you refuse to make many of the changes and claim the reviewers did not know what they were talking about. Vague and broad responses, such as "the manuscript is now much improved," won't cut it either. Your responses need to be very specific and thorough. Consider presenting your responses to reviewers in table format. (p. 47)

24.10 A Few Final Points

MTL strives to maintain a high standard of scholarship. It is to be hoped that the points presented in this chapter assist authors who are interested in submitting their papers to the journal. The advice included here is by no means exhaustive. Queries regarding the suitability of an article prior to submission are always welcome. We encourage a range of submissions that address the aims and scope of the journal, and that adhere to the journal guidelines. As we almost never receive commentaries on published *MTL* articles, we encourage interested readers to submit their thoughts on issues raised. Submissions for special issues are also appreciated.

It is important to keep in mind that *MTL* is an international journal, and as such, has readers and submissions from many nations. Authors who only cite research or curriculum development in their own country need to also consider what is happening elsewhere.

Submissions from beginning researchers are always welcomed, and we try to offer as much support as we can. Likewise, we welcome young researchers as reviewers and even recommend that competent doctoral students undertake reviews under the guidance of their advisor or supervisor. Some of the better reviews I have received for *MTL* submissions have come from young researchers and doctoral students nearing completion of their studies.

Lastly, as founding editor, I wish to thank and acknowledge the valuable contributions from a range of authors and reviewers, over two decades. Without such support the journal would not be where it is today. The assistance from the journal publishers, Taylor & Francis, is also appreciated.

References

American Educational Research Association (2006). Standards for reporting on empirical social science research. *Educational Researcher, 35*(6), 33–40).
American Psychological Association. (2013). *Publication manual of the American Psychological Association* (6th ed.). Washington, DC: American Psychological Association.
Bol, L., & Hacker, D. J. (2014). Publishing in high quality journals: Perspectives from overworked and unpaid reviewers. *Journal of Computing in Higher Education, 26,* 39–53.
Journal for Research in Mathematics Education (2015). Characteristics of a high quality *JRME* manuscript. Retrieved from 16 Feb 2015. https://www.nctm.org/publications/write-review-referee/journals/Characteristics-of-a-High-Quality-JRME-Manuscript/.
Robinson, D. H., Levin, J. R., Schraw, G., Patall, E. A., & Hunt, E. B. (2013). On going (way) beyond one's data: A proposal to restrict recommendations for practice in primary educational research journals. *Educational Psychology Review, 25,* 291–302.
Saracho, O. N. (2013). Writing research articles for publication in early childhood education. *Early Childhood Education Journal, 41,* 45–54.

Open Access This chapter is licensed under the terms of the Creative Commons Attribution 4.0 International License (http://creativecommons.org/licenses/by/4.0/), which permits use, sharing, adaptation, distribution and reproduction in any medium or format, as long as you give appropriate credit to the original author(s) and the source, provide a link to the Creative Commons license and indicate if changes were made.

The images or other third party material in this chapter are included in the chapter's Creative Commons license, unless indicated otherwise in a credit line to the material. If material is not included in the chapter's Creative Commons license and your intended use is not permitted by statutory regulation or exceeds the permitted use, you will need to obtain permission directly from the copyright holder.

Chapter 25
ZDM Mathematics Education—Its Development and Characteristics

Gabriele Kaiser

Abstract This chapter provides a description of *ZDM Mathematics Education*, one of the oldest journals in mathematics education. Although *ZDM Mathematics Education* was founded in Germany, it was oriented internationally since its beginning. The historical development of *ZDM Mathematics Education* and its characteristics are described, namely the exclusive publishing of thematic issues by invited guest editors, who invite the contributors of the papers. This feature distinguishes *ZDM Mathematics Education* from many other journals in mathematics education. Despite the invitation-only submission basis, all papers undergo a rigorous peer-review process. The review criteria, the reviewing processes, and the editorial decision process are described, which are currently common to the major mathematics education journals. The journal's foci and orientation have evolved significantly since its founding in 1969, with a strong inclusion of empirical research oriented towards a broad international audience, but adhering to its roots by emphasising subject-based themes.

Keywords Journals in mathematics education · ZDM Mathematics Education · Academic publishing · Review criteria · Editorial decisions

---

The first part is a reprinted and enriched version of the following papers: Kaiser, G. (2017). On the occasion of the decennial publication of *ZDM Mathematics Education* by Springer. *ZDM Mathematics Education*, 49(1), 1–3; Kaiser, G. (2018). Celebration of fifty years of *ZDM Mathematics Education*. *ZDM Mathematics Education*, 50(1), 1–3.

G. Kaiser (✉)
University of Hamburg, Hamburg, Germany
e-mail: gabriele.kaiser@uni-hamburg.de

© The Author(s) 2019
G. Kaiser and N. Presmeg (eds.), *Compendium for Early Career Researchers in Mathematics Education*, ICME-13 Monographs,
https://doi.org/10.1007/978-3-030-15636-7_25

25.1 Development and Scope of *ZDM Mathematics Education*

ZDM Mathematics Education has a distinguished lineage, reaching back to the origins of mathematics education as a discipline in the 1960s. First published in 1969 under the name *Zentralblatt für Didaktik der Mathematik*, abbreviated *ZDM*, the journal then highlighted important international events in mathematics education, with a largely German readership.

The journal was originally founded as an informational and encyclopaedic review on mathematics education. It was initiated by Emmanuel Röhrl, who at that time was the head of the editorial staff for mathematics and physics at Klett Publishing House, and Hans-Georg Steiner, who was at that time working at the Centre for Didactics of Mathematics at the University of Karlsruhe. The Internationale Mathematische Unterrichtskommission (IMUK)—International Commission on Mathematical Instruction (ICMI)—supported the journal as co-publisher. In June 1969 the first edition of the new journal, with the abbreviated name '*ZDM*', came out.

The journal was characterised by its division into two parts, according to the twofold function of *ZDM*: the documentation section, which was defined as the main part of *ZDM*, and the analysis section. The documentation section gave an overview of new publications and was printed on cards that could be detached. The analysis section was meant to reflect on the current discussion in mathematics education. Therefore, the analysis section mainly consisted of papers devoted to a specific theme edited by invited mathematics educators. With a few exceptions the early issues of *ZDM* consisted of thematically oriented issues, which we call nowadays special issues. Hans-Georg Steiner, who had in 1973 moved to the recently founded Institute for Didactics of Mathematics in Bielefeld, devoted his time to the internationalisation of the documentation section and it attained a significant degree of success. In his capacity as chair of the programme committee of the 3rd International Congress on Mathematics Education (ICME-3), which had taken place in 1976 in Karlsruhe, Hans-Georg Steiner had seen the necessity of international publication possibilities in mathematics education as well as the need to review the growing body of publications in this area. He was supported by Heinz Kunle from Karlsruhe, who had served as chair of the local organising committee of ICME-3. Until his death in 2004, Hans-Georg Steiner remained closely connected with *ZDM* and participated actively in the internationalisation process of *ZDM*. Thanks to him, *ZDM* had an English title '*International Reviews on Mathematical Education*' from its very beginning.

In 1976, the responsibility for the journal was delegated to the *Zentralstelle für Atomkernenergie-Dokumentation* (ZAED)—Nuclear Energy Documentation Centre. In 1978 the journal was taken over by the Fachinformationszentrum Energie, Physik, Mathematik (FIZ)—the Leibniz Institute for Information—in connection with the demand for modernisation and internationalisation. Gerhard König, who had originally worked for the publishing house Klett became Managing Editor of *ZDM* and *ZAED* and kept these positions until his retirement in 2004 (for details on Gerhard König see the obituary by Kaiser 2016). He officially represented *ZDM* at all leading conferences in mathematics education and caused the journal to become well known already very early in the history of the international community on mathematics education.

ZDM was supported by the *Verein zur Förderung der Didaktik der Mathematik* (Organization for the promotion of didactics of mathematics) under the chairmanship of Heinz Kunle and Hans-Georg Steiner and the *FIZ*. There the relevant international journals were evaluated for the documentation section, and, based on co-operation with various national and international institutions, many non-German publications were included in the database on mathematics education. In 1998 the former documentation section of *ZDM* was integrated into the *European Mathematical Information Service* so that it became available electronically as a web-based database.

In 2001 the analysis section was excluded from the *ZDM* print version due to budgetary reasons. Since then the analysis section has been available only electronically. The new electronic journal was published and edited under the auspices of the *Fachinformationszentrum Karlsruhe* (FIZ Karlsruhe), together with the *European Society for Mathematics* (ESM) and the *Gesellschaft für Didaktik der Mathematik* (GDM)—Society of Didactics of Mathematics—which took over the rights and responsibilities of the dissolved and above mentioned organisation *Verein zur Förderung der Didaktik der Mathematik*.

In 2006 further changes followed, which resulted in an official separation of the two parts of *ZDM*, namely the reviews and the analysis sections, a fact formerly reflected by the two names. The original documentation section of *ZDM*, the actual database, was distributed under the name *MATHDI/MATHEDU—International Reviews in Mathematical Education*, while the former analysis section was published under the title *Zentralblatt für Didaktik der Mathematik*. At the same time the international nature of the journal was developing further, which became obvious from the international editorial board and the exclusive use of the English language in its publications.

In the year 2007, the 39th volume of *ZDM*, Springer started to publish the journal. The original abbreviation of the journal *ZDM* was maintained, in order to refer to its origin. However, with the implementation of a new sub-title *The International Journal on Mathematics Education*, the opening to an international audience became clear, offering new opportunities, both in scope and reach. The core idea was to continue to publish focused thematic volumes on issues of central importance, such as curricula, assessment, problem solving, and professional development. Authors and editors were to represent the best of mathematics education around the world, and the readership was intended to be equally broad.

With Springer entering the stage, an international editorial board was implemented, thus integrating international scholars with those who were German-speaking, including the continuing editor-in-chief, Gabriele Kaiser, who had already worked in this capacity since 2004. The bimonthly frequency of publication was maintained, with six issues per year. However, in contrast to the previous publication form, the journal was published both in printed format and in a web-based online version, the latter offering access to a much broader international readership via the worldwide presence of Springer.

The first issue published by Springer was dedicated to the memory of Hans-Georg Steiner and his efforts to establish mathematics didactics as a scientific discipline. With this issue *ZDM* went back to its roots in honour of Hans-Georg Steiner, whose constant endeavour made the existence of *ZDM* possible.

The structure of *ZDM*, which had been developed during the last decade, was not changed. Thematically based issues, edited by invited guest-editors with invited papers, still characterised the journal, representing topical mathematics educational approaches and the current state in mathematics education. This practice allowed the publishing of coherent issues describing the state-of-the-art on selected topics and reflecting topical trends of the discussion on mathematics education by invited well-known scholars.

The themes of the issues in the last decade were multifaceted; however, there were recurrent topics, which can be grouped around the following broader themes:

- **Comparative studies, especially between East Asian and Western countries**:
  - Effective mathematics teaching in East and West
  - Asia Pacific focus on mathematics classrooms
  - Exemplary mathematics instruction in East Asia
  - Curriculum research in China and the US
  - Values in East Asian mathematics education
  - Cross-national studies on teaching and learning mathematics
  - Lesson study in mathematics: an international perspective.

- **Teacher education and teacher's professional development**:
  - Empirical research on mathematics teacher education
  - Creating and using representations of mathematics teaching in teacher development
  - Developing teachers' expertise
  - Measuring teacher knowledge from a cross-national perspective
  - Theoretical frameworks in research on and with teachers
  - Re-sourcing teacher work and interaction
  - Promoting professional development of didacticians and mathematics teachers
  - Evidence-based continuous professional development
  - Perception, interpretation and decision making
  - Impact of university teacher education programs
  - Bridging teachers' professional knowledge and instructional quality.

- **Psychological topics**:
  - Flexible/adaptive use of strategies and representations
  - Metacognition in mathematics education
  - Cognitive neuroscience and mathematics learning
  - Cognitive neuroscience and mathematics learning—revisited after five years

- Mathematical thinking and learning
- Beliefs and beyond
- Creativity in mathematics education/Mathematical creativity and psychology
- New perspectives on learning and cognition
- Inhibitory control in mathematics education
- Emotions and motivation in mathematics education
- Applying (cognitive) theory-based instructional design principles in mathematics teaching and learning
- Mathematical word problem solving: psychological and educational perspectives
- Assessment and understanding young children's mathematical minds.

- **New technology and New media**:

  - Usage of dynamic mathematics technologies
  - Historical aspects of the use of technology and devices
  - Handheld technology in mathematics classrooms
  - Interoperable interactive geometry
  - Online mathematics education and e-learning
  - Digital curricula in mathematics education.

- **Mathematics-specific topics**:

  - Learning, teaching and using measurement
  - Whole number arithmetic and its teaching and learning
  - Research on early childhood mathematics teaching and learning
  - Probability in reasoning about data and risk
  - Innovations in statistical modelling to connect data, chance and context
  - Teaching and learning of calculus
  - Research on teaching and learning in linear algebra
  - From patterns to generalization: development of algebraic thinking
  - Geometry in primary school
  - Numeracy/Numeracy and vulnerability in adult life.

- **Research on classroom activities**:

  - Problem solving around the world
  - Didactical and epistemological perspectives on mathematical proof
  - Mathematical evidence and argument
  - Interdisciplinarity in mathematics education
  - 21st century skill and STEM teaching and learning
  - Implementation of inquiry-based learning
  - Visualization as epistemological learning tool
  - Classroom-based interventions in mathematics education
  - Scaffolding and dialogic teaching
  - Textbook research in mathematics education and its recent advancement
  - Language and communication: empirical research and theoretical frameworks
  - Empirical research on the teaching and learning of mathematical modelling

- Studying instructional quality in mathematics through different lenses
- Mathematical tasks and the student.

- **General aspects on mathematics education**:
  - Didactics of mathematics as a scientific discipline—in memoriam Hans-Georg Steiner
  - Turning points in the history of mathematics teaching
  - New perspectives on gender
  - Enacted mathematics curriculum
  - Material ecologies of teaching and learning
  - Socio-economic influences on mathematical achievements
  - New perspectives on the didactic triangle
  - Survey on research on mathematics education
  - Mathematical working spaces in schooling
  - Identity in mathematical education
  - The role of mathematicians' practice in mathematics education research.

- **Methodological issues**:
  - Networking strategies for connecting theoretical approaches
  - Enactivist methodology
  - Design research with a focus on learning processes
  - Assessment in mathematics education: issues regarding methodology, policy and equity.

- **Country-specific issues**:
  - Nordic issue on research
  - South American tapestry of trends
  - Turkish issue on research developments
  - Features of Korean mathematics education.

Since 2010, seven issues per year have been published. Each issue published is comprised of about 12–14 original papers, and additionally one survey paper on the state-of-the-art on the topic of this issue, and one or two commentary papers. As a result of this format, about 90 manuscripts are published per year, covering around 1100 pages (in standard paper-size and two-column format). With the introduction of a survey paper on the state-of-the-art in 2014, ZDM Mathematics Education aimed to give even more concisely an overview of the latest developments concerning the topic of the specific issue. Commentary papers, which were introduced a few years earlier, aimed to provoke a discussion on the theme of the issue, which could not always be achieved. Therefore, the practice of including commentary papers was discontinued in recent years.

A further milestone in the development of *ZDM The International Journal on Mathematics Education* was the change of the subtitle in 2015 leading to the current title of the journal as **ZDM Mathematics Education**. The main reason behind this decision was the ambiguity of the original subtitle *The International Journal on*

Mathematics Education, which led to diverse perceptions of the thrust of the journal, which was not helpful for shaping a clear identity for this journal. It was therefore an obvious consequence to choose a distinct sub-title complementing *ZDM* and keeping the original roots. With the current name *ZDM Mathematics Education*, the aim is an unambiguous title preserving the roots as *Zentralblatt für Didaktik der Mathematik*.

Furthermore, *ZDM Mathematics Education* is characterised by strong support with an editorial office and language editing for papers of non-native speakers of English. This strong support by Springer allowed the establishment of a journal with a broad range of themes and topics reaching as readers not only European or North American mathematics educators. In contrast *ZDM Mathematics Education* is now widely accepted in many Asian countries. The strong German roots of *ZDM Mathematics Education* are apparent in the high importance of subject-specific issues and subject-related analyses in many issues, reflecting the appreciation for and priority given to the subject mathematics and content-related reflections.

Currently *ZDM Mathematics Education* is accepted widely and listed as one of the seven leading journals in mathematics education (see Nivens and Otten 2017; Williams and Leatham 2017) and included in many indexing services, amongst others the *Emerging Sources Citation Index, Scopus, Google Scholar,* and *ERIC System Database*.

With more than 200,000 downloads per year, papers in *ZDM Mathematics Education* receive remarkable recognition. Overall, the impact of *ZDM* Mathematics Education measured by various impact factors confirms that *ZDM Mathematics Education* is one of the leading journals in mathematics education (see the journal's website for more information, https://www.springer.com/education+%26+language/mathematics+education/journal/11858).

Although *ZDM Mathematics Education* publishes only invited papers, all these papers have to follow the guidelines now usual for all major journals in mathematics education. They undergo a rigorous peer-review process, which is described in the next section, and which is similar to the review system in other relevant journals in mathematics education.

25.2 The Submission, Review and Decision Process

A manuscript submitted to *ZDM Mathematics Education* should be of high quality and make a significant contribution to the field. In addition, the article should be an original paper and not have been published elsewhere. *ZDM Mathematics Education* provides guidelines for papers, as do all major journals in mathematics education, which need to be followed by the provisional authors. The main restriction is the length of the submitted manuscript: manuscripts should be no shorter than 40,000 characters including spaces and no longer than 60,000 characters including spaces, and covering abstract, references and a possible appendix. The papers have to be written in English (either American or British English).

The guidelines for the authors are displayed in the website of *ZDM Mathematics Education*.

The papers are submitted electronically via an editorial system, *ZDM Mathematics Education* uses the *Editorial Manager* provided by Springer. The editorial office checks the manuscripts for their compliance with the guidelines.

The papers submitted to the journal undergo a peer-review process by the guest editors and external review by invited experts. Three reviewers are invited to evaluate the paper according to the following criteria, which are displayed in the website of *ZDM Mathematics Education*. Based on these criteria the reviewers are asked to write a commentary on the paper analysing the strengths, weaknesses and limitations of the paper and the research reported. The reviewers are asked to make their comments as explicit, detailed and constructive as possible, in order to provide the editor-in-chief and the guest editors with a sound basis for their decision and to help the author to revise the paper, if necessary. Reviewers have the discretion to differentiate between a commentary to the editors and comments to the authors.

The scientific quality of the paper is evaluated along the following criteria:

* Is the paper a meaningful contribution to mathematics education research and is it distinct from other work of the author(s)?
* Is the approach or the argumentation original and does the paper develop new insights into relevant research questions on mathematics education?
* Does the paper review previous studies and does it consider the relevant literature in the field? Does it avoid unnecessary self-references?
* Is the theoretical frame adequate, i.e., is there an appropriate alignment between the theoretical framework and the questions asked or the problems tackled?
* Is the methodological approach adequate, i.e., do the research methods and analyses match the problem or question?
* Are the argumentations consistent, are the claims and conclusions justified in an acceptable way, do they follow logically from the data or other information presented?"

The quality of the presentation is assessed along these criteria:

* Is the title suitable and is the abstract distinct and adequate?
* Is the writing lucid, clear, and well-organised?
* Is the quality of the figures and tables adequate?"

Finally, the reviewers are asked to make one of the following recommendations:

* Accept without changes
* Accept with minor changes
* Accept with significant changes
* Rewrite the paper
* Reject the paper.

(Source: Information for Reviewers https://www.springer.com/education+&+language/mathematics+education/journal/11858).

Based on the recommendations of the reviewers a decision letter is sent out by the editor-in-chief, which contains a decision and summarises the necessary changes. This decision is sent out on average 60 days after submission, which is quite fast. As *ZDM Mathematics Education* deals only with invited papers by carefully selected authors, the quality of most papers is already quite high at the first submission. The most frequent decision is therefore accept with significant changes, which requires the authors to revise the paper strongly, but allows them to keep the core of the paper. Revision time is usually two months. The authors are asked to submit not only their revised manuscript, additionally they have to provide a letter to the reviewers and the editor-in-chief, in which the changes made are described, in point form. This practice has been established by nearly all academic journals in recent years and allows the authors to explain which changes have been made, and to justify why required changes have not been done, for example due to space restrictions or conflicting requirements by the reviewers. The revised paper is reviewed another time by the same reviewers (usually only two are invited) and after two months at the latest, the next decision is sent out. Usually two to three rounds of revision are needed before the paper can be accepted. For non-native speakers *ZDM Mathematics Education* provides language editing, in which the correctness and adequacy of the academic expressions is checked. On average 16 days after acceptance of the manuscript the paper is available online at Springer Link and can be quoted with its DOI.

This fast and transparent process has led to high satisfaction of the authors, who rated their publishing experience with *ZDM Mathematics Education* as excellent or good.

To close this description of *ZDM Mathematics Education* I would like to summarise common errors being made by many authors who submit their paper to this journal or to others, and which should be avoided, when publishing in *ZDM Mathematics Education* or elsewhere.

Overall, a manuscript has to be based on accepted scientific standards; it should report new scientific results based on high-level research and avoid providing anecdotal evidence.

Furthermore, a clear structure of the paper is necessary, which is quite often not the case for the first submission of the manuscript. The following structure is advisable for papers based on empirical research; theoretically oriented papers or papers oriented towards constructive aims such as the development of learning environments or teaching approaches may follow another structure. This structure is advisable for papers, or at least a paper has to contain these parts:

- Introduction, in which the research question or research aim is roughly described functioning as advance organiser;
- Literature review on the state-of-the-art on the research question or research aim;
- Development of the detailed research questions or research aims referring to the literature review;

- Description of the theoretical framework on which the study is based, the important theoretical conceptualisations or constructs;
- Description of the underlying methodology;
- Display of the results;
- Summary of the results and interpretations;
- Discussion of the limitations of the study, conclusions, potential to generalise and further prospects.

One central error often made within the first version of a manuscript is that a clear research question or research aim is missing, so that the central argumentation of the manuscript remains vague or unclear. It is indispensable to develop a clear research question or, if that is not possible, to formulate at least a precise research aim. A rough research question should be formulated at the beginning of the paper and should already be mentioned in the abstract. Details of the research question should follow after the literature review, in which a clear research gap has been pointed out, which the paper intends to close.

A common problem of the literature review is the usage of outdated literature or non-consideration of the most recent literature, which means that the literature review is not really covering the current state-of-the-art. Furthermore, the literature review is quite often too narrow and focused only on the country or the culture of the author. An international journal such as *ZDM Mathematics Education* cannot accept such a narrow focus and the reviewers will usually ask for a broader view.

A strong theoretical framework is the indispensable part of a scientific manuscript. This does not need to be a framework developed by oneself; in contrast, it is nowadays usual to refer to grand theories of mathematics education developed by others, which are then narrowed down to the specific research goal of the study. It is essential to develop carefully all theoretical constructs used and to embed these constructs in the overall framework. To a certain extent, in contrast to the above remarks, one can state that is important to focus the literature survey on the research question and avoid a too general overview of the field, only loosely connected to the research questions and aims of the paper. The balance between broadness and focus is important.

For empirical papers the methodological part of a manuscript is indispensable and quite often not satisfactory, which leads to requests for revision. The embedding of the chosen methodological approach in a research paradigm is indispensable, i.e., it must become clear to which paradigm the study is referring, to a qualitative or quantitative design, or design-based research, the mixed method paradigm, variations of the interpretative paradigm or other theoretical references. It must be convincingly explained why the chosen methodology and/or methodical approach is adequate and necessary. Especially the reflection of the adequacy of the methods is of strong importance for a high-quality paper.

Furthermore, the description of the chosen sample and sampling procedure is necessary. The description of the data evaluation process in detail can be seen as the heart of the methodological section, which is often quite poor. A short reference to a grand theory such as Grounded Theory or Text Analysis is not sufficient; in contrast, a description of the coding structure, the development of codes and a short example is necessary to display. It is advisable to include parts of the coding manual in the appendix as well as worked out examples. These details are needed for various empirical methods, including case studies. Within the interpretative design, a careful translation of verbatim transcripts is needed, while in a quantitative design the usual quality indicators should be given. Overall, the evaluation process needs to be transparent enough for a critical reader to follow.

Many qualitatively oriented studies aim for the description of the variability of the data, which is in contrast to quantitatively oriented studies aiming for uniformity. The variability of the data should be described and should not be restricted to extremely small-scale studies.

A clear description of the results is necessary, i.e., the results should be described and discussed. In detail, interpretations referring to the original theoretical framework and the state-of-the-art of the scientific discussion should be provided. Apart from the problems mentioned above, a further problem is the missing connection between an ambitious theoretical framework and the results of study, which is caused, amongst other reasons, by the lack of intensive interpretation of the results. A connection of the achieved results and their interpretation to the theoretical framework is indispensable. However, one can state as a common mistake that an ambitious framework is used and only minor results are achieved.

Although most studies do not use representative samples the potential to generalise or to transfer to other samples or topics is important as this increases the relevance and scope of the study. Fine-grained studies are of high relevance, but at the end of the day one wishes to know how far these results hold in general or can be transferred to the context of broader research questions.

Overall, these recommendations and descriptions are not only focused on *ZDM Mathematics Education*, but on papers in mathematics educational journals in general. However, they are based on the editor's personal experience and reflect the specific features of *ZDM Mathematics Education*.

To conclude, it is hoped that *ZDM Mathematics Education* will continue to grow in its international acceptance and reach and will contribute to the further development of mathematics education as a scientific discipline.

References

Kaiser, G. (2016). On the death of Gerhard König. *ZDM Mathematics Education, 48*(1), 247.
Nivens, R. A., & Otten, S. (2017). Assessing journal quality in mathematics education. *Journal for Research in Mathematics Education, 48*(4), 348–368.
Williams, S. R., & Leatham, K. R. (2017). Journal quality in mathematics education. *Journal for Research in Mathematics Education, 48*(4), 369–396.

Open Access This chapter is licensed under the terms of the Creative Commons Attribution 4.0 International License (http://creativecommons.org/licenses/by/4.0/), which permits use, sharing, adaptation, distribution and reproduction in any medium or format, as long as you give appropriate credit to the original author(s) and the source, provide a link to the Creative Commons license and indicate if changes were made.

The images or other third party material in this chapter are included in the chapter's Creative Commons license, unless indicated otherwise in a credit line to the material. If material is not included in the chapter's Creative Commons license and your intended use is not permitted by statutory regulation or exceeds the permitted use, you will need to obtain permission directly from the copyright holder.

Part V
Looking Ahead

Chapter 26
What Makes for Powerful Classrooms, and How Can We Support Teachers in Creating Them? A Story of Research and Practice, Productively Intertwined

Alan H. Schoenfeld

Abstract This article, and my career as an educational researcher, are grounded in two fundamental assumptions: (1) that research and practice can and should live in productive synergy, with each enhancing the other; and (2) that research focused on teaching and learning in a particular discipline can, if carefully framed, yield insights that have implications across a broad spectrum of disciplines. This article begins by describing in brief two bodies of work that exemplify these two fundamental assumptions. I then elaborate on a third example, the development of a new set of tools for understanding and supporting powerful mathematics classroom instruction—and by extension, powerful instruction across a wide range of disciplines.

Keywords Educational research · Practice · Synergy · Mathematics classroom instruction

---

This paper is based on my 2013 AERA Distinguished Researcher lecture, presented at the AERA annual meeting, Philadelphia, April 6, 2014.

The work reported in this paper was made possible by generous support from the National Science Foundation for the Algebra Teaching Study (Grant DRL-0909815 to PI Alan Schoenfeld, U.C. Berkeley, and Grant DRL-0909851 to PI Robert Floden, Michigan State University), and the Bill and Melinda Gates Foundation for the Mathematics Assessment Project (Grant OPP53342 to PIs Alan Schoenfeld, U. C Berkeley, and Hugh Burkhardt and Malcolm Swan, The University of Nottingham). I am deeply indebted to the members of both the ATS and MAP teams for their essential contributions to the work reported here.

A. H. Schoenfeld (✉)
University of California, Berkeley, USA
e-mail: alans@berkeley.edu

26.1 Introduction

I am honored and grateful to have been awarded the 2013 AERA Distinguished Researcher award. I am gratified as well that the timing of the award allows me to unveil a new set of tools for understanding and supporting powerful classroom instruction. This article also allows me to reflect on, and exemplify, two themes that have been central to my work from my beginnings in educational research almost forty years ago:

(1) research and practice can and should live in productive synergy, with each enhancing the other;
(2) research focused on teaching and learning in one particular discipline can, if carefully framed, yield insights that have implications across a broad spectrum of disciplines.

In what follows I shall briefly review two main lines of my work over the years: a decade of work on problem solving, and two decades of work on modeling the teaching process. My focus in those reviews will be on elaborating the research-practice dialectic, and showing how results first derived in mathematics apply more generally. Having done so, I will turn my attention to work I have been involved with over the past half dozen years, which has been focused on understanding the attributes of powerful mathematics classrooms. Here too, I will show how an expanding R&P agenda has enriched both the research and the practices with which it has lived in happy synergy. Then, having elaborated on the nature of the work and framed it within mathematics, I will indicate how it yields a set of hypotheses for understanding and enhancing teaching in all disciplines.

26.2 Case 1: Problem Solving in Mathematics and Beyond

Perhaps the best way to summarize my problem solving work (see, e.g., Schoenfeld 1985, 1992) is that it consisted of a decade-long series of design experiments aimed at understanding and enhancing students' mathematical problem solving.

Here a brief theoretical detour on the nature of design experiments is in order—my impression is that a significant number of researchers take "design experiment" to mean something like "cycles of design and implementation that result in an improved educational intervention." While design experiments do include such cycles, there is more to them than that. They are about improving both theory and practice.

So, just what is a design experiment? As I understand it (see, e.g., Cobb et al. 2003; Schoenfeld 2006),

a. One has a "local theory" about learning, which suggests some aspects of design.
b. One crafts a theory-based intervention ("the local theory says that *this* intervention ought to work in the following ways, to enhance understanding in *these ways*").
c. On the basis of implementing the intervention and carefully observing its impact, one (i) refines the local theory and (ii) refines the intervention.

That is, design experiments are as much about theory as they are about design. That said, let me briefly recap the evolution of my problem solving work. Prior to building my first problem solving course, I had conducted some experimentation, and done some theorizing, about what it would take to make effective use of particular problem solving strategies. I took these ideas into the first version of the course, where I found that some things seemed to work, but some didn't. Close observations of my students' struggles provided a refined understanding of aspects of metacognition, which I could then better theorize. The same was the case for laboratory studies and ongoing instruction, aimed at understanding and then having an impact on belief systems. Over the course of a decade, my evolving understanding resulted in the following theoretical perspective:

If one seeks the reason(s) for someone's success or failure in a mathematical problem solving attempt, the cause of that success or failure will be located in one or more of that person's

A. mathematical knowledge and resources
B. access to productive "heuristic" strategies for making progress on challenging problems
C. monitoring and self-regulation (aspects of metacognition), and
D. belief systems regarding mathematics, and one's sense of self as thinker in general and a doer of mathematics in particular (in more current language, one's mathematical identity). (See, e.g., Schoenfeld 1985).

At the same time, the problem solving course improved, both profiting from the research and contributing to it. In that way, then, research and practice lived in productive synergy. (This is fundamental assumption 1.)

It goes without saying that the problem solving work was not conducted in a theoretical vacuum. There was, of course, a large body of research on domain-specific knowledge in a wide variety of content areas. As I was elaborating on productive strategies (heuristics) for engaging in mathematics, others were elaborating on productive strategies in other domains (e.g., in reading (Palincsar and Brown 1984), writing (Scardamalia and Bereiter 1983), science (diSessa 1983), and artificial intelligence (Newell 1983)). Clearly, metacognition has a domain-specific component (that is, the more knowledge you have, the more effective one can be in monitoring and self-regulation), but aspects of it are domain-general (e.g., Brown 1987). Similarly, some beliefs about self may be general, some mathematics-specific; but there are surely analogs in other domains. Thus, when the mathematical problem solving work was well established, I could claim with confidence that A through D above were essential components of mathematical problem solving. But, given parallel work in other domains, I could already suggest the following with some confidence:

If one seeks the reason(s) for someone's success or failure in a problem solving attempt in any knowledge-rich domain, the cause of that success or failure will be located in one or more of that person's

A. domain-specific knowledge and resources
B. access to productive "heuristic" strategies for making progress on challenging problems in that domain
C. monitoring and self-regulation (aspects of metacognition), and
D. belief systems regarding that domain, and one's sense of self as thinker in general and a doer of that domain in particular (in more current language, one's domain-specific identity).

That conjecture has held, in that resources, strategies, metacognition, and beliefs are generally acknowledged to be essential parts of sense making in every field, and no additional arenas have been declared as essential[1] (see, e.g., Collins et al. 1989). I take this to be a case in point of fundamental assumption 2, that the research originally done in mathematics had direct analogues in other content domains.

26.3 Case 2: Decision Making in Mathematics Teaching and Beyond

My second example concerns the theory of decision making put forth in my book *How We Think* (Schoenfeld 2010). My research group, known as the "Functions Group," had been conducting a series of studies of mathematics tutoring (see, e.g., Schoenfeld et al. 1992) in order to develop the tools for studying teaching. My first case study of teaching occurred when a student in our teacher preparation program was dissatisfied with a lesson he had taught, but couldn't figure out why things had gone wrong. The coordinator of the program, who was also a member of Functions Group, suggested that he bring a video of his lesson to us for analysis.

My goal was to do more than help the student, though that was important. Ultimately, my intention was to be able to model this mathematics teacher's classroom decision making, on a moment-by moment basis—and then others'.

Let me unpack the central ideas in the previous sentence. First, my intention was to build an analytical model of the student's teaching. The reason for modeling is that modeling is a rigorous way to test theoretical ideas. It's one thing to say "I think this is why the teacher did what he did;" it's quite something else to say "here is a general model of the decision making process during teaching, into which

---

[1]That is not to say that refinements have not been made—e.g., discussions of individual identity and its evolution in social interactions are much more rich than they were a quarter century ago. However, the core categories still stand.

I insert a characterization of the key aspects of this teacher's teaching. The model makes the same decisions that the individual did." Models are falsifiable, which means that one's explanations are put to the test.[2] Second, the state of the art had advanced to the point where we might have a chance of understanding and modeling teaching as it happens, rather than studying behavior in the laboratory. When the state of the art allows for it, the idea is to push the theory-practice dialectic. Third, yes, I began by modeling mathematics teaching—because my grounding is in mathematics and it is what I know best—but, it was reasonable to expect that the essentials of teachers' decision making (if framed the right way) would be akin to teachers' decision making in other fields.[3]

To summarize a book in a paragraph, the key idea in *How We Think* (Schoenfeld 2010) is that people's moment-by-moment decision making in: teaching; in medicine; in fact, in *all* knowledge-rich domains, can be modeled as a function of their:

- Resources (especially their knowledge, but also the tools at their disposal);
- Orientations (a generalization of beliefs, including values and preferences); and
- Goals (which are often chosen on the basis of orientations and available resources).

I will note, as before, that the theoretical ideas summarized above evolved in productive dialectic with practice. The first attempt at modeling was motivated by a problem from practice, and potential limits to the scope of our models were posed by other cases of "real world" teaching. Moreover, as our understandings evolved, we embarked on experimental work related to professional development (see, e.g., Arcavi and Schoenfeld 2008). It is one thing to say, theoretically, that orientations are central and belief change is slow; it is quite something else to try to achieve belief change. In attempting to do so and studying what happens, one develops a more nuanced understanding of the growth and change of belief systems. Thus, the work modeling decision making during mathematics teaching was, again, a case example of the productive research-and practice synergy (that is, fundamental assumption 1).

Re fundamental assumption 2, I will note again that while I was focused on mathematics teaching in the early phases of modeling, the architecture of the decision making process was constructed so as to be general. As in the case of problem solving, what was known about decision making in a wide range of knowledge-intensive fields (e.g., teaching in other domains, but also medical decision making; see, e.g., Groopman 2007; Szolovits et al. 1988) was entirely consistent with what was known in mathematics; it stood to reason that with the

---

[2]For those who are philosophically inclined, I will note that I use falsifiability as a design heuristic: the idea is to frame my claims in ways that they can be falsified, which then allows for theory testing and refinement. I am not making claims about falsifiability in general.

[3]Clearly, the content being taught is different, so teachers in different disciplines will have different knowledge bases, and even within a discipline teachers will have different epistemological stances with regard to the content. The question is to frame things so that there are important generalities despite the domain-specific particulars.

right framing, a theory of decision making during mathematics teaching could be seen as an instance of something more general (and, the applications to other fields would be straightforward). *How We Think* makes a plausibility case, with ties to the broader literature and some fully worked out examples. Time will tell how robust the claims will be.

26.4 Case 3: Documenting and Supporting Productive Teaching in Mathematics

26.4.1 (3A): What Counts in Mathematics Teaching?

Here we come to the core example of this paper. The question here is: can one identify the key aspects of powerful mathematics classrooms—classrooms that produce students who do well on tests of mathematical content and problem solving?

The motivation for this work was the observation (a half dozen years ago, before the MET study (Bill and Melinda Gates Foundation 2012) was conducted) that, although many of us have strong opinions about what makes for 'good teaching' in mathematics and other classrooms, there was precious little evidence to support those beliefs. Ideally, one would like to have tools to measure classroom practices, and tools to measure student performance, to explore the relationship between the two: do classrooms that score high on the dimensions of purported importance produce students who score high on tests of mathematical thinking?

To explore this issue, we needed a classroom measure that (a) was comprehensive, (b) focused on key aspects of mathematical sense making, (c) contained a relatively small number of important dimensions (so that, among other things, the implications for professional development would be clear), and (d) could be used in perhaps twice real time to code classroom data (that is, an hour of observations and note-taking would require an additional hour to code the score), so that large-scale data analysis would be feasible. As explained in Schoenfeld (2013), although there were many schemes for classroom analysis—e.g., Beeby et al. 1980; Danielson 2011; Institute for Research on Policy Education and Practice 2011; Junker et al., 2004; Marder and Walkington 2012; PACT Consortium 2012; Pianta et al. 2008; University of Michigan 2006—no schemes with attributes (a) through (d) above were available. Thus we set about building a theoretical framework and a classroom analysis rubric to match. The details of how we arrived at the theoretical frame are given in Schoenfeld (2013). In Table 26.1, I set forth our hypotheses regarding the key dimensions of powerful mathematics classrooms.[4] Again, this distillation is

---

[4]Table 26.1 describes the domain-general part of our work. The Algebra Teaching Study has also focused on what it takes for students to develop proficiency working with contextual algebraic tasks, and crafted materials to support algebra teachers. Those materials are part of the "TRU Math Suite," described below.

Table 26.1 The five dimensions of mathematically powerful classrooms

The Five Dimensions of Mathematically Powerful Classrooms
1. The Mathematics: The extent to which the mathematics discussed is focused and coherent, and to which connections between procedures, concepts and contexts (where appropriate) are addressed and explained. Students should have opportunities to learn important mathematical content and practices, and to develop productive mathematical habits of mind. (See, e.g., Common Core State Standards Initiative 2010; National Council of Teachers of Mathematics 1989, 2000)
2. Cognitive Demand: The extent to which classroom interactions create and maintain an environment of productive intellectual challenge that is conducive to students' mathematical development. There is a happy medium between spoon-feeding mathematics in bite-sized pieces and having the challenges so large that students are lost at sea. (See, e.g., Henningsen and Stein 1997; Stein et al. 2008; Stein et al. 1996)
3. Access to Mathematical Content: The extent to which classroom activity structures invite and support the active engagement of all of the students in the classroom with the core mathematics being addressed by the class. No matter how rich the mathematics being discussed, a classroom in which a small number of students get most of the "air time" is not equitable. (See, e.g., Cohen and Lotan 1997; Oakes et al. 2001)
4. Agency, Authority, and Identity: The extent to which students have opportunities to conjecture, explain, make mathematical arguments, and build on one another's ideas, in ways that contribute to their development of agency (the capacity and willingness to engage mathematically) and authority (recognition for being mathematically solid), resulting in positive identities as doers of mathematics. (See, e.g., Cobb et al. 1997; Engle 2011)
5. Uses of Assessment: The extent to which the teacher solicits student thinking and subsequent instruction responds to those ideas, by building on productive beginnings or addressing emerging misunderstandings. Powerful instruction "meets students where they are" and gives them opportunities to move forward. (See, e.g., Black and Wiliam 1998)

grounded in the literature (see Schoenfeld 2013; Schoenfeld et al. 2014). The key feature here is the distillation into a small number of dimensions.

To explore the hypothesis that these are indeed (one productive organization of) the dimensions of powerful classrooms, one needs a rubric for classroom observations. The team has produced such a rubric, called the "Teaching for Robust Understanding of Mathematics" (or TRU Math) rubric.[5] Before summarizing its

---

[5]The TRU Math Rubric and all of the other documents discussed in this article—known collectively as the TRU Math Suite—can be downloaded from http://ats.berkeley.edu/tools.html and http://map.mathshell.org/materials/trumath.php.

essence I must emphasize that this rubric was developed a research tool, and that it is not intended for administrative use in evaluating teachers. This is for at least three reasons: (1) validation of the rubric through research is in its very early stages; (2) although the summary rubric given below seems straightforward, the actual use of the rubric requires training; and (3) we would much rather focus on working productively with teachers, as opposed to rating them. As seen later in this paper, we have an approach to professional development that focuses on engaging teachers in productive activities and conversations concerning the five dimensions of TRU Math.

The full TRU Math rubric contains sub-rubrics for characterizing episodes of: whole-class instruction; small group work; student presentations; and individual student work. Using the rubric involves parsing classroom activities into a sequence of 'episodes' of no more than five minutes each in duration, assigning scores to each episode using the relevant sub-rubric, and then computing a weighted average of scores. The summary rubric, which is not used for scoring, is given in Fig. 26.1. The summary rubric does provide a clear sense of the kinds of classroom activities that will score high or low along each of the dimensions.

As noted above, to explore the relationship between classroom practices and student performance, one needs robust measures of student performance—in particular, measures of content, concepts, reasoning and problem solving. This, fortunately, has been a focus of our work since the early 1990s. The Balanced Assessment Project (Hugh Burkhardt, Alan Schoenfeld, Judah Schwartz, and Sandra Wilcox, principal investigators) was first funded in 1992 to construct assessments in line with the 1989 NCTM Standards, and versions of the project (the Mathematics Assessment Resource Service and the Toolkit for Change, with Burkhardt, Schoenfeld, and Wilcox as PIs, and the Mathematics Assessment Project) have continued to the present day.[6] In sum, we now have a set of tools—both independent and dependent measures—for the empirical exploration of research-based hypotheses regarding powerful instruction and its impact. (See the left hand side of Fig. 26.3.) Very preliminary data analyses suggest that the relationship exists, but large n studies are really what is called for.

26.4.2 (3B): Supporting Effective Mathematics Teaching

The next logical question is how to enhance teachers' proficiency along those five dimensions (and study the impact of that work on teachers and students). Here the Mathematics Assessment Project and the Algebra Teaching Study have produced two sets of tools. The first is a set of "Classroom Challenges" or "Formative Assessment Lessons" designed to support teachers engagement in formative

---

[6] I note that tasks developed by the Balanced Assessment group were used as the dependent measures for the Gates Foundation's (2012) Measures of Effective Teaching study.

	The Mathematics	Cognitive Demand	Access to Mathematical Content	Agency, Authority, and Identity	Uses of Assessment
	How accurate, coherent, and well justified is the mathematical content?	To what extent are students supported in grappling with and making sense of mathematical concepts?	To what extent does the teacher support access to the content of the lesson for all students?	To what extent are students the source of ideas and discussion of them? How are student contributions framed?	To what extent is students' mathematical thinking surfaced; to what extent does instruction build on student ideas when potentially valuable or address misunderstandings when they arise?
1	Classroom activities are unfocused or skills-oriented, lacking opportunities for engagement in key practices such as reasoning and problem solving.	Classroom activities are structured so that students mostly apply memorized procedures and/or work routine exercises.	There is differential access to or participation in the mathematical content, and no apparent efforts to address this issue.	The teacher initiates conversations. Students' speech turns are short (one sentence or less), and constrained by what the teacher says or does.	Student reasoning is not actively surfaced or pursued. Teacher actions are limited to corrective feedback or encouragement.
2	Activities are primarily skills-oriented, with cursory connections between procedures, concepts and contexts (where appropriate) and minimal attention to key practices.	Classroom activities offer possibilities of conceptual richness or problem solving challenge, but teaching interactions tend to "scaffold away" the challenges, removing opportunities for productive struggle.	There is uneven access or participation but the teacher makes some efforts to provide mathematical access to a wide range of students.	Students have a chance to explain some of their thinking, but "the student proposes, the teacher disposes": in class discussions, student ideas are not explored or built upon.	The teacher refers to student thinking, perhaps even to common mistakes, but specific students' ideas are not built on (when potentially valuable) or used to address challenges (when problematic).
3	Classroom activities support meaningful connections between procedures, concepts and contexts (where appropriate) and provide opportunities for engagement in key practices.	The teacher's hints or scaffolds support students in productive struggle in building understandings and engaging in mathematical practices.	The teacher actively supports and to some degree achieves broad and meaningful mathematical participation; OR what appear to be established participation structures result in such engagement.	Students explain their ideas and reasoning. The teacher may ascribe ownership for students' ideas in exposition, AND/OR students respond to and build on each other's ideas.	The teacher solicits student thinking and subsequent instruction responds to those ideas, by building on productive beginnings or addressing emerging misunderstandings.

Fig. 26.1 The TRU Math Summary Rubric

assessment focused on core content. To put things simply, doing formative assessment is hard: it calls for a set of pedagogical habits of mind and pedagogical content knowledge that most teachers do not have, and which are not simple to acquire. For that reason the Mathematics Assessment Project developed a series of 100 Formative Assessment Lessons (FALs) whose purpose it is to scaffold teachers in teaching formatively. The content-oriented FALs are grounded in research on what students find difficult. They begin with tasks designed to elicit student thinking—to reveal bases of understanding that can be built upon, and to reveal misunderstandings that need to be addressed. The lessons indicate common patterns of student responses to the tasks, and ways to deal with them; they also contain activities that support the teacher in further assessing student understanding, and building on it.

It is worth discussing the project's design methodology here, for it too reflects a form of research-and-practice dialectic. Project designers based at the University of Nottingham craft a draft version of a lesson, which is then piloted in local schools. Team members observe the lessons (using a feedback rubric) and make suggestions for refinement to the design team, which then modifies the draft. When the draft is deemed solid, it is sent to three observation centers in the US (in California, Michigan, and Rhode Island). The lessons are taught in a range of classrooms, and the observers document how they are working (or not) using a standard protocol. Observation forms are returned to Nottingham, where they are compiled by and discussed by the team. Revisions are then made by a team member other than the person who designed the lesson. This results in an "alpha" version. The alpha version is then distributed to the observation centers in the US, where the observation process is repeated and the compiled feedback is used in the creation of a beta version. See Mathematics Assessment Project (2014) for detail.

To date there have been more than two million Formative Assessment Lesson downloads from the project website, http://map.mathshell.org/.

The second set of materials we offer by way of support for teachers is the "TRU Math Conversation Guide" (Baldinger and Louie 2014). This tool, intended for teacher-coach conversations (or, better, professional learning communities), addresses each of the five dimensions of TRU Math by raising a series of questions that teachers might consider with regard to lesson planning, debriefing, and thoughts about where to go next. In the conversation guide, the approach to the five dimensions is reframed as in Table 26.2.

These framing questions are mere overtures to conversations; the questions are elaborated in the Conversation Guide. Figure 26.2 shows the conversational elaboration of the third dimension, *Access to Mathematical Content*.

The Formative Assessment Lessons and the TRU Math Conversation Guide constitute the Professional Development part of the TRU Math Suite. As discussed below, they constitute the right hand side of Fig. 26.3.

Table 26.2 Framing questions in the TRU Math Conversation Guide

Framing Questions in the TRU Math Conversation Guide
The Mathematics: How do mathematical ideas from this unit/course develop in this lesson/lesson sequence?
Cognitive Demand: What opportunities do students have to make their own sense of mathematical ideas?
Access to Mathematical Content: Who does and does not participate in the mathematical work of the class, and how?
Agency, Authority, and Identity: What opportunities do students have to explain their own and respond to each other's mathematical ideas?
Uses of Assessment: What do we know about each student's current mathematical thinking, and how can we build on it?

Access to Mathematical Content

Core Question: Who does and does not participate in the mathematical work of the class, and how?

All students should have access to opportunities to develop their own understandings of rich mathematics, and to build productive mathematical identities. For any number of reasons, it can be extremely difficult to provide this access to everyone, but that doesn't make it any less important! We want to challenge ourselves to recognize who has access and when. There may be mathematically rich discussions or other mathematically productive activities in the classroom—but who gets to participate in them? Who might benefit from different ways of organizing classroom activity?

Access to Mathematical Content

Pre-observation	Reflecting After a Lesson	Planning Next Steps
What opportunities exist for each student to participate in the mathematical work of the class?	Who did and didn't participate in the mathematical work of the class, and how?	How can we create opportunities for each student to participate in the mathematical work of the class?

Think about:

- What range of ways students can and do participate in the mathematical work of the class (talking, writing, leaning in, listening hard; manipulating symbols, making diagrams, interpreting graphs, using manipulatives, connecting different strategies, etc.).
- Which students participate in which ways.
- Which students are most active when, and how we can create opportunities for more students to participate more actively.
- What opportunities various students have to make meaningful mathematical contributions.
- Language demands and the development of students' academic language.
- How norms (or interactions, or lesson structures, or task structure, or particular representations, etc.) facilitate or inhibit participation for particular students.
- What teacher moves might expand students' access to meaningful participation (such as modeling ways to participate, providing opportunities for practice, holding students accountable, pointing out students' successful participation).
- How to support particular students we are concerned about (in relation to learning, issues of safety, participation, etc.).

Fig. 26.2 Access to mathematical content, in the TRU Math Conversation Guide

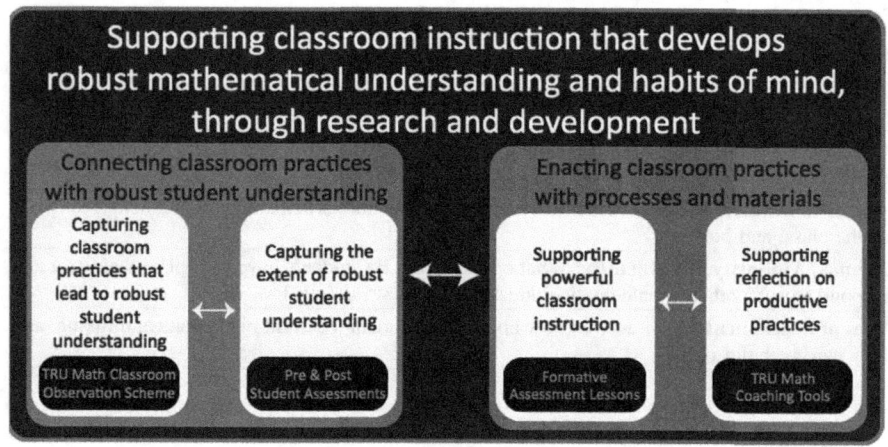

Fig. 26.3 The research, practice, and development dialectic in mathematics

26.5 Discussion: The Current State, and Possibly Productive Next Steps

Figure 26.3 offers the "big picture" view of the enterprise as I have described it thus far.

In concluding I would like to review the enterprise described in Fig. 26.3 with regard to the framing assumptions outlined at the beginning of this article.

Framing Assumption 1: Research and practice can and should live in productive synergy, with each enhancing the other.

The examples discussed in this article provide substantial backing for this assumption. In the problem solving work, the course and the theory I was developing were mutually enriching, with the theory suggesting ideas for implementation and, at times, my intuitions as a teacher suggesting things for me to explore theoretically. The result was a 'virtuous cycle' of discovery, including the refinement of ideas about strategy implementation, metacognition, and belief systems. The work on teacher modeling was inspired by problems of practice, and refined by it; in turn, the theoretical work suggested avenues for the improvement of practice. In the current body of work, it is worth noting that every object and every arrow in Fig. 26.3 represents or embodies a productive dialectic between theory and practice.

Framing Assumption 2: research focused on teaching and learning in one particular discipline can, if carefully framed, yield insights that have implications across a broad spectrum of disciplines.

As indicated above, the problem solving work was done in mathematics but had obvious analogues in other disciplines. The theoretical claims with regard to generality have stood the test of time. Similarly, the decision making work was done in the context of a vast literature on decision making; mathematics teaching was the focus of my core examples, but the modeling was framed in ways that could be abstracted. I believe the same is the case with regard to the issues encapsulated in Fig. 26.3. The TRU Math scheme is, of necessity, grounded in the specifics of mathematics teaching and learning. Thus, dimension 1 ("the mathematics") is fundamentally mathematical, just as the "resources" in the original problem solving work and teacher modeling were fundamentally mathematical. But the other dimensions of TRU Math—cognitive demand; access to meaningful engagement with the content; agency, authority, and identity; and the uses of assessment—while 'tinged' with mathematics when one looks at mathematics instruction, are general. That is, in a writing (or literature, or physics) class they would be 'tinged' with writing (or literature, or physics) in the same ways.

Hence, to use mathematical language, one can think of "The Mathematics" in the TRU Math work as a variable—call it X, where X = "any particular discipline." In the new scheme, called the "TRU X framework," the first dimension, "The X," would be "the extent to which this discipline ("X") comes alive in the classroom as described in content standards or other documents, with students having the opportunity to develop productive disciplinary habits of mind." The other three tools (represented by the dark boxes) in Fig. 26.3 would be fleshed out analogously, resulting in Fig. 26.4.

This, of course, is just a conjecture at this point. I do think, however, that working on it will be a productive enterprise. I look forward to doing so, with colleagues from across the educational spectrum, in the years to come.

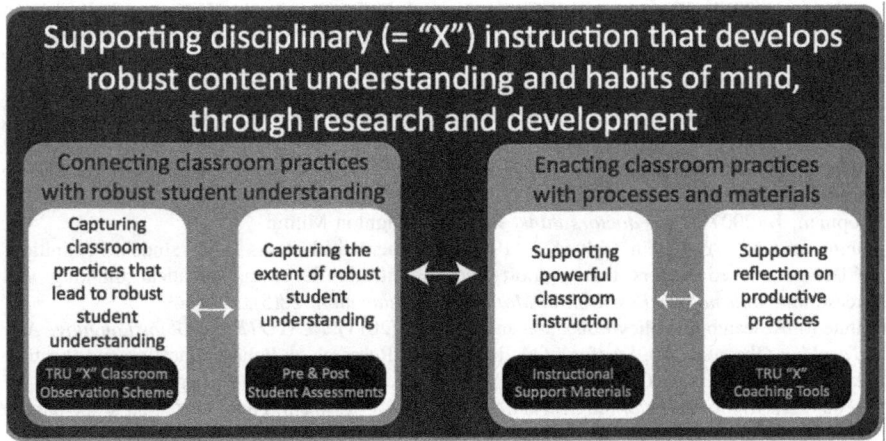

Fig. 26.4 The research, practice, and development dialectic in general

References

Arcavi, A., & Schoenfeld, A. H. (2008). Using the unfamiliar to problematize the familiar. *Canadian Journal of Science, Mathematics and Technology Education, 8*(3), 280–295.

Baldinger, E., & Louie, N. (2014). TRU Math conversation guide: A tool for teacher learning and growth. Berkeley, CA & E. Lansing, MI: Graduate School of Education, University of California, Berkeley & College of Education, Michigan State University. Retrieved from http://ats.berkeley.edu/tools.html and/or http://map.mathshell.org/materials/pd.php.

Beeby, T., Burkhardt, H., & Caddy, R. (1980). *SCAN: Systematic classroom analysis notation for mathematics lessons*. England Shell Centre for Mathematics Education: Nottingham.

Bill and Melinda Gates Foundation. (2012). *Gathering feedback for teaching: Combining high-quality observations with student surveys and achievement gains*. Seattle, WA: Bill and Melinda Gates Foundation.

Black, P., & Wiliam, D. (1998). Assessment and classroom learning. *Assessment in Education, 5*(1), 7–74.

Brown, A. (1987). Metacognition, executive control, relf-regulation, and other more mysterious mechanisms. In F. Reiner & R. Kluwe (Eds.), *Metacognition, motivation, and understanding* (pp. 65–116). Hillsdale, NJ: Erlbaum.

Cobb, P., Gravemeijer, K., Yackel, E., McClain, K., & Whitenack, J. (1997). Mathematizing and symbolizing: The emergence of chains of signification in one first-grade classroom. In D. Kirschner & J. A. Whitson (Eds.), *Situated cognition: Social, semiotic and psychological perspectives* (pp. 151–233). Mahwah, NJ: Erlbaum.

Cobb, P., Confrey, J., diSessa, A., Lehrer, R., & Schauble, L. (2003). Design experiments in educational research. *Educational Researcher, 32*(1), 9–13.

Cohen, E. G., & Lotan, R. A. (Eds.). (1997). *Working for equity in heterogeneous classrooms: Sociological theory in practice*. New York: Teachers College Press.

Collins, A., Brown, J. S., & Newman, S. (1989). Cognitive apprenticeship: Teaching the craft of reading, writing, and mathematics. In L. B. Resnick (Ed.), *Knowing, learning, and instruction: Essays in honor of Robert Glaser* (pp. 453–494). Hillsdale, NJ: Erlbaum.

Common Core State Standards Initiative (2010). Common core state standards for mathematics. Downloaded June 4, 2010, from http://www.corestandards.org/the-standards.

Danielson, C. (2011). The framework for teaching evaluation instrument (2011 ed.). Downloaded April 1, 2012, from http://www.danielsongroup.org/article.aspx?page=FfTEvaluationInstrument.

diSessa, A. (1983). Phenomenology and the evolution of intuition. In D. Gentner & A. Stevens (Eds.), *Mental models* (pp. 15–33). Hillsdale, NJ: Erlbaum.

Engle, R. A. (2011). The productive disciplinary engagement framework: Origins, key concepts, and continuing developments. In D. Y. Dai (Ed.), *Design research on learning and thinking in educational settings: Enhancing intellectual growth and functioning* (pp. 161–200). London: Taylor & Francis.

Groopman, J. (2007). *How doctors think*. Boston: Houghton Mifflin.

Henningsen, M., & Stein, M. K. (1997). Mathematical tasks and student cognition: Classroom-based factors that support and inhibit high-level mathematical thinking and reasoning. *Journal for Research in Mathematics Education, 28*(5), 524–549.

Institute for Research on Policy Education and Practice. (2011). *PLATO (Protocol for Language Arts Teaching Observations)*. Stanford, CA: Institute for Research on Policy Education and Practice.

Junker, B., Matsumura, L. C., Crosson, A., Wolf, M. K., Levison, A., Weisberg, Y., & Resnick, L. (2004, April). *Overview of the Instructional Quality Assessment*. Paper presented at the annual meeting of the American Educational Research Association, San Diego, CA.

Marder, M., & Walkington, C. (2012). UTeach teacher observation protocol. Downloaded April 1, 2012, from https://wikis.utexas.edu/pages/viewpageattachments.action?pageId=6884866&sortBy=date&highlight=UTOP_Physics_2009.doc&.

Mathematics Assessment Project. (2014). Lesson revision from feedback: An analysis of the process. Downloaded April 1, 2014, from http://map.mathshell.org/.

National Council of Teachers of Mathematics. (1989). *Curriculum and evaluation standards for school mathematics*. Reston, VA: NCTM.

National Council of Teachers of Mathematics. (2000). *Principles and standards for school mathematics*. Reston, VA: NCTM.

Newell, A. (1983). The heuristic of George Pólya and its relation to artificial intelligence. In R. Groner, M. Groner, & W. Bischof (Eds.), *Methods of heuristics* (pp. 195–243). Hillsdale, NJ: Erlbaum.

Oakes, J., Joseph, R., & Muir, K. (2001). Access and achievement in mathematics and science. In J. A. Banks & C. A. McGee Banks (Eds.), *Handbook of research on multicultural education* (pp. 69–90). San Francisco: Jossey-Bass.

PACT Consortium. (2012). Performance Assessment for California Teachers (2012). A brief overview of the PACT assessment system. Downloaded April 1, 2012, from http://www.pacttpa.org/_main/hub.php?pageName=Home.

Palincsar, A., & Brown, A. (1984). Reciprocal teaching of comprehension-fostering and comprehension-monitoring activities. *Cognition and Instruction, 1*(2), 117–175.

Pianta, R., La Paro, K., & Hamre, B. K. (2008). *Classroom assessment scoring system*. Baltimore: Paul H. Brookes.

Scardamalia, M., & Bereiter, C. (1983). Child as co-investigator: Helping children to gain insight into their own mental processes. In S. G. Paris, M. Olson, & H. W. Stevenson (Eds.), *Learning and motivation in the classroom* (pp. 61–82). Hillsdale, NJ: Erlbaum.

Schoenfeld, A. H. (1985). *Mathematical problem solving*. Orlando, FL: Academic Press.

Schoenfeld, A. H. (1992). Learning to think mathematically: Problem solving, metacognition, and sense-making in mathematics. In D. Grouws (Ed.), *Handbook for research on mathematics teaching and learning* (pp. 334–370). New York: MacMillan.

Schoenfeld, A. H. (2006). Design experiments. In P. B. Elmore, G. Camilli, & J. Green (Eds.), *Handbook of complementary methods in education research* (pp. 193–206). Washington, DC and Mahwah, NJ: American Educational Research Association and Lawrence Erlbaum Associates.

Schoenfeld, A. H. (2010). *How we think: A theory of goal-oriented decision making and its educational applications*. New York: Routledge.

Schoenfeld, A. H. (2013). Classroom observations in theory and practice. *ZDM, The International Journal of Mathematics Education, 45*, 607–621. https://doi.org/10.1007/s11858-012-0483-1.

Schoenfeld, A., Gamoran, M., Kessel, C., Leonard, M., Orbach, R., & Arcavi, A. (1992). Toward a comprehensive model of human tutoring in complex subject matter domains. *Journal of Mathematical Behavior, 11*(4), 293–320.

Schoenfeld, A. H., Floden, R. E., & the Algebra Teaching Study and Mathematics Assessment Project. (2014). An introduction to the TRU Math Dimensions. Berkeley, CA & E. Lansing, MI: Graduate School of Education, University of California, Berkeley & College of Education, Michigan State University. Retrieved from http://ats.berkeley.edu/tools.html and/or http://map.mathshell.org/materials/pd.php.

Stein, M. K., Grover, B., & Henningsen, M. (1996). Building student capacity for mathematical thinking and reasoning: An analysis of mathematical tasks used in reform classrooms. *American Educational Research Journal, 33*(2), 455–488.

Stein, M. K., Engle, R. A., Smith, M. S., & Hughes, E. K. (2008). Orchestrating productive mathematical discussions: Five practices for helping teachers move beyond show and tell. *Mathematical Thinking and Learning, 10*(4), 313–340.

Szolovits, P., Patil, R., & Schwartz, W. (1988). Artificial intelligence in medical diagnosis. *Annals of Internal Medicine, 108*(1), 80–87.

Open Access This chapter is licensed under the terms of the Creative Commons Attribution 4.0 International License (http://creativecommons.org/licenses/by/4.0/), which permits use, sharing, adaptation, distribution and reproduction in any medium or format, as long as you give appropriate credit to the original author(s) and the source, provide a link to the Creative Commons license and indicate if changes were made.

The images or other third party material in this chapter are included in the chapter's Creative Commons license, unless indicated otherwise in a credit line to the material. If material is not included in the chapter's Creative Commons license and your intended use is not permitted by statutory regulation or exceeds the permitted use, you will need to obtain permission directly from the copyright holder.

Chapter 27
If We Want to Get Ahead, We Should Transcend Dualisms and Foster Paradigm Pluralism

Thorsten Scheiner

Abstract In this chapter, I argue for the importance of transcending dualisms and using multi-paradigm perspectives when examining phenomena and issues in mathematics education. I begin by exploring the philosophical bases—ontological, epistemological, axiological, and methodological—underlying three major paradigms in mathematics education research: the modernist (post-)positivist paradigm, the post-modernist interpretive paradigm, and the post-modernist transformative paradigm. Then, I present three modes of thinking that enable researchers to deal with multiple paradigms: dualistic thinking, dialogical thinking, and dialectical thinking. I adopt the dialectical mode of thinking to blend the modernist and post-modernist paradigms with respect to an ontological opposition (mind-world duality) and an epistemological opposition (objectivity-subjectivity duality) prevalent in the literature. A new paradigm begins to emerge from this blend, one which transcends these dualities to better interpret phenomena and issues in mathematics education.

Keywords Paradigm · Mathematics education research · Pluralism · Multi-paradigm inquiry · Blending · Transcending dualisms

---

Following diSessa (1991) and Schoenfeld (2014) this chapter takes as its point of departure Karmiloff-Smith and Inhelder's (1974/75) well-known paper *If you want to get ahead, get a theory*. In his paper, *If we want to get ahead, we should get some theories*, diSessa (1991) argued for serious dedication toward theory advancement in mathematics education, as we have not yet reached deep theoretical understanding of knowledge or the learning process. In his paper, *If you really want to get ahead, get a bunch of theories … and data to test them*, Schoenfeld (2014) called for approaching complex issues in mathematics education from multiple theoretical perspectives and at multiple levels of granularity. In this chapter, I intend to contribute to this conversation by arguing for conducting multi-paradigm inquiry and blending paradigmatic controversies. Such an approach moves the field beyond dualisms that hinder theoretical discourse.

T. Scheiner (✉)
Institute for Learning Sciences & Teacher Education, Australian Catholic University, Brisbane, Australia
e-mail: thorsten.scheiner@acu.edu.au

The University of Auckland, Auckland, New Zealand

© The Author(s) 2019
G. Kaiser and N. Presmeg (eds.), *Compendium for Early Career Researchers in Mathematics Education*, ICME-13 Monographs,
https://doi.org/10.1007/978-3-030-15636-7_27

27.1 Introduction

Mathematics education has become an independent research field that draws insights, perspectives, and methods from a variety of other fields, including anthropology, cognitive science, education, history, linguistics, mathematics, philosophy, psychology, semiotics, and sociology. Thus, it is not surprising that a diversity of theoretical and philosophical bases underpins mathematics education research. Indeed, this diversity of theoretical and philosophical bases serves to strengthen the field (Cobb 2007). Nevertheless, when conducting mathematics education research, it is necessary to carefully select and justify appropriate theoretical and philosophical bases. Indeed, mathematics education research is undertaken for a variety of reasons, including understanding and explaining phenomena in mathematical knowing, learning, and teaching; exposing and challenging the social and political frames in which mathematics education come about; and empowering individuals involved in the broader educational context. The exact purpose and nature of research are influenced by the researcher's ways of looking at the world: that is, they are influenced by the researcher's paradigm. A paradigm is a way of viewing the world that reflects fundamental philosophical assumptions that guide and direct thinking and action.

The perspective taken here is that our paradigms frame our inquiries, and indeed lives, by giving shape and meaning to the world we experience and act within. Indeed, a researcher's worldview not only underlies his or her choice of what phenomena to study but has implications for the choice of method when studying the phenomena. Such choices are based on fundamental assumptions about the nature of the phenomena and the nature of knowledge about the phenomena. Some researchers do not explicitly acknowledge the fundamental philosophical assumptions underlying their research; this does not mean that such assumptions do not exist, but rather that their research relies on implicit, and partially unrecognized or unexamined, assumptions. However, in order to make sensible decisions when planning and conducting research, be mindful in reading and critiquing research, and contribute productively to the theoretical and methodological debates in the research community, one needs to recognize and understand the fundamental philosophical assumptions underpinning one's study. In summary, researchers should identify their views of the world and acknowledge the way these views "orient and constrain the types of questions that are asked about the learning and teaching of mathematics, and thus the nature of the phenomena that are investigated and the forms of knowledge produced" (Cobb 2007, p. 7). Being explicit in recognizing one's own paradigm enables a researcher to become a more reflective practitioner and allows researchers to recognize the constraints of their sense-making of phenomena under consideration.

Over the past few decades there has been a remarkable growth, within the mathematics education research community, in the recognition of and discussion about: diverse theoretical and philosophical positions (Ernest 1991; Sierpinska and Kilpatrick 1998; Sriraman and English 2010); various methodologies

(Bikner-Ahsbahs et al. 2015; Kelly and Lesh 2000; Schoenfeld 2008); and central educational dimensions (e.g., critical, cultural, political, and social) (Jablonka et al. 2013; Rogers and Kaiser 1995; Skovsmose 1994). Scholars in our field have been debating the distinctive contributions of, and to, knowledge that arise from different research paradigms (Ernest 1998). This debate is perhaps most succinctly characterized by examining different fundamental assumptions about the nature of the world (ontology), the nature of knowledge about the world (epistemology), the nature of ways of studying phenomena in the world (methodology), and the value of knowledge, including ethical concerns (axiology). These fundamental philosophical assumptions (ontological, epistemological, methodological, and axiological) are arguably the core bases used (and disputed) amongst different paradigms (Lincoln et al. 2011). Ernest (2012), for example, positioned ethics as a first philosophy for mathematics education, as it "enters into mathematics education research in several ways" (p. 13) and enables one "to rethink and reevaluate some of the taken-for-granted commonplaces of our practices" (p. 14), which opens up new possibilities for the advancement of the field.

Mathematics education research today is "very multi-faceted and highly diverse" (Niss 2018, p. 41) and is "decidedly not in a period of normal science" (Schoenfeld 1992, p. 180), but instead is shaped and underpinned by a variety of different paradigms. Trying to identify all the paradigms that underpin and shape research and practice in mathematics education is impossible, and conceivably less useful than identifying the major paradigms within which many researchers, knowingly or unknowingly, situate themselves. In this chapter I consider three such paradigms that embody fundamental differences in understanding the nature of inquiry in mathematics education.

The purpose of this chapter is to provide researchers with an opportunity to reflect on and reframe their own paradigms (see Schön and Rein 1994) and, even more importantly, an opportunity to bring diverse paradigms into productive interplay. In Sect. 27.2, I outline three major paradigms in mathematics education research, allowing researchers to identify the paradigm most aligned with their own, as well as to examine dominant worldviews and how they shape the way researchers think. Rather than encouraging researchers to choose from these seemingly-opposed paradigms, I propose in Sect. 27.3 different ways of dealing with these paradigms. In particular, three modes of thinking are outlined: dualistic thinking, dialogical thinking, and dialectical thinking. Dualistic thinking divides philosophical assumptions underlying different paradigms into polar opposite positions and allows privileging one side of the dualism. Dialogical thinking entertains different—even opposing—views simultaneously, and thereby develops richer accounts of phenomena that better reflect their complexity, paradoxes, and ambiguities. Dialectical thinking seeks to transcend dualism by blending opposing positions to arrive at a comprehensive view of the phenomena under consideration.

In Sect. 27.4, I coordinate seemingly opposing philosophical assumptions underlying critical paradigms in such a way as to provide new possibilities for reframing our view of the world. Finally, I conclude in Sect. 27.5 with some reflections and further considerations of these modes of thinking—for better understanding the complexities, recognizing the paradoxes, and appreciating the ambiguities inherent in the multi-faceted phenomena and diverse issues in mathematics education.

27.2 Delineating Major Paradigms That Underpin Mathematics Education Research

Paradigms are overarching frameworks that shape our whole approach to being in the world (Kuhn 1962): they shape our perceptions, conceptions, and actions. Kuhn (1962), for instance, showed that normal scientific research takes place within such an overarching framework and that various forces work to cohere (consciously and unconsciously) the fundamental philosophical assumptions of the framework. However, from time to time the overarching framework shifts in revolutionary fashion as new philosophical assumptions are used to make better sense of particular phenomena.

Nowadays various such overarching frameworks underpin mathematics education research. The purpose here is not to judge, but to elucidate the philosophical assumptions of these paradigms. The overarching frameworks under consideration in this section are the positivist paradigm and its successor the post-positivist paradigm (that are often referred to as modernist worldviews) as well as the interpretive paradigm and the transformative paradigm (that are often referred to as post-modernist worldviews).[1]

Higginson (1980) argued that

> [a]ll [human] intellectual activity is based on some set of assumptions of a philosophical type. [...] Reduced to their essence these assumptions deal with concerns such as the nature of 'knowledge', 'being', 'good', 'beauty', 'purpose' and 'value'. More formally we have, respectively, the fields of epistemology, ontology, ethics, aesthetics, teleology and axiology. More generally we have issues of truth, certainty and logical consistency. (p. 4)

---

[1] Indeed, there is a variety of paradigmatic strands in mathematics education research. Focusing on the (post-)positivist, interpretive, and transformative paradigms is not meant exhaustively list all possible paradigms underpinning mathematics education research, but rather to accentuate major, seemingly opposing positions in the literature. These paradigms represent broad camps within which many schools of thought and subtle variations flourish. These paradigms also indicate decisive shifts and historical moments of mathematics education research, including the process-product moment (with its aim of predicting phenomena), the interpretivist-constructivist moment (with its aim of understanding phenomena), the social-turn moment (with its aim of understanding the situatedness of phenomena), and the socio-political-turn moment (with its aim of emancipation and deconstruction) (Stinson and Bullock 2012).

Notice that there is no universally agreed upon way to divide up the schools of thought; neither the labels (or terms) of these paradigms nor the lines between them are altogether clear. Different terms have been used for describing each paradigm. For example, the (post-)positivist paradigm has been referred to as the "conventional paradigm" (Galbraith 1993) or the "scientific paradigm" (Habermas 1972).

For the purposes of this chapter, the focus is on the ontological, epistemological, axiological, and methodological bases of a paradigm. In summary:

- the *ontological* base concerns issues about the nature of reality or being in itself (e.g., 'What is the nature of reality?');
- the *epistemological* base concerns issues about the nature of knowledge (including what forms of knowledge are considered as 'scientific') (e.g., 'What is the nature of knowledge and the relation between the knower and what can be known?');
- the *axiological* base concerns issues about values and ethics (e.g., 'What knowledge is intrinsically worthwhile and what is it about it that is valuable as an end in itself?'); and
- the *methodological* base concerns issues about ways of studying phenomena in the world (e.g., 'How can the knower obtain knowledge?').

These four methodological bases are intricately related and mutually informing.

In the following subsections, the (post-)positivist, interpretive, and transformative paradigms are contrasted on the basis of their ontological, epistemological, axiological, and methodological assumptions. To do so, the more radical philosophical assumptions within each paradigm are foregrounded, not only because the controversies concerning their intellectual legitimacy often take place at the edges of those paradigms, but also because those edges are the intellectual, theoretical, and practical space for dialogue.

Table 27.1 lists assumptions that the (post-)positivist, interpretive, and transformative paradigms make about the nature of reality (ontology), the nature of knowledge (epistemology), the value of knowledge (axiology), and the nature of inquiry (methodology).

Table 27.1 Overview of fundamental philosophical assumptions underlying major paradigms[a]

	Modernist	Post-modernist	
	(Post-)Positivist	*Interpretive*	*Transformative*
Ontology	Realism—'real' reality that is independent of and external to the knower Positivist: naïve realism (reality is knowable) Post-positivist: critical realism (reality is only imperfectly and probabilistically knowable)	Relativism—multiple, locally constructed realities (or: reality as an intersubjective social construction)	Relativism—various versions of reality based on, and shaped by, cultural, social, political, ethnic, and gender values crystallized over time

(continued)

Table 27.1 (continued)

	Modernist		Post-modernist
Epistemology	Reality is discovered (or uncovered); findings are (probably) true; striving for objectivity	Reality is (socially) constructed; findings are created; acknowledging subjectivity (or inter-subjectivity)	Knowledge is socially and historically situated; value mediated findings; seeking objective multi-perspectival knowledge of all participants
Axiology	Knowledge about the world is an end in itself; need to minimize harm; informed consent; respect for privacy	Multi-perspectival knowing is valuable as a means for balancing representations of views and raising participants' awareness	Knowing is valuable as a means for promoting human rights and increasing social justice; need to address issues of power and trust; respect for cultural norms
Methodology	(Quasi-)experimental; seeking general laws; hypotheses-testing (verification or falsification of hypotheses); mainly quantitative methods	Hermeneutical, generative approaches; case-study design; mainly qualitative methods	Critical, reflexive, and deconstructive approaches; mainly qualitative methods

[a]Adapted, modified, and extended from Guba and Lincoln (1994), Heron and Reason (1997), and Lincoln et al. (2011)

27.2.1 (Post-)Positivist Paradigm

Positivism and its successor, post-positivism, view the world as external to humans and independent of human experience. This view relies on the existence of reliable knowledge about the world that research strives to gain. In this perspective, there is a world independent of human experience, containing objects which behave in accordance with a set of natural laws. Positivist researchers can discover knowledge about these real things (knowledge that is certain, valid, and accurate), and determine the mechanisms and relations governing their behavior, through the use of the scientific method of reason, logic, and empirical inquiry (that is, experimentation and measurement of what can be observed). As there are many critical human phenomena that are not observable (e.g., mathematical thinking), post-positivists reject the positivist position that what can be studied is limited to the observable. Post-positivists are similar to positivists in that they believe the social world, like the natural world, can be studied in a value-free way that provides causal explanations for phenomena (Phillips and Burbules 2000). However, they differ from positivists in their belief that researchers should base claims regarding truth on probability rather than certainty.

In both a positivist and post-positivist view, researchers strive for uncovering a single view of reality, a reality that is separated from the mind: the rational researcher can come to know the objective world by employing analytical thought and experimental methods. This is the cornerstone of a modern worldview concerned with objectivity, prediction, generalizability, linearity, and absolute truth (Harvey 1990).

Ontology Post-positivists hold that the world is real, is structured, and that this structure can be modeled. The positivists hold that a 'real' reality exists and that it is the researchers' job to discover that reality (naïve realism) (Guba and Lincoln 1994). Post-positivists concur, but add the qualification that reality can merely be known imperfectly because of the human limitations of researchers (critical realism) (Maxwell 2012). Therefore, researchers can discover reality only within a certain degree of probability. By eliminating alternative explanations for phenomena, they can strengthen existing theories that account for these phenomena, but never prove them beyond doubt.

Epistemology (Post-)positivists hold that there is an objective reality that researchers are expected to 'mirror' or 'replicate' in their models and theories. The role of research is to discover or uncover the real world and its structure. This position assumes that knowledge about the world is (or should be) objective and scientific findings can be determined reliably and validly, given that biases and values of the researcher and others involved in the research process are eliminated.

Axiology The (post-)positivist paradigm regards knowing the 'truth' in propositional form as an end in itself—and as the only end in itself (Lincoln et al. 2011). The role of the researcher is to be as objective as possible in order to ensure that scientific findings are obtained through a neutral process; that is, the research process is seen as largely apolitical and separate from a world of individual and group interests. The researcher has an ethical obligation to conduct research that is intellectually honest, suppresses personal bias, and avoids harm. Such research should entail careful collection and accurate reporting of data, as well as candid evaluation of the limitations of the study.

Methodology In general, researchers in this paradigm assume that they can obtain an accurate portrait of the 'true' nature of reality through the scientific methods of reason, logic, and empirical inquiry. The research designs used to accomplish this goal are largely deductive, with an emphasis on determining which variables explain or predict outcomes for a phenomenon of interest. Positivists borrow their experimental methods from the natural sciences. Post-positivists, in contrast, modify these methods in order to apply them to people, developing quasi-experimental methods. These predominantly quantitative methods privilege experimental, randomized-sample, hypothesis-testing studies.

27.2.2 Interpretive Paradigm

The interpretive paradigm (or constructivist paradigm) views all meaning, including the meaning of research findings, as fundamentally interpretative. This paradigm assumes that all knowledge and meaning is constructed by those active in the research process (including participants and observers) and that researchers should attempt to understand the complex world of lived experiences from the viewpoint of those who live it (Schwandt 2000). The interpretive paradigm emphasizes that research is a product of the theories and values of researchers and cannot be independent of them. As Schoenfeld (2007) underlined: "One's explicit or implicit theoretical biases frame what one looks at, how one characterizes it, how one analyzes it, and how one interprets what one has analyzed" (p. 93).

Ontology Interpretivists reject the notion that there is one 'real' reality that can be known, but take a relativistic stance: that is, reality is a social construction that is experienced subjectively by different individuals. As there might be multiple socially constructed realities, "truth is the best-informed construction about which there is presently consensus" (Galbraith 1993, p. 74). Researchers in this paradigm try to understand the knowledge of others, as the others perceive it. In its most trivial version, interpretivism (or constructivism) takes the stance that the mind is active, not passive, in the construction of meaning and knowledge (von Glasersfeld 1995). Interpretivists do not so much discover knowledge but construct it.

Epistemology As there are multiple possible versions of reality (depending on the perspectives and values of individuals) in the interpretive paradigm, this paradigm replaces the concept of objectivity that is prominent in the (post-)positivist paradigm with the acknowledgement of subjectivity, inter-subjectivity, and live truth (i.e., truth in human terms) (Ernest 1998). The interpretive paradigm "challenges the traditional projection of epistemology, that of identifying a universal method for determining whether a particular theory or conceptual scheme matches or corresponds with external reality" (Cobb 2007, p. 10). The goal instead is, "to identify the variety of constructions that exist and bring them into as much consensus as possible" (Guba 1990, p. 26).

Axiology Interpretivists concern themselves with the meaning people derive from social interaction (Bryman 2016). The interpretive paradigm recognizes that experience is shaped by culture and context and filtered through individuals, and that there is not a singular reality that can be captured through research. Thus, multi-perspectival knowing is valuable as a means for balancing representations of diverse views. Interpretivists differ from (post-)positivists in that their model of 'reality' is contextual and situational. As such, alternative criteria are used to assess the validity of results, such as trustworthiness and authenticity.

Methodology In order to obtain contextual knowledge and to create a shared sense of reality, researchers in this paradigm typically use inductive research designs, which provide opportunities for findings to reflect context-specific, constructed meanings. Ethnography, case studies, and mostly qualitative forms of inquiry are used in this paradigm, with attempts made to better interpret meaning by obtaining, comparing, and contrasting multiple perspectives. The resultant exchange of conflicting ideas forces the reconsideration of previous positions and assists in the triangulation of multiple viewpoints (Ernest 1998).

27.2.3 Transformative Paradigm

The transformative paradigm (or critical paradigm) arose in response to the historical disadvantage, oppression, or discrimination faced by individuals belonging to minority groups, and seeks the intellectual, ideological, and spiritual liberation of such individuals (Tyson 2015). As such, it centers on the lives and experiences of those who experience oppression, discrimination, or inequality, including the following: women; people of color; immigrants; indigenous and postcolonial people; lesbian, gay, bisexual, transgender, and queer individuals; members of minority religious groups; and people with disabilities. Transformative researchers place priority on empowering those without power to bring about social transformation (see Horkheimer 1972; Mertens 2009).

The philosophical basis of the transformative paradigm is diverse, reflecting multiple approaches, theories, and positions represented in that paradigm, such as critical theory, critical race theory, feminist theory, queer theory, disability theory, and Indigenous theory (see Tyson 2015). For instance, feminist theory studies the systems and means employed by one group of people to structure and legitimize their domination of another group of people, and the strategies employed by the latter to resist this domination (see Hesse-Biber 2014; Lather 1991). Kaiser and Rogers (1995), drawing on McIntosh's (1983) phase theory of curriculum reform, argued for "loosen[ing] curriculum from a male-dominated, Eurocentric world view and to evolve a more inclusive curriculum to which all may have access" (pp. 1–2). On the other hand, queer theory challenges the binary notions of male and female that facilitate dichotomous conceptions of gender and sexual identity (see Dodd 2009; Mertens et al. 2008).

Ontology Similar to the interpretive paradigm, the transformative paradigm recognizes multiple versions of what is perceived to be real. However, those working within a transformative paradigm argue that "those working within an interpretative framework are too passive in that the framework itself is not critically examined for distortion and bias, i.e., crucial problems of conflict and change, are passed by through the acceptance of existing reference points" (Galbraith 1993, p. 76). That is, the transformative paradigm stresses that accepting different perceptions of reality as equally legitimate is dangerous, because it ignores the damage done by the social, political, cultural and economic factors that help privilege one version of reality over another. Besides, the transformative ontological position emphasizes that what seems 'real' may instead be an abstraction that was reified due to the influence of social and historical factors. Thus, before accepting something as 'real', those using the transformative paradigm critically examine that thing's role in perpetuating oppressive social structures and policies.

Epistemology The transformative epistemological assumption centers on the meaning of knowledge, as viewed through a variety of cultural lenses, and the power issues involved in determining what knowledge is legitimate. Objectivity in the transformative paradigm is achieved by reflectively examining the values and social positions implicit in research questions, hypotheses, and definitions.

Axiology The transformative paradigm emerged as a consequence of dissatisfaction with research conducted within other paradigms, which was perceived to be irrelevant to, or a misrepresentation of, the lives of people who experience oppression, discrimination, or inequality. Valuable research in this paradigm is defined by its fostering of social justice and human rights, and the role of a researcher is to be an agent of prosocial change. Transparency and reciprocity are essential principles of the axiological position in the transformative paradigm. An explicit connection is made between the process and outcome of research and the fostering of a social agenda.

Methodology Transformative researchers use a diversity of methodologies to understand and analyze the experiences of study participants. Many use qualitative methods such as critical hermeneutics, as well as reflexive and deconstructive ethnography (see Kincheloe and McLaren 2002): critical hermeneutics seeks to understand how research works to maintain existing power relations and reflexive and deconstructive ethnography seeks "to free the object of analysis from the tyranny of fixed, unassailable categories and to rethink subjectivity itself as a permanently unclosed, always partial, narrative engagement with text and context" (Kincheloe and McLaren 2002, p. 121).

While some researchers working within this paradigm use quantitative and mixed methods, they stress the importance of being cautious in following existing methods to avoid racist, sexist, or otherwise biased results. Despite some variety, a common theme in transformative methodology is the inclusion of diverse voices from the marginalized. This inclusion takes the form of the involvement of participants in all stages of the research process, including planning, conducting, analyzing, interpreting, using, and benefiting from research.

27.3 Ways of Dealing with Different Paradigms

Traditional approaches in mathematics education have produced valuable but partial insights into critical issues in mathematics education, primarily because they have been grounded almost exclusively in the tenets of a narrow set of paradigmatic perspectives. Schoenfeld (2007) stated that around the mid-1970s, "the field's primary research methods (in the United States, at least) were statistical, but their use was often unsophisticated, and the field as a whole suffered from a reductive form of what has been called 'science envy'" (p. 103). Nowadays, however, the field recognizes that the use of any single paradigm produces too narrow a view to reflect the multi-faceted nature of the issues and phenomena under consideration. Over the past decades, mathematics education has increasingly veered away from modernist worldviews (in particular the (post-)positivist paradigm) toward post-modernist worldviews (in particular the interpretive and transformative paradigm) (Ernest 1998). This shift from modernist worldviews to post-modernist worldviews have resulted in a dynamic field, with a growing body of research from diverse, often contentious theoretical and philosophical positions that may enrich understandings of the complexity and the diverse concerns of mathematics education.

Increasing recognition and acknowledgment of the uncertainty and fluidity of knowledge are energizing the so-called 'paradigm debate' (see Gage 1989), fueling arguments over the superiority of certain paradigms as well as the commensurability (or incommensurability) and permeability (or impermeability) of paradigms (Cobb 2007; Lincoln et al. 2011). As the paradigm debate continues, education research appears increasingly fragmented and reflexive. Mathematics education offers a case in point. The field has become marked by numerous, deep-seated divisions, illustrated by dichotomous conceptualizations concerning mathematics (e.g., Platonism versus constructivism), mathematical meaning (e.g., referential versus shared; universal versus contextual; objective versus subjective), knowledge (e.g., formal versus intuitive; stable versus emergent; hierarchical versus decentralized), knowledge development (e.g., the ascension from the concrete to the abstract versus the ascension from the abstract to the concrete), and the unit of analysis (e.g., the individual versus the collective; the cognitive versus the social), among many others. Steen (1999) remarked that mathematics education is "a field in disarray, a field whose high hopes for a science of education have been overwhelmed by complexity and drowned in a sea of competing theories" (p. 236).

Mathematics education researchers have begun to explore strategies for dealing with the increasing multiplicity and diversity of theories in mathematics education (Bikner-Ahsbahs and Prediger 2014; Prediger et al. 2008). These efforts have indicated that at times different lenses might offer alternative perspectives of the phenomenon under consideration and at times fundamentally new viewpoints are needed to account for these different lenses (see Presmeg 2018, p. 281). Though the field has made substantial progress in coping with the diversity of theories, ways of dealing with different paradigms have been underexplored, and the benefits of examining a research problem from multiple paradigms seem to have not been explicitly investigated yet. This section puts forth three modes of thinking for dealing with various paradigms (and their respective philosophical assumptions) in mathematics education research: dualistic thinking, dialogical thinking, and dialectical thinking. Certainly, this is not an exhaustive list of modes of thinking concerning various paradigms. In fact, researchers in mathematics education, including Gravemeijer (1994), Lester (2005), and Cobb (2007) explicated that we often act as *bricoleurs* (in the sense of Lévi-Strauss 1966), by adopting ideas from a variety of theoretical sources and paradigms—in a variety of complex and at times conflicting ways—to conform to our intentions and own biases, an approach that cannot be easily subsumed under any of the three modes of thinking presented here.

27.3.1 Dualistic Thinking: Toward an Oppositional Standpoint

The now-ubiquitous diversity of philosophical bases underpinning mathematics education research proliferates and polarizes paradigms, biasing researchers against opposing standpoints, and framing debates in terms of pairs of opposites, such as objectivity *versus* subjectivity and world *versus* mind. (Post-)positivist, interpretive, and transformative stances are often framed as competing paradigms from which one must choose. Dewey (1938/1997) reminded us:

> Mankind likes to think in terms of extreme opposites. It is given to formulating its beliefs in terms of Either-Ors, between which it recognizes no intermediate possibilities. (p. 17)

Perhaps because of our predisposition "to think in terms of extreme opposites" (Dewey 1938/1997, p. 17), we are likely to look at the relationship between fundamental philosophical assumptions underpinning different paradigms as poles of an 'either-or' opposition. Such an oppositional standpoint encourages dualistic thinking that follows either-or logic for cognizing phenomena in the world. Such dualistic thinking compels researchers (by comparison, opposition, and differentiation of poles) to choose one paradigm while disregarding other paradigms as irrelevant. It prioritizes one side of a dualism (e.g., subjectivity over objectivity) and consequently takes a rather restricting frame of reference (e.g., mind over matter). It champions one-sidedness in the research process. For example, if one maintains that the world is real, one disregards the importance of the mind for the construction of reality, yielding a positivist position. On the other hand, if one thinks the mind determines what is real, one disregards the importance of the world in a similar way, favoring a relativist viewpoint, which is presupposed, for example, in the interpretive position. Either position commits itself to reductionism and determinism: a positivist position assumes that what dictates reality is the world itself, while an interpretive position advocates an individual's mind as the determinant of what is real.

27.3.2 Dialogical Thinking: Toward a Pluralistic Standpoint

An either-or logic that prioritizes one side of a dualism and marginalizes the other, fails to account for the complexity of reality. Accounting for the complexity of reality requires a pluralistic view that offers a "metaphysically perspicuous" approach (Turner 2010, p. 8).

In contrast to dualistic thinking, which follows either-or logic, dialogical thinking follows 'both-and' logic, in which two or more seemingly opposing perspectives can co-exist. This is not to say that dialogical thinking conflates or integrates different paradigms existing in the field; instead, dialogical thinking facilitates an interplay between paradigms, accentuating their differences and interconnections and fostering an appreciation of how paradigm insights and limitations are most apparent from opposing views. This sort of interplay of paradigms relates to multi-paradigm inquiry, in which different paradigm lenses are employed to cultivate diverse insights and contrast their various representations (see Gioia and Pitre 1990; Lewis and Grimes 1999).[2] Lewis and Keleman (2002), for instance, stressed: "Multi-paradigm researchers apply an accommodating ideology, valuing paradigm perspectives for their potential to inform each other toward more encompassing theories" (p. 258).

Researchers might use various paradigms (including their respective foci and methods) to collect, analyze, and interpret data for recognizing complexities involved in, and acknowledging multiple understandings of, phenomena under consideration (see Lewis and Grimes 1999). By using paradigms other than their usual paradigm, a researcher might unfreeze and liberate initial assumptions, and eventually foster more creative and comprehensive insights as they continuously elaborate on and question previous analyses.

Whereas use of a single paradigm can produce a valuable but narrow view, multi-paradigm inquiry can generate multi-faceted accounts that portray the complexity and ambiguity of phenomena in mathematics education—accounts that reveal different yet interwoven facets of these phenomena.

Dualistic thinking fosters belief in an either-or dichotomous relationship to explain phenomena and ignores the possibility that facets of seemingly opposing accounts may be dependent on one another. Dialogical thinking, in contrast, might foster a more comprehensive portrayal of tensions and interdependencies, one that reflects complexity, plurality, and paradox—preventing researchers from falling into one-sided and partial claims about knowledge.

27.3.3 Dialectical Thinking: Toward an Emerging Standpoint

Dualistic thinking sidesteps paradoxes by privileging one side of a dualism, and dialogical thinking preserves conflicts between fundamental philosophical assumptions in order to grasp the disparate yet complementary focal points. Dialectical thinking, as suggested here, reconciles paradoxes to arrive at a richer and more comprehensive view of phenomena under consideration.

Lincoln et al. (2011) asked: "Are paradigms commensurable? Is it possible to blend elements of one paradigm into another, so that one is engaging in research that represents the best of both worldviews?" (p. 174). It is assumed here that paradigms (and their respective philosophical assumptions) can be blended to

---

[2]Researchers in the field of organizational theory use multi-paradigm approaches to capitalize on the strengths of different paradigms, in areas such as the formation of research questions, determination of methods, and analysis of validity of data.

provide novel insights and understandings that were not evident in each isolated paradigm. As Tall (2013) indicated:

> [...] frameworks may benefit from a broader theory that is a blend of both, explicitly revealing the nature of aspects that are supportive in some contexts yet problematic in others, yet at the same time, these aspects may blend together so that an apparent dichotomy has the potential to offer new insights. (pp. 410–411)

Blending[3] is a high level of coordinating paradigms (or their underlying philosophical assumptions) that does not imply synthesis or unification, but instead seeks to transcend dualisms. This is the level of coordinating perspectives that diSessa et al. (2016) described as 'deep synergy':

> [the level] at which things pass beyond being 'interesting' to being 'fundamental for the field' [...], where the intellectual support for at least some of the most important ideas comes from both perspectives. This is the regime where retaining the identity of the two perspectives begins to become questionable. Genuinely new intellectual territory has been reached that is not construable from within only one perspective. (p. 5)

Blending is considered here as a rich resource for dealing with different paradigms that provides a productive way of producing novel insights that may not be manifest in the original paradigms. The goal is to arrive at an account that would make it possible to link diverse paradigms without reducing one to the other. What is important here is the recognition that different paradigms might have conflicting philosophical assumptions, but those conflicting assumptions can contribute to the blend, with the resulting blend being a worldview of higher explanatory power, flexibility, and greater insight.

In the following section, such a worldview is outlined: this worldview emerges from blending the modernist and post-modernist worldviews.

27.4 Blending Modernism and Post-modernism: Towards an Emerging Paradigm

The modern *versus* post-modern duality can be re-conceptualized as a blend of these two worldviews, forming a new worldview, one that has different, but related, underlying assumptions. The next two subsections explore such a blend with

---

[3]The term 'blending' has its origin in the work of Fauconnier and Turner (2002) on 'conceptual blending', who built a detailed framework of blending knowledge domains, where new elements result in the blend that were not evident in either domain on its own. According to Fauconnier and Turner (2002): "In conceptual blending, frames from established domains (known as *inputs*) are combined to yield a hybrid frame (a *blend* or *blended model*) comprised of structures from each of the inputs, as well as unique structure of its own" (p. 115). Turner (2014) specified that "[t]he blend is not an abstraction, or an analogy, or anything else already named and recognized in common sense. A blend is a new mental space that contains some elements from different mental spaces in a mental web but that develops new meaning of its own that is not drawn from those spaces. This new meaning emerges in the blend" (p. 6).

respect to an ontological opposition (mind-world duality) and an epistemological opposition (objectivity-subjectivity duality) prevalent in the literature.

27.4.1 Beyond Ontological Opposites: Transcending the Duality of Mind and World

Modernism advocates a viewpoint in which the world surrounding us is seen as independent of our thought, a position that conflicts with post-modernism, which asserts that there is nothing but the constructions of our minds. A fundamental problem of the objective mind of modernism is that it cannot acknowledge that the ground, on which it stands to frame the world, is its own creation. It confuses the given world with the worldview it has generated for interpreting the given world. A basic problem with the subjective mind of post-modernism, on the other hand, is that it both allows any grounds as valid because it proposes a multiplicity of realities but offers no way to distinguish which is more legitimate. It confuses relative truth with nihilistic skepticism (Heron and Reason 1997): it postulates that because no ground is final, no ground has any claim to truth. While these perspectives help us in seeing the strengths and limitations of each of the paradigms, they do not help us in moving beyond the confusion they have produced. The alienation from experience created by the separation of mind and world is compounded when the world is reduced to multiple relativist constructions. Starting from this confusion, we can blend various aspects of modern and post-modern worldviews that are usually kept separate.

Such a blend accepts that there is a given world that the human mind actively interacts with (Skolimowski 1994). Mind and given world are engaged in a co-creative interaction so that what emerges as reality is an artifact of a complex, on-going interaction between the given world and the way mind engages with it (see Abram 1996; Heron and Reason 1997). Such a view seems to share certain aspects with Radford's (2013) theory of objectification. It shares the assumption that 'objective knowledge' exists independently of each one of us and that we meet what is other. However, while Radford (2013) emphasizes the idea that we objectify what meets (or objects) us, the view advanced here is that we do not only meet or objectify the other, but we also actively shape the other in mutually influencing ways: we shape the other and the other shapes us. This co-shaping brings about a subjectively articulated world, whose objectivity is relative to how the knower shapes it. Reality is *subjective-objective*, always called into being and shaped by the complex participation of the knower in what is known (see Reason 1998).

This ontology is thus subjective-objective: "It is subjective because it is only known through the form the mind gives it; and it is objective because the mind interpenetrates the given cosmos which shapes it" (Heron 1996, p. 11).[4]

27.4.2 Beyond Epistemological Opposites: Transcending the Duality of Objectivity and Subjectivity

Modernism seems trapped in a Cartesian epistemology, a position in which our representations must conform to an objective world in order to constitute knowledge. This objectivity derives from the Enlightenment perspective for knowledge of the physical world, which is postulated to be separate and distinct from those who know. Kant (1787/2003) set out to reverse these assumptions, arguing we should see any possible object as having to conform to conditions of our knowledge before it can become an object for us. Thus, from a post-modernist perspective, knowledge cannot be separated from the knower, but is instead rooted in the knower's mental construction of that world. In post-modernism, the relativist concept of (socially constructed) reality leads to a subjectivist view of epistemology, in which individuals construct multiple (even competing and contradicting) realities.

Modernism and post-modernism struggle to maintain the balance between objectivity and subjectivity, and thus encounter the paradox of seeing objective subjectivity (or subjective objectivity). The blended view overcomes the epistemological limitations of modernism and post-modernism: reality is not pre-given or deterministically pre-defined but co-created. With the view of humans being an integral part of the world, the mind is meeting given reality through complex participating in its being, and the mind makes its world by meeting the given (see Abram 1996). Thus, knowledge is co-created by mind and environment.

Such a view agrees with post-modernist perspectives that it is impossible to give any definitive account of what exists: this view recognizes the subjective articulation of being in the world and accepts that our knowing is from a particular perspective—authentic and valuable but also restricted and biased. In this view,

---

[4]One might misunderstand these assertions, confusing this view with mentalistic or representationist approaches in which individuals construct internal representations of external representations. Though the view advocated here suggests that what can be known about an objective world is always known as a subjectively articulated world, it differs from mentalistic or representationist approaches in at least three critical characteristics: (1) it views the individual as an integral part of the world rather than isolated and against matter (or the 'outer world'), (2) it views individuals as self-determining rather than being determined by the 'outer world', and (3) it acknowledges rather than denies individuals in the creation of their world. It views the world as a 'living whole', a "complex system of interrelated entities of which we are part" (Reason 1998, p. 42). The notion of world as a living whole emphasizes that the given world that surrounds us is complex and dynamic. As such, not only 'the subjective' but also 'the objective' evolve and change over time, in the interaction with the mind. Such a view echoes Burger and Starbird's (2005) suggestion to construe disciplines such as mathematics as "a living, breathing, changing organism" (p. xi).

an individual is critically reflective to the ground on which she or he stands; as echoed in what Torbert (1987) called a *reframing mind* that "continually overcomes itself, divesting itself of its own presuppositions" (p. 211).

27.5 Reflections and Further Considerations

Paradigms offer distinct, yet limited, insights into phenomena under consideration; they are contestable and provisional accounts that reveal certain facets of phenomena while overlooking others. Different paradigm lenses might contribute various, at times opposing and at times complementary, understandings. Taking a critical stance toward one's own underlying (and often taken-for-granted) assumptions is vital because "what we know of as 'reality' is an active projection of our own cognitive structure […] we see the world in terms of ourselves" (Brocklesby 1997, p. 195).

Paradigm insights and biases are most recognizable from opposing viewpoints. Section 27.2 specified sets of fundamental philosophical assumptions used to delineate major paradigms underpinning much of mathematics education research, namely the (post-)positivist paradigm, the interpretive paradigm, and the transformative paradigm. By making opposing views and tensions explicit, one might distinguish the value and constraints of different paradigm lenses, identify unnoticed anomalies, and recognize how each lens distorts the phenomena observed and explanations proffered. Reflecting on the focus and limitations of different paradigm lenses may encourage researchers to "question, possibly for the first time, the veracity of the claim that the social consensus surrounding a paradigm's body of knowledge somehow represents proof of the truth" (Brocklesby 1997, p. 200). Such a critical reflection opens space for questioning, valuing, and including alternative paradigms in the research process. Cobb (2007) remarked that, "in coming to understand what adherents to an alternative perspective think they are doing, we develop a more sensitive and critical understanding of some of the taken-for-granted aspects of our own perspectives" (p. 32).

Section 27.3 outlined various potential ways for dealing with alternative paradigms, such as the following: privileging one side of a dualism; taking a multi-paradigm approach that aims to generate multi-sided accounts reflecting complexity, paradox, and ambiguity; and blending opposing positions to arrive at an expanded view that transcends dualisms. The intention was not to argue that the field should aim for conflation, integration, synthesis, or unification of competing paradigms. Instead, this chapter argued that phenomena and issues in mathematics education should be considered from a multi-paradigm perspective, and that paradigms could be blended to account creatively for a multi-faceted reality that is "in perpetual flux and transformation and hence unrepresentable through any static conceptual framework or paradigm of thought" (Chia 1996, p. 46). As Kilpatrick (1993) reminded us, "researchers in mathematics education should never become wedded to a single approach, epistemology, paradigm, means of representation or method. All are partial and provisional, none can tell the whole story" (p. 17).

It is suggested here that it is critical to hold a pluralist view when it comes to "understand[ing] the balancing of the complex human worlds involved in mathematics education" (Presmeg 1998, p. 63). When we consider each paradigm as a valid perspective and hold, use, or blend various paradigms, we are better able to cope with the "dilemmas, tensions, and contradictions of mathematical classrooms" (Presmeg 1998, p. 63). To better understand the complexities, recognize the paradoxes, and appreciate the ambiguities of phenomena and issues in mathematics education, we must often embrace seemingly contradictory views about the world. Hence, Sect. 27.4 attempted to blend modernism and post-modernism to articulate an emerging paradigm that acknowledges the co-creative interaction between mind and world, recasting the subjectivity-objectivity divide by viewing the world as subjectively articulated, in that its objectivity is relative to how it has been shaped by the knower (see Heron and Reason 1997). Such an account promotes a different way of conceptualizing paradoxical tensions across paradigms, which acknowledges the interrelationships between oppositions.

Interrelating seemingly conflicting worldviews might eventually foster recognition of the viewpoints that alternative paradigms provide additional layers of meaning (Morgan 1983) and that tensions between paradigms act as sense-making heuristics (Lewis and Grimes 1999). Such a recognition might then give rise to the view that the multi-vocality, contested meanings, and paradigmatic controversies existing in our field are rich resources for emancipation—emancipation from being framed by a single worldview, from being subject to a single voice, and from being trapped by dualistic perspectives. Eventually, this might provoke a 'transforming in the being' of the researchers themselves (Mason 1998): "it is their questions that change, their sensitivities that develop, their attention that is restructured, their awarenesses that are educated, their perspectives that alter. In short, it is their being that develops" (p. 358).

It is hoped that this chapter might prove helpful in reframing researchers' stances toward research in mathematics education, shifting them from a search for 'the' truth to a search for more critical, multi-faceted understandings stemming from diverse and partial worldviews—understandings that acknowledge the diversity and interdependencies of theoretical accounts and that reflect the complexity, ambiguity, and conflicts experienced by different individuals in the research process and beyond.

References

Abram, D. (1996). *The spell of the sensuous: Perception and language in a more than human world*. New York, NY: Pantheon.
Bikner-Ahsbahs, A., Knipping, C., & Presmeg, N. C. (Eds.). (2015). *Approaches to qualitative research in mathematics education: Examples of methodology and methods*. New York, NY: Springer.

Bikner-Ahsbahs, A., & Prediger, S. (Eds.). (2014). *Networking of theories as a research practice in mathematics education.* New York, NY: Springer.

Brocklesby, J. (1997). Becoming multimethodology literate: An assessment of the cognitive difficulties of working across paradigms. In J. Mingers & A. Gills (Eds.), *Multimethodology* (pp. 189–216). New York, NY: Wiley.

Bryman, A. (2016). *Social research methods* (5th ed.). Oxford, UK: Oxford University Press.

Burger, E. B., & Starbird, M. (2005). *The heart of mathematics: An invitation to effective thinking.* Emeryville, CA: Key College Publishing.

Chia, R. (1996). *Organizational analysis as deconstructive practice.* New York, NY: Walter de Gruyter.

Cobb, P. (2007). Putting philosophy to work: Coping with multiple theoretical perspectives. In F. K. Lester (Ed.), *Second handbook of research on mathematics teaching and learning* (Vol. 2, pp. 3–38). Greenwich, CT: Information Age Publishing.

Dewey, J. (1938/1997). *Experience and education* (Original published 1938 by Kappa Delta Pi). New York, NY: Touchstone.

diSessa, A. A. (1991). If we want to get ahead, we should get some theories. In R. G. Underhill (Ed.), *Proceedings of the 13th Annual Meeting of the North American Chapter of the International Group for the Psychology of Mathematics Education* (Vol. 1, pp. 220–239). Blacksburg, VA: PME-NA.

diSessa, A. A., Levin, M., & Brown, N. J. (Eds.). (2016). *Knowledge and interaction: A synthetic agenda for the learning sciences.* New York, NY: Routledge.

Dodd, S. (2009). LGBTQ: Protecting vulnerable subjects in all studies. In D. M. Mertens & P. E. Ginsberg (Eds.), *The handbook of social research ethics* (pp. 474–488). Thousand Oaks, CA: Sage.

Ernest, P. (1991). *The philosophy of mathematics education.* London, UK: Routledge.

Ernest, P. (1998). A postmodern perspective on research in mathematics education. In A. Sierpinska & J. Kilpatrick (Eds.), *Mathematics education as a research domain: A search for identity* (pp. 71–85). Dordrecht, The Netherlands: Kluwer.

Ernest, P. (2012). What is our first philosophy in mathematics education? *For the Learning of Mathematics, 32*(3), 8–14.

Fauconnier, G., & Turner, M. (2002). *The way we think: Conceptual blending and the mind's hidden complexities.* New York, NY: Basic Books.

Gage, N. L. (1989). The paradigm wars and their aftermath a "historical" sketch of research on teaching since 1989. *Educational Researcher, 18*(7), 4–10.

Galbraith, P. (1993). Paradigms, problems and assessment: Some ideological implications. In M. Niss (Ed.), *Investigations into assessment in mathematics education* (pp. 73–86). Dordrecht, The Netherlands: Springer.

Gioia, D. A., & Pitre, E. (1990). Multiparadigm perspectives on theory building. *Academy of Management Review, 15*(4), 584–602.

Gravemeijer, K. (1994). Educational development and developmental research. *Journal for Research in Mathematics Education, 25*(5), 443–471.

Guba, E. G. (1990). The alternative paradigm dialog. In E. G. Guba (Ed.), *The paradigm dialog* (pp. 17–27). Newbury Park, CA: Sage.

Guba, E. G., & Lincoln, Y. S. (1994). Competing paradigms in qualitative research. In N. K. Denzin & Y. S. Lincoln (Eds.), *Handbook of qualitative research* (pp. 105–117). Thousand Oaks, CA: Sage.

Habermas, J. (1972). *Knowledge and human interests.* London, UK: Heinemann.

Harvey, D. (1990). *The condition of postmodernity.* Oxford, UK: Blackwell.

Heron, J. (1996). *Co-operative inquiry: Research into the human condition.* London, UK: Sage.

Heron, J., & Reason, P. (1997). A participatory inquiry paradigm. *Qualitative Inquiry, 3*(3), 274–294.

Hesse-Biber, S. N. (Ed.). (2014). *Feminist research practice: A primer.* Thousand Oaks, CA: Sage.

Higginson, W. (1980). On the foundations of mathematics education. *For the Learning of Mathematics, 1*(2), 3–7.
Horkheimer, M. (1972). *Critical theory.* New York, NY: Seabury Press.
Jablonka, E., Wagner, D., & Walshaw, M. (2013). Theories for studying social, political and cultural dimensions of mathematics education. In J. Clements, C. Keitel, A. J. Bishop, J. Kilpatrick, & F. K. S. Leung (Eds.), *Third international handbook of mathematics education* (pp. 41–67). Dordrecht, The Netherlands: Springer.
Kaiser, G., & Rogers, P. (1995). Introduction: Equity in mathematics education. In P. Rogers & G. Kaiser (Eds.), *Equity in mathematics education: Influences of feminism and culture* (pp. 1–10). London, UK: Routledge.
Kant, I. (1787/2003). *Critique of pure reason* (N. K. Smith, Trans.). New York, NY: St. Marin's Press.
Karmiloff-Smith, A., & Inhelder, B. (1974/75). If you want to get ahead, get a theory. *Cognition, 3*(3), 195–212.
Kelly, A. E., & Lesh, R. A. (2000). *Handbook of research design in mathematics and science education.* Mahwah, NJ: Lawrence Erlbaum Associates.
Kilpatrick, J. (1993). Beyond face value: Assessing research in mathematics education. In G. Nissen & M. Blomhøj (Eds.), *Criteria for scientific quality and relevance in the didactics of mathematics* (pp. 15–34). Denmark: Danish Research Council for the Humanities, Roskilde University.
Kincheloe, J. L., & McLaren, P. (2002). Rethinking critical theory and qualitative research. In Y. Zou & E. T. Trueba (Eds.), *Ethnography and schools: Qualitative approaches to the study of education* (pp. 87–138). Oxford, UK: Rowman & Littlefield.
Kuhn, T. S. (1962). *The structure of scientific revolutions.* Chicago, IL: The University of Chicago Press.
Lather, P. (1991). *Getting smart: Feminist research and pedagogy with/in the postmodern.* New York, NY: Routledge.
Lester, F. K. (2005). On the theoretical, conceptual, and philosophical foundations for research in mathematics education. *ZDM—The International Journal on Mathematics Education, 37*(6), 457–467.
Lévi-Strauss, C. (1966). *The savage mind.* Chicago, IL: University of Chicago Press.
Lewis, M. W., & Grimes, A. J. (1999). Metatriangulation: Building theory from multiple paradigms. *Academy of Management Review, 24,* 672–690.
Lewis, M. W., & Kelemen, M. L. (2002). Multiparadigm inquiry: Exploring organizational pluralism and paradox. *Human Relations, 55*(2), 251–275.
Lincoln, Y. S., Lynham, S. A., & Guba, E. G. (2011). Paradigmatic controversies, contradictions, and emerging confluences, revisited. In N. K. Denzin & Y. S. Lincoln (Eds.), *The Sage handbook of qualitative research* (4th ed., pp. 97–128). Thousand Oaks, CA: Sage.
Mason, J. (1998). Researching from the inside in mathematics education. In A. Sierpinska & J. Kilpatrick (Eds.), *Mathematics education as a research domain: A search for identity* (pp. 357–377). Dordrecht, The Netherlands: Kluwer.
Maxwell, J. A. (2012). The importance of qualitative research for causal explanation in education. *Qualitative Inquiry, 18*(8), 655–661.
McIntosh, P. (1983). *Phase theory of curriculum reform.* Wellesley, MA: Center for Research on Women.
Mertens, D. M. (2009). *Transformative research and evaluation.* New York, NY: Guilford.
Mertens, D. M., Foster, J., & Heimlich, J. E. (2008). M or F? Gender, identity and the transformative research paradigm. *Museums and Social Issue, 3*(1), 81–92.
Morgan, G. (Ed.). (1983). *Beyond method: Strategies for social research.* Newbury Park, CA: Sage.
Niss, M. (2018). The very multi-faceted nature of mathematics education research. In E. Bergqvist, M. Österholm, C. Granberg, & L. Sumpter (Eds.), *Proceedings of the 42nd Conference of the International Group for the Psychology of Mathematics Education* (Vol. 1, pp. 35–50). Umeå, Sweden: PME.

Phillips, D. C., & Burbules, N. C. (2000). *Postpositivism and educational research*. New York, NY: Rowman & Littlefield.

Prediger, S., Bikner-Ahsbahs, A., & Arzarello, F. (2008). Networking strategies and methods for connecting theoretical approaches: First steps towards a conceptual framework. *ZDM—The International Journal on Mathematics Education, 40*(2), 165–178.

Presmeg, N. C. (1998). Balancing complex human worlds: Mathematics education as an emergent discipline in its own right. In A. Sierpinska & J. Kilpatrick (Eds.), *Mathematics education as a research domain: A search for identity* (pp. 57–70). Dordrecht, The Netherlands: Kluwer.

Presmeg, N. C. (2018). Communication, cooperation and collaboration: ERME's magnificent experiment. In T. Dreyfus, M. Artigue, D. Potari, S. Prediger, & K. Ruthven (Eds.), *Developing research in mathematics education: Twenty years of communication, cooperation and collaboration in Europe* (pp. 276–286). New York, NY: Routledge.

Radford, L. (2013). Three key concepts of the theory of objectification: Knowledge, knowing, and learning. *Journal of Research in Mathematics Education, 2*(1), 7–44.

Reason, P. (1998). Toward a participatory worldview. *Resurgence, 168,* 42–44.

Rogers, P., & Kaiser, G. (Eds.). (1995). *Equity in mathematics education: Influences of feminism and culture*. London, UK: Routledge.

Schön, D. A., & Rein, M. (1994). *Frame reflections: Toward the resolution of intractable policy controversies*. New York, NY: Basic Books.

Schoenfeld, A. H. (1992). On paradigms and methods: What do you do when the ones you know don't do what you want them to? Issues in the analysis of data in the form of videotapes. *The Journal of the Learning Sciences, 2*(2), 179–214.

Schoenfeld, A. H. (2007). Method. In F. K. Lester (Ed.), *Second handbook of research on mathematics teaching and learning* (pp. 69–107). Greenwich, CT: Information Age Publishing.

Schoenfeld, A. H. (2008). Research methods in (mathematics) education. In L. D. English, M. Bartolini-Bussi, G. A. Jones, R. A. Lesh, B. Sriraman, & D. Tirosh (Eds.), *Handbook of international research in mathematics education* (pp. 467–519). Mahwah, NJ: Erlbaum.

Schoenfeld, A. H. (2014). If you *really* want to get ahead, get a bunch of theories … and data to test them. *The Mathematics Enthusiast, 11*(1), 7–40.

Schwandt, T. A. (2000). Three epistemological stances for qualitative inquiry: Interpretivism, hermeneutics, and social constructionism. In N. K. Denzin & Y. S. Lincoln (Eds.), *Handbook of qualitative research* (pp. 189–213). Thousand Oaks, CA: Sage.

Sierpinska, A., & Kilpatrick, J. (Eds.). (1998). *Mathematics education as a research domain: A search for identity*. Dordrecht, The Netherlands: Kluwer.

Skolimowski, H. (1994). *The participatory mind*. London, UK: Arkana.

Skovsmose, O. (1994). *Towards a philosophy of critical mathematics education*. Dordrecht, The Netherlands: Kluwer.

Sriraman, B., & English, L. (Eds.). (2010). *Theories of mathematics education*. New York, NY: Springer.

Steen, L. A. (1999). Theories that gyre and gimble in the wabe. *Journal for Research in Mathematics Education, 30*(2), 235–241.

Stinson, D. W., & Bullock, E. C. (2012). Critical postmodern theory in mathematics education research: A praxis of uncertainty. *Educational Studies in Mathematics, 80*(1–2), 41–55.

Tall, D. O. (2013). *How humans learn to think mathematically. Exploring the three worlds of mathematics*. Cambridge, UK: Cambridge University Press.

Torbert, W. R. (1987). *Managing the corporate dream: Restructuring for long-term success*. Homewood, IL: Dow Jones-Irwin.

Turner, J. (2010). Ontological pluralism. *Journal of Philosophy, 107*(1), 5–34.

Turner, M. (2014). *The origin of ideas*. Oxford, UK: Oxford University Press.

Tyson, L. (2015). *Critical theory today* (3rd ed.). New York, NY: Routledge.

von Glasersfeld, E. (1995). *Radical constructivism: A way of knowing and learning*. London, UK: Falmer Press.

Open Access This chapter is licensed under the terms of the Creative Commons Attribution 4.0 International License (http://creativecommons.org/licenses/by/4.0/), which permits use, sharing, adaptation, distribution and reproduction in any medium or format, as long as you give appropriate credit to the original author(s) and the source, provide a link to the Creative Commons license and indicate if changes were made.

The images or other third party material in this chapter are included in the chapter's Creative Commons license, unless indicated otherwise in a credit line to the material. If material is not included in the chapter's Creative Commons license and your intended use is not permitted by statutory regulation or exceeds the permitted use, you will need to obtain permission directly from the copyright holder.